Copyright ©1991 The Creative Black Book, a Division of
Macmillan Information Company, Inc. All rights reserved.
We are not responsible for errors or omissions.
The Creative Black Book, 115 Fifth Avenue, New York, NY 10003
(212) 254-1330, Facsimile (212) 598-4497
Telex 230199 SWIFT UR Attn: CBB
Publisher: John P. Frenville
Assistant: Karen Price
Sales:
Director: Rob Drasin
Assistant: Linda Anne Braunstein
Account Representatives: Katie Adams, Roxanne Brown, Diane Casey, Francoise
DuBois, Merrit Hartblay, Sue Ellen McMaster, Amy Wheeler, Ginger Wheeler, Juliette Wolf
Administrative Staff: Corby Barnett, Mark Coffey, Danna Markson, Dana White
Creative:
Director: Joseph S. Napolitano
Assistant: Ellyn Moran
Art Directors: Lori McDaniel, Peter Del Pesce
Production:
Director: Meggin Chinkel
Senior Coordinator: Carol Schultheiss
Coordinators: Cathy Citarella, Lynn Feinberg, Katherine S. Spadoni
Assistant: Kirk Oliphant
Traffic: Terri Jackson
Studio Manager: Paul Turzio
Artists: Laura Hayes, Annette Namaroff
Listings & Distribution:
Director: Maria Ragusa
Assistant Listings Manager: Me'Shel Riedel
Staff: Kip Azzoni Longinotti-Buitoni, Brian Celiberti, Rosa Munguia, Robert Sefcik, Woody Stevenson
Promotion:
Director: Mitchell Engelmeyer
Coordinator: Lecia Wood
Art Director: Janet Giampietro
Administrative:
Business Manager: Christopher E. Lenzi
Controller: Irving Wiener
Staff: Judy Chin, Cynthia Riley, Michael Rispoli, Steve Schmidt

Special Thanks for their support and contribution:
Sharon Ames, Faye Balestro, Adrian Hessel, Christina Holbrook, Susan Sgueglia, Shirona Sheffer, Jason Taback

Advertising Sales Offices:
The Creative Black Book, 212 W. Superior St., Ste 203, Chicago, IL 60610 (312) 944-5115
The Creative Black Book, 5619 W. Fourth St., #7, Los Angeles, CA 90036 (213) 939-0085

Divider Artwork by: Jack Perno

The Creative Black Book is distributed in the US and Canada by:
The Creative Black Book, 115 Fifth Avenue, New York, NY 10003
(212) 254-1330, Telex 230199 SWIFT UR Attn: CBB.
The Creative Black Book is distributed outside of the US and Canada by:
Hearst Books International, 105 Madison Avenue, New York, NY 10016, Facsimile (212) 481-3826.

THE CREATIVE BLACK BOOK 1991

The Creative Black Book
is a trademark of The Creative Black Book,
a Division of Macmillan Information Company, Inc.,
which is registered in the U.S. Patent and Trademark Office.
ISBN (2-Volume Set) 0-916098-50-8
ISBN (Volume II) 0-916098-52-4
ISSN (2-Volume Set) 0738-9000
Much of the artwork contained in this publication
is protected by prior copyright in the name of the artist,
and is reproduced here with permission.
No art shown in this publication may be reproduced in any form
without first obtaining the permission of the artist.

Printed in Italy by Arnoldo Mondadori Editore, Verona.

1991

JANUARY
S	M	T	W	T	F	S
		1	2	3	4	5
6	7	8	9	10	11	12
13	14	15	16	17	18	19
20	21	22	23	24	25	26
27	28	29	30	31		

FEBRUARY
S	M	T	W	T	F	S
					1	2
3	4	5	6	7	8	9
10	11	12	13	14	15	16
17	18	19	20	21	22	23
24	25	26	27	28		

MARCH
S	M	T	W	T	F	S
					1	2
3	4	5	6	7	8	9
10	11	12	13	14	15	16
17	18	19	20	21	22	23
24	25	26	27	28	29	30
31						

APRIL
S	M	T	W	T	F	S
	1	2	3	4	5	6
7	8	9	10	11	12	13
14	15	16	17	18	19	20
21	22	23	24	25	26	27
28	29	30				

MAY
S	M	T	W	T	F	S
			1	2	3	4
5	6	7	8	9	10	11
12	13	14	15	16	17	18
19	20	21	22	23	24	25
26	27	28	29	30	31	

JUNE
S	M	T	W	T	F	S
						1
2	3	4	5	6	7	8
9	10	11	12	13	14	15
16	17	18	19	20	21	22
23	24	25	26	27	28	29
30						

JULY
S	M	T	W	T	F	S
	1	2	3	4	5	6
7	8	9	10	11	12	13
14	15	16	17	18	19	20
21	22	23	24	25	26	27
28	29	30	31			

AUGUST
S	M	T	W	T	F	S
				1	2	3
4	5	6	7	8	9	10
11	12	13	14	15	16	17
18	19	20	21	22	23	24
25	26	27	28	29	30	31

SEPTEMBER
S	M	T	W	T	F	S
1	2	3	4	5	6	7
8	9	10	11	12	13	14
15	16	17	18	19	20	21
22	23	24	25	26	27	28
29	30					

OCTOBER
S	M	T	W	T	F	S
		1	2	3	4	5
6	7	8	9	10	11	12
13	14	15	16	17	18	19
20	21	22	23	24	25	26
27	28	29	30	31		

NOVEMBER
S	M	T	W	T	F	S
					1	2
3	4	5	6	7	8	9
10	11	12	13	14	15	16
17	18	19	20	21	22	23
24	25	26	27	28	29	30

DECEMBER
S	M	T	W	T	F	S
1	2	3	4	5	6	7
8	9	10	11	12	13	14
15	16	17	18	19	20	21
22	23	24	25	26	27	28
29	30	31				

HOLIDAYS

JAN 1/NEW YEAR'S DAY
JAN 21/MARTIN LUTHER KING, JR. DAY
FEB 12/LINCOLN'S BIRTHDAY
FEB 14/VALENTINE'S DAY
FEB 18/PRESIDENT'S DAY
MARCH 17/ST. PATRICK'S DAY

MARCH 24/PALM SUNDAY
MARCH 29/GOOD FRIDAY
MARCH 30/PASSOVER BEGINS
MARCH 31/EASTER SUNDAY
MAY 12/MOTHER'S DAY
MAY 27/MEMORIAL DAY—OBSVD

JUNE 16/FATHER'S DAY
JULY 4/INDEPENDENCE DAY
SEPT 2/LABOR DAY
SEPT 9/ROSH HASHANAH
SEPT 18/YOM KIPPUR
OCT 14/COLUMBUS DAY—OBSVD

OCT 31/HALLOWEEN
NOV 5/ELECTION DAY
NOV 11/VETERANS DAY
NOV 28/THANKSGIVING DAY
DEC 2/HANUKKAH
DEC 25/CHRISTMAS DAY

AIRLINE GUIDE

ATLANTA (AC 404)
American . . . 800-433-7300
Continental . . . 436-3300
Delta . . . 765-5000
Delta Connection . . . 765-2000
Eastern . . . 435-1111
Metro . . . 800-327-8376
Midway . . . 800-621-5700
Midwest Express . . . 800-452-2022
Northwest . . . 800-225-2525
Pan Am . . . 800-221-1111
TWA . . . 522-5738
United . . . 394-2234
USAir . . . 681-3100

BOSTON (AC 617)
American . . . 800-433-7300
Continental . . . 569-8400
Delta . . . 567-4100
Eastern . . . 262-3700
Enterprise . . . 800-343-7300
First Air . . . 800-468-8292
Hub Express . . . 800-962-4744
Midway . . . 800-621-5700
Midwest Express . . . 800-452-2022
Mohawk . . . 800-252-2144
Northwest . . . 800-225-2525
Pan Am . . . 800-221-1111
Trump Shuttle . . . 800-247-8786
TWA . . . 367-2800
United . . . 482-7900
USAir . . . 482-3160

CHICAGO (AC 312)
Alaska . . . 800-426-0333
American . . . 800-433-7300
America West . . . 372-2402
Continental . . . 686-6500
Delta . . . 346-5300
Eastern . . . 467-2900
Great Lakes . . . 800-554-5111
Midway . . . 767-3400
Northwest . . . 346-4900
Pan Am . . . 800-221-1111
Southwest . . . 922-1221
TWA . . . 938-9000
United . . . 569-3000
USAir . . . 726-1201

DALLAS (AC 214)
Alaska . . . 800-426-0333
American . . . 267-1151
Continental . . . 263-0523
Delta . . . 630-3200
Exec. Express II . . . 800-877-3932
Midwest Express . . . 800-452-2022
Northwest . . . 800-225-2525
Pan Am . . . 800-221-1111
Southwest . . . 640-1221
TWA . . . 741-6741
United . . . 988-1004
USAir . . . 647-8823

DENVER (AC 303)
American . . . 800-433-7300
American West . . . 571-0738
Continental . . . 396-3000
Delta . . . 696-1322
Eastern . . . 398-3333
Mesa . . . 800-637-2247
Midway . . . 800-621-5700
Midwest Express . . . 800-452-2022
Northwest . . . 800-225-2525
Pan Am . . . 800-221-1111
TWA . . . 629-7878
United . . . 398-4141
USAir . . . 800-428-4322

DETROIT (AC 313)
American . . . 800-433-7300
Continental . . . 963-4600
Delta . . . 355-3200
Eastern . . . 800-327-8376
Midway . . . 800-621-5700
Northwest . . . 962-2002
Pan Am . . . 800-221-1111
Southwest . . . 562-1221
TWA . . . 962-8650
United . . . 336-9000
USAir . . . 963-8340

HOUSTON (AC 713)
Alaska . . . 800-426-0333
American . . . 800-433-7300
Conquest . . . 800-722-0860
Continental . . . 821-2100
Delta . . . 448-3000
Northwest . . . 800-225-2525
Pan Am . . . 447-0088
Southwest . . . 237-1221
TWA . . . 222-7273
United . . . 650-1055
USAir . . . 757-9707

KANSAS CITY (AC 816)
American . . . 800-433-7300
Continental . . . 471-3700
Delta . . . 471-1828
Eastern . . . 800-327-8376
Midway . . . 800-621-5700
Northwest . . . 474-1104
Pan Am . . . 800-221-1111
Southwest . . . 474-1221
TWA . . . 842-4000
United . . . 471-6060
USAir . . . 800-428-4322

AIRLINE GUIDE

LOS ANGELES (AC 213)
Alaska . . . 800-426-0333
American . . . 935-6045
America West . . . 746-6400
Continental . . . 772-6000
Delta . . . 386-5510
Eastern . . . 772-5800
MGM Grand Air . . . 414-0163
Midway . . . 800-621-5700
Northwest . . . 380-1511
Pan Am . . . 800-221-1111
Southwest . . . 485-1221
TWA . . . 484-2244
United . . . 772-2121
USAir . . . 935-5005

MIAMI (AC 305)
American . . . 800-433-7300
Continental . . . 871-1400
Delta . . . 448-7000
Eastern . . . 873-3000
Midway . . . 800-621-5700
Northwest . . . 377-0311
Pan Am . . . 874-5000
TWA . . . 800-371-7471
United . . . 377-3461
USAir . . . 358-3396

MONTREAL (AC 514)
American . . . 397-9635
Canadian Airlines . . . 286-1212
City Express . . . 636-3456
Delta . . . 337-5520
Eastern . . . 483-6363
First Air . . . 931-4411
Mall Airways . . . 800-453-3001
Nationair . . . 476-3387
Northwest . . . 800-225-2525
Skycraft . . . 800-263-7753
USAir . . . 671-0017
Voyageur . . . 800-461-1636
Wardair . . . 288-9231

NEW YORK (AC 212)
American . . . 800-433-7300
Continental . . . 319-9494
Delta . . . 239-0700
Eastern . . . 986-5000
Mall Airways . . . 800-342-9803
MGM Grand Air . . . 800-422-1101
Midway . . . 800-621-5700
Midwest Express . . . 800-452-2022
Northwest . . . 800-225-2525
Pan Am . . . 800-221-1111
Trump Air . . . 972-4444
Trump Shuttle . . . 800-247-8786
TWA . . . 290-2121
United . . . 867-3000
USAir . . . 736-3200

SAN FRANCISCO (AC 415)
Alaska . . . 931-8888
American . . . 800-433-7300
Continental . . . 397-8818
Delta . . . 552-5700
Eastern . . . 474-5858
Northwest . . . 392-2163
Pan Am . . . 800-221-1111
Southwest . . . 885-1221
TWA . . . 864-5731
United . . . 397-2100
USAir . . . 956-8636

SEATTLE (AC 206)
Alaska . . . 433-3100
American . . . 800-433-7300
American West . . . 763-0737
Chartair . . . 800-237-1101
Coastal . . . 800-547-5022
Continental . . . 624-1740
Delta . . . 433-4711
Eastern . . . 622-1881
Harbor . . . 800-521-3450
Horizon Air . . . 800-547-9308
Lake Union . . . 800-826-1890
Northwest . . . 433-3500
Pan Am . . . 800-221-1111
TWA . . . 447-9400
United . . . 441-3700
USAir . . . 587-6229

TORONTO (AC 416)
American . . . 283-2243
Canadian Airlines . . . 675-2211
City Express . . . 800-387-2664
Delta Connection . . . 868-1717
Eastern . . . 362-3461
Mall Airways . . . 800-453-3001
Northwest . . . 800-225-2525
United . . . 362-5000
USAir . . . 361-1560
Wardair . . . 620-9800

VANCOUVER (AC 604)
Air Canada . . . 688-5515
Alaska . . . 800-426-0333
American . . . 222-2532
Canadian Airlines . . . 682-1411
Continental . . . 222-2442
Delta . . . 682-5933
United . . . 683-7111

WASHINGTON D.C. (AC 202)
Alaska . . . 800-426-0333
American . . . 800-433-7300
American West . . . 800-247-5692
Continental . . . 478-9700
Delta . . . 301-468-2282
Eastern . . . 393-4000
Midway . . . 800-621-5700
Midway Express . . . 800-452-2022
Northwest . . . 737-7333
Pan Am . . . 845-8000
Trump Shuttle . . . 800-247-8786
TWA . . . 737-7400
United . . . 742-4600
USAir . . . 783-4500

DIALING INTERNATIONALLY

When dialing a European country, dial the international access code (below), drop the initial "0" of the phone number ("9" for Finland), then dial the remainder of the number.

TO (YOU WANT TO CALL) ▶
FROM (YOU ARE IN) ▼

	Austria	Belgium	Canada	Denmark	Finland	France	Germany	Gr. Britain	Greece	Ireland	Italy	Japan	Netherlands	Norway	Portugal	Spain	Sweden	Switzerland	USA
Austria	—	0032	001	0045	00358	0033	06	0044	0030	00353	040	9008	0031	0047	00351	0034	0046	050	001
Belgium	0043	—	001	0045	00358	0033	0049	0044	0030	00353	0039	0081	0031	0047	00351	0034	0046	0041	001
Canada	01143	01132	—	01145	011358	01133	01149	01144	01130	011353	01139	01181	01131	01147	011351	01134	01146	01141	1
Denmark	00943	00932	0091	—	009358	00933	00949	00944	00930	009353	00939	00981	00931	00947	009351	00934	00946	00941	0091
Finland	99043	99032	9901	99045	—	99033	99049	99044	99030	990353	99039	99081	99031	99047	990351	99034	99046	99041	9901
France	1943	1932	191	1945	19358	—	1949	1944	1930	19353	1939	1981	1931	1947	19351	1934	1946	1941	191
Germany	0043	0032	001	0045	00358	0033	—	0044	0030	00353	0039	0081	0031	0047	00351	0034	0046	0041	001
Gr. Britain	01043	01032	0101	01045	010358	01033	01049	—	01030	0001	01039	01081	01031	01047	010351	01034	01046	01041	0101
Greece	0043	0032	001	0045	00358	0033	0049	0044	—	00353	0039	0081	0031	0047	00351	0034	0046	0041	001
Ireland	1643	1632	161	1645	16358	1633	1649	03	1630	—	1639	1681	1631	1647	16351	1634	1646	1641	161
Italy	0043	0032	001	0045	00358	0033	0049	0044	0030	00353	—	0081	0031	0047	00351	0034	0046	0041	001
Japan	00143	00132	0011	00145	001358	00133	00149	00144	00130	001353	00139	—	00131	00147	001351	00134	00146	00141	0011
Netherlands	0943	0932	091	0945	09358	0933	0949	0944	0930	09353	0939	0981	—	0947	09351	0934	0946	0941	091
Norway	09543	09532	0951	09545	095358	09533	09549	09544	09530	095353	09539	09581	09531	—	095351	09534	09546	09541	0951
Portugal	0743	0732	071	0745	07358	0733	0749	0744	0730	07353	0739	09781	0731	0747	—	0734	0746	0741	0971
Spain	0743	0732	071	0745	07358	0733	0749	0744	0730	07353	0739	0781	0731	0747	07351	—	0746	0741	071
Sweden	00943	00932	0091	00945	009358	00933	00949	00944	00930	009353	00939	00981	00931	00947	009351	00934	—	00941	0091
Switzerland	0043	0032	001	0045	00358	0033	0049	0044	0030	00353	0039	0081	0031	0047	00351	0034	0046	—	001
USA	01143	01132	—	01145	011358	01133	01149	01144	01130	011353	01139	01181	01131	01147	011351	01134	01146	01141	—

If your exchange is not equipped to dial direct internationally, dial "0" and give the operator the number.

12 NOON
DUBLIN
LISBON
LONDON

1 PM
AMSTERDAM MILAN
BRUSSELS MUNICH
COPENHAGEN OSLO
DUSSELDORF PARIS
FRANKFURT ROME
HAMBURG STOCKHOLM
MADRID VIENNA

2 PM
ATHENS
HELSINKI

8 PM
HONG KONG

9 PM
TOKYO

2 AM
ANCHORAGE
HONOLULU

4 AM
LOS ANGELES
SAN FRANCISCO
SEATTLE
VANCOUVER

5 AM
DENVER

6 AM
CHICAGO KANSAS CITY
DALLAS MEXICO CITY
DETROIT NASHVILLE
HOUSTON NEW ORLEANS
ST. LOUIS

7 AM
ATLANTA NEW YORK
BOSTON PHILADELPHIA
MIAMI TORONTO
MONTREAL
WASHINGTON D.C.

9 AM
BUENOS AIRES

ABOUT COPYRIGHT . . . The 1991 Creative Black Book *includes current information on copyright as a service to all members of the creative community.* Excerpts are from Assigning Advertising Photography: A Buyer's Guide, Revised Edition copr. 1988, prepared by the Advertising Photographers of America, New York Chapter based on a survey of APA/NY membership. We have also quoted Ellen M. Kozak's article, "U.S. Joins Berne Convention" and Margaret J. Vergeront's "Supreme Court Decision Strengthens Freelancer's Copyright Ownership" both for Wisconsin Lawyer in October 1989. Confirming information and insight were supplied by the Graphic Artists Guild and from a 3-column series by Alan J. Hartnick for The NY Law Journal during December 1989 and "Determining Copyright Ownership: The Supreme Court's new litmus test" by Scott W. Pink for Los Angeles Lawyer's September 1989 issue.

There have been three copyright acts in the United States. The 1909 Copyright Act was revised effective January 1, 1978 under the 1976 Copyright Act. As of March 1, 1989, the Berne Convention Implementation Act of 1988 took effect. The Berne treaty contains a "moral rights" provision which reads as follows: "independently of the author's economic rights, and even after the transfer of said rights, the author shall have the right to claim authorship in the work and to object to any distortion, mutilation or other modification of, or other derogatory action in relation to, the said work, which would be prejudicial to his honor or reputation." According to Ms. Kozak, Congress managed to slip past the "moral rights" provision by including language in the ratification to the effect that an author's rights "to object to any distortion, mutilation, or other modification of" a work that currently exists are neither enlarged nor reduced by ratification of the Berne treaty. Ms. Kozak asserts that state laws in NY and CA as well as libel and trademark decisions "have paralleled moral rights law as it exists in other countries," and that moral rights may be further asserted "through contracts restricting editorial changes."

Among other changes, the Berne Convention officially eliminates the formalities of copyright registration and notice in order to preserve copyright ownership–but only on work first published after March 1, 1989. In the event notice was omitted from work first published before January 1, 1978, the 1909 Copyright Act causes the work to enter the public domain. From January 1, 1978 to February 28, 1989, omission of notice *could* mean lapse of copyright protection, though remedy can be made for a limited time period following publication. In order to safely use works created by others, public domain status of the copyright can be assumed only if the work was published over 75 years ago.

Placement of notice provides "evidentiary weight" in the event of infringement as well as warns viewers that the work is protected. Generally, copyright registration is a prerequisite to filing such a suit under the 1976 Copyright Act. Without doubt, registration prior to an infringement provides additional legal remedies if a violation occurs.

Ms. Kozak urges creators always to **1)** affix proper copyright notice on all published and public works; **2)** register works within a preferred three months after first publication (though registering as late as five years after first publication is possible); and, **3)** assume everything from which you might quote or derive is protected under copyright law, unless there is proof to the contrary.

Additionally, from the APA/NY's Buyer's Guide: "When considering the application of the Copyright notice, keep in mind these additional points. **1)** Overall copyright notices in magazines, newspapers, and other periodicals cover only the editorial content of the publication and do not protect the advertising it carries. To protect the creator's rights, each advertisement must include its own separate notice. **2)** The separate notice protects not only the overall advertisement, but also each of its component elements, including photographs, drawings, design, copy, and typography. **3)** The correct form for a copyright notice includes the word Copyright [Copr.] or the symbol @, the year [of first publication], and the name of the copyright holder (who may be the client, the advertising agency, or the photographer, depending upon the arrangement made between the parties). As a rule, the advertiser's name appears in the notice, because it's in his interest to protect the whole advertisement..."

Another legacy of multiple Copyright Acts is increased complexity in determining whether a given work is protected or whether protection may have lapsed. Schedules for renewal of copyright protection differ given the window in which the work was created. For example, works published before 1978 required renewal after 28 years in order to extend protection for another 28 years. That second term was extended to 47 years by the 1976 Copyright Act. Works published after January 1, 1978 are generally protected during the creator's life and for 50 years following the death of the last surviving creator.

Under current copyright law–and as stated by Ms. Vergeront–a work is a work for hire when either one of the following applies. **1)** The work is prepared by an employee within the scope of his or her employment; **2)** The work is specially ordered or commissioned for use as a contribution to a collective work, a part of a motion picture or other audio-visual work, a translation, a supplementary work, a compilation, an instructional text, a test, answer material for a test or an atlas, if the parties expressly agree in a written instrument signed by them that the work shall be considered a work made for hire.

In June 1989, the U.S. Supreme court decided CCNV v. Reid. The decision clarified the issue of employment and strengthened the freelancer's right to retain copyright ownership. In reaching its decision, the Court applied "the common law definition of agency" and "set forth a nonexhaustive list of factors relevant to determining whether or not an artist is an employee: the source of the instruments and tools, the location of the work, the duration of the relationship between the parties, whether the hiring party has the right to assign additional projects to the hired party, the extent of the hired party's discretion over when and how long to work, the method of payment, the hired party's role in hiring and paying assistants, whether the work is part of the regular business of the hiring party, whether the hiring party is in business, the provision of employee benefits, and the tax treatment of the hired party." (taken from Ms. Vergeront's article)

Thus, if the hiring party desires copyright ownership, one of two things is required: **1)** a written work for hire agreement if the work is commissioned for one of the uses stated in the second work for hire option of the Copyright Act, **2)** a transfer of copyright from the freelancer to the commissioner. Copyright transfers must be written, with signatures of the creator, or authorized agent. Notarization is not necessary.

Of course, it may not be necessary to buy or sell 100% of the rights to any work. Detailed information follows on the concept of multiple rights, according to the APA/NY's Buyer's Guide. Though directed to buyers and sellers of photography, the information is applicable to other creative media.

"Almost any type of use, in any place, and for any time period, can be treated as a separate right independent of other uses, places, and periods. All these uses would be paid for as separate items. What the Copyright Law does is set in motion a sometimes complicated bargaining process, whereby the photographer licenses or grants specific use and reproduction rights to the client, while retaining all other rights and the ownership of the underlying photographs. The client must gauge which rights are actually needed, so as to avoid either paying more than he has to (by buying what he doesn't need) or getting less than he needs (by not buying the necessary rights).

"To avoid trouble which may occur in the event of a misunderstanding, it becomes very important to settle all questions of use and reproduction rights in advance. More often than not, the client does not need full ownership of all rights. Moreover, when exclusivity is of competitive concern to the client, it is customary for the photographer to agree to reasonable restrictions on the exercise of other rights the client is not buying. For the photographer to refrain from licensing the same photograph to one of the client's competitors, or to refrain from using the photograph for self-promotion until the client has enjoyed the exclusive use of the image for a reasonable period of time, is just common sense and good business, as well as industry custom. Nevertheless, there is no substitute for spelling out all restrictions and licenses in writing before the work begins. This can be accomplished by a process of free-marketplace negotiations.

"...The subject of categories of advertising usage easily can be organized around four questions...

1) What is the distribution? 2) What's the specific (or primary) use? 3) What's the period of use? 4) Are there multiple usages involved?

"**What's the distribution?** There are three classes of distribution: national, regional, and local. By and large, fees are based on the population in the area or areas of exposure.

National Distribution includes 'spot' exposure in widely separated population centers (for example, an advertisement published in New York, Miami, Chicago, Dallas, and Los Angeles). Certain 'regional' publications, such as *The New York Times* or *The Washington Post*, are really national in their distribution and readership.

Regional Distribution is exposure in a limited geographic area in one state or a group of nearby states, or in the regional edition of a national magazine. New England, for example, or all of New Jersey, or the 'Southeast Edition' of *ADWEEK*, would be considered regional distributions.

Local Distribution is normally understood as limited to a single city or tightly defined geographic area–for example, Tulsa, Oklahoma, together with a few of its suburbs.

"**What's the specific (or primary) use?** There are many more categories of use than of distribution, reflecting the perception that the more precisely the use can be specified, the more fairly the fee can be related to client benefit.

Consumer Advertisements are published in those magazines and newspapers of substantial circulation directed at the general public, and which are most often available at newsstands and other retail outlets and through paid subscriptions.

Trade Advertisements appear in publications directed at specific professional, trade, business, or special interest groups. They are not usually available through newsstands and retail outlets, and often, a percentage of their circulation is made up of complimentary subscriptions to qualified professionals in a defined audience.

Circulation is generally smaller than for consumer magazines. Examples of trade publications include *Chain Store News*, *American Bookseller*, *Industrial Launderer*, *Photo District News*, and *Backstage*. (Some trade publications have attained distribution and readership approximating those of general interest 'consumer' publications. They are no longer considered 'trade,' but 'consumer' publications. Examples include business, fashion, and entertainment magazines such as *Forbes*, *Fortune*, *Business Week*, *Billboard*, and *Women's Wear Daily*.)

Free-Standing Inserts are marketing advertisements–usually for packaged goods–which are most commonly circulated by insertion in newspapers. Inserts may have clip-out coupons offering a product discount, and they may be 'tipped' in to several different magazines and newspapers, which will afford them extremely broad exposure.

Billboards/Out-of-Home displays are commonly defined as 12-, 24-, or 30-sheet outdoor posters along roads, sides of building, or in other high-traffic 'out-of-home' locations such as a sports stadium.

Transit Posters/Out-of-Home displays are usually smaller than billboards, and are used in subway and train stations or on the outside or inside of public transportation vehicles. They are sometimes lumped together with billboards in the larger category referred to as 'out-of-home' advertising.

Point-of-Sales/Point-of-Purchase materials are displayed in retail stores or other locations where consumers can purchase the products. Examples include in-store signs, shopping cart posters, illuminated clocks and transparencies, countertop displays, self-contained dump displays, shelf-shockers, leaflets, and brochures and catalogs distributed in retail outlets.

Direct Mail Pieces include brochures, fliers, and cards, alone or in combination, whose primary distribution is direct to consumers through the mail. These items usually feature a single product or line, and are sometimes used for in-store point of sales as well as for direct mail.

Direct Mail Catalogs include bound booklets listing a large number of products. Primary distribution is directly to consumers through the mail, although this material is sometimes also used at the point of sale.

Packaging includes any box, container, or wrapper placed around or attached to a product. 'Hang tags'–often attached to products or garments–are usually considered part of the packaging.

Television Stills are single-frame photographs produced to be broadcast as elements of a TV commercial.

Photomatics are photographic 'storyboards' for television commercials. They are usually reproduced for use in presenting, testing, and refining a concept prior to production of the final commercial.

Presentation and Research Use. The terms 'presentation,' 'research,' and 'comp use' all refer to developmental, inside-agency, or company use, and specifically exclude the grant of any publication rights.

Test Market Use refers to photographs produced for testing proposed advertisements in a small, tightly defined segment of a potentially larger market.

Artist's Reference refers to photographs by an illustrator for reference or detail information. Normally, reference photographs are not easily recognizable in the final illustration.

"**What's the period of use?** ...Time period is usually the simplest to resolve. The client buys the use for whatever time...seems likely to be useful, which, in...advertising, is often not very long...The photographer can contribute very little input to this decision.

"**Are multiple usages involved?** From the client's standpoint, it's rarely efficient to buyout all rights to a photograph, or it's copyright. Because the breakouts of distribution, usage, and time period lend themselves to so many combinations...the process of tailoring the optimum combination may take some time and effort... But, it is usually a lot less costly than going for a 'buyout,' and...may have the added value of sharpening the concept for client and photographer.

Nevertheless, when clients do feel it necessary to buyout most–or all–of the rights of ownership,...there are two...types to consider. A Complete Buyout covers every right the photographer owns as the creator of the work, excluding...copyright itself. A Limited Buyout covers all possible usage and reproduction rights for a specified period of time, or the specified usage and reproduction rights for an unlimited period of time. Either way, the photographer retains the copyright. Expectedly, limited buyouts are usually not as expensive as...complete buyouts."

For Ten Years

Mondadori Has Helped The Black Book

Maintain The Highest Standards

Of Print Production.

It Has Been A Decade

Of Friendship And Excellence.

Luigi Sterzi
Roberto Voltolina

Elio Dorigatti
Rolando Aratri

Enrico Battei
Gianfranco Zanoni

Riccardo Rimini
Antonio Bovo

Alfredo Dal Ben
Pier Luigi Campagnari

Raffaele Salvaro
Massimo Cauchioli

Renzo Calafà
Bruno Pasini

Gianluigi Boscaini
Mario Pollini

Laura Brancato
Walter Weintz, NY

Nancy English, NY
Lois Turel, NY

Aresu, Paul/NYC/(212) 334-9494 . . . . **pages 348-349**
Aresu/Goldring Studio/NYC/(212) 334-9494 . . . . **pages 348-349**
Ariav, Haim . . . . (212) 689-7579
Aristo, Donna/80 Wheeler Ave., Pleasantville . . . . (914) 747-1422
Arky, David/140 Fifth Ave., NYC . . . . (212) 242-4760
Arlak, Victoria/40 E. End Ave., NYC . . . . (212) 879-0250
Arma, Tom/38 W. 26th St., NYC . . . . (212) 243-7904
Armbruster, Paul/153 Norfolk, NYC . . . . (212) 529-8690
Armstrong, Christine/5002 Pilgrim Rd., Balt. . . . . (301) 426-3069
Aromando, Tony/111 Cedar St., New Rochelle . . . . (914) 576-3965
Aronson, Barry/Boston . . . . (617) 542-1480
Arslanian, Ovak/344 W. 14th St., NYC . . . . (212) 255-1519
Art & Commerce/108 W. 18th St., NYC . . . . (212) 206-0737
Art Porta/333 Park Ave. S., NYC . . . . (212) 353-0488
Arts Counsel, The/NYC/(212) 725-3806 . . . . **pages 41-43, 220-221**
Arvyst Group/10555 Guilford Rd., Jessup . . . . (301) 470-4046
Ash, Michael/NYC/(212) 807-6286 . . . . **pages 230-231, 472-473, 496-497**
Ashe, Bill/534 W. 35th St., NYC . . . . (212) 695-6473
Ashley White, Brian/559 Broome St., NYC . . . . (212) 925-6465
Aslan, Steve/2900 Milton Pl., Bronx . . . . (212) 792-8826
Astor, Josef/NYC . . . . (212) 633-2050
Atkin, Jonathan/23 E. 17th St., NYC . . . . (212) 242-5218
Aubry, Daniel/NYC . . . . (212) 598-4191
Austin, Miles/253 W. 73rd St., NYC . . . . (212) 496-1820
Ava, Beth/87 Franklin St., NYC . . . . (212) 966-4407
Avatar Studio/One Grace Dr., Cohasset . . . . (617) 383-1099
Avedis Studio/130 East 65th St., NYC . . . . (212) 472-3615
Avid Productions/10 Terhune Ave., Hackensack . . . . (201) 343-1060
Avis, Paul/Manchester/(603) 627-2659 . . . . **page 197-199**
Azzi, Robert/116 E. 27th St., NYC . . . . (212) 481-6900
Baasch Maio, Dianne/124 W. 73rd St., NYC . . . . (212) 724-2123
Babchuk, Anne Marie R./NYC/(212) 929-8811 . . . . **pages 334-335**
Babchuk, Jacob/NYC/(212) 929-8811 . . . . **pages 334-335**
Badin, Andy/NYC . . . . (212) 532-1222
Baehr, Sarah/708 South Ave., New Canaan . . . . (203) 966-6317
Baitz, Otto/130 Maple Ave., Red Bank . . . . (201) 530-8809
Baker, Chuck, Inc./1630 York Ave., NYC . . . . (212) 517-9060
Bakerman, Nelson/220 E. Fourth St., NYC . . . . (212) 777-7321
Balaban, Steve/2 Tudor City Pl., NYC . . . . (212) 697-6792
Baldwin, Joel/NYC/(212) 727-1400 . . . . **pages 420-421**
Bale, J.R./1283 Cambridge Ave., Plainfield . . . . (201) 561-9762
Baleno, Ralph Studio, Inc./192 Newtown Rd., Plainview . . . . (516) 293-3399
Ballerini, Albano/NYC . . . . (212) 486-9575
Banks, Don/133 W. 19th St., NYC . . . . (212) 255-7465
Bantry, Bryan/Four W. 58 St. Penthouse, NYC . . . . (212) 935-0200
Baraban, Joe/NYC/(212) 758-4545 . . . . **pages 256-257**
Baras, Lloyd/37 W. 20th St., NYC . . . . (212) 255-8279
Barash, Howard/349 W. 11th St, NYC . . . . (212) 242-6182
Baratta, Nick/450 W. 31st St., NYC . . . . (212) 239-0999
Barba, Dan/305 Second Ave., NYC . . . . (212) 420-8611
Barbara, Vincent/2426 Lemoine Ave., Fort Lee . . . . (201) 585-1874
Barber, Jim/873 Broadway, NYC . . . . (212) 598-4500
Barboza, Anthony/853 Broadway, NYC . . . . (212) 529-5027
Barboza, Ken Assoc./853 Broadway, NYC . . . . (212) 505-8635
Barchus-Ferrari, Sara/251 W. 19th St., NYC . . . . (212) 255-6663
Barclay, Robert W. Studios, Inc./5 W. 19th St., NYC . . . . (212) 255-3440
Bard, Rick/61 W. 62nd St., NYC . . . . (212) 265-7970
Barkentin/15 W. 18th St., NYC . . . . (212) 243-2174
Barker, Robert/35 Buffard Dr., Rochester . . . . (716) 383-8850
Barns, Larry/21 W. 16th St., NYC . . . . (212) 242-8833
Barocas, Melanie Eve/78 Hart Rd., Guilford . . . . (203) 457-1717
Barr, Neal/222 Central Park S., NYC . . . . (212) 765-5760
Barr, Paula/144 E. 24th St., NYC . . . . (212) 473-4191
Barrett & MacKay/Charlottetown . . . . (902) 675-3383
Barrick, Rick/12 E. 18th St., NYC . . . . (212) 741-2304
Barrow, Scott/Garrison/(914) 265-4242 . . . . **pages 380-381**
Barrows, Wendy/205 E. 22nd St., NYC . . . . (212) 685-0799
Bartels, Ceci/NYC/(212) 912-1877 . . . . **pages 526-527**
Bartlett, Chris/21 E. 37th St., NYC . . . . (212) 213-2382
Bartlett, Linda/3316 Runnymede Pl. N.W., Wash. D.C. . . . . (202) 362-4777
Barton, Paul/NYC/(212) 691-1999 . . . . **pages 134-135**
Barutha, Mitchell S. Photography/565 Broadway, NYC . . . . (212) 431-0895
Basile, Joseph/448 W. 37th St., NYC . . . . (212) 564-1625

Basilion, Nicholas/150 Fifth Ave., NYC	(212) 645-6568
Baskin, Gerry/12 Union Park St., Boston	(617) 482-3316
Bassman, Lillian/117 E. 83rd St., NYC	(212) 737-4737
Bates, Carolyn L./174 Battery St., Burlington	(802) 862-5386
Baumann, Jennifer/179 Prospect Park S.W., Bklyn.	(718) 854-3834
Baumgartner, Peter/1905 William, Montréal	(514) 989-1484
Bava, John/13-17 Laight St., NYC	(212) 274-0515
Beall, Kathleen R./Wash.	(202) 298-6584
Bean, Jeremiah/96 North Ave., Garwood	(201) 789-2200
Bean, John Inc./Five W. 19th St., NYC	(212) 242-8106
Beardsley, John/322 Summer St., Boston	(617) 482-0130
Bebirian, Walter Paul/70-02 Nansen St., Forest Hills	(718) 268-6935
Bechtold, John A./117 E. 31st St., NYC	(212) 679-7630
Beck, Arthur/NYC	(212) 691-8331
Becker Studios, Inc./500 Broadway, NYC	(212) 925-3974
Becker, Jonathan/NYC	(212) 929-3180
Becker, Noel/150 W. 55th St., NYC	(212) 757-8987
Becker, Rick/500 Broadway, NYC	(212) 925-3974
Begleiter, Steven/38 Greene St., NYC	(212) 334-5262
Behal, Steve/123 Alton Ave., Toronto	(416) 463-7022
Bell, Bert/52 Shaftesbury Ave., Toronto	(416) 961-9304
Bell, James A./119-20 Union Tpk., Kew Gardens	(718) 263-8418
Bell, Karen/139 W. 19th St., NYC	(212) 255-5527
Beller, Janet/225 Varick, NYC	(212) 727-0188
Belott, Robert/236 W. 26th St., NYC	(212) 924-1503
Belushin, Blandon/56 W. 22nd St., NYC	(212) 691 0301
Bender, Rhoda/29 Arista Dr., Dix Hills	(516) 549-9158
Benjamin, Judy A./150 W. 87th St., NYC	(212) 580-1633
Benoit Photography/31 Blackburn Center, Gloucester	(508) 281-3079
Benson, Hank/NYC/(212) 727-1400	**pages 422-423**
Benveniste, Kathleen/104 W. 17th St., NYC	(212) 242-4153
Bercow, Larry/344 W. 38th St., NYC	(212) 629-9000
Berenholtz, Richard/NYC	(212) 222-1302
Bergami/NYC/(212) 242-0942/979-2930	**pages 104-105**
Bergen, Michael/167 E. 87th St., NYC	(212) 876-0235
Berger, Joseph/121 Madison Ave., NYC	(212) 685-7191
Berinstein, Martin A./215 A St., Boston	(617) 268-4117
Berkwit, Lane/262 Fifth Ave., NYC	(212) 889-5911
Berlin, Ron/145 W. 28th St., NYC	(212) 564-0606
Berman, Howard/NYC/(212) 925-2999	**pages 119-122**
Berns, Judith D./75 E. End Ave., NYC	(212) 249-8291
Bernson, Carol/NYC	(212) 473-3884
Bernstein & Andriulli, Inc./NYC/(212) 682-1490	**pages 76-87**
Bernstein, Alan/6766 N.W. 43rd Pl., Coral Springs	(305) 753-1071
Bernstein, Bill/38 Greene St., NYC	(212) 334-3982
Bernstein, David M./67 Columbia St., NYC	(212) 477-1983
Bersell, Barbara/12 E. 86th St., NYC	(212) 734-9049
Berzins, Normunds/516 Wellington St. W., Toronto	(416) 593-0526
Bessler, John/503 Broadway, NYC	(212) 941-6179
Bester, Roger, Inc./NYC	(212) 645-5810
Bevan, David/8 Shepard Rd., Hewitt	(201) 728-1149
Bevan, Paul/NYC/(212) 645-5832	**pages 414-415**
Bevilacqua Photography/202 E. 42nd St., NYC	(212) 490-0355
Bezahler, Alysse/14 E. 17th St., NYC	(212) 242-5081
Bezushko/1311 Irving St., Phila.	(215) 735-7771
Bibikow, Walter/Boston	(617) 451-3464
Biegun, Richard/56 Cherry Ave., W. Sayville	(516) 567-2645
Big City Productions/NYC/(212) 473-3366 .... pages 174-185, 578-579, Vol. I pages 272-277	
Bindas Studio/205 A St., Boston	(617) 268-3050
Birdsell, Doreen/297 Third Ave., NYC	(212) 213-4141
Bishop, David/NYC/(212) 929-4355	**pages 244-245**
Bishop, Lynn/NYC	(212) 517-4886
Bittner, Peter Studios/36 E. 20th St., NYC	(212) 242-4150
Blachut, Dennis/NYC/(212) 953-0088	**pages 438-439**
Black, Fran/NYC	(212) 725-3806
Black, Pamela/NYC/(212) 385-0667	**pages 112-113**
Black Star/NYC	(212) 679-3288
Blackburn, Joseph Mark/568 Broadway, NYC	(212) 966-3950
Blackfan Studio/286 Meetinghouse Rd., New Hope	(215) 862-3403
Blackman, Barry/NYC/(212) 627-9777	**pages 340-341**
Blackman, Jeffrey E./Bklyn.	(718) 769-0986
Blake, Mike/35 Drummer Rd., Acton	(508) 264-9099
Blake, Rebecca/584 Broadway, NYC	(212) 925-1290

Blanche, Andrea/434 E. 52nd St., NYC	(212) 888-7912
Blank, Bruce/228 Clearfield Ave., Norristown	(215) 539-6166
Blate, Samuel R. Assoc./Wash. D.C.	(301) 840-2248
Blecker, Charles/NYC/(212) 242-8390	**pages 238-239**
Blevins, Burgess/Baltimore/(301) 685-0740	**pages 52-53**
Blinkoff, Richard, Inc./147 W. 15th St., NYC	(212) 620-7883
Block, Ira/215 W. 20th St., NYC	(212) 242-2728
Block, Ray/458 W. 20th St., NYC	(212) 691-9375
Bloncourt, Nelson/666 Greenwich St., NYC	(212) 924-2255
Bloncourt, Nelson/NYC/(212) 924-2255	**pages 272-275**
Bloom, Teri/300 Mercer St., NYC	(212) 475-2274
Bobbé, Leland/51 W. 28th St., NYC	(212) 685-5238
Bodi Productions/340 W. 39th St., NYC	(212) 947-7883
Bogertman, Inc./34 W. 28th St., NYC	(212) 889-8871
Boghosian, Marty/201 E. 21st St., NYC	(212) 353-1313
Bohm, Linda/Montclair/(201) 746-3434	**pages 306-307**
Bohm, Linda/NYC/(212) 349-5650	**pages 306-307**
Boisseau, Joseph/3520 Herring Ave., N. Bronx	(212) 519-8672
Bolesta, Alan/11 Riverside Dr., NYC	(212) 873-1932
Boljonis, Steven J./555 Ft. Washington Ave., NYC	(212) 740-0003
Bolster, Mark/502 W. North Ave., Pittsburgh	(412) 231-3757
Bondellio, John E./606 Driggs Ave., Bklyn	(718) 963-0207
Booth, Tom, Inc/425 W. 23rd St., NYC	(212) 243-2750
Bordnick, Barbara/39 E. 19th St., NYC	(212) 533-1180
Borea, Raimondo/245 W. 104 th St., NYC	(212) 663-4463
Borg, Erik/Drew La., Middlebury	(802) 388-6302
Borkoski, Matthew/1506 Noyes Dr., Silver Spring	(301) 589-4858
Borowski, Steve/36 W. 20th St., NYC	(212) 627-7642
Bosch, Peter/NYC	(212) 925-0707
Bostrom, Thor & Bie/239 Park Ave. S., NYC	(212) 475-8211
Boszko, Ron/140 W. 57th St., NYC	(212) 541-5504
Bovo, Thomas J./7218 Seventh Ave., Bklyn.	(718) 833-8465
Boyer, Susan/NYC	(212) 533-3113
Bowden, John/528 F. Street Terr. S.E., Wash. D.C.	(202) 543-5151
Bowman, Ron/Lancaster	(717) 898-7716
Boyd, Gus/130 E. 75th St., NYC	(212) 988-5095
Boyd, William Jr./3707 California Ave., Pittsburgh	(412) 761-4571
Brack, Dennis/318 Third St. N.E. (Rear), Wash. D.C.	(202) 547-1176
Bradley, Roy/113 S. Brandywine, Schenectady	(518) 377-9457
Bradshaw Photography, Inc./56 The Esplanade, Toronto	(416) 363-7081
Brady, Steve/NYC/(212) 941-6093	**pages 210-211**
Brandt, Peter/73 Fifth Ave., NYC	(212) 242-4289
Brant Group, The/25 Brant St., Toronto	(416) 864-1858
Brauné, Peter/13 Laight St., NYC	(212) 219-2489
Braune, Peter/127 W. 26th St., NYC	(212) 255-2220
Braverman, Ed/337 Summer St., Boston	(617) 423-3373
Breitrose, Howard/NYC/(212) 242-7825	**pages 240-241**
Brello, Ron Jr./400 Lafayette St., NYC	(212) 982-0490
Brenner/Lennon Photo Prods., Inc./24 S. Mall, Plainview	(516) 752-0610
Breskin, Michael/133 Second Ave., NYC	(212) 979-8245
Bridges, Kiki Studio/147 W. 26th St., NYC	(212) 807-6563
Brigitte, Inc./NYC	(212) 243-6811
Brill, James/108 5th Ave., NYC	(212) 645-9414
Britz Fotograf/2619 Lovegrove St., Balt.	(301) 338-1820
Brizzi, Andrea/405 W. 23rd St., NYC	(212) 627-2341
Brodsky, Joel/321 W. 13th St., NYC	(212) 645-5484
Brody, Bob/NYC/(212) 741-0013	**pages 56-59**
Brody, Sam/NYC	(212) 758-0640
Bronstein Berman/NYC/(212) 925-2999	**pages 114-125**
Bronstein, Steve/NYC/(212) 925-2999	**pages 115-118**
Brooks, Bill/19 MacDuff Cres., Scarborough	(416) 261-3626
Brosan, Roberto/NYC/(212) 473-1471	**pages 60-61**
Brown, Blain/32 W. 31st St., NYC	(212) 279-0162
Brown, Constance/133 Rochambeau Ave., Providence	(401) 274-2712
Brown, Curtis/130 W. 20th St., NYC	(212) 807-1511
Brown, Cynthia/448 W. 37th St., NYC	(212) 564-1625
Brown, Deborah/NYC/(212) 463-7732	**pages 52-53, 346-347**
Brown, Doug/NYC/(212) 953-0088	**pages 438-445**
Brown, Ed/146 W. 29th St., NYC	(212) 563-2084
Brown, Ed Studios/7410 La Grange Rd., Louisville	(502) 426-9693
Brown, George/39 Spring St., NYC	(212) 941-1786
Brown, Gerald/1929 Chestnut St., Harrisburg	(717) 236-4698
Brown, Jim/Salem	(508) 741-2783

Brown, Marc B./4 Jones St., NYC . . . . (212) 691-6045
Brown, Nancy/NYC/(212) 924-9105 . . . . **page 358**
Brown, Owen/134 W. 29th St., NYC . . . . (212) 947-9470
Brown, Skip/1720 21st St., N.W., Wash. D.C. . . . . (202) 234-3187
Brown, Steven/465 W. 23rd St., NYC . . . . (212) 243-2474
Brown, Thomas Toohey/Penllyn . . . . (215) 628-3332
Browne, Robert/NYC . . . . (212) 601-5191
Brownell, David/Main St., Andover . . . . (603) 735-6440
Brt Photo Illustrations/911 State St., Lancaster . . . . (717) 393-0918
Bruce, Brad, Inc./Beaver Falls . . . . (412) 846-2776
Bruderer, Rolf/NYC/(212) 535-2751 . . . . **pages 172-173**
Bruel, Jean-Yves Inc./400 McGill St., Montréal . . . . (514) 398-9595
Bruml, Kathy/201 W. 77th St., NYC . . . . (212) 874-5659
Brundage, Kip/NYC . . . . (212) 725-3806
Bruno Photography, Inc./NYC/(212) 925-2929 . . . . **pages 282-283**
Bry, Knut/NYC . . . . (212) 925-8333
Bryan, Bob/10 W. 18th St., NYC . . . . (212) 989-2595
Bryant, Bob Jr./270 Convent Ave., NYC . . . . (212) 368-9392
Bryce, Sherman/NYC . . . . (212) 475-0292
Bubbenmoyer, Kevin/Orefield . . . . (215) 395-9167
Buceta, Jaime/56 W. 22nd St., NYC . . . . (212) 807-8485
Buchanan, Robert/56 Lafayette Ave., White Plains . . . . (914) 948-9260
Buchler, Raphaël/NYC . . . . (212) 260-0112
Buck, Bruce/39 W. 14th St., NYC . . . . (212) 645-1022
Buckler, Susanne/NYC . . . . (212) 279-0043
Buckley, Dana/156 Waverly Pl., NYC . . . . (212) 206-1807
Buckmaster, Adrian/332 W. 87th St., NYC . . . . (212) 799-7318
Buckner, Bill/38 Green St., NYC . . . . (212) 941-1204
Budde, John/NYC . . . . (212) 533-3138
Bugzester, Mark/NYC . . . . (212) 925-8333
Buhl Studio, Inc./114 Green St., NYC . . . . (212) 274-0100
Building Images/153 W. 18th St., NYC . . . . (212) 255-1723
Bullaty, Sonja/336 Central Park W., NYC . . . . (212) 663-2122
Burdick, Garry/Nine Parker Hill, Brookfield . . . . (203) 775-2894
Burke, John/60 K St., Boston . . . . (617) 269-6677
Burklin, Bruno/873 Broadway, NYC . . . . (212) 420-0208
Burnett, David/NYC/(212) 683-2002 . . . . **pages 288-289**
Burns, Tom/534 W. 35th St., NYC . . . . (212) 927-4678
Burquez, Felizardo/22-63 38th St., Astoria . . . . (718) 274-6139
Burrell, Fred/25 Shadyside Ave., Nyack . . . . (914) 358-4902
Burtnett, James/12221 Cedar Hill Dr., Silver Spring . . . . (301) 622-3366
Bush, Nan/135 Watts St., NYC . . . . (212) 226-0814
Buss, Gary/NYC . . . . (212) 663-8330
Buzoianu, Peter/32-15 41st St., L.I.C. . . . . (718) 278-2456
Byers, Bruce/NYC/(212) 242-5846 . . . . **pages 50-51**
Byrnes, Charles/NYC/(212) 473-3366 . . . . **pages 174-185, 578-579, Vol. I pages 272-276**
Cabrera, Alejandro/NYC . . . . (212) 925-8333
Cadge, Jeff/NYC/(212) 563-0547 . . . . **pages 106-107**
Cahill, Joseph/636 Ave. of the Americas, NYC . . . . (212) 751-0529
Cailor/Resnick/NYC/(212) 977-4300 . . . . **pages 226-227**
Cal, Mario Photography/31 W. 21st St., NYC . . . . (212) 366-5047
Cala, Tony/NYC/(212) 447-0666 . . . . **page 337**
Callis, Chris/NYC . . . . (212) 243-0231
Camera Communications/130 E. 67th St., NYC . . . . (212) 371-6770
Camera Five, Inc./Six W. 20th St., NYC . . . . (212) 989-2004
Camp, Woodfin & Assocs./NYC . . . . (212) 481-6900
Campbell, Barbara/NYC/(212) 929-5620 . . . . **pages 148-149**
Campos, John Studio, Inc./NYC . . . . (212) 675-0601
Cannon, Gregory/51 MacDougal St., NYC . . . . (800) 727-1807
Cantor, Fredrich/338 W. 11th St., NYC . . . . (212) 691-2502
Cantor, Phil/75 Ninth Ave., NYC . . . . (212) 243-1143
Cape Scapes/542 Higgins Crowell Rd., W. Yarmouth . . . . (617) 362-8222
Caplan, Skip/NYC/(212) 463-0541 . . . . **pages 364-365**
Capri, Frank/3201 Wisconsin N.W., Wash. D.C. . . . . (202) 362-1885
Caputo, Elise & Assocs./NYC/(212) 725-0503 . . . . **pages 208-211**
Caravaglia, Tom/830 Broadway, NYC . . . . (212) 260-4840
Carbone's, Fred Studio Six/1041 Buttonwood St., Phila. . . . . (215) 236-2266
Cardacino, Michael/20 Ridge Rd., Douglaston . . . . (718) 224-0426
Carlson Emberling Studio/Nine E. 19th St., NYC . . . . (212) 473-5130
Carlton, Chuck/1041 Buttonwood, Phila. . . . . (215) 236-2266
Carol, David J./Glen Cove . . . . (516) 674-9534
Carmel/NYC . . . . (212) 925-6216
Carp, Stan/NYC/(212) 362-4000 . . . . **pages 160-161**

Carr, E.J./236 W. 27th St. E., NYC .... (212) 242-0818
Carraway, Tommy/34 E. 30th St., NYC .... (212) 213-2092
Carroll, Don/NYC .... (212) 219-2824
Carroll, Mary Claire/Richmond .... (802) 434-2312
Carron, Les/15 W. 24th St., NYC .... (212) 255-8250
Carstens, Don/2121 N. Lovegrove St., Balt. .... (301) 385-3049
Casanas, Richard/73 W. 82nd St., NYC .... (212) 874-2445
Case, Derek/60 Sumach St., Toronto .... (416) 864-1314
Casey, Judith Inc./96 Fifth Ave., NYC .... (212) 255-3252
Casey, Marge & Assocs./NYC/(212) 486-9575 .... **pages 137-145**
Cashin, Art/Five W. 19th St., NYC .... (212) 627-9476
Cass, Bob Studio/40 W. 17th St., NYC .... (212) 727-9302
Castelli, Charles/41 Union Sq. W., NYC .... (212) 620-5536
Castronovo, John/147 Fairview Ave., Boonton .... (201) 227-4646
Cates, Gwendolen/NYC .... (212) 633-2050
Cattan Photograpics/20 W. 20th St., NYC .... (212) 243-3281
Cattoni, Renzo/One Gorevale Ave., Toronto .... (416) 364-6534
Cattroll Ritcey Photo/335 Catherine ST., Ottawa .... (613) 235-3686
Caverly, Kat/504 W. 48th St., NYC .... (212) 757-8388
Cazzaniga, Luigi/393 W. Broadway, NYC .... (212) 219-8567
Celnick, Eddie/36 E. 12th St., NYC .... (212) 420-9326
Cenicola, Tony/325 W. 37th St., NYC .... (212) 695-0773
Center for Nature Photography/P.O. Box 118, Riverdale .... (914) 968-7163
Century Reproductions/682 Howard Ave., New Haven .... (203) 777-7288
Cerniglio, Tom/1115 E. Main, Rochester .... (716) 654-8561
Chadman Studios/595-603 Newbury St., Boston .... (617) 262-3800
Chakmakjian, Paul/35 W. 36th St., NYC .... (212) 563-3195
Chalifour, Benoît/4297 Redwood, Montréal .... (514) 620-6487
Chalkin, Dennis/NYC .... (212) 929-1036
Chan, Amos T.S./NYC .... (212) 219-0574
Chan, John/225 E. 49th St., NYC .... (212) 755-3816
Chan, Michael/22 E. 21st St., NYC .... (212) 460-8030
Chaney, Scott/NYC/(212) 924-8440 .... **pages 290-291**
Chanteau, Pierre/80 Warren St., NYC .... (212) 227-4931
Chapman, Peter/254 W. Foster St., Melrose .... (617) 662-5462
Chappell, Eric J./Hampton Falls .... (603) 772-6026
Charles, Bill/148 W. 23rd St., NYC .... (212) 627-8012
Charles, F./254 Park Ave. S., NYC .... (212) 505-0686
Charles, Lisa/NYC .... (212) 807-8600
Charlus/NYC .... (212) 260-0112
Chatelain, Alex/Suffern .... (212) 924-0750
Chen, Paul C., Inc./133 Fifth Ave., NYC .... (212) 674-4100
Chen, Ray/1420 Notre Dame St. W., Montréal .... (514) 931-2203
Chernush, Kay/3855 N. 30th St., Arlington .... (703) 528-1195
Chesnut, Richard/236 W. 27th St., NYC .... (212) 255-1790
Chevallier, Pascal/NYC .... (212) 260-0112
Chin, Mark/251 W. 19th St., NYC .... (212) 243-0864
Chin, Ted/NYC/(212) 947-3858 .... **pages 404-405**
Chin, Walter/NYC .... (212) 924-6760
Chokel, Dan/147 W. 25th St., NYC .... (212) 989-0944
Choroszewski, Walter J./1310 Orchard Dr., Somerville .... (201) 369-3555
Christensen, Paul/NYC/(212) 279-2838 .... **pages 300-301**
Christie, Chris/119 W. 22nd St., NYC .... (212) 691-8331
Chrynwski, Walter/154 W. 18th St., NYC .... (212) 675-1906
Chwatsky, Ann/85 Andover Rd., Rockville Centre .... (516) 766-2417
Cicero-Donnelly/854 N. Prince St., Lancaster .... (717) 392-5752
Cipolla, Karen/NYC/(212) 619-6114 .... **pages 100-101**
City Limit Productions/80 Wheeler Ave., Pleasantville .... (914) 747-1422
Clark, Kevin/900 Broadway, NYC .... (212) 460-9360
Clark, Sandy/4414 Millstone Ct., Jacksonville .... (904) 268-1736
Clarke, Jeff/266 Pine St., Burlington .... (802) 863-4393
Clarke, John Patrick/St. James .... (516) 584-6115
Clarke, Kevin/900 Broadway, NYC .... (212) 460-9360
Clarke, Marna G./140 Huyshope Ave., Hartford .... (203) 247-8228
Cleff, Bernie/715 Pine St., Phila. .... (215) 922-4246
Clemens, Clint/256 Marginal St., Boston .... (617) 567-0303
Clemens, Peter Russell/153 Sidney St., Oyster Bay .... (516) 922-1759
Clifford, Geoffrey/NYC/(212) 486-9575 .... **pages 144-145**
Clough, Terry/147 W. 25th St., NYC .... (212) 255-3040
Clymer, Jonathan/180 F Central Ave., Englewood .... (201) 568-1760
Cobb, Jan/NYC/(212) 255-1400 .... **page 196**
Cobin, Martin, Inc./145 E. 49th St., NYC .... (212) 758-5742
Cockrell, Jeré/13-17 Laight St., NYC .... (212) 925-6314

Coggin, Roy/64 W. 21st St., NYC ... (212) 929-6262
Cohen, James/36 E. 20th St., NYC ... (212) 533-4400
Cohen, Ken/441 Park Ave. S., NYC ... (212) 779-4861
Cohen, Leonard/130 E. Glenside Ave., Wyncote ... (215) 886-1625
Cohen, Marc David/NYC ... (212) 741-0015
Cohen, Rena/NYC ... (212) 420-0133
Cohn, Ric/NYC/(212) 924-4450 ... **pages 98-99**
Colabella, Vincent/304 E. 41st St., NYC ... (212) 949-7456
Colavecchio, Bob/3 Parkside Dr., Belleville ... (201) 759-2711
Cole, Randy/NYC/(212) 679-5933 ... **pages 190-193**
Cole, Vicki, Inc./134 Spring St., NYC ... (212) 431-1212
Coleman, Gene/250 W. 27th St., NYC ... (212) 691-4752
Colen, Corinne/NYC/(212) 431-7425 ... **pages 258-259**
Collier, Terry/441 Queen St. E., Toronto ... (416) 869-3155
Collins, Benton/NYC/(212) 925-8750 ... **pages 218-219**
Collins, Chris/NYC/(212) 297-0041 ... **pages 168-169**
Collins, Fred Studios, Inc./300 W. Main St., Stamford ... (203) 348-1010
Collins, Joe Jefferson/208 Garfield Pl., Bklyn. ... (212) 965-4836
Color Express/8 E. 36th St., NYC ... (212) 689-0002
Colton, Bob/1700 York Ave., NYC ... (212) 831-3953
ComPixCo Inc./45 W. 17th St., NYC ... (212) 675-1202
Comet, Renée/410 Eighth St. N.W., Wash. D.C. ... (202) 347-3408
Commercial Graphics, Inc./257 Park Ave. S., NYC ... (212) 477-9100
Comte, Michael/NYC ... (212) 243-5340
Conaty, Jim/Robins St., Hanscom Field E., Bedford ... (617) 274-8200
Conter, Holt/2016 Franklin Pl., Wyomissing ... (215) 678 0131
Conlon, Jean/NYC/(212) 966-9897 ... **pages 60-63**
Contarsy, Ron/275 W. 96th St., NYC ... (212) 678-0660
Contrino, Tom/NYC ... (212) 947-4450
Cook, Angie/NYC ... (212) 260-0112
Cook, Rod/NYC/(212) 995-0100 ... **pages 368-369**
Cooke, Colin/380 Lafayette St., NYC ... (212) 254-5090
Coolidge, Jeffrey/322 Summer St., Boston ... (617) 338-6869
Cooper, John F. Photography, Inc./One Bank St., Summit ... (201) 273-0368
Cooper, Steve/5 W. 31st St., NYC ... (212) 279-4543
Coppes, Michael/Pittsburgh ... (412) 372-1395
Corbett, Jane/303 Park Ave. S., NYC ... (212) 505-1177
Corbo, Sal/18 E. 18th St.., NYC ... (212) 242-3748
Cordoza, Tony/15 W. 18th St., NYC ... (212) 243-8441
Cornelia & Friends/NYC/(212) 732-6240 ... **pages 354-355**
Cornish, Dan/222 Valley Pl., Mamaroneck ... (914) 698-4060
Cornu, Alain/3704 Laval Ave., Montréal ... (514) 845-5888
Cornwell, David/NYC ... (212) 772-0346
Corona Productions /N.Y., Inc./Ten W. 33rd St., NYC ... (212) 239-4990
Coshof, Karen/63 Prince Arthur St. E., Montréal ... (514) 842-1393
Cosimo/43 W. 13th St., NYC ... (212) 206-1818
Cosm Studio, Inc./NYC/(212) 691-1000 ... **page 372**
Coté, Sylvain/1435 Bleury, Montréal ... (514) 845-8828
Coughlin, Suki/Main St., New London ... (603) 526-4645
Coulter, David W./Delaware Water Gap ... (717) 424-1357
Coupon, William/69 Murray St., NYC ... (212) 619-7473
Couzens, Larry/16 E. 17th St., NYC ... (212) 620-9790
Cowan, Frank Studio, Inc./Patterson ... (914) 878-6104
Cox, David/25 Mercer St., NYC ... (212) 925-0734
Craig, Stuart/381 Fifth Ave., NYC ... (212) 683-5475
Crane, Chris/31 W. 31st St., NYC ... (212) 206-0966
Crane, Hyla/119 W. 22nd St., NYC ... (212) 255-2330
Crane, Tom/113 Cumberland Pl., Bryn Mawr ... (215) 525-2444
Crawford, Neelon/Ten E. 23rd St., NYC ... (212) 475-7808
Creative Club of Boston, The/155 Massachusetts Ave., Boston ... (617) 536-8999
Crecco, Michael/NYC/(212) 682-3422 ... **pages 74-75**
Creighton, Kathleen/102 Hall St., Bklyn. ... (718) 857-9267
Crespo, David/34-15 12th St., L.I.C. ... (718) 937-4579
Criterion Photo/31 E. 28th St., NYC ... (212) 725-2627
Croes, Larry/256 Charles St., Waltham ... (617) 894-4897
Cronin, Casey/115 Wooster St., NYC ... (212) 334-9253
Croydon, Peter/70 McGee St., Toronto ... (416) 463-6230
Crum, John R./124 W. 24th St., NYC ... (212) 463-8663
Crum, Lee/NYC/(212) 953-0088 ... **pages 440-441**
Crutchfield, Karl V., Inc./301 W. 125th St., NYC ... (212) 662-8225
Cruz, John J./539 Bergen St., Bklyn ... (718) 783-0517
Cuesta, Michael/NYC/(212) 929-5519 ... **pages 294-295**
Cuevas, Robert/118 E. 28th St., NYC ... (212) 679-0622

Cuington & Wier/36 W. 25th St., NYC	(212) 691-1901
Culberson, Earl/NYC/(212) 473-3366	**pages 174-177**
Cullom, Ellen/55 E. Ninth St., NYC	(212) 777-1749
Cunningham, Christopher/Nine East St., Boston	(617) 542-4640
Cunningham, Daniel/304 E. 81st. St., NYC	(212) 772-1942
Cunningham, Peter/214 Sullivan St., NYC	(212) 475-4866
Curatola, Tony Studio/18 E. 17th St., NYC	(212) 243-5478
Curtis, John/50 Melcher St., Boston	(617) 451-9117
Cushner, Susie Photography/354 Congress St., Boston	(617) 542-4070
Cutler, Craig/39 Walker St., NYC	(212) 966-1652
Czepiga, David J./101 Fitzrandolph Ave., Hamilton	(609) 396-2976
D'Innocenzo, Paul/568 Broadway, NYC	(212) 925-9622
D'Orio, Tony/NYC/(212) 473-3366	**pages 184-185**
D.A.C Photography/62A E. Blackwell St., Dover	(201) 989-1421
DE Paul, Raymond/529 W. 42nd St., NYC	(212) 967-0831
Dagrosa, Terry/NYC/(212) 254-4254	**pages 368-369**
Dale Camera Graphics/12 W. 27th St., NYC	(212) 696-9440
Daley, James Dee/568 Broadway, NYC	(212) 925-7192
Daley, Katie/245 W. 29th St., NYC	(212) 465-2420
Danello, Peter Jr./386 Kerrigan Blvd., Newark	(201) 371-5899
Dantuono, Paul F./433 Park Ave. S., NYC	(212) 683-5778
Datoli, Michael/121 W. 17th St., NYC	(212) 633-1672
Dauman, Henri/4 E. 88th St., NYC	(212) 860-3804
Davidson, Bruce/NYC	(212) 475-7600
Davidson, Cameron/5316 Admirality Ct., Alexandria	(703) 922-3922
Davidson, Rob & Associates/390 Dupont St., Toronto	(416) 922-5212
Davies, Nora/370 E. 76th St., NYC	(212) 628-6657
Davis, Dick/400 E. 59th St., NYC	(212) 751-3276
Davis, Harold/299 Pavonia Ave., Jersey City	(201) 659-4554
Davis, James/159 Walnut St., Montclair	(201) 746-6972
Davis, Micheal/49 Summit Rd., Holbrook	(617) 767-0780
Davis, Richard/17 E. 16th St., NYC	(212) 675-2428
Davis, Rick/9-210 Carter Dr., West Chester	(215) 436-6050
Davis, Rik/151 W. 19th St., NYC	(212) 206-9333
Day, Donna/486 Broadway, NYC	(212) 219-8632
Day, Joel/421 W. Walnut St., Lancaster	(717) 291-7228
Day, Michael/264 Seaton St., Toronto	(416) 920-9135
Day, Olita/239 Park Ave. S., NYC	(212) 673-9354
De Leon, Martin/286 Fifth Ave., NYC	(212) 714-9777
De Lorenzo, Bob/211 Stewart St., Princeton	(609) 586-2421
De Melo Studio, Inc./126 W. 22nd St., NYC	(212) 929-0507
De Vlieger, Mary/2109 Broadway, NYC	(212) 903-4321
De Zitter, Harry/Six Jane St., NYC	(212) 989-7074
DeCunzo, Michael/5 West 19th St., NYC	(212) 741-0015
DeFever Productions, Ltd./157 Chambers St., NYC	(212) 227-3587
DeGrado, Drew/37 Midland Ave., Elmwood	(201) 797-2890
DeLeon, Katrina/NYC	(212) 279-2838
DeLessio, Len/121 E. 12th St., NYC	(212) 353-1774
DeLucia, Ralph/120 E. Hartsdale Ave., Hartsdale	(914) 472-2253
DeMicco, David Studio/40 W. 17th St., NYC	(212) 627-4074
DeMilt, Ronald/873 Broadway, NYC	(212) 228-5321
DePra, Nancy/15 W. 24th St., NYC	(212) 242-0252
DeSantis, Stephen/85 E. Tenth St., NYC	(212) 228-7315
DeSanto, Thom/116 W. 29th St., NYC	(212) 967-1390
DeVito, Bart J./Ninham Rd., Carmel	(914) 225-7464
DeVito, Michael Studio Ltd./NYC	(212) 243-5267
DeVoe, Marcus/34 E. 81st St., NYC	(212) 737-9073
DeWan, Michael/NYC	(212) 371-0739
Dean, Floyd, Inc./2-B S. Poplar St., Wilmington	(302) 655-7193
Deane, John/529 W. 42nd St., NYC	(212) 563-3054
Delmas, Didier/1 Mill St., Burlington	(802) 862-0120
Delp, David/230 Central Park S., NYC	(212) 245-8849
Delsol, Michel/250 W. 26th St., NYC	(212) 807-8370
Demarchelier, Patrick/Four W. 58th St., NYC	(212) 935-0200
Dempsey-Hart, Jonathan/241 A St., Boston	(617) 338-6661
Denbo, Robert Forox Photography Studio/135 W. 29th St., NYC	(212) 465-2297
Denison, Bill/302 Thornhill Rd., Balt.	(301) 323-1114
Denker, Deborah/460 Greenwich St., NYC	(212) 219-9263
Denner, Manuel/249 W. 29th St., NYC	(212) 947-6220
Denson, Walt/70 W. 83rd St., NYC	(212) 496-7305
Denuto, Ellen/NYC	(212) 663-8330
Derr, Stephen/420 W. 45th St., NYC	(212) 246-5920
Des Fontaines, Thierry/NYC	(212) 925-5909

Des Verges, Diana/NYC . . . . (212) 691-8674
Deschamps, Pierre-Oliver/NYC . . . . (212) 260-0112
Dessarzin, John/40 Riverside Dr., NYC . . . . (212) 769-1787
Desvergers, Diana/73 Fifth Ave., NYC . . . . (212) 691-8674
Devine, Dan/Leesport . . . . (215) 926-6631
Devlieger, Mary/2109 Broadway, NYC . . . . (212) 903-4321
Di Micco, David/40 W. 17th St., NYC . . . . (212) 627-4074
DiBartolo, Joe/NYC/(212) 297-0041 . . . . **pages 46-47, 168-171, 562-563, 664-667**
DiBartolo/Lemkowitz/NYC/(212) 297-0041 . . . . **pages 46-47, 168-171, 562-563, 664-667**
DiMaggio, Joe/512 Adams St., Centerport . . . . (516) 271-6133
DiPetto, John/245 E. 54th St., NYC . . . . (212) 935-4762
Diamant, Rouge/519 Broadway, NYC . . . . (212) 614-0435
Diamond, Joe/915 West End Ave., NYC . . . . (212) 316-5295
Diaz, Jorge/142 W. 24th St., NYC . . . . (212) 675-4783
Dibue, Robert Studio, Inc./NYC . . . . (212) 206-0860
Dick, David/138 W. 25th St., NYC . . . . (212) 633-1780
Dickson, Nigel/60 Sumach St., Toronto . . . . (416) 864-1314
Dictenberg, Robin/NYC/(212) 473-3366 . . . . **pages 174-185, 578**
Diebold, George/416 Bloomfield Ave., Montclair . . . . (201) 744-5789
Diparisi, Peter/250 W. 99th St., NYC . . . . (212) 663-8330
Dodge, Jeff/133 Eighth Ave., NYC . . . . (212) 620-9652
Dojc, Yuri/74 Bathurst St., Toronto . . . . (416) 366-8081
Dole, Jody/NYC/(212) 953-0088 . . . . **pages 442-443**
Dolgins, Alan/1390 Market St., S.F. . . . . (415) 626-7905
Dollard, Bob/6 Hull Ave., Annapolis . . . . (301) 268-3331
Dominion-Wide Photographs Ltd./Ottawa . . . . (613) 725-2151
Dominis, John/252 W. 102nd St., NYC . . . . (212) 222-9890
Dorf, Myron/205 W. 19th St., NYC . . . . (212) 255-2020
Dorman, Paul/NYC . . . . (212) 826-6737
Dorot, Didier/48 W. 21st St., NYC . . . . (212) 206-1608
Dorr, Chuck/291 Church St., NYC . . . . (212) 727-7300
Dorrance, Scott/131 E. 23rd St., NYC . . . . (212) 529-4030
Dorskind, Cheryl Machat/15A Baycrest Ave., Westhampton . . . . (516) 288-0829
Douglass, Jim/5161 River Rd., Bethesda . . . . (301) 652-1303
Dresner, Harvey/202-26 45th Ave., Bayside . . . . (718) 225-2332
Drexler, Steven/175 Woodard Ave., Buffalo . . . . (716) 834-1344
Dreyer, Peter/916 Pleasant St., Norwood . . . . (617) 762-8550
Drivas, Joe/15 Beacon Ave., Staten Island . . . . (718) 667-0696
Duane, Dick/48 Great Jones St., NYC . . . . (212) 260-0230
Dubin, Nancy/347 E. 58th St., NYC . . . . (212) 355-5887
Dubler, Douglas Photography/162 E. 92nd St., NYC . . . . (212) 410-6300
Duchaine, Randy/200 W. 18th St., NYC . . . . (212) 243-4371
Ducoté, Kim/NYC/(212) 989-3680 . . . . **pages 328-329**
Dugaw, Susi/8 S. Main St., Portchester . . . . (914) 939-4459
Duke, Dana/NYC . . . . (212) 260-3334
Dunas, Jeff/NYC/(212) 242-1266 . . . . **page 337**
Dunn, Paul/28 Southpoint Dr., S. Sandwich . . . . (508) 420-5511
Dunn, Phoebe/20 Silvermine Rd., New Canaan . . . . (203) 966-9791
Dunning, Hank/50 W. 22nd St., NYC . . . . (212) 627-1880
Dunning, Robert/57 W. 58th St., NYC . . . . (212) 688-0788
Dunoff, Rich/1313 Delmont Ave., Phila. . . . . (215) 642-6137
Dunwell, Steve/20 Winchester St., Boston . . . . (617) 423-4916
Durrance, Dick II/NYC . . . . (212) 749-6382
Dvonch & Seger/1325 Fifth Ave., Pittsburgh . . . . (412) 471-4884
Dwiggins, Gene/204 Westminster St., Providence . . . . (401) 421-6466
Ealovega, Chuck/NYC . . . . (212) 683-2002
Earle, John/Cambridge . . . . (617) 628-1454
Eastep, Wayne/443 Park Ave. South, NYC . . . . (212) 686-8404
Eastern Light Photography/113 Arch St., Phila. . . . . (215) 238-0655
Eaton, Roger/NYC . . . . (212) 598-4473
Ecclef, Andre/NYC . . . . (212) 779-3600
Eckerle, Tom/32 Union Sq. East, NYC . . . . (212) 677-3635
Eckstein, Ed/234 Fifth Ave., NYC . . . . (212) 685-9342
Edahl, Ed/236 W. 27th St., NYC . . . . (212) 929-2002
Edelman IV, Harry R./2790 McCully Rd., Allison Park . . . . (412) 486-8822
Edge, Dennis/235 Peel St., Montréal . . . . (514) 871-1936
Edgeworth, Anthony/130 Madison Ave., NYC . . . . (212) 679-6031
Edmunds, Douglas/126 W. 22nd St., NYC . . . . (212) 627-4040
Edson, Franz/26 Watch Way, Huntington . . . . (516) 692-4345
Edson, Steve/Boston/(617) 924-2212 . . . . **pages 108-109**
Egan, Jim/150 Chestnut St., Providence . . . . (401) 331-6220
Egermayer, Michael/292 Clinton Ave., Brooklyn . . . . (718) 398-6844
Eggers, Claus/900 Broadway, NYC . . . . (212) 243-6811

Eguiguren, Carlos/139 E. 57th St., NYC .... (212) 888-6732
Ehrlich, George/New Hampton .... (914) 355-1757
Einzig Photographers, Inc./236 W. 26th St., NYC .... (212) 246-4074
Eisenberg, Leonard J./85 Wallingford Rd., Brighton .... (617) 787-3366
Eisenberg, Steve, Inc./448 W. 37th St, NYC .... (212) 563-2061
Ekmekji, Raffi/377 Park Ave South, NYC .... (212) 696-5577
Elkins, Joel/Eight Minkel Rd., Ossining .... (212) 941-0168
Ella, Inc/Boston/(617) 266-3858 .... **pages 430-433**
Ellman, Faye/270 W. 25th St., NYC .... (212) 243-3759
Elmore, Steve/60 E. 42nd St., NYC .... (212) 472-2463
Elmy, Ron/56 The Esplanade, Toronto .... (416) 363-7081
Elness, Jack/236 W. 26st St., NYC .... (212) 242-5045
Elson, Paul/NYC .... (212) 692-9254
Elz, Barry/68 Thomas St., NYC .... (212) 962-0037
Emerson, John/511 W. 33rd St., NYC .... (212) 268-1704
Emmott, Bob/700 S. Tenth St., Phila. .... (215) 925-2773
Emrich, Bill/448 W. 19th St., NYC .... (212) 889-7482
Endress, John Paul/254 W. 31st St., NYC .... (212) 736-7800
Engel, Mary/NYC .... (212) 580-1051
Englander, Maury/43 Fifth Ave., NYC .... (212) 242-9777
Englert, Michael/142 W. 24th St., NYC .... (212) 243-3446
Ephemara, Inc./Rowley .... (617) 926-7987
Epstein Photography, Inc./295 Silver St., Agawam .... (413) 789-3320
Erika Groeschel, Inc./114 E. 32nd St., NYC .... (212) 685-3291
Errico, Jerry/80 Wheeler Ave., Pleasantville .... (914) 747-1422
Erwitt, Elliott/88 Central Park W., NYC .... (212) 799-6767
Essel, Robert/39 W. 71st St., NYC .... (212) 877-5228
Evans, Lance/330 E. 63rd St., NYC .... (212) 752-8316
Evans, Richard/25 Lafayette Ave., Brooklyn .... (718) 797-0379
Everett, Michael Photog., Ltd./27 W. 15th St., NYC .... (212) 243-0627
Excalibur Photo Graphics, Inc./300 E. 42nd St., NYC .... (212) 949-1300
Exley, Jonathan/NYC .... (212) 447-2500
Exit Productions/NYC/(212) 925-8750 .... **pages 218-219**
Eyle, Nicolas/205 Onondaga Ave., Syracuse .... (315) 422-6231
Eyre, Susan/Brooklyn .... (718) 282-5034
F-90, Inc./60 Sindle Ave., Little Falls .... (201) 785-9090
F/Stop Pictures, Inc./283 Kirk Meadow Rd., Springfield .... (802) 885-5261
Fallon, Kevin/2586 Fernwood Ave., Abington .... (215) 885-2222
Famighetti, Thomas/40 W. 24th St., NYC .... (212) 255-8334
Fanelli, Robert/2276 Mt. Carmel Ave., Glenside .... (215) 572-7399
Faraghan, George/940 N. Delaware Ave., Phila. .... (215) 928-0499
Farber, Enid/1770 Church St. Station, NYC .... (201) 451-6744
Farber, Robert/207A E. 62nd St., NYC .... (212) 486-9090
Faria, Rui/304 Eighth Ave., NYC .... (212) 929-2993
Farrell, Bill/343 E. 30th St., NYC .... (212) 683-1425
Farrell, John William/189 Second Ave., NYC .... (212) 460-9001
Fatta, C. Studio/25 Dry Dock Ave., Boston .... (617) 423-6638
Faulkner, Robert I./14 Elizabeth Ave., East Brunswick .... (201) 390-6650
Fay, Stephen Studios/128 Roaring Brook Rd., Chappaqua .... (914) 238-3122
FayFoto, Inc./45 Electric Ave., Boston .... (617) 267-2000
Feder, Ted/65 Bleecker St., NYC .... (212) 505-8700
Feiling, Dave/1941 Teall Ave., Syracuse .... (315) 437-7059
Feinstein, Gary/NYC .... (212) 242-3373
Feldman, Robert/NYC/(212) 243-7319 .... **pages 54-55**
Fellerman, Stan/NYC .... (212) 243-0027
Fellman, Sandi/548 Broadway, NYC .... (212) 925-5187
Feraulo, Richard/760 Plain St., Marshfield .... (617) 837-9563
Fernsell, Robin/Boston/(617) 720-4400 .... **pages 360-363**
Ferorelli, Enrico/50 W. 29th St., NYC .... (212) 685-8181
Ferrari, Maria/37 W. 20th St., NYC .... (212) 924-1241
Ferri, Mark/463 Broome St., NYC .... (212) 431-1356
Ferrino, Paul/Milford .... (203) 878-4785
Fery, Guy/NYC/(212) 371-9771 .... **pages 242-243**
Fetter, Frank/232 Spring St., Redbank .... (201) 530-8613
Feurer, Hans/NYC .... (212) 924-6760
Fidner, David/NYC .... (212) 243-2750
Field, Pat/16 E. 23rd St., NYC .... (212) 477-9016
Fields, Bruce/71 Greene St., NYC .... (212) 431-8852
Figliozzi, Stephen M./1733 20th St. N.W., Wash. D.C. .... (202) 328-9304
Filipe, Tony/239 A St., Boston .... (617) 542-8330
Findel, Stefan/286 Fifth Ave., NYC .... (212) 279-2838
Findlay, Christine/Hazlet .... (201) 264-2211
Fine, Peter M./115 Crosby St., NYC .... (212) 431-9776

Fine, Ron/8600 Long Acre Ct., Wash. D.C.	(301) 469-7960
Finkelman, Allan/118 E. 28th St., NYC	(212) 684-3487
Finlay, Alastair/13-17 Laight St., NYC	(212) 334-8001
Firestein, Conrad/Eight E. 96th St., NYC	(212) 831-4846
Firman, John/434 E. 75th St., NYC	(212) 794-2794
First Impressions/Morgantown	(215) 286-6500
First Light Assoc./78 Rusholme Rd., Toronto	(416) 532-6108
Fischer, Bob/135 E. 54th St., NYC	(212) 755-2131
Fischer, Carl/NYC/(212) 794-0400	**pages 186-187**
Fischer, Ken/NYC/(212) 794-0400	**pages 186-187**
Fishbein Studio/50 W. 17th St., NYC	(212) 675-4900
Fisher, Al Photography, Inc./601 Newbury St., Boston	(617) 536-7126
Fisher, Bob Inc./14406 Madison Ave., Pierrefonds	(514) 620-4040
Fishman, Robert/153 W. 27th St., NYC	(212) 620-7976
Fiterman Studio/1415 Bayard St., Balt.	(301) 625-1265
Flanigan, Jim/1325 N. Fifth St., Phila.	(215) 236-4448
Flatow, Carl/20 E. 30th St., NYC	(212) 683-8688
Flowers, Morocco/520 Harrison Ave., Boston	(617) 426-3692
Flynn, Matt/99 W. 27th St., NYC	(212) 627-2985
Foldes, Peter/250 St. Paul E., Montréal	(514) 397-9202
Foley, Paul/791 Tremont St., Boston	(617) 266-9336
Folio, Inc./3417 ½ M. St. N.W., Wash. D.C.	(202) 965-2410
Fonteyne, Carel/NYC	(212) 370-4300
Fonyo, Andrea/350 E. 57th St., NYC	(212) 759-5089
Foote, James/22 Tomac Ave., Old Greenwich	(203) 637-3228
Forastieri, Marili/426 W. Broadway, NYC	(212) 431-1840
Forbes, Peter/916 N. Charles St., Balt.	(301) 727-8800
Ford, Carol/NYC	(212) 779-3600
Ford, Charles/NYC	(212) 925-8333
Forelli, Chip/NYC/(212) 564-1835	**pages 102-103**
Fornuff, Doug Studios, Inc./323 Park Ave. S., NYC	(212) 529-4440
Forrest, Bob/273 Fifth Ave., NYC	(212) 288-4458
Forsyth, Alfred W./19 W. 21st St., NYC	(212) 627-4060
Foster, Frank/61 North Rd., W. Harwich	(617) 432-1270
Foster, Nicholas/143 Claremont Rd., Bernardsville	(201) 766-7526
Foster, Peter/870 United Nations Plz., NYC	(212) 593-0793
Fotiades, Bill & Assoc./952 Rose Hill Rd., Water Mill	(516) 726-4773
Foto Expression International/27 St. Clair E., Toronto	(416) 665-8459
Fotowerke Int'l./4064 St. Lawrence Blvd., Montréal	(514) 288-6693
Foulke, Douglas/NYC/(212) 243-0822	**pages 252-253**
Fournier, Frank/NYC	(212) 725-3806
Fox, Jeffrey/Six W. 20th St., NYC	(212) 620-0147
Frakes, Bill/NYC/(212) 905-8400	**pages 146-147**
Frame, Bob/225 Lafayette, NYC	(212) 431-6707
Francekevich, Al/73 Fifth Ave., NYC	(212) 691-7456
Frances, Leslie/41 Vickson Ct., Islington	(416) 237-1452
Francisco, Thomas/21 Quine St., Cranford	(201) 272-1155
Francki, Jo/NYC	(212) 838-3170
Frank, Dick/11 W. 25th St., NYC	(212) 242-4648
Franzos, Stan/5261 Forbes Ave., Pittsburgh	(412) 687-8850
Fraser, Gaylene/211 Thompson St., NYC	(212) 475-5911
Fraser, Renee/1260 Boylston St., Boston	(617) 267-9299
Fraser, Rob/211 Thompson St., NYC	(212) 677-4589
Frattolillo, Rinaldo/360 E. 55th St., NYC	(212) 486-1901
Fredric Studios, Inc./907 Broadway, NYC	(212) 673-3070
Freeze Frame Studio/255 Leonia Ave., Bogota	(201) 343-1233
Freson, Robert/881 7th Ave., NYC	(212) 246-0679
Freund, Bud/1435 Bedford St., Stamford	(203) 359-0147
Fried, Richard/145 E. 22nd St., NYC	(212) 473-9521
Friedman, Benno/26 W. 20th St., NYC	(212) 255-6038
Friedman, Bill/Stamford	(203) 348-8114
Friedman, Carol	(212) 925-4951
Friedman, Jerry/NYC	(212) 505-5600
Friedman, Stuart/1905 N.W. 80th Ave., Margate	(305) 977-4820
Friess, Susan/NYC	(212) 675-3021
Friscia, Salmon/NYC	(212) 228-4134
Froomer, Brett/NYC/(212) 533-3113	**pages 78-81**
Fuhrer, Chuck/339 Blvd. of the Allies, Pittsburgh	(412) 261-4046
Fulton, George/1237 Gadsden St., Columbia	(803) 779-8249
Funk, Mitchell/500 E. 77 St., NYC	(212) 988-2886
Furman, Michael/Phila./(215) 925-4233	**pages 72-73**
Furst, Franz/NYC	(212) 684-0492
Furst, Ina/4670 Waldo Ave., Riverdale	(212) 548-6464

12 **NORTHEAST**

Fuss, Philipp/NYC	(212) 260-0112
G/Q Studios/1217 Spring Garden St., Phila.	(215) 236-7770
Galante, Dennis/NYC	(212) 463-0938
Galante, Jim/676 Broadway, NYC	(212) 529-4300
Gale, Howard/Judy/712 Chestnut St., Phila.	(215) 629-0506
Gallery, Bill/86 South St., Boston	(617) 542-0499
Gallitelli, Michael A./4-A and B Vatrano Rd., Albany	(518) 459-8050
Gallo, Peter/1238 Callowhill St., Phila.	(215) 440-9752
Gallucci, Ed/568 Broadway, NYC	(212) 226-2215
Galton, Beth/NYC/(212) 242-2266	**pages 64-65**
Gamarge Studios/32 Studley St., Brentwood	(516) 273-3390
Gamba, Mark/NYC/(212) 727-8313	**pages 96-97**
Gang, Julie/NYC/(212) 925-3351	**pages 274-275**
Ganges, Halley/370 E. 76th St., NYC	(212) 628-6657
Gannon, Barbara/7 Sleepy Hollow Rd., Essex Jct.	(802) 899-2143
Garbarini Studio/594 Broadway, NYC	(212) 925-1408
Garber Truck Photos/2110 Valley Dr., W. Chester	(215) 692-9076
Garber, Ira/150 Chestnut St., Providence	(401) 274-3723
Garcia, Ray/60 E. 11th St., NYC	(212) 674-5494
Gardner, Charles/12 N. Fourth St., Reading	(215) 376-8086
Gardner, Derek/NYC/(212) 683-2002	**page 287**
Garfield, Peter/7370 MacArthur Blvd., Glen Echo	(301) 229-6800
Garrett, William/NYC	(212) 243-2750
Gaskins, Bill/Phila.	(215) 879-0283
Gaynin, Gail/NYC/(212) 580-3141	**pages 100-101**
Geaney, Tim/NYC	(212) 838-3170
Gebbia, Doreen/312 W. 88th St., NYC	(212) 496-1279
Geiger, Michael/P.O. Box 946, Tillson	(212) 431-5205
Geller, Bonnie S./57 W. 93rd St., NYC	(212) 864-5922
Gelsobello, Paul/245 W. 29th St., NYC	(212) 947-0317
Gemmell, Bill/531 W. 45th St., NYC	(212) 265-2343
Generico, Tony/130 W. 25th St., NYC	(212) 627-9755
Geng, Maud/25 Gray St., Boston	(617) 236-1920
Gensheimer, Frank/Five Lawrence St., Bloomfield	(201) 743-4305
Gensheimer, Rich/3730 Zuck Rd., Erie	(814) 833-8739
George, Michael/525 Hudson St., NYC	(212) 924-5273
George, Sammy/39 83 45th St., Sunnyside	(718) 706-6053
Gerardi, Marcia/NYC	(212) 243-8400
Gershman, Neil/135 W. 29th St., NYC	(212) 629-5877
Gerstein, Jesse/249 W. 29th St., NYC	(212) 370-4300
Gesar Productions/250 W. 57th St., NYC	(212) 713-5164
Gescheidt, Alfred/175 Lexington Ave., NYC	(212) 889-4023
Getz, Jacob/87 Franklin St., NYC	(212) 925-7376
Giandomenico Inc./13 Fern Ave., Collingswood	(215) 625-0322
Giant Photo Inc./200 Park Ave. S., NYC	(212) 477-1792
Gidley, E. Fenton/NYC	(212) 772-0846
Gierszewski, John/1515 Matheson Blvd., Mississauga	(416) 624-1668
Giese, Al/RR1 Box 302, Pound Ridge	(914) 764-4639
Gigli, Ormond/327 E. 58th St., NYC	(212) 758-2860
Giglio, Harry Photography, Inc./925 Penn Ave., Pittsburgh	(412) 261-3338
Gilbert, Gil Inc./29 E. 22nd St., NYC	(212) 254-3096
Gilbert, Thom/NYC	(212) 243-2750
Gillardin, André/Six W. 20th St., NYC	(212) 675-2950
Gillette, Rick/NYC	(212) 925-8333
Ginsburg, Michael/245 E. 19th St., NYC	(212) 677-0167
Giraldi/54 W. 39th St., NYC	(212) 840-8225
Giraldo, Anita/83 Canal St., NYC	(212) 431-1193
Gladstone Studio, The, Ltd./237 E. 20th St., NYC	(212) 777-7772
Glancz, Jeff/NYC	(212) 741-2504
Glaviano, Marco/NYC	(212) 924-6760
Glick, Roberta/126 E. 7th St., NYC	(212) 254-5385
Glinn, Burt/41 Central Park W., NYC	(212) 877-2210
Globus Studios/NYC/(212) 243-1008	**page 264**
Goble, Brian/NYC/(212) 219-0887	**page 265**
Goell, Jon/535 Albany St., Boston	(617) 423-2057
Gold, Bernie/873 Broadway, NYC	(212) 677-0311
Gold, Charles, Inc./56 W. 22nd. St., NYC	(212) 242-2600
Goldberg, Jeff/Mamaroneck	(914) 698-4060
Goldblatt, Steven/32 S. Strawberry St., Phila.	(215) 925-3825
Golden, Bob/Ten Terhune Dr., Hackensack	(201) 343-1060
Goldman, Mel Studio, Inc./329 Newbury, Boston	(617) 536-0539
Goldman, Richard/36 W. 20th St., NYC	(212) 675-3021
Goldmann Management/349 W. 29th St., NYC	(212) 549-5018

Goldring, Barry/NYC/(212) 334-9494 . . . . **pages 348-349**
Goldsmith, Bruce/1 Clayton Ct., Park Ridge . . . . (201) 391-4946
Goldsmith, Lynn/241 W. 36th St., NYC . . . . (212) 736-4602
Goldstein, Alan/702 Gist Ave., Silver Spring . . . . (301) 589-1690
Goldstein, Art/NYC/(212) 966-2682 . . . . **page 376**
Goldstein, Michael/107 W. 69th St., NYC . . . . (212) 874-6933
Goll, Charles R./NYC . . . . (212) 628-4881
Golob, Stanford/10 Waterside Plz., NYC . . . . (212) 532-7166
Gonzalez Studio, Inc./127 W. 26th St., NYC . . . . (212) 242-2202
Gonzalez, Gustavo/13 W. 17th St., NYC . . . . (212) 206-1043
Goodman, Howard/424 Central Ave., Peekskill . . . . (914) 737-1162
Goodman, John D./1 Mill St., Burlington . . . . (802) 864-0200
Goodman, Lou/322 Summer St., Boston . . . . (617) 542-8254
Goodwin, Phyllis/NYC/(212) 570-6021 . . . . **pages 430-433**
Gorchev & Gorchev, Inc./11 Cabot Rd., Woburn . . . . (617) 933-8090
Gordon, David A./1413 Hertel Ave., Buffalo . . . . (716) 833-2661
Gordon, Elliot/165 E. 32nd St., NYC . . . . (212) 686-3514
Gordon, Joel/112 Fourth Ave., NYC . . . . (212) 254-1688
Gorin, Bart/1160 Broadway, NYC . . . . (212) 683-3743
Gosso, Chris/67 Mowat Ave., Toronto . . . . (416) 534-4301
Gotman, John/111 W. 24th St., NYC . . . . (212) 255-0569
Gottlieb, Dennis M./NYC/(212) 620-7050 . . . . **pages 44-45**
Gottschalk, George III/173 Massachusetts Ave., Boston . . . . (617) 267-4724
Gould, Harrison/NYC/(212) 929-9001 . . . . **pages 48-49**
Gould, Stephen/222 E. 44th St., NYC . . . . (212) 867-4030
Gove, Geoffrey/117 Waverly Pl., NYC . . . . (212) 260-6051
Gozo/NYC . . . . (212) 620-8115
Grace, Arthur/1928 35th Pl. N.W., Wash. D.C. . . . . (202) 333-6568
Graff, Randolph/636 Broadway, NYC . . . . (212) 420-6011
Graham, Donald/NYC/(212) 459-4767 . . . . **pages 388-389**
Grande, Carla/NYC . . . . (212) 691-1015
Grant, Gail/43 S. Third St., Phila. . . . . (215) 922-4378
Grant, Jarvis J./1650 Harvard St. N.W., Wash. D.C. . . . . (202) 387-8584
Grant, Rob/262 W. 22nd St., NYC . . . . (212) 727-1038
Grant, Robert/62 Greene St., NYC . . . . (212) 925-1121
Graves, Tom/136 E. 36th St., NYC . . . . (212) 683-0241
Gray, Mitchel/1160 Fifth Ave., NYC . . . . (212) 722-6228
Gray, Sam/23 Westwood Rd., Wellesley . . . . (617) 237-2711
Grayson, Jay/NYC . . . . (212) 490-6490
Green, Anita/718 Broadway, NYC . . . . (212) 674-4788
Green, Jeremy/4128 Westview Rd., Balt. . . . . (301) 366-0123
Green-Armytage, Stephen/171 W. 57th St., NYC . . . . (212) 247-6314
Greenberg, David/54 King St., NYC . . . . (212) 243-7351
Greenberg, Steven/560 Harrison Ave., Boston . . . . (617) 423-7646
Greene, Jim/20 W. 20th St., NYC . . . . (212) 741-3764
Greene, Joshua/NYC . . . . (212) 243-2750
Greene, P.A./Baltimore . . . . (301) 298-3437
Greene, Richard/56 W. 22nd St., NYC . . . . (212) 242-5282
Greenfield, Lois/NYC/(212) 686-6883 . . . . **page 366**
Greenfield-Sanders, Timothy/135 E. Second St., NYC . . . . (212) 674-7888
Greenwald, Scott T./200 Portland Rd., Highlands . . . . (201) 872-1184
Gregory, John/NYC . . . . (212) 581-5766
Gregory, Kevin/237 W. 26th St., NYC . . . . (212) 807-9859
Gregory, Mark/10615 Duvall St., Glenn Dale . . . . (301) 262-8646
Grehan, Farrell/Five E. 22nd St., NYC . . . . (212) 677-3999
Greniers, The, Inc./127 Mill St., Springfield . . . . (413) 532-9440
Greyshock, Caroline/578 Broadway, NYC . . . . (212) 226-7113
Grieve, Anne Jane/366 Adelaide E., Toronto . . . . (416) 362-7793
Griffen, Charles/NYC . . . . (212) 598-4473
Griffin, Gregory/109 W. 26th St., NYC . . . . (212) 807-7385
Griffiths-Belt, Annie/1301 Noyes Dr., Silver Springs . . . . (301) 495-3127
Grill, Tom/NYC . . . . (212) 889-9700
Grimes, Patti/77 W68th St., NYC . . . . (212) 877-1453
Groeschel, Erika/114 E. 32nd St., NYC . . . . (212) 685-3291
Grohe, Steve/451 D St., Boston . . . . (617) 426-2871
Groskinsky, Alma/5 Woodcleft Ave., Pt. Washington . . . . (516) 883-3294
Gross, Cy/59 W. 19th St., NYC . . . . (212) 243-2556
Gross, David/922 Third Ave., NYC . . . . (212) 688-4729
Gross, Garry/235 W. Fourth St., NYC . . . . (212) 807-7141
Gross, Geoffrey/40 W. 27th St., NYC . . . . (212) 685-8850
Gross, Lee/366 Madison Ave., NYC . . . . (212) 682-5240
Gross, Stuart/111 W. 19th St., NYC . . . . (212) 255-2770
Grotell, Al/170 Park Row, NYC . . . . (212) 349-3165

Gruber, Terry/885 West End Ave., NYC . . . . (212) 749-2840
Guarneri, Vincent/236 Fifth Ave., NYC . . . . (212) 696-8019
Gudnason, Torkil/58 W. 15th St., NYC . . . . (212) 929-6680
Guice, Brad/31 W. 31st St., NYC . . . . (212) 206-0966
Guilburt, David/NYC/(212) 677-8600 . . . . **pages 310-311**
Gurovitz, Judy/207 E. 74th St., NYC . . . . (212) 988-8685
Guyaux, Jean-Marie/29 E. 19th St., NYC . . . . (212) 529-5395
Guyette, John/5120 Wyffels Rd., Canandalgua . . . . (716) 394-5210
H/O Photographers, Inc./197 Main St., Hartford . . . . (802) 295-6321
Haak, Ken/122 E. 30th St., NYC . . . . (212) 679-6284
Haas, David/7-A Heritage Hills, Somers . . . . (914) 277-4415
Haas, Ed/130 W. 25th St., NYC . . . . (212) 463-0998
Haas, Ken, Inc./15 Sheridan Sq., NYC . . . . (212) 255-0707
Haft, Emily/435 E. 65th St., NYC . . . . (212) 517-5123
Hagen, Boyd B./448 W. 37th St., NYC . . . . (212) 244-2436
Haggerty, David/17 E. 67th St., NYC . . . . (212) 879-4141
Hagle, Bob /Lord Corp./2000 W. Grandview, Erie . . . . (814) 868-3611
Hahn, Bob/3522 Skyline Dr., Bethlehem . . . . (215) 868-0339
Haiman, Merritt Todd/NYC/(212) 391-0810 . . . . **pages 352-353**
Hainy, Barry/82 Jane St., NYC . . . . (212) 645-9335
Halard, Francois/NYC . . . . (212) 370-4300
Haling, George/231 W. 29th St., NYC . . . . (212) 736-6822
Halsband, Michael/1200 Broadway, NYC . . . . (212) 889-2994
Hamilton Vm. H., Keith/749 F.D.R Dr., NYC . . . . (212) 982-3375
Hamilton, Mark/119 W. 23rd St., NYC . . . . (212) 242-9814
Hammond, Maury/Nine E. 19th St., NYC . . . . (212) 460-9990
Hampton Studios/515 Broadway, NYC . . . . (212) 431-4320
Handelman, Dorothy/10 Gay St., NYC . . . . (212) 242-3058
Hankin, Jamie/Phila. . . . . (215) 238-9076
Hansen, Constance/31 W. 31st St., NYC . . . . (212) 643-9375
Hansen, Wendy/126 Madison Ave., NYC . . . . (212) 684-7139
Hanson, Kent/147 Bleecker St., NYC . . . . (212) 777-2399
Harbinger, Inc./1400 16th St. N.W., Wash. D.C. . . . . (202) 628-0053
Harmon, Rodd/NYC . . . . (212) 929-9001
Harper, Sharon/Battell Block, Middlebury . . . . (802) 388-3402
Harquail, John/67 Mowat Ave., Toronto . . . . (416) 535-1620
Harrington III, Blaine/2 Virginia Ave., Danbury . . . . (203) 798-2866
Harrington, Collen/27 Hallvard Ter., Rockaway . . . . (201) 625-0409
Harris, Alan/NYC . . . . (212) 877-8003
Harris, Brownie/McGuire Ln., Croton on Hudson . . . . (914) 271-6426
Harris, Michael/NYC . . . . (212) 255-3377
Harris, Ronald G./NYC . . . . (212) 255-2330
Harrison, Alec/45 First Ave., NYC . . . . (212) 995-8181
Hart, Steve/411 Bergen St., Bklyn . . . . (718) 857-1454
Harting, Christopher/327 Summer St., Boston . . . . (617) 451-6330
Hartney, Joe/NYC . . . . (212) 242-8106
Haruo/37 W. 20th St., NYC . . . . (212) 505-8800
Hashi/NYC/(212) 675-6902 . . . . **pages 418-419**
Hathon, Elizabeth/NYC/(212) 219-0685 . . . . **pages 330-331**
Hausman, George/NYC . . . . (212) 686-4810
Hauss, Friedemann/NYC . . . . (212) 219-0707
Haviland, Brian/34 E. 30th St., NYC . . . . (212) 481-4132
Hawkes, Michael/346 E. 20th St., NYC . . . . (212) 254-6281
Hayes, Barry C.P.P./53 Main St., St. Johnsbury . . . . (802) 748-8916
Hayes, Kerry/318 Willow Ave., Toronto . . . . (416) 698-0511
Haynes, G. Paul/50 Charles St., NYC . . . . (212) 206-7085
Haywood, Alan/39 Westmoreland Ave., White Plains . . . . (914) 946-1928
Head, Olive/155 Riverside Dr., NYC . . . . (212) 580-3323
Healey, Doug/9 E. 75th St., NYC . . . . (212) 472-0263
Heayn, Mark/17 W. 24th St., Balt. . . . . (301) 235-1608
Hecker, David/568 Broadway, NYC . . . . (212) 925-1233
Heiberg, Milton/71 W. 23rd St., NYC . . . . (212) 741-6405
Heinlein, David/56 W. 22nd St., NYC . . . . (212) 645-1158
Heisler, Gregory/NYC/(212) 777-8100 . . . . **pages 230-231**
Heist, H. Scott & Co./Durham . . . . (215) 965-5479
Heleotis, Harry/16 Jane St., NYC . . . . (212) 675-6951
Hellerstein, Steve/NYC/(212) 645-0508 . . . . **pages 247-251**
Helmar Advertising Photograpy, Inc./46 Midway St., S. Boston . . . . (617) 269-7410
Helms, Bill/1175 York Ave., NYC . . . . (212) 759-2079
Henderson, Gayle/NYC . . . . (212) 689-6783
Henning, Diane/NYC . . . . (212) 879-8787
Henry, John/NYC/(212) 686-6883 . . . . **page 366**
Henze, Don/39 W. 29th St., NYC . . . . (212) 689-7375

Herail, Laurent/NYC	(212) 260-0112	
Herholdt, Frank/NYC/(212) 682-1490		**pages 76-77**
Hermsdorf, Conrad/810 Canyon Crest Dr., Sierra Madre	(818) 355-1898	
Heron, Pat/80 Madison Ave., NYC	(212) 683-9039	
Herr, H. Buff/56 W. 82nd St., NYC	(212) 595-4783	
Herron, Pat/80 Madison Ave., NYC	(212) 683-9039	
Hess, Trudee/333 E. 49th St., NYC	(212) 755-0532	
Heuberger, William/NYC/(212) 242-1532		**pages 112-113**
Heyert, Elizabeth/NYC	(212) 594-1008	
Heyl, Fran/NYC	(212) 581-6470	
Hickman, Louis (HPNS)/Plainfield	(201) 561-2696	
Hideoki Studio/236 W. 26th St., NYC	(212) 255-6116	
Hill, David/128 Berkeley, Toronto	(416) 362-8285	
Hill, Fred G./165 Cherry St., Burlington	(802) 864-4385	
Hill, Jonathan/NYC/(212) 627-5460		**pages 280-281**
Hill, John T./388 Amity Rd., Bethany	(203) 393-0035	
Hill, Pat/37 W. 26th St., NYC	(212) 679-0884	
Hill, Richard/1179-A King St. W., Toronto	(416) 533-6634	
Hiller, David/Stamford	(203) 975-7676	
Hine, Skip/NYC/(212) 529-6100		**pages 188-189**
Hing/Norton/NYC/(212) 683-4258		**pages 190-191**
Hiro Studio, Inc./NYC	(212) 580-8000	
Hirsch, Butch/NYC	(212) 807-7498	
Hirshfeld, Max/1027 33rd St. N.W., Wash. D.C.	(202) 333-7450	
Hispard, Marc/NYC	(212) 370-4300	
Hoban, Tana/105 E. 16th St., NYC	(212) 477-6071	
Hochman, Richard, Inc./210 Fifth Ave., NYC	(212) 532-7766	
Hoebermann Studio, Inc./49 W. 44th St., NYC	(212) 840-2678	
Hoeye, Michael/NYC	(212) 222-2012	
Holden, Chris Ltd./118 E. 28th St., NYC	(212) 685-4655	
Holderer, John/37 W. 20th St., NYC	(212) 620-4260	
Holloway, Jim/1301 Briggs-Chaney Rd., Silver Springs	(301) 604-1758	
Hollyman, Tom/300 E. 40th St., NYC	(212) 867-2383	
Holniker, Barry/400 E. 25th St., Balt.	(301) 889-1919	
Holographic Studios, Inc./240 E. 26th St., NYC	(212) 686-9397	
Holography: Casdin-Silver Studios/51 Melcher St., Boston	(617) 739-6869	
Holt, John Studios, Inc./25 Drydock Ave., Boston	(617) 426-4658	
Holt, Rita Assocs., Inc./NYC/(212) 683-2002		**pages 287-289**
Holtz, Ron/9153 Brookville Rd., Silver Spring	(301) 589-7900	
Holtzman, Jeffrey/201 E. 21st St., NYC	(212) 353-8517	
Holz, George/400 Lafayette St., NYC	(212) 505-5607	
Hone, Stephen, Inc./859 N. 28th St., Phila.	(215) 765-6900	
Hooper, Thomas/NYC/(212) 691-0122		**pages 140-141**
Hopkins, Douglas/NYC	(212) 243-1774	
Hopson, Gareth/22 E. 21st St., NYC	(212) 475-7391	
Hornick/Rivlin/25 Drydock Ave., Boston	(617) 482-8614	
Horowitz, Irwin, Inc./1200 Broadway, NYC	(212) 889-8098	
Horowitz, Ryszard/137 W. 25th St., NYC	(212) 243-6440	
Horowitz, Ted/214 Wilton Rd., Westport	(203) 454-8766	
Horst/188 E. 64th St., NYC	(212) 751-4937	
Horth, Anthony/NYC	(212) 925-8333	
Horton, Debbie/93 Lexington Ave., Bklyn.	(212) 638-0797	
Horvath & Assoc. Studios, Ltd./95 Charles St., NYC	(212) 741-0300	
Horvath Studios/95 Charles St., NYC	(212) 741-0300	
Horvath, J. Productions/335 W. 12th St., NYC	(212) 741-0300	
Houck/Holt Studio/535 Albany St., Boston	(617) 338-4009	
Houston Studio/Bayside	(718) 224-7806	
Hovde, Nob/1438 3rd Ave., NYC	(212) 753-0462	
Howard, Davis/19 E. 21st St., Baltimore	(301) 625-3838	
Howard, Rosemary/902 Broadway, NYC	(212) 473-5552	
Hoyt, Wolfgang/NYC/(212) 686-2569		**pages 236-237**
Hubbell, William/99 E. Elm St., Greenwich	(203) 629-9629	
Hudgins, Stephen/5200 Montgomery Ave., Phila.	(215) 878-0991	
Huet, John/NYC	(212) 219-0707	
Hughes, Judy/Boston/(617) 426-9111		**pages 384-385**
Hui, Norisa/NYC	(212) 221-7490	
Huibregtse, Jim/NYC/(212) 925-3351		**pages 272-273**
Huntzinger, Robert/76 Ninth Ave., NYC	(212) 929-9001	
Hurd, Michael/774 Wilcoxson Ave., Stratford	(203) 378-8766	
Hurewitz, Gary/NYC/(212) 925-2999		**pages 114-125**
Hurwitz, Harrison/14 Horatio, NYC	(212) 989-4113	
Husak, John/NYC	(212) 463-7025	
Husebye, Terry/NYC	(212) 633-2050	

Huss, John W./Wethersfield	(203) 728-0545
Huss, W. John/Wethersfield	(203) 728-0545
Husted, Daniel/143 Sagamore Rd., Millburn	(201) 761-1348
Huston, Larry/40 E. 21st St., NYC	(212) 777-7541
Huszar, Steven/377 Park Ave. S., NYC	(212) 532-3772
Huchings, Richard/24 Pinebrook Dr., Larchmont	(914) 834-9633
Hutchinson, Gardiner/239 Causeway St., Boston	(617) 523-5180
Hyman, Paul/124 W. 79th St., NYC	(212) 580-6501
Iacovelli, Richard/560 Harrison Ave., Boston	(617) 451-0966
Ian, Michael/214 W. 30th St., NYC	(212) 947-0583
Iannazzi, Robert F./450 Smith Rd., Rochester	(716) 624-1285
Ichi Studio/303 Park Ave. S., NYC	(212) 254-4810
Ideas & Images/292 City Island Ave., City Is.	(212) 885-0753
Iglarsh, Gary/855 Tyson St., Baltimore	(301) 383-1208
Iglesias, Jose/830 N. 24th St., Philadelphia	(212) 236-3156
Ihara Studio, Inc./568 Broadway, NYC	(212) 219-9363
Ikeda, Shig/636 Ave. of the Americas, NYC	(212) 924-4744
Image Bank N.Y., The/111 Fifth Ave., NYC	(212) 529-6700
Image Factory/200 W. North Ave., Baltimore	(301) 539-1300
Image Group, The/5 Hummingbird Lne., Enfield	(203) 749-8147
Image Photographic Services/96 Walnut St., Montclair	(201) 746-9133
Images Unlimited/Meriden	(203) 634-6633
Imouye, Kaz/6568 Beachview Dr., Rancho Palos Verdes	(213) 544-2044
Impact Studios/614 S. Ninth St., Phila.	(800) 726-3988
Impact Studios, Ltd./1084 N. Delaware, Phila.	(215) 426-3988
In Focus Assocs./21 E. 40th St., NYC	(212) 779-3600
Infinity Multi-Media/100-18 DeKruif Pl., NYC	(212) 671-7432
Ing, Francis/112 W. 31st St., NYC	(212) 279-5022
Inouye, Yosh/155 Broadview Ave., Toronto	(416) 469-1733
Insight Photography/55 Gill Ln., Iselin	(201) 283-4727
Inventive Eye Ltd./160 Fifth Ave., NYC	(212) 741-3128
Iooss, Walter/NYC/(212) 727-1400	**pages 426-429**
Ishimuro Studio/130 W. 25th St., NYC	(212) 255-9198
Israel, Anthony/566 Ninth St., Brooklyn	(718) 832-1976
Izu, Kenro/NYC/(212) 254-1002	**pages 62-63**
J&M Studio/NYC/(212) 627-5460	**pages 280-281**
Jackson, Thom/NYC	(212) 838-3170
Jacobs, Martin/34 E. 23rd St., NYC	(212) 475-1160
Jacobs, Raymond/119 E. 17th St., NYC	(212) 777-4779
Jacobs, Richard B./138 Chatsworth Ave., Larchmont	(914) 834-0722
Jacobs, Robert/NYC/(212) 967-6883	**pages 154-155**
Jacobson, Alan J./370 Riverside Dr., NYC	(212) 222-7548
James, Francis/6954 Edgerton Ave., Pittsburgh	(412) 362-4499
Jamiak, Sebstien/NYC	(212) 260-0112
Janeart, Ltd./Landgrove	(802) 824-4135
Janiak, Sebastien/NYC	(212) 260-0112
Janovsky, Paul/Santa Monica	(213) 394-5031
Jawitz, Louis H./13 E. 17th St., NYC	(212) 929-0008
Jean, Eddy/Rockefeller Center, NYC	(212) 468-2889
Jean, Philip/175 Fifth Ave., NYC	(212) 969-8522
Jedell, Joan/NYC/(212) 861-7861	**pages 384-385, 624-625**
Jefferds, Bob/NYC	(212) 779-3600
Jeffery, Richard/119 W. 22nd St., NYC	(212) 255-2330
Jeffrey, Lance/30 E. 21st St., NYC	(212) 674-0595
Jenkins, Hank/234 Arlington Ave, Paterson	(201) 956-7244
Jenshel, Len/309 W. 93rd St., NYC	(212) 316-7809
Jim, Billy/54 Catherine St., NYC	(212) 233-8635
Joachim, Bruno Studio, Inc./Boston	(617) 451-6156
Joel, Seth/12 E. 20th St., NYC	(212) 674-0852
Joern, James/125 Fifth Ave., NYC	(212) 260-8025
Joester, Steve/15 W. 26th St., NYC	(212) 545-9255
Johansky, Peter/27 W. 20th St., NYC	(212) 242-7013
Johnson, Arlene/NYC/(212) 725-4520	**pages 204-207**
Johnson, Catherine/41 Union Sq. W., NY	(212) 989-4325
Johnson, Eric Glenn/583 Leonard St., Bklyn.	(718) 383-4161
Jones, Chris/240 E. 27th St., NYC	(212) 685-0679
Jones, Lou/Boston/(617) 426-6335	**pages 402-403**
Jones, Lou/NYC/(212) 463-8971	**pages 402-403**
Jones, Peter/43 Charles St., Boston	(617) 227-6400
Jones, Spencer/23 Leonard St., NYC	(212) 941-8165
Jones, Steven/120 W. 25th St., NYC	(212) 929-3641
Judkis, Jim/1602 King James Dr., Pittsburgh	(412) 366-2242
Juliano, Vincent/Douglaston	(718) 423-6187

Jung/Lee/132 W. 21st St., NYC	(212) 807-8107
Jurado, Louis/126 W. 22nd St., NYC	(212) 242-7480
Jurak, Dan/10330-104 St., Edmonton	(403) 423-2494
Kachaturian, Armen/330 Broome St., NYC	(212) 334-0986
Kahan, Eric/NYC	(212) 243-9727
Kahn, Harvey Assoc./14 E. 52nd St., NYC	(212) 752-8490
Kakizaki, Seiji/611 Broadway, NYC	(212) 674-8878
Kalan, Mark R./922 President St., Bklyn	(718) 398-0165
Kalish, JoAnne/512 Adams St., Centerport	(516) 271-6133
Kalisher, Bonnie G./NYC	(212) 586-6300
Kalisher, Simpson/North St., Roxbury	(203) 354-8893
Kaliski, Arthur/66 Gilbert St., Northport	(516) 261-8804
Kaltman, Naomi/NYC	(212) 219-0707
Kamar, David, Inc./1165 Broadway, NYC	(212) 685-4784
Kammler, Frederic/345 E. 93rd St., NYC	(212) 757-2676
Kamper, George/15 W. 24th St.., NYC	(212) 627-7171
Kan Photography/NYC	(212) 989-1083
Kan, Toshi/153 W. 27th St., NYC	(212) 645-2684
Kana, Titus/876 Broadway, NYC	(212) 473-5550
Kane, Art/568 Broadway, NYC	(212) 925-7334
Kane, Odette/NYC	(212) 807-8730
Kane, Peter T./236 W. 26th. St., NYC	(212) 924-4968
Kane, Rich/NYC/(212) 496-9670	**page 685**
Kannair, Jonathan/91 Quaker Ln., Bolton	(508) 799-2266
Kaplan, Alan/NYC/(212) 982-9500	**pages 86-87**
Kaplan, Barry/40 Webb Ave., N. Kingstown	(401) 295-0922
Kaplan, Carol/Boston/(617) 720-4400	**pages 360-363**
Kaplan, Holly/NYC/(212) 925-2929	**pages 282-283**
Kaplan, Peter B./Seven E. 20th St., NYC	(212) 995-5000
Kaplan, Peter J./924 West End Ave., NYC	(212) 222-1193
Kapner, Ronnie/166 E. 34th St., NYC	(212) 725-8450
Karales, James H./147 W. 79th St., NYC	(212) 799-2483
Karnow, Catherine/1707 Columbia Rd., N.W., Wash. D.C.	(202) 332-5656
Karzen, Marc/185 E. 85, NYC	(212) 722-5347
Kassabian, Ashod/127 E. 59th St., NYC	(212) 222-1116
Kassimir, Owen/10 Grace Ave., Great Neck	(516) 773-3067
Kasten, Barbara/251 W. 19th St., NYC	(212) 627-5229
Katrina/NYC/(212) 279-2838	**pages 302-303**
Katz, Howard R./400 E. 89th St., NYC	(212) 722-1940
Katz, Paul/65-61 Saunders St., Queens	(718) 275-3615
Katzenstein, David/21 E. Fourth St., NYC	(212) 529-9460
Kaufman, Jeff/27 W. 24th ST., NYC Pk.	(212) 627-1878
Kaufman, Mickey/144 W. 27th St., NYC	(212) 255-1976
Kaufman, Ted/121 Madison Ave., NYC	(212) 685-0349
Kauss, Jean Gabriel/235 E. 40th St., NYC	(212) 370-4300
Kawachi, Yutaka/NYC/(212) 929-4825	**pages 260-261**
Kawalerski, Ted/7 Evergreen Way, N. Tarrytown	(212) 242-0198
Keegan, Marcia/140 E. 46th St., NYC	(212) 953-9023
Keeve, Douglas/50 Ave. A, NYC	(212) 777-5405
Kelemen, Paul/11 W. 30th St., NYC	(212) 947-0788
Keller, Michael/145 E. 16th St., NYC	(212) 869-1711
Keller, Tom/440 E. 78th St., NYC	(212) 472-3667
Kelley, Charles W. Jr./649 Second Ave., NYC	(212) 686-3879
Kelley, Patsy/70 Atlantic Ave., Marblehead	(617) 639-1147
Kellner, Jeff/16 Waverly Pl., NYC	(212) 475-3719
Kelly, Bill/NYC/(212) 989-2794	**pages 338-339**
Kelly/Mooney	(212) 268-6936
Kelsh/Marr Studios/211 N. 13th St., Phila.	(215) 242-3395
Ken Buris Location Photography/Green Hills Drive, Shelburne	(802) 985-3263
Kendrick, Robb/NYC	(212) 633-2050
Kenik, David/16 Atlantic Ave., West Warwick	(401) 823-3080
Kennedy, David Michael/Cerrillos	(505) 473-2745
Kennedy, Donald/160 Fifth Ave., NYC	(212) 924-6760
Kenner, Fred/494 Broadway, NYC	(212) 226-7171
Kenney, John/NYC/(212) 758-4545	**pages 256-257, 260-261**
Kent, Karen/NYC	(212) 962-6793
Kentz, Mike/323 W. 14th St., NYC	(212) 645-0539
Keowon, Sandra/4301 Massachusetts Ave. N.W., Wash.	(202) 244-5906
Kern, Karen/17 Park Ave., NYC	(212) 683-9216
Kerr, Barbara & Justin/14 W. 17th St., NYC	(212) 741-1731
Kerr, Ralph/Phila./(215) 592-1359	**pages 228-229**
Kerson, Larry/539 Amity Rd., Woodbridge	(203) 393-3752
Khornak, Lucille/NYC/(212) 593-0933	**page 157**

Kiernan, James/348 West End Ave., NYC	(212) 874-2736
Kim/NYC	(212) 679-5628
Kimmel, Lily & Assocs./NYC/(212) 794-1542	**pages 240-241**
King, William Douglas/1766 E. 32nd St., Bklyn.	(718) 998-8351
Kingsford, Michael/NYC	(212) 475-0553
Kipp, Bill/One Fitchburg St., Somerville	(617) 666-2344
Kirk, Malcolm/12 E. 72nd St., NYC	(212) 744-3642
Kirk, Russell/NYC	(212) 206-1446
Kirschner, Stan/8 Scotsdale Rd., S. Burlington	(802) 862-3768
Kisch, John/Box 114, Hyde Park	(212) 489-1518
Kiss, Bob/315 Seventh Ave., NYC	(212) 243-1328
Kitchen, Dennis/NYC/(212) 674-7658	**pages 160-161**
Klauss, Cheryl/463 Broome St., NYC	(212) 431-3569
Klein, Les/222 W. 23rd St., NYC	(212) 490-1460
Klein, Matthew/NYC/(212) 255-6400	**pages 74-75**
Klesenki, Deborah/NYC/(212) 627-7006	**pages 266-267**
Klesenki-Ward Studio Inc./NYC/(212) 627-7006	**pages 266-267**
Kligge, Robert/578 Broadway, NYC	(212) 226-7113
Kligman, Fred/9153 Brookville Rd., Silver Spring	(301) 589-7900
Klinefelter, Eric/10963 Hickory Rdg. Rd., Columbia	(301) 964-0273
Knight, Harrison/NYC/(212) 288-9777	**pages 148-149**
Knowles, Eugene/365 Wilden Pl., S. Orange	(201) 763-9355
Knowles, Robert M./525 Ellendale Ave., Rye Brook	(914) 934-2619
Kobrin, Hal/Otis	(800) 243-3113
Koenig, Lisa/Five W. 19th St., NYC	(212) 929-5210
Koenig, Phil/49 Market St., NYC	(212) 964-1590
Kohli, Eddy/NYC	(212) 924-6760
Kohn, Michael Photography/67 Mowat Ave., Toronto	(416) 588-1889
Kojima, Tak/NYC/(212) 889-3337	**Vol. I pages 64-65**
Kolansky, Palma/NYC/(212) 727-7300	**pages 342-343**
Kontaxis, George/8 Washington Ct., Stamford	(203) 327-9921
Kooyker, Valerie/201 E. 12th St., NYC	(212) 673-4333
Kopelow, Paul/135 Madison Ave., NYC	(212) 689-0685
Korman, Alison/NYC/(212) 633-8407	**pages 244-245**
Korn, Elaine Associates Ltd./234 Fifth Ave., NYC	(212) 679-6739
Korsh, Ken/118 E. 28th St., NYC	(212) 685-8864
Kosoff, Brian/28 W. 25th St., NYC	(212) 243-4880
Koudis, Nick/NYC/(212) 475-2802	**pages 128-129**
Kouirinis, Bill/381 Park Ave. S., NYC	(212) 696-5674
Kozan, Dan/127 W. 25th St., NYC	(212) 691-2288
Kozlowski, Mark Productions/48 Fourth Street, Troyny	(518) 274-8512
Kozyra, James/NYC/(212) 431-1911	**pages 208-209**
Kramer, Daniel/110 W. 86th St., NYC	(212) 873-7777
Kramer, Phil/NYC	(212) 477-2255
Kramer, Phil/30 S. Bank St., Philadelphia	(215) 928-9189
Kramer, Roger E./305 Cherry St., Phila.	(215) 627-3062
Kranzler, Dick/162 W. 21st St., NYC	(212) 242-4167
Kraus, Brian/126 W. 22nd St., NYC	(212) 691-3364
Kraus, Gerald/46 Janet St., Pt. Jefferson	(516) 473-9105
Krein, Jeffrey/NYC	(212) 741-5207
Kreis, Ursula G./63 Adrian Ave., NYC	(212) 562-8931
Krementz, Jill/228 E. 48th St., NYC	(212) 688-0480
Krims, Les/187 Linwood Ave., Buffalo	(716) 883-8593
Krinke, Michael/NYC/(212) 627-5460	**pages 280-281**
Krist, Bob/333 So. Irving St., Ridgewood	(201) 585-9464
Kristofik, Robert/334 E. 90th St., NYC	(212) 534-5541
Krohn, Lee A./P.O. Box 909, Manchester Center	(802) 362-4824
Krongard, Paula/NYC/(212) 683-1020	**pages 252-255**
Krongard, Steve/NYC/(212) 689-5634	**pages 46-47**
Kuehn, Karen/49 Warren St., NYC	(212) 406-3005
Kugler, Dennis/43 Bond St., NYC	(212) 677-3826
Kuhn, Ann/107 W. 86th St., NYC	(212) 595-7611
Kuklin, Susan/436 W. 23rd St., NYC	(212) 620-8125
Kuzmanoff, Leon/508 La Guardia Pl., NYC	(212) 673-0169
LaBua, Frank/37 N. Mountain Ave., NYC	(201) 783-6318
LaCroix, Pat/25 Brant St., Toronto	(416) 864-1858
LaMonica, Chuck/NYC	(212) 727-7884
LaPlaca Productions/873 Broadway, NYC	(212) 725-4949
Lachenauer, Paul/876 Broadway, NYC	(212) 529-7059
Lada, Joe/NYC	(212) 254-0253
Laird, Richard/414 W. 22nd St., NYC	(212) 675-2138
Lallemand, Sylvain Lawrence/NYC	(212) 260-0112
Lambert, Robert Michael/48 E. 66th St., NYC	(212) 486-9575

Lambray, Maureen/NYC	(212) 879-3960
Lamonica, Chuck/NYC	(212) 727-7884
Lamont, Mary	(212) 242-1087
Lander, Jane/NYC	(212) 679-1358
Landsman, Gary/12115 Parklawn Dr., Rockville	(301) 468-2588
Landwehrle, Don/9 Hother Ln., Bay Shore	(516) 665-8221
Lane, Morris/212-A E. 26th St., NYC	(212) 696-0498
Lane, Whitney/109 Somerstown Rd., Ossining	(914) 762-5335
Lange, Paul/157 Chambers St., NYC	(212) 513-1400
Langley, David/NYC/(212) 581-3933	**pages 304-305**
Lanker, Brian/NYC/(212) 944-2853	**pages 406-409**
Lanzano, Louis/49 W. 19th St., NYC	(212) 929-7668
Laperruque Photography, Inc./157 Chambers St., NYC	(212) 962-5200
Lapides, Susan/451 Huron Ave., Cambridge	(617) 864-7793
Larkin, Mary/NYC	(212) 832-8116
Larrabee, R./Donegal	(412) 423-6871
Larrain, Gilles, Inc./95 Grand St., NYC	(212) 925-8494
Larrimore, Walter/916 N. Charles St., Balt.	(301) 727-8800
Larson, Susan/56 W. 22nd St., NYC	(212) 929-8980
Lashue, Sonja/NYC	(212) 929-5701
Laszlo Studio, Inc./179 E. 80th St., NYC	(212) 737-1620
Latour/Rossel Comm., Inc./10812 Connecticut Ave., Kensington	(301) 933-5111
Lattari, Anthony/NYC	(212) 598-4473
Lauber, Christopher/108 Grozier Rd., Cambridge	(617) 864-3367
Laurance, Bruce/NYC/(212) 947-3451	**page 286**
Lavine, Arthur/1361 Madison Ave., NYC	(212) 348-2642
Lawfer, Larry/27 Drydock Ave., Boston	(617) 439-4349
Lawrence, Christopher/NYC	(212) 807-8028
Lawrence, Stephanie/3000 Chestnut Ave., Baltimore	(301) 235-2454
Layman, Alex Studio Inc./142 W. 14th St., NYC	(212) 989-5845
Lazzarini, Bob/25 Park Pl., NYC	(212) 513-7163
Le Baube, Guy/310 E. 46th St., NYC	(212) 986-6981
LeBlond, Jerry/7 Court Sq., Rutland	(802) 775-5367
LeMieux, Charles P./Fairfield	(203) 259-4987
Leach, David/NYC/(212) 288-1234	**pages 204-205**
Leach, Peter/802 Sansom St., Phila.	(215) 574-0230
Leaman, Chris/42 Old Lancaster Rd., Malvern	(215) 647-8455
Lecash, Leon/284 Fifth Ave., NYC	(212) 967-0827
Ledds, Karen/219 Henry St., Stamford	(203) 847-3155
Leduc, Lyle/320 E. 42nd St., NYC	(212) 697-9216
Lee, Daniel/550 W. 43rd St., NYC	(212) 239-4646
Lee, Schecter/13 Laight St., NYC	(212) 431-0088
Lee, Vincent B./155 Wooster St., NYC	(212) 254-7888
Leech, Ian & Assoc./140 E. 56th St., NYC	(212) 751-0022
Leeming, Bill/222 Richmond St., Providence	(401) 421-1916
Lefkowitz, Jay Alan/Five E. 16th St., NYC	(212) 929-1036
Legrand, Jean-Yves/41 W. 84th St., NYC	(212) 724-5981
Legrand, Michel/152 W. 25th St., NYC	(212) 807-9754
Lei, John/222 Park Ave. S., NYC	(212) 674-7695
Leighton/322 Summer St., Boston	(617) 426-2099
Leighton, Thomas/321 E. 43rd St., NYC	(212) 370-1835
Leinwand, Freda/463 West St., NYC	(212) 691-0997
Leith, Ian Assocs./1515 Matheson Blvd., Mississauga	(416) 274-3778
Lemkowitz, Laura/NYC/(212) 297-0041	**pages 46-47, 168-171, 562-563, 664-667**
Lennard, Erica/214 E. 12th St., NYC	(212) 254-2377
Lens 14, Inc./234 Forbes Ave., Pittsburgh	(412) 471-1445
Leo, Donato/866 Ave. of the Americas, NYC	(212) 685-5527
Leonard, Barney/134 Cherry Lane, Wynnewood	(215) 664-2525
Leone, Mindy/381 Park Ave. S., NYC	(212) 696-5674
Leonian, Edith/NYC	(212) 989-7670
Leonian, Phillip/220 E. 23rd St., NYC	(212) 989-7670
Lerman, Gary/NYC/(212) 683-5777	**page 196**
Lerman, Peter M./37 E. 28th St., NYC	(212) 685-0053
Lerner, Ira/74 Fifth Ave., NYC	(212) 989-5462
Leroy, Philippe/NYC	(212) 260-0112
Lesinski, Martin/40 W. 17th St., NYC	(212) 463-7857
Lesnick, John M./221 Ellis Rd., Bloomington	(812) 876-6479
Lesnick, Steve/28 W. 25th St., NYC	(212) 929-1078
Leung, Jook P./35 S. Van Brunt St., Englewood	(201) 894-5881
Levin, Bruce Assocs./NYC/(212) 832-4053	**pages 714-715**
Levin, Dan/520 E. 76th St., NYC	(212) 861-3269
Levin, James/45 W. 21st St., NYC	(212) 481-3676
Levine, Allen/B-2 Merry Ln., E. Hanover	(201) 884-1154

Levine, Jonathan/366 Broadway, NYC	(212) 791-7578
Levinson, Ken/35 E. 10th St., NYC	(212) 254-6180
Levy, Franck/NYC	(212) 557-8256
Levy, Peter/119 W. 22nd St., NYC	(212) 691-6600
Levy, Richard/Five W. 19th St., NYC	(212) 243-4220
Lewin, Ralph/154 W. 74th St., NYC	(212) 580-0482
Lewin, Samantha/NYC/(212) 228-5530	**pages 128-129**
Lewis Studios, Inc./344 Kaplan Dr., Fairfield	(201) 227-1234
Lewis, Robert/333 Park Ave. S., NYC	(212) 475-6564
Lewis, Ross/415 W. 23rd St., NYC	(212) 691-4929
Ley, Russell/103 Ardale St., Boston	(617) 325-2500
Li, Liz/260 Fifth Ave., NYC	(212) 889-7067
Lieberman, Allen H./NYC	(212) 925-8874
Lieberman, Ellen/135 W. 29th St., NYC	(212) 967-8359
Ligeti, Pete/415 W. 55th St., NYC	(212) 246-8949
Lightstruck Studio/613 N. Eutaw St., Baltimore	(301) 727-2220
Lilley, Weaver/2107 Chancellor, Phila.	(215) 567-2881
Linck, Tony/2100 Linwood Ave., Fort Lee	(201) 944-5454
Lindkvist, Anders/200 Clermont Ave., Bklyn	(718) 858-0593
Lindley, Thomas/133 Fifth Ave., NYC	(212) 505-0966
Lindner, Steve/18 W. 27th St., NYC	(212) 683-1317
Lippisch, Alex/36 Bartlett St., Beverly	(508) 927-8966
Lipshutz, Ellen/Buckhill Farm Rd., Arlington	(802) 375-6316
Littell, Dorothy/74 Lawn St., Boston	(617) 739-5196
Littlehales, Breton/6856 Eastern Ave. N.W., Wash. D.C.	(202) 291-2422
Littlewood, John/Woodville	(617) 435-5778
Litwin, Richard/23 E. 11th St., NYC	(212) 620-7144
Lloyd, Harvey/310 E. 23rd St., NYC	(212) 777-5318
Lobell, Richard/536 West Chester St., Long Beach	(516) 431-8899
Loew, Anthony/503 Broadway, NYC	(212) 226-1999
Lofaro, Juliet/NYC	(212) 595-6696
Logan, Kevin/NYC/(212) 206-0539	**pages 278-279**
Lohr, Richard/NYC	(212) 219-0707
Lomeo, Angelo/336 Central Park W., NYC	(212) 663-2122
Londoner, Hank/1921 N. Hobart Blvd., LA	(213) 462-1717
Long Beach Photo Center, Ltd./255 W. Park Ave., Long Beach	(516) 431-6900
Longcor, W.K./Bear Pond, Andover	(201) 398-2225
Longcore, Bill/Riley Rd., New Windsor	(914) 564-6972
Lönninge, Lars/NYC/(212) 627-0100	**pages 374-375**
Loomis, Just/NYC	(212) 924-6760
Lorenz, Robert/80 Fourth Ave., NYC	(212) 505-8483
Lotta, Tom/1337 Beach Ave., Rochester	(716) 461-1390
Lowe, Jacques/NYC/(212) 227-3298	**pages 234-235**
Lubman, David/7 E. 17th St., NYC	(212) 741-1042
Luftig, Allan/873 Broadway, NYC	(212) 533-4113
Lulow, William/126 W. 22nd St., NYC	(212) 675-1625
Luppino, Michael/NYC/(212) 633-9486	**pages 142-143**
Luria, Dick/NYC/(212) 929-7575	**pages 150-153**
Lusk, Frank/25 E. 37th St., NYC	(212) 679-1441
Lydon, Kevin/250 Goodman St. N., Rochester	(716) 473-6930
Lysohir, Chris/80 Eigtht Ave., NYC	(212) 741-3187
Maas, Rita/40 W. 27th St.., NYC	(212) 447-0410
MacHenry, Kate/5 Colliston Rd., Brookline	(617) 277-5736
MacKenzie, Maxwell/2641 Garfield St. N.W., Wash. D.C.	(202) 232-6686
MacWeeney, Alen/171 First Ave., NYC	(212) 473-2500
Macedonia, Carmine/866 Ave. of the Americas, NYC	(212) 889-8520
Macia, Rafael/55 W. 82nd St., NYC	(212) 799-4441
Macpherson, Andrew/NYC	(212) 924-6760
Madris, Stephen/NYC/(212) 744-6668	**page 156**
Maglott, Larry/249 A St., Boston	(617) 482-9347
Maisel, David/NYC/(212) 228-2288	**pages 206-207**
Maisel, Jay/NYC	(212) 431-5157
Malabrigo, Mark/NYC/(212) 420-8087	**page 246**
Malignon, Jacques/NYC/(212) 532-7727	**pages 436-437**
Malitsky, Ed/337 Summer St., Boston	(617) 451-0655
Malka, Daniel/1030 St. Alexandre, Montréal	(514) 397-9704
Mallo, Luis/8525 53rd Ave., Elmhurst	(718) 446-3283
Malyszko, Mike/Boston/(617) 426-9111	**pages 384-385**
Mandarino, Tony/114 E. 32nd St., NYC	(212) 686-2866
Mandelkorn, Richard/309 Waltham St., W. Newton	(617) 332-3246
Mandell, Ilene/NYC	(212) 860-3148
Mann, Ken/NYC/(212) 944-2853	**pages 406-411**
Manna, Lou/347 E. 53rd St., NYC	(212) 826-3150

NORTHEAST

Manno, John/NYC/(212) 243-7353 . . . . **pages 350-351**
Maquere, Alain/NYC . . . . (212) 260-0112
Marc Bryan-Brown Photography/534 W. 35th St., NYC . . . . (212) 691-6045
Marchese, Jim . . . . (212) 242-1087
Marcus, Helen/120 E. 75th St., NYC . . . . (212) 879-6903
Marek & Assocs., Inc./NYC . . . . (212) 924-6760
Maresca, Frank/NYC/(212) 620-0955 . . . . **pages 296-297**
Margerin, Bill/41 W. 25th St., NYC . . . . (212) 645-1532
Margolies, John/222 Valley Pl., Mamaroneck . . . . (914) 698-4060
Mariucci, Marie A./NYC . . . . (212) 944-9590
Mark, Mary Ellen/134 Spring St., NYC . . . . (212) 925-2770
Maroon, Fred/2725 P St. N.W., Wash. D.C. . . . . (202) 337-0337
Marquet, Francois/NYC . . . . (212) 260-0112
Marsell, Steve/NYC . . . . (212) 633-2050
Marshall, Alec/287 Ave. C, NYC . . . . (212) 995-0153
Marshall, Bette/250 W. 26th St., NYC . . . . (212) 463-7884
Marshall, James/20 Jay St., Bklyn . . . . (718) 797-9458
Marshall, John/24 Chester St., Somerville . . . . (617) 628-2475
Marshall, Lee/201 W. 89th St., NYC . . . . (212) 799-9717
Marshall, Mel Assocs./40 W. 77th St., NYC . . . . (212) 877-3921
Marsico, Dennis/110 Fahnestock Rd., Pittsburgh . . . . (412) 781-6349
Martel, Maureen/5 Union Sq. W., NYC . . . . (212) 727-1400
Martens, Wayne/112 31st St., NYC . . . . (212) 239-0283
Martin, Bard/142 W. 26th St., NYC . . . . (212) 929-6712
Martin, Bill/110 W. 17th St., NYC . . . . (212) 929-2071
Martin, Bruce/266A Pearl St., Cambridge . . . . (617) 492-8009
Martin, Dennis/11 W. 25th St., NYC . . . . (212) 929-2221
Martin, Marilyn/Boston . . . . (617) 262-5507
Martinez, Oskar/303 Park Ave. S., NYC . . . . (212) 673-0932
Marvullo/141 W. 28th St., NYC . . . . (212) 564-6501
Marx, Richard/130 W. 25th St., NYC . . . . (212) 929-8880
Marzena/NYC . . . . (212) 772-2522
Masca/109 W. 26th St., NYC . . . . (212) 929-4818
Masiello, Frank/Woodcliff Lake . . . . (201) 573-0965
Mason, Don/111 W. 19th St., NYC . . . . (212) 675-3809
Mason, Kathy/111 W. 19th St., NYC . . . . (212) 675-3809
Mason, Phil/15 St. Mary's Ct., Brookline . . . . (617) 232-0908
Mason, Tom/117 Van Dyke Rd., Hopewell . . . . (609) 466-0911
Massar, Ivan/296 Bedford St., Concord . . . . (508) 369-4090
Massey, David/NYC/(212) 473-3366 . . . . **pages 180-181**
Masterminds/Gordons Alley Mall, Atlantic City . . . . (609) 347-0007
Masters, Charles/NYC . . . . (212) 688-9510
Mastri, Len/1 Mill St., Burlington . . . . (802) 862-4009
Masullo, Ralph/NYC/(212) 727-1809 . . . . **pages 378-379**
Matsuo, Toshi/105 E. 29th St., NYC . . . . (212) 532-1320
Matt, Phil/Rochester . . . . (716) 461-5977
Mattei, George/179 Main St., Hackensack . . . . (201) 342-0740
Matthews, Barbara Lynn/16 Jane St., NYC . . . . (212) 691-0823
Matthews, Cynthia B./200 E. 78th St., NYC . . . . (212) 288-7349
Matura, Nedjeljko/119 W. 23rd St., NYC . . . . (212) 463-9692
Mauss, Peter/222 Valley Pl., Mamaroneck . . . . (914) 698-4060
Mayernik, George/41 Wolfpit Ave., Norwalk . . . . (203) 864-1406
Mayhon, Linda/200 W. 86th St., NYC . . . . (212) 903-4127
Mazzeo, Michael/NYC/(212) 226-7113 . . . . **pages 324-325**
McAfee, Toby/80 Ridge Dr., Yonkers . . . . (914) 423-1836
McCabe, David/NYC . . . . (212) 874-7480
McCabe, Robert/NYC . . . . (212) 677-1910
McCants, Solomon D. III/Queens Village . . . . (718) 776-3673
McCarthy, Joanna/535 Greenwich St., NYC . . . . (212) 675-2757
McCash, Scott W./7213 16th St., Takoma Park . . . . (301) 889-1780
McCavera, Tom/NYC/(212) 682-1490 . . . . **pages 84-85**
McCormick, Ned/55 Hancock Street, Lexington . . . . (617) 862-2552
McDermott, Brian P./48 W. 21st St., NYC . . . . (212) 675-7273
McFarland, Lowell & Nancy/128 E. 28th St., NYC . . . . (212) 686-6346
McGill, Cutty/174 W. 89th St., NYC . . . . (212) 362-8030
McGrail, John/6576 Senator Ln., Bensalem . . . . (215) 750-6070
McKay, Colleen/229 E. Fifth St., NYC . . . . (212) 598-0469
McLaren, Lynn/105 Charles St., Boston . . . . (617) 227-7448
McLaughlin, Glenn/NYC/(212) 645-7028 . . . . **page 359**
McLeod, William/33 Jefferson Ave., Toronto . . . . (416) 535-1955
McLoughlin, James/NYC/(212) 206-8207 . . . . **pages 276-277**
McMullen, Mark/25 Monroe St., Albany . . . . (518) 426-9284
McMullin, Forest/183 St. Paul St., Rochester . . . . (716) 262-3944

McNamara, Jeff/NYC	(212) 779-3600
McNeil, Pierre/550 De Mortagne, Boucherville	(514) 449-1050
McQueen, Ann/791 Tremont St., Boston	(617) 267-6258
Meacham, Joseph/601 N. Third St., Phila.	215) 925-8122
Mead, Bob/NYC/(212) 758-4545	**pages 256-257, 260-261**
Mead, Chris Inc./108 Reade St., NYC	(212) 619-5616
Mecca, Jack/1508 72nd St., N. Bergen	(201) 869-7956
Meier, Raymond/532 Broadway, NYC	(212) 219-0120
Meillier, Henri Studio, Inc./1026 Wood St., Phila.	(215) 922-1525
Meinecke, Gordon/198 Merton St., Toronto	(416) 484-1580
Melford, Michael/Mt. Kisco/(914) 666-6244	**pages 346-347**
Melford, Michael/NYC/(212) 473-3095	**pages 346-347**
Mellor, D.W./1020 Mt. Pleasant Rd., Bryn Mawr	(215) 527-9040
Melnick, Steve/NYC	(212) 219-0707
Melo, Michael/Winterport	(207) 223-8894
Meltzer, Irwin & Assoc., Ltd./50 W. 17th St., NYC	(212) 807-7464
Memo Studio/39 W. 67th St., NYC	(212) 787-1658
Menashe, Abraham/306 E. Fifth St., NYC	(212) 254-2754
Menda Studio/NYC/(212) 675-5561	**page 377**
Mendelsohn, David/Sky Farm Rd., Northwood	(603) 942-7622
Mendelsohn, Richard/353 W. 53rd St., NYC	(212) 682-2462
Mendlowitz, Benjamin/Brooklin	(207) 359-2131
Menken, Howard/NYC/(212) 924-4240	**pages 430-431**
Mennemeyer & Co./NYC/(212) 279-2838	**pages 298-303**
Meo, Frank/NYC/(212) 353-0907	**pages 200-203**
Meola, Eric/NYC/(212) 255-5150	**pages 416-417**
Mercer, Ralph/451 D St., Boston	(617) 957-4604
Meringolo, Thomas/7504 Fifth Ave., Bklyn.	(212) 238-8976
Merle, Michael G./54 W. 16th St., NYC	(212) 741-3801
Mermelstein, Jeff/98 Riverside Dr., NYC	(212) 496-9427
Merrick, Tad/64 Main St., Middlebury	(802) 388-9598
Mervar, Louis/29 W. 38th St., NYC	(212) 354-8024
Mesdon, Randall/NYC	(212) 219-0707
Mesmer, Jerry/1523 22nd St. N.W., Wash. D.C.	(202) 785-2188
Mesopotamia Productions/NYC/(212) 989-2794	**pages 338-339**
Metzger, Richard/Five Tsienneto Rd., Derry	(615) 357-9679
Meyer, Mary Ellen/13 Laight St., NYC	(212) 226-7560
Meyer, Rich/13 Laight St., NYC	(212) 226-7560
Meyerowitz, Joel/817 West End Ave., NYC	(212) 666-6505
Meyers, Karen/7527 Rosemary Road, Pittsburgh	(412) 731-8608
Michael, Pamela/36 Riverside Dr., NYC	(212) 799-8281
Michaels, Darren/4440 Sepulveda Blvd., Sherman Oaks	(818) 788-1041
Michaels, Duane/109 E. 19th St., NYC	(212) 473-1563
Michelson, Eric/37 E. 63rd St., NYC	(212) 633-1660
Mikoleski, Pete/86-13 55th Rd., Elmhurst	(718) 478-4133
Milbauer, Dennis/15 W. 28th St., NYC	(212) 532-3702
Milens, Sanders H./P.O. Box 805, Shelburne	(802) 985-8577
Milewicz, Marck/160 Fifth Ave., NYC	(212) 924-6760
Milisenda, John/424 56th St., Bklyn.	(718) 439-4571
Miller, Ann/130 W. 86th St., NYC	(212) 496-6159
Miller, Donald L./295 Central Park W., NYC	(212) 496-2830
Miller, J.T./12 Forrest Edge Dr., Titusville	(609) 737-3116
Miller, Josh/126 W. 22nd St., NYC	(212) 645-5420
Miller, Judith/20 E. 35th St., NYC	(212) 213-1772
Miller, Michael S./Three Clayton Rd., Morganville	(201) 536-9459
Miller, Myron/23 E. 17th St., NYC	(212) 242-3780
Miller, Robert/430 W. 14th St., NYC	(212) 242-2118
Miller, Roger/1411 Hollins, Balt.	(301) 566-1222
Miller, Sue Ann/115 W. 27th St., NYC	(212) 645-5172
Miller, Susan/NYC/(212) 905-8400	**pages 158-159, 480-481, 598-599**
Milne, Bill/140 W. 22nd St., NYC	(212) 255-0710
Milovich, Dan/590 Summit Dr., Carlisle	(717) 249-0045
Mindell, Doug/811 Boylston St., Boston	(617) 262-3968
Minh Studio/NYC	(212) 477-0649
Mirando, Gary/27 Cleveland St., Valhalla	(914) 997-6588
Mistretta, Martin, Inc./220 W. 19th St., NYC	(212) 675-1547
Mitchell & Witchell Associates/122 Parkview Avenue, NYC	(201) 617-9320
Mitchell, Benn/75 Bank St., NYC	(212) 255-8686
Mitchell, Eric/Saint Peters	(215) 469-4690
Mogerly, Jean/220 E. 65th St., NYC	(212) 758-4068
Molacek, Rudy/NYC	(212) 598-4473
Molinaro, Neil R./15 Walnut Ave., Clark	(201) 396-8980
Monaco Reps./NYC	(212) 979-5533

Montaine, Allan/61 W. Eighth St., NYC	(212) 674-0241
Monteith's Countryhouse Studios/Annville	(717) 867-2278
Moody, Glenn/444 S. Union St., Burlington	(802) 862-1984
Moore, Anthony Photography Ltd./56 The Esplanade, Toronto	(416) 363-7081
Moore, Christopher/20 W. 22nd St., NYC	(212) 242-0553
Moore, Cliff/30 Skillman, Rocky Hill	(609) 921-3754
Moore, Marvin Photograghy/5240 Blowers St., Halifax	(902) 420-1559
Moore, Robert/11 W. 25th St., NYC	(212) 691-4373
Moore, Steven/311 Church St., NYC	(212) 431-8742
Moore, Truman/873 Broadway, NYC	(212) 533-3655
Moran, Nancy/143 Greene St., NYC	(212) 529-8425
Morehand Photography Inc./200 Highpoint Ave., Weehawken	(201) 867-8025
Morello, Joe/NYC	(212) 684-2340
Moretz, Charles/529 W. 42nd St., NYC	(212) 714-1357
Moretz, Eileen P./NYC	(212) 254-3766
Morgan, Jeff/NYC/(212) 924-4000	**pages 320-321**
Morrin, John/140 W. 57th St., NYC	(212) 245-8435
Morris, Bill/NYC/(212) 685-7354	**page 373**
Morris, Leonard Prods., Inc./200 Park Ave South, NYC	(212) 473-8485
Morrison, Rick/NYC	(212) 473-3366
Morrison, Ted/NYC/(212) 279-2838	**pages 298-299**
Morrow, Christopher/163 Pleasant St., Arlington	(617) 648-6770
Morse, Lauren/NYC	(212) 807-1551
Morsillo, Les/13 Laight St., NYC	(212) 219-8009
Mosel, Sue/310 E. 46th St., NYC	(212) 599-1806
Moser, Trixie/NYC	(212) 929-7962
Moses, Janice/NYC/(212) 475-4010	**pages 446-451**
Moss & Meixler/36 W. 37th St., NYC	(212) 868-0078
Moss, Eileen/NYC	(212) 980-8061
Moss, Susan/NYC	(212) 354-8024
Mougin, Claude/227 W. 17th St., NYC	(212) 691-7895
Move Art Productions/117 E. 24th St., NYC	(212) 260-0112
Mozo Photo/Design/282 Shelton Rd., Monroe	(203) 261-7400
Mucchi, Fabio/Five W. 20th St., NYC	(212) 620-0167
Mucci, Tina/119 W. 23rd St., NYC	(212) 206-9402
Mudersbach, Gary/640 Hadley Ave., Dayton	(513) 293-6158
Mueller, Robert D./140 Seventh Ave., NYC	(212) 691-3855
Muir, Steve/Raleigh	(919) 851-0458
Mulaire, Douglas W./135 Hudson St., NYC	(212) 334-9863
Mullen, Dan/110 Madison Ave., NYC	(212) 725-8753
Muller, Rick/23 W. 31st St., NYC	(212) 967-3177
Muller, Rudy/NYC	(212) 679-8124
Mulligan, Joseph/Phila./(215) 592-1359	**pages 228-229**
Munson, Russell/458 Broadway, NYC	(212) 226-8875
Murphy, Dennis/NYC/(212) 725-3806	**pages 220-221**
Murphy, Francis/NYC	(212) 760-0057
Murray, Bob/54 Greenwich Ave, NYC	(212) 255-4410
Murray, Ric/232 W. Exchange St., Providence	(401) 751-8806
Musser, Jerry King/932 N. Second St., Harrisburg	(717) 233-4411
Muth, John/NYC	(212) 532-3479
Myers, Gene/250 N. Goodman St., Rochester	(716) 244-4420
Myers, Steve/110 S. Main, Almond	(607) 276-6400
Myriad Communications/208 W. 30th St., NYC	(212) 564-4340
Myron/127 Dorrance St., Providence	(401) 421-1946
Naar, Larry/71 E. Seventh St., NYC	(212) 254-1884
Nabe Studio/153 W. 27th St., NYC	(212) 807-6024
Nadelson, Jay/116 Mercer St., NYC	(212) 226-4266
Nagy, Andy/28 Caswell Ave., Fords	(201) 636-2965
Nahoum, Ken/NYC/(212) 924-8880	**pages 268-271**
Naideau, Harold/233 W. 26th St, NYC	(212) 691-2942
Nakamura, Tohru/112 Greene St., NYC	(212) 334-8011
Nakano, George/8 ½ McDougal Alley, NYC	(212) 228-9370
Namuth, Hans/20 W. 22nd St., NYC	(212) 691-3220
Napaer, Michele/NYC	(212) 219-0325
Naples, Elizabeth/210 Fifth Ave., NYC	(212) 889-1476
Nardiello, Carl/143 W. 20th St., NYC	(212) 242-3106
Nasmith, Peter/29 Sackville St., Toronto	(416) 362-3770
Nathan, Eunice/NYC/(212) 772-1776	**pages 56-59**
Nathan, Simon/175 Prospect St., E. Orange	(201) 675-5026
Needham, Steven Mark/111 W. 19th St., NYC	(212) 206-1914
Neenan, Michael/NYC	(212) 860-8280
Neil, Joe/150 Fifth Ave., NYC	(212) 691-1881
Neill, Michael/418 Beresford Ave., Toronto	(416) 766-3928

Neleman, Hans/NYC/(212) 645-5832 .... **pages 414-415**
Nelken, Dan Studio, Inc./43 W. 27th St., NYC .... (212) 532-7471
Nemeth, Bruce/441 E. Arrowood Rd., Charlotte .... (704) 525-6531
Nemeth, Judy/930 N. Poplar St., Charlotte .... (704) 375-9292
Nerney, Dan/5 Vincent Pl., Rowayton .... (203) 853-2782
Nesbit, Charles/NYC/(212) 925-0225 .... **pages 386-387**
Neumann, Peter/30 E. 20th St., NYC .... (212) 420-9538
Neumann, William/119 W. 23rd St., NYC .... (212) 691-7405
Newirth, Scott/104 W. 17th St., NYC .... (212) 242-7303
Newler, Michael/135 W. 29th St., NYC .... (212) 643-0022
Newman, Arnold/39 W. 67th St., NYC .... (212) 877-4510
Newman, Marvin E./561 Broadway, NYC .... (212) 219-1228
Nexvisions, Inc./NYC/(212) 371-9771 .... **pages 242-243**
Ney, Nancy/NYC .... (212) 260-4300
Ng, Kaimen Norman/405 E. 92nd St., NYC .... (212) 860-2168
Ngo, Meng H./21 Village Commons, Fishkill .... (914) 897-2836
Niagara Studio, The/41 Niagara St., Toronto .... (416) 865-1868
Niccolini, Dianora/356 E. 78th St., NYC .... (212) 288-1698
Nicholas, Peter/29 Bleecker St., NYC .... (212) 529-5560
Nichols, Don Studio, Inc./1241 University Ave., Rochester .... (716) 461-9666
Nicolaysen, Ron/448 W. 37th St., NYC .... (212) 947-5167
Nicotera, Doug/8 Roller Dr., Harrisburg .... (717) 939-4908
Niefield, Terry/NYC/(212) 686-8722 .... **pages 54-55**
Nigro, Giorgio/80 Spadina Ave., Toronto .... (416) 363-3287
Nilsen, Geoffrey/2565 Third St., S.F. .... (415) 648-7090
Niwa Studio, Inc./NYC/(212) 627-4608 .... **pages 370-371**
Nivelle, Serge Studio, Inc./145 Hudson St., NYC .... (212) 226-6200
Nobart-New York, Inc./110 Leroy St., NYC .... (212) 633-0033
Noble, Inc./2313 Maryland Ave., Baltimore .... (301) 235-5235
Noel, Claude/409 Front St. W., Toronto .... (416) 366-0142
Nones, Leonard/Five Union Sq. W., NYC .... (212) 741-3990
Norman & Cheek/3000 Chestnut Ave., Balt. .... (301) 235-4771
Norma, Helen/NYC .... (212) 486-9575
Norstein, Marshall/399 Sackett St., Bklyn. .... (718) 522-4909
North Light Photographics, Ltd./332 Dante Ct., Holbrook .... (516) 585-2900
Northlight Visual Comm. Group, Inc./21 Quine Street, Cranford ... (201) 272-1155
Norwood, Nick/15 W. 18th St., NYC .... (212) 645-8220
Noto, Rino/276 Carlaw Ave., Toronto .... (416) 465-8094
Nozik, Ira/50-A Wintonbury Mall, Bloomfield .... (203) 243-2800
O'Baitz, Otto/130 Maple Ave., Red Bank .... (201) 530-8809
O'Brien, Michael/Brooklyn/(718) 398-2235 .... **pages 412-413**
O'Connell, Bill/791 Tremont St., Boston .... (617) 437-7556
O'Connor, Kelly/Los Gatos .... (408) 378-5600
O'Connor, Thom/74 Fifth Ave., NYC .... (212) 620-0723
O'Neal, Charles T./416 W. 20th St., NYC .... (212) 691-7768
O'Neill, Michael/134 Tenth Ave., NYC .... (212) 807-8777
O'Rourke, J. Barry/578 Broadway, NYC .... (212) 226-7113
O'Rourke, Randy/578 Broadway, NYC .... (212) 226-7424
O'Rourke-Page Assocs./NYC .... (212) 772-0346
O'Toole, Terence Images/104 Union Park St., Boston .... (617) 426-6357
Oberdorf, Elizabeth Joy/724 Northbrook Rd., Kennett Square ..... (215) 347-0370
Obremski Studio/1200 Broadway, NYC .... (212) 684-2933
Ochi, Toru/NYC .... (212) 807-7711
Ockenga, Starr/68 Laight St., NYC .... (212) 431-5158
Odor, Lou/288 Kerrigan Blvd-1, Newark .... (201) 371-2669
Oelbaum, Zeva/NYC .... (212) 486-9575
Oesterreicher, Albert/488 Seventh Ave., NYC .... (212) 643-3100
Ogden, Perry/47 E. 19th St., NYC .... (212) 505-2660
Ogilvy, Stephen/876 Broadway, NYC .... (212) 505-9005
Ogrudek, Robert/NYC/(212) 645-8008 .... **pages 68-71, 110-111**
Okada, Tom/81 Park Ter. W., NYC .... (212) 304-4645
Oliver, Clifford/79 Fourth St., Troy .... (518) 274-0160
Oliver-McConnel Photography, Inc./Eight Adler Dr., E. Syracuse .. (315) 433-1005
Olivo, John, Inc./545 W. 45th St., NYC .... (212) 765-8812
Olman, Bradley/15 W. 24th St., NYC .... (212) 243-0649
Olmsted Studio/118 South St., Boston .... (617) 542-2024
Olof/NYC/(212) 929-9067 .... **pages 344-345**
Onaya-Ogrudek/NYC/(212) 645-8008 .... **pages 110-111**
Onyx/NYC .... (212) 633-2050
Orenstein, Ronn/511 W. 33rd St., NYC .... (212) 967-6075
Oristaglio, Susan/155 W. 81st St., NYC .... (212) 877-8495
Orrico, Chas. J./72 Barry Ln., Syosset .... (516) 364-9826
Ortiz, Gilbert/19 W. 21st St., NYC .... (212) 620-7936

Ortner, Jon/64 W. 87th St., NYC .... (212) 873-1950
Osborn, Jim/3330 Emerson Ave., Parkersburg .... (304) 428-1631
Osentoski, Rick/13 E. 31st St., NYC .... (212) 679-5919
Osonitsch, Robert/112 Fourth Ave., NYC .... (212) 533-1920
Oudi/33 Bleecker St., NYC .... (212) 777-0847
Owen, Sigrid/221 E. 31st St., NYC .... (212) 686-5190
Owens, Frank/NYC/(212) 686-2535 .... **page 367**
Paccione Photography, Inc./73 Fifth Ave., NYC .... (212) 691-8674
Pace Ltd./560B Central Ave., Cedarhurst .... (516) 295-5000
Padys, Diane/NYC/(212) 941-8532 .... **pages 41-43**
Page Assocs./NYC/(212) 772-0346 .... **pages 584-585**
Page, Lee/NYC/(212) 286-9159 .... **pages 332-333**
Pagliuso, Jean/315 Central Park W., NYC .... (212) 580-7044
Paige, Peter/269 Parkside Rd., Harrington Park .... (201) 767-3150
Pajluiso, Jean/315 Central Park W., NYC .... (212) 873-6594
Pallat, Caroline M./506 NInth St., Bklyn .... (718) 965-0894
Palmer, Gabe/Fire Hill Farm, W. Redding .... (203) 938-2514
Palmer-Smith, Glenn/NYC/(212) 769-3940 .... **pages 350-351, 356,357, 386-387**
Palmer/Kane, Inc./30 Rockledge Rd., W. Redding .... (203) 938-2514
Palubniak, Jerry & Nancy/144 W. 27th St., NYC .... (212) 645-2838
Panaro, Adrian/440 E. 75th St., NYC .... (212) 988-0398
Panopoulos, Gerald/458 W. 20th St., NYC .... (212) 242-3132
Papadopolous, Peter/NYC .... (212) 675-8830
Papadoullos, Jeannie/Whitestone/(718) 767-0573 .... **pages 166-167**
Paras, Michael N./309 Fifth Ave., NYC .... (212) 779-9135
Parkes, Ted/264 Seaton St., Toronto .... (416) 923-6025
Parks, Peggy/21 Broadview Dr., San Rafael .... (415) 457-5300
Parnell, John/125 Eastern Pkwy., Bklyn. .... (718) 398-8204
Parsekian, John/Five Lawrence St., Bloomfield .... (201) 748-9717
Parsons, Andy/59 Wareham St., Boston .... (617) 542-9071
Parvis, Frank/78 Fifth Ave., NYC .... (212) 473-5868
Pasley,Richard/21 Erie St., Cambridge .... (617) 864-8386
Pastor, Mariano/20 W. 22nd St., NYC .... (212) 242-0553
Pateman, Michael/155 E. 35th St., NYC .... (212) 685-6584
Paterson Photographic Works, Inc./6 Croft St., Toronto .... (416) 968-6696
Paul, Richard/2011 Noble St., Pittsburgh .... (412) 271-6609
Paulin-Gilmore Studios, Inc./NYC .... (212) 477-2047
Payne, Carol/NYC .... (212) 481-6433
Payne, John J./43 Brookfield Pl., Pleasantville .... (914) 747-1282
Pease, Greg & Assocs., Inc./23 E. 22nd St., Baltimore .... (301) 332-0583
Peck, Joseph/878 Lexington Ave., NYC .... (212) 472-1929
Peden, John/155 W. 19th St., NYC .... (212) 255-2674
Pederson, Lane/NYC/(212) 929-9001 .... **pages 132-133**
Pehlman, Barry/542 Merioneth Dr., Exton .... (215) 524-1444
Peirce, George E./133 Ramapo Ave., Pompton Lakes .... (201) 831-8418
Peluso, Frank/15 Caspar Berger Rd., Whitehouse Sta. .... (201) 534-9637
Penn, Irving/NYC .... (212) 246-0679
Penny, Donald/NYC/(212) 633-9650 .... **pages 126-127**
Peoples, Joe/11 W. 20th St., NYC .... (212) 633-0026
Pereg, Larry/NYC .... (212) 645-9136
Perkell, Jeff/36 W. 20th St., NYC .... (212) 645-1506
Perno, Jack/NYC/(212) 679-5933 .... **pages 192-193**
Perron, Bea/35 E. 38th St., NYC .... (212) 953-9046
Perweiler Studio, Inc./873 Broadway, NYC .... (212) 925-8750
Peterson, Gosta/200 E. 87th St., NYC .... (212) 876-0560
Peterson, Grant/NYC .... (212) 219-0004
Peterson, Rick/NYC .... (212) 772-0346
Petku, Diane/385 Sumner Ave., Whitehall .... (215) 439-1577
Petöe, Dénes/NYC/(212) 213-3311 .... **pages 392-399**
Petrie, Jack/28 Vesey St., NYC .... (212) 301-5196
Petrucelli, Tony/NYC .... (212) 490-9269
Petters, Fredric/241 W. 36th St., NYC .... (212) 629-0868
Pettinato, Anthony/42 Greene St., NYC .... (212) 226-9380
Pfizenmaier, Edward/236 W. 27th St., NYC .... (212) 627-5659
Philiba, Allan A./3408 Bertha Dr., Baldwin .... (212) 286-0948
Philippeaux, Eddy J./220 Anchor Way, Uniondale .... (516) 483-3745
Phillips, Bernard/3100 Stonybrook Dr., Raleigh .... (919) 878-1611
Phillips, Jamie/82 Greene St., NYC .... (212) 219-1799
Phillips, Robert Ltd./101 W. 57th St., NYC .... (212) 757-5190
Phoebe/68 Thomas St., NYC .... (212) 962-0038
Photo Arts/282 4th St., Jersey City .... (201) 795-3448
Photo Forum/110 W. 17th St., NYC .... (212) 924-9460
Photo Shuttle: Japan/47 Greene St., NYC .... (212) 966-9641

PhotoGraphic Images/39 Westmoreland Ave., White Plains	(914) 761-8885
PhotoPros/90 Earhart, Williamsville	(716) 632-2810
Photographers & Co., The/760 State St., Schenectady	(518) 377-9457
Photographic House, Inc./158 W. Clinton St., Dover	(201) 366-3000
Photographic Illus., Ltd./7th & Ranstead Sts., Phila.	(215) 925-7073
Photographic Studio, The, Inc./150 Clearbrook Rd., Elmsford	(914) 592-7788
Piaget, John/520 Nepperhan Ave., Yonkers	(914) 376-7401
Pickerell, James Howard/110-E Frederick Ave., Rockville	(301) 251-0720
Picturesques Studios/1879 Old Cuthbert Rd., Cherry Hill	(609) 354-1903
Picturewise, Inc./Ten Terhune Pl., Hackensack	(201) 343-1060
Pierce, Barbara L./Main St., Pittsford	(802) 483-2283
Pierce, Jennifer/1376 York Ave., NYC	(212) 744-3810
Pierce, Richard/NYC/(212) 947-8241	**pages 354-355**
Pilgreen, John/140 E. 13th St., NYC	(212) 982-4887
Pilon, Michel/141 Shannon, Montréal	(514) 861-6169
Pilossof, Judd/NYC/(212) 989-8971	**pages 434-435**
Pinderhughes Studio/122 W. 26th St., NYC	(212) 989-6706
Pinney, Doris/22 Covewood Dr., Rowayton	(203) 853-3314
Pioppo, Peter/50 W. 17th St., NYC	(212) 243-0661
Piscioneri, Joseph/333 Park Ave. S., NYC	(212) 533-7982
Pite, Jonathan E./244 E. 21st St., NYC	(212) 777-5484
Pizzarello, Charlie/15 W. 18th St., NYC	(212) 243-8441
Pizzolorusso, Christopher/NYC	(212) 686-7175
Plank, David/Cherry & Carpenter St., Reading	(215) 376-3461
Plauto/343 W. Fifth St., NYC	(212) 254-9618
Plessner International/121 W. 27th St., NYC	(212) 645-2121
Plotkin, Bruce/NYC/(212) 691-6185	**pages 292-293**
Plotkin, Burt/141 Wooster St., NYC	(212) 995-0300
Plum Studios Inc./1209 King St. W., Toronto	(416) 535-4484
Pobereskin, Joseph/453 Washington Ave., NYC	(212) 619-3711
Pobiner, Ted Studios, Inc./381 Park Ave. S., NYC	(212) 679-5911
Pocock, Philip/330 E. 19th St., NYC	(212) 460-5683
Poggenpohl, Eric/12 Walnut St., Amherst	(413) 256-0948
Pohuski, Michael/36 S. Paca St., Balt.	(301) 962-5404
Poinot, Remy/NYC	(212) 260-0112
Polansky, Allen/1431 Park Ave., Baltimore	(301) 383-9021
Pollack, David/132 W. 15th St., NYC	(212) 242-2115
Pollack, Pamela/5775 Big Tree Rd., NYC	(716) 662-6002
Pollard, Pat/24 Spring Ln., Farmington	(203) 677-9557
Polott, Mark/324 E. 34th St., NYC	(212) 679-0047
Polsky, Herb/1024 Ave. of the Americas, NYC	(212) 730-0508
Polumbaum, Ted/326 Harvard St., Cambridge	(617) 491-4947
Pool, Penny/22 Barker Ave., White Plains	(914) 997-2200
Pope-Lance, Elton Photography/125 Stock Farm Rd., Sudbury	(508) 443-4393
Popp, Wendy/NYC	(212) 807-0840
Popper, Andrew/330 First Ave., NYC	(212) 982-9713
Porges, Danny/37 W. 39th St., NYC	(212) 391-4117
Porta, Art/333 Park Ave. S., NYC	(212) 353-0488
Porto, James/NYC/(212) 966-4407	**pages 170-171**
Postal, Jonathan/280 Mulberry St., NYC	(212) 226-2799
Poster, James/210 Fifth Ave., NYC	(212) 206-4065
Potter, Anthony/509 W. Fayette St., Syracuse	(800) 344-2019
Potter, Lincoln/NYC	(212) 772-0346
Pottle, Jock/222 Valley Pl., Mamaroneck	(914) 698-4060
Powers, Guy/534 W. 43rd St., NYC	(212) 563-3177
Powers, James M./15 Jerome Pl., Leominster	(508) 534-3664
Powers, Lisa/Hollywood	(213) 874-5877
Powers-Trupp, Elizabeth/16 W. 22nd St., NYC	(212) 463-8302
Pressman, Herb/225 Rector Pl., NYC	(212) 945-4228
Prete, Laura/57 Whitfield St., Guilford	(203) 458-8680
Prete, Ralph/346 Coe Ave., E. Haven	(203) 469-9269
Prezant, Steve/666 Greenwich St., NYC	(212) 727-0590
Pribula, Barry/59 First Ave., NYC	(212) 777-7612
Price, Clayton/205 W. 19th St., NYC	(212) 929-7721
Price, David/Four E. 78th St., NYC	(212) 794-9040
Price, M. Paul/NYC	(212) 629-1864
Price, Shirlee/165 Ave. A, NYC	(212) 254-3530
Prigent, Roger/253 E. 74th St., NYC	(212) 288-7569
Priggen, Leslie/215 E. 73rd St., NYC	(212) 772-2230
Proulx, Matthew/27 Willard Ter., Stamford	(203) 322-6430
Pruitt, David/NYC	(212) 807-0767
Pruzan, Michael/NYC/(212) 686-5505	**pages 450-451**
Pszenica, Judith/Two Scribner Ave., Norwalk	(203) 866-2929

NORTHEAST 27

Purvis, Charles/84 Thomas St., NYC .... (212) 619-8028
Putterman, Jaydie/NYC .... (212) 260-0112
Quartuccio, Dom/410 W. 24th St., NYC .... (212) 727-7329
Quat, Daniel/380 Rector Pl., NYC .... (212) 945-1814
RS Photography/48 Union St., Stamford .... (203) 967-4438
Raab, Michael/NYC .... (212) 533-0030
Rabanne, Roberto/1560 Broadway, NYC .... (212) 869-3050
Rabdau, Yvonne/Stormville .... (914) 221-4643
Ragsdale, Robert C. Ltd./21 Avenue Rd., Toronto .... (416) 967-3326
Rajs, Jake/252 W. 30th St., Apt. #10-A, NYC .... (212) 947-9403
Rapoport, David/55 Perry St., NYC .... (212) 691-5528
Rapp, Gerald & Cullen, Inc./NYC/(212) 889-3337 .... **pages 92-95**
Raso, Peter/1940 Mayflower Ave., Bronx .... (212) 829-4992
Rattner, Robert/106-15 Jamaica Ave., Richmond Hill .... (718) 441-0826
Raupp, Gunther/NYC/(212) 682-1490 .... **pages 82-83**
Ravid, Joyce/NYC .... (212) 633-2050
Ray, Bill/350 Central Park W., NYC .... (212) 222-7680
Ray, Marlys/NYC .... (212) 222-7680
Raycroft, Jim/326 A St., Boston .... (617) 542-7229
Red Circle Studios/Five W. 19th St., NYC .... (212) 924-4545
Redmond, Calvin/Five W. 20th St., NYC .... (212) 675-4946
Reed, Robert/NYC .... (212) 243-2750
Reed, Tom/9505 Adelphi Rd., Silver Springs .... (301) 439-2912
Reese, Kay & Assoc., Inc./225 Central Park W., NYC .... (212) 799-1133
Reichman, Amy/348 W. 14th St., NYC .... (212) 691-6711
Reid, Pamela/66 Crosby St., NYC .... (212) 925-5909
Reiff, Hal/129 E. 19th St., NYC .... (212) 533-0699
Reiher, Jim/31 W. 31st St., NYC .... (212) 736-3131
Reinhardt, Mike/881 Seventh Ave., NYC .... (212) 541-4787
Reinmiller, Mary Ann/163 W. 17th St., NYC .... (212) 243-4302
Reis, Jon/141 The Commons, Ithaca .... (607) 272-1966
Renard, Jean/142 Berkley St., Boston .... (617) 266-8673
Rentmeester, Co/68 Griffing Avenue, W. Hampton Beach .... (516) 288-1310
Ressmeyer, Roger Inc./61 Hill St., Southampton .... (516) 283-6183
Reuben, Martin/1231 Superior, Cleveland .... (216) 781-8644
Revette, David/111 Sunset Ave., Syracuse .... (315) 422-1558
Reynolds, Vee Prods./245 E. 19th St., NYC .... (212) 420-5955
Reznicki, Jack/568 Broadway, NYC .... (212) 925-0771
Rezny, Aaron/NYC/(212) 691-1894 .... **pages 88-89**
Rezny, Abe/28 Cadman Plz W., Brooklyn .... (212) 226-7747
Richards, Jim/75 Park Ave., Garden City Pk. .... (516) 248-2359
Richards, Mark/58 Falcon St., Needham .... (617) 449-7135
Richman, Susan/119 W. 25th St., NYC .... (212) 929-8801
Richmond, Jack/Boston .... (617) 482-7158
Rickard, Pierce/241 W. 36th St., NYC .... (212) 947-8241
Rieb, Robert Communications/24 Narrow Rocks Rd., Westport .... (203) 227-0061
Riemer, Ken/180 St. Paul St., Rochester .... (716) 232-5450
Ries, Henry/204 E. 35th St., NYC .... (212) 689-3794
Ries, Stan/48 Great Jones St., NYC .... (212) 533-1852
Right Image, The, Inc./Five W. 20th St., NYC .... (212) 620-0167
Riley, Carin & David/152 W. 25th St., NYC .... (212) 741-3662
Riley, Jon/12 E. 37th St., NYC .... (212) 532-8326
Riley, Laura/Hidden Spring Farm, Pittstown .... (201) 735-7707
Rioux, Paul Emile/1850 rue Notre Dame O., Montréal .... (514) 935-8749
Ritter, Robin/NYC .... (212) 645-1177
Rivelli, William/303 Park Ave. S., NYC .... (212) 254-0990
Rizzo, Alberto/188 Grand St., NYC .... (212) 941-1012
Rizzo, John/146 Halstead St., Rochester .... (716) 288-1102
Robb, Steve/535 Albany St., Boston .... (617) 542-6565
Roberts, Grant/NYC .... (212) 242-2000
Roberts, Terence/1909 N. Market St., Wilmington .... (302) 658-8854
Robins, Lawrence/50 W. 17th St., NYC .... (212) 206-0436
Robins, Susan/124 N. Third St., Phila. .... (215) 238-9988
Robinson, George A./A-4 Stonehedge Dr., S. Burlington .... (802) 862-6902
Robinson, Herb/11 W. 25th St., NYC .... (212) 627-1478
Robinson, James/NYC/(212) 580-1793 .... **page 156**
Robinson, Madeleine/NYC/(212) 243-3138 .... **pages 570-571**
Robledo, Maria I./43 W. 29th St., NYC .... (212) 213-1517
Roderick, Jennifer/NYC/(212) 268-1788 .... **pages 265-267**
Rodowitz, Nancy/31 Jane St., NYC .... (212) 620-9052
Rody Productions/205 E. 78th St., NYC .... (212) 584-3887
Rokach, Allen/NY Botanical Gardens, Bronx .... (212) 220-8698
Rooney, Lawrence/32 W. 40th St., NYC .... (212) 869-9038

Roos, Warren/135 Somerset St., Portland .... (207) 773-3771
Rose Studios/11 Westport Rd., Wilton .... (203) 762-9408
Rose, Uli/NYC/(212) 988-8890 .... **pages 316-317**
Roseman, Shelly/1238 Callowhill St., Phila. .... (215) 922-1430
Rosen, Trix/810 Broadway, NYC .... (212) 228-8100
Rosenberg, Arlene/377 W. 11th St., NYC .... (212) 675-7983
Rosenberg, Arnold T./14 Georgica Close Rd., E. Hampton .... (516) 324-1227
Rosenberg, Ken/514 West End Ave., NYC .... (212) 362-3149
Rosenberg, Len/2077 Clinton Ave. S., Rochester .... (716) 244-6910
Rosenthal, Barry/NYC/(212) 645-0433 .... **pages 216-217**
Rosenthal, Ben/20 E. 17th St., NYC .... (212) 807-7737
Rosenthal, Marshal M./231 W. 18th St., NYC .... (212) 807-1247
Rosner, Eric/314 N. 13th St., Phila. .... (215) 629-1240
Ross Productions/310 E. 46th St., NYC .... (212) 986-5122
Ross, Bob /E.C.V. & Forensic/98 Riverside Dr., NYC .... (212) 799-1040
Ross, Douglas/610 Eighth Ave., E. Northport .... (516) 754-2023
Ross, Ken/80 Madison Ave., NYC .... (212) 213-9205
Ross, Steve/Ten Montgomery Pl., Bklyn. .... (718) 783-6451
Rossi, Dave/121 Central Ave., Westfield .... (201) 232-8300
Rossignol, Lara/NYC .... (212) 243-2750
Rossum, Cheryl/310 E. 75th St., NYC .... (212) 628-3173
Roth, Seth D./NYC/(212) 620-7050 .... **pages 44-45**
Roth, Eric/337 Summer St., Boston .... (617) 338-5358
Roth, Joan/215 E. 80th St., NYC .... (212) 628-8160
Roth, Peter/270 Riverside Dr., NYC .... (212) 222-7748
Rotman, Jefferey/14 Cottage Ave., Somerville .... (617) 666-0874
Rousseau, Will/1068 Second Ave., NYC .... (212) 755-5330
Rovtar, Ron/49 Walhalla Rd., Columbus .... (614) 261-6083
Rowin, Stanley/791 Tremont St., Boston .... (617) 437-0641
Rozsa, Nick/NYC .... (212) 734-5629
Rubenstein, Raeanne/Eight Thomas St., NYC .... (212) 964-8426
Rubin, Al/250 Mercer St., NYC .... (212) 674-4535
Rubin, Daniel/126 W. 22nd St., NYC .... (212) 989-2400
Rubin, Elaine/322 Eigth Ave., NYC .... (212) 645-0700
Rubin, J. Ivan/NYC/(212) 645-0020 .... **page 136**
Ruderman, Linda/1245 Park Ave., NYC .... (212) 369-7531
Rudnick, James .... (212) 466-6337
Rudnick, Michael/16 W. 22nd St., NYC .... (212) 463-8302
Rudnicki, Stefan/NYC .... (212) 228-3762
Rugen-Kory/27 W. 20th St., NYC .... (212) 242-2772
Ruggeri, Francesco/71 St. Marks Pl., NYC .... (212) 505-8477
Ruggeri, Lawrence W./Ten Post Office Rd., Silver Spring .... (301) 588-3131
Ruggiero, Marie/185 E. 85th St., NYC .... (212) 534-3071
Rumbough, Stan/154 W. 18th St., NYC .... (212) 206-0183
Runyon, Paul/113 Arch St., Phila. .... (215) 238-0655
Ruschak, Robert P./3633 Forest Ave., Munhall .... (412) 462-3072
Russell Studios/103 Ardale, Boston .... (617) 325-2500
Russell Studios/14 Hawk St., Scotia .... (518) 370-3600
Russell, Patrick/NYC .... (212) 243-2750
Russo, Karen/NYC .... (212) 749-6382
Russo, Rich Adv. Photography, Inc./11 Clinton St., Morristown .... (201) 538-6954
Rusten, Shelly/225 First Ave., NYC .... (212) 982-7063
Rutherford, H. John Jr./646 Amsterdam Ave., NYC .... (212) 580-4171
Ryan, Will/NYC .... (212) 242-6270
Rysinski, Edward/NYC .... (212) 807-7301
Sabal, David/20 W. 20th St., NYC .... (212) 242-8464
Sacco, Vittorio/126 Fifth Ave., NYC .... (212) 929-9225
Sacha, Bob/370 Central Park W., NYC .... (212) 749-4128
Sachs, Arthur/200 Park Ave. S., NYC .... (212) 777-6993
Sachs, Joseph/Six W. 28th St., NYC .... (212) 685-1441
Sacramone, Dario/NYC/(212) 929-0487 .... **pages 284-285**
Sahaida, Michael/Five W. 19th St., NYC .... (212) 924-4545
Sailors, David/123 Prince St., NYC .... (212) 505-9654
Sakas, Peter/400 Lafayette St., NYC .... (212) 254-6096
Sakmanoff, George/179 Massachusetts Ave., Boston .... (617) 262-7227
Salaff, Fred/322 W. 57th St., NYC .... (212) 246-3699
Salamon, Londa/2634 Parrish, Phila. .... (215) 765-6632
Salant, Robin/317 Elm St., Westfield .... (201) 654-6847
Salaverry, Philip/NYC .... (212) 807-0896
Salmolraghl, Franco/NYC .... (212) 772-0346
Salsbery, Lee/14 Seventh St. N.E., Wash. D.C. .... (202) 543-1222
Saltiel, Ron/78 Fifth Ave., NYC .... (212) 627-0003
Salzano Studio, Inc./29 W. 15th St., NYC .... (212) 242-4820

NORTHEAST 29

Samara Photography, Inc./713 Erie Blvd. W., Syracuse	(315) 476-4984
Samardge, Nick/302 W. 86th St., NYC	(212) 226-6770
Samuels, Charlie/216 W. 99th St., NYC	(212) 865-5044
Samuels, Rosemary/NYC/(212) 477-3567	**pages 64-67**
Sanchez-Weber Photography/635 Chili Ave., Rochester	(716) 436-8329
Sander, Vicki/155 E. 29th St., NYC	(212) 683-7835
Sanders, Chris/NYC/(212) 645-6111	**pages 66-67**
Sanderson, John/2310 Penn Ave., Pittsburgh	(412) 263-2121
Sandone, A.J./132 W. 21 St., NYC	(212) 807-6472
Sands, Mark/57 E. 77th St., NYC	(212) 288-6152
Sangirardi, Joyce/43 E. 19th St., NYC	(212) 420-9738
Santos, Antonio Photography/202 E. 21st St., NYC	(212) 477-3514
Sapienza, Louis A./1344 Martine Ave., Plainfield	(201) 756-9200
Sarner, Sylvia/Ten E. 78th St., NYC	(212) 744-5943
Sartan, Edward/488 Seventh Ave., NYC	(212) 643-3100
Sartor, Vittorio/10 Bleecker St., NYC	(212) 674-2994
Sasahara, Mark T./91-93 N. Union St., Burlington	(802) 864-4992
Sato, Susumu/NYC/(212) 741-0688	**pages 382-383**
Satterthwaite, Victoria/Phila./(215) 925-4233	**pages 72-73**
Satterwhite, Al/NYC/(212) 219-0808	**pages 162-163**
Satterwhite, Steve/13 Avenue A, NYC	(212) 254-8844
Sauer, Max Studio, The/1010 Ste. Catherine W., Montréal	(514) 861-6666
Saunders, Daryl-Ann/NYC	(212) 242-0942
Saunders, T. & Assocs./163-A Manning Ave., Toronto	(416) 368-1611
Sauter, Ron/183 St. Paul St., Rochester	(716) 232-1361
Savage, Bob/10 Sycamore St., Pt.Jeff. Sta.	(516) 474-3375
Savage, Clinton/Five W. 19th St., NYC	(212) 924-4545
Savell, Becky/204 River Rd., Grand View	(914) 359-1222
Saylor, H. Durston/14 E. 4th St., NYC	(212) 620-7122
Scanlon, Henry/30 Irving Pl., NYC	(212) 353-8600
Scarbrough, Carl W./20 Beacon St., Boston	(617) 720-4400
Scarlett, Nora/37 W. 20th St., NYC	(212) 741-2620
Scavullo, Francesco/212 E. 63rd St., NYC	(212) 838-2450
Schaeffer, Bruce/631 N. Pottstown Pike, Exton	(215) 363-5230
Schafer, Jim/109 Forest Hills Rd., Pittsburgh	(412) 371-2491
Schatten, Diane/NYC	(212) 688-3262
Schein, Barry/6W 20th St., NYC	(212) 432-6844
Schenk, Fred/112 Fourth Ave., NYC	(212) 677-1250
Scher, Dorothea/235 E. 22nd St., NYC	(212) 689-7273
Scherzi, James/Syracuse	(315) 455-7961
Schiavone, Carmen/271 Central Park W., NYC	(212) 496-6016
Schiff, Nancy Rica/24 W. 30th St., NYC	(212) 679-9444
Schild, Irving/34 E. 23rd St., NYC	(212) 475-0090
Schiller-Ogrudek/NYC/(212) 645-8008	**pages 68-71**
Schinz, Marina/222 Central Park W., NYC	(212) 246-0457
Schlachter, Trudy/NYC	(212) 741-3128
Schleipman, Russell/298 A. Columbus Ave., Boston	(617) 267-1677
Schlowsky Photography/73 Old Rd., Weston	(617) 899-5110
Schnakenberg, Eric/Whitestone/(718) 767-0573	**pages 166-167**
Schneider Studio Assocs., Inc./135 W. 36th St., NYC	(212) 695-3620
Schneider, Josef/119 W. 57th St., NYC	(212) 265-1223
Schneider, Peter/31 W. 21st St., NYC	(212) 366-6242
Schochat, Kevin R./150 E. 18th St., NYC	(212) 475-7068
Schoon, Tim/Lancaster	(717) 291-9483
Schramm, F. Emily/167 Perry St., NYC	(212) 620-0284
Schreck, Bruno/873 Broadway, NYC	(212) 254-3078
Schreiber, Martin H./611 Broadway, NYC	(212) 460-9744
Schreyer, Mark/One S. Portland Ave., Bklyn.	(718) 596-7745
Schroers, Kenneth/188 Highland Ave., Clifton	(201) 472-8395
Schub & Bear/136 E 57 St., NYC	(212) 246-0679
Schulman, Martin/12023 Coldstream Dr., Potomac	(202) 928-1300
Schulze, Fred/38 W. 21st St., NYC	(212) 242-0930
Schupf, John Studio, Inc./580 Broadway, NYC	(212) 226-2250
Schwartz, Andy/11 W. 30th St., NYC	(212) 947-0485
Schwartz, Linda L./One Franklin Dr., Mays Landing	(609) 625-7617
Schweikardt, Eric/Southport	(203) 221-7132
Schwerin, Ron/889 Broadway, NYC	(212) 228-0340
Science Source/60 E. 56th St., NYC	(212) 758-3420
Sclight, Greg/322 Second Ave., NYC	(212) 677-5146
Scocozza, Victor/42 W. 24t St., NYC	(212) 627-2177
Scott, James/210 N. Fillmore St., Arlington	(703) 522-8261
Scully, Michael/122 W. 71st St., NYC	(212) 496-0650
Sculnick, Herb/611 Warren St., Hudson	(518) 828-2178

Sea, Gerard/568 Broadway, NYC .... (212) 941-9777
Secunda, Shel/112 Fourth Ave., NYC .... (212) 477-0241
Sederowsky, Ben/308 E. 49th St., NYC .... (212) 752-7466
Seftel, Tobi/166 W. 22nd St., NYC .... (212) 243-6815
Segerstrom, Rebecca/NYC/(212) 242-0181 .... **pages 382-383**
Seghers II, Carroll/441 Park Ave. S., NYC .... (212) 679-4582
Seidman, Barry/85 Fifth Ave., NYC .... (212) 255-6666
Seitz & Seitz/1006 N. Second St., Harrisburg .... (717) 232-7944
Seitz, Sepp/12 E. 22nd St., NYC .... (212) 505-9917
Sekita, Mikio/44 Lispenard St., NYC .... (212) 925-6717
Selkirk, Neil/NYC/(212) 243-6778 .... **pages 322-323**
Sellentin, Greg/NYC/(212) 645-0508 .... **pages 247-251**
Seltzer, Abe/NYC/(212) 807-0660 .... **pages 444-445**
Seltzer, Laura/NYC/(212) 334-9494 .... **pages 348-349**
Seng, Walt/810 Penn Ave., Pittsburgh .... (412) 391-6780
Sessa, Stephen/78 Exchange Pl., Port Chester .... (914) 939-7405
Severi, Robert/Wash. D.C. .... (301) 585-1010
Shacter, Susan/NYC .... (212) 598-4473
Shaffery, Nancy/Lincroft .... (201) 830-1261
Shames, Martin/140 Water St., S. Norwalk .... (203) 853-4888
Shames, Stephen/P.O. Box 77, Wynnewood .... (215) 642-0770
Shamilzadeh, Sol/214 E. 24th St., NYC .... (212) 532-1977
Shanoff, Nancy & Assocs./688 Richmand St. W., Toronto .... (416) 863-1774
Shapiro, Pam/11 W. 30th St., NYC .... (212) 967-2363
Sharko, Greg/103-56 103rd, Ozone Park .... (212) 738-9694
Sharp, Ivor/80 Front St., Toronto .... (416) 363-3991
Sharp, Steve/153 N. Third Ave., Phila. .... (215) 925-2890
Sharpshooter Studios/387 Richmond St. E., Toronto .... (416) 860-0300
Shaw, Rik Assocs./525 W. 52nd St., NYC .... (212) 757-3988
Shawn, John/129 Sea Girt Ave., Manasquan .... (201) 233-1190
Sheldon Buckman Studios/17 Kiley Dr., Randolph .... (617) 986-4773
Sheldon, John S./197 Main St., Hartford .... (802) 295-6321
Shelley, George/873 Broadway, NYC .... (212) 473-0519
Shepherd, Judith & Assocs./NYC/(212) 242-6554 .... **pages 434-435**
Sherman, Guy/108 E. 16th St., NYC .... (212) 675-4983
Shiansky, Harry/118 E. 28th St., NYC .... (212) 889-5489
Shiki/119 W. 23rd. St., NYC .... (212) 929-8847
Shim/NYC/(212) 691-1000 .... **page 372**
Shin, Judy/NYC/(212) 997-1103 .... **pages 352-353**
Shiraishi, Carl/137 E. 25th St., NYC .... (212) 679-5628
Shooting Star/NYC/(212) 447-0666 .... **page 337**
Shopper, David Photography/409 W. Broadway, Boston .... (617) 268-2044
Shotwell, John/12 Farnsworth, Boston .... (617) 357-7456
Shung, Ken/220 E. 49th St., NYC .... (212) 807-1449
Shutterbugs/149 W. 27th St., NYC .... (212) 627-5999
Sid-Hoeltzell Photog. Ltd./156 Fifth Ave., NYC .... (212) 255-0303
Siegel Studio/59 Main St., Brattleboro .... (802) 257-0691
Silano/Lumber La., Bridgehampton .... (516) 537-2338
Sillas, Lorraine/71 W. 23rd St., NYC .... (212) 243-6690
Silva-Cone Studios Ltd./260 W. 36th St., NYC .... (212) 279-0900
Silver, Larry/NYC/(212) 807-9560 .... **pages 262-263**
Silvera, Alfred/370 W. 30th St., NYC .... (212) 268-8522
Silvia, Peter Jr./20 Burdick Ave., Newport .... (401) 841-5076
Simain, George/566 Commonwealth Ave., Boston .... (617) 267-3558
Simhoni, George/33 Jefferson Ave., Toronto .... (416) 535-1955
Simko, Robert/395 South End Ave., NYC .... (212) 912-1192
Simmons, Erik Leigh/Boston .... (617) 268-4650
Simon, Debra/NYC/(212) 988-8890 .... **pages 316-317**
Simon, Peter Angelo/568 Broadway, NYC .... (212) 925-0890
Simone, Bill/Lebanon/(717) 274-3621 .... **page 164**
Simons, Stuart/71 Highland St., Paterson .... (201) 278-5050
Simpson, Jerry Studio/244 Mulberry St., NYC .... (212) 941-1255
Singer, Michele/9161 Hazen Dr., L.A. .... (213) 858-0821
Singer, Shirley/1185 Greacen Point Rd., Mamaroneck .... (914) 698-1240
Sing-Si/NYC/(212) 475-9222 .... **pages 312-313**
Sippel, Rick/118 Manton Ave., Providence .... (401) 331-8825
Sirdofsky, Arthur/112 W. 31st St., NYC .... (212) 279-7557
Sirota, Peggy/13 Gramercy Park S., NYC .... (212) 598-4473
Siteman Studios/136 Pond St., Winchester .... (617) 729-3747
Skalski, Ken/866 Broadway, NYC .... (212) 777-6207
Skelley, Ariel/80 Varick St., NYC .... (212) 226-4091
Sklute, Kenneth/1740 E. Jericho Tnpke., Huntington .... (516) 462-6100
Skogsbergh, Ulf/NYC/(212) 255-7536 .... **pages 410-411**

Skolnick-Chany/106 E. 19th St., NYC	(212) 254-3409
Skolnik, Lewis/135 W. 29th St., NYC	(212) 239-1455
Skott, Michael/244 Fifth Ave., NYC	(212) 686-4807
Slade, Chuck/12 E. 14th St., NYC	(212) 807-1153
Slavin, Fred/43 W. 24th St., NYC	(212) 627-2652
Slavin, Neal/62 Greene St., NYC	(212) 925-8167
Sleppin, Jeff/Three W. 30 St., NYC	(212) 947-1433
Slome, Nancy/121 Madison Ave., NYC	(212) 685-8185
Slotnick, Jeff Photography/225 Lafayette St., NYC	(212) 966-5162
Small, John/400 Second Ave., NYC	(212) 725-9733
Smilow, Stanford Productions/333 E. 30th St., NYC	(212) 685-9425
Smith, Bill/498 West End Ave., NYC	(212) 877-8456
Smith, David B./178 Mitchell Ave., East Meadow	(516) 565-2631
Smith, Emily/30 E. 21st St., NYC	(212) 674-8383
Smith, Gene /Profoto Inc./6312 Westfield Ave., Pennsauken	(609) 622-8045
Smith, J. Frederick/400 E. 52nd St., NYC	(212) 838-9797
Smith, Jeff/30 E. 21st St., NYC	(212) 674-8383
Smith, Kevin B./446 W. 55th St., NYC	(212) 757-4812
Smith, Maurice/NYC	(212) 260-0112
Smith, Philip W., Inc./Pennington	(609) 737-3370
Smith, Ronald Baxter/39 Parliament St., Toronto	(416) 365-1429
Smith, Sam/3280 Cedar St., Allentown	(215) 395-5447
Smith, Sean/NYC	(212) 505-5688
Smith, Stuart/68 Raymond Lane, Wilton	(203) 762-3158
Smyth, Kevin/23 Walnut Ave., Clark	(908) 388-8831
Sochurek, Howard/680 Fifth Ave., NYC	(212) 582-1860
Sokolik, Jim/NYC/(212) 241-4014	**page 527**
Solomon, Paul R./440 W. 34th St., NYC	(212) 760-1203
Somekh, Ric N./13 Laight St., NYC	(212) 219-1613
Soodak, Arlene Represents/11135 Korman Dr., Potomac	(301) 983-2343
Soorenko, Barry/5161 River Rd., Bethesda	(301) 652-1303
Soot, Olaf/419 Park Ave. S., NYC	(212) 686-4565
Sorel, Elaine/NYC/(212) 873-4417	**pages 72-73**
Sorensen, Chris/NYC	(212) 684-0551
Spadoni, Gildo Nicolo/24-41 26th St., Astoria	(718) 728-7180
Spear, Geoff/NYC	(212) 243-2750
Speier, Len/190 Riverside Dr., NYC	(212) 595-5480
Speliotis, Steven/114 E. 13th St., NYC	(212) 529-4765
Spelman, Steve/NYC/(212) 889-3337	**Vol. I pages 64-65**
Spencer, Michael J./735 Mt. Hope Ave., Rochester	(716) 475-6817
Sperduto, Stephen/18 Willett Ave., Port Chester	(914) 939-0296
Spiegel, Meryl/East Hampton	(516) 324-8602
Spiegel, Ted/Laurie Ln., S. Salem	(914) 763-3668
Spierman, Shelley/NYC/(212) 749-8911	**pages 364-365**
Spindel, David M./NYC/(212) 989-4984	**pages 314-315**
Spinelli, Frank/NYC	(212) 243-8318
Spinelli, Phil/12 W. 21st St., NYC	(212) 243-7718
Spiro, Don/137 Summit Rd., Sparta	(201) 729-6535
Spiro, Edward/340 WE. 39th St., NYC	(212) 947-7883
Spreitzer, Andy/225 E. 24th St., NYC	(212) 685-9669
St. John, Lynn/NYC	(212) 308-7744
Staedler, Lance/154 W. 27th St., NYC	(212) 370-4300
Stage, John Lewis/Iron Mountain Rd., New Milford	(914) 986-1620
Stahl, Bill/87 Mulberry Ave., Garden City	(516) 741-5709
Stahman, Robert/1200 Broadway, NYC	(212) 679-1484
Staller, Jan/37 Walker St., NYC	(212) 966-7043
Standart, Joe/Five W. 19th St., NYC	(212) 924-4545
Stanitz Photography/305 Second Ave., NYC	(212) 477-1633
Stanton, Brian/175 Fifth Ave., NYC	(212) 678-7574
Stapleton, John/6854 Radbourne Rd., Upper Darby	(215) 626-0920
Star, Scott/452 W. 19th St., NYC	(212) 627-5299
Stark, Philip/245 W. 29th St., NYC	(212) 868-5555
States, Randall Taylor/3016 Weaver Ave., Balt.	(301) 426-6910
Stayner, Becky Luigart/3060 Williston Rd., S. Burlington	(802) 865-3477
Steedman, Richard/214 E. 26th St., NYC	(212) 679-6684
Steele, Kim/640 Broadway, NYC	(212) 777-7753
Steer, John/37 King St., Norwalk	(203) 853-0485
Stegemeyer, Werner/377 Park Ave. S., NYC	(212) 686-2247
Steigelman, Glenn, Inc./873 Broadway, NYC	(212) 533-6080
Stein, Geoffrey/Boston/(617) 536-8227	**pages 318-319**
Stein, Jonathan/579 Sagamore Ave., Portsmouth	(603) 436-6365
Stein, Larry/568 Broadway, NYC	(212) 219-9077
Stein, Lisa J./321 E. 12th St., NYC	(212) 777-4483

Steiner, Charles/61 Second Ave., NYC	(212) 777-0813
Steiner, Laurie/101 W.23rd St., NYC	(212) 627-9711
Steiner, Peter/183 Saint Paul St., Rochester	(716) 454-1012
Steinmetz, George/NYC	(212) 633-2050
Stember, John/NYC	(212) 730-4300
Stemrich & Associates/213 N. 12th St., Allentown	(215) 776-0825
Stephanie Studios/277 W. 10th St., NYC	(212) 929-1029
Stephens, Antonio/45 E. 20th St., NYC	(212) 674-2350
Sterling Commercial Photography/310 Eigth St., New Cumberland	(717) 774-0967
Stern, Anna/261 Broadway, NYC	(212) 349-1134
Stern, Bert/NYC	(212) 925-5909
Stern, Bob/12 W. 27th St., NYC	(212) 889-0860
Stern, Cynthia/NYC	(212) 925-2677
Stern, Edward E./312 W. 23rd St., NYC	(212) 627-0436
Stern, Laszlo/NYC	(212) 691-7696
Stetson, David/NYC	(212) 279-1515
Stettner, Bill, Inc./118 E. 25th St., NYC	(212) 460-8180
Stevensen, Jeff/496 Congress St., Portland	(207) 773-5175
Stewart, Craig/1900 W Alabama Rd., Houston	(713) 529-5959
Stewart, David Harry/100 Chambers St., NYC	(212) 619-7783
Stier, Kurt/451 D. St., Boston	(617) 330-9461
Stierer, Dennis/443 Albany St., Boston	(617) 357-9488
Still, John/17 Edinboro St., Boston	(617) 451-8178
Stillings, Jamey/87 N. Clinton Ave., Rochester	(716) 232-5296
Stockland Martel/NYC/(212) 727-1400	**pages 416-429**
Stockwell, Jehremy L./307 W. 82nd St., NYC	(212) 595-5757
Stoecker Studios/34 W. 15th St., NYC	(212) 929-6393
Stogo, Don/310 E. 46th St., NYC	(212) 490-1034
Stokes, Stephanie/40 E. 68th St., NYC	(212) 744-0655
Stoller, Ezra/222 Valley Pl., Mamaroneck	(914) 698-4060
Stone, Erika/327 E. 82nd St., NYC	(212) 737-6435
Stone, Pete/NYC/(212) 473-3366	**pages 182-183**
Stott, Raymond/RD 2, Miller Rd., Ballston Lake	(518) 899-5256
Stratos, Jim/176 Madison Ave., NYC	(212) 696-1133
Strauss, Steve/43 W. 39th St., NYC	(212) 354-7828
Strock, Carren/1380 E. 17th St., Brooklyn	(718) 375-8519
Stroller, Ezra/Mamaroneck	(914) 698-4060
Strongin, Jeanne/61 Irving Pl., NYC	(212) 473-3718
Ströube, Greg/NYC/(212) 912-1877	**pages 528-529**
Struan Photographic, Inc./Four New St., Toronto	(416) 923-9311
Stuart, John/80 Varick St., NYC	(212) 966-6783
Studer, Lillian/305 E. 24th St., NYC	(212) 683-2082
Studio 514 Photographix/514 Merrick Rd., Baldwin	(516) 546-2766
Studio Associates/30-6 Plymouth St., Fairfield	(201) 575-2640
Studio C/22 Industrial Park Rd., Hingham	(617) 749-7771
Studio L'Image/251A Brooklyn Ave., Bklyn.	(718) 771-7464
Studio Z/Cranberry Commons, Eatontown	(212) 406-9590
Studio, The, Inc./938 Penn Ave., Pittsburgh	(412) 261-2022
Stupakoff, Bico/NYC	(212) 219-0707
Stupakoff, Otto/80 Varick St., NYC	(212) 490-1034
Sturdevant, Erica/NYC/(212) 242-0840	**pages 90-91**
Sued, Yamil R./Stamford	(203) 353-8865
Sugarman, Lynn/40 W. 22nd St., NYC	(212) 691-3245
Sun Photography/19 E. 21st St., NYC	(212) 505-9585
Super, Drew Photography/Hicksville	(516) 935-9595
Susse, Ed/NYC	(212) 243-1126
Sussman, Daniel/369 Seventh Ave., NYC	(212) 947-5546
Sutton, Jane/Manchester/(603) 627-2659	**page 197-199**
Svensson, Steen/52 Grove St., NYC	(212) 242-7272
Swann/Niemann/1258 Wisconsin Ave. N.W., Wash. D.C.	(202) 342-6300
Swanson, Neil/6 Ricky Lne., South Norwalk	(203) 853-7126
Swedowsky, Ben/381 Park Ave. S., NYC	(212) 684-1454
Swertfager, Amy I./343 Manville Rd., Pleasantville	(516) 747-1900
Swett, Jennifer/N. Sutton	(603) 927-4648
Swick, Danille A./276 First Ave., NYC	(212) 777-0653
Switzer, Maynard/215 E. 68th St., NYC	(212) 988-8298
Swoger, Arthur/61 Savoy St., Providence	(401) 331-0440
Szabo, Art/156 Deport Rd., Huntington Sta.	(516) 549-1699
TDF Artists Ltd./291 Lakeshore Blvd. E., Toronto	(416) 924-3371
Tadder, Morton & Assocs., Inc./1010 Morton St., Balt.	(301) 837-7427
Tahari, Ltd./525 Seventh Ave., NYC	(212) 921-3600
Tamin Productions, Inc./440 West End Ave., NYC	(212) 807-6691
Tanaka, Ron/67 Mowat Ave., Toronto	(416) 536-9440

Tannenbaum, Dennis/NYC . . . . (212) 279-2838
Tannenbaum, Ken, Inc./16 W. 21st St., NYC . . . . (212) 675-2345
Tanous, Dorothy/652 Hudson St., NYC . . . . (212) 255-9409
Tanteri, Matthew Laserman/10-63 Jackson Ave., L.I.C. . . . . (718) 937-4480
Tara Universal Studios/34 E. 23rd St., NYC . . . . (212) 673-6730
Tarantola, Kathy/187 St. Botoloph St., Boston . . . . (617) 353-0756
Tardio, Robert Photography, Ltd./19 W. 21st St., NYC . . . . (212) 463-9085
Tartaglia, Victor/23 Dodd St., Bloomfield . . . . (201) 429-4983
Tasca, Sandra/72 Pauline Ave., Toronto . . . . (416) 532-1716
Taylor, Curtice/29 E. 22nd St., NYC . . . . (212) 473-6886
Taylor, John Bigelow/162 E. 92nd St., NYC . . . . (212) 410-5300
Taylor, Jonathan/NYC . . . . (212) 741-2805
Tcherevkoff Studio, Ltd./873 Broadway, NYC . . . . (212) 228-0540
Tedesco, Frank/Nine W. 31st St., NYC . . . . (212) 629-4353
Teicholz, Leslie S./320 Central Park W., NYC . . . . (212) 362-7252
Tenin, Barry/Westport . . . . (203) 226-9396
Terk, Harold/170 Quarry Rd., Stamford . . . . (203) 329-1360
Terzis, Cornelia/448 W. 37th St., NYC . . . . (212) 564-7533
Tesi, Mike/12 Kulick Rd., Fairfield . . . . (201) 575-7780
Tessler, Stefan/115 W. 23rd St., NYC . . . . (212) 924-9168
Tessy, Mike/12 Kulick Rd., Fairfield . . . . (201) 575-7780
Teuwen, Geert/NYC/(212) 929-9001 . . . . **page 165**
Thayer, Mark/25 Drydock Ave., Boston . . . . (617) 542-9532
Thiery, Franck/NYC . . . . (212) 925-5909
Thomas, Lee/Lexington . . . . (606) 268-1264
Thomas, Mark/141 W. 26th St., NYC . . . . (212) 741-7252
Thomas, Ted/Teaneck . . . . (201) 837-6682
Thomas, Wes/140 Bradley St., New Haven . . . . (203) 624-1996
Thompson, Eleanor/NYC . . . . (212) 675-6773
Thornton Studio/18 W. 27th St., NYC . . . . (212) 685-1725
Thornton, John/NYC . . . . (212) 772-0346
Tighe, Michael/425 W. 23rd St., NYC . . . . (212) 243-2750
Till, Tom/Moab . . . . (801) 259-5327
Tillinghast, Paul/20 W. 20th St., NYC . . . . (212) 741-3764
Tillman, Denny/39 E. 20th St., NYC . . . . (212) 674-7160
Timpone, Bob/126 W. 22nd St., NYC . . . . (212) 989-4266
Titcomb, Jeffery/423 W. Broadway, Boston . . . . (617) 269-8777
Tkatch, James/2307 18th St. N.W., Wash. D.C. . . . . (202) 462-2211
Togashi Studio, Inc./36 W. 20th St., NYC . . . . (212) 929-2290
Tokerud, Camille/NYC . . . . (212) 766-1193
Tolbert, Brian R./911 State St., Lancaster . . . . (717) 393-0918
Toma, Kenji/NYC . . . . (212) 925-8333
Tomalin, Norman Owen/381 Fifth Ave., NYC . . . . (212) 683-5227
Tomba, Jany/NYC/(212) 570-2189 . . . . **pages 172-173**
Tornberg/Coghlan Assoc./Six E. 39th St., NYC . . . . (212) 685-7333
Toscannis, Nick/10 Hubert St., NYC . . . . (212) 966-0357
Toshi, Otsuki/241 W. 36th St., NYC . . . . (212) 594-1939
Toto, Joe/NYC/(212) 966-7626 . . . . **pages 202-203**
Tracey, Olga/33 Jefferson Ave., Toronto . . . . (416) 535-1955
Trachman, Emanuel/63 Haven Esplanade, Staten Island . . . . (718) 447-1393
Trafidlo Communications/17 Stillings St., Boston . . . . (617) 338-9343
Transtock/15 S. Grand Ave., Baldwin . . . . (516) 223-9649
Traub, Charles/NYC . . . . (212) 505-8152
Travers, David Inc./980 St. Paul St. W., Montréal . . . . (514) 861-9107
Treiber, Peter/917 Highland Ave., Bethlehem . . . . (215) 867-3303
Trian, George/Hartford . . . . (203) 647-1372
Troha, John/Washington . . . . (301) 340-7220
Truman, Gary T./Charleston . . . . (304) 755-3078
Trumbo, Keith/221 W. 78th St., NYC . . . . (212) 580-7104
Truslow, Bill/118 W. 27th St., NYC . . . . (212) 691-7612
Trzoniec, Stanley/58 W. Main St., Northboro . . . . (617) 842-6721
Tsufura, Satoru/48 Bently Rd., Cedar Grove . . . . (201) 239-4870
Tsunokawa, Mas/417 St. Pierre, Montréal . . . . (514) 849-8404
Tsutsumi, Edward Studio/56 W. 22nd St., NYC . . . . (212) 645-3070
Tullis, Marcus/NYC . . . . (212) 966-8511
Tully, Roger/344 W. 38th St., NYC . . . . (212) 947-3961
Tung, Matthew/Five Union Sq. W., NYC . . . . (212) 741-0570
Turbeville, Deborah/NYC . . . . (212) 924-6760
Turbitt, Ann-Marie/NYC/(212) 925-8750 . . . . **pages 218-219**
Turner, Pete/154 W. 57th St., NYC . . . . (212) 765-1733
Turo, Peter/Sarasota . . . . (813) 351-5351
Turpan, Dennis P./25 Amsterdam Ave., Teaneck . . . . (201) 837-4242
Tuthill, Thomas/34 E. 30th St., NYC . . . . (212) 685-7734

Tutino, Aldo/407 N. Washington, Alexandria	(703) 549-8014
Tweel, Ron/241 W. 36th St., NYC	(212) 563-3452
Uher, John/NYC/(212) 594-7377	**page 336**
Uhl, Phil/NYC	(212) 772-0346
Ultimate Image/47 Alden St., Cranford	(201) 272-4455
Umans, Marty/NYC/(212) 929-0487	**pages 284-285**
Umlas, Barbara & Assocs./NYC/(212) 534-4008	**pages 102-105**
Unangst, Andrew/381 Park Ave. S., NYC	(212) 889-4888
Underhill, Ray/568 Broadway, NYC	(212) 925-2250
Unger, Trudi/116 Pinehurst Ave., NYC	(212) 740-7678
Unitas, Joseph C./314 E. McMurray Rd., McMurray	(412) 941-9009
Urbina, Walt/7208 Thomas Blvd., Pittsburgh	(412) 242-5070
Uzzell, Steve/1419 Trap Rd., Vienna	(703) 938-6868
Uzzle, Burk/7 W. 22nd St., NYC	(212) 933-2468
Vaeth, Peter/295 Madison Ave., NYC	(212) 685-4700
Vail, Baker/111 W. 24th St., NYC	(212) 463-7560
Valada, M.C./204 Park Terrace Ct. S.E., Vienna	(703) 938-0324
Valente. Jerry/193 Meserole Ave., Bklyn.	(718) 389-0469
Valentine, Gloria/NYC	(212) 725-1596
Valentino, Thom/25 Navaho St., Cranston	(401) 946-3020
Valeska, Shonna/140 East 28 St., NYC	(212) 683-4448
Van Arnam, Lewis/881 Seventh Ave., NYC	(212) 541-4787
Van Camp, Louis & Assoc./713 San Juan Rd., New Bern	(919) 633-6081
Van Dezendorf, Garry/NYC	(212) 924-6760
Van Nes, Hans/427 E. 90th St., NYC	(212) 876-4900
Van Otteren, Juliet/568 Broadway, NYC	(212) 627-1958
Van Petten, Rob/Boston/(617) 426-8641	**pages 222-223**
Van Petten, Rob/NYC/(212) 869-2190	**pages 222-223**
Van Wormer, Mark/192 Main St., Guiderland Ctr.	(518) 861-7233
Vance, Philip/NYC/(212) 645-6677	**pages 234-235**
Vano, Robert/NYC	(212) 924-6760
Varnedoe, S./12 W. 27th St., NYC	(212) 679-1230
Varriale, Jim/36 W. 20th St., NYC	(212) 807-0088
Vartoogian, Jack/262 W. 107th St., NYC	(212) 663-1341
Vassiliev, Nina/135 E. 17th St., NYC	(212) 473-0190
Vaughan, Ted/423 Doe Run Rd., Manheim	(717) 665-6942
Vecchio, Dan/129 E. Water St., Syracuse	(315) 471-1064
Vecchione, Jim/9153 Brookville Rd., Silver Spring	(301) 589-7900
Vega, Julio/417 Third Ave., NYC	(212) 889-7568
Vegam, Keith/Linden	(201) 486-9257
Veldenzer, Alan/160 Bleecker St., NYC	(212) 420-8189
Vendikos, Tasso Photography, Inc./59 W. 19th St., NYC	(212) 206-6451
Verde, Anthony/133 Mulberry St., NYC	(212) 219-1152
Vericker, Joseph/60 E. 42nd St., NYC	(212) 863-9801
Veronsky, Frank/1376 York Ave., NYC	(212) 744-3810
Vest, Michael/40 W. 27th St., NYC	(212) 532-8331
Vhandy Productions, Inc./401 E. 57th St., NYC	(212) 759-6150
Vicari, Jim/Stockton	(609) 397-4231
Vickers, Camille/200 W. 79th St., NYC	(212) 580-8649
Vidal, Bernard/450 W. 31st St., NYC	(212) 629-3764
Vincent, Chris/119 W. 23rd St., NYC	(212) 691-1894
Vincenzo/NYC	(212) 564-4100
Vine, David/873 Broadway, NYC	(212) 505-8070
Viola, Philip F./37 Thompson Ave., White Plains	(914) 428-4875
Visions/36 Hillcrest Rd., Martinsville	(201) 469-7450
Visual Impact Productions/15 W. 18th St., NYC	(212) 243-8441
Visual Studies Workshop/31 Prince St., Rochester	(716) 442-8676
Vogel, Allen/348 W. 14th St., NYC	(212) 675-7550
Vogue Photographic Svcs./214 Oakdale Rd., Downsview	(416) 741-9889
Volkmann, Roy/NYC	(212) 594-8204
von Hoffmann/Madison	(201) 377-0317
von Hoffman, Trip/Madison/(201) 377-0317	**pages 130-131**
von Hoffman, Trip/NYC/(212) 575-1041	**pages 130-131**
von Hohenberg, Christophe/114 Greene St., NYC	(212) 274-0100
Von Schreiber, Barbara/315 Central Park W., NYC	(212) 580-7044
von Ulfeldt, Garrett Korfitz/119 W 23rd St., NYC	(212) 254-1798
Von Ulfeldt Photography/119 W. 23rd St., NYC	(212) 727-1444
Waggaman, John/2746 N. 46th St., Phila.	(215) 473-2827
Wagner, Daniel/50 W. 29th St., NYC	(212) 532-8255
Wagner, David A./NYC/(212) 925-5149	**pages 232-233**
Wagner, Donald E./2101 Nottinghill Lne., Trenton	(609) 586-3399
Wagoner, Robert/5775 Big Tree Rd., NYC	(716) 662-6002
Wahlund, Olof/NYC/(212) 929-9067	**pages 344-345**

Wainman, Rick & Assoc./360 W. 36th St., NYC	(212) 512-9118
Waldinger Photographic Group/3158 Webster Ave., NYC	(212) 547-0555
Waldo, Maje/NYC	(212) 353-9868
Waldron, William/463 Broome St., NYC	(212) 226-0356
Walker, John/245 E. 11th St., NYC	(212) 995-5959
Wallace, Randall/43 W. 13th St., NYC	(212) 242-2930
Wallach, Louis/NYC/(212) 260-5393	**pages 138-139**
Walle, Christopher/9518 Donnan Castle Ct., Laurel	(301) 470-4046
Wallen, Jonathan/41 Lewis Pkwy., Yonkers	(914) 476-8674
Walsh, Robert/360 N. Midler Ave., Syracuse	(315) 437-2034
Waltzer, Bill/110 Greene St., NYC	(212) 925-1242
Waltzer, Carl/873 Broadway, NYC	(212) 475-8748
Walz, Barabar/NYC	(212) 633-2050
Wang, Harvey/574 Argyle Rd., Brooklyn	(718) 282-2800
Wang, John/30 E. 20th St., NYC	(212) 982-2765
Wang, Tony/NYC/(212) 213-4433	**pages 390-391**
Ward, Bob/NYC/(212) 627-7006	**pages 266-267**
Ward, Jack/221 Vine St., Phila.	(215) 627-5311
Ward, Michael/916 N. Charles St., Balt.	(301) 727-8800
Ward, Tony/704 S. Sixth St., Phila.	(215) 238-1208
Warinsky, Jim/38 W. 26th St., NYC	(212) 206-6448
Warren, George W./NYC/(212) 929-8231	**page 326**
Warsaw Photographic Assoc./36 E. 31st St., NYC	(212) 725-1888
Warshaw, Peter/85 Strong St., Bronx	(212) 601-1007
Warwick, Cindy/NYC	(212) 663-8330
Wasserman, Cary/Six Porter Rd., Cambridge	(617) 492-5621
Wasserman, Ted Assocs./51 E. 42nd St., NYC	(212) 867-5360
Watanabe, Nana/130 W. 25th St., NYC	(212) 741-3248
Waterfall, William/NYC	(212) 772-0346
Watson, Michael/133 W. 19th St., NYC	(212) 620-3125
Watson, Ross H./Frog Hollow Studio/Bryn Mawr	(215) 353-9898
Watson, Tom/2172 W. Lake Rd., Skaneateles Lake	(315) 685-6033
Watt, Elizabeth/141 W. 26th St., NYC	(212) 929-8504
Watts, Cliff/360 W. 36th St., NYC	(212) 629-8116
Watts, Todd/167 Spring St., NYC	(212) 226-6136
Waxman, Dani/242 E. 19th St., NYC	(212) 995-2221
Wayne, Meri/134 E. 22nd St., NYC	(212) 730-1188
Wayne, Philip/NYC/(212) 696-5215	**pages 392-399, 400-401**
Weaks, Dan/NYC/(212) 473-3366	**pages 178-179**
Weber, Bruce/135 Watts St., NYC	(212) 226-0814
Webster, Clive/56 The Esplanade E., Toronto	(416) 363-7081
Weckler, Chad/NYC	(212) 355-1135
Weckler, Charles/NYC	(212) 861-7861
Weems, Al/14 Imperial Pl., Providence	(401) 455-0484
Weese, Carl/140-50 Huyshope Ave., Hartford	(203) 246-6016
Weidlein, Peter King/122 W. 26th St., NYC	(212) 989-5498
Weidman, H. Mark/2112 Goodwin Ln., N. Wales	(215) 646-1745
Weigand, Tom/707 N. Fifth St., Reading	(215) 374-4431
Weinberg, Carol/40 West 17th St., NYC	(212) 206-8200
Weinberg, Michael S./Five E. 16th St., NYC	(212) 691-1000
Weinrebe, Steve/225 Arch St., Phila.	(215) 625-0333
Weinstein, Michael/508 Broadway, NYC	(212) 925-2612
Weinstein, Todd Productions/47 Irving Pl., NYC	(212) 254-7526
Weisbrot, Rick/NYC/(212) 477-3333	**pages 212-215**
Weiser, Barry/336 W. 11th St., NYC	(212) 620-4525
Weiss, David/NYC/(212) 924-1030	**pages 224-225**
Weiss, Michael/Ten W. 18th St., NYC	(212) 929-4073
Weissberg, Elyse/NYC	(212) 406-2566
Weissman, Walter/463 W. St., NYC	(212) 989-9694
Weldon, Mort/473 Winding Rd. N., Ardsley	(914) 693-4005
Welles, Harris/NYC	(212) 725-3806
Welling, James/NYC	(212) 966-3253
Welling, Kathy/NYC/(212) 575-1041	**pages 130-131**
Welsch, Urike/4 Dunns Lane, Marblehead	(617) 631-1641
Welsh, Bob Jr./158 Forest St., Manchester	(203) 647-8025
West, Bonnie/156 Fifth Ave., NYC	(212) 929-3338
West, Jerry/530 W. 58th St., NYC	(212) 245-2416
West, Melanie/126 Ruane St., Fairfield	(203) 255-3590
Westerman, Charlie/NYC/(212) 353-1235	**pages 510-511**
Westheimer, Bill/167 Spring St., NYC	(212) 431-6360
Wexler, Ira/4911 V St. N.W., Wash. D.C.	(202) 337-4886
Wheeler, Ed/1050 King of Prussia Rd., Radnor	(215) 964-9294
Wheeler, Paul/50 W. 29th St., NYC	(212) 696-9832

Whipple III, George Carrol/NYC/(212) 219-0202 .... **pages 356-357**
White Light Inc./186 Greenwood Ave., Bethel .... (203) 743-3834
White Light Studios, Inc./24-41 26th St., L.I.C. .... (718) 728-7180
White, Bill/NYC/(212) 243-1780 .... **pages 254-255**
White, David/31 W. 21st St., NYC .... (212) 938-1211
White, Joel/135 W. 26th St., NYC .... (212) 929-1777
White, John/11 W. 20th, NYC .... (212) 691-1133
White, Keith/330 W. 22nd St., NYC .... (212) 941-0435
White, Timothy/448 W. 37th St., NYC .... (212) 971-9039
Whitehead, Buz/NYC .... (212) 460-8572
Whitehurst, William/32 W. 20th St., NYC .... (212) 206-8825
Whitman, Robert/1181 Broadway, NYC .... (212) 213-6611
Whyte, Douglas/NYC/(212) 431-1667 .... **pages 400-401**
Wick, Walter/NYC .... (212) 243-3448
Wickrath, Claus/NYC .... (212) 925-8333
Wien, Jeffrey/160 Fifth Ave., NYC .... (212) 243-7028
Wiener, Mark/49 W. 23rd St., NYC .... (212) 675-6902
Wilby, Dan/NYC/(212) 929-8231 .... **page 326**
Wild Inc./6 Church St., Toronto .... (416) 863-6875
Wild, Terry/Morgan Valley Rd., Williamsport .... (717) 745-3257
Wilkes, Stephen/NYC/(212) 475-4010 .... **pages 446-449**
Wilkings, Steve/NYC .... (212) 772-0346
Wilkins, Doug/33 Church St., Canton .... (617) 828-2379
Willardt, Kenneth/NYC .... (212) 725-3806
Willer, Brian Photography, Inc./Caledon .... (416) 266-8989
Williams, Larry/315 Rue St-Sacrement, Montréal .... (514) 849-0260
Williams, Lawrence S., Inc./9101 W. Chester Pike, Upper Darby ... (215) 789-3030
Williford Studios/873 Broadway, NYC .... (212) 995-8806
Wills, Bret/NYC/(212) 925-2999 .... **pages 123-125**
Wilson, John G./2416 Wynnefield Dr., Havertown .... (215) 446-4798
Wilson, Kevin/11231 Bybee St., Silver Spring .... (301) 649-3151
Wilson, Michael/441 Park Ave. S., NYC .... (212) 683-3557
Wing, Peter/56-08 138th St., Flushing .... (718) 762-3617
Winkler, Robert S./Seven Woodland Way, Weston .... (203) 227-7139
Winstead, Jimmy/453 Washington Ave., Bklyn. .... (718) 789-2997
Wojcik, James/256 Mott St., NYC .... (212) 431-0108
Wolf, Bruce/NYC/(212) 633-6660 .... **pages 424-425**
Wolf, Henry/167 E. 73rd St., NYC .... (212) 472-2500
Wolf, Lloyd/5710 S. First St., Arlington .... (703) 671-7668
Wolff, Nancy/125 Gates Ave., Montclair .... (201) 746-7415
Wolff, Randolph/5811 Edson Ln., Rockville .... (301) 468-0833
Wolff, Timmi/Baltimore/(301) 383-7059 .... **pages 52-53**
Wolfson Inc./NYC .... (212) 924-1510
Wolfson, Bob/NYC .... (212) 682-1490
Wolfson, Jeffrey/13-17 Laight St., NYC .... (212) 226-0077
Wolosker, Steven/19 E. 65th St., NYC .... (212) 288-8989
Wolvovitz, Ethel/305 Ocean Pky., Bklyn. .... (718) 851-3162
Wong, Leslie/303 W. 78th St., NYC .... (212) 595-0434
Wood, Richard/169 Msgr. O'Brien Hwy., Cambridge .... (617) 661-6856
Woods, Patrick/41-15 45th St., Sunnyside .... (718) 786-5742
Woodward, Herbert/555 Third Ave., NYC .... (212) 685-4385
Workman, Bob/18 W. 27th St., NYC .... (212) 684-0019
Worrall, David/2107 Chancellor, Phila. .... (215) 567-4030
Wright, William P./545 NE 80th St., Seattle .... (206) 522-2658
Wu, Ron/179 St. Paul St., Rochester .... (716) 454-5600
Wyatt, Chad Evans/3625 Everett St. N.W., Wash. D.C. .... (202) 244-7117
Wyley, Bill/146 W. 17th St., NYC .... (212) 627-1007
Wylie, Bill/134 W. 32nd St., NYC .... (212) 924-7770
Wylie, Camie/NYC/(212) 721-2865 .... **pages 370-372**
Wyman Studios/36 Riverside Dr., NYC .... (212) 799-8281
Wynn, Dan/170 E. 73rd St., NYC .... (212) 535-1551
Wyville, Mark/25-40 31st. Ave., Long Island City .... (718) 204-2816
Yamashiro, Tad/224 E. 12th St., NYC .... (212) 473-7177
Yeager, Richard/1000 Lenola Rd., Moorestown .... (609) 235-3482
Yee, Henry/473 Cosburn Ave., Toronto .... (416) 423-4883
Yee, Tom/141 W. 28th St., NYC .... (212) 947-5400
Yellen/Lachapelle, Inc./NYC/(212) 838-3170 .... **pages 342-345**
Ynocencio, Anthony J./F.D.R Sta., NYC .... (212) 753-0154
Young, James/56 W. 22nd St., NYC .... (212) 924-5444
Young, Rick/27 W. 20th St., NYC .... (212) 929-5701
Young, Steve/NYC .... (212) 691-5860
Young, Tom/181 Westchester Ave., Port Chester .... (914) 939-7722
Z, Taran/528 F St. Terr. S.E., Wash. D.C. .... (202) 543-5322

Zaccaro, Jim/116 E. 78th St., NYC ... (212) 744-4000
Zager, Howard/450 W. 31st St., NYC ... (212) 239-8082
Zan Productions/NYC/(212) 477-3333 ... **pages 212-215**
Zander, Peter/312 E. 90th St., NYC ... (212) 246-2300
Zanetti, Gerry/NYC/(212) 767-1717 ... **pages 308-309**
Zapp, Carl/NYC/(212) 924-4240 ... **pages 432-433**
Zarember, Sam/26 Old S. Salem Rd., Ridgefield ... (203) 438-4472
Zari Int'l./NYC/(212) 765-8220 ... **pages 502-503**
Zebra Island Studios/333-66 King St., Winnipeg ... (204) 943-7553
Zegre, Francois/124 E. 27th St., NYC ... (212) 684-6517
Zehnder, Bruno/NYC/(212) 840-1234 ... **pages 194-195**
Zelea Photography/15 Sherman Ave. S., Hamilton ... (416) 549-1616
Zelea Photography/334 King St. E., Toronto ... (416) 361-0204
Zelman, Elyn/NYC/(212)645-0433 ... **pages 216-217**
Zenreich, Alan/78 Fifth Ave., NYC ... (212) 807-1551
Zeppetello, Michael/NYC ... (212) 219-0707
Zeray, Peter/113 E. 12th St., NYC ... (212) 674-0332
Zeschin, Elizabeth/50 White St., NYC ... (212) 219-0326
Zhimin, Shi/25-17 39th Ave., LIC ... (718) 361-6768
Zimmerman, David/NYC/(212) 206-1000 ... **pages 158-159**
Zipkowitz, Harold/240-23 66th Ave., Douglaston ... (718) 423-5036
Zitz, Peter/NYC ... (212) 543-7896
Zoda, Michele/13 E. 31st St., NYC ... (212) 679-5919
Zoiner, John/12 W. 44th St., NYC ... (212) 972-0357
Zwiebel, Michael/42 E. 23rd St., NYC ... (212) 477-5629

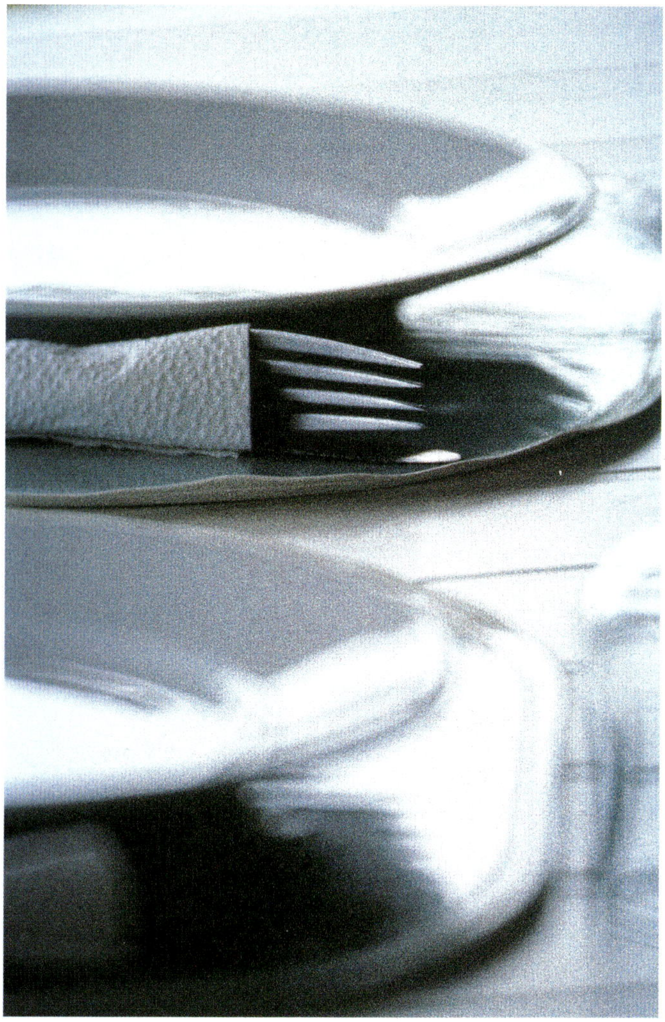

Wamsutta

Haagen Daz

Century Windows

Honda

DIANE

PADYS

STUDIO

212.941.8532

PRINT/FILM

Representation:
New York City
The Arts Counsel
212.725.3806

43

Gottlieb

Dennis M. Gottlieb &

associate Seth D. Roth

137 West 25 Street

NewYork, N.Y. 10001

Tel:212-620-7050

Fax:212-633-9842

Stock available

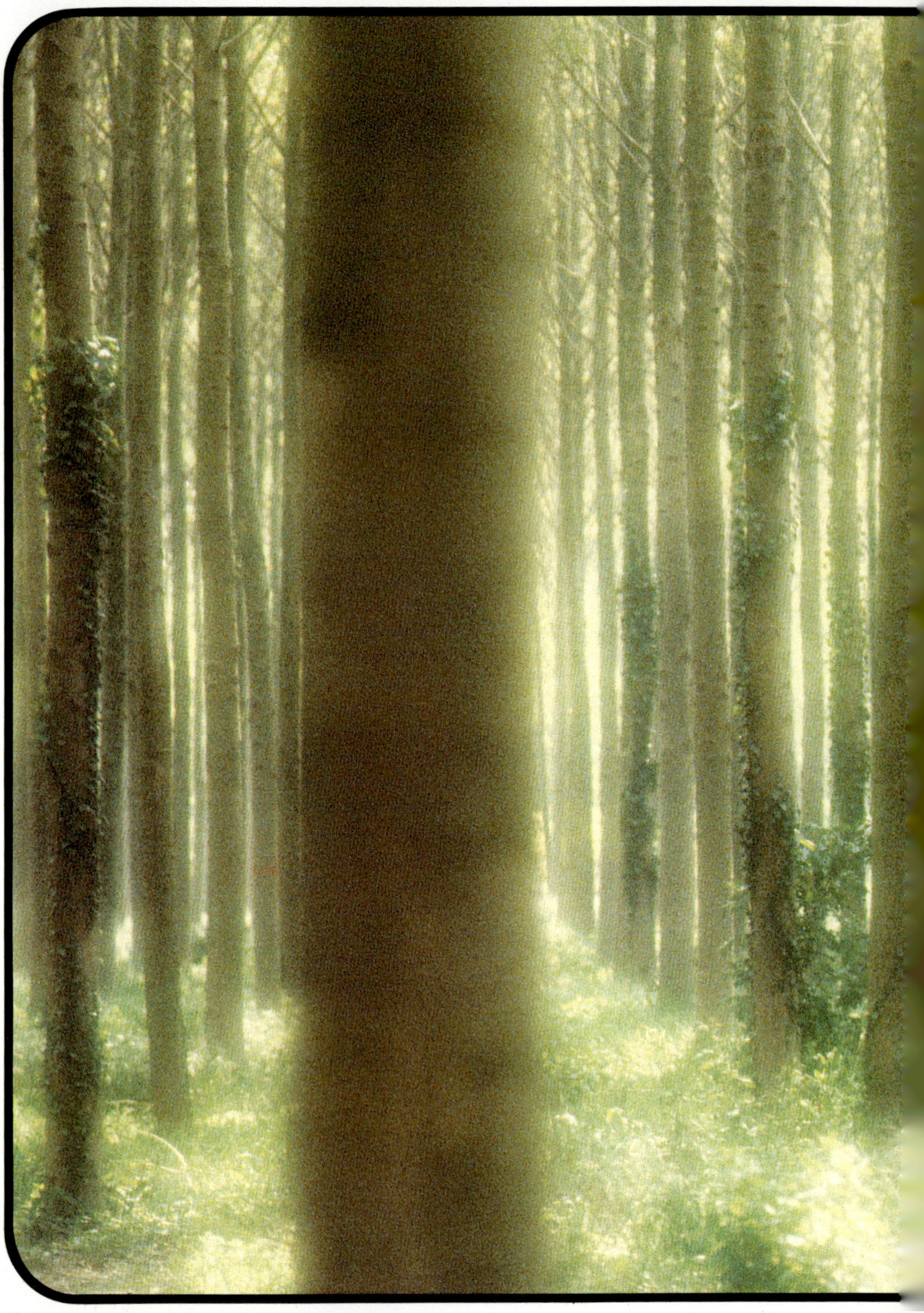
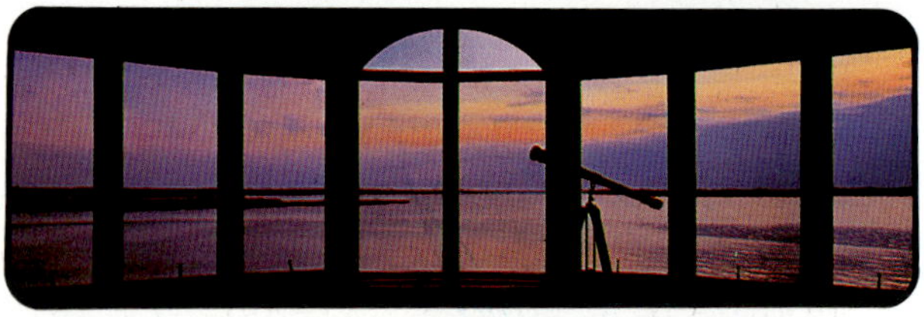
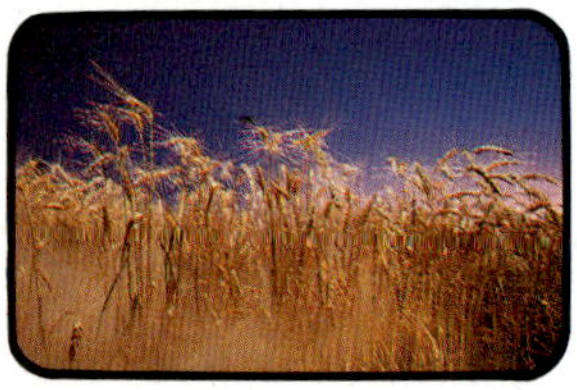
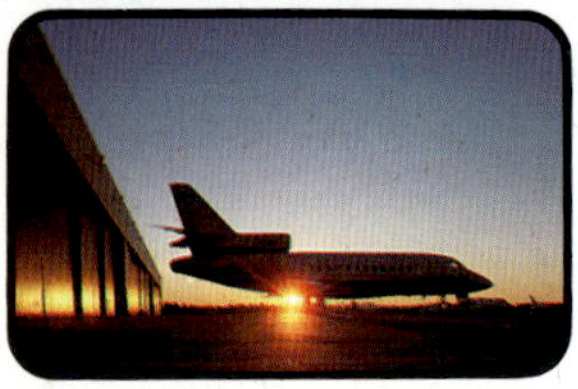

© 1991 STEVE KRONGARD

STEVE KRONGARD

PHONE: 212-689-5634 FAX: 212-689-8811

REPRESENTED BY JOE DiBARTOLO AND LAURA LEMKOWITZ PHONE: 212-297-0041 FAX: 212-297-0043

HARRISON

GOULD

76 NINTH AVENUE
PENTHOUSE WEST
NEW YORK, N.Y. 10011

212•929•9001

BRUCE BYERS PHOTOGRAPHY

11 West 20th St • New York, NY 10011 • 212-242-5846

BRUCE BYERS PHOTOGRAPHY

11 West 20th St • New York, NY 10011 • 212-242-5846

BURGESS

BLEVINS

urgess Blevins
01 685 0740
epresented by
ew York: Deborah Brown 212 463 7732
hicago: Ken Feldman 312 337 0447
outheast: Timmi Wolff 301 383 7059

Represented by
Robert Feldman
212-243-7319

N I E F

Terry Niefield Studio
12 West 27th Street
New York, NY 10001
212-686-8722

I E L D

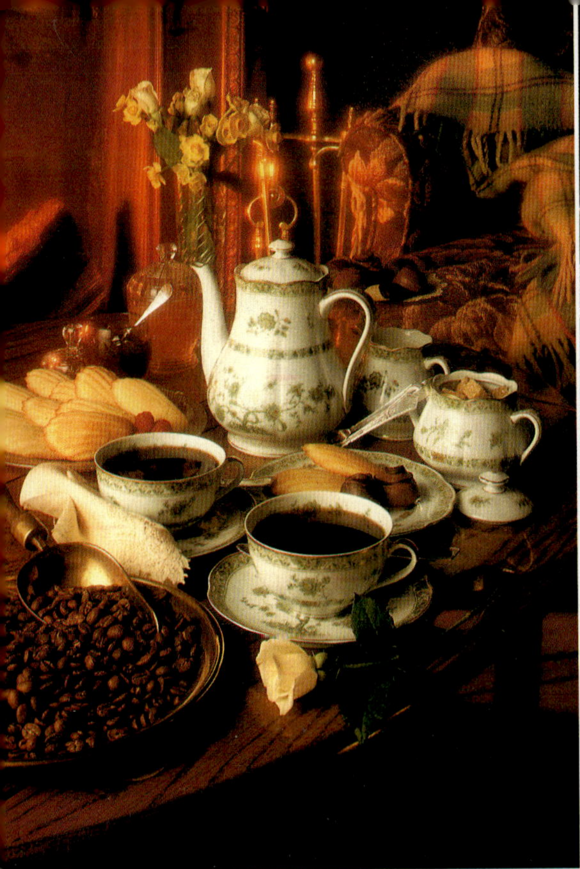
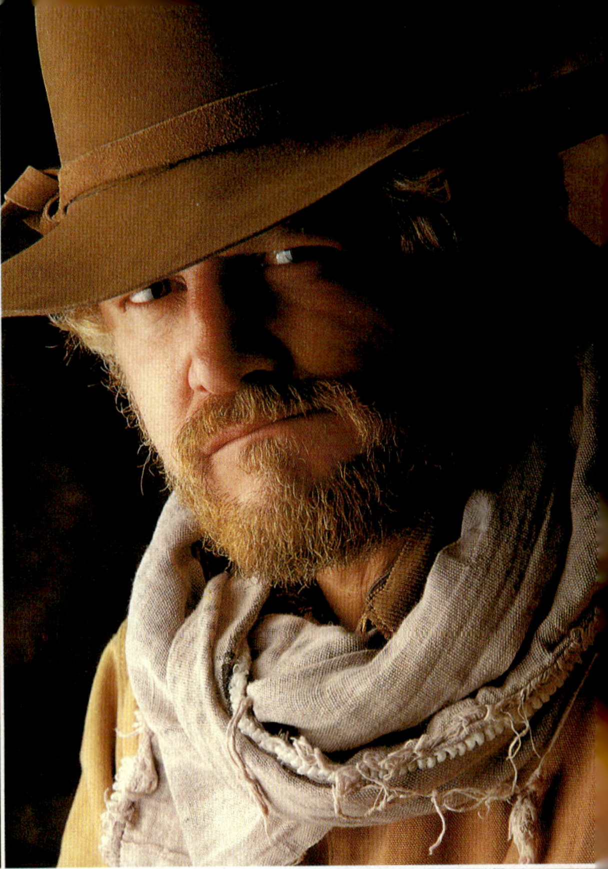
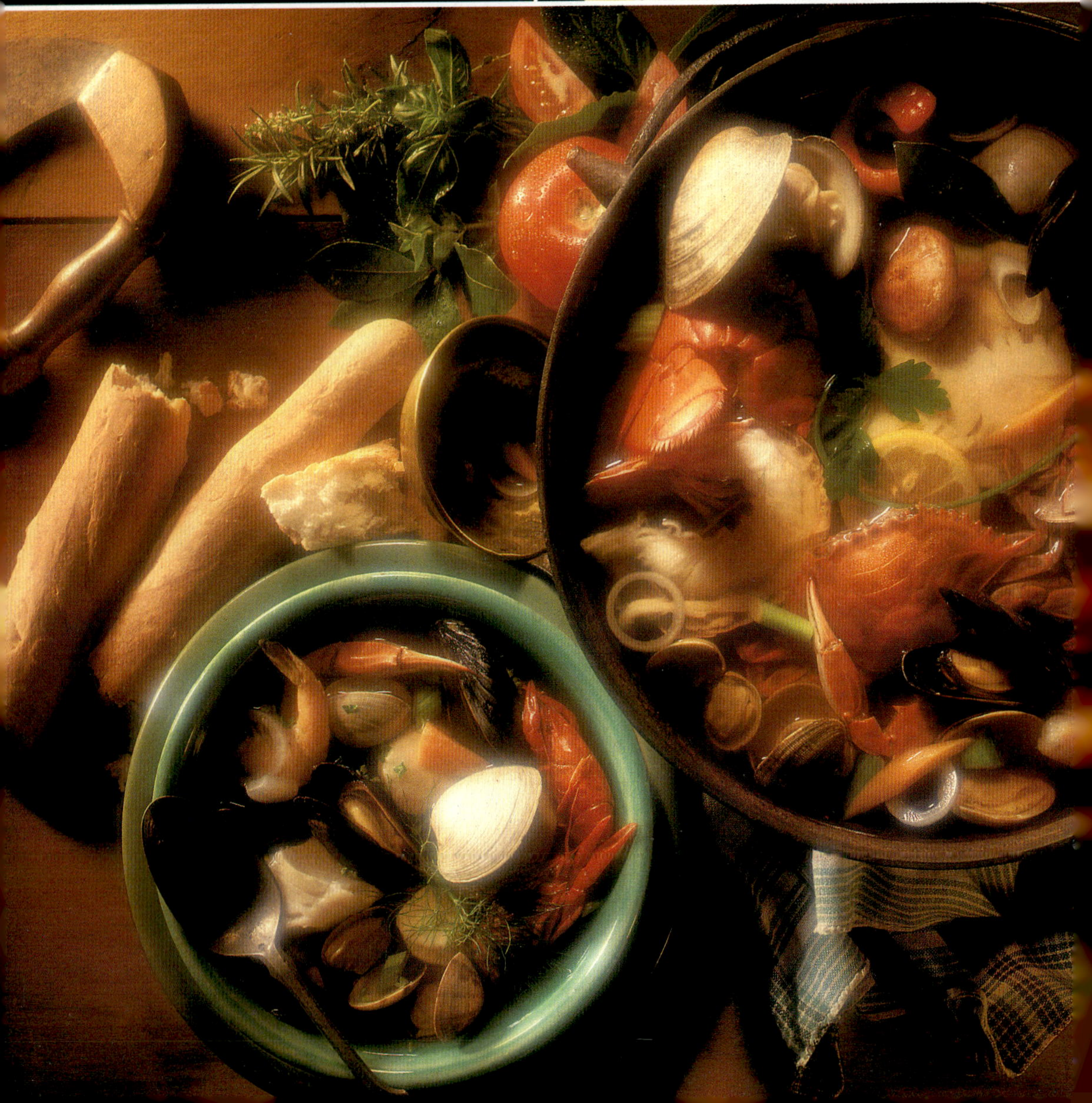

Brody

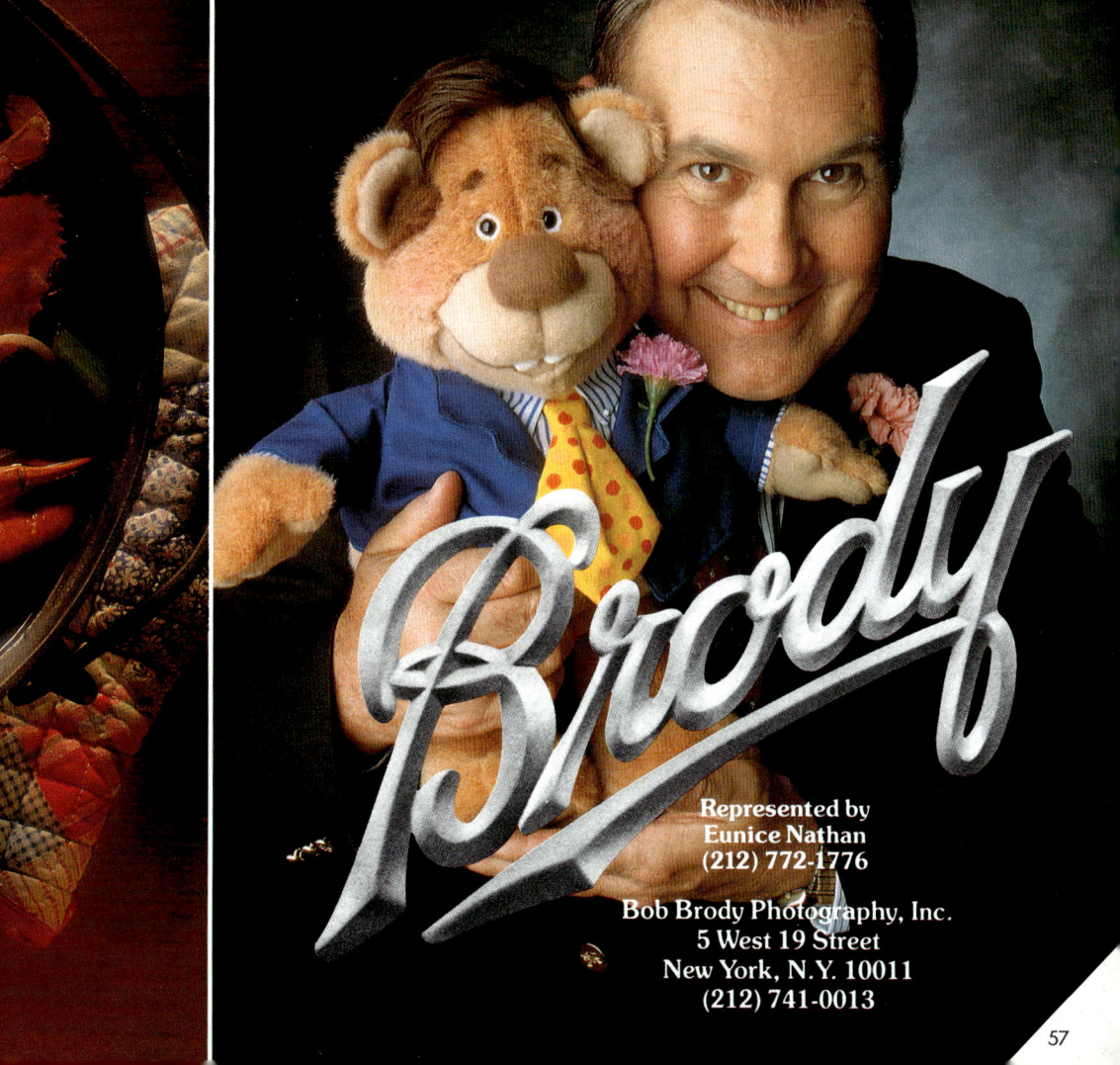

Represented by
Eunice Nathan
(212) 772-1776

Bob Brody Photography, Inc.
5 West 19 Street
New York, N.Y. 10011
(212) 741-0013

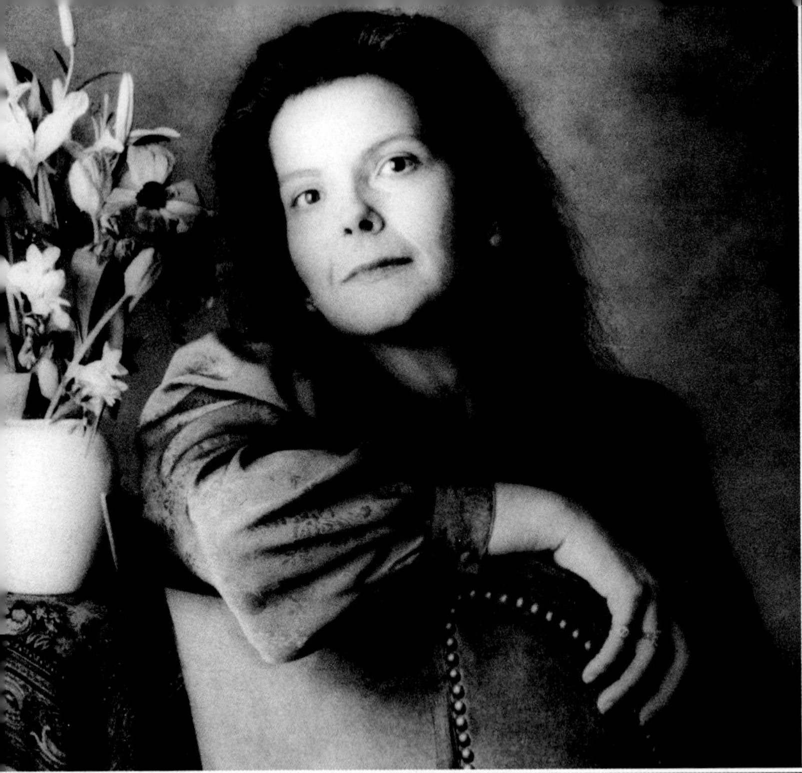
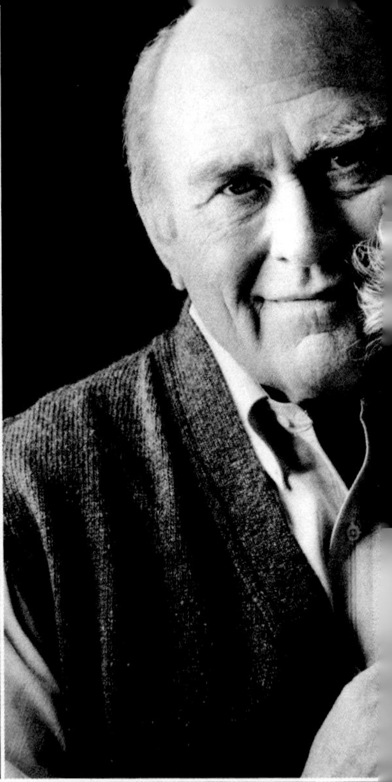
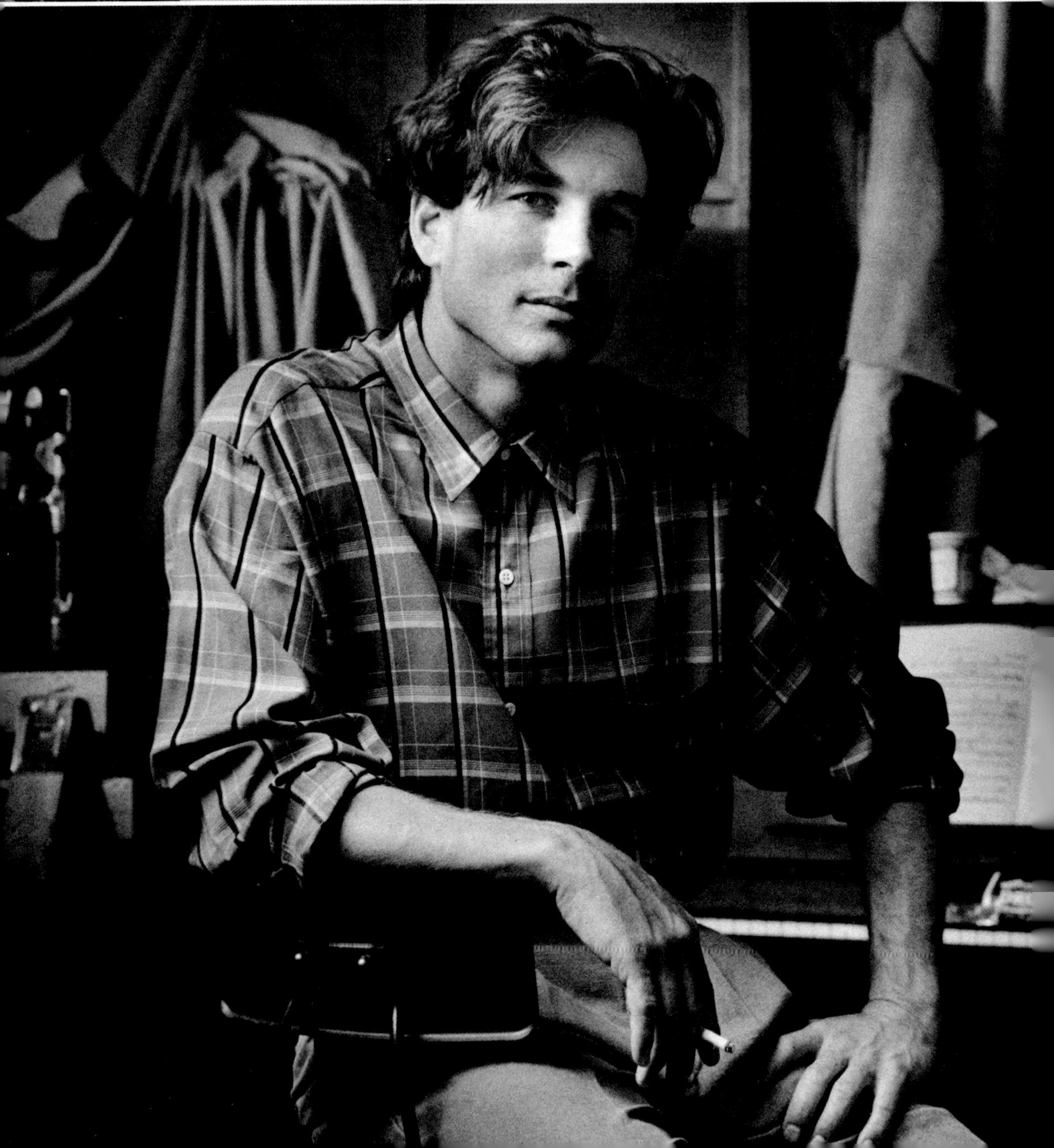

Brody

Represented by
Eunice Nathan
(212) 772-1776

Bob Brody Photography, Inc.
5 West 19 Street
New York, N.Y. 10011
(212) 741-0013

Kirk Lake
Mahopac, NY

ROBERTO BROSAN

873 BROADWAY NEW YORK NY 10003 212.473.1471

REPRESENTED BY JEAN CONLON 212.966.9897

KENRO IZU · PHOTOGRAPHY / JEAN CONLON · REPRESENTATIVE · 140 WEST 22nd STREET NEW YORK, NY 10011 · 212-254-10

KENRO IZU

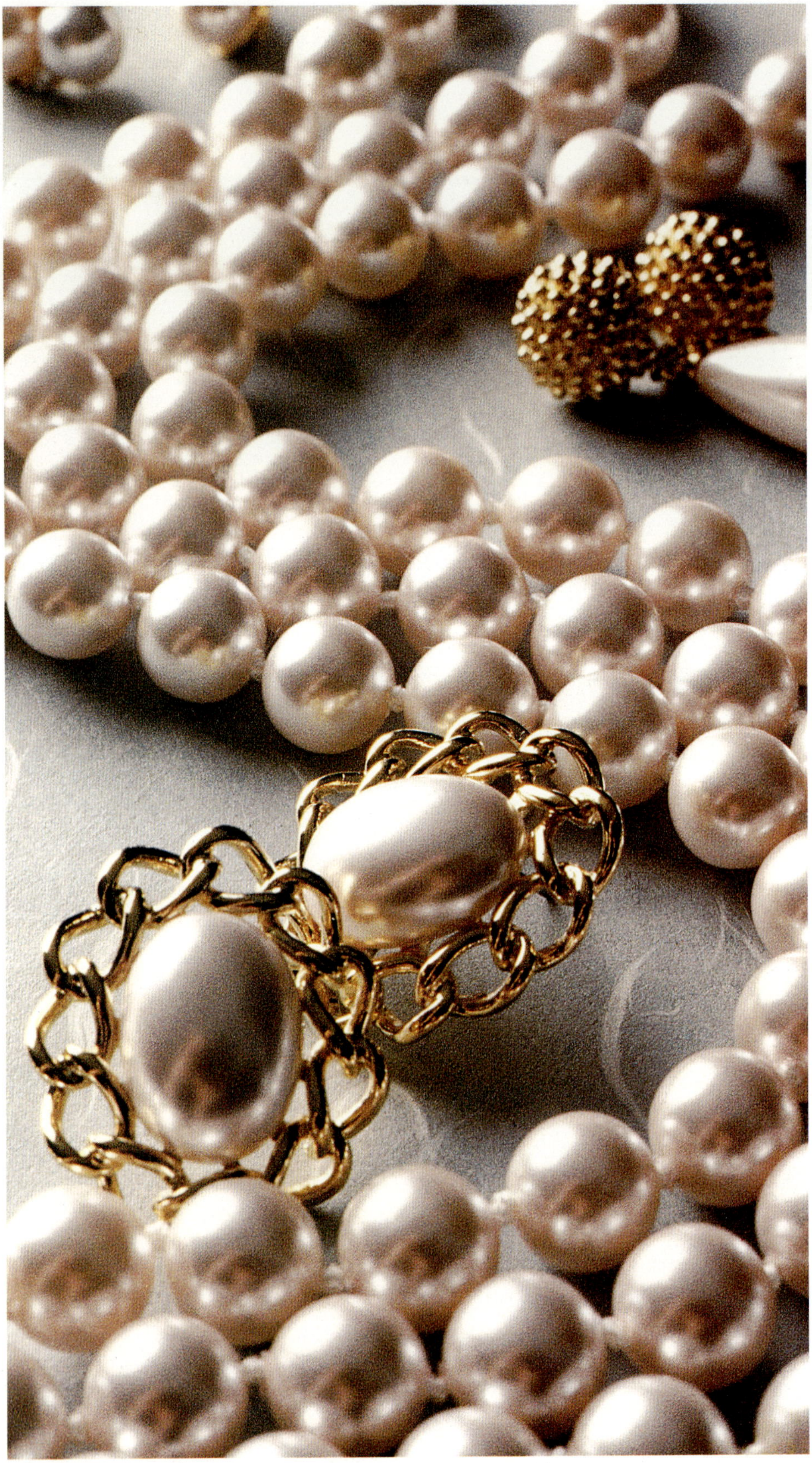

Beth Galton
Photography
236 West 26th Street 12E
New York, NY, 10001
(212) 242-2266
Fax: 691-1705

Represented By
Rosemary Samuels
(212) 477-3567

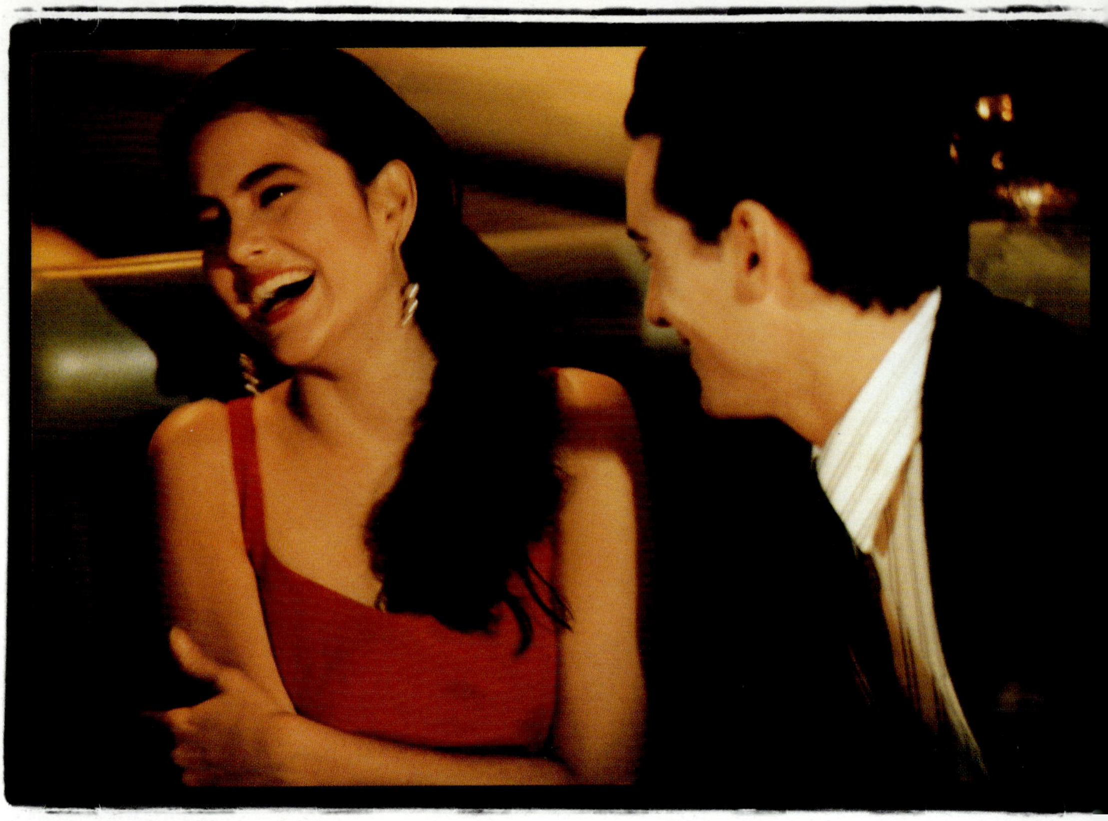
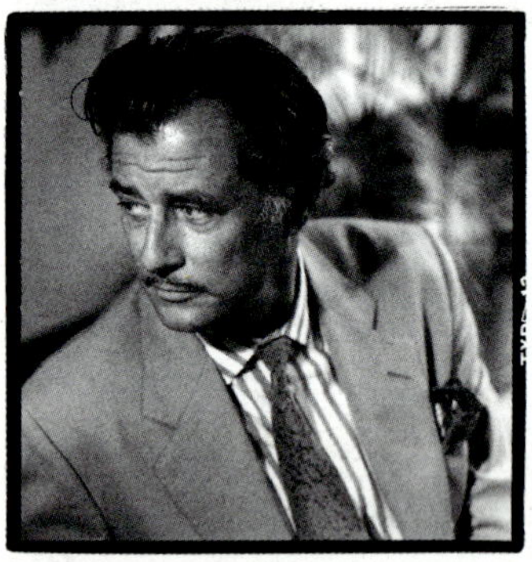
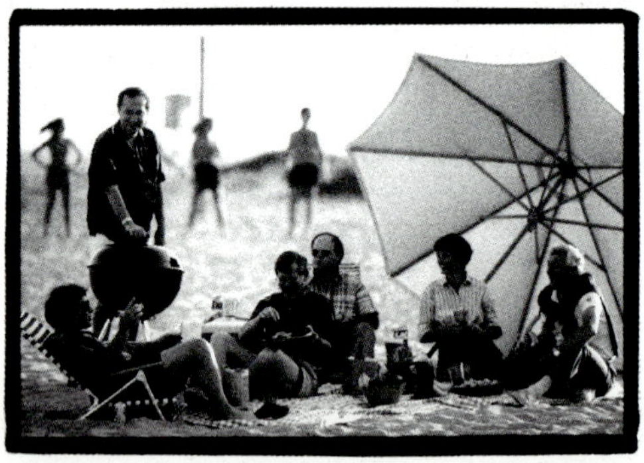
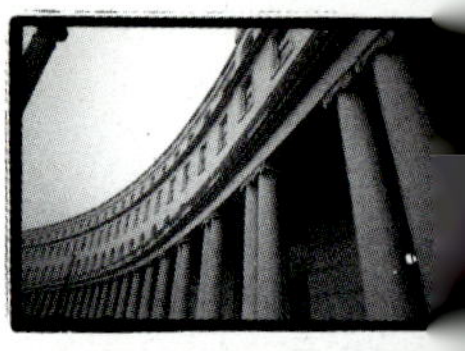
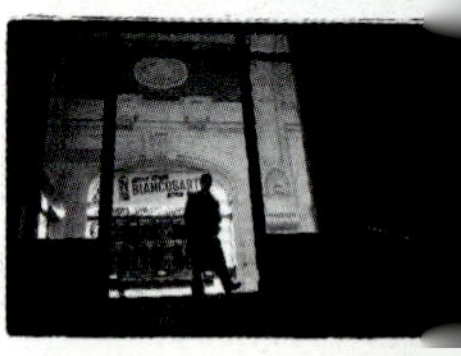
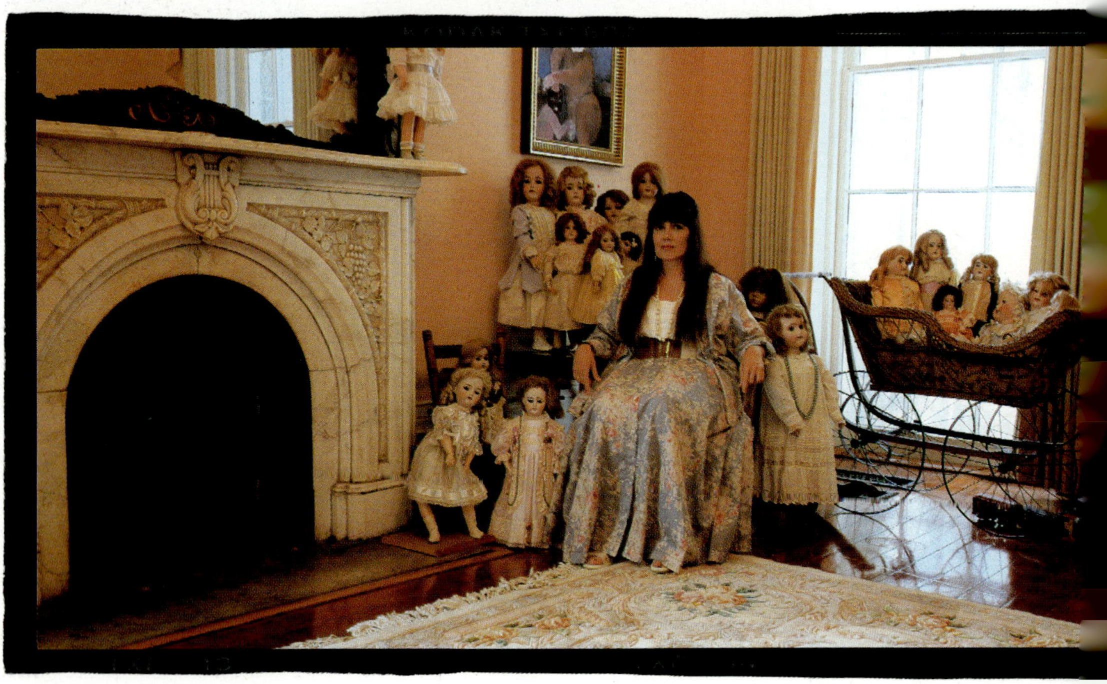

CHRIS SANDERS

130 WEST 23RD STREET   NEW YORK CITY 10011   212 645 6111
REPRESENTED BY ROSEMARY SAMUELS   212 477 3567

SCHILLER

SCHILLER-OGRUDEK:
17 WEST 17 STREET
NEW YORK, NY 10011
212.645.8008

SCHILLER

SCHILLER-OGRUDEK:
17 WEST 17 STREET
NEW YORK, NY 10011
212.645.8008

MICHAEL FURMAN

PRESENTED BY

ELAINE SOREL
212.873.4417
FAX 212.874.0831

VICTORIA SATTERTHWAITE
215.925.4233
FAX 215.925.6108

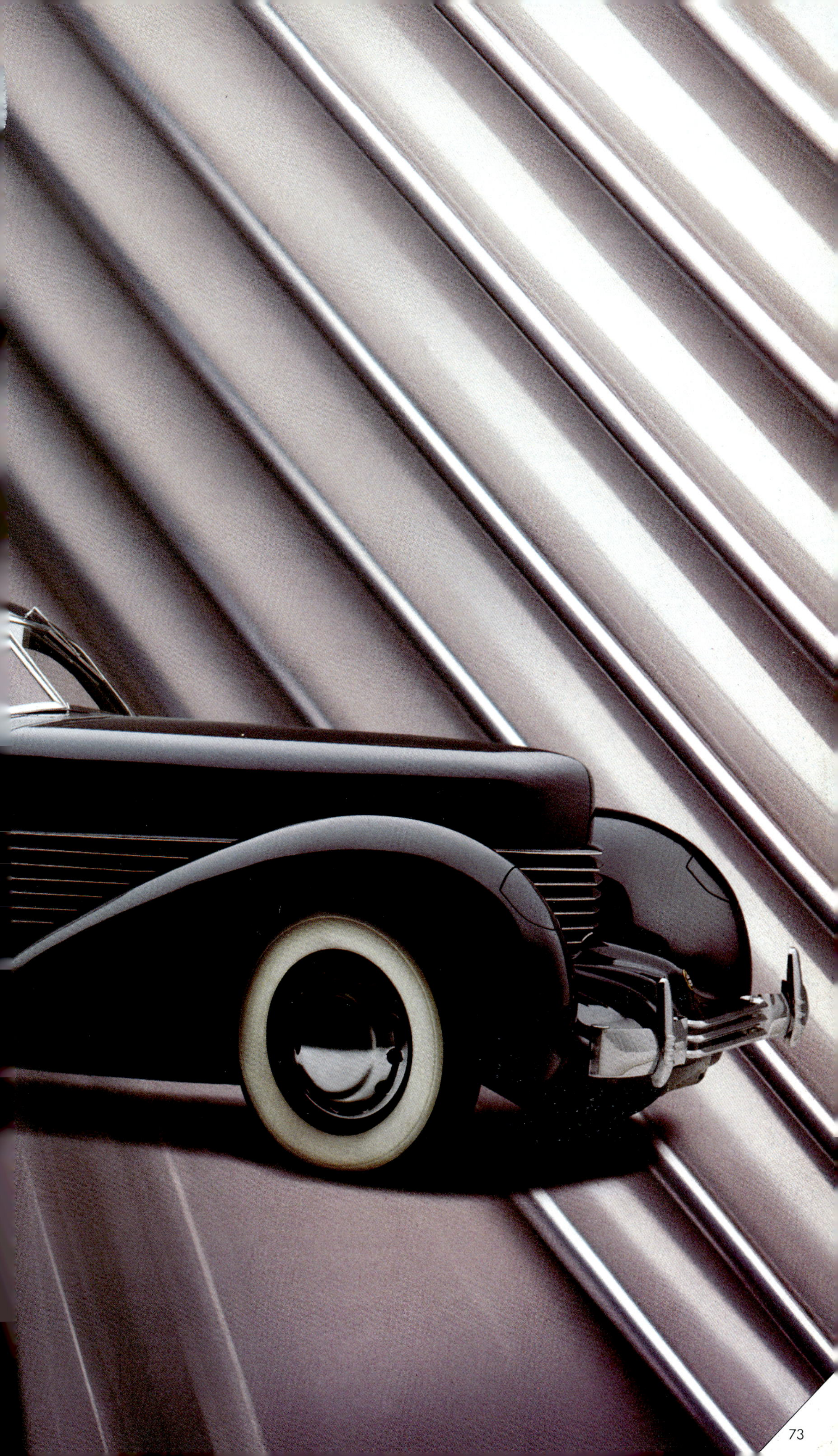

Matthew Klein   Phone (212) 255-6400   Fax (212) 242-6149

"*Matthew Klein has done virtually every food photograph*

Represented by Michael Crecco (212) 682-3422

I've needed for the past 19 years. Perfectly."—Milton Glaser

FRANK

H

ERHOLDT

73 LEONARD STREET   LONDON EC2   TEL 071 739 7359

REPRESENTED IN THE UNITED STATES BY BERNSTEIN & ANDRIULLI, INC.   TEL 212 682 1490   FAX 212 286 1890

77

© 1991 BRETT FROOMER

BRETT FROOMER
REPRESENTED BY
BERNSTEIN & ANDRIULLI INC
FAX 212-286-1890
212-682-1490
STUDIO 212-533-3113

FROOMER

© 1991 Brett Froomer

Brett Froomer
Represented By
Bernstein & Andriulli Inc
Fax 212-286-1890
212-602-1490
Studio 212-533-3113

FROOMER

GUNTHER RAUPP IS REPRESENTED
IN THE UNITED STATES BY
BERNSTEIN & ANDRIULLI, INC.
CALL 212/682-1490, FAX 212/286-1890

IN EUROPE BY
BOB TOAY, LONDON
CALL 071/379-8111, FAX 071/240-5600

IN GERMANY
CALL 07144/25800, FAX 07144/207978

R A U

FERRARI: CALENDAR EDITION

FERRARI: CALENDAR EDITION

GM EUROPE: OPEL VECTRA BROCHURES

FORD: CONCEPT CAR CALENDAR

BUICK: U.S. REATTA CAMPAIGN

ALL PHOTOGRAPHS © 1991 GUNTHER RAUPP

83

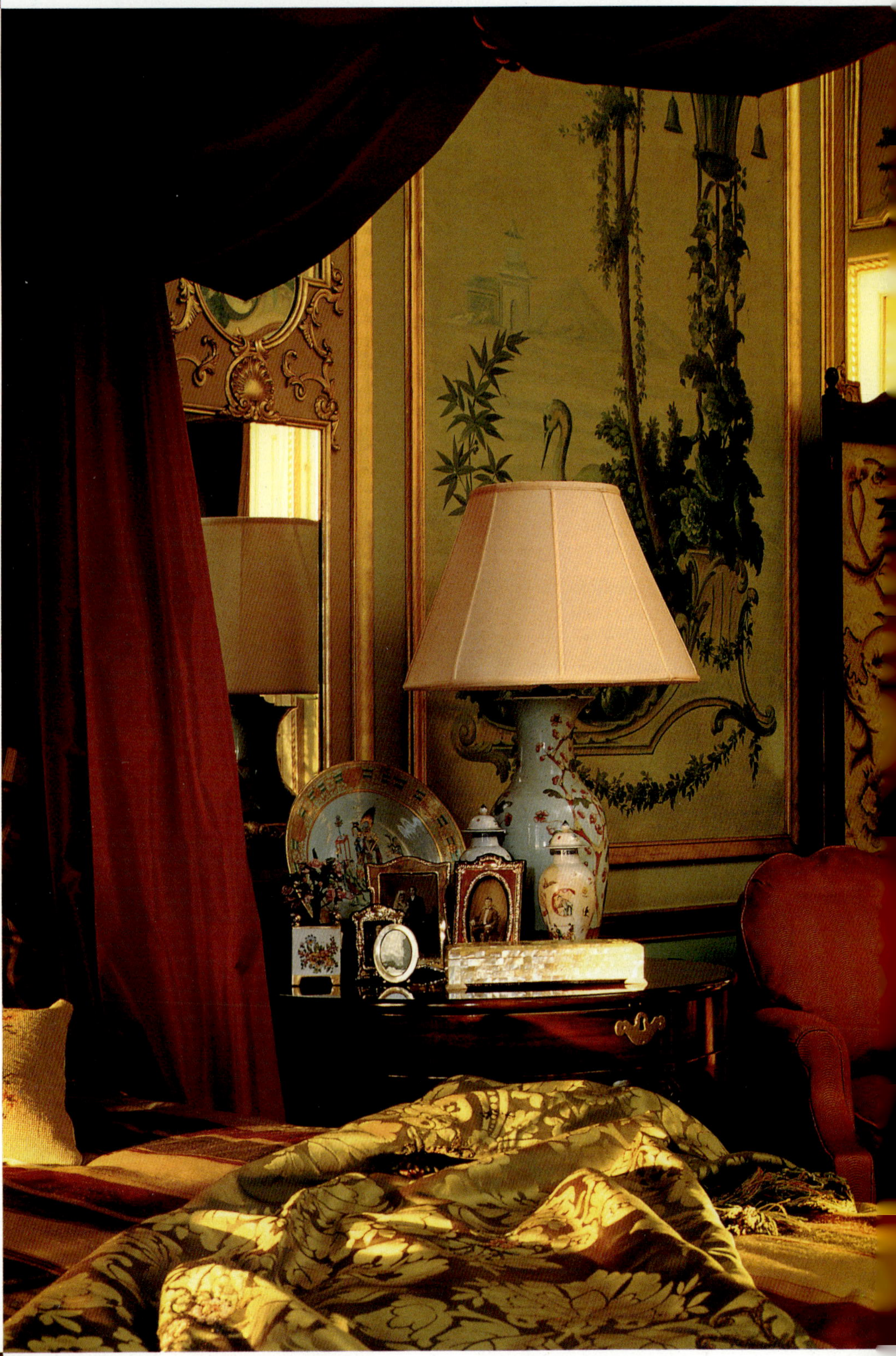
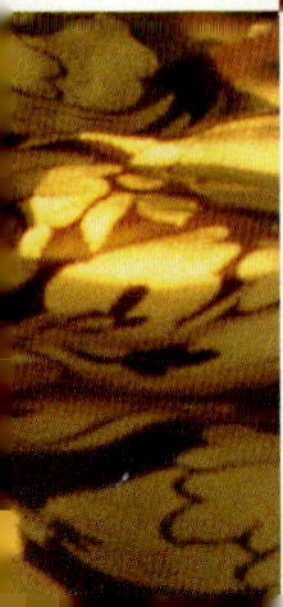

M^cCAVERA

TOM M^cCAVERA REPRESENTED BY **BERNSTEIN & ANDRIULLI**, 60 EAST 42ND STREET, NEW YORK, NY 10165, FAX (212) 286-1890 (212) 682-1490

85

Alan Kaplan 212.982.9500 Fax 212.614.0732

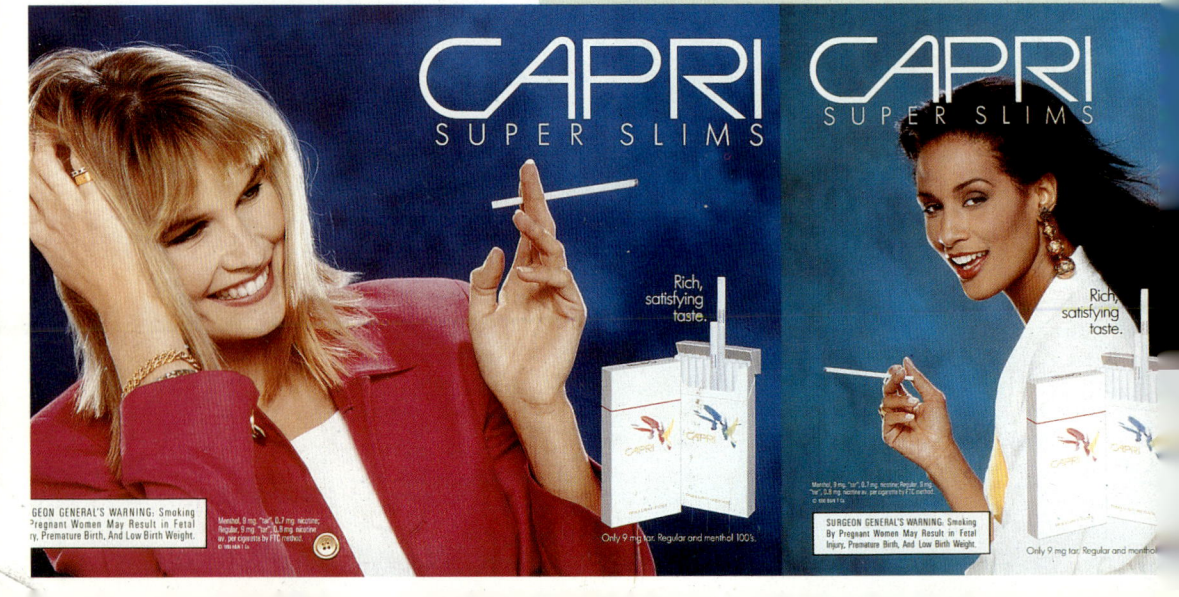

ALAN KAPLAN

CAPRI SUPER SLIMS

Rich, satisfying taste.

CAPRI SUPER SLIMS

Rich, satisfying taste.

SURGEON GENERAL'S WARNING: Smoking By Pregnant Women May Result in Fetal Injury, Premature Birth, And Low Birth Weight.

Only 9 mg tar. Regular and menthol 100's.

© Copyright ALAN KAPLAN 1991

Represented by Bernstein & Andriulli: 212.682.1490   Represented in Chicago by Carolyn Potts: 312.944.1130

87

LIPTON SOUP WILL GET YOU A GO[OD]

REZNY

AARON REZNY, INC • 119 WEST 23RD STREET • NEW YORK CITY, NY 10011 • 212 691 1894

OUS HUNK.

vith Lipton.

REPRESENTED BY JERRY ANTON 212·633·9880 FAX 691·1685

REPRESENTED BY: ERICA STURDEVANT 212.242.0840

PRINT & FILM

JADE
59 WEST 19TH STREET
ALBERT
NEW YORK, NY 10011
STUDIO
PHONE 212.242.0840

TAK KOJIMA

TAK-E AD-VANTAGE, DO IT AD-VENTURE.

25 WEST 23RD STREET, NEW YORK, N.Y. 10010 · PHONE 212 243-2243 FAX 212 929-3985
Rep by Rapp GERALD & CULLEN RAPP, Inc. Phone 212 889-3337, Fax 212 889-3341

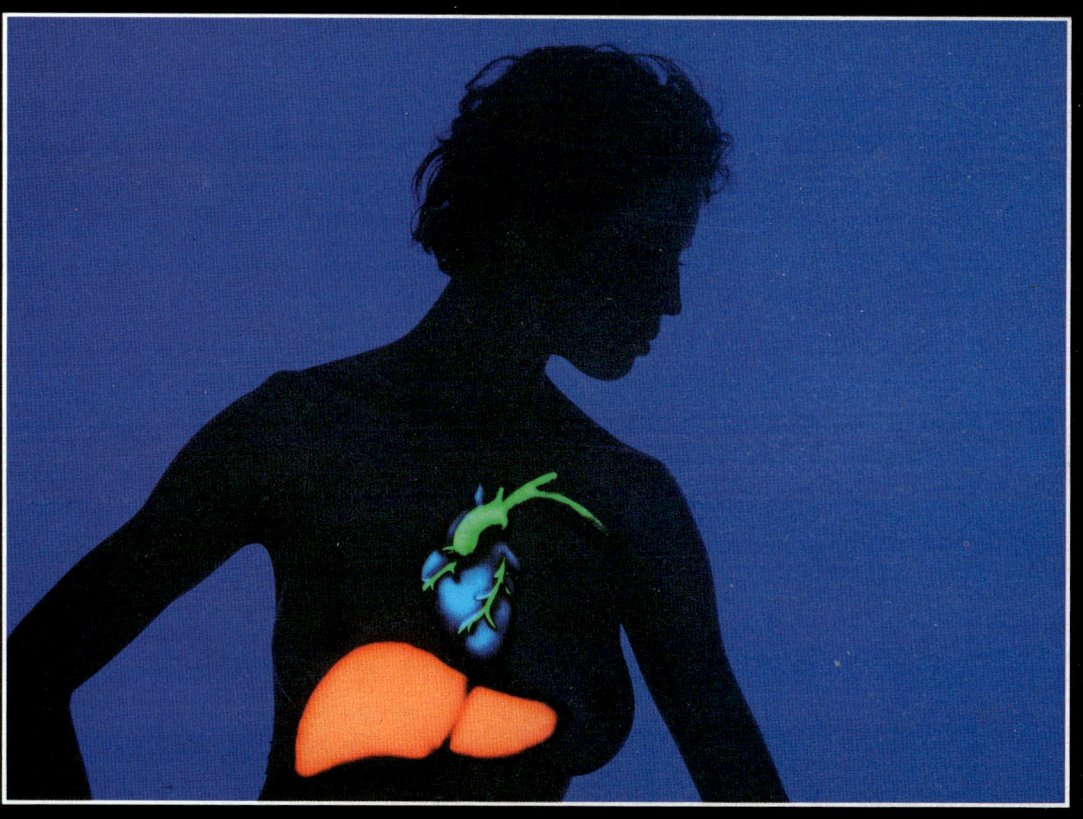

TAK KOJIMA

TAK-E AD-VANTAGE, DO IT AD-VENTURE.

25 WEST 23RD STREET, NEW YORK, N.Y. 10010 · PHONE 212 243-2243 FAX 212 929-3985
Rep by Rapp   GERALD & CULLEN RAPP, Inc.   Phone 212 889-3337, Fax 212 889-3341

SPEL·MAN

Steve Spelman Photography · New York City · 212 242 9381

GAMBA

MARK GAMBA
PHOTOGRAPHY
212·727·8313
FAX 212·645·9520

GAMBA

97

AND NOW,
SOME COLOR
MASCARA
And still,
no raccoon eyes.
SOME COLOR
SOME COLOR
MAX FACTOR

Canon
FAXPHONE 23

SENSITIVE SOLUTIONS
SHAMPOOS AND CONDITIONERS SPECIALLY FORMULATED FOR YOUR TYPE OF HAIR
ALMAY
Shampoo
ALMAY
Shampoo
ALMAY
HYPO-ALLERGENIC
Shampoo
For Dry, Damaged Hair

FLAWLESS SKIN.
Love Pat indulges it with
moisturizing color and coverage.
Love Pat
REVLON
UNFORGETTABLE

RIC COHN

137 WEST 25 STREET NEW YORK, N.Y. 10001
STUDIO 212/924-4450 FAX 212/645-2059

CALL FOR PORTFOLIO OR T.V. REEL

K A R E N

PHOTOGRAPHY 103 READE ST

C I P O L L A

NEW YORK NY 10013   (212) 619-6114

REPRESENTED BY GAIL GAYNIN   (212) 580-3141

Chip Forelli

REPRESENTED BY
BARBARA UMLAS
212.534.4008

STUDIO

529
WEST
42ND
STREET

NEW
YORK,

NEW
YORK

10036

TEL
212
564
1835

FAX
212
564
2109

BERGAMI

5 WEST 20TH ST.
NY, NY 10011
(212) 242-0942/
(212) 979-2930

REPRESENTED BY
BARBARA UMLAS
& ASSOCIATES
(212) 534-4008

AGENCY: FCB/LKP   CLIENT: RJ REYNOLDS

AGENCY: LGFE   CLIENT: HENNESSY

BERGAMI

5 WEST 20TH ST.
NY, NY 10011
(212) 242-0942/
(212) 979-2930

REPRESENTED BY
BARBARA UMLAS
& ASSOCIATES
(212) 534-4008

JEFF

CADGE

New York City 212•563•0547

STEVE EDSON

617.924.2212

Copyright 1991 Steve Edson
See work in Creative Black Book 88/89/90

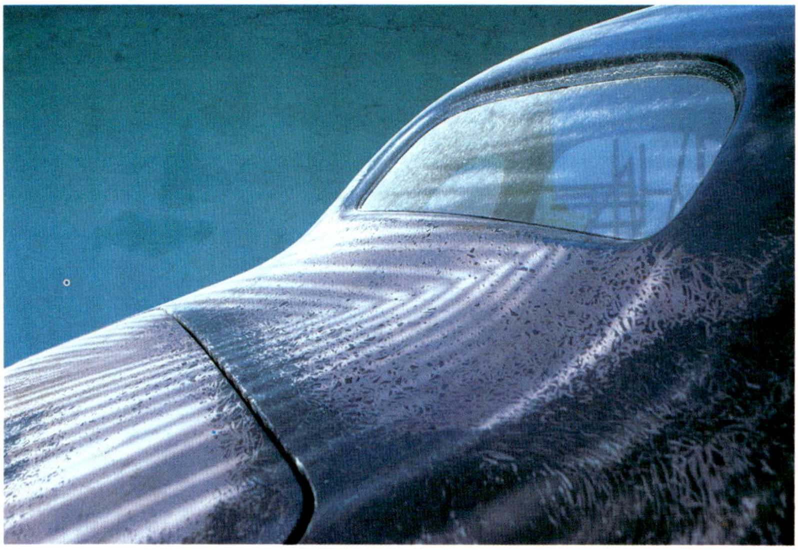

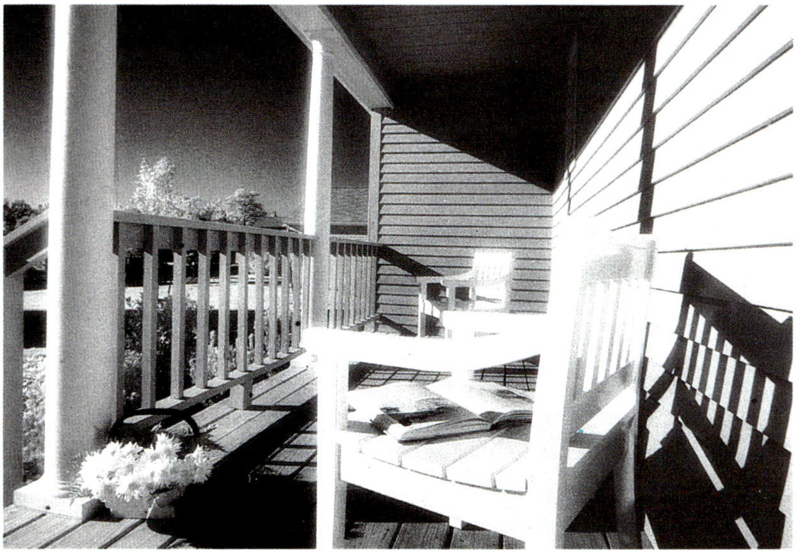

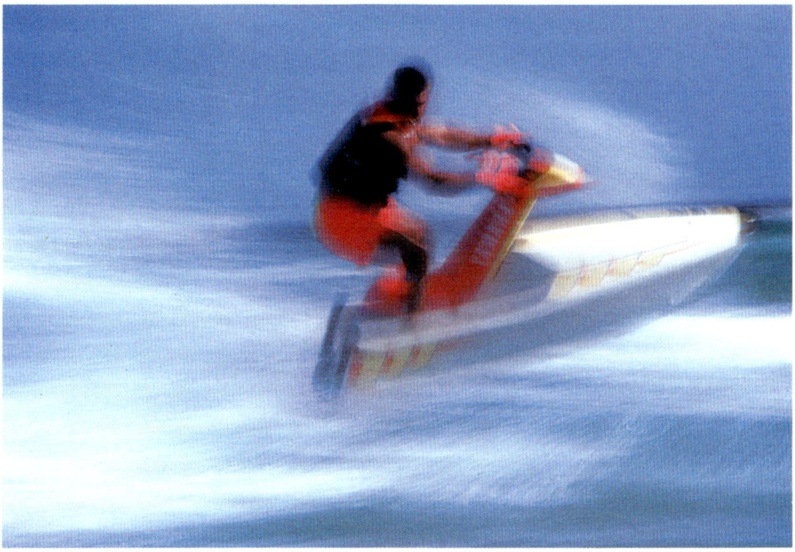

ONAYA

ONAYA-OGRUDEK: 17 WEST 17 STREET NEW YORK, NY 10011   212.645.8008

ONAYA

ONAYA-OGRUDEK: 17 WEST 17 STREET NEW YORK, NY 10011

REPRESENTED BY PAMELA BLACK
212-385-0667   212-242-1532
REEL AVAILABLE

WILLIAM HEUBERGER

BRONSTEIN BERMAN

STEVE BRONSTEIN, HOWARD BERMAN, BRET WILLS. PHOTOGRAPHERS. REPRESEN

© BRONSTEIN/BERMAN & ASSOC. INC.

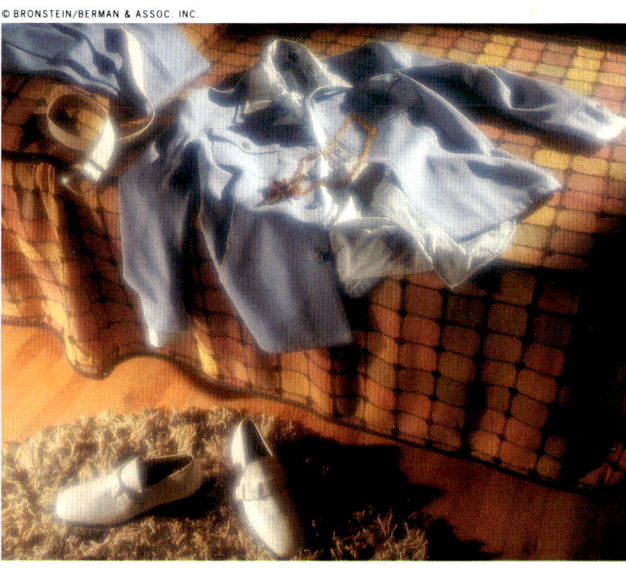

LEISURE SUIT *by* Steve Bronstein

WE CAN MAKE *Almost* ANYTHING LOOK GOOD ON FILM.

STEVE BRONSTEIN
38 GREENE ST. *(212) 925-2999*

GARY HUREWITZ. 38 GREENE ST. N.Y. N.Y. 10013 *(212) 925-2999*

STEVE BRONSTEIN. PHOTOGRAPHER. REPRESENT

y Gary Hurewitz. 38 Greene St. *(212) 925-2999*

MINIATURE SET

STEVE BRONSTEIN. PHOTOGRAPHER. REPRESENTED BY GARY HUREWITZ.

38 GREENE ST. *(212) 925-2999*

© BRONSTEIN/BERMAN & ASSOC. INC.

JERRY DELLA FEMINA *by Howard Berman*

WE CAN MAKE *Almost* ANYONE LOOK GOOD ON FILM.

HOWARD BERMAN
38 GREENE ST. *(212) 925-2999*

HOWARD BERMAN. PHOTOGRAPHER. REPRESENTED BY GARY HUREWITZ.
38 GREENE ST. *(212) 925-2999*

HOWARD BERMAN. PHOTOGRAPHER. REPRESENT

Gary Hurewitz. 38 Greene St. *(212) 925-2999*

HOWARD BERMAN. PHOTOGRAPHER. REPRESENTED BY GARY HUREWITZ.
38 GREENE ST. *(212) 925-2999*

DINNER by Bret Wills

WE CAN MAKE *Almost* ANYTHING LOOK GOOD ON FILM.

BRET WILLS
38 GREENE ST. *(212) 925-2999*

BRET WILLS. PHOTOGRAPHER. REPRESENTED BY GARY HUREWITZ.
38 GREENE ST. *(212) 925-2999*

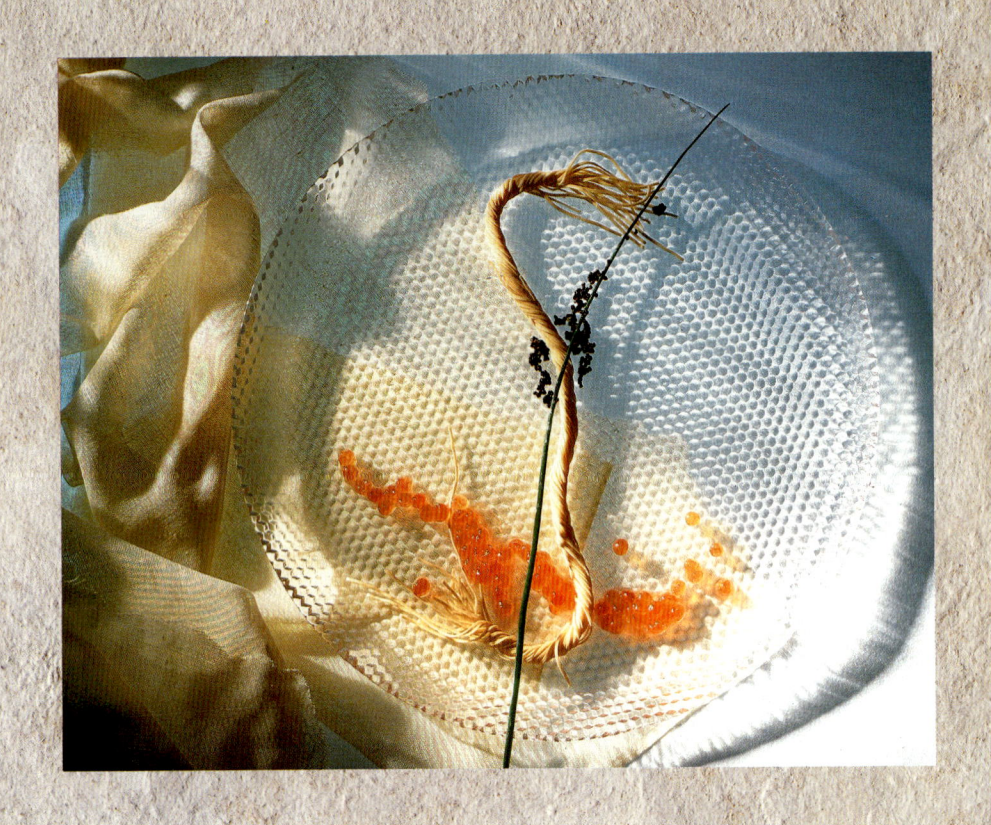

BRET WILLS. PHOTOGRAPHER. REPRESENTED

ARY HUREWITZ. 38 GREENE ST. *(212) 925-2999*

125

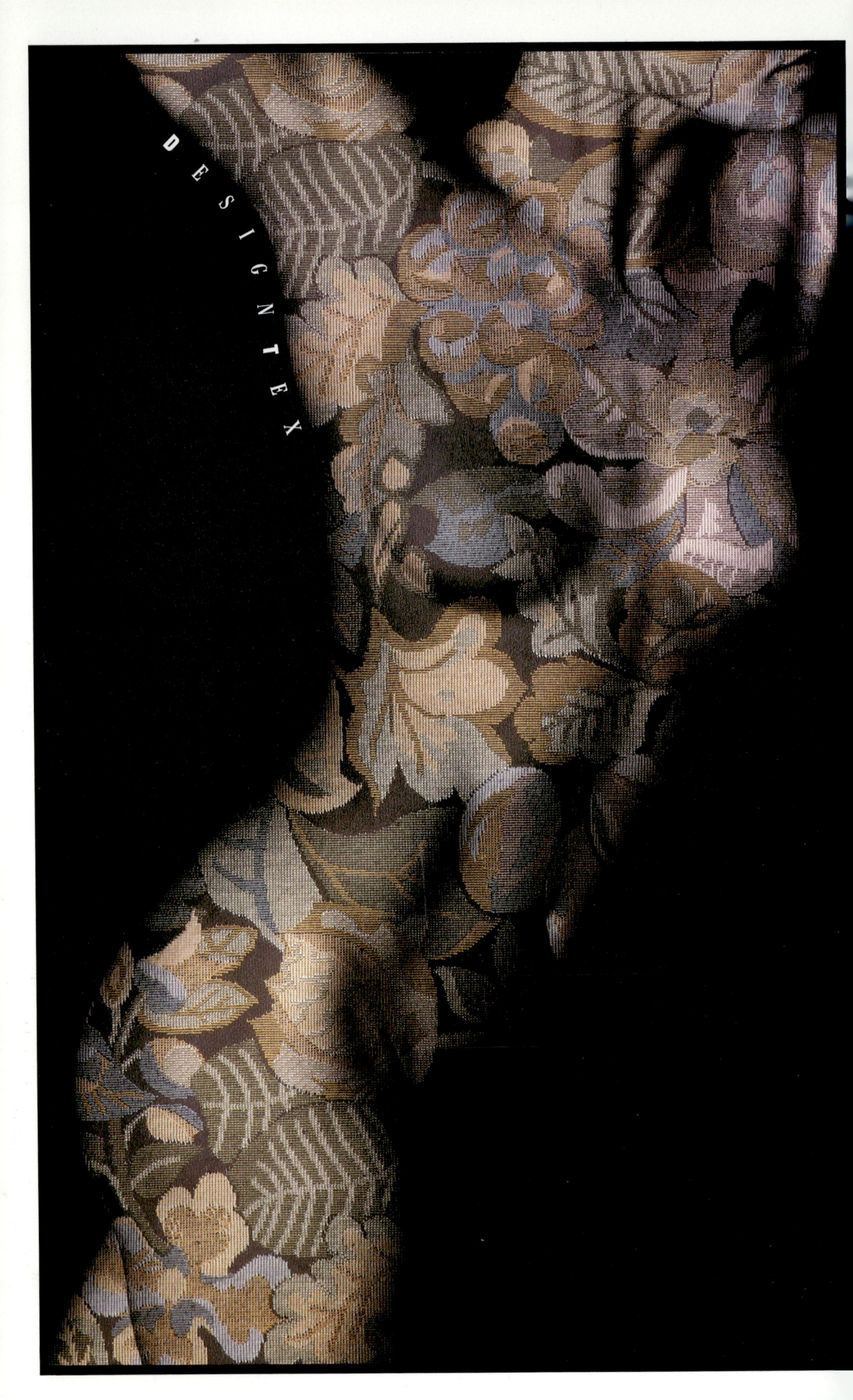

DONALD PENNY PHOTOGRAPHY 10 WEST 18 STREET NEW YORK 10011 (212) 633-9650 /FAX 675-6721

PENNY

40 East 23rd St. New York NY 100

•REPRESENTED BY SAMANTHA LEWIN (212) 228-5530•

(212) 475-2802•

Anything is Possible

Nick Koudis

PHOTOGRAPHER • MODELMAKER

©1991 Trip von Hoffmann

VON HOFFMAN TRIP

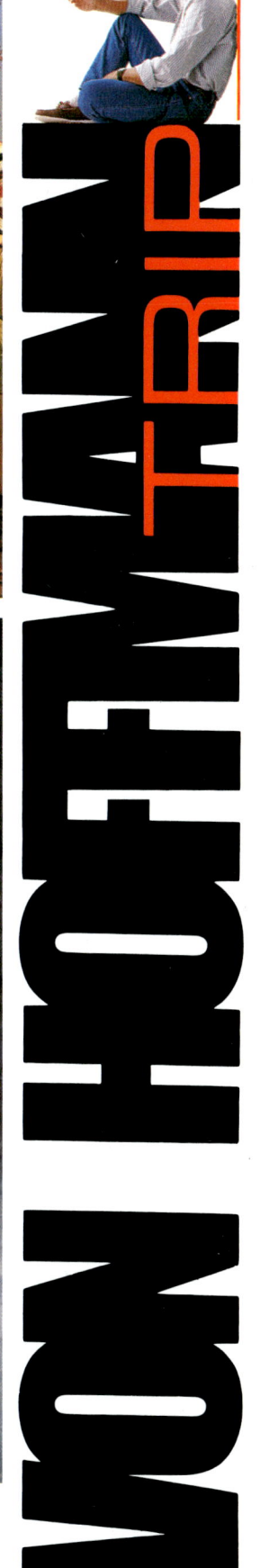

ASSOCIATE KATHY WELLING (212) 575-1041
(201) 377-0317

131

LANE PEDERSON

LANE PEDERSON
PHOTOGRAPHY

76 NINTH AVENUE PH
NEW YORK, NY 10011

212 • 929 • 9001

smart. beautiful.
Maybelline

smart. beautiful.
Maybelline

smart. beautiful.
Maybelline

PAUL
BARTON
PHOTOGRAPHY

111 W. 19TH ST, NYC 10011, 212. 691.1999

A FINE SELECTION OF STOCK PHOTOGRAPHY AVAILABLE

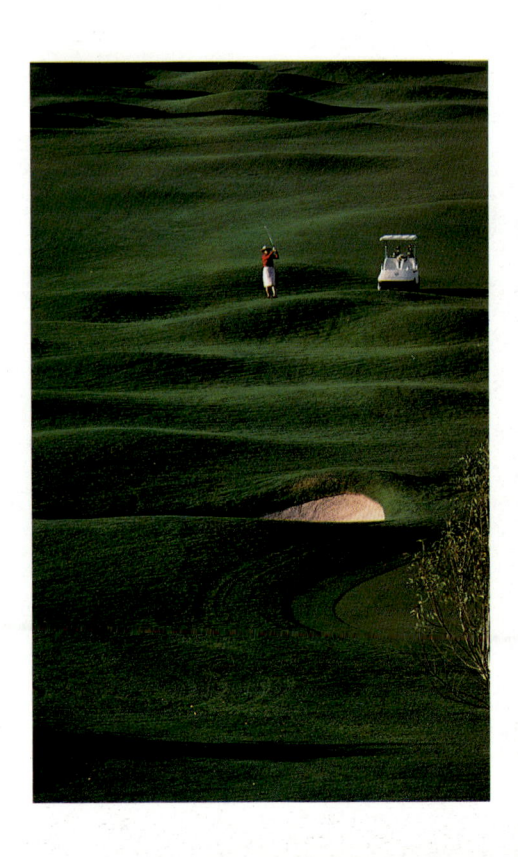

PAUL
BARTON
PHOTOGRAPHY

111 W. 19TH ST, NYC 10011, 212. 691.1999

A FINE SELECTION OF STOCK PHOTOGRAPHY AVAILABLE

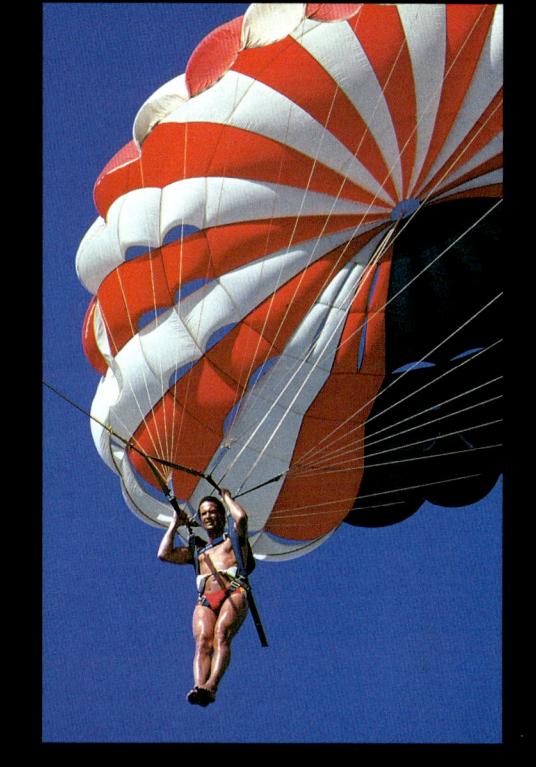

© Paul Barton 1991

135

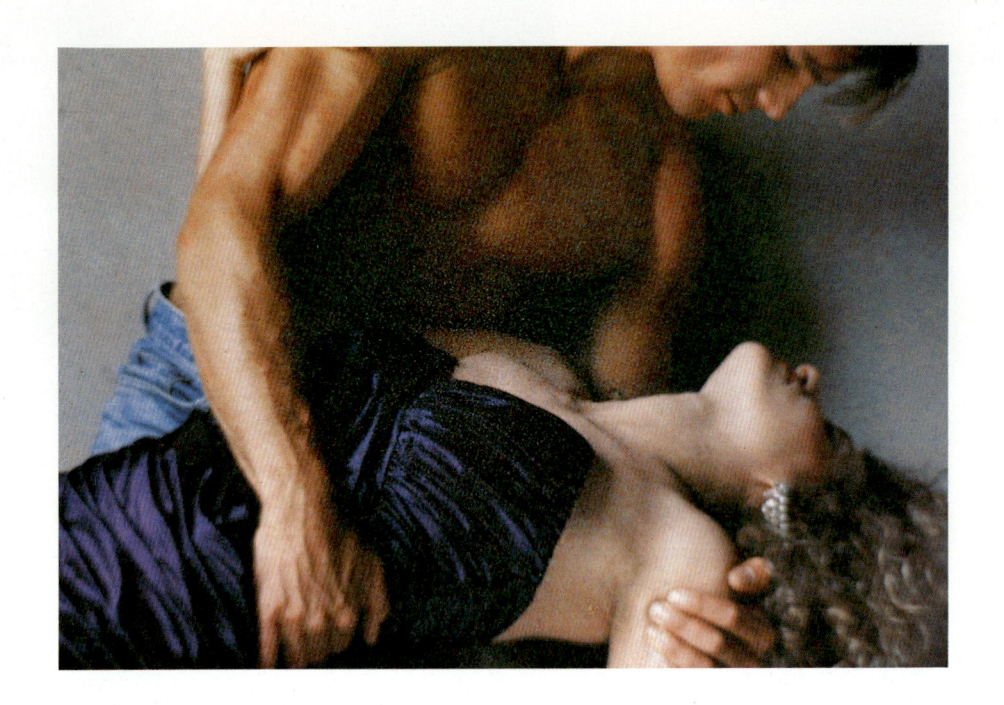

J. IVAN RUBIN PHOTOGRAPHY
240 West Twenty-Third Street, New York City, 10011

212/645/0020

MARGE CASEY ASSOCIATES

REPRESENTS

On The Following Pages:

Lou Wallach

Thomas Hooper

Michael Luppino

Geoffrey Clifford

•

And Also:

Albano Ballerini

Helen Norman

Zeva Oelbaum

212.486.9575　FAX　212.838.5751

245 EAST 63RD STREET, NEW YORK, NY 10021

LOUIS WALLACH
PHOTOGRAPHY
212.260.5393
FAX 529.2848
REPRESENTED BY
MARGE CASEY
212.486.9575

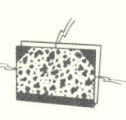

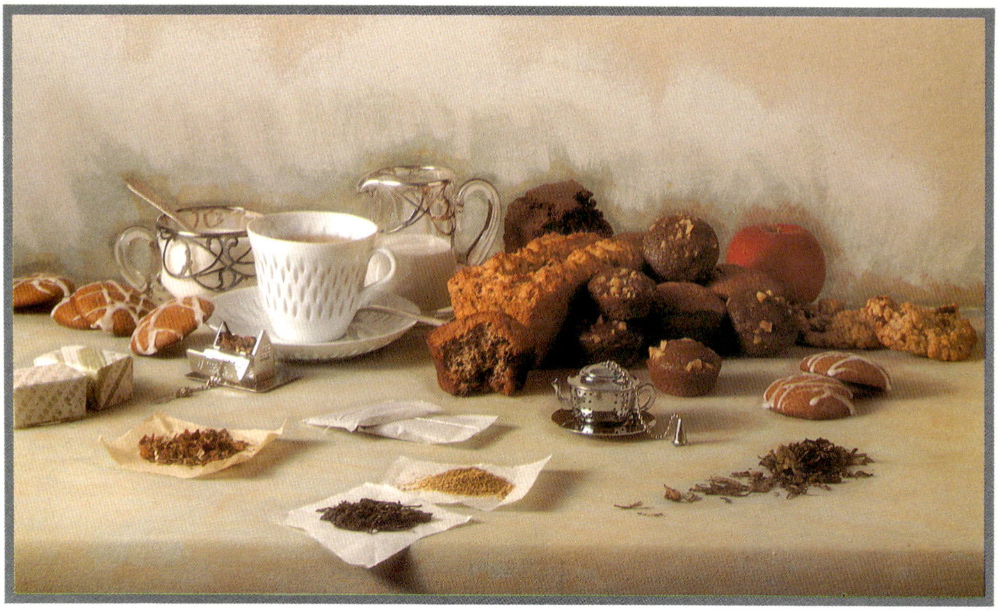

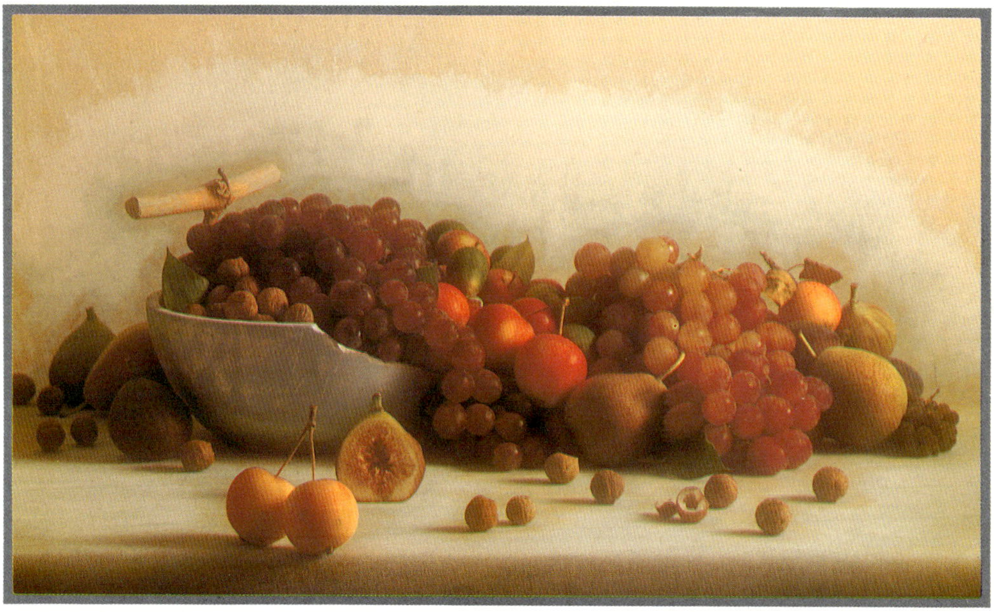

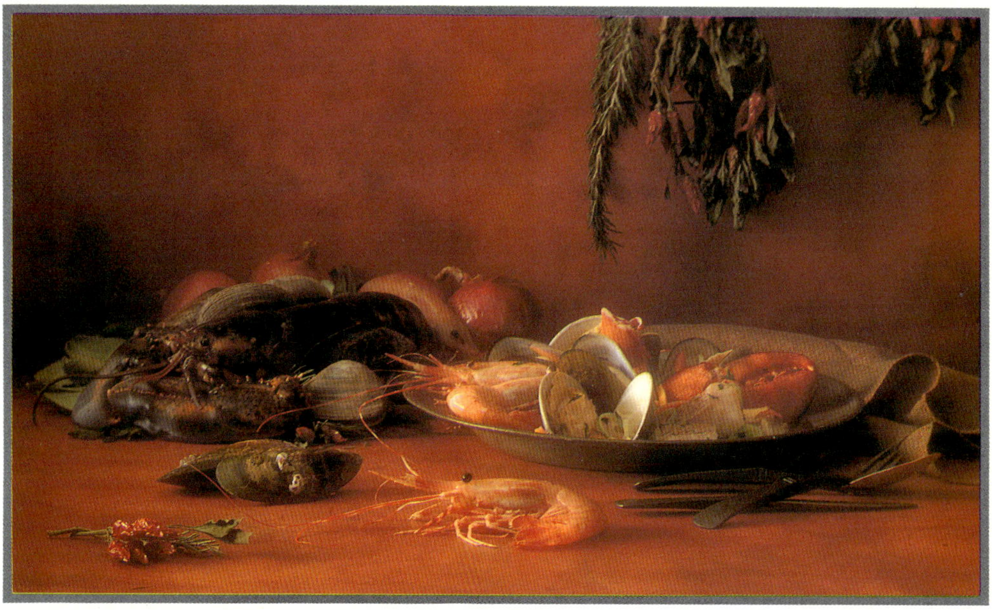

HOOPER

THOMAS HOOPER
MARGE CASEY ASSOCIATES 212·486·9575
STUDIO: 126 FIFTH AVENUE, NEW YORK 10011 212·691·0122

141

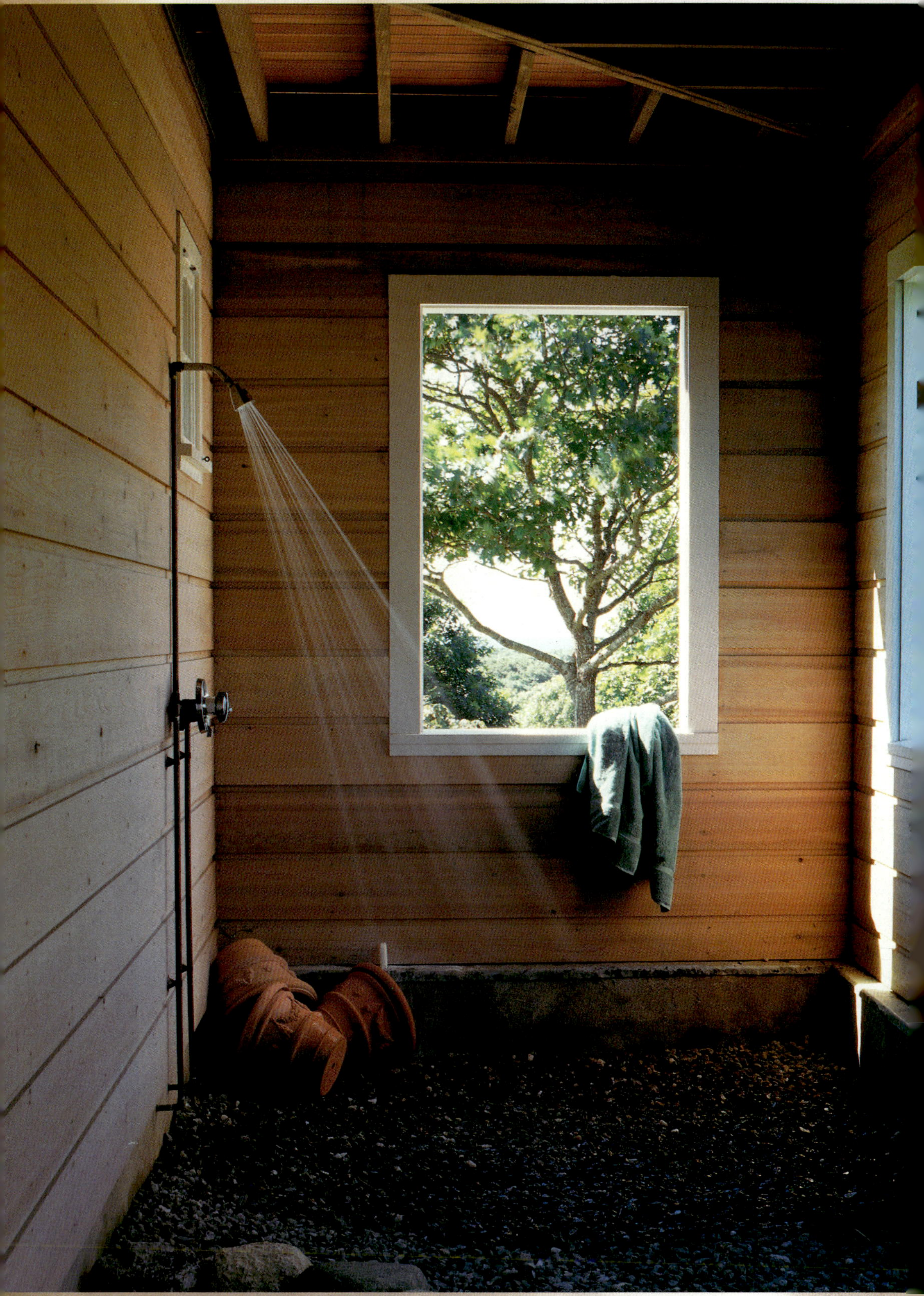

MICHAEL LUPPINO

126 WEST 22ND STREET, NEW YORK, NY 10011
PHONE: 212/633-9486   FAX: 212/727-9096

REP. BY MARGE CASEY ASSOC.   212/486-9575   FAX 212/838-5751

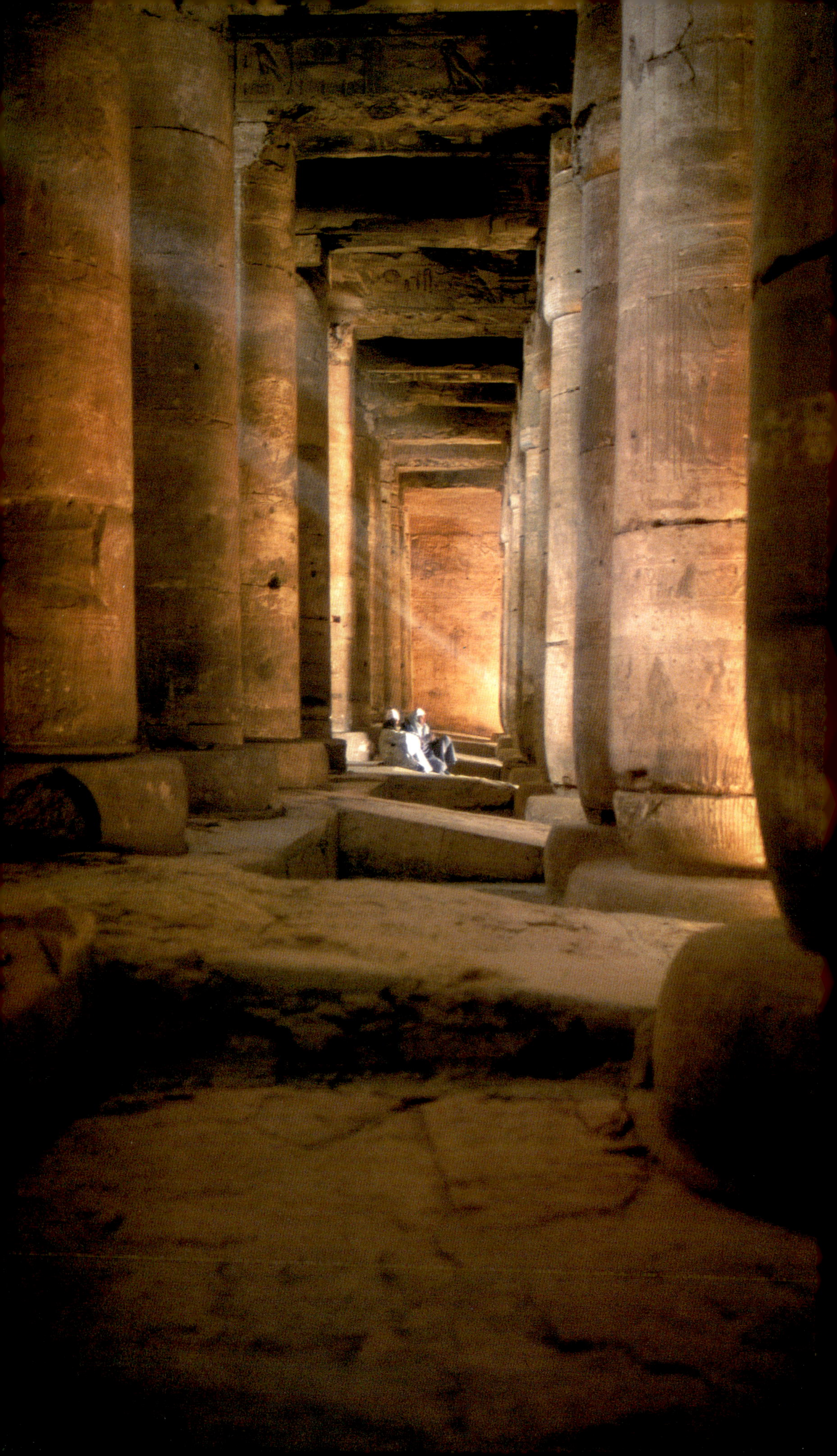

GEOFFREY CLIFFORD
LOCATION PHOTOGRAPHY

REPRESENTED BY MARGE CASEY

IN NEW YORK:

212/486-9575

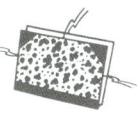

IN THE WEST:

602/577-6439

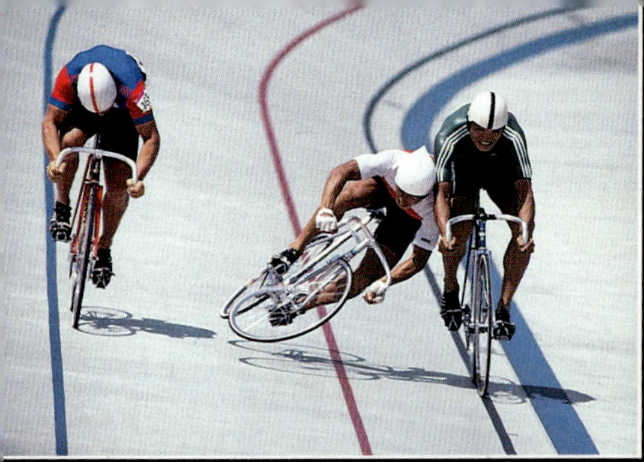

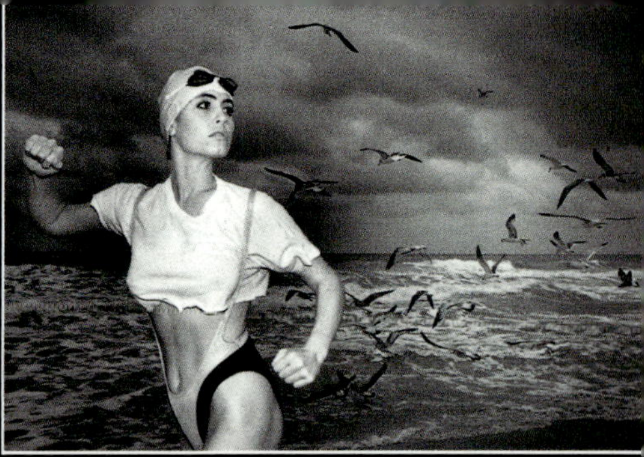

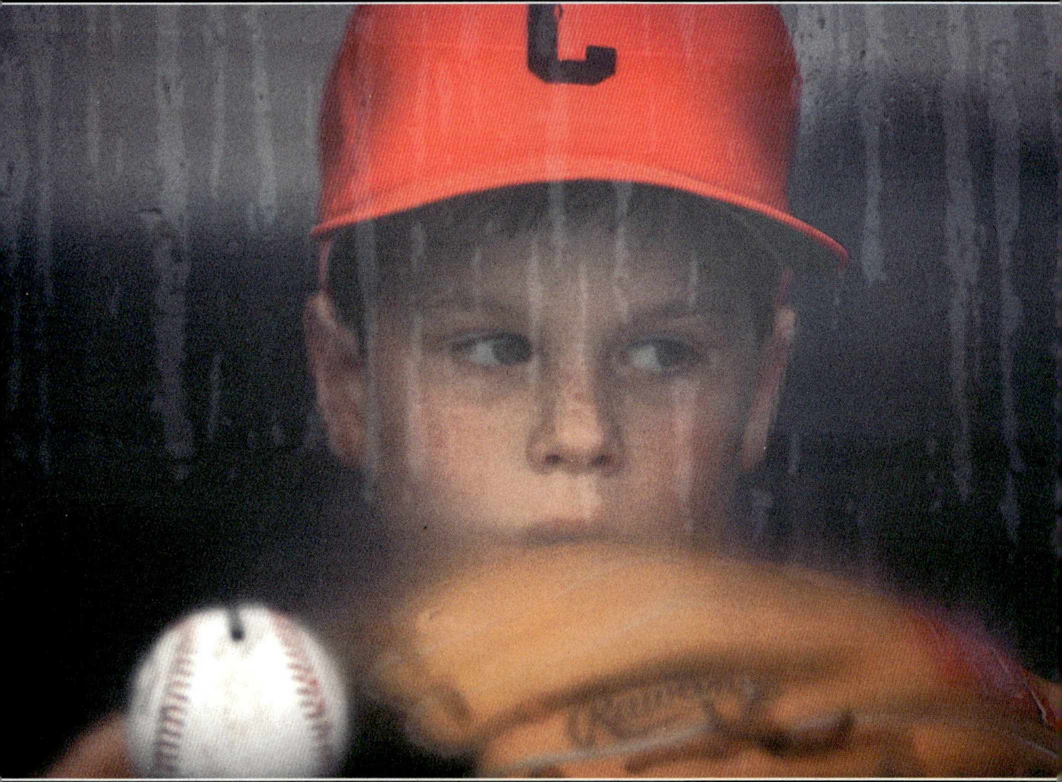

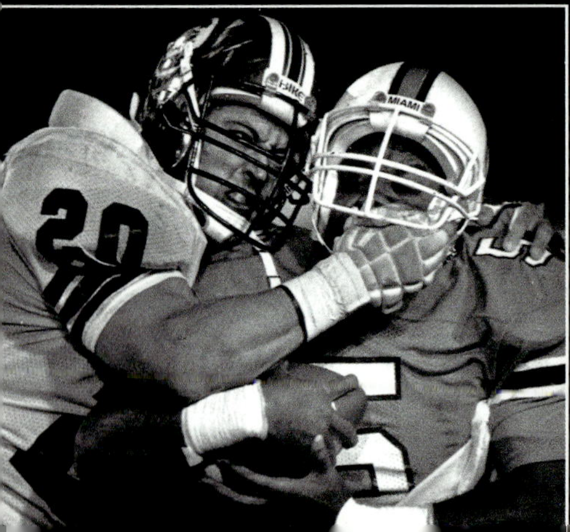
MIAMI

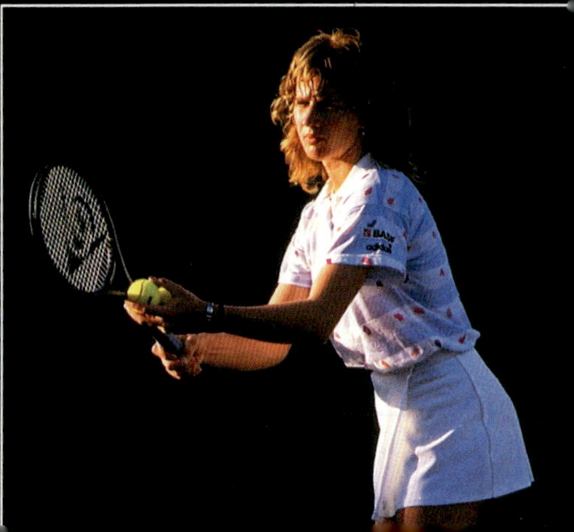

Bill Frakes

Represented by:
Susan Miller
(212) 905-8400
(212) 427-7777 Fax

Miami Studio (305) 441-9048

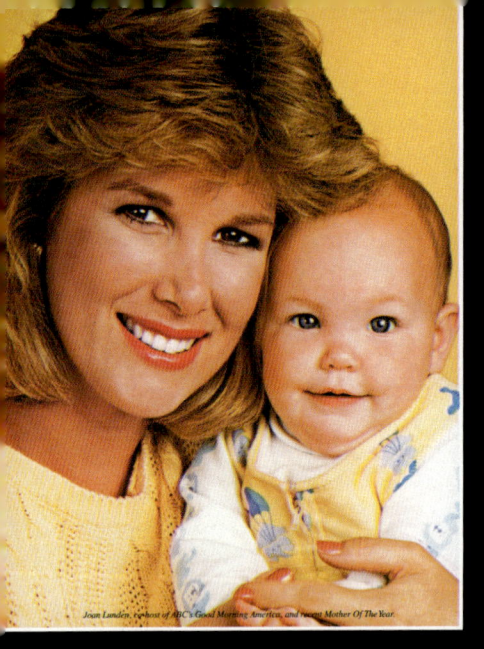

Joan Lunden, co-host of ABC's Good Morning America, and recent Mother Of The Year.

Kids don't wear adult-size clothes. Why should they wear adult-size bandages?

Finally, bandages that fit kids. New Curad® Kid Size.™

Kids are smaller than adults. So smaller bandages fit them better.
Finally, there's a complete selection of bandages that fit kids. New Curad® Kid Size™ bandages.
They're smaller than adult-size bandages.
And they're bigger in fun — featuring Happy Strips,™ with Ronald McDonald® and other great McDonaldland® characters.

Plus McDonaldland Feel Better Activity Cards to help put a smile on your kid's face again.
Next time you go shopping, pick up new Curad® Kid Size™ bandages.
Then when your kid gets a cut or scrape, you'll be able to put on a bandage that fits better.
And you'll have Ronald McDonald and friends to help your kid feel better.

PLAYSKOOL PROMISES FUN!

Come inside and discover the wonderful world of Playskool toys! Boys and girls of all ages will surely find fascinating and exciting ways to have fun. In fact, we promise it!

Questions? Call: 1-800-PLAYSKL

BARBARA CAMPBELL

138 WEST 17TH STREET NYC 10011 212/929-5620
REPRESENTED BY HARRISON KNIGHT 212/288-9777 FAX 212/288-9846
PHOTOMATIC AND TV REELS AVAILABLE

149

DICK LURIA

PHOTOGRAPHY
212-929-7575
FAX: 212-255-4657

151

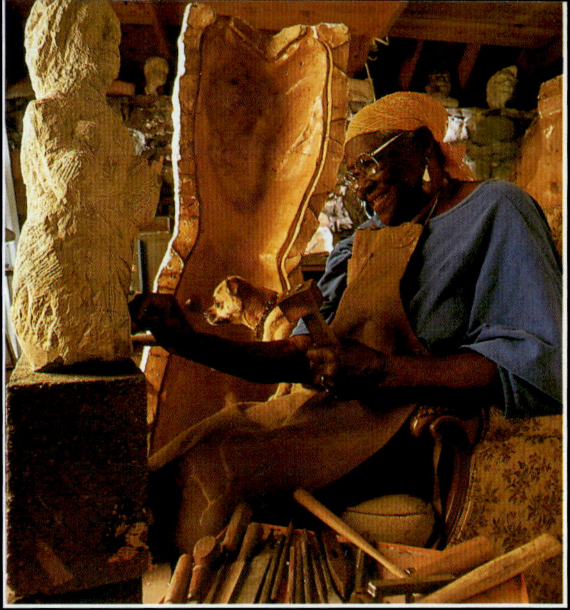

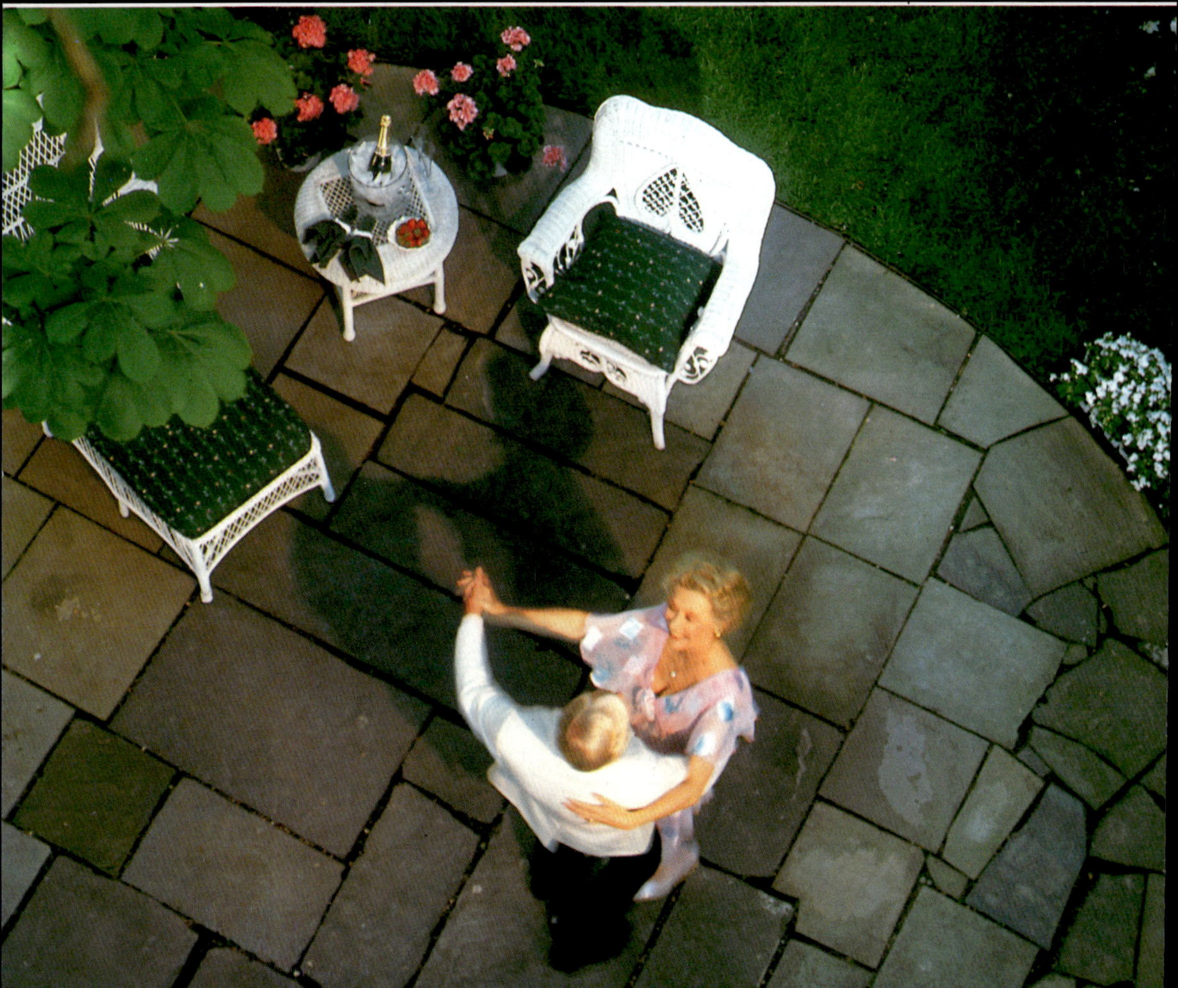

PHOTOGRAPHY
212-929-7575

ROBERT JACOBS

448 WEST 37TH STREET, NYC 10018, 212-967-6883

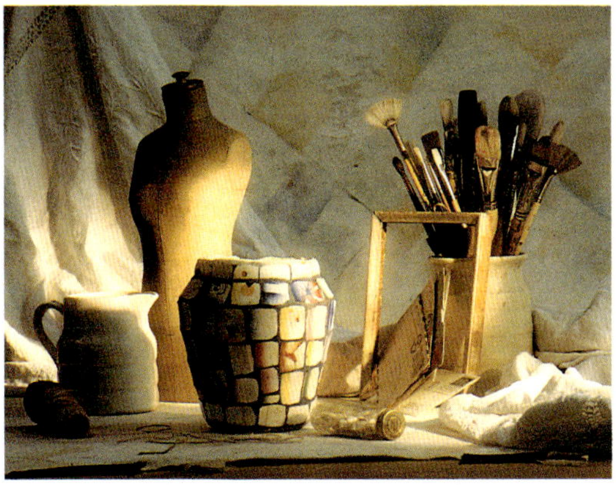

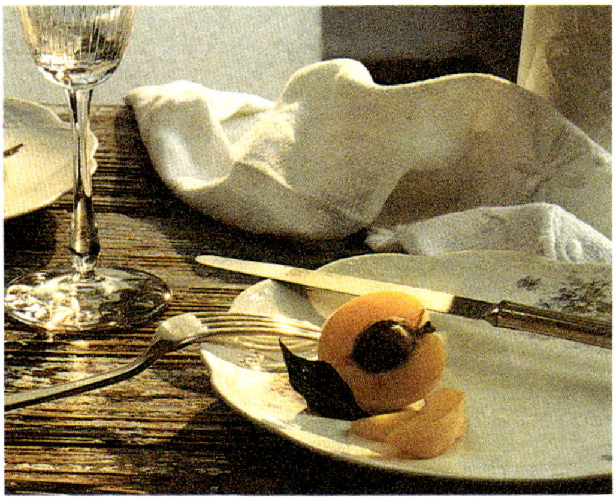

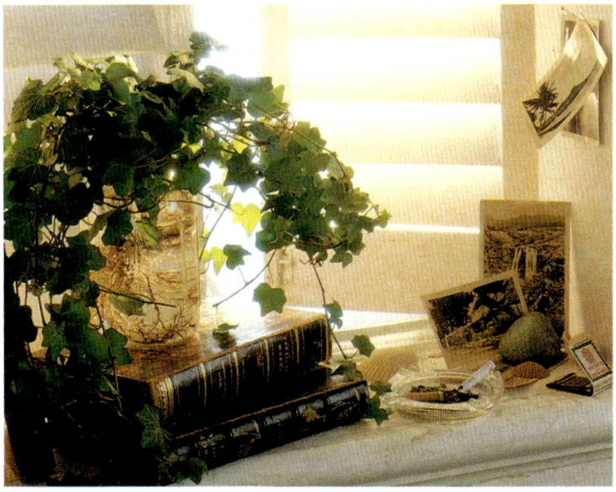

"OOPS!"

PENTAX

NISSAN

MAINE TOURISM

R O B I N S O N

JAMES ROBINSON

212 • 580 • 1793

155 RIVERSIDE DRIVE

NEW YORK CITY 10024

REPRESENTED BY

STEPHEN MADRIS

212 • 744 • 6668

STOCK AVAILABLE

LUCILLE KHORNAK

PHOTOGRAPHY
425 East 58th Street ■ New York, N.Y. 10022
212 593 0933

SPILL LIFE®

David Zimmerman Studio, Inc.
36 West 20th Street
New York, NY 10011
212-206-1000
Fax 212-929-6385

London:
Suzana Podolska
011-4471-624-4989

ZIMMERMAN

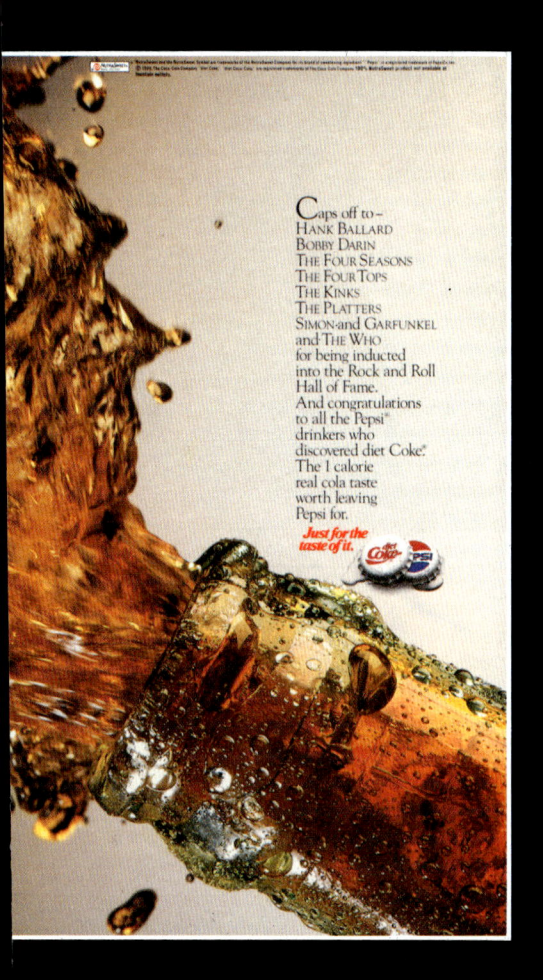

**REPRESENTED BY:
SUSAN MILLER**
212.905.8400   Fax 212-427-7777

kitchen

DENNIS KITCHEN STUDIO
80 FOURTH AVENUE • NY, NY 10003
212 674-7658   FAX 212 995-8090
REP: STAN CARP 212 362-4000

© ALL PHOTOS DENNIS KITCHEN

161

JOHNSON OUTBOARD MOTORS

SAAB

WER DIE WELT KENNT, KENNT TUBORG.

WER DIE WELT KENNT, KENNT TUBORG.

satterwhite

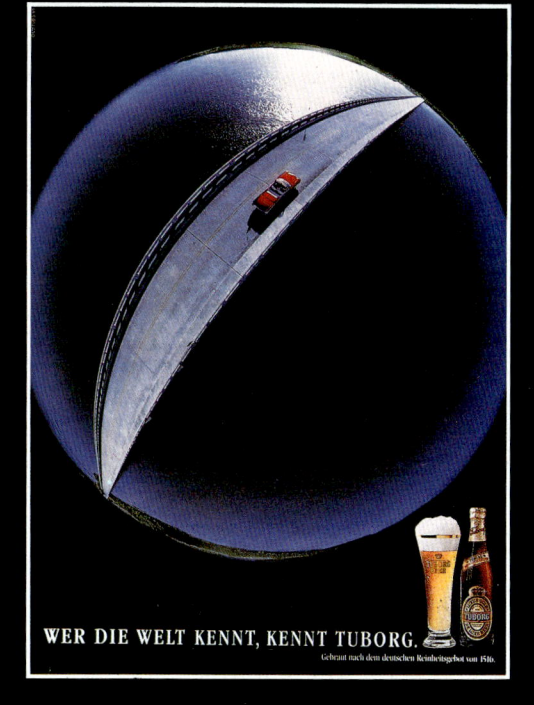

AL SATTERWHITE 80 Varick Street/NYC 10013 TEL: (212) 219-0808.

© SATTERWHITE PRODUCTIONS INC.

163

STILL LIFE.
PEOPLE.
FOOD.

PHOTOGRAPHY BY
SIMONE

GIV'EM
A CALL.
HE'LL
BRING
THE
GUM.

BILL SIMONE
717-274-3621
FAX 717-274-2286

LEBANON, PA 17042

Geert Teuwen
Photography

212.929.9001

76 Ninth Avenue West Penthouse New York, New York 10011

ERIC SCHNAKENBERG

© 1991 Eric Schnakenberg

Represented by Jeannie Papadopoullos

Phone (718) 767-0573   Fax (718) 767-0423

ERIC SCHNAKENBERG

© 1991 Eric Schnakenberg

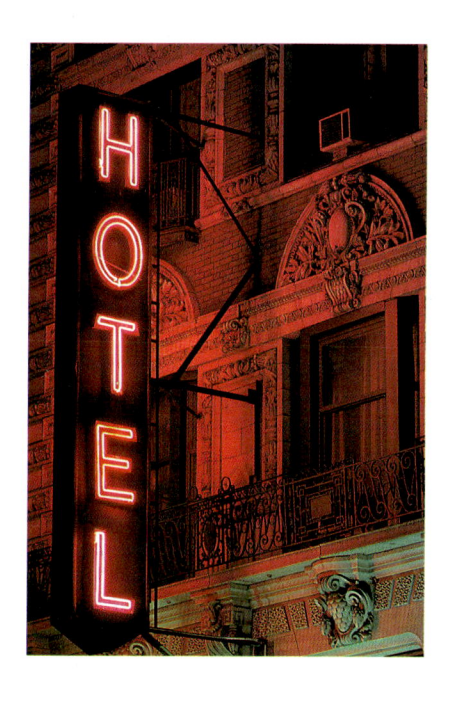

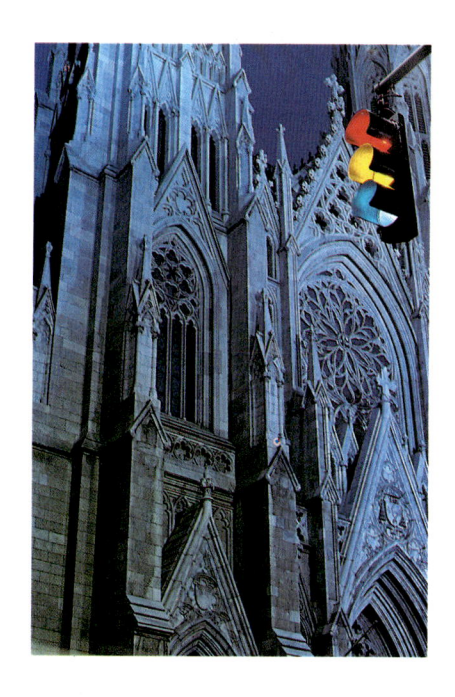

Represented by Jeannie Papadopoullos

Phone (718) 767-0573 Fax (718) 767-0423

167

CHRIS C

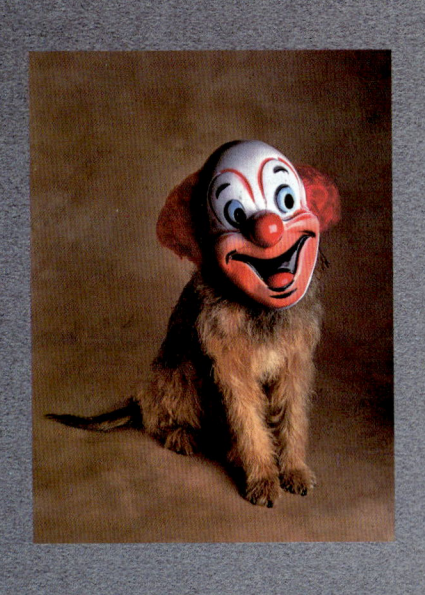

ONEIDA

REPRESENTED BY JOE DiBARTOLO & LAURA L

OLLINS

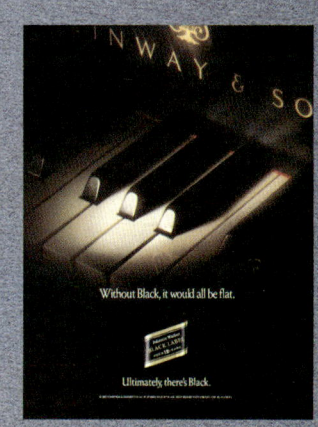

OWITZ (212) 297-0041 FAX: (212) 297-0043

James Porto
Photographer

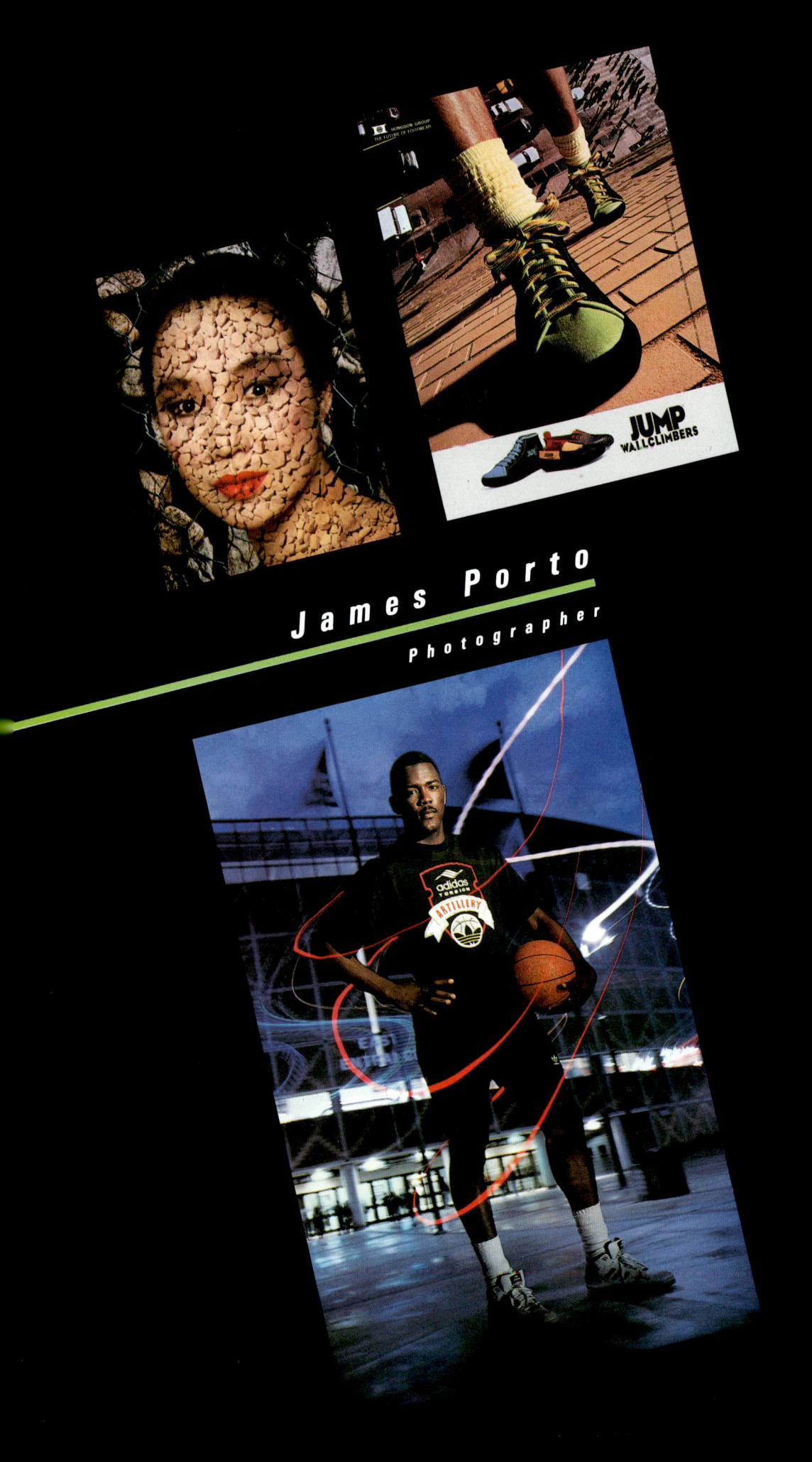

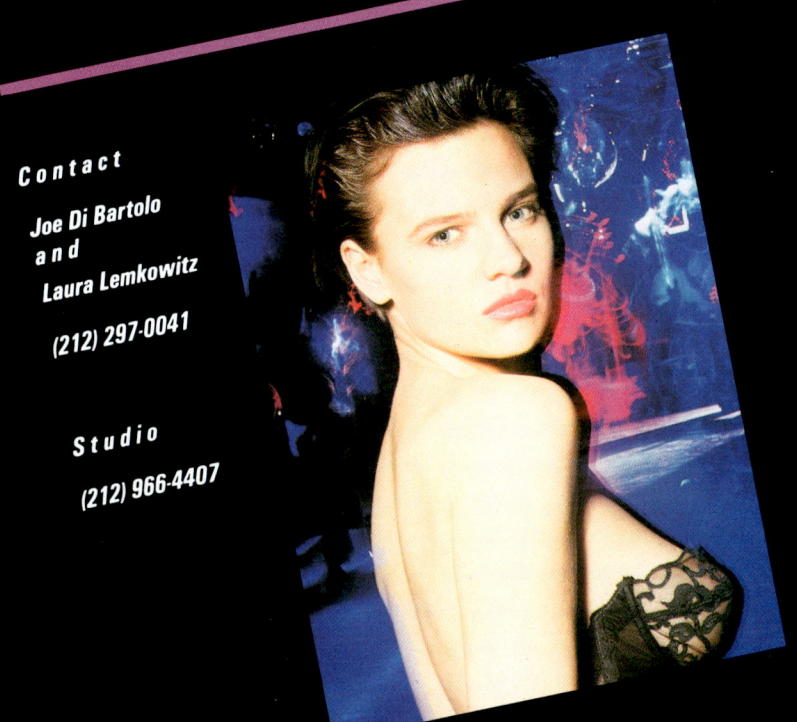

Contact

**Joe Di Bartolo
and
Laura Lemkowitz**

(212) 297-0041

Studio

(212) 966-4407

REPRESENTED
IN NEW YORK BY
JANY TOMBA
212.570.2189
IN HAMBURG BY
AGENCY
40.422.5923

Rolf Bruderer
NYC 212.535.2751

E.C.

EARL CULBERSON REPRESENTED BY ROBIN DICTENBERG AND CHARLES BYRNES

BIG CITY PRODUCTIONS · 5 E 19TH STREET · NYC 10003   212·473·3366

EARL CULBERSON REPRESENTED BY ROBIN DICTENBERG AND CHARLES BYRNES

E.C.

BIG CITY PRODUCTIONS · 5 E 19TH STREET · NYC 10003   212·473·3366

DAN WEAKS

REPRESENTED BY ROBIN DICTENBERG AND CHARLES BYRNES

BIG CITY PRODUCTIONS · 5 E 19TH STREET NYC 10003   212·473·3366

DAVID MASSEY

REPRESENTED BY ROBIN DICTENBERG AND CHARLES BYRNES

BIG CITY PRODUCTIONS · 5 E 19TH STREET · NYC 10003 212·473·3366

PETE STONE

REPRESENTED BY ROBIN DICTENBERG AND CHARLES BYRNES

BIG CITY PRODUCTIONS · 5 E 19TH STREET · NYC 10003   212·473·3366

D'ORIO

REPRESENTED BY ROBIN DICTENBERG AND CHARLES BYRNES

BIG CITY PRODUCTIONS · 5 E 19TH STREET · NYC 10003   212·473·3366

Ken & Carl Fischer

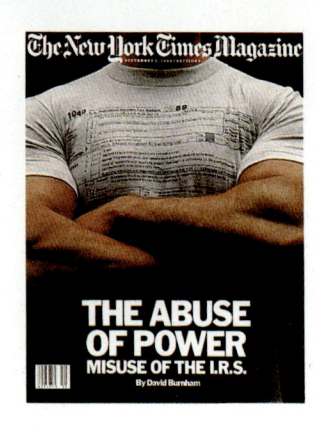

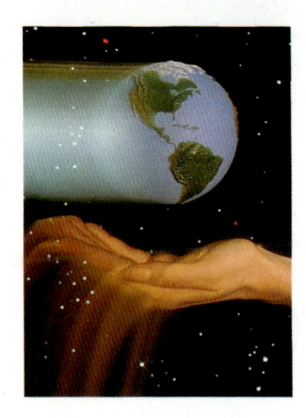

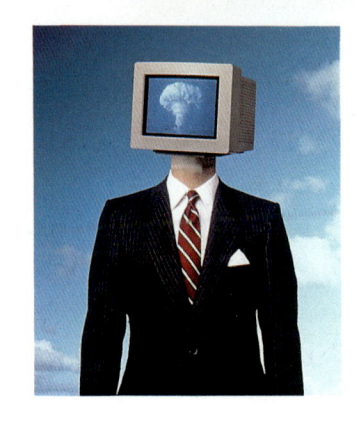

Ken & Carl Fischer Photography
121 East 83rd Street, New York, NY 10028-0821
(212) 794-0400 Fax (212) 794-0959

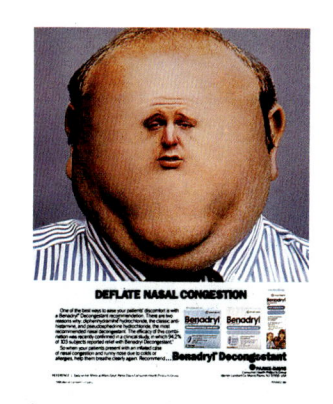

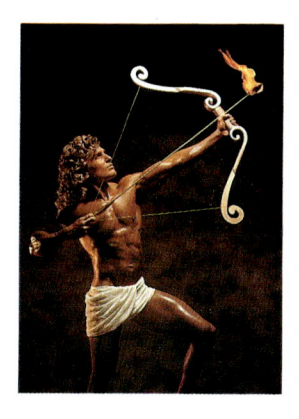

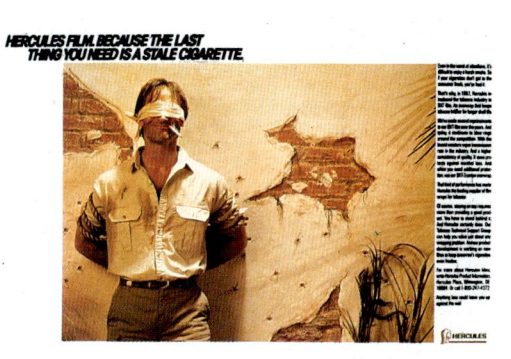

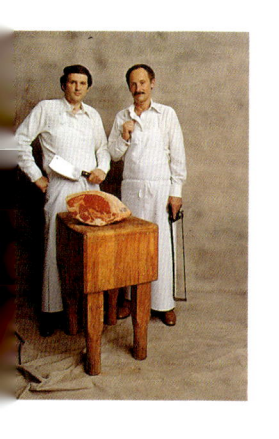

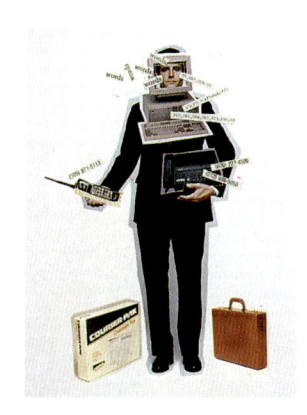

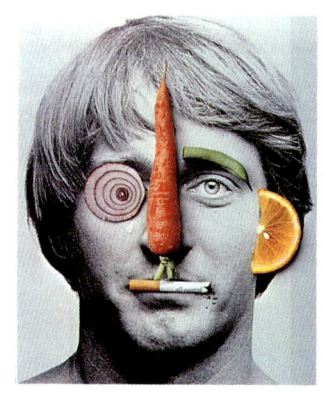

Copyright 1991 Ken & Carl Fischer

187

Tropicana
PURE PREMIUM
Florida Squeezed
Orange Juice
Tropicana
PURE PREMIUM
Florida Squeezed
Orange Juice

SKIP HINE
PHOTOGRAPHY

117 E. 24 St., Suite 4B, NY, NY 10010 212-529-6100
FAX 212-529-6288

© 1991 Skip Hine

189

studio 212 683 4258
fax 212 481 3812

client commodore **ad** ed evangelista

hing/norton

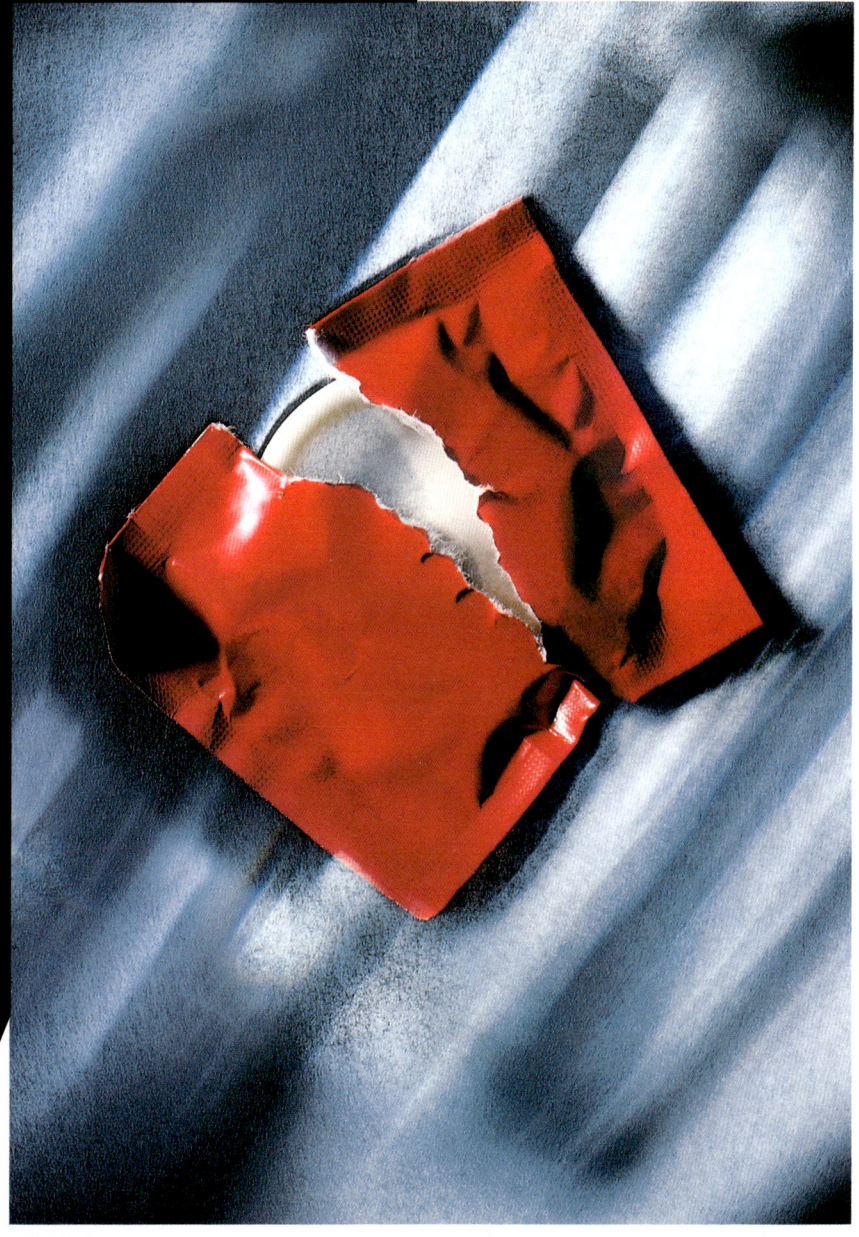

©1990 hing/norton

represented by randy cole
212 679 5933

client rodale press **ad** d. jewett

REPRESENTED BY
RANDY COLE 212 679-5933
ELIZABETH ALTMAN ASSOC. 312 935-9007

PERNO

STUDIO 312 666-4345

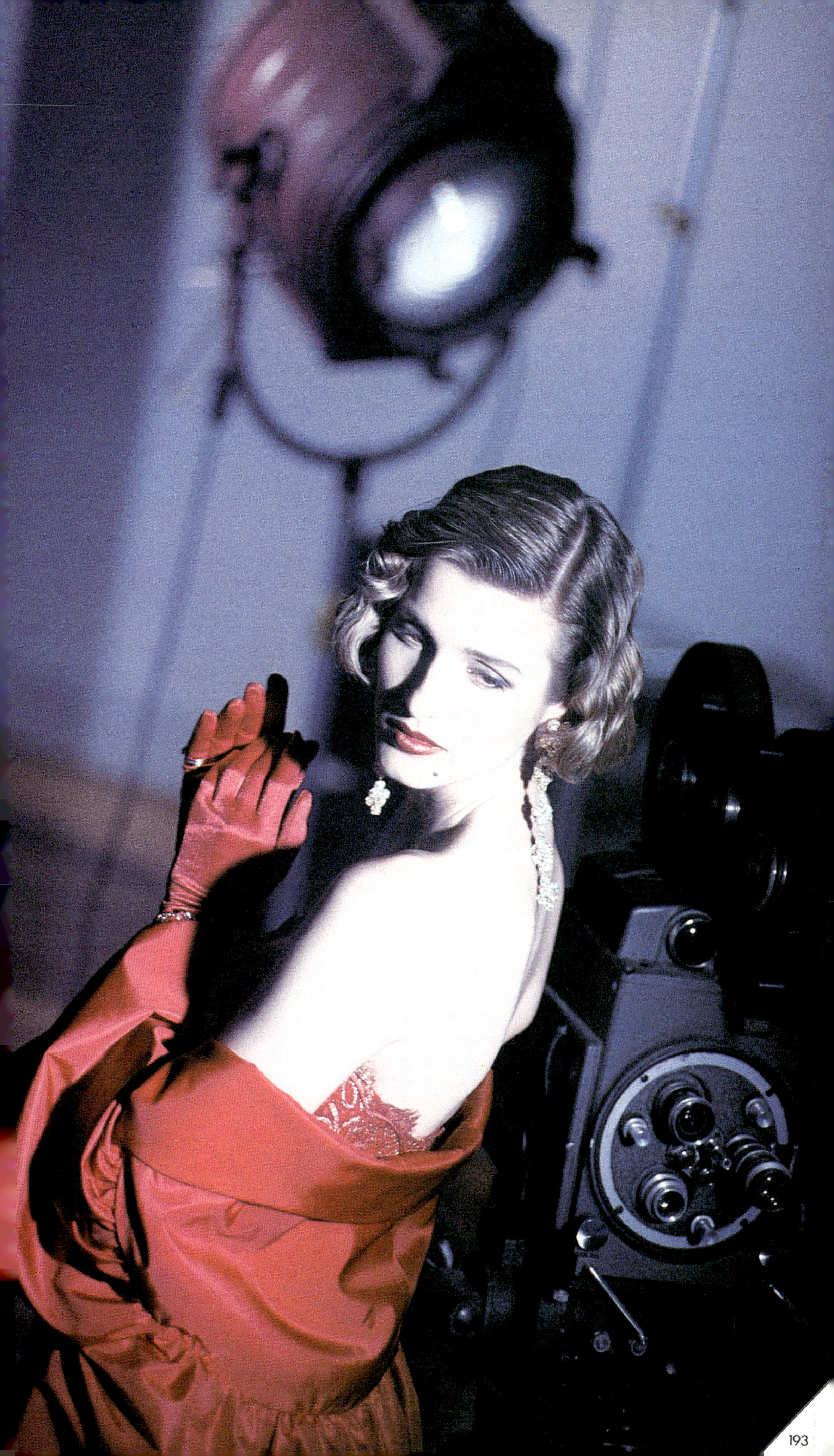

BRUNO ZEHNDER

Bruno Zehnder's Antarctica™

The World's Best Penguin Photographer

Copyright, Bruno Zehnder 1991

New York, New York 10163-5996 U.S.A. Phone 212•840•1234

Jan Cobb Photography Ltd.

Represented
by
Gary Lerman
(212) 683-5777
Fax: 779-3697

Black
&
White

Studio:
5 West 19
NYC 10011
(212) 255-1400
Fax: 627-1962

196

avis

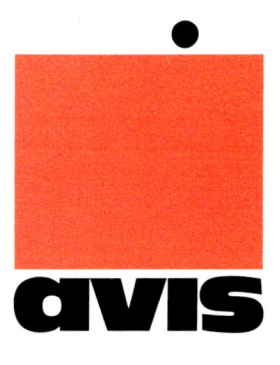

For additional samples
see the 1989 and 1990 Black Book.
Mini Portfolio available upon request.
Contact Jane 603/627-2659
Fax 603/627-4854
Paul Avis Photographer, Inc.

avis

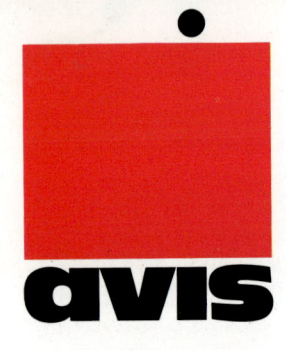

avis

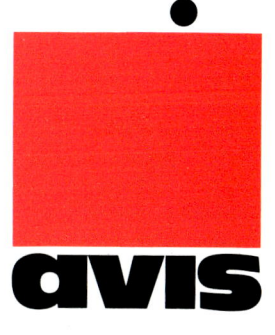

For additional samples
see the 1989 and 1990 Black Book.
Mini Portfolio available upon request.
Contact Jane 603/627-2659
Fax 603/627-4854
Paul Avis Photographer, Inc.

Roberta

Robert Ammirati Studio, 66 Crosby Street N.Y., N.Y. 10012 (212) 925-58

AMMIRATI

epresented by Frank Meo

TOTO
LOVES TO SHOOT PEOPLE

JOE TOTO/13-17 LAIGHT STREET/NY 10013/212-966-7626/FAX 212-966-7

REPRESENTATIVE: FRANK MEO/212-353-0907/FAX 212-673-8679

203

RICK CARPENTER • DELLA FEMINA, MCNAMEE WCRS, INC., • LOS ANGELES.

ED MCGRADY • EARLE PALMER BROWN & SPIRO • PHILADELPHIA.

David Leach

© David Leach 1991

JIM MILLER • THE PHELPS GROUP • LOS ANGELES.

KAREN SIMON • FCB/LEBER KATZ PARTNERS • NEW YORK CITY.

PHOTOGRAPHY

75 Spring St.
New York, N.Y. 10012
(212) 288-1234
East coast, Arlene Johnson: (212) 725-4520
West/Midwest, Randi Fiat & Associates: (312) 784-2343

16 East 23rd Street

New York, New York 10010

212-228-2288

© 1991

DAVID MAISEL | PHOTOGRAPHY

REPRESENTED BY

ARLENE JOHNSON

212-725-4520

JAMES KOZYRA, 568 BROADWAY, NEW YORK, NY 10012/(212) 431-1911, 12/FAX 966-90

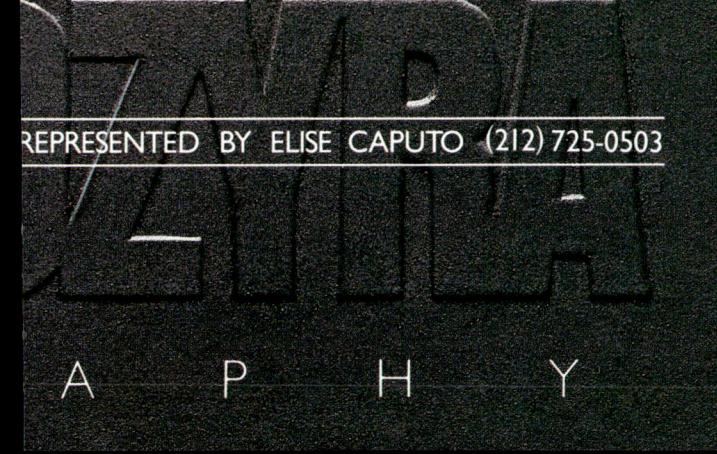

REPRESENTED BY ELISE CAPUTO (212) 725-0503

209

STEVE BRADY

STEVE BRADY PHOTOGRAPHY INC. Studio 212-941-6093 713-660-6663 FAX 212-925-6171

New York, Elise Caputo & Assoc. 212-725-0503 Midwest, Michelle Clayborne & Assoc. 312-421-2265 Southwest, Those 3 Reps 214-871-1316

211

ZAN/BEAUTY

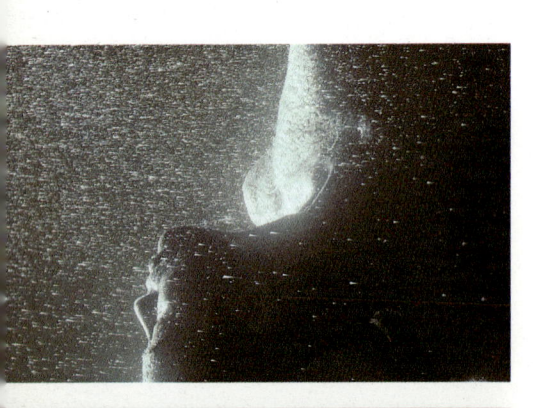

ZAN PRODUCTIONS/35 E 20 STREET/NYC 10003/REPRESENTATIVE—RICK WEISBROT

ZAN/STILL-LIFE

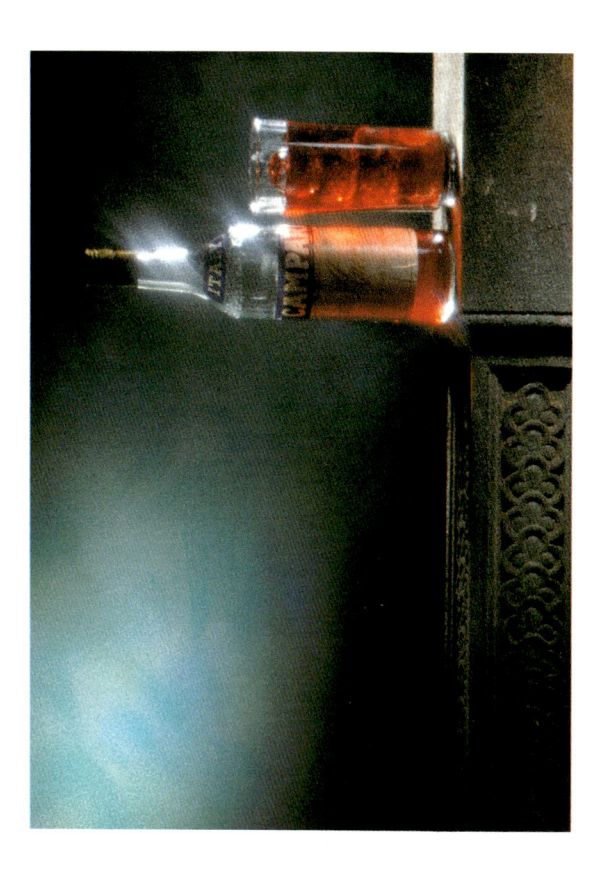

212-477-3333/FAX-212-477-3337

ZAN

ZAN/FOOD

ZAN PRODUCTIONS/35 E 20 STREET/NYC 10003/REPRESENTATIVE—RICK WEISBROT

ZAN/STILL-LIFE

212-477-3333/FAX-212-477-3337

RUDI DE HARAK · GRAPHIC DESIGNER, NYC

MICHELE + WILSON

FRANCISCO FERNANDEZ — MOLD MAKER

RICHARD IRVING — TRINITY CHURCH

Rosenthal BARRY ROSENTHAL

LOLA - MILLINER

ARMAND GILANYI - SCULPTOR

© 1991 BARRY ROSENTHAL

TIMES SQUARE BOXING CLUB

CHEE JAP - AMEX BANK, LONDON

REPRESENTED BY ELYN ZELMAN 205 W 19TH ST NEW YORK 10011 212.645.0433

BENTON COLLINS

bijan nights

LESS FILLING. TASTED GREAT.

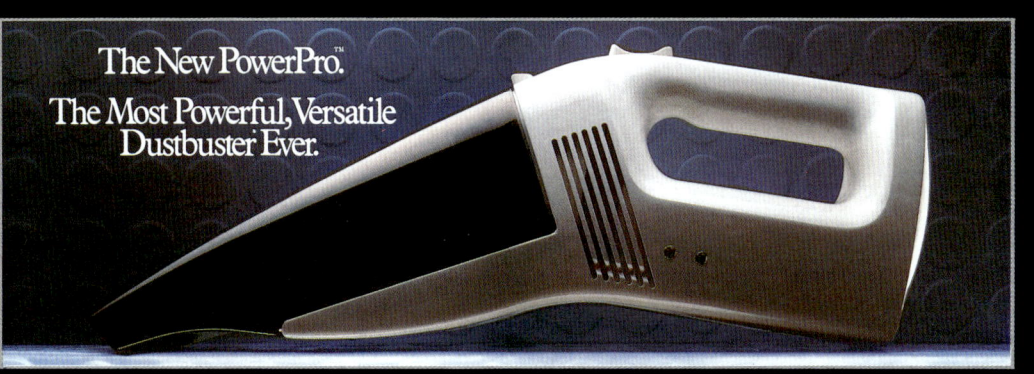

The New PowerPro.™
The Most Powerful, Versatile Dustbuster Ever.

REPRESENTED BY: ANN-MARIE TURBITT • EXIT PRODUCTIONS • 212 925 8750

219

Dennis Mu

Represented in New York by The Arts Counsel. 212-725-3806. Fax 212-779-9589.
101 Howell, Dallas, Texas 75207, 214-651-7516. Fax 214-748-0856. Call Katie.

rphy

221

unlawful to allow any Animal
create a nuisance on public school
Failure to comply with this
will result in legal action in
with Section
Angeles Municipal Code

Rob Van Petten
PHOTOGRAPHER

617-426-8641   212-869-2190

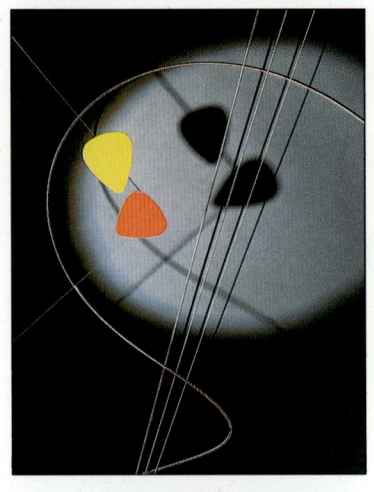

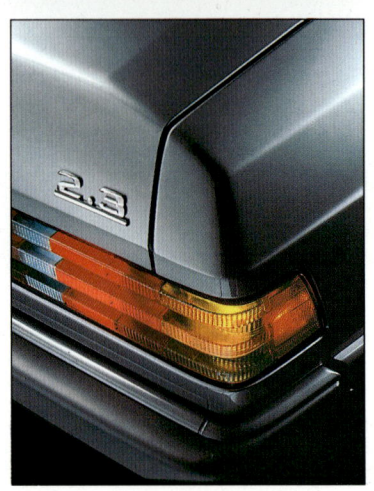

DAVID WEISS

STUDIO
15 W 24 Street
New York City
1 0 0 1 0
212.924.1030
FAX 989.1531

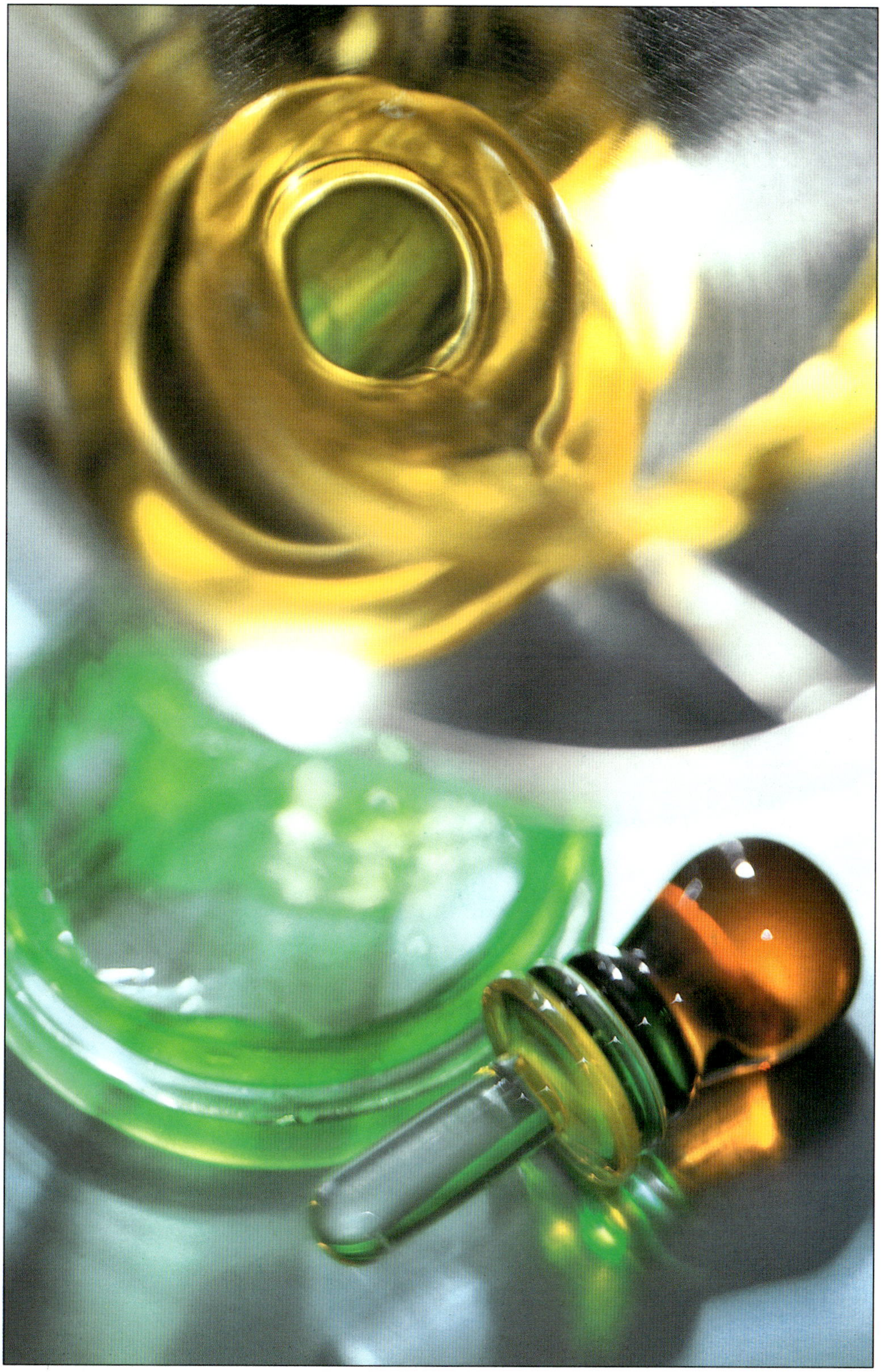

See One Show, Art Directors Club, Andy Awards And Clio Winners, All In One Book.

The book belongs to Jerry Cailor and Elliott Resnick. They're photographers who still get excited about doing great advertising. The ads in it belong to some of the best art directors in the business today. If you'd like to see it, call Bob Altamore, studio representative at (212) 977-4300. FAX (212) 247-2815. Like most award books, you'll find it hard to put down.

Cecile Resnick Studio

237 WEST 54TH STREET, NEW YORK, NEW YORK 10019, (212) 977-4300

JOSEPH MULLIGAN

239 CHESTNUT STREET
PHILADELPHIA, PA 19106
215 592-1359

REPRESENTED BY
RALPH KERR

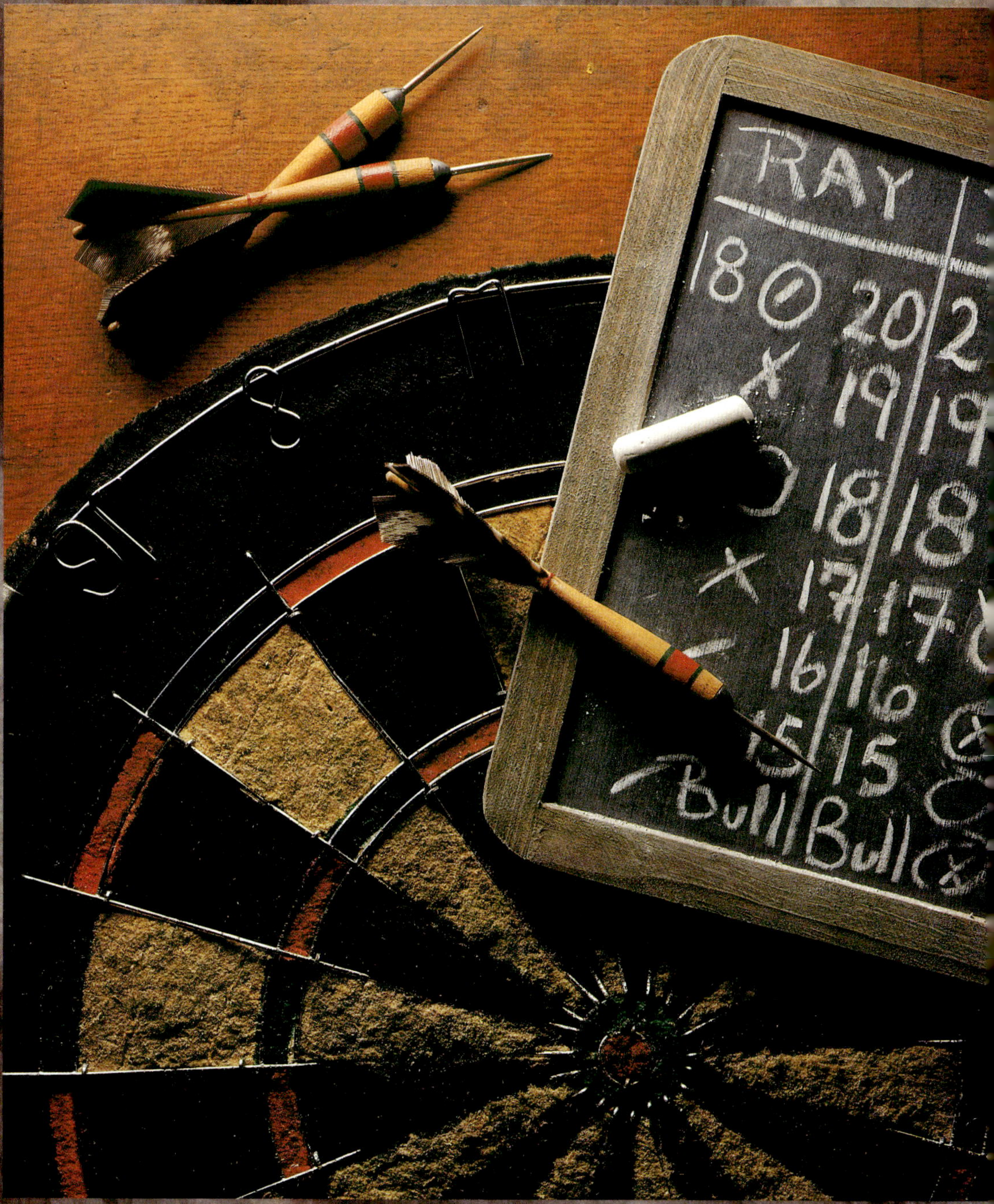
RAY
20 20
19 19
18 18
17 17
16 16
15 15
Bull Bull

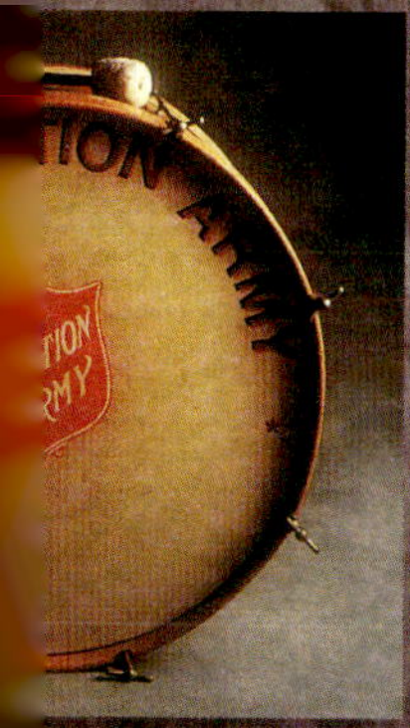

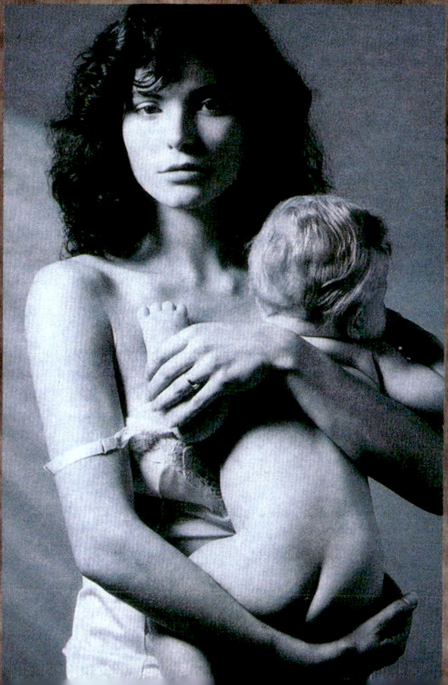

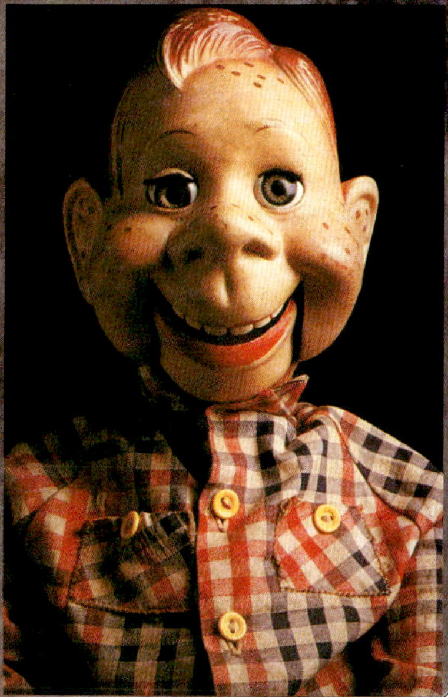

Milton Glaser for Lightolier

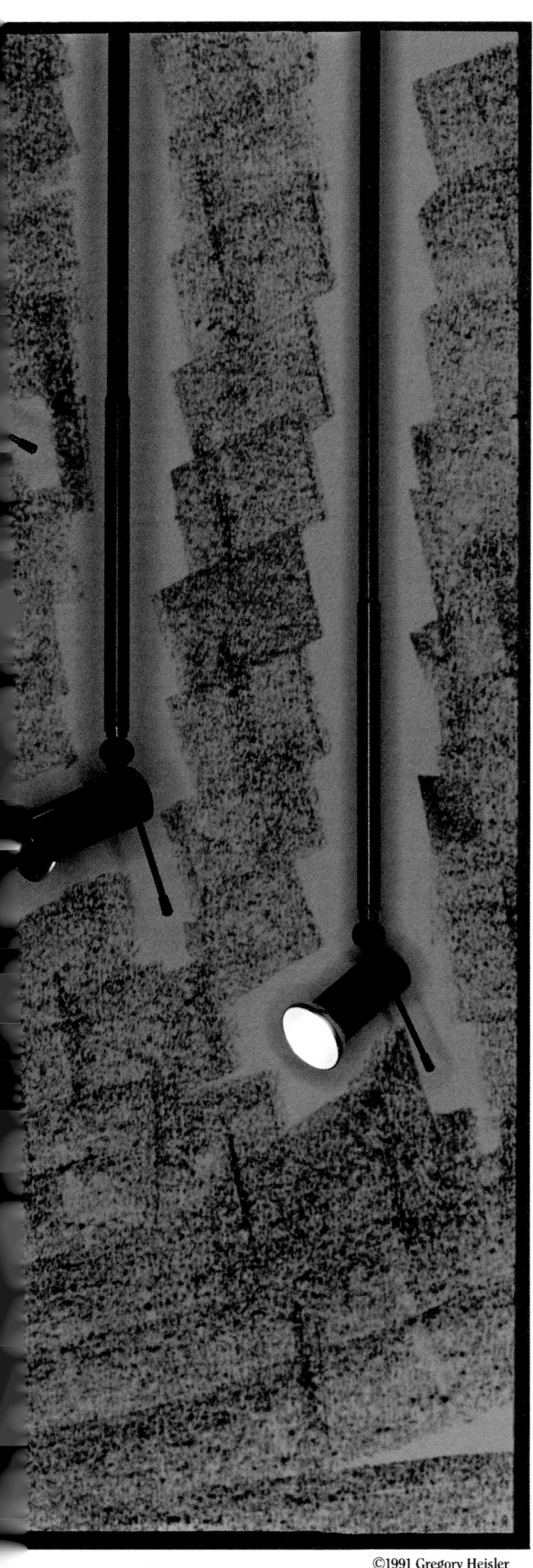

©1991 Gregory Heisler

Heisler

568 Broadway | Represented by
New York 10012 | Michael Ash
212 777 8100 | 212 807 6286

DAVID A. WAGNER
PHOTOGRAPHY
568 BROADWAY
SUITE 103
NEW YORK, NY 10012
(212) 925 • 5149
FAX (212) 219 • 9629

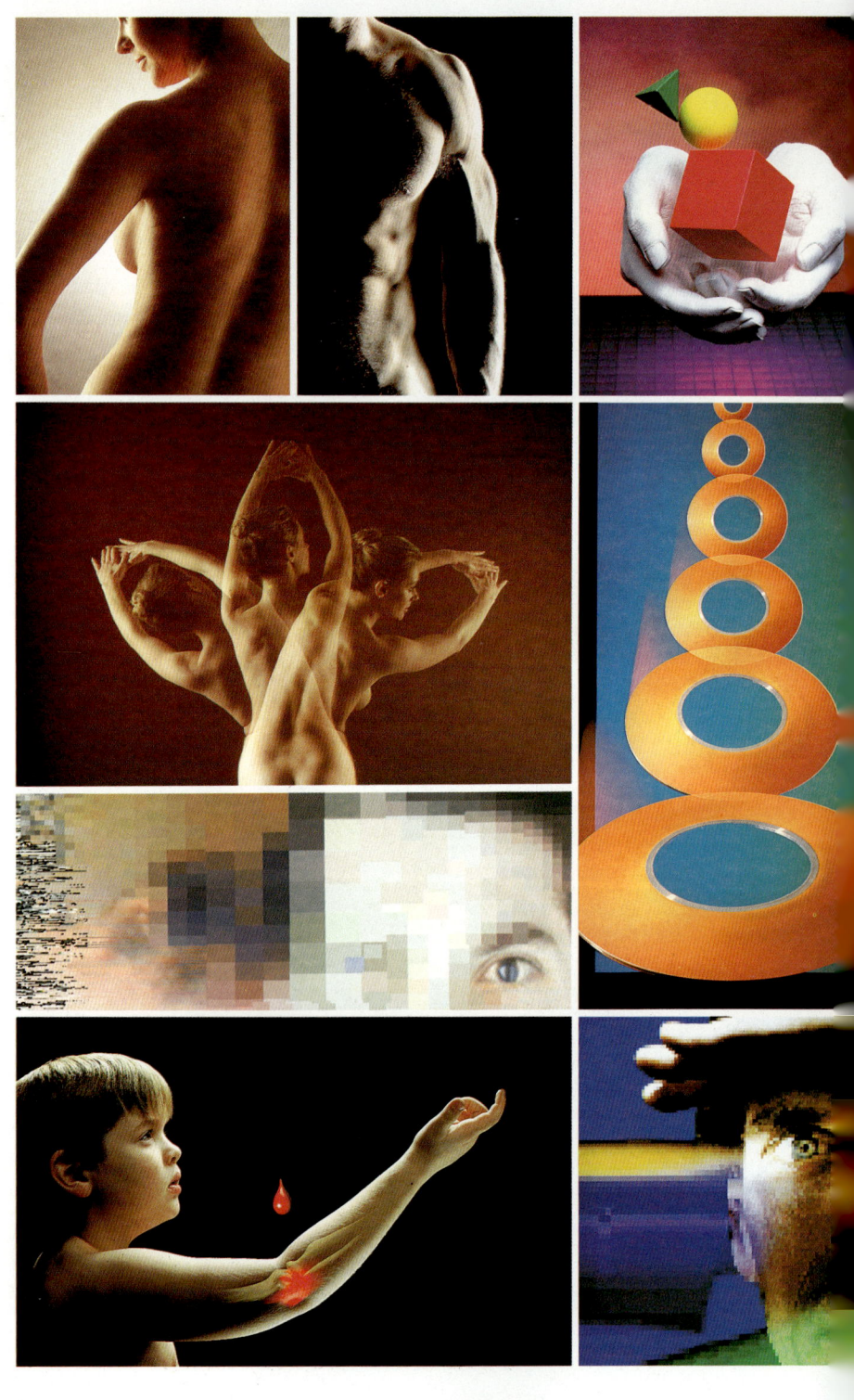

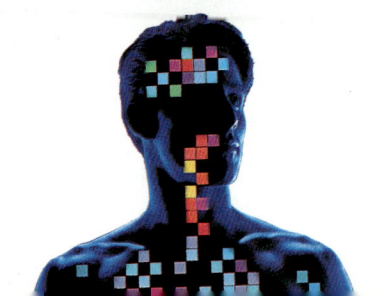

WAGNER

JACQUES LOWE
138 DUANE ST.
N.Y., N.Y. 10013
TEL./FAX (212) 227-3298

REPRESENTED BY:
PHILIP VANCE
ARTISTS REPRESENTATIVES, INC.
27 W. 24 ST.
N.Y., N.Y. 10010
(212) 645-6677

JACQUES LOWE

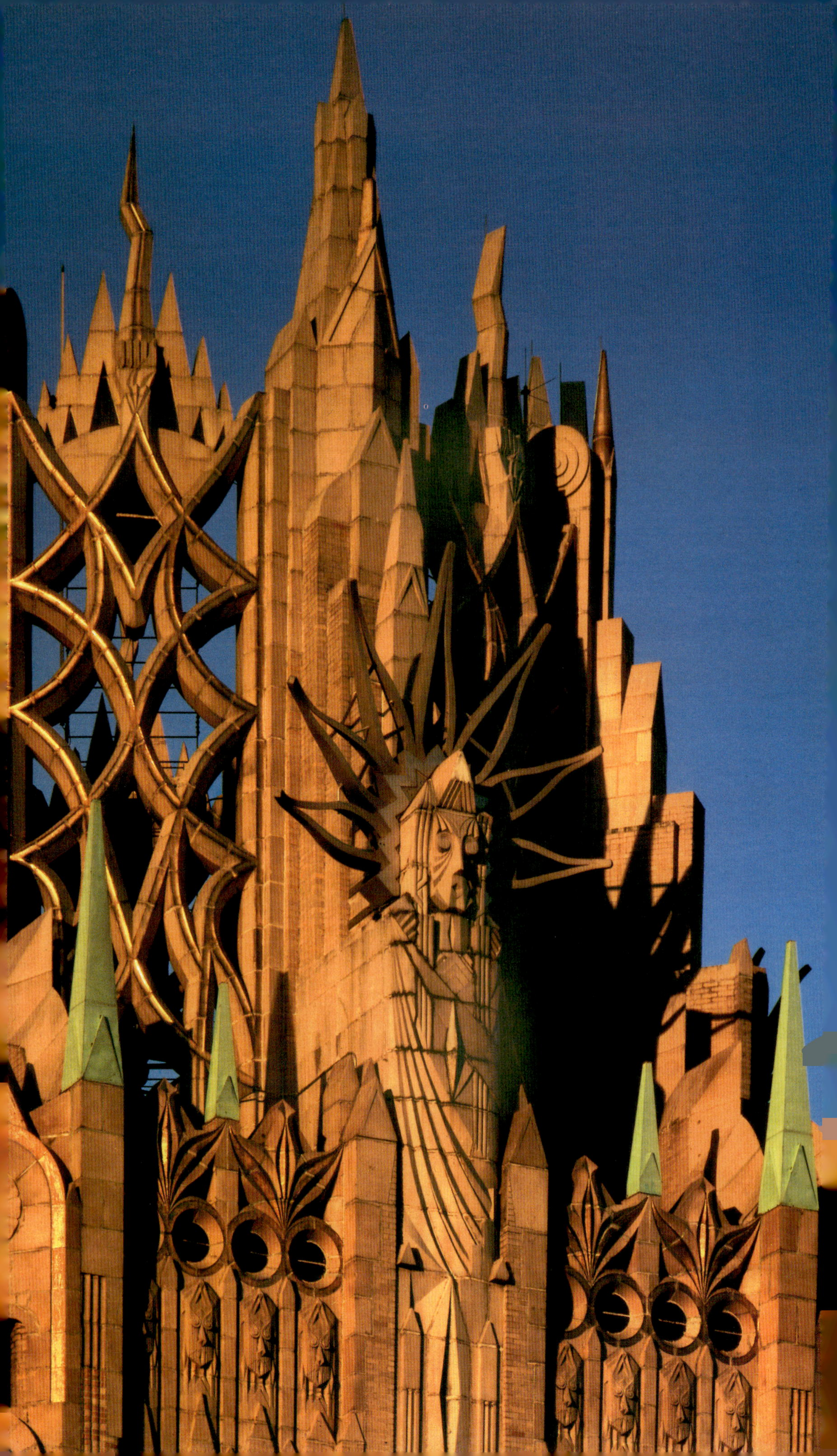

18 West 27 Street
New York, NY 10001
212.686.2569

Wolfgang Hoyt
Photography

237

CHARLES
BLECKER

(212) 242-8390

380 BLEECKER ST., #140, NEW YORK, NY 10014

ON LOCATION • ADVERTISING
• CORPORATE • STOCK •

© 1991 CHARLES BLECKER

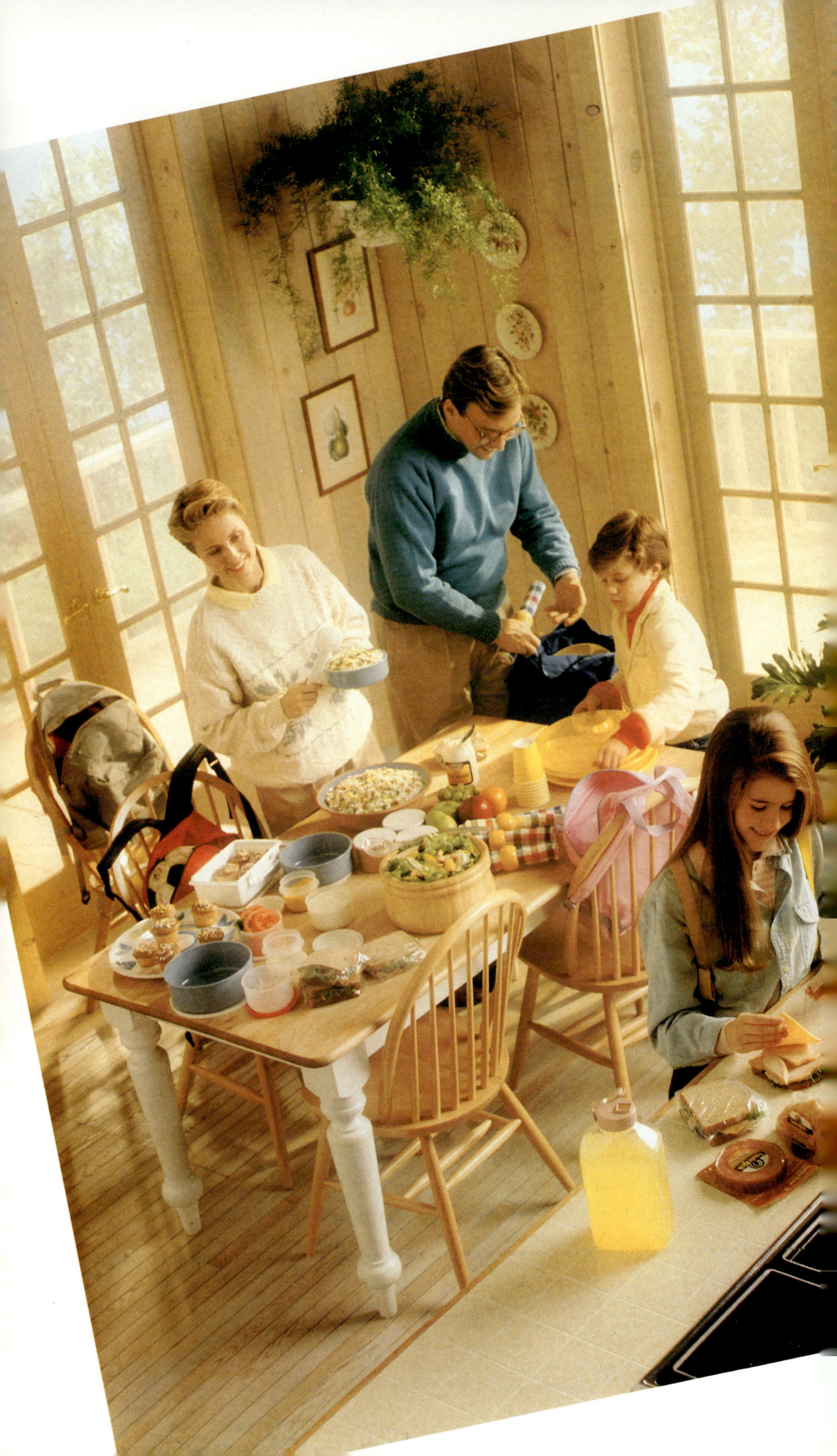

Represented by:
New York: Lily Kimmel & Associates (212) 794 1542
California: Ostan Prentice Ostan Inc. (213) 826 1332
Stock Photography Available: 1 (800) 873 7862

Howard Breitrose
STUDIO
443 West 18th Street
New York, New York 10011
212 242 7825
Fax: 212 691 3357

NEXVISIONS, INC.
&
GUY A. FERY
212 371 9771

243

DAVID BISHOP

251 West 19th Street, New York 10011 212/929/4355 Represented by Alison Korman 212/633/8407 Korman & Company

DAVID BISHOP

251 West 19th Street, New York 10011 212/929/4355 Represented by Alison Korman 212/633/8407 Korman & Company

mark malabrigo
new york
212 429-8087

Police 374-5000
Fire 627-2900
Ambulance 326-0600
Hellerstein 645-0508

In New York. Ask for Greg or Steve.   212.645.0508

249

There's only one drawback to comparing Sony's Video Hi8 Dockable Camcorder to our competitors.

They leave us very little room.

As modest as our new camcorder might appear, it's easy to underestimate its considerable capabilities.

Introducing the Sony DXC-325 3CCD Camera with the EVV-9000 video Hi8 Dockable VTR. At 19 inches long and just over 13 pounds, it combines the compactness of 8mm with professional quality and features previously found only in larger configurations.

Small in scale but highly regarded, the MultiCam™ DXC-325 camera has an electronic shutter for extended dynamic range and cableless interchangeable lenses for convenience.

The EVV-9000 Dockable VTR features over 400 lines of resolution, built-in time code, two-hour record time and weather-resistant construction.

Together, the camera and back provide Y/C recording for excellent color reproduction, "in viewfinder" review, 3-channel audio and 60 minutes recording time on a single battery.

To learn more, call 1-800-523-SONY, Extension 362.

The Sony video Hi8 Dockable Camcorder. In its own small way, it establishes a new standard.

SONY PROFESSIONAL VIDEO

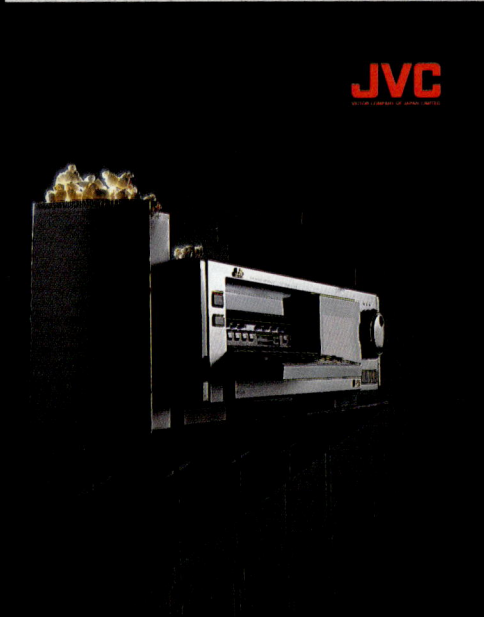

JVC

Would you still drink it?

SURGEON GENERAL'S WARNING: Quitting Now Will Greatly Reduce Serious Risks to Your Health

Then why do you still smoke? New York Lung Association.

Will This Become America's Number-One Pain Killer?

TIME ALONE WILL TELL.

In New York. Ask for Greg or Steve. 212.645.0508

255

BARABAN

JOE BARABAN
REPRESENTED BY
JOHN KENNEY &
BOB MEAD
IN NEW YORK
212-758-4545

JOE BARABAN
2426 BARTLETT #2
HOUSTON, TEXAS
77098
713-526-0317

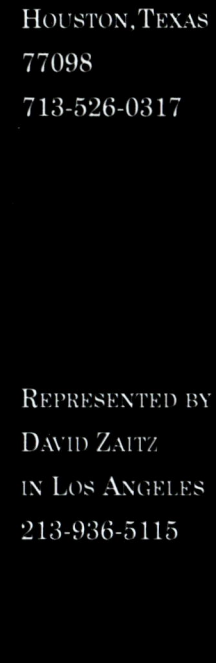

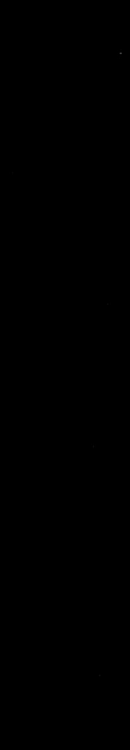

REPRESENTED BY
BILL RABIN
IN CHICAGO
312-944-6655

REPRESENTED BY
DAVID ZAITZ
IN LOS ANGELES
213-936-5115

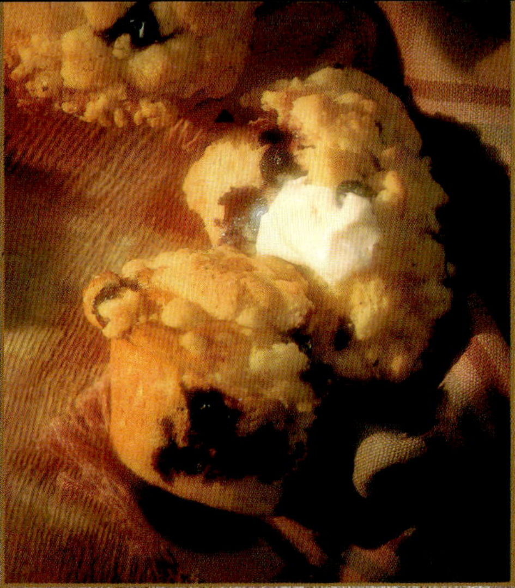

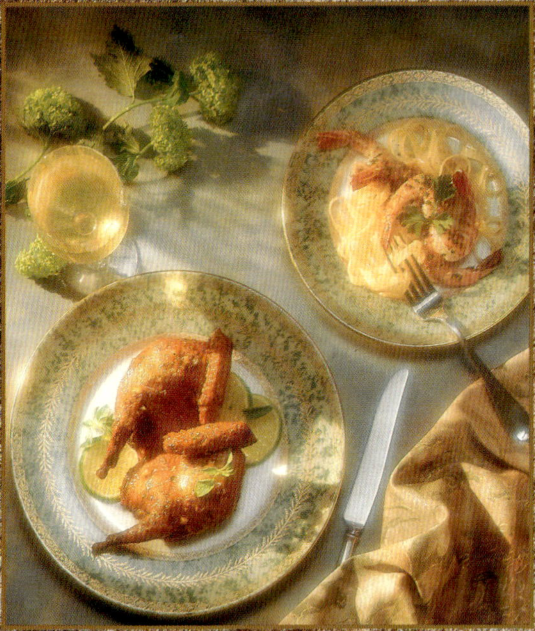

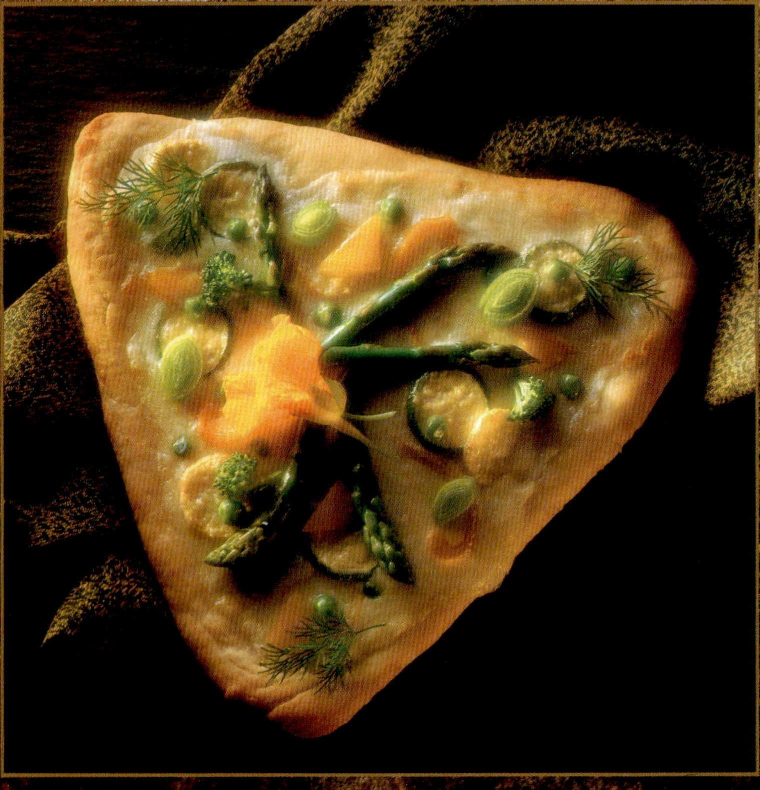

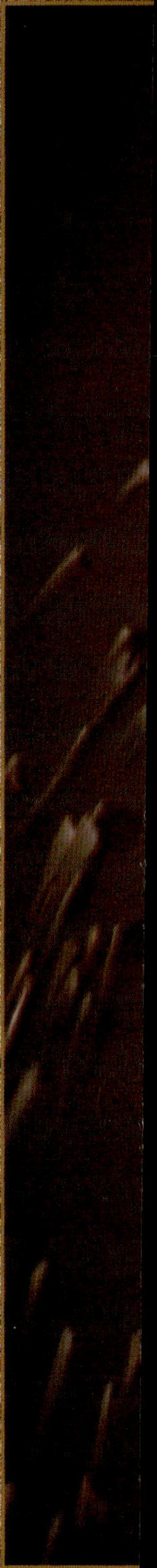

Corinne

Corinne Colen Photography
519 Broadway, NYC
212/431-7425

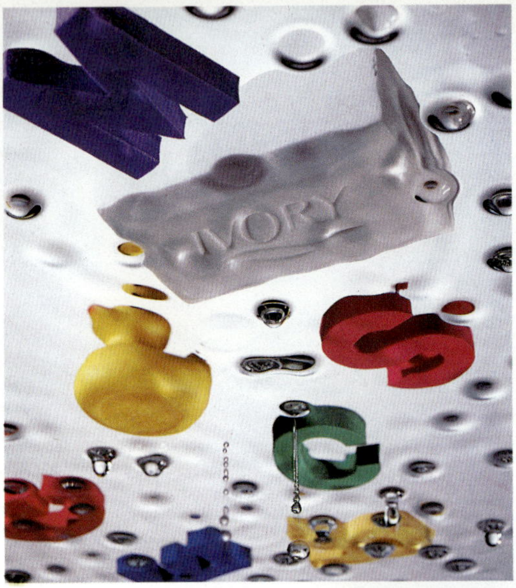
IVORY

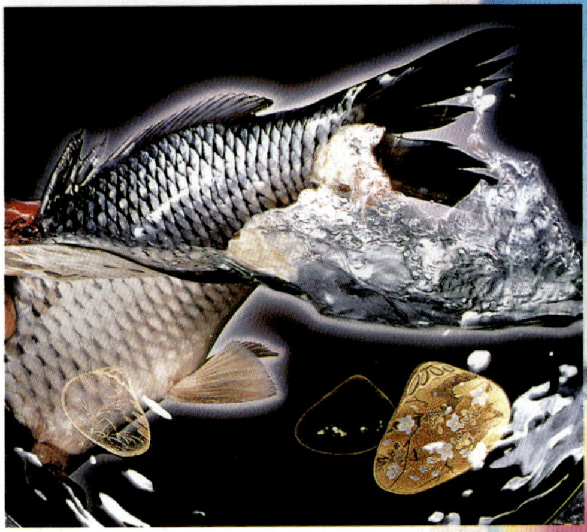

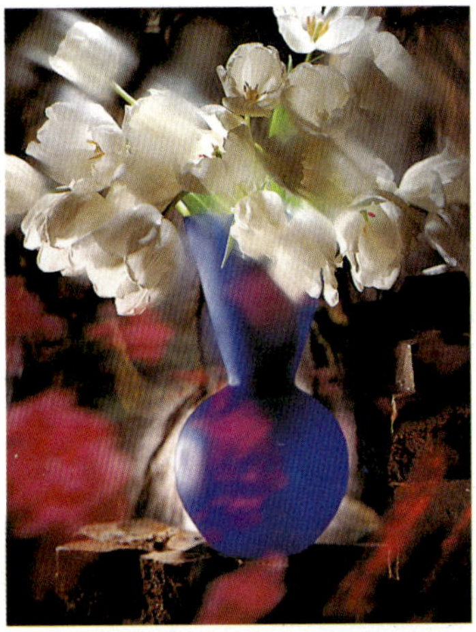

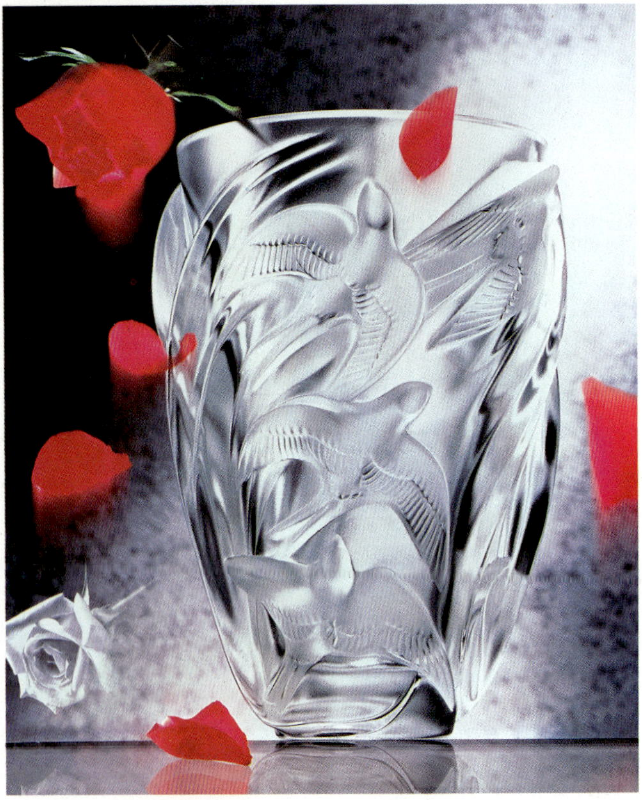

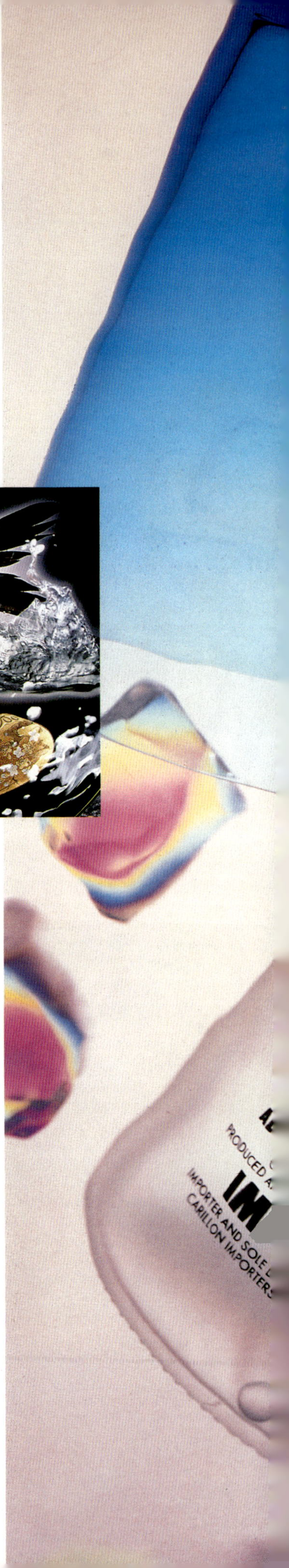
CARILLON IMPORTERS

YUTAKA KAWACHI STUDIO, INC.   33 WEST 17 STREET NEW YORK 10011
212.929.4825   FAX 212.627.1462

REPRESENTED BY A.I.S.   CONTACT BOB MEAD OR JOHN KENNEY
212.758.4545   FAX 212.832.2296

Four of the 187 images
by Larry Silver
in permanent collections
of the following museums:

Addison Gallery of American Art
Boston Museum of Fine Art
Brooklyn Museum
George Eastman House
High Museum Atlanta
Housatonic Museum of Art
Houston Museum of Fine Art
Int'l. Center of Photography "ICP"
Metropolitan Museum of Art
Museum of the City of New York
New Britain Museum
Philadelphia Museum of Art
Queensboro Community College Art Gallery
RISD Museum of Art
Rochester Institute of Technology
Museum of Art, St. Petersburg
Tampa Museum of Art
William Benton Museum of Art
Yale University Art Gallery

Larry Silver 1991

For your private showing call
212 807-9560

L A R R Y

A PARTIAL LIST OF COMMERCIAL CLIENTELE: AETNA AMERICAN HOME AMERICAN TOURISTER AMERICAN EXPRESS
B.F. GOODRICH BRISTOL MYERS CANON CASIO CHASE MANHATTAN CITIBANK EASTERN AIRLINES FORBES MAGA
GORDON'S GIN GREYHOUND HERTZ HOLIDAY INN HUMANA IBM LIPTON MARS CANDY MEMBERS ONLY MERRILL LY

SILVER

NSANTO MTA NABISCO NESTLES NIKON NY TEL PANASONIC PELLON PINCH SCOTCH PROCTER & GAMBLE
 LOBSTER SEARS & ROEBUCK SOLOMON BROS. SONY SOUTHEAST BANK S.T.P. TIME INC. U.S. ARMED FORCES
KSWAGON WINS WYETH AYERST XEROX • 236 WEST 26 STREET, NEW YORK, N.Y. 10001 FAX 212-807-9562

263

Globus Studios

Strobe & Motion
(212) 243-1008

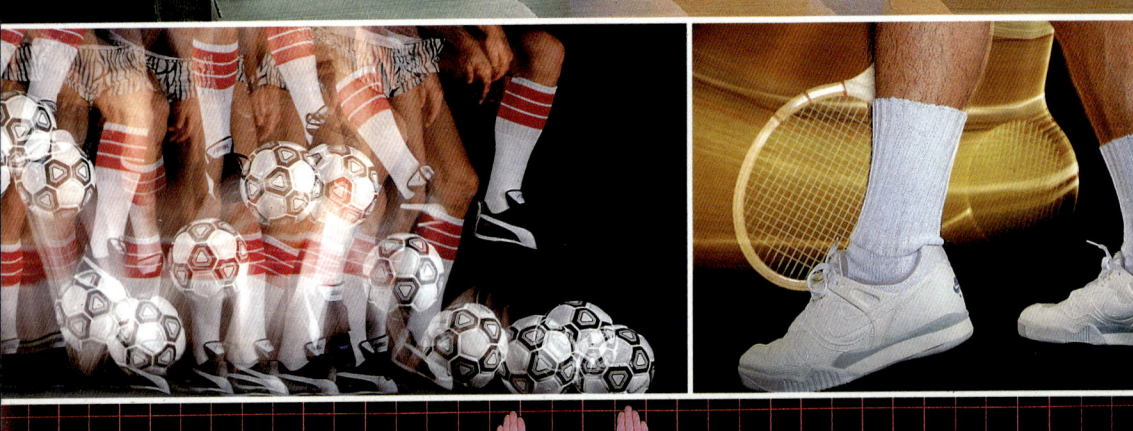

264

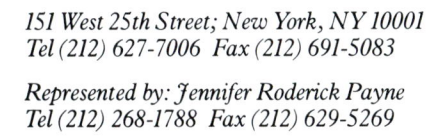

151 West 25th Street; New York, NY 10001
Tel (212) 627-7006 Fax (212) 691-5083

Represented by: Jennifer Roderick Payne
Tel (212) 268-1788 Fax (212) 629-5269

DEBORAH KLESENSKI
of Klesenski-Ward Studio Inc.

KEN NAHOUM   212·924·8880

PRINT & FILM

KEN NAHOUM 212·924·8880

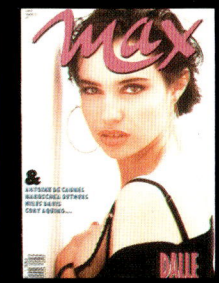

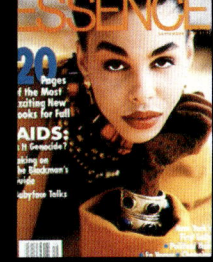

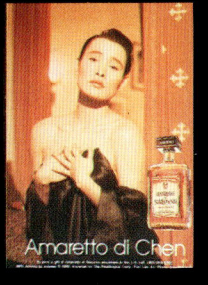

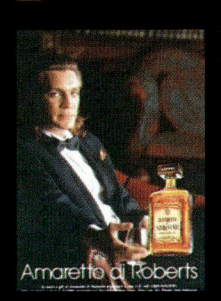

PRINT & FILM

Dressed for success.
Johnnie Walker Black Label for the Holidays.

Stock your shelves with the best dressed gift of the year—
the Johnnie Walker Black Label pinstriped gift tin.
It's tailor-made for holiday profit.

SMITH GREENLAND ADVERTISING
GLENN SCHEUER, SENIOR ART DIRECTOR

DCA ADVERTISING
KEITH BENNETT, SENIOR ART DIRECTOR

HUIBREGTSE

JIM HUIBREGTSE PHOTOGRAPHY

54 GREENE STREET, NYC 10013 · 212-925-3351 · FAX 212-941-1738
REPRESENTED BY NELSON BLONCOURT · 212-924-2255 · FAX 212-727-0565

Your Favorite Person's Favorite Six-Pack

Kids are smart. They only eat what they like, and taste tests show that kids prefer the taste of the Light n' Lively® six-pack to the Dannon® six-pack.* It's fruity, creamy and already mixed.

Light n' Lively lowfat yogurt has the goodness you like to give them and the taste they like best. Light n' Lively lowfat yogurt. The six-pack kids like best.

Eat Smart

Save 30¢ When you buy any six-pack Light n' Lively lowfat yogurt

Manufacturer's Coupon Expiration 3-31-89

*Based on taste tests of common flavors by 6-12 year olds.
© Kraft, Inc. 1987

Your Favorite Person's Favorite Six-Pack

Kids are smart. They only eat what they like, and taste tests show that kids prefer the taste of the Light n' Lively® six-pack to the Dannon® six-pack.* It's fruity, creamy and already mixed.

Light n' Lively lowfat yogurt has the goodness you like to give them and the taste they like best.

Light n' Lively lowfat yogurt. The six-pack kids like best. **Eat Smart**

*Based on taste tests of common flavors by 6-12 year olds.

Julie Gang

54 GREENE
4th FLOOR
NEW YORK
N. Y. 10013
• • •
212-925-3351

REPRESENTED BY NELSON BLONCOURT: 212·924·2255

275

McLou

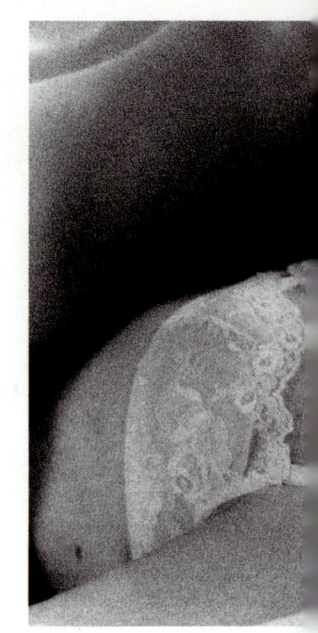

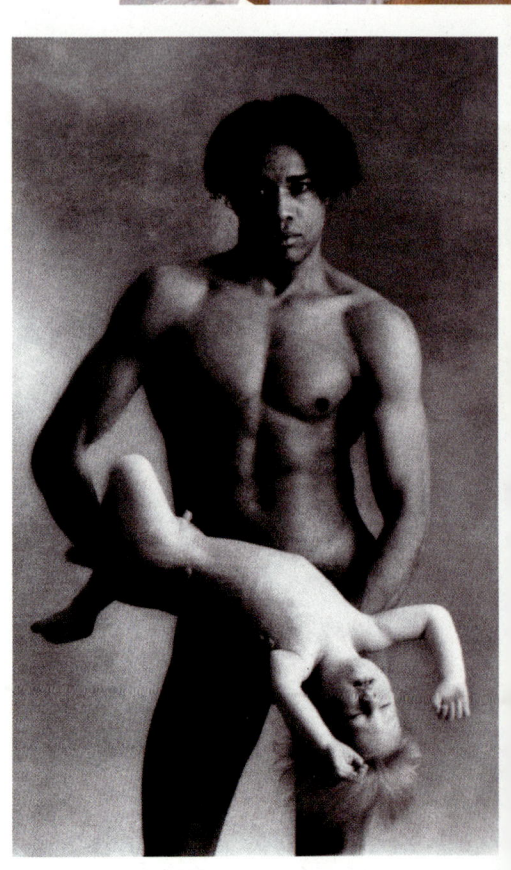

James McLoughlin Photography
New York City

Tel. 212.206.8207   Fax 212.206.9339

ghlin

dditional work: • NY Gold • Select Magazine • Single Image • Workbook •

277

119 West 23rd Street New York, N.Y. 10011 (212) 206-0539

Kevin A. Logan

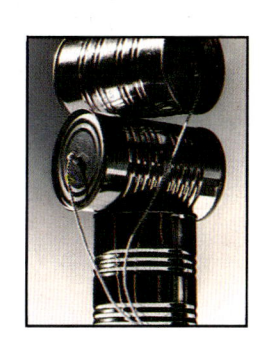

J&M STUDIO
PHOTOGRAPHY

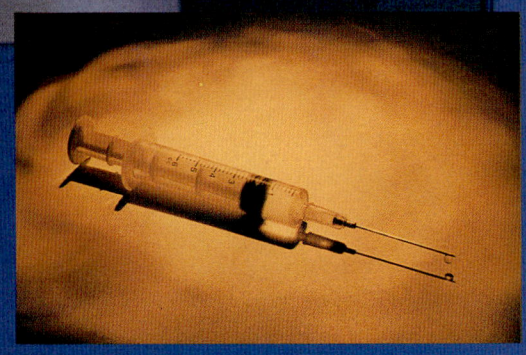

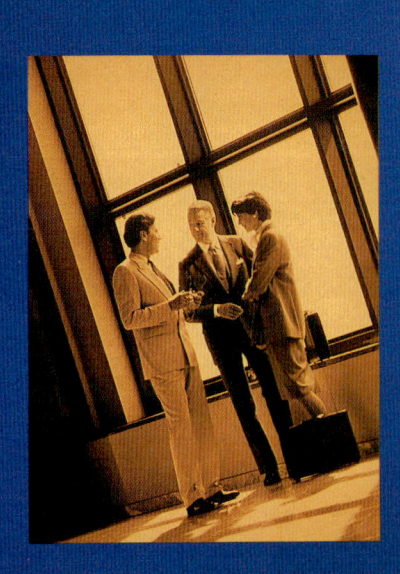

Jonathan Hill

Michael Krinke

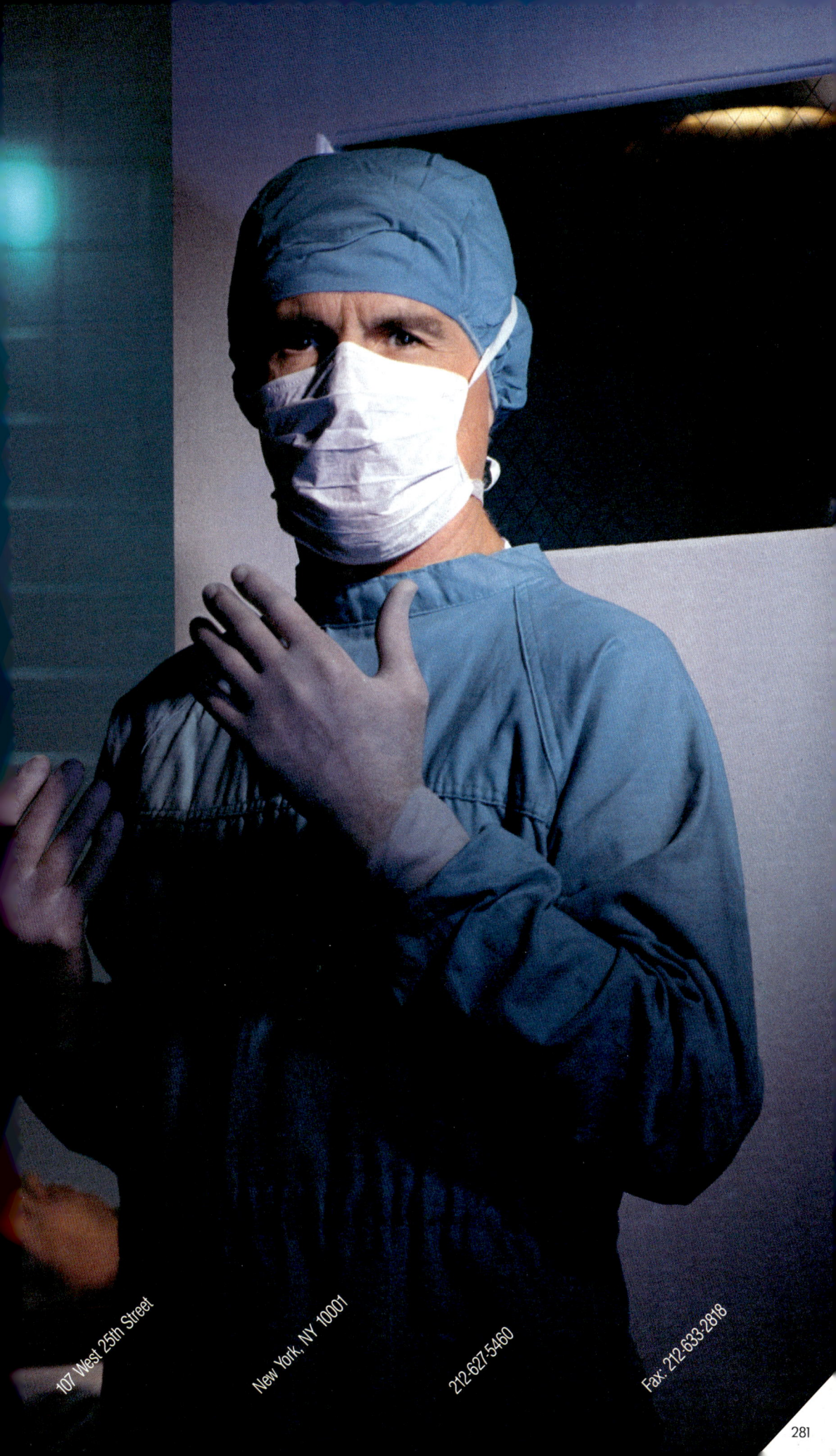

107 West 25th Street   New York, NY 10001   212-627-5460   Fax: 212-633-2818

Not all men dream of castles.

To send a gift of Chivas Regal, dial 1-800-243-3787. Void where prohibited.
12 YEARS OLD WORLDWIDE • BLENDED SCOTCH WHISKY • 86 PROOF • © 1986 375 SPIRITS COMPANY, NEW YORK, N.Y.

BRUNO

J&B on the rocks.

Bruno Photography Incorporated 43 Crosby Street New York, NY 10012
Represented by Holly Kaplan 212-925-2929

HUMANS BY UMANS

MARTY UMANS PHOTOGRAPHY
REPRESENTED BY DARIO SACRAMONE
TEL: 212.929.0487   FAX: 212.529.3801

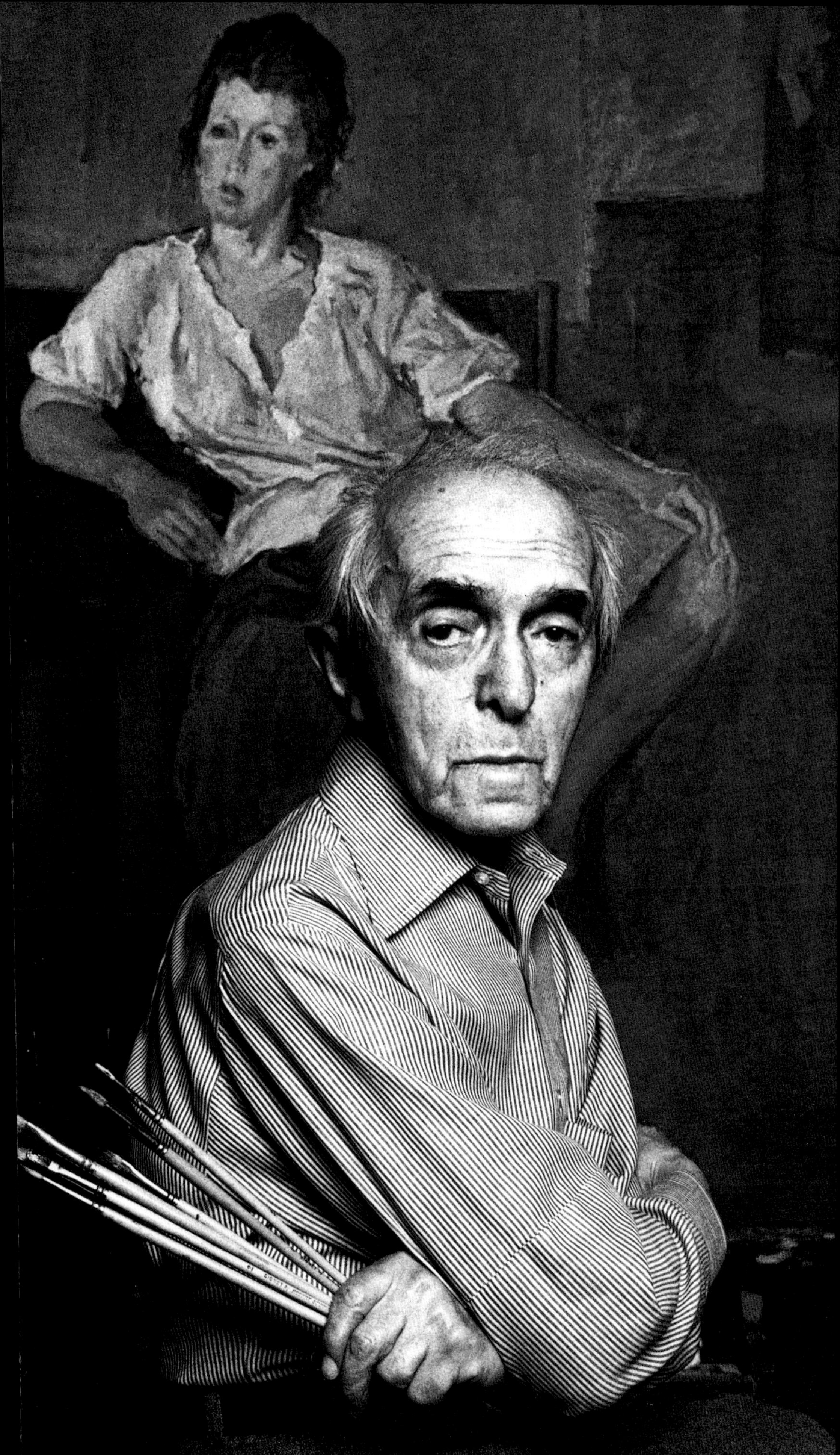

253
W. 28
ST.
NEW
YORK
NY
10001
(212)
947-
3451

BRUCE LAURANCE

Derek Gardner

RITA HOLT & ASSOCIATES, INC.
(212) 683-2002 FAX: (201) 738-5499

David Burnett

RITA HOLT & ASSOCIATES, INC.
(212) 683-2002   FAX: (201) 738-5499

New York City
212 924-8440
Fax: 691-8690

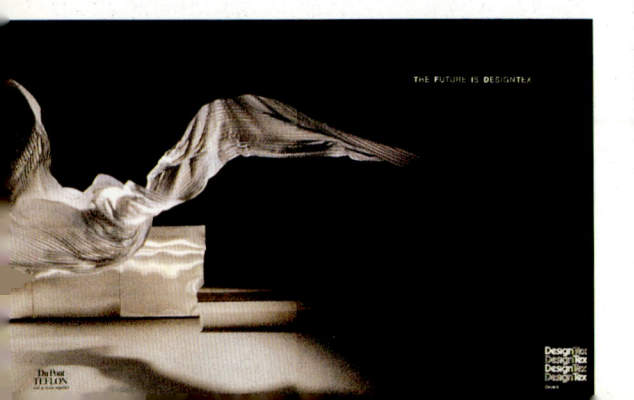

THE FUTURE IS DESIGNTEX

SCOTT CHANEY

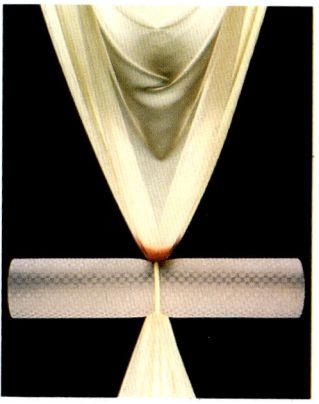

PHOTOGRAPHY

291

Bruce PLOTKIN

Bruce PLOTKIN

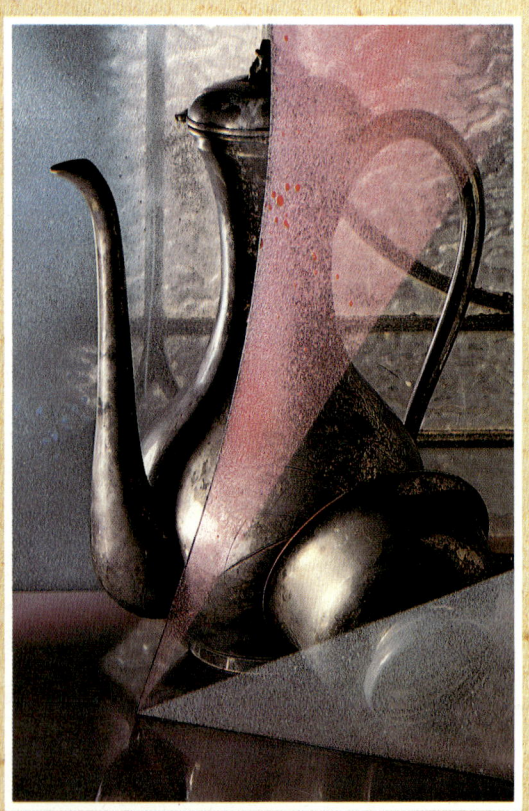

Michael Cuesta

Film Reel
Available
Upon Request

(212) 929-5519

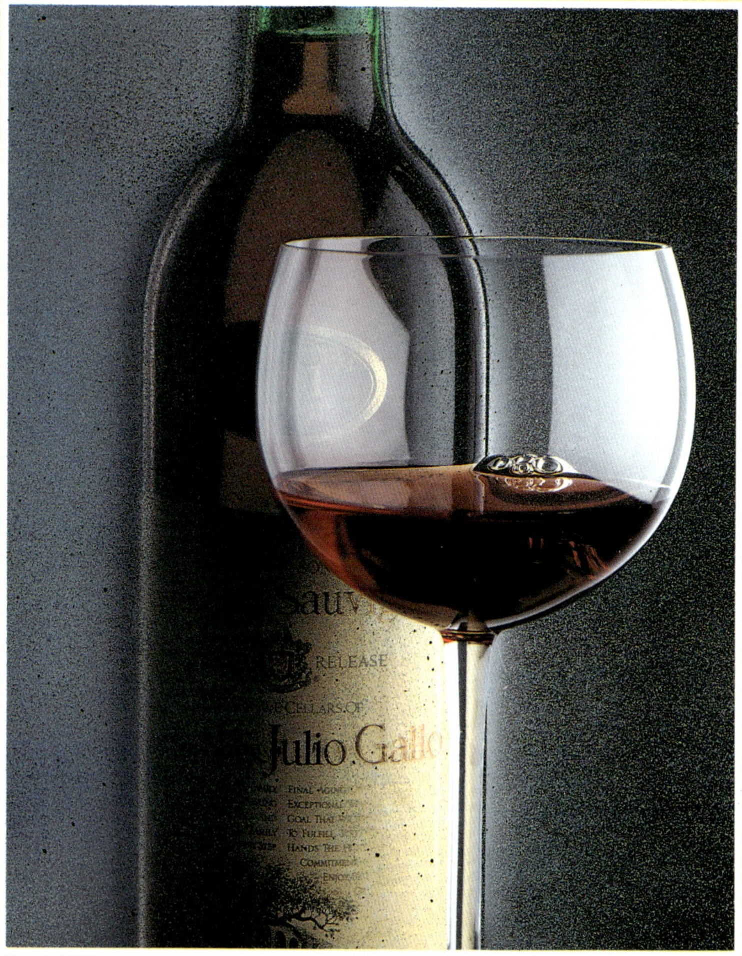
RELEASE
CELLARS OF
Julio

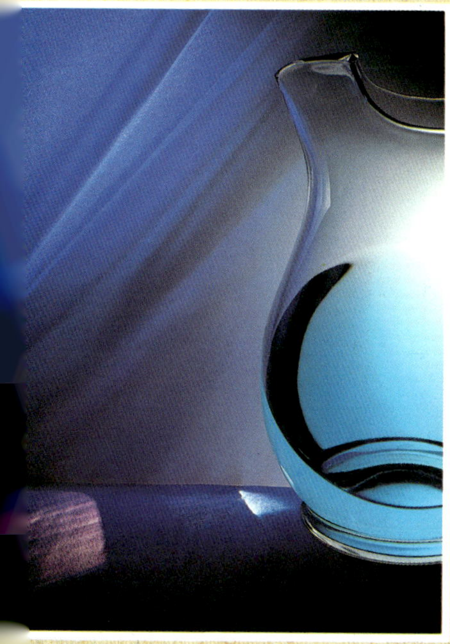

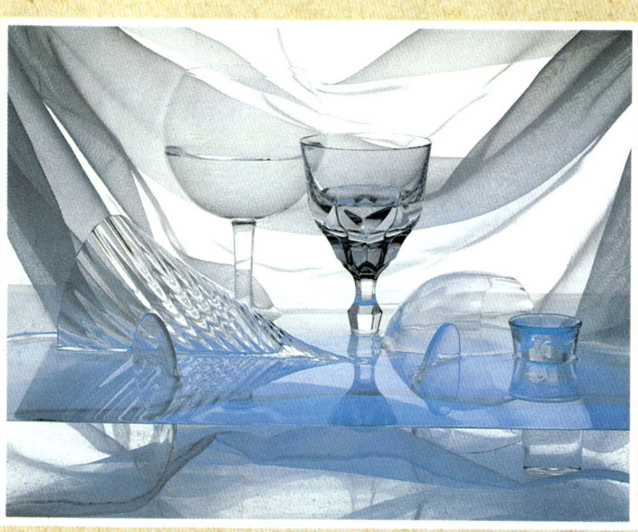

236 W. 26TH ST.
NEW YORK, N.Y. 10001
212·620·0955
FAX·212·620·0961

FOR ADDITIONAL IMAGES PLEASE REFER TO THE GOLD BOOK

MARESCA

297

TED

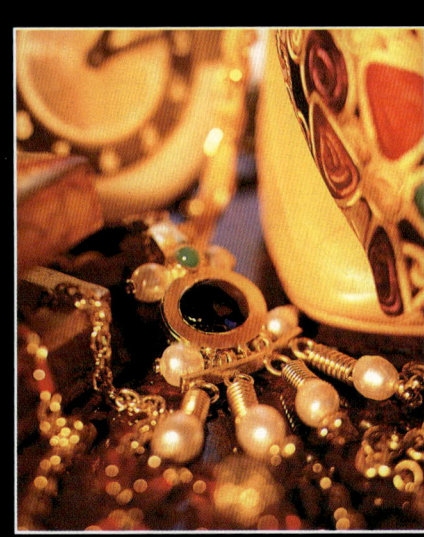

MORRISON

Ted Morrison Photography   286 Fifth Avenue, New York, NY 10001

Represented by Mennemeyer & Co.   212-279-2838   fax 212-563-0402

Still life. Real life.
CHRISTE

Represented by:
MENNEMEYER & COMPANY
286 Fifth Avenue · NYC · 10001   (212) 279-2838

Kat

Represented by:
MENNEMEYER & COMPANY
286 Fifth Avenue • NYC • 10001   (212) 279-2838

rina

Courtesy: Victoria Magazine

303

© 1991 DAVID LANGLEY STUDIO

DAVID ANGELO: DDB Needam Worldwide · GTE Sylvania

Sometimes it's nice to have a little extra cash to play with.

When it's time to sell your servicing packages to get extra cash to play with, the last thing you need is a buyer who likes to play games.

At Marine Midland, straightforward business is our first rule of thumb.

So, for example, when we say we'll buy a wide range of servicing packages, we mean what we say.

Conventional or ARM's. Securitized or non-securitized. Large, small or in between. Whatever size your servicing packages, we've got the purchasing power to offer an aggressive price.

Our long experience makes our response time short.

And when you entrust your servicing packages to us, you can expect nothing less than professional service.

So the next time you need money to play with, set Marine Midland to work. We'll put you ahead of the game.

If we can help you, call your **Wholesale** Mortgage Banking Group representative. Ray Morris in the Northeast at 617-849-5440. Rod Linder in the Midwest at 312-706-2140. Doris Kirby in the South at 704-542-1593. Doug Miller in all other areas at 704-542-1593.

MARINE MIDLAND MORTGAGE CORPORATION
We mean what we say.

JIM NEALEY: Doyle Graf Mabley

DAVID L
S T U
536 W. 50TH STREET · NEW YORK 1001

AND THE WALLS CAME TUMBLIN' DOWN.

DESIGN: MIKE QUON DESIGN OFFICE, NYC

PAT PEDUTO: Young & Rubicam

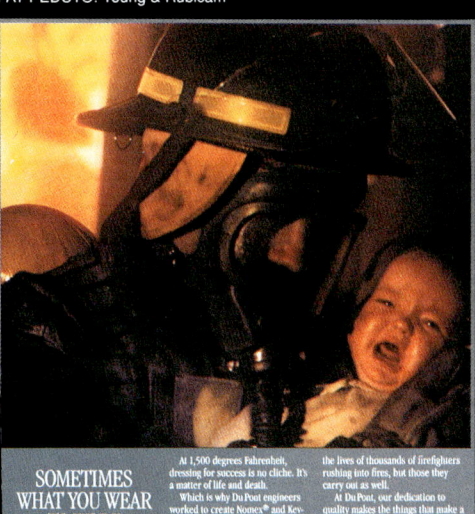

HERB LEVITT: Ally & Gargano

LEN McCARRON: BBDO

PHOTOMATIC REEL
ON REQUEST

SPECIALTY PORTFOLIOS
AVAILABLE:
KIDS, CARS, SETS,
ANIMALS, LOCATION

ANGLEY
D I O

TEL: 212 581 3933 • FAX: 212 265 8205

305

LINDA BOHM

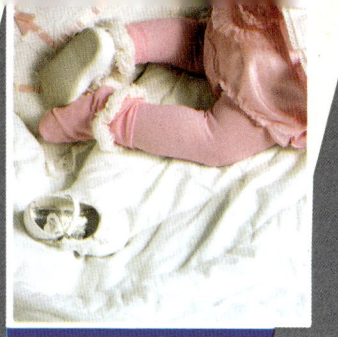

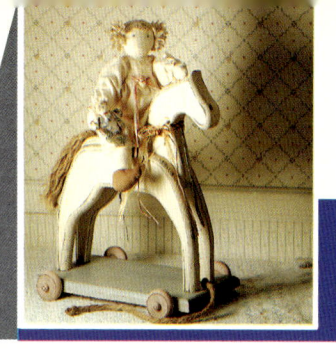

L.D. BOHM STUDIOS, INC.
7 PARK STREET
MONTCLAIR, NJ 07042

201 746-3434
212 349-5650
FAX 201 746-4905

307

zanetti

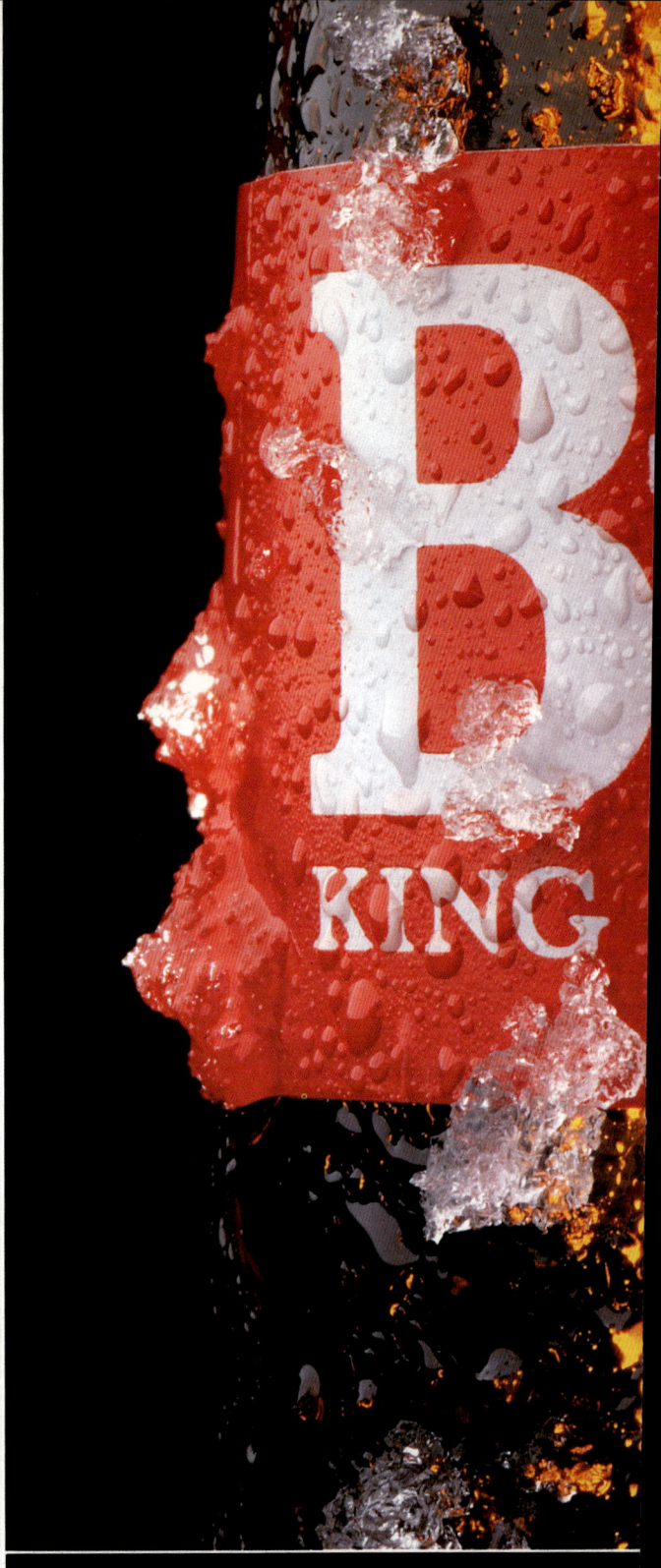

B KING

Nature promises the taste of ripe, luscious strawberries.

Breyers keeps nature's promise.

ALL NATURAL BREYERS

Colombian. And nothing but Colombian.
Gourmet Coffee That Comes In a Can.

Yuban

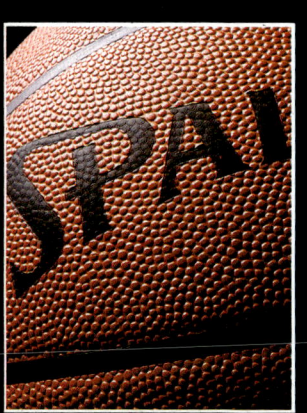

GERRY ZANETTI

TEL: 212 767-1717

FAX: 212 265-8205

DAVID G
PHOTO

DGP / N.Y.

212 · 677 · 8600

DGP / L.A.

213 · 930 · 1898

🚫 FLASH

UILBURT
RAPHY

15 Gramercy Park South / NY, NY 10003 / FAX: 212-228-4466 / TEL: 212-475-9222

Jay Leno

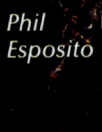

Phil Esposito

Sing-Si

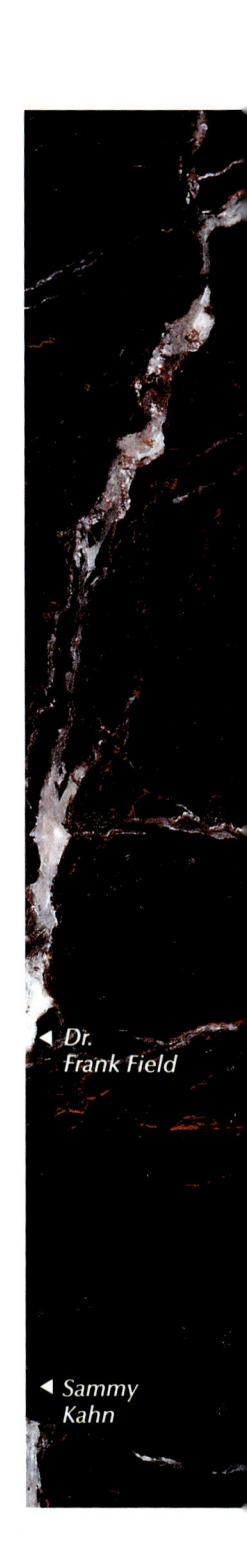

◀ Dr. Frank Field

◀ Sammy Kahn

313

DAVID M.

18 EAST 17TH ST., NEW YORK

SPINDEL

NY 10003 · 212·989·4984

Make yourself comfortable.
HEAD
Shoes for all walks of life.

LIVE IN IT
AND YOU OWN THE WORLD.
METROPOLIS
A LAUDER FOR MEN FRAGRANCE

Scent matters.
LAUDER FOR MEN
FRAGRANCE

"I never thought I'd get a wrinkle...
until I got a wrinkle."
don't panic.
A sheer greaseless fluid,
amazingly like your own skin's fluid,
is soaking into your skin.
Replenishing.
Reassuring your skin that its youthful
moisture will be long maintained.
Helping to smooth the tiniest teeniest
line or wrinkle.
under control.

Sensitive skin has something to celebrate.
Oil of Olay Sensitive Skin Beauty Fluid
is so compatible with your own
sensitive skin,
it absorbs almost instantly, without being irritating.
Helps restore moisture levels so well,
so thoroughly, sensitive skin, too,
can become softer, smoother, more radiant.
And isn't that really something to celebrate?
fragrance free.
Color free. Dermatologist tested. Hypo-allergenic.

Why grow old gracefully?
Fight it with Oil of Olay
Sensitive Skin Beauty Fluid.

OIL of OLAY
BEAUTY FLUID
SENSITIVE SKIN

ULI ROSE
Debra Simon (212) 988-8890

GEOFFREY STEIN STUDIO, INC

348 Newbury Street, Boston, Massachusetts 02115 617-536-8227 FAX 617-536-7113

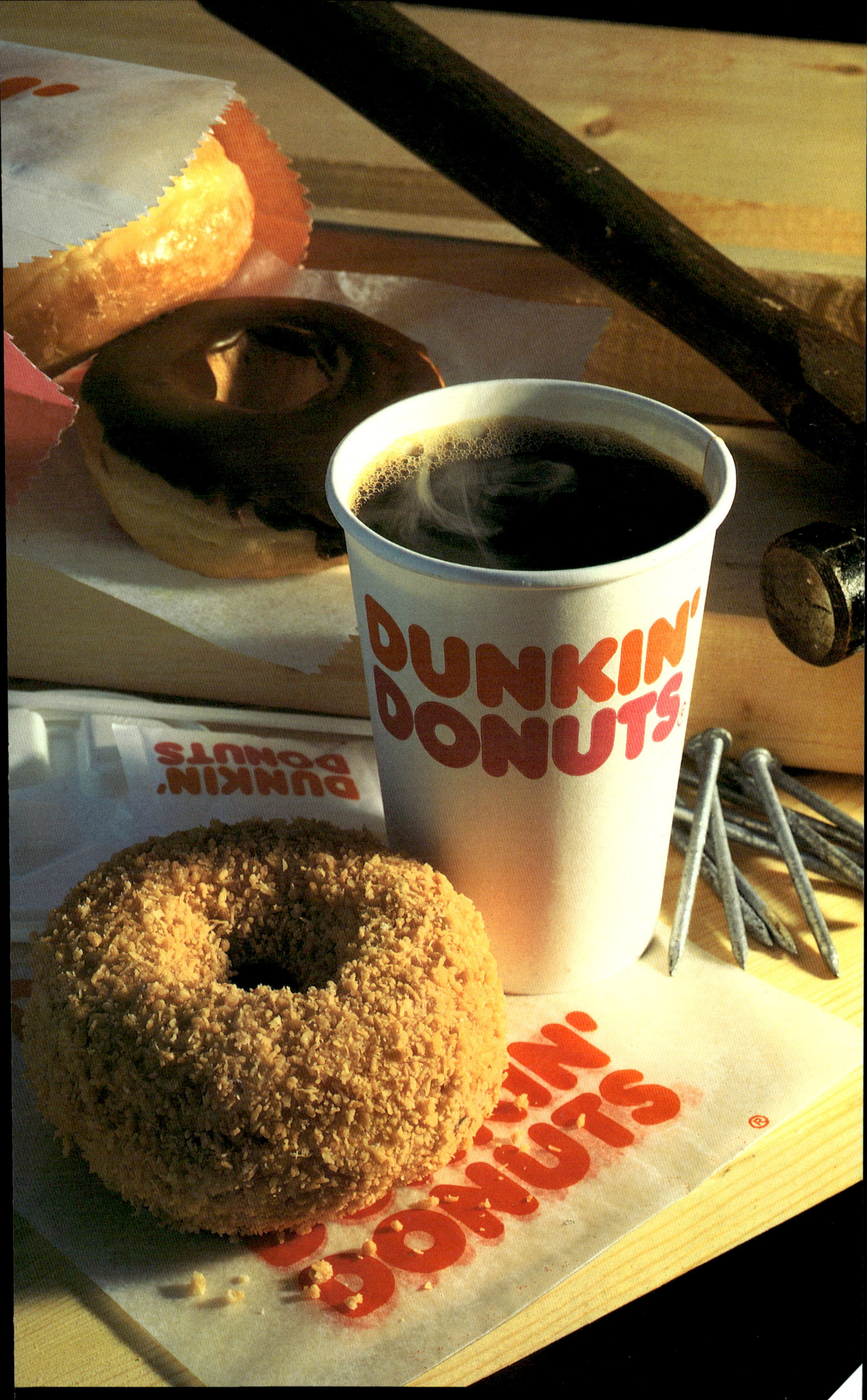
DUNKIN'
DONUTS

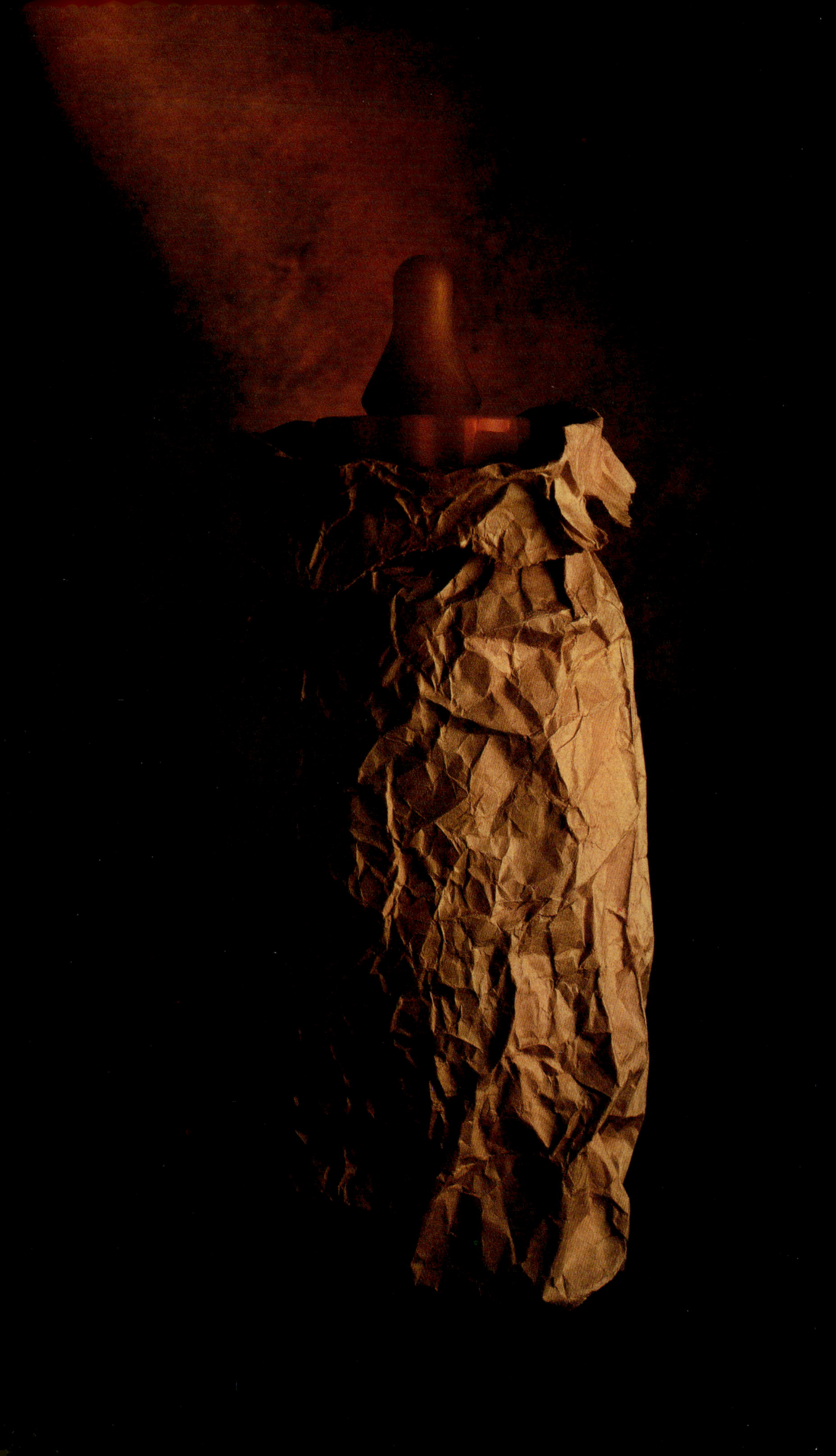

Morgan

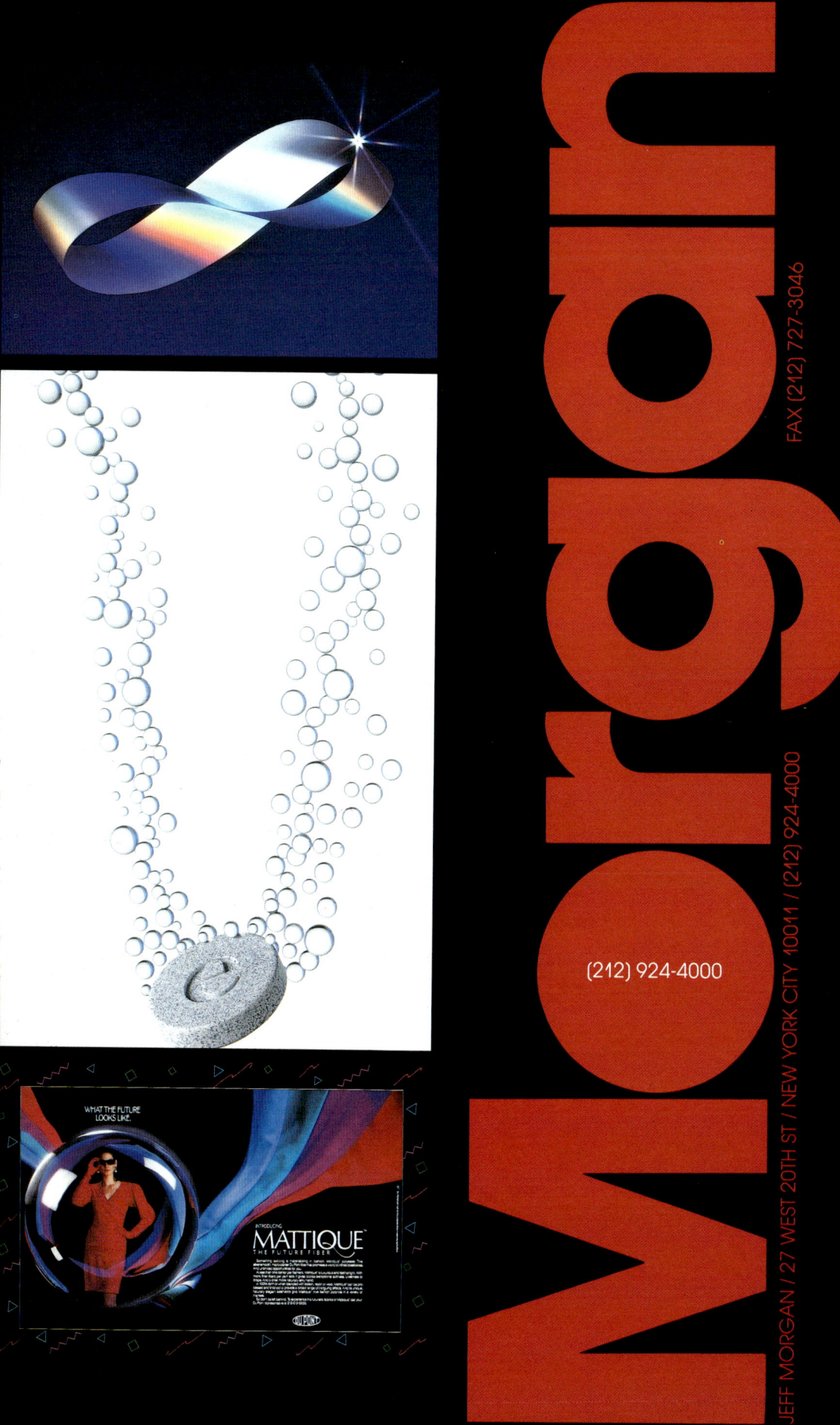

FAX (212) 727-3046

(212) 924-4000

JEFF MORGAN / 27 WEST 20TH ST / NEW YORK CITY 10011 / (212) 924-4000

NEIL SELKIRK   212 243-6778

NEIL SELKIRK 212 243-6778

MICHAEL MAZZEO   NEW YORK CITY   212·226·7113

Mazzeo

Michael Mazzeo   New York City   212·226·7113

DAN WILBY

45 WEST 21ST ST. FIFTH FLOOR NEW YORK 10010

TEL 212 929-8231

FAX 212 929-8249

Represented by George W. Warren

WILBY

JEFFREY APOIAN

66 CROSBY STREET, NEW YORK CITY 10012 • (212) 431-5513

327

SCHOOL BUS

TIME

IS COLOR.

KIM DUCOTE

PHOTOGRAPHY

445 W 19 ST.

NEW YORK CITY

10011

212·989·3680

Elizabeth Hathon Photography

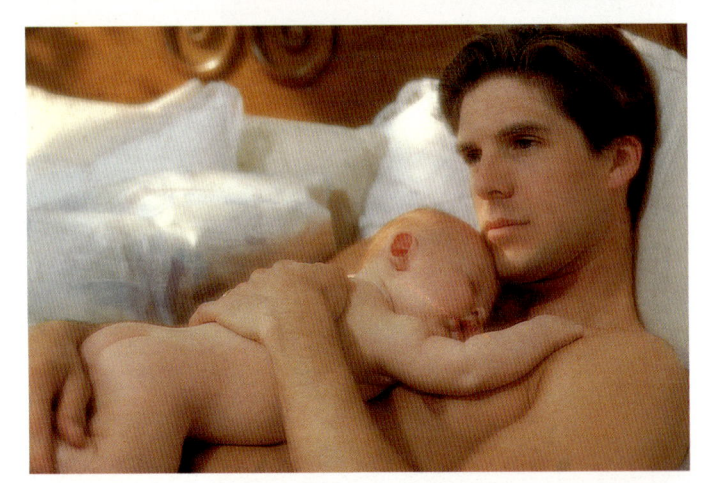

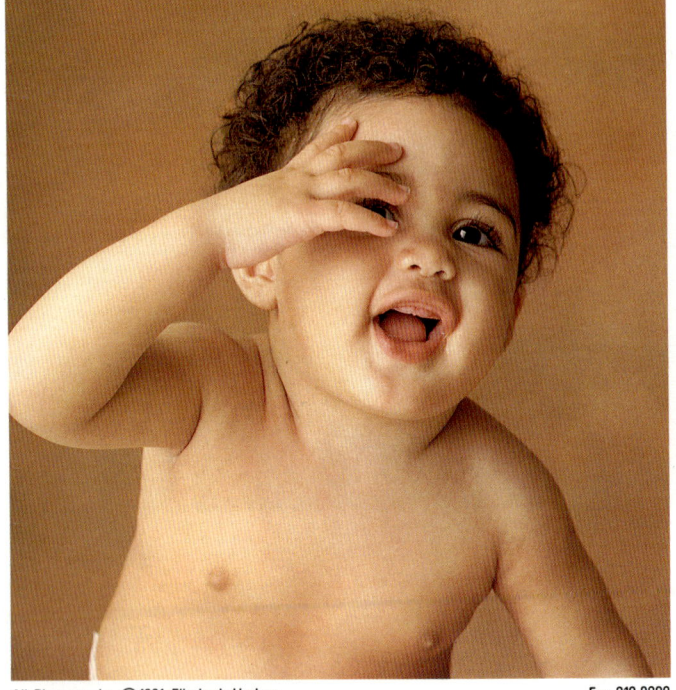

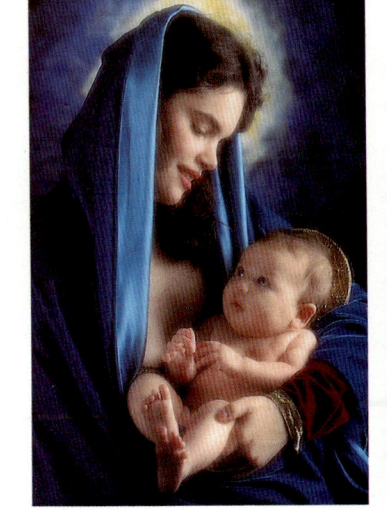

All Photographs ©1991 Elizabeth Hathon Fax 219.0289 Stock Available

8 Greene St NY, NY 10013 212.219.0685

Elizabeth Hathon Photography

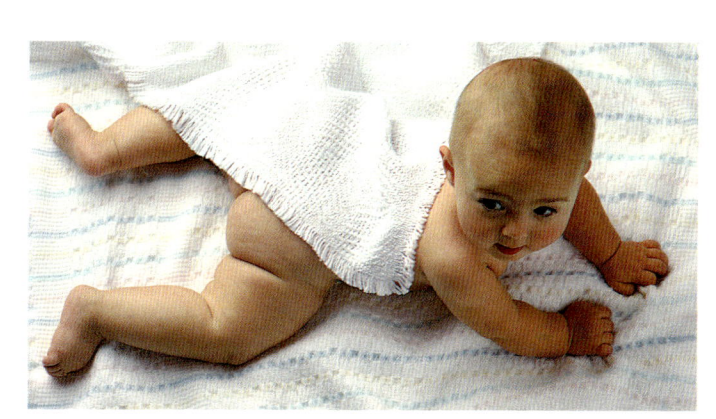

All Photographs ©1991 Elizabeth Hathon   Fax 219.0289   Stock Available

8 Greene St NY, NY 10013 212.219.0685

LEE PAGE

2 1 2 - 2 8 6 - 9 1 5 9

LEE PAGE

212-286-9159

BABCHUK

CONTACT ANNE MARIE BABCHUK 132 W 22 ST NYC 10011 212 929 8811 FAX 212 929 8817

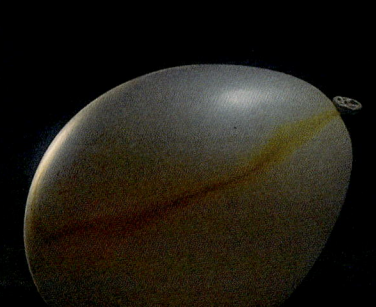

335

John UHER Photography

529 WEST
42ND STREET,
NEW YORK,
N.Y. 10036
(212) 594-7377

JEFF DUNAS

JEFF DUNAS
212 242-1266

Represented By
Tony Cala

Shooting Star   1181 Broadway   New York, N.Y. 10001   Phone:(212) 447-0666   Fax:(212) 779-7056

©1991 BILL KELLY

BILL KELLY

MESOPOTAMIA PRODUCTIONS
140 SEVENTH AVENUE, NY, NY 10011
(212) 989-2794   FAX (212) 989-8472

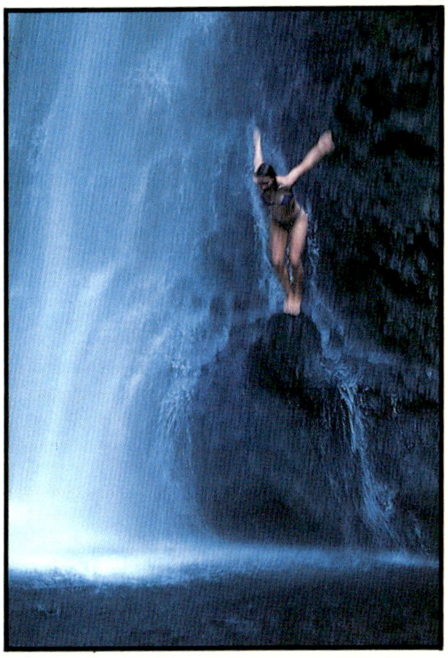
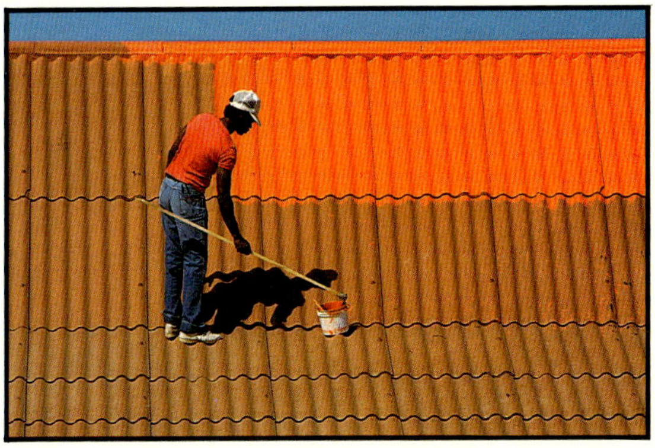
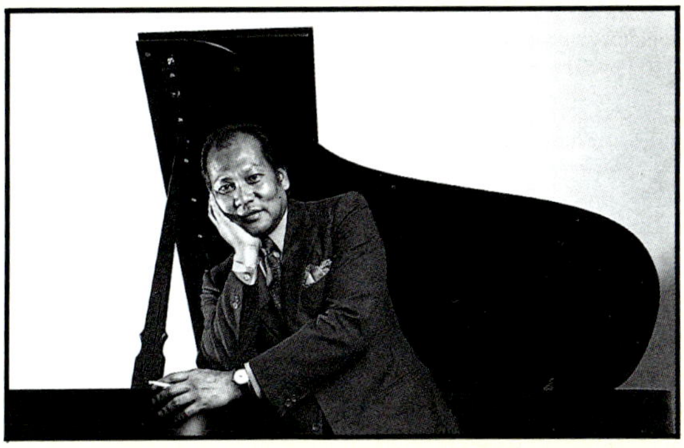
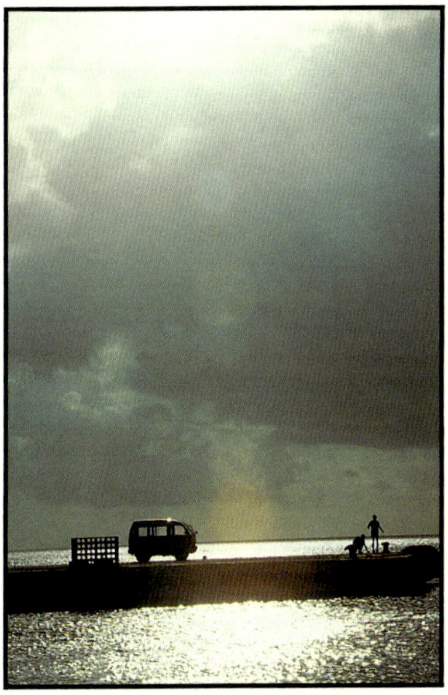
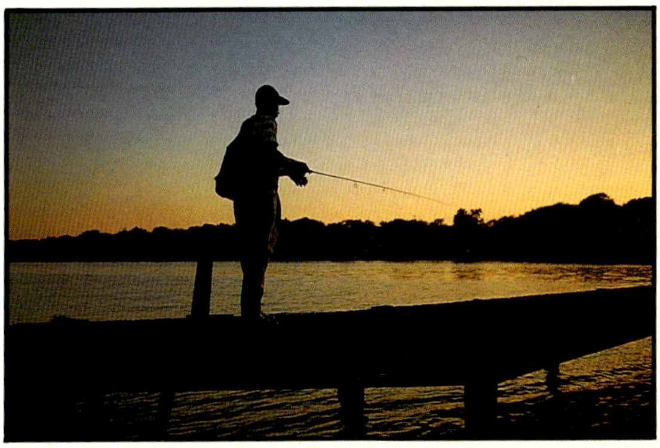
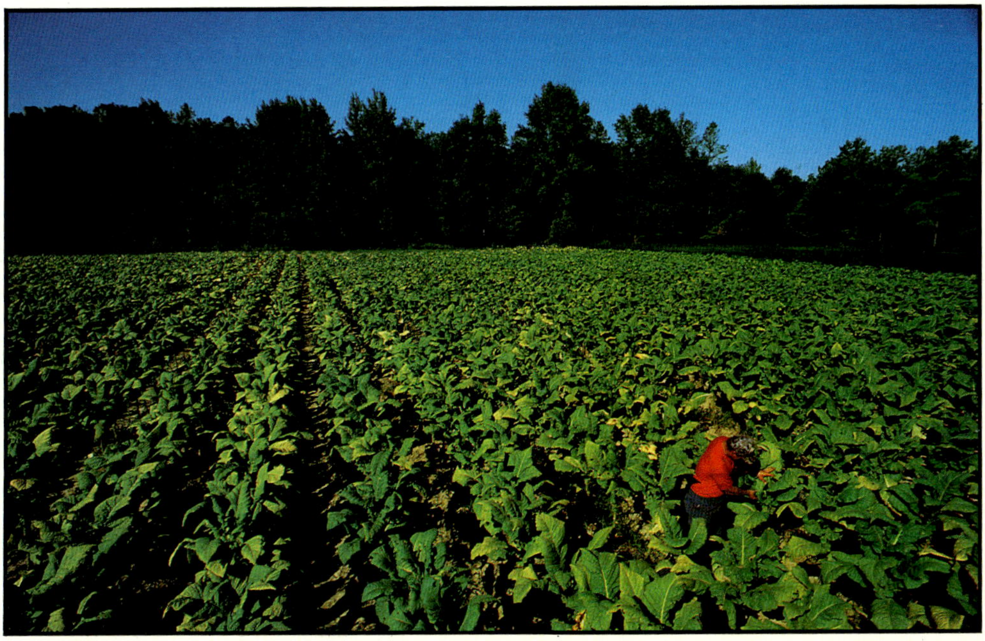

"...If you can

"See the wires, there is no magic!"

Control and communication are the bottom lines for creative problem solving. Drawing on seven years of experience as an illustrator and art director, Barry speaks your language and understands your problems. Most importantly, he has the expertise to solve them. Whether it's creating an image in a unique way or executing an image the desired message in a unique way or executing an image that has already been sold to the client, you get to see it on Barry's high resolution computer screen and can make your changes before it is turned into the final chrome. There are no last minute surprises!

No gimmicks, no fabricated models, no additional retouching or expense. Just skill, talent, 20 years of creative photographic experience and an in-house high resolution "Creator 2600" graphic computer to turn your concept into reality in the form of a perfect transparency.

Call for a studio demonstration or Barry Blackman's portfolio.

The only thing you see is the magic.

Barry Blackman
Very Special Photography

1 212 627 9777
150 Fifth Avenue
Suite # 220
New York, N.Y.
10011

Represented by Yellen/Lachapelle
212-838-3170 • Fax 212-758-6199
Palma Kolansky 212-727-7300

Palma Kolansky

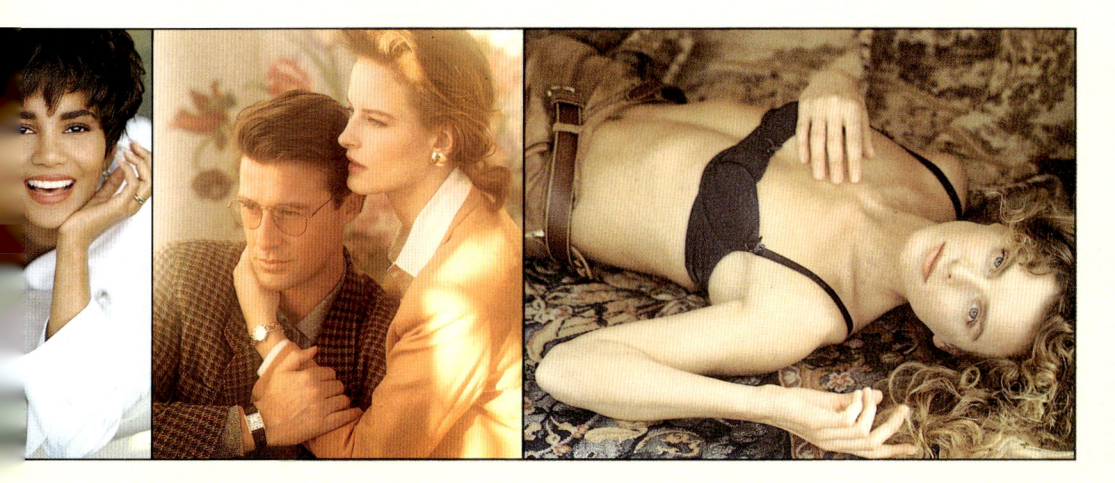

OLOF

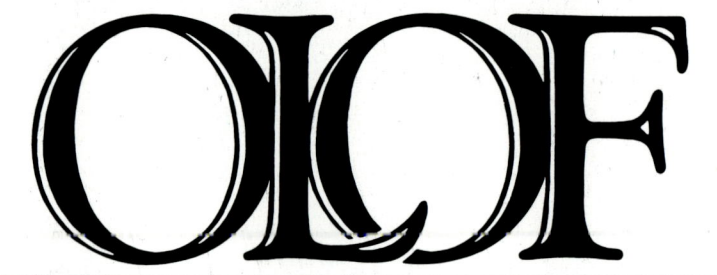

Olof Wahlund Photography Inc.   7 East 17th Street, New York 10003   (212) 929 9067   Fax: (212) 929 7299

Represented by Yellen/Lachapelle, Inc.   420 East 54th Street, New York 10022   (212) 838 3170   Fax: (212) 758 6199

OLOF

Olof Wahlund Photography Inc.   7 East 17th Street, New York 10003   (212) 929 9067   Fax: (212) 929 7299

Represented by Yellen/Lachapelle, Inc.   420 East 54th Street, New York 10022   (212) 838 3170   Fax: (212) 758 6199

Michael
PHOTOGRAPHER • PETERSVILLE FARM • MT. KISCO • NEW YORK • 10549 • 212-473-3095 • 914-666-62
Melford

© MICHAEL MELFORD 1991

REPRESENTED BY DEBORAH BROWN • 212-463-7732 • FAX 212-645-7951

Aresu-Goldring
Studio
568 Broadway
Suite 608
NY, NY 10012
Contact
Laura Seltzer
Barry Goldring
212-334-9494
FAX 212-431-9858

PAUL ARESU

MANNO

© 1991 JOHN MANNO

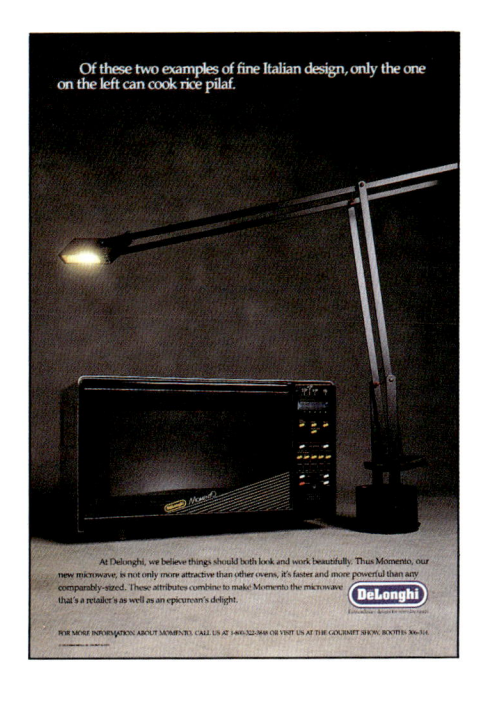

JOHN MANNO PHOTOGRAPHY
20 WEST 22ND STREET
NEW YORK, NEW YORK 10010
212 243 7353
FAX 212 243 7876

REPRESENTED BY GLENN PALMER-SMITH
212 769 3940

twenty
six
west
thirty
eighth
street

telephone
2 1 2
3 9 1
0 8 1 0

FAX
2 1 2
7 6 8
3 7 7 5

*new
york
city*

*haiman
photo
graphy*

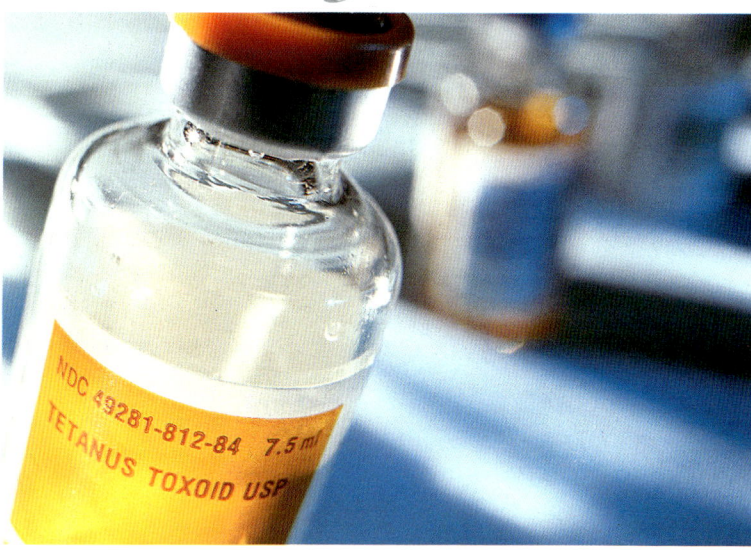

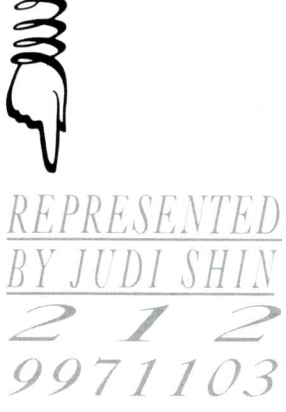

REPRESENTED
BY JUDI SHIN
*2 1 2
9971103*

Richard Pierce
241 West 36th Street
New York, NY 10018
(212) 947-8241

HARPERS BAZAAR

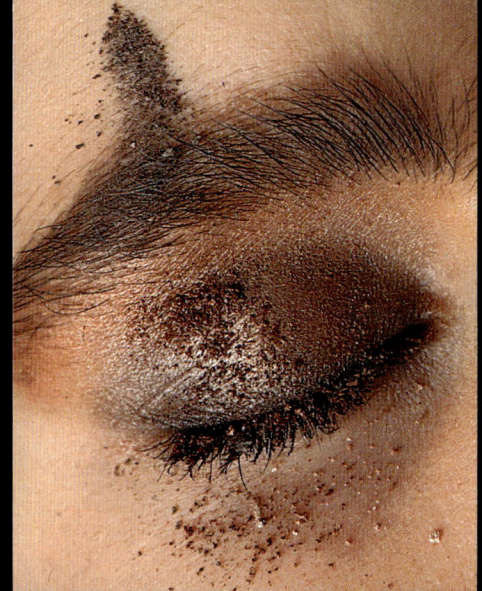

HARPERS BAZAAR

Represented by Glenn Palmer-Smith
212.769.3940   Fax 212.787.6968

C R O W D

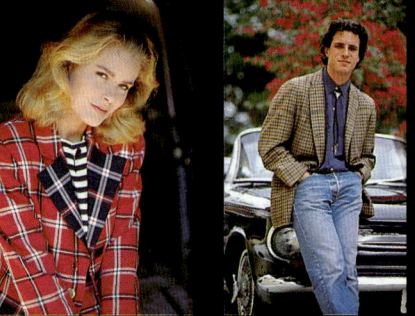

PALL MALL BELONGS

George Carroll Whipple III
212.219.0202

C O N T R O L

357

NANCY BROWN

APA ASMP
STOCK: IMAGE BAN
SELECT STOCK IN STU
SEE MORE WORK I
'91 GOLD BOOK
6 W. 20 ST
NY, NY 100
(212) 924-910
(212) 633-09
FAX

© 1990 NANCY BROW

PHOTOGRAPHY

Not every professional can see the difference. We make it for those who can.

Professional
Not Just Different, Better.

GLENN **MCLAUGHLIN** 6W 20ST NY NY 10011

(212) 645 7028　　　　　FAX (212) 633 0911

Carol Kaplan Studio, Inc.
20 Beacon Street
Boston, MA 02108
617·720·4400   FAX 617·720·1311
Represented by Robin Fernsell

Kaplan

Carol Kaplan Studio, Inc.
20 Beacon Street
Boston, MA 02108
617·720·4400   FAX 617·720·1311
Represented by Robin Fernsell

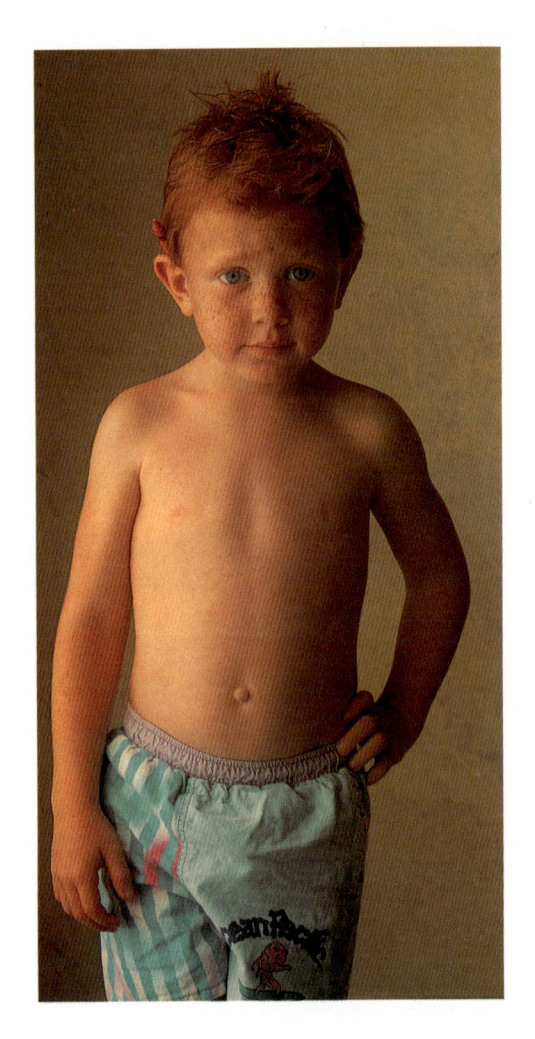

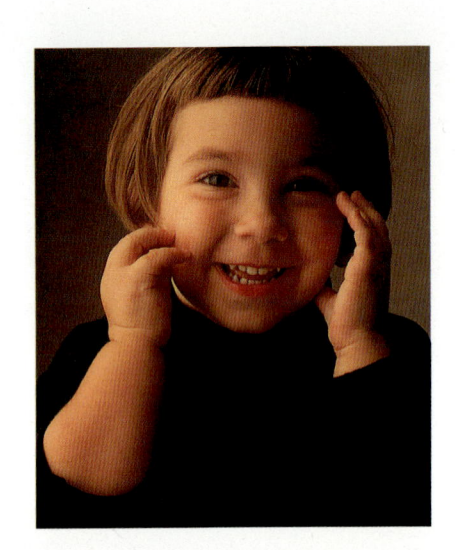

Kaplan

represented by • SHELLEY SPIERMAN • *212.749.8911*

Skip Caplan • *studio*

124 West 24 Street • New York, NY 10011

Telephone: *212.463.0541* • Fax: *212.627.1956*

John Henry

represents

•

Lois Greenfield

52 White Street · N.Y.C.

•

686·6883

Frank OWENS

11 WEST 29TH ST. N.Y, N.Y. **(212) 686-2535**

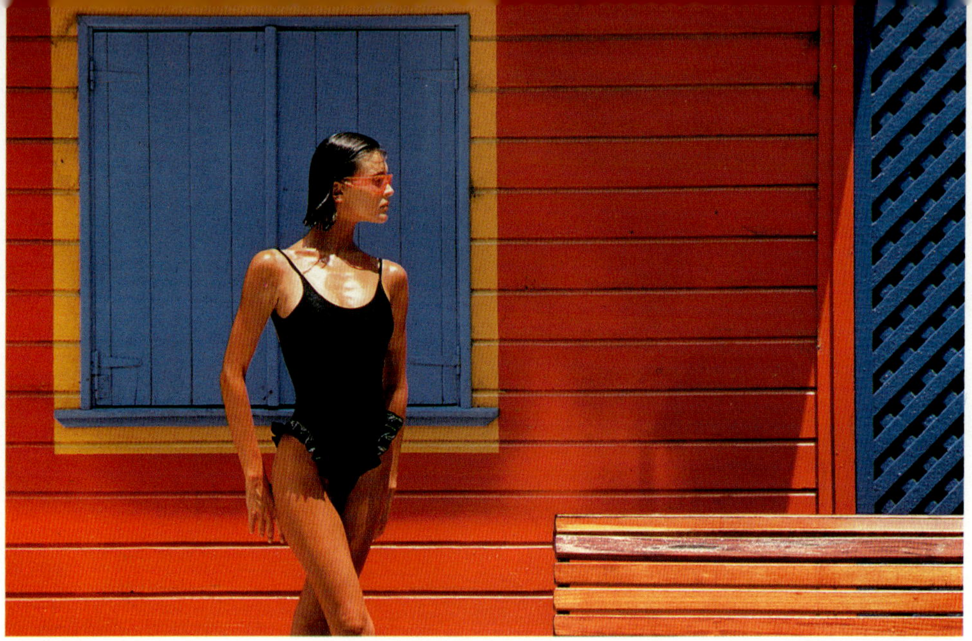

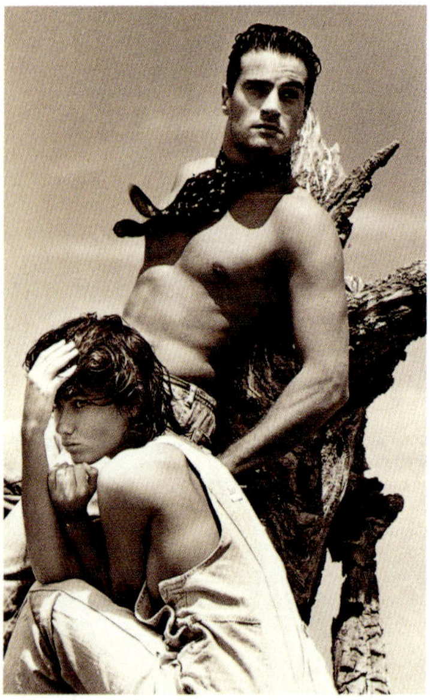

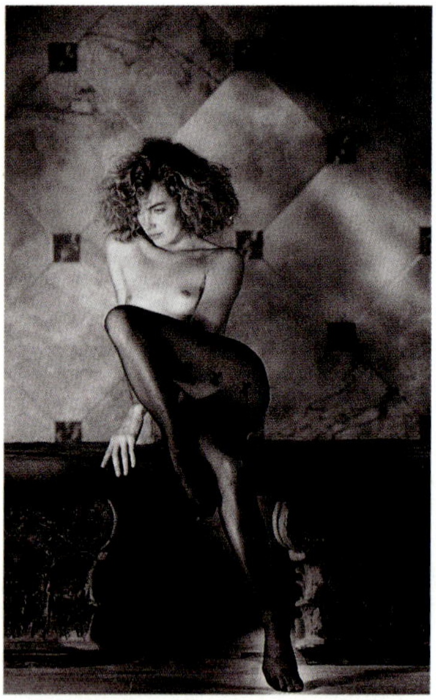

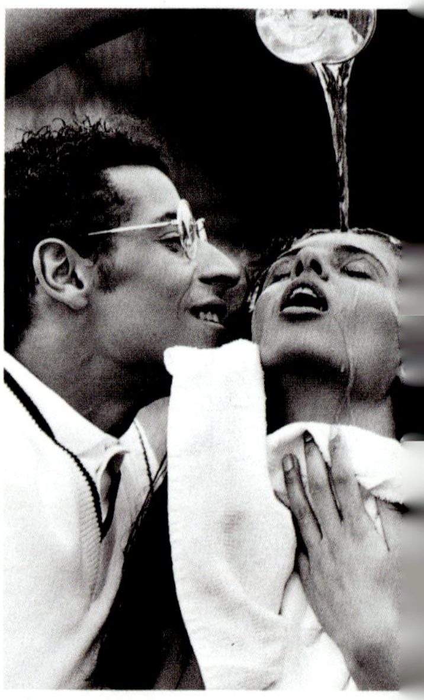

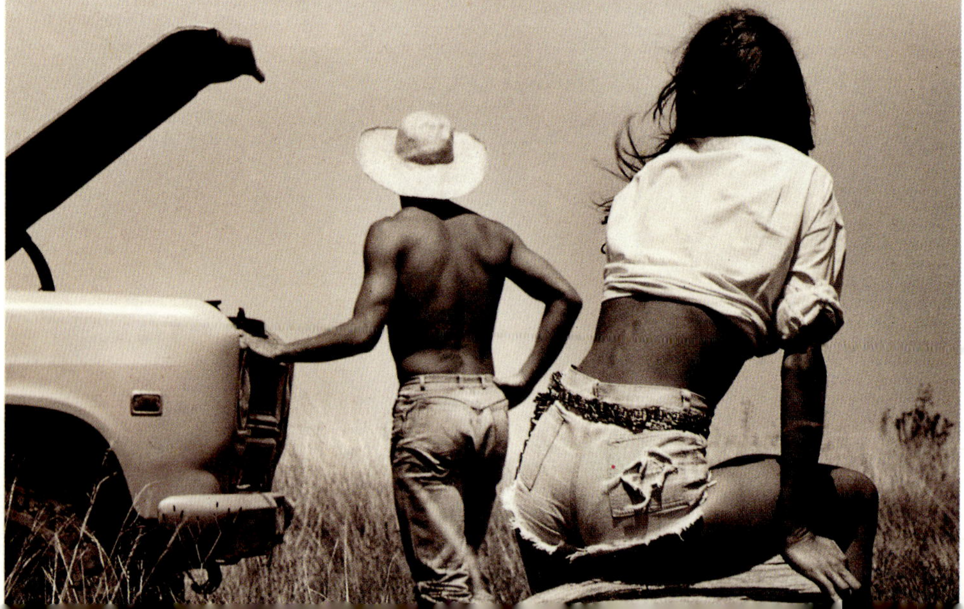

ROD COOK

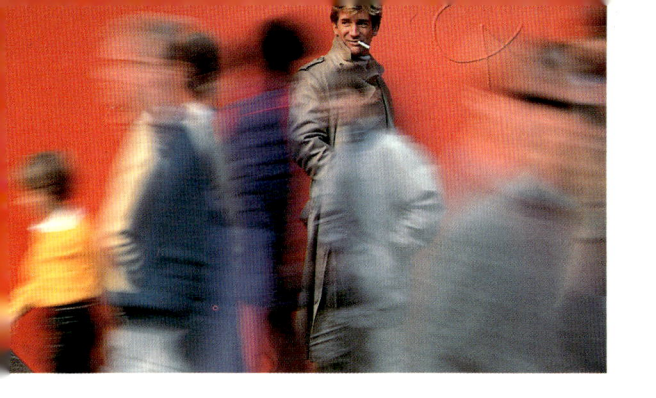

29 EAST 19TH STREET

NEW YORK, NY 10003

(212) 995-0100

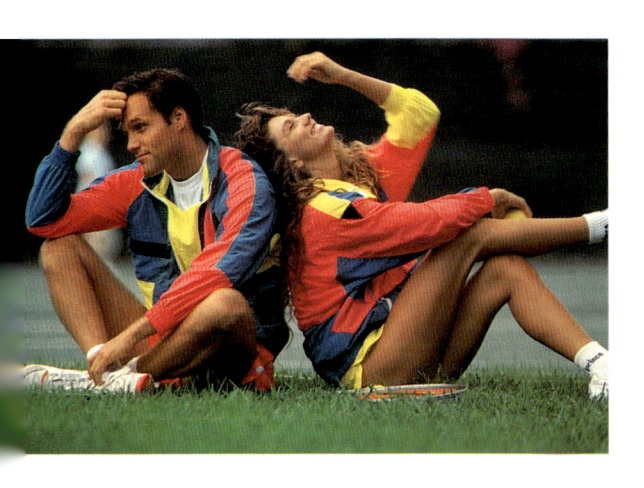

FOR ROD COOK'S

PORTFOLIO

CONTACT: TERRY DAGROSA

(212) 254-4254

Niwa Studio, Inc.

5 East 16 Street

New York, NY 10003

(Just off Union Square)

Tel. 212.627.4608

Fax. 212.691.9570

Represented by

Camie Wylie

Tel. 212.721.2865

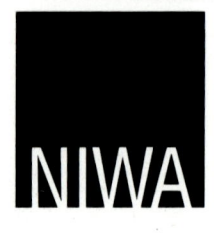

NIWA

Niwa Studio, Inc.
5 East 16 Street
New York, NY 10003
(Just off Union Square)
Tel.212.627.4608
Fax.212.691.9570

Represented by
Camie Wylie
Tel.212.721.2865

NIWA

COSM

COSM STUDIO INC

5 E. 16TH. ST. NY. NY. 10003

REPRESENTATIVE

CAMIE WYLIE

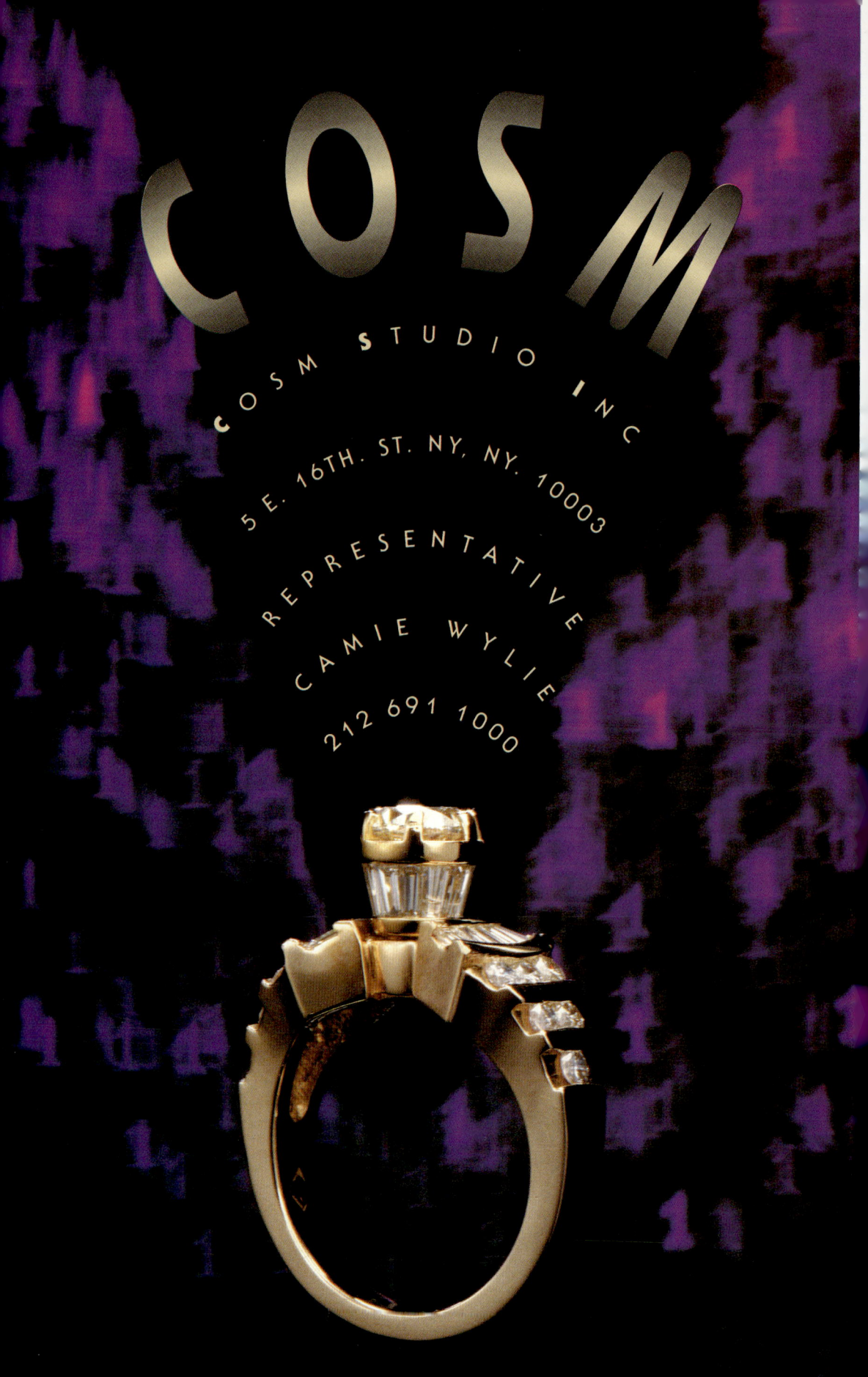

212 691 1000

PHOTO: SHIM

BILL MORRIS
34 EAST 29 STREET • NEW YORK CITY 10016 • (212) 685-7354

ERICSSON

LÖNNINGE

LARS LÖNNINGE STUDIO INC.

NEW YORK TELEPHONE: 212-627-0100, TELEFAX: 212-633-8144,

LONDON TEL: +44-71-379-4755, COPENHAGEN TEL: +45-35-822-616.

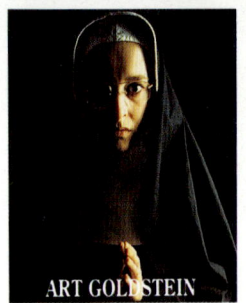

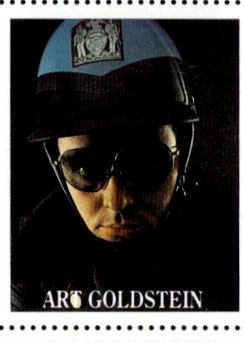

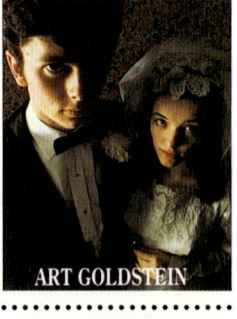

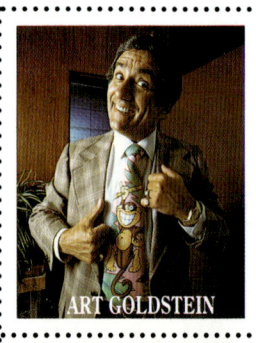

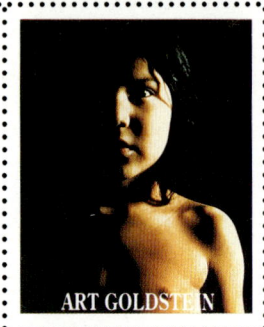

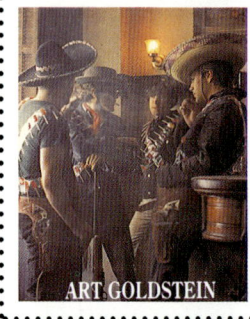

ART GOLDSTEIN
66 CROSBY STREET
NEW YORK, NY 10012
(212) 966-2682
REPRESENTATIVE:
ANGELINE

MENDA
STUDIO

MENDA STUDIO/36 WEST 20TH STREET/NEW YORK, N.Y. 10011/(212) 675-5561

MASULLO

RALPH MASULLO PHOTOGRAPHY, INC.

111 WEST 19TH ST., STUDIO 2B

NEW YORK, N.Y. 10011

212•727•1809   FAX: 212•924•4936

Sony • RC Cola • Scali, McCabe, Sloves • AT&T • Lowe Marschalk • Lorillard • Saatchi & Saatchi • Grey Advertising • Time Life

Champion • Hertz • Chase Manhattan • Pluzynski Associates • J. Walter Thompson • Sony • RC Cola • Scali, McCabe, Sloves • AT&T

RALPH MASULLO PHOTOGRAPHY, INC.

111 WEST 19TH ST., STUDIO 2B

NEW YORK, N.Y. 10011

212•727•1809   FAX: 212•924•4936

• RCA Records

M A S U L L O

SCOTT BARROW. 914-265-4242. FAX 914-265-2046

AEROMEXICO
AMERICAN EXPRESS
AT&T
BAHAMAS
CANCUN
CONTINENTAL AIRLINES
FORD MOTOR COMPANY
GENERAL MOTORS
HERTZ
HILTON INTERNATIONAL
MASTERCARD
MEXICO
NORTHWEST AIRLINES
SOUTHWESTERN BELL
TWA
ETC.

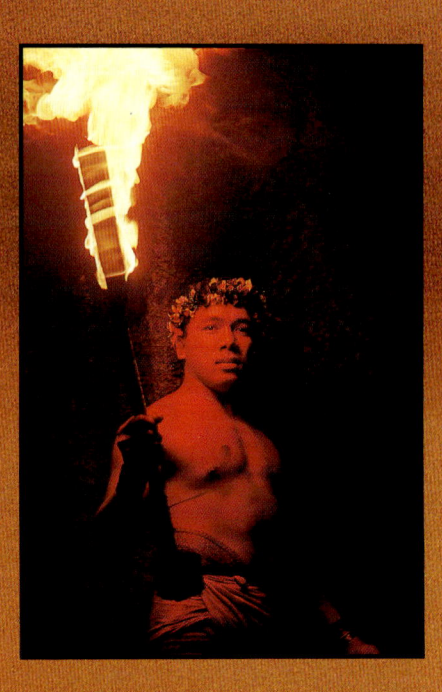

When you want your work to have a strong individual style.

© Copyright 1991 Scott Barrow, Inc.

BARROW

381

SUSUMU SATO

SUSUMU SATO PHOTOGRAPHY INC.
109 WEST 27TH STREET
NEW YORK, NEW YORK 10001
FAX: 212 633-9235

TEL: 212 741-0688

REPRESENTED BY:
REBECCA SEGERSTROM
IN GERMANY BY **KNOW HOW**
FAX: 0211 75-41-40

TEL: 212 242-0181
TEL: 0211 75-40-35

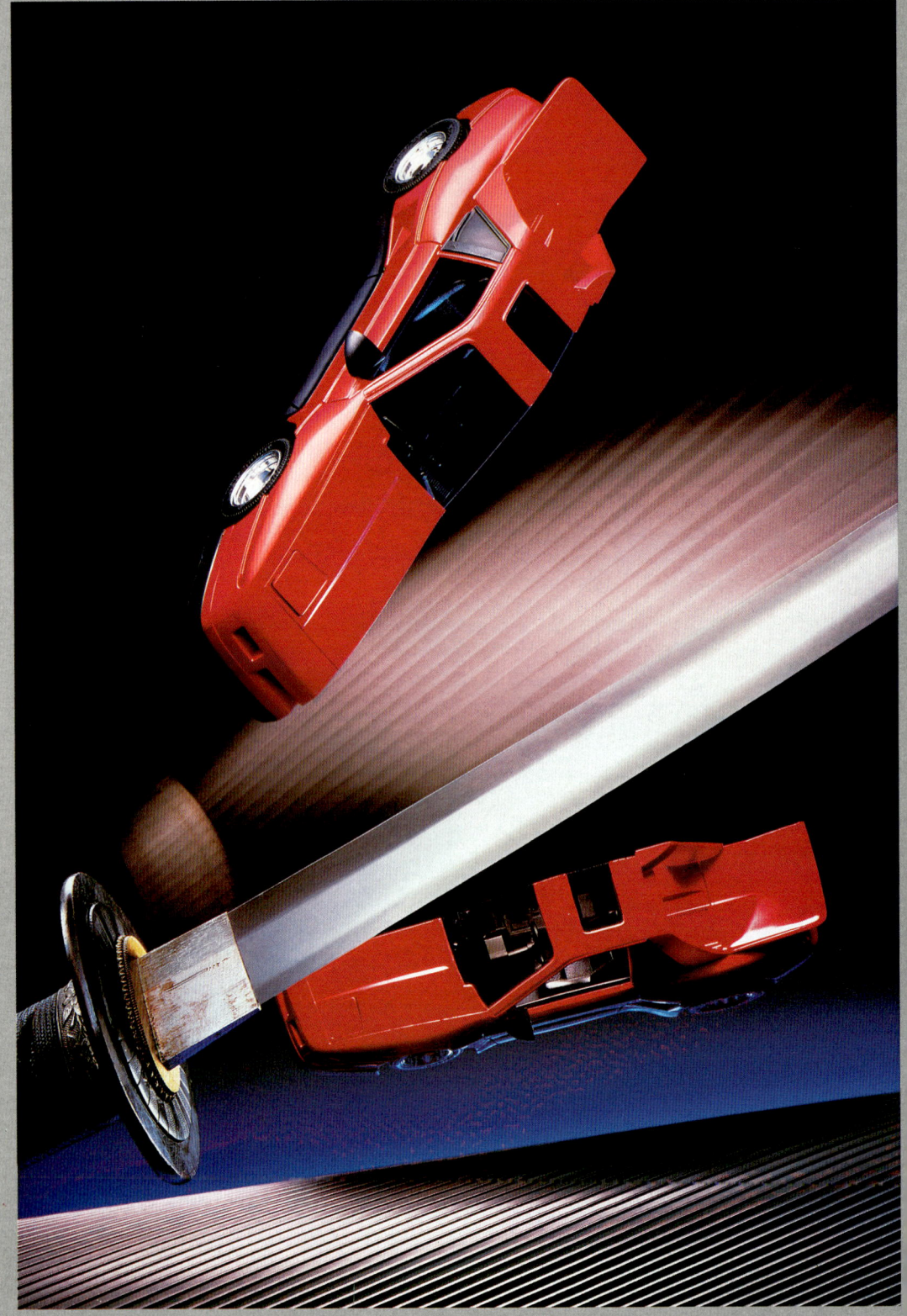

CHUCK DAVIDSON / SUSUMU SATO

CI: LABATT U.S.A.

SUSUMU SATO

CI: CHIQUITA BRANDS

383

MALYSZKO

Mike Malyszko

Judy Hughes

90 South Street

Boston, Massachusetts 02111

617 426 9111

In New York, represented by Joan Jedell 212 861 7861

385

Charles Nesbit

represented by
Glenn Palmer-Smith
212-769-3940
fax 212-787-6968

Charles Nesbit

64 greene street,

new york, ny 10012

212-925-0225   fax 212-274-1650

represented by Glenn Palmer-Smith
212-769-3940   fax 212-787-6968

donald graham

new york city:
(212)459-4767

los angeles:
(213)656-7117

DONALD GRAHAM

TONY WAANG

American Express

Anne Klein

AT&T

A&W Rootbeer

Changing Times

Chase Manhattan Bank

Chemical Bank

Continental Technology

Courvoisier

Deloitte & Touche

Francesco Smalto

IBM

Johnson & Johnson

Longevity

Macy's

McGraw-Hill

Med-Chek

Mobil

Nabisco

New York Telephone

Panasonic

Pantone

Riunite

STP

TWA

DÉNES PETÖE 22 WEST 27TH STREET

© 1991, Dénes Petöe

NEW YORK, NY 10001   (212) 213-3311

Dénes Petöe
REPRESENTED BY PHILIP WAYNE 212·696·5215

DÉNES PETÖE 22 WEST 27TH STREET

© 1991, Dénes Petöe

NEW YORK, NY 10001 (212) 213-3311

© 1991, Dénes Petöe

Dénes Petöe

REPRESENTED BY PHILIP WAYNE 212·696·5215

DÉNES PETÖE 22 WEST 27TH STREET

© 1991, Dénes Petöe

NEW YORK, NY 10001   (212) 213-3311

Dénes Petöe

REPRESENTED BY PHILIP WAYNE 212·696·5215

DÉNES PETÖE 22 WEST 27TH STREET

© 1991, Dénes Petöe

NEW YORK, NY 10001   (212) 213-3311

© 1991, Dénes Petöe

Dénes Petöe

REPRESENTED BY PHILIP WAYNE 212-696-5215

W H Y

DOUGLAS WHYTE, 519 BROADWAY, NEW YORK, NY 10012

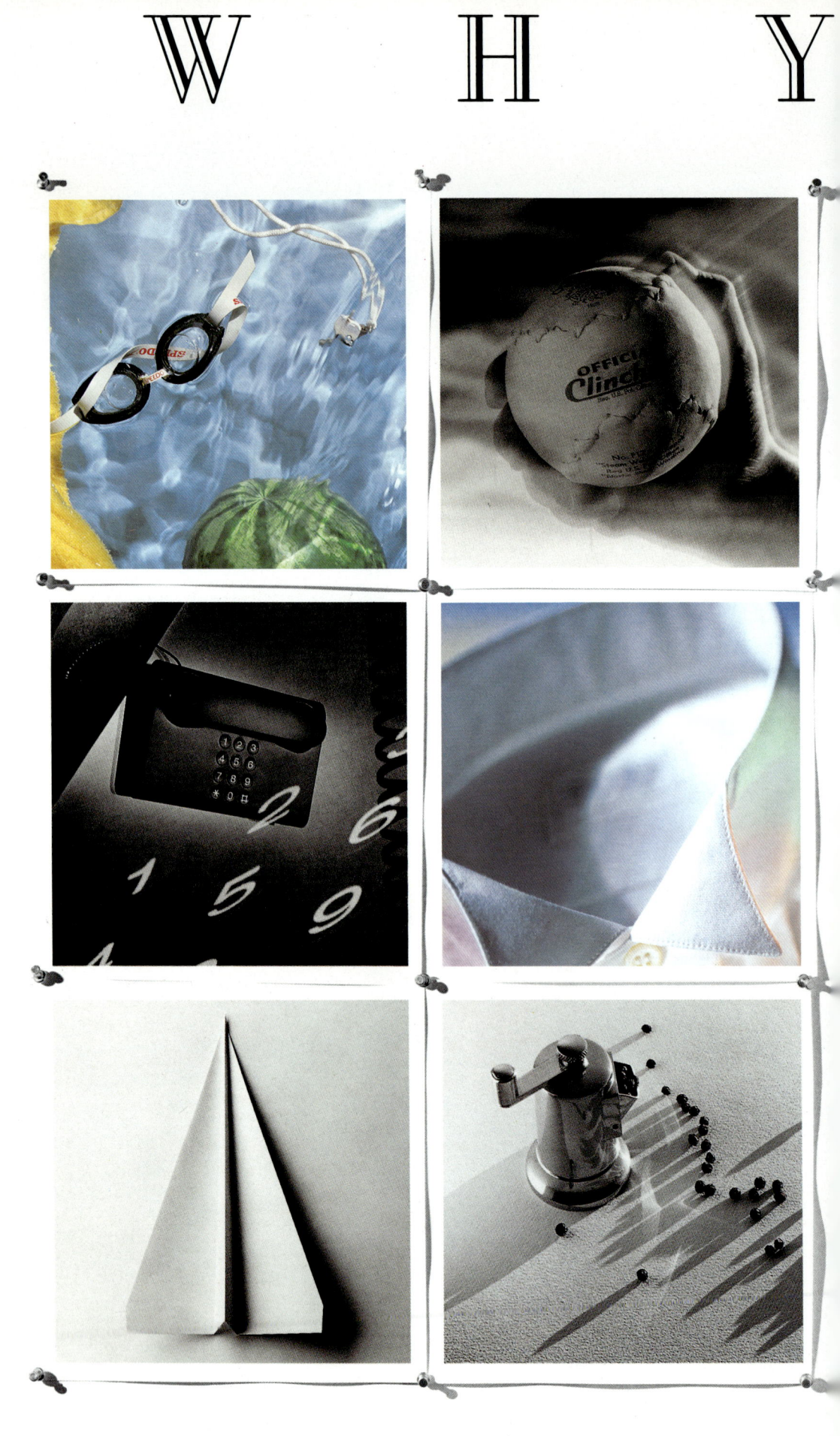

T E

(212) 431-1667 • REPRESENTED BY PHILIP WAYNE • 212-696-5215

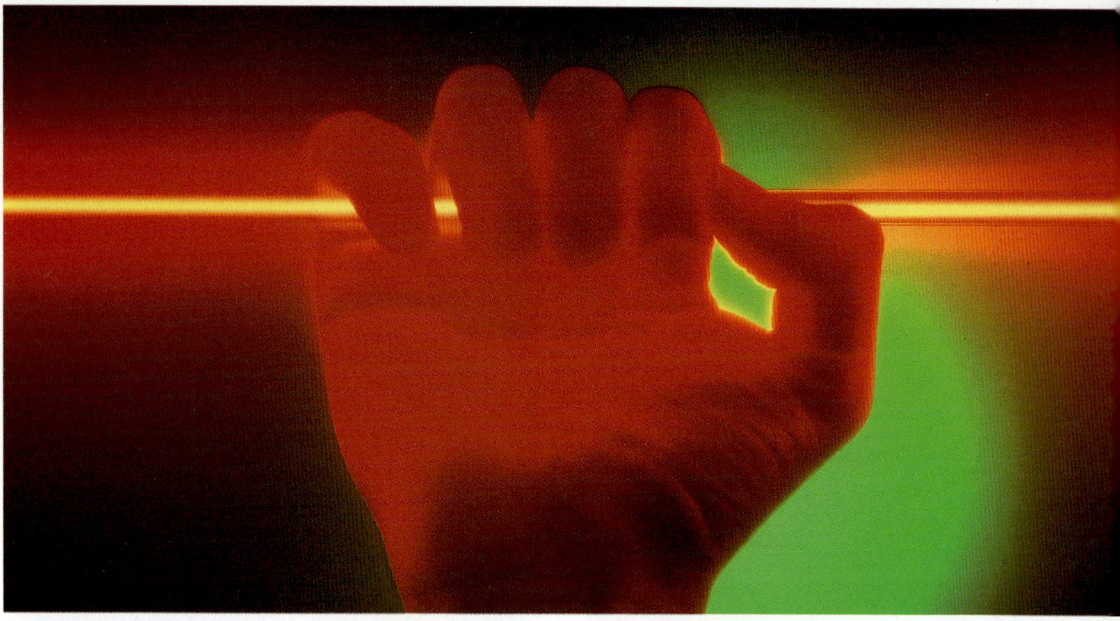

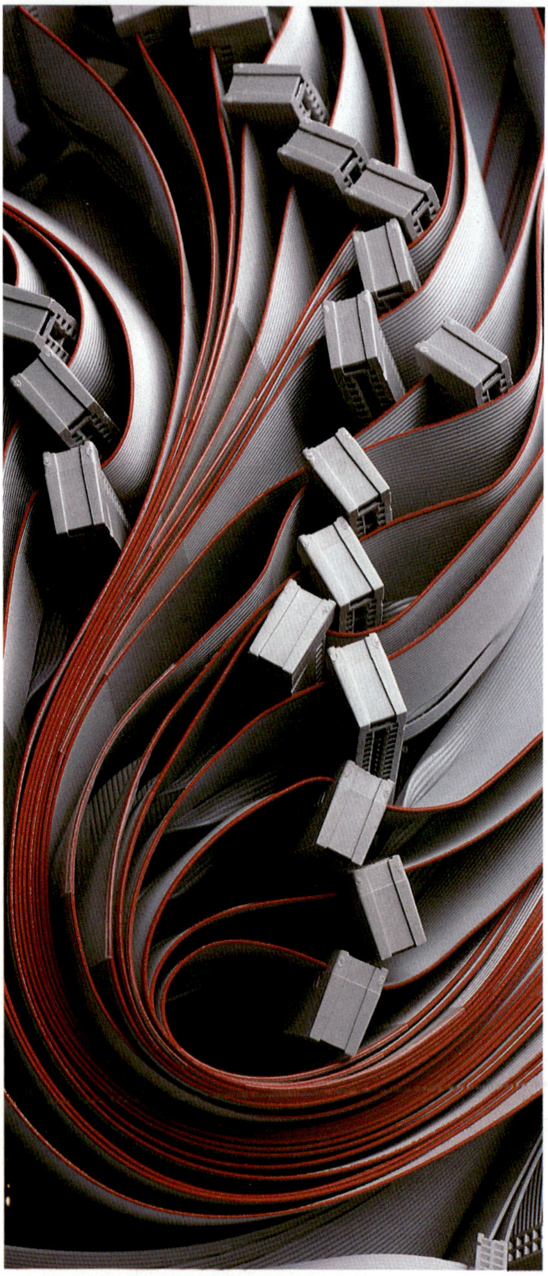

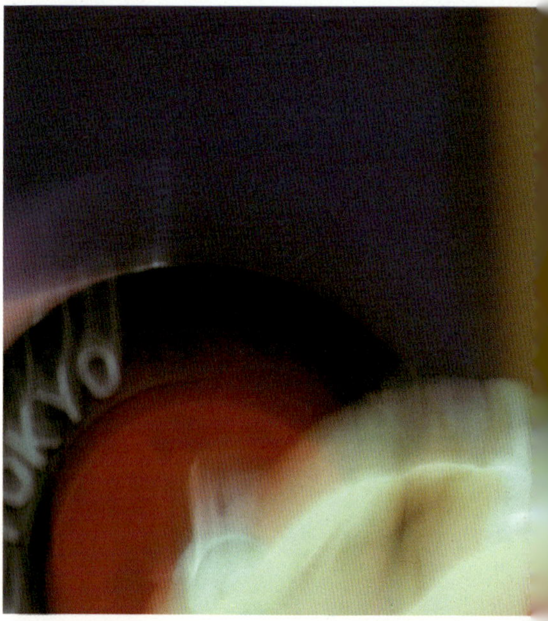

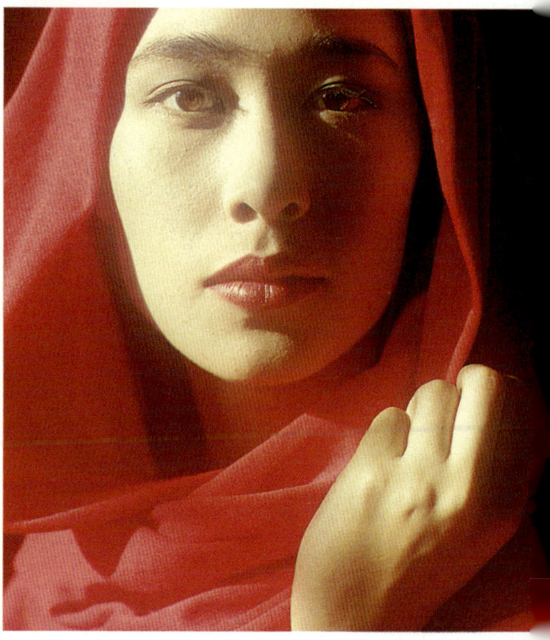

© jones

lou jones
22 randolph street
boston 02118 usa
617/426 6335
212/463 8971

clients:
klm
boeing
nikon
sd warren
boise cascade
at&t
dun & brad street
citibank
chase
red cross

403

TCHIN TCHIN   9 West 31 Street · (212) 947-3858 · FAX (212) 563-1194

TED CHIN

Brian
Lanker

Represented by Ken Mann 212/944-2853

PHYSICAL THERAPY
FROM NIKE.
Just do it.

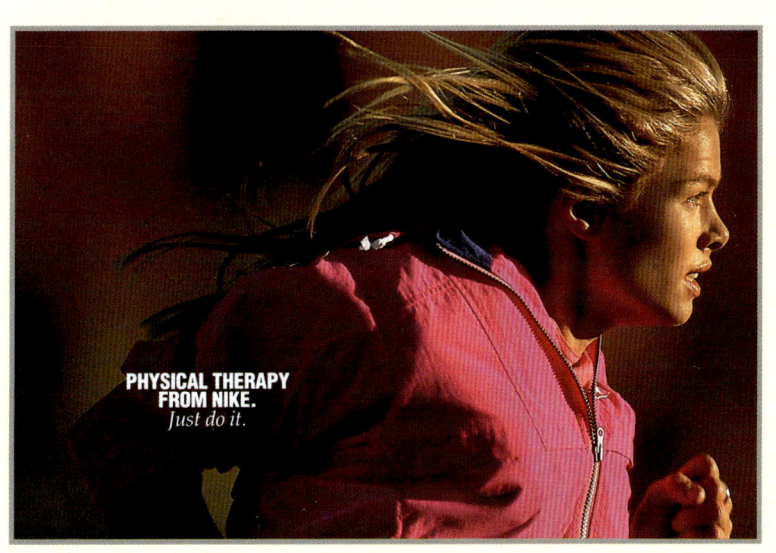

Brian
Lanker

Represented by
Ken Mann
212/944-2853

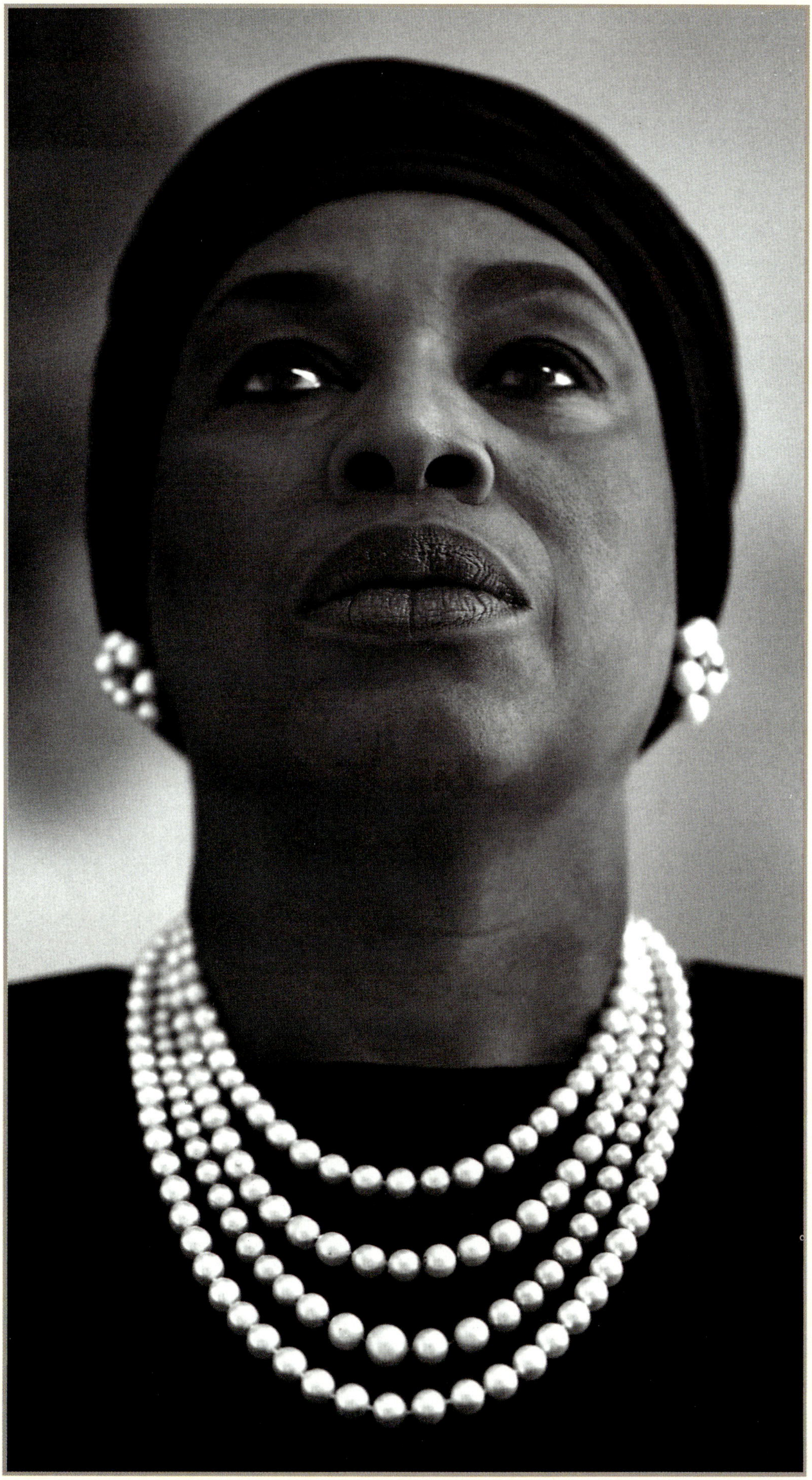

ULF SK

5 East 16th Street, New
Represented by K
Print a

SBERGH

Y 10003 · 212 255 7536
nn · 212 944 2853
vision

411

Randy Travis for *Warner Bros. Records Inc.*

Archie Moore for *Sports Illustrated*

Australians for *National Geographic*

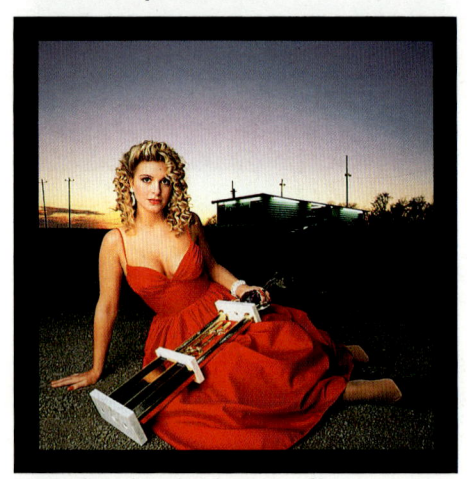

Miss Devil's Bowl Speedway for *Texas Monthly*

Hal Riney for *Esquire*

Willie Nelson for *National Geographic*

MICHAEL O'BRIEN

P·H·O·T·O·G·R·A·P·H·E·R

41 EASTERN PARKWAY, BROOKLYN, NY 11238
718-398-2235

NELEMAN

NEW YORK

HANS NELEMAN
STUDIO

LONDON

HAMILTONS
PHOTOGRAPHERS LTD.

PAUL BEVAN
212.645.5832

FIONA COWAN
071.259.2106

ERIC MEOLA

535 GREENWICH STREET NYC 10013 212-255-5150
REPRESENTED BY STOCKLAND MARTEL 212-727-1400

417

HASHI

212 • 675 • 6902   Fax 212 • 633 • 0163

Represented by

Stockland   Martel

212 • 727 • 1400   Fax 212 • 727 • 9459

419

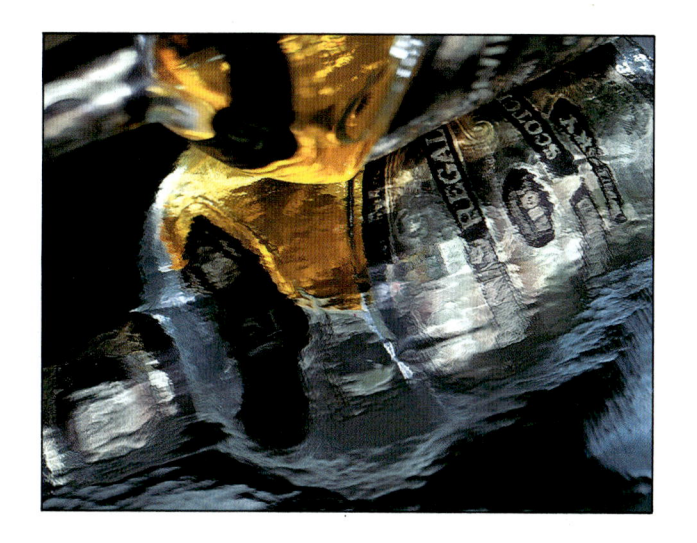

JOEL BALDWIN

REPRESENTED BY STOCKLAND MARTEL
5 UNION SQUARE WEST, NEW YORK, NY 10003
TELEPHONE: 212·727·1400 ~ FAX: 212·727·9459

Kronenbourg
Corning
Michelob
Meridian Hotels
Amtrak
Fuji Film
American Express
Lorillard
L'Oreal
ABC
Irving Trust
Kodak
Chevrolet
Johnnie Walker
Coca-Cola
Nikon
Pepsi
Anheuser Busch
Sanyo
Procter & Gamble
Lever Brothers
Maxwell House
JC Penny
Bank Of America
Warner Lambert
Eastern Airlines
Spiegel
Coors
Bacardi
Dewars
U.S. Trust
Seagrams
Adidas
General Foods
Colombian Coffee
Budget Rent-A-Car
N.Y. Telephone
AT&T
Johnson & Johnson
Paco Rabanne
Sheraton Hotels
Canon
Gucci
Freddie Mac
Citibank
Hyatt Hotels
Morgan Bank
Concord Watches
Manufacturers Hanover
American Airlines
Visa
Hallmark
Martex
Delta Airlines
Bristol Meyers
Cheseborough Ponds
Milton Bradley
Commodore

© JOEL BALDWIN 1991

New York:

Stockland Martel, Inc.

212 727 1400

Chicago:

Bill Rabin & Associates

312 944 6655

San Francisco

415 543 8153

Fax 415 543 8244

Film reel available

COLOR SEPARATIONS: BALZER/SHOPES, INC.

DESIGN: COURTNEY D. REESER

423

Bruce Wolf

136 West 21 Street

New York City

10011

212 633 6660

Facsimile

212 633 0484

Representation

Stockland Martel

212 727 1400

film reel available

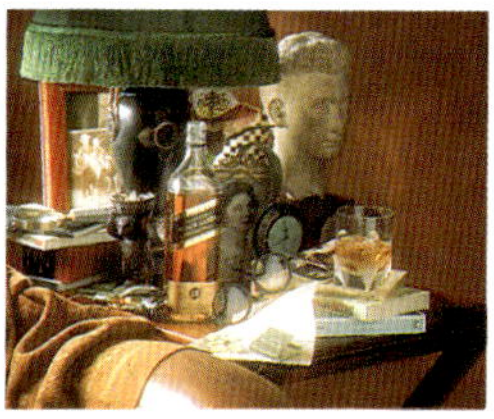

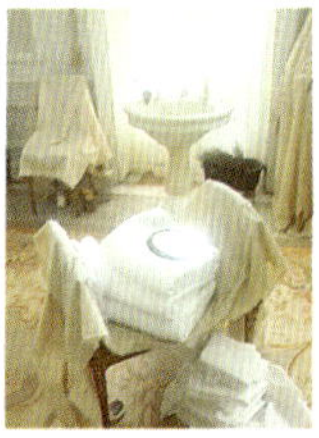

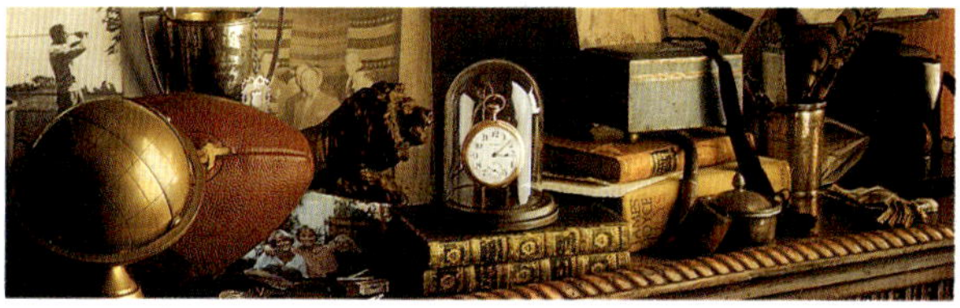

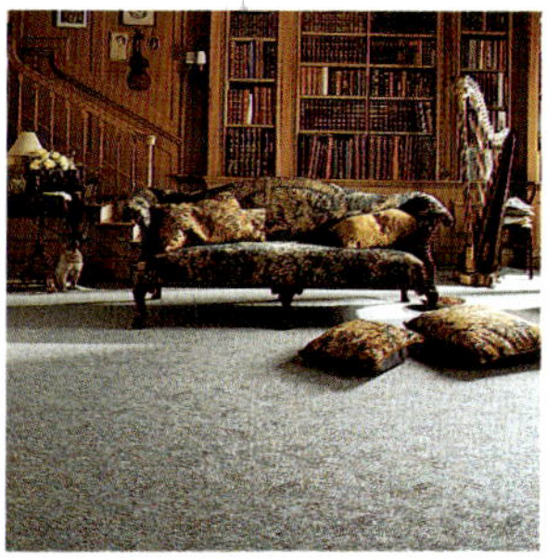

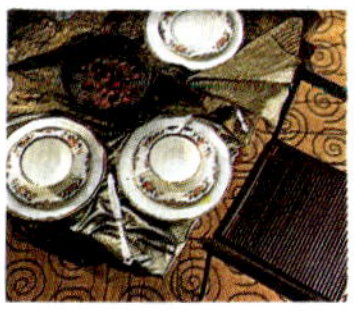

Walter Iooss

*Represented by
Stockland Martel
5 Union Square West
New York, NY 10003
Tel: 212.727.1400
Fax: 212.727.9459*

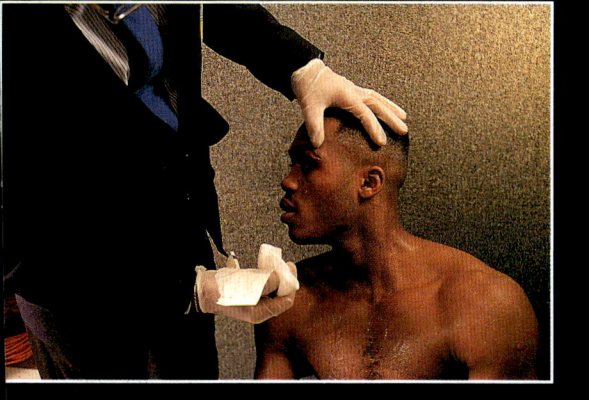

Film reel available

WALTER IOOSS JR. 1991

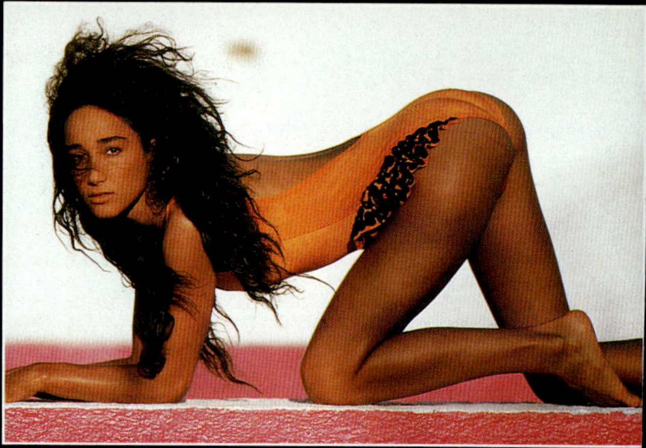

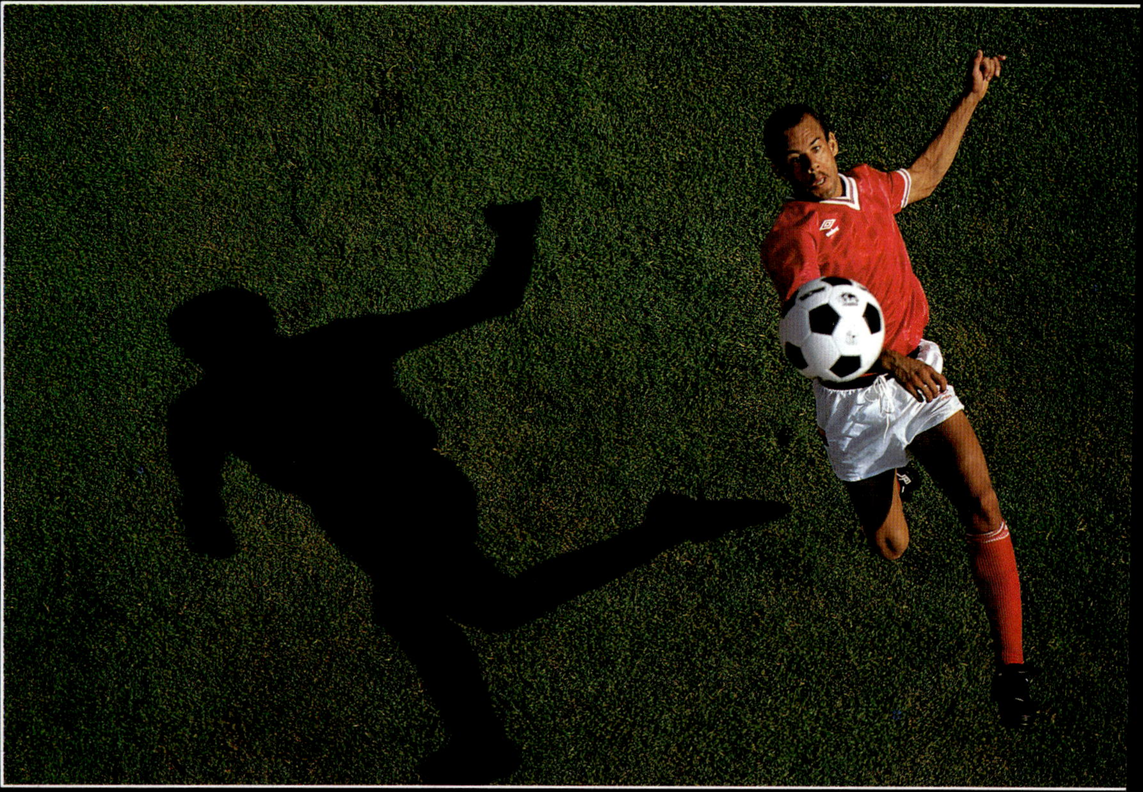

Walter Iooss

Represented by
Stockland Martel
5 Union Square West
New York, NY 10003
Tel: 212.727.1400
Fax: 212.727.9459

Film reel available

MENKEN STUDIOS
119 WEST 22 STREET
NEW YORK, N.Y. 10011
(212) 924-4240
(212) 463-7276 FAX

HOWARD

PHYLLIS GOODWIN•NEW YORK
(212) 570-6021
VICKI PETERSON•CHICAGO
(312) 467-0780
ELLA•BOSTON
(617) 266-3858

M E N K E N

C A R L

CARL ZAPP
IN ASSOCIATION WITH
MENKEN STUDIOS
119 WEST 22 STREET
NYC 10011
(212) 924-4240
(212) 463-7276 FAX

PHYLLIS GOODWIN
NEW YORK
(212) 570-6021

ELLA
BOSTON
(617) 266-3858

VICKI PETERSON
CHICAGO
(312) 467-0780

INGE METZGER
GERMANY
211/575053

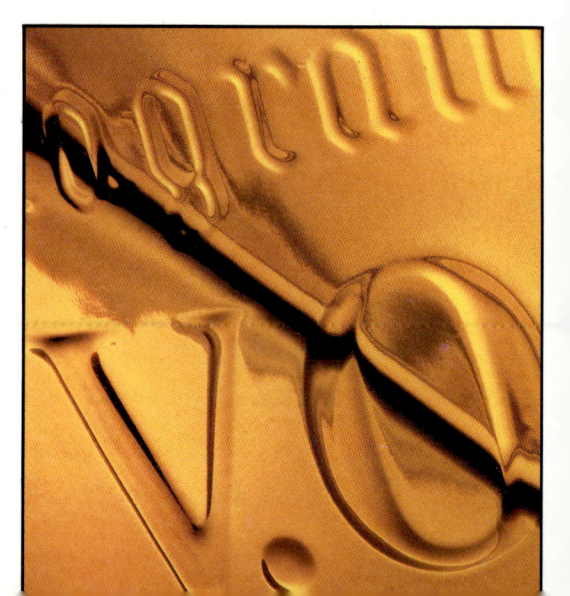

ZAPP

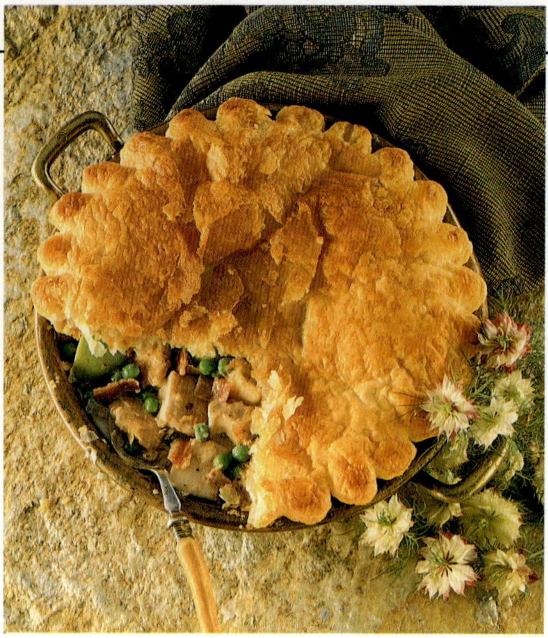

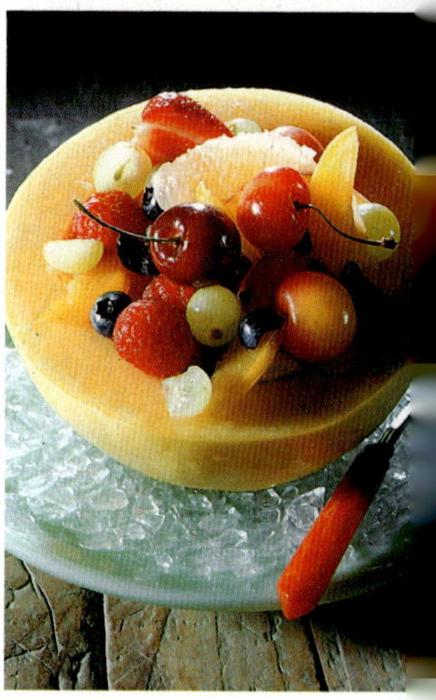

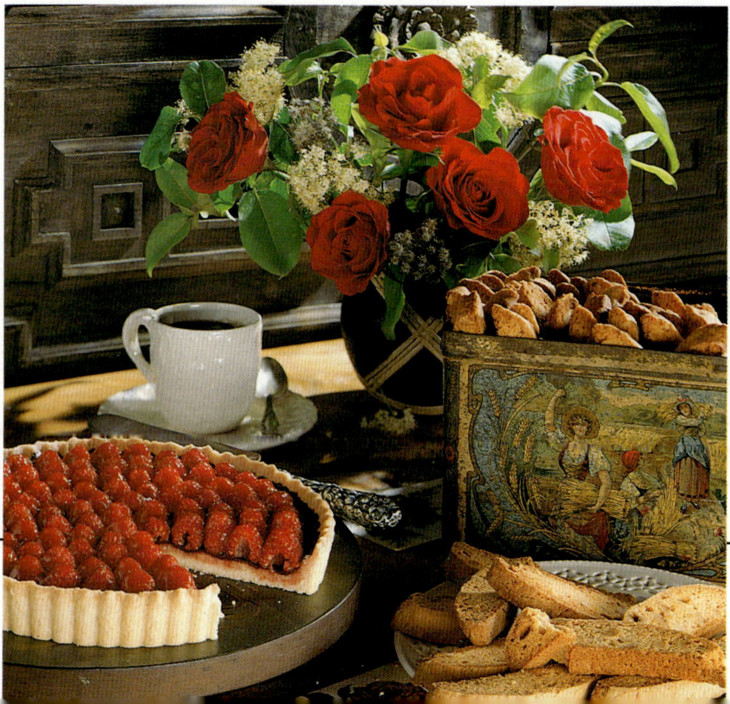

Judd

Pilossof

142 West 26th Street • New York City • (212) 989-8971
Represented by Judith Shepherd & Associates • (212) 242-6554 • Fax: (212) 242-6580

New York Times Magazine Cover, Sept. 15

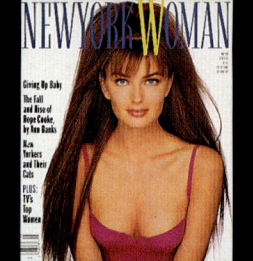

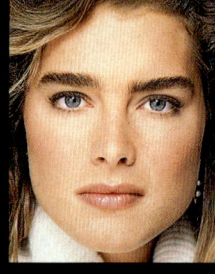

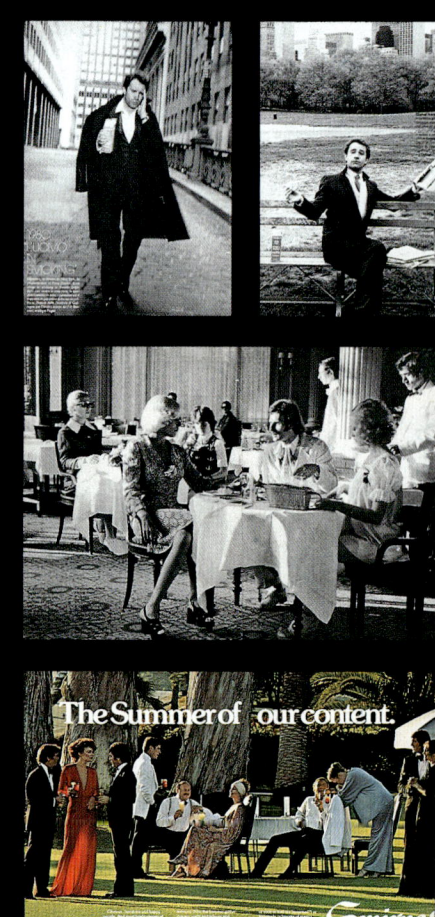

JACQUES MALIGNON

JACQUES MALIGNON

JM Studio 34 West 28th Street, New York, N.Y. 10001 (212) 532-7727 Fax (212) 481-8549

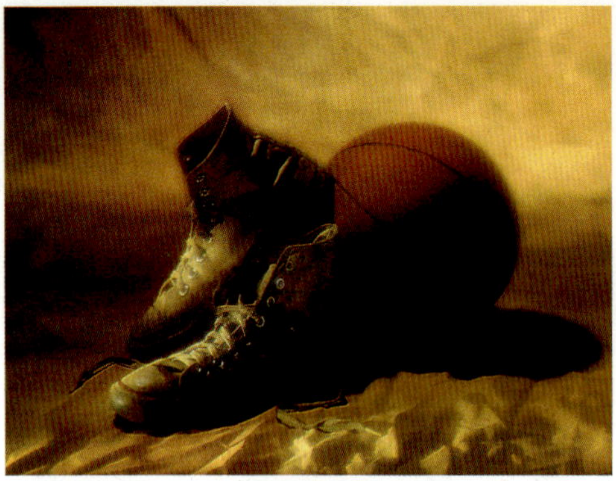
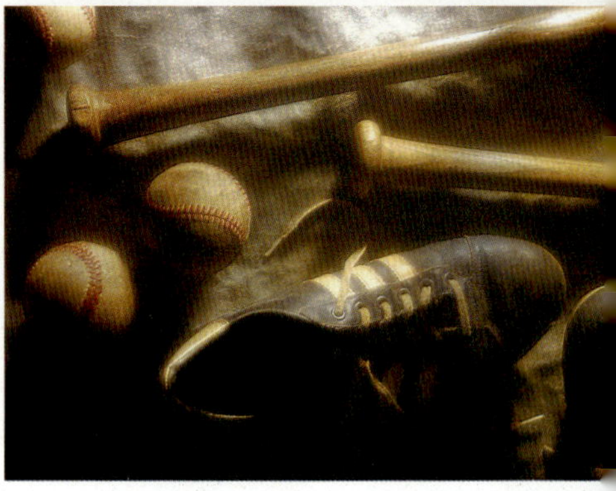
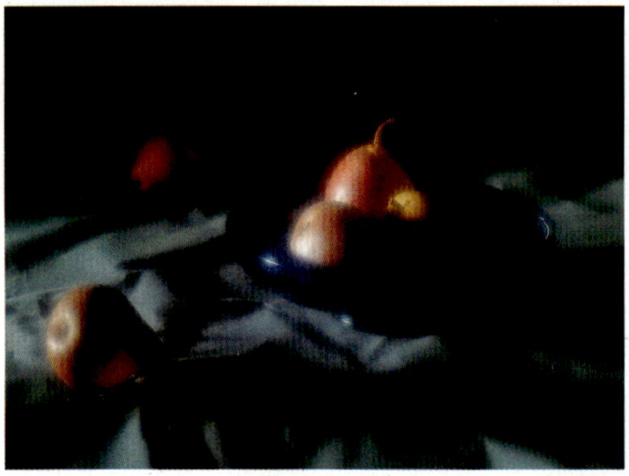
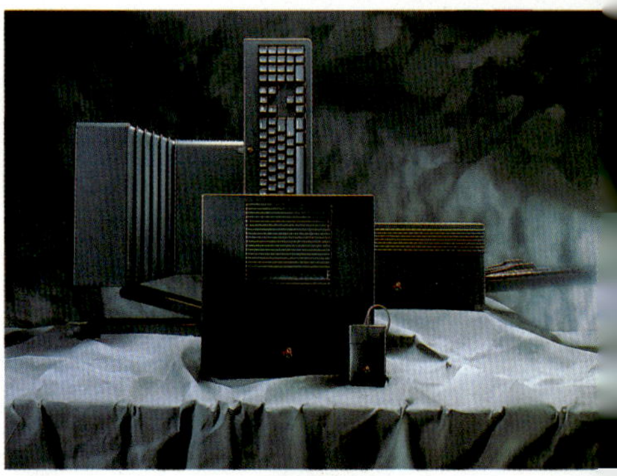
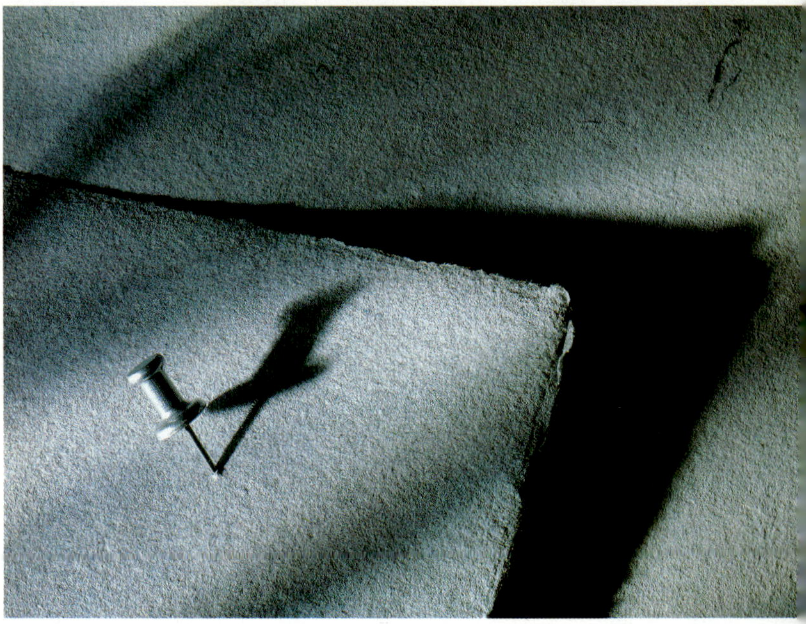

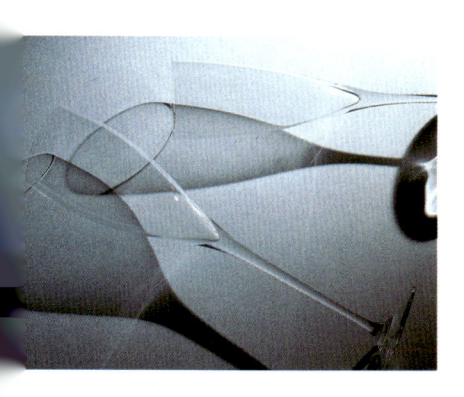

Dennis Blachut
Represented By Doug Brown
(212) 953-0088

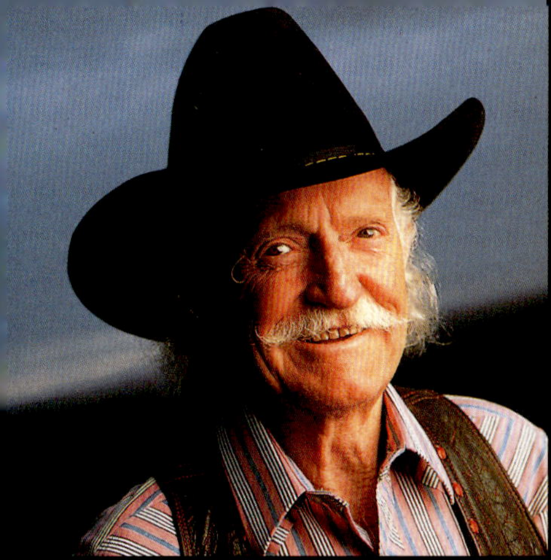
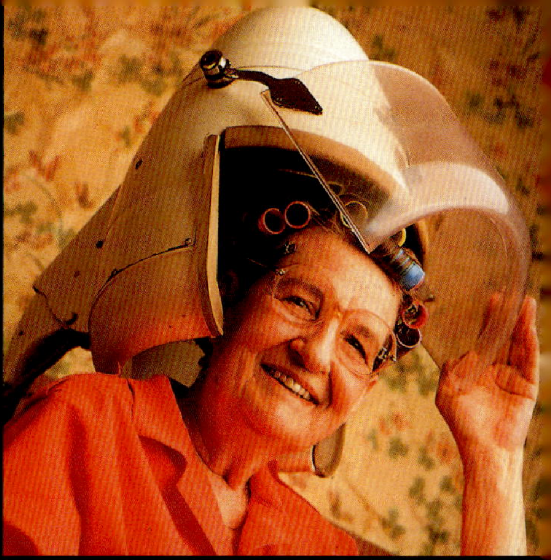
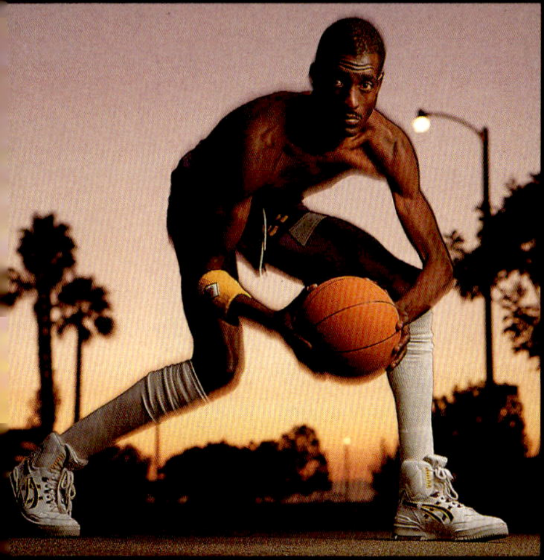
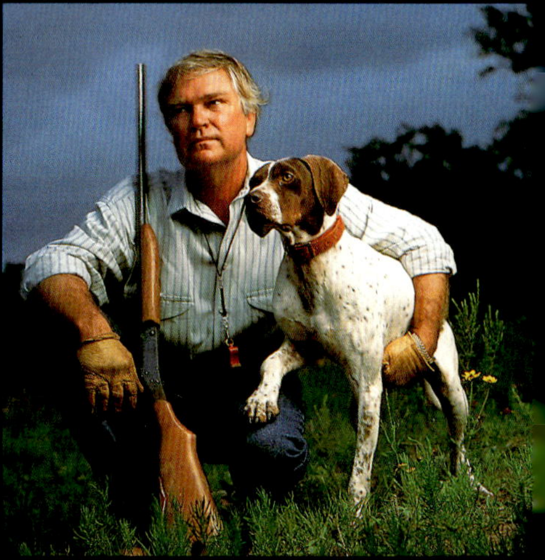
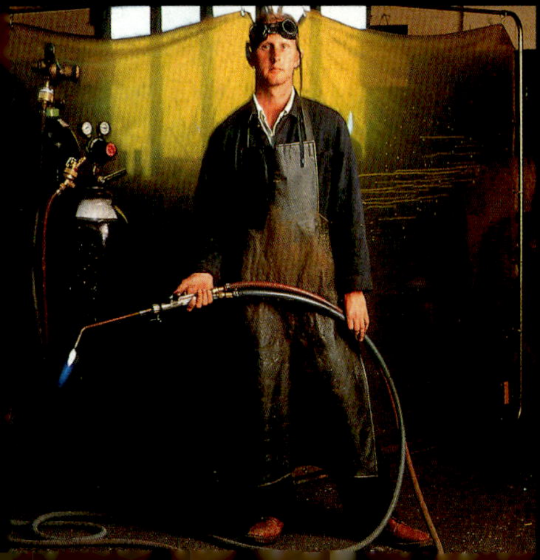
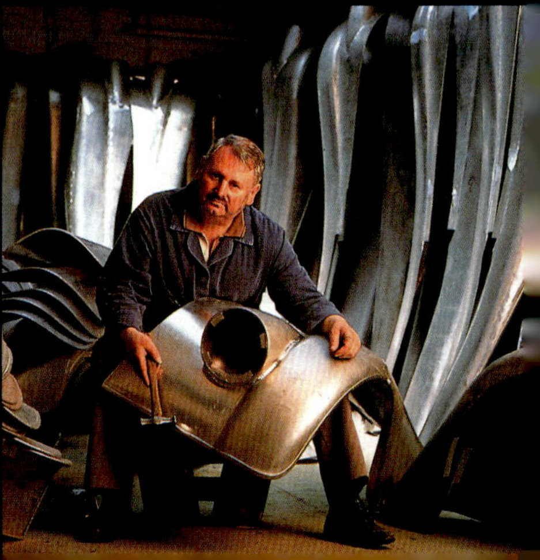

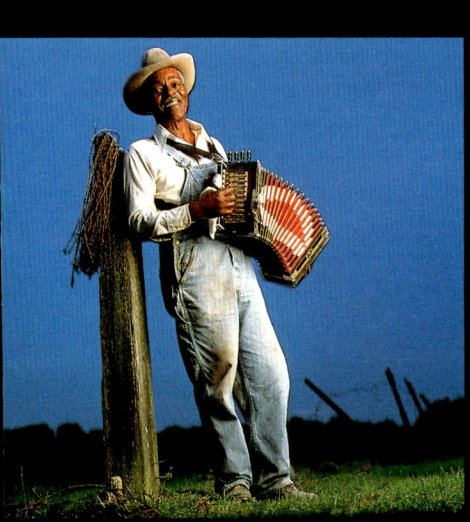

© LEE CRUM
REPRESENTED BY DOUG BROWN
(212) 953-0088
STUDIO (504) 529-2156

JODY DOLE • REPRESENTED B

DOUG BROWN • 212-953-0088

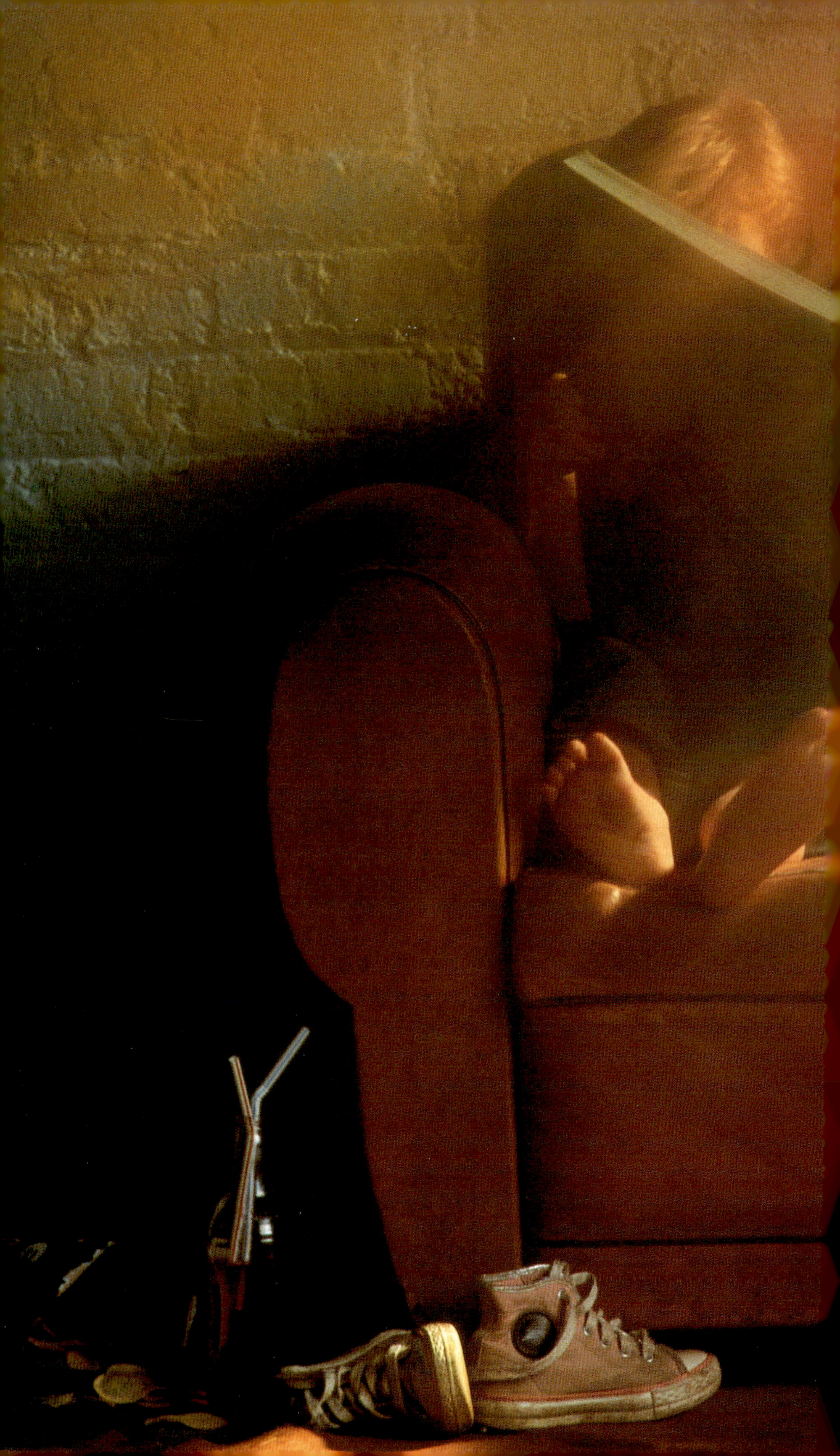

Abe Seltzer Represented By Doug Brown (212) 953-0088. Studio (212) 807-0660.

445

Stephen Wilkes

48 East 13th Street, New York, NY 10003
Phone 212·475·4010

TIME WARNER

Represented by
Janice Moses

Assignments for both advertising
and corporate photography.

TIME WARNER

All Photos © Stephen Wilkes 1990

447

Stephen Wilkes

48 East 13th Street, New York, NY 10003
Phone 212·475·4010

ESTÉE LAUDER

AMTRAK

Represented by
Janice Moses

Assignments for both advertising
and corporate photography.

NIKE

ESTÉE LAUDER

NIKE

All Photos © Stephen Wilkes 1990

449

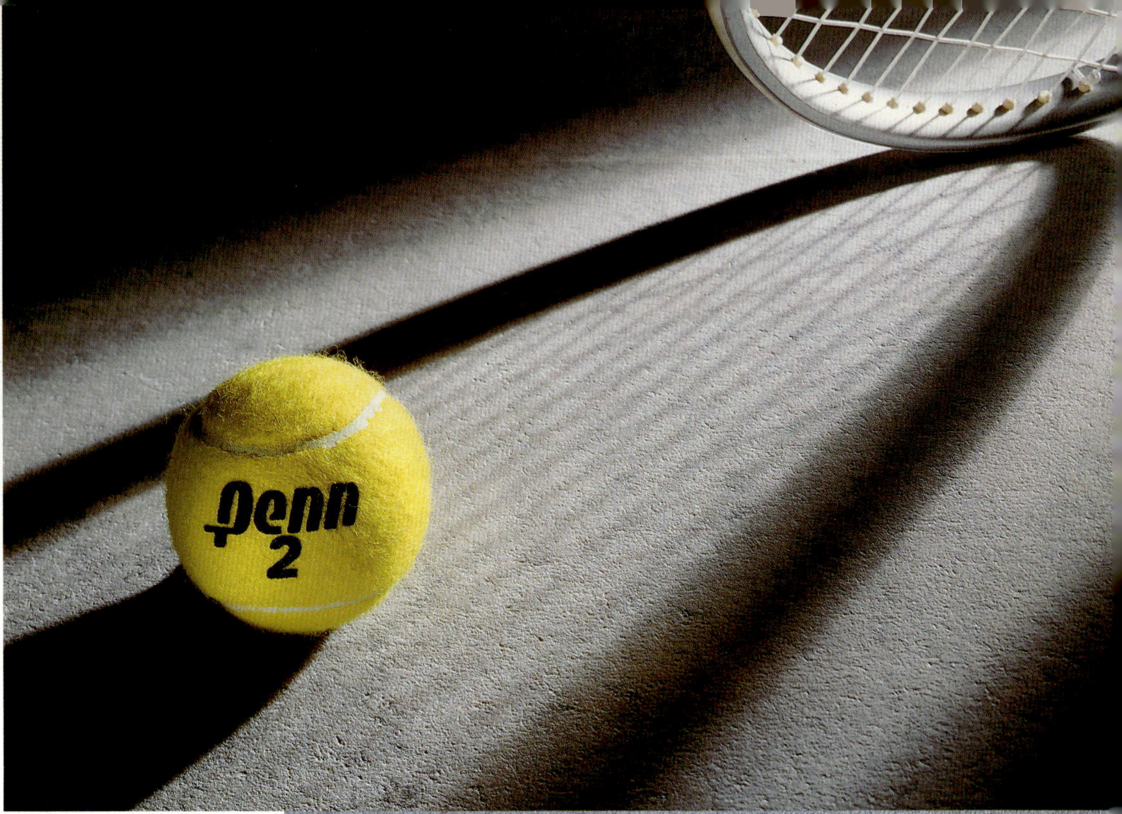
Penn
2

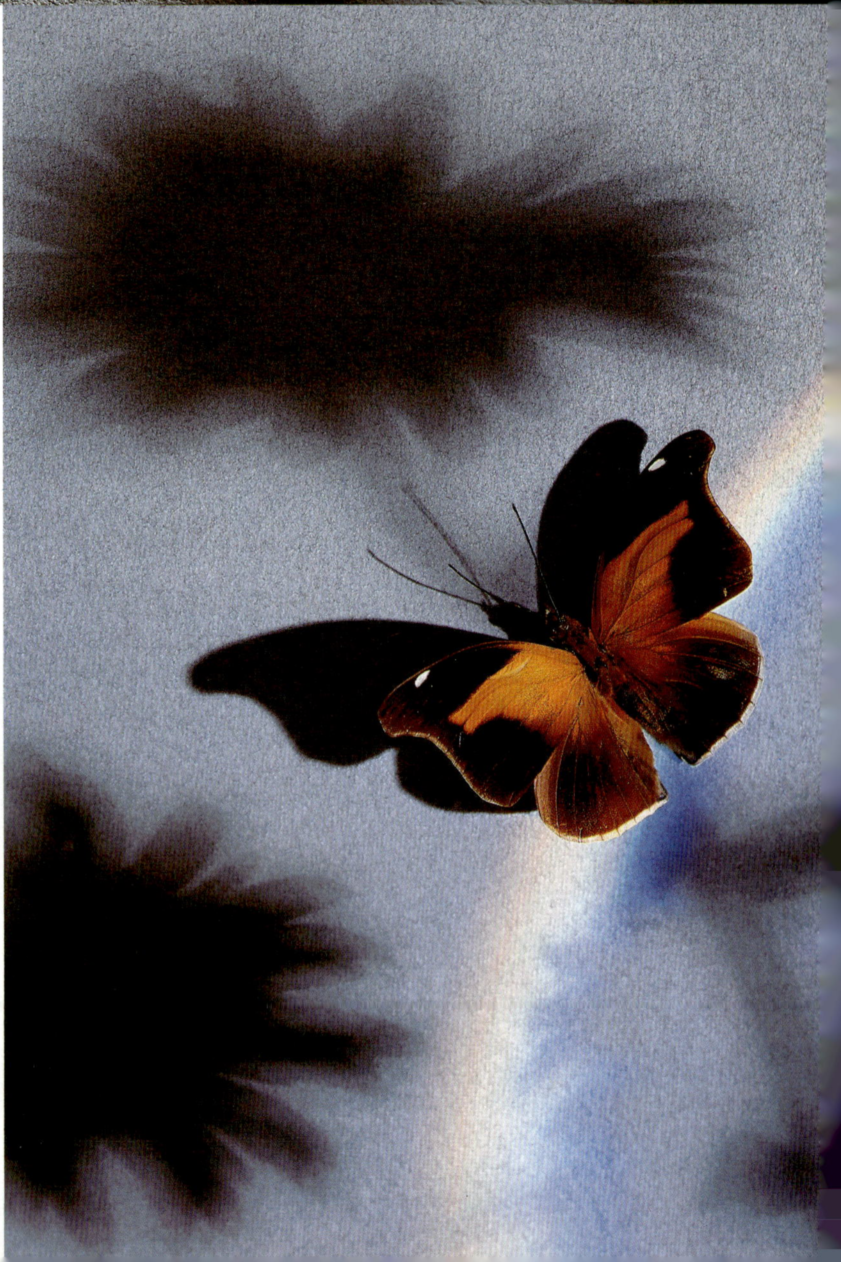

P

MICHAEL PRUZAN
1181 BROADWAY
NEW YORK CITY
NEW YORK 10001
212 686-5505
FAX 779-3688

**REPRESENTED BY
JANICE MOSES**
212 779-7929

**MIDWEST
PHOTOGRAPHY**

Listings 454
Ads 469

ILLINOIS
INDIANA
IOWA
KANSAS
MICHIGAN
MINNESOTA
MISSOURI
NEBRASKA
NORTH DAKOTA
OHIO
SOUTH DAKOTA
WISCONSIN

MIDWEST
PHOTOGRAPHY

AGS&R Communication/314 W. Superior, Chicago . . . . (312) 649-4500
AGS&R Communications/1835 S. Calhoun, Ft. Wayne . . . . (219) 744-4255
Abramson, Michael L./3312 W. Belle Plaine, Chicago . . . . (312) 267-9189
Accents Studios/611 N. State, Chicago . . . . (312) 664-1311
Adams Group, The, Inc./703 E. 30th St., Indpls. . . . . (317) 924-2400
Adams, Janet L./1199 Franklin Ave., Columbus . . . . (614) 252-7922
Adams, Steve/3101 S. Hanley Rd., St. Louis . . . . (314) 781-6667
Adcock, Gary/70 W. Huron, Chicago . . . . (312) 943-6917
Advertising Photography & Art/1921 S. 17th St., Lincoln . . . . (402) 476-9864
Albright Photography/23395 Middlebelt, Farmington Hills . . . . (313) 473-2556
Alderson, John/3806 N. Kenmore, Chicago . . . . (312) 281-2228
Alexander, Mark/Cincinnati/(513) 651-5020 . . . . **page 507**
Allan-Knox Studios/450 S. 92nd St., Milwaukee . . . . (414) 774-7900
Allen, Carter/8081 Zionsville Rd., Indpls. . . . . (317) 872-7220
Altman, Ben/Chicago . . . . (312) 404-0133
Altman, David Photograpy, Inc/400 N. Broadway, Milwaukee . . . . (414) 224-9735
Altman, Elizabeth Assoc./Chicago/(312) 935-9007 . . . . **pages 192-193**
Amberlight Photography/5040 Antioch, Shawnee . . . . (816) 471-1201
Ambrosi & Assoc./1100 W. Washington Blvd., Chicago . . . . (312) 666-9200
Amenta, Joseph/555 W. Madison,, Chicago . . . . (708) 248-2488
Anderson, Kevin/404 N. New Jersey, Indpls. . . . . (317) 632-9405
Anderson, Rob Photo./900 W. Jackson, Chicago . . . . (312) 942-0551
Anderson, Whit/650 W. Lake St., Chicago . . . . (312) 993-7644
Andre, Bruce Photography, Inc./Chicago . . . . (312) 661-1060
Andrews, Bruce/1546 N. Orleans, Chicago . . . . (312) 642-8715
Anton, Jerry/Chicago . . . . (312) 606-0633
Apex Photographic/7001 Orchard Lake Rd., W. Bloomfield . . . . (313) 737-2460
Apolinski, John/735 N. Oriole Ave., Park Ridge . . . . (312) 696-3156
Apple Studio, Ltd./2301 W. Nordale Dr., Appleton . . . . (414) 733-9001
Arciero, Anthony Photography Street/19745 Purlingbrook, Livonia . . . . . . (313) 477-9944
Arello, Frank/35 S. Van Brunt St., Englewood . . . . (201) 894-5120
Armour, Tony Photography/1726 N. Clybourn, Chicago . . . . (312) 733-7338
Arndt, David MacTavish/4620 N. Winchester, Chicago . . . . (312) 334-2841
Arndt, Jim/Mpls./(612) 332-5050 . . . . **pages 496-497**
Arsenault, Bill/1105 W. Chicago Ave., Chicago . . . . (312) 421-2525
Ascherman, Herbert Jr./1846 Coventry Rd., Cleveland Hts. . . . . (216) 321-0055
Atevich, Alex/325 N. Hoyne Ave., Chicago . . . . (312) 942-1453
Atkinson Image/St.Louis/(314) 535-6484 . . . . **page 520**
Atols, Mary/Chicago/(312) 222-0504 . . . . **pages 480-483**
Baartman, Doug/311 N. Des Plaines, Chicago . . . . (312) 337-2101
Bachnick Photography Inc./650 Taft St. N.E., Mpls. (612) 623-0406
Baer, Gordon/18 E. Fourth St., Cincinnati . . . . (513) 381-4466
Bafile, Patrick/5955 E. 14 Mile Rd., Sterling Heights . . . . (313) 795-8370
Bahm, Bob/4191 Pearl Rd., Cleveland . . . . (216) 398-1338
Balterman, Lee/910 Lake Shore Dr., Chicago . . . . (312) 642-9040
Baltz, Bill/3615 Superior Ave., Cleveland . . . . (216) 431-0979
Banner & Burns, Inc./153 W. Ohio, Chicago . . . . (312) 644-4770
Bannister, Will/849 W. Lill, Chicago . . . . (312) 327-2143
Barasa, Mary Ann/Chicago/(312) 464-7815 . . . . **pages 470-471**
Barnett, Jim/5580 N. Dequincy, Indpls. . . . . (317) 257-7177
Barrett, Bob/3733 Pennsylvania, Kansas City . . . . (816) 753-3208
Bart Harris Photography, Inc./70 W. Hubbard St., Chicago . . . . (312) 751-2977
Bartels, Ceci Assocs./Chicago/(312) 786-1560 . . . . **pages 526-529**
Bartels, Ceci Assocs./St. Louis/(314) 241-4014 . . . . **pages 526-529**
Bartz, Carl/1307 Washington Ave., St. Louis . . . . (314) 231-8690
Basdeka, Peter/1254 N. Wells, Chicago . . . . (312) 944-3333
Bass Photo/308 S. New Jersey St., Indpls. . . . . (317) 632-4545
Battrell, Mark/1611 N. Sheffield, Chicago . . . . (312) 642-6650
Bausman, David/5500 Feltl Rd., Minnetonka . . . . (612) 933-2042
Bayles, Dal/4431 N. 64th St., Milwaukee . . . . (414) 464-8917
Beach & Barnes/25 N. Fifth Ave., Maywood . . . . (312) 345-8340
Beasley Photography/126 N. Third St., Mpls. . . . . (612) 339-0991
Beasley, Michael/1210 W. Webster Ave., Chicago . . . . (312) 248-5769
Beaulieu, Allen/400 First Ave. N., Mpls. . . . . (612) 338-2327

Beck, Peter Photography/718 Washington Ave. N., Mpls. (612) 338-5712
Beck, Thom/N. 16 W. 22033 Jericho Dr., Waukesha . . . . (414) 549-4566
Beckett/Beckett Photography/117 S. Morgan St., Chicago . . . . (312) 733-6550
Bellville, Cheryl Walsh/2823 Eighth St. S., Mpls. . . . . (612) 333-5788
Belter Photography, Inc./640 N. La Salle St., Chicago . . . . (312) 337-7676
Bender & Bender Photography/281 Klingel Rd., Waldo . . . . (614) 726-2470
Bender/Luce Studio/1547 St. Clair Ave., Cleveland . . . . (216) 781-1547
Benkert, Christine/27 N. Fourth St., Mpls. . . . . (612) 340-9503
Benoit, Bill/1708½ Washington Ave., Wilmette . . . . (708) 251-7634
Bentley, David/208 W. Kinzie, Chicago . . . . (312) 836-0242
Bentley, Gary/1611 N. Sheffield, Chicago . . . . (312) 642-6650
Berg, Ron/Kansas City . . . . (816) 471-5488
Berglund, Peter/718 Washington Ave. N., Mpls. . . . . (612) 371-9318
Berlin/Chicago Photography/708 W. School St., Chicago . . . . (312) 327-2266
Berr, Keith/1220 W. Sixth St., Cleveland . . . . (216) 566-7950
Better Be Bass/824 N. Racine, Chicago . . . . (312) 666-6111
Bevacqua, Alberto/3012 S. Archer, Chicago . . . . (312) 247-4773
Bewsey, Austin Studios, Inc./675 Wilmer Ave., Cincinnati . . . . (513) 871-8660
Bidak, Lorne/827 N. Milwaukee, Chicago . . . . (312) 733-3997
Bieber, Tim/Chicago/(312) 463-3590 . . . . **pages 472-473**
Big Deahl Photography/443 N. Clark, Chicago . . . . (312) 644-3187
Bilisko, Norm/314 W. Institute Pl., Chicago . . . . (312) 280-1909
Bishop Photographics/5200 Prospect Ave., Cleveland . . . . (216) 881-6565
Bishop, G. Robert/5622 Delmar, St. Louis . . . . (314) 367-8787
Bjornson, Howard, Inc./300 N. Ashland Ave., Chicago . . . . (312) 243-8200
Blair, John/1019 Bellemeede Ave., Evansville . . . . (812) 464-5663
Block, Ernie Studio, Inc./1138 Cambridge Cir. Dr., Kansas City . . . . (913) 321-3080
Block, Stuart/1242 W. Washington Blvd., Chicago . . . . (312) 733-3600
Blue Sky Pictures, Inc./1237 Chicago Rd., Troy . . . . (313) 583-2828
Bock, Edward/400 N. First Ave., Mpls. . . . . (612) 332-8504
Bojarski, Jerome S./535 N. 27th St., Milwaukee . . . . (414) 342-6363
Bonnen, Edwin/444 Lentz Ct., Lansing . . . . (517) 371-3086
Boschke, Les/1839 W. Fulton St., Chicago . . . . (312) 666-8819
Bosek, George/1301 S. Wabash Ave., Chicago . . . . (312) 939-0777
Bosy, Peter/120 N. Green, Chicago . . . . (312) 243-9220
Boulevard Photographic, Inc./591 Executive Dr., Troy . . . . (313) 868-2200
Braddy, Jim/Chicago . . . . (312) 337-5664
Bradley Photographics/329 10th Ave. S.E., Cedar Rapids . . . . (319) 365-5071
Brahm, Timothy J./522 W. Eugenie, Chicago . . . . (312) 943-8616
Brandenburg, Jim/708 N. First St., Mpls. . . . . (612) 341-0166
Brandt & Assoc., Ltd./Barrington Hills . . . . (708) 428-6363
Braun Photography/1245 S. Cleveland-Massillon Rd., Akron . . . . (216) 666-4540
Brayne, T.W./326 W. Kalamazoo Ave., Kalamazoo . . . . (616) 344-0283
Bretheim, Mark/5429 Woodcrest Dr., Edina . . . . (612) 927-8062
Brimacombe, Gerald/7112 Mark Ter. Dr., Edina . . . . (612) 941-5860
Brodersen, Fred Photography, Inc./935 W. Chestnut, Chicago . . . . (312) 226-0622
Brooke Lemburg Photography, Inc./6515-17 N. Sheridan Rd., Peoria . . . . (309) 691-8133
Brooks & Assocs./855 W. Blackhawk, Chicago . . . . (312) 642-3208
Brooks, Joseph/1800 N. Wolcott, Chicago . . . . (312) 227-5641
Brown, James F./1349 E. McMillan St., Cincinnati . . . . (513) 221-1144
Brown, Ron/1546 S. First St., Lincoln . . . . (402) 476-1760
Brown, Steve/107 W. Hubbard, Chicago . . . . (312) 467-4666
Browne, Warren Photography/1012 W. Randolph, Chicago . . . . (312) 733-8134
Brus, David/420 N. Fifth St., Mpls. . . . . (612) 338-2041
Bruton, Jon/3842 W. Pine Blvd., St. Louis . . . . (314) 533-6665
Bullicant, Robert/935 W. Chestnut, Chicago . . . . (312) 738-3757
Bundt, Nancy/1908 Kenwood Pky., Mpls. . . . . (612) 377-7773
Burd, Paul E./300 E. Hydraulic, Yorkville . . . . (708) 553-7510
Burkat, Stan/3910 W. Wrightwood, Chicago . . . . (312) 278-3072
Burlingham, William/1506 Dempster Ave., Evanston . . . . (708) 864-9027
Burns, Harold Photography, Inc./2333 St. Clair Ave., Cleveland . . . . (216) 566-0004
Burris, Zachary/407 N. Elizabeth, Chicago . . . . (312) 666-0315
Bush, Tim/360 W. Erie, Chicago . . . . (312) 337-0414
CR Studio/1101 Auburn, Cleveland . . . . (216) 861-5360
Cable, Gary/9201 E. Bloomington Fwy., Richfield . . . . (612) 888-6642
Cable, Wayne Studios/401 W. Superior, Chicago . . . . (312) 951-1799
Cain, C.C./420 N. Clark St., Chicago . . . . (312) 644-2371
Callahan, Lawrence/600 Washington Ave. N., Mpls. . . . . (612) 333-0133
Camlen Studios/300 N. State St., Brookfield . . . . (414) 781-9477
Campbell, Bob/722 Prestige St., Joliet . . . . (815) 725-1862
Carlson, Bill/2750 Bryant Ave. S., Mpls. . . . . (612) 827-7132
Carney, Joann/401 N. Racine, Chicago . . . . (312) 829-2332
Carosella, Tony/4138A Wyoming, St. Louis . . . . (314) 664-3462

MIDWEST

Casalini, Tom/Zionsville	(305) 666-1266
Cascarano, John/657 W. Ohio, Chicago	(312) 733-1212
Casemore/Damon Productions/Detroit/(313) 645-0741	**pages 616-617**
Caswell Photography/700 Washington Ave. N., Mpls.	(612) 332-2729
Center for Communications, Inc./954 Springer Dr., Lombard	(708) 620-8886
Chadwick, Taber/617 W. Fulton St., Chicago	(312) 454-0855
Chambers, Tom/153 W. Ohio, Chicago	(312) 828-9488
Chapman, Cam/126 W. Kinzie, Chicago	(312) 222-9242
Chapman, John S./900 Elmwood Ave., Wilmette	(708) 251-7080
Chare, Dave Photography/1045 N. Northwest Hwy., Park Ridge	(708) 696-3188
Charlie Company, Inc./Cleveland	(216) 566-7464
Chauncey, Paul, Inc./388 N. Hydraulic, Wichita	(316) 262-6733
Chicago Photographers/430 W. Erie St., Chicago	(312) 944-4828
Chobot, Dennis J./2857 E. Grand Blvd., Detroit	(313) 875-6617
Christian Studios, Inc./5408 N. Main St., Dayton	(513) 275-3775
Clarke, Jim/3721 Grandel Sq., St. Louis	(314) 652-6262
Clay, Willard/2976 E. 12th Rd., Ottawa	(815) 433-1472
Clayton, Curt/2655 Guoin, Detroit	(313) 567-3897
Coats & Assocs./2928 Fifth Ave. S., Mpls.	(612) 827-4676
Cockerill, J.M./1636 Chase Ave., Cincinnati	(573) 541-1200
Cocose Studios/445 E. Ohio, Chicago	(312) 527-9444
Coha, Dan/Nine W. Hubbard, Chicago	(312) 664-2270
Coil, Ron/15 W. Hubbard, Chicago	(312) 321-9021
Coit, Ken/1531 Grand, Kansas City	(816) 421-4755
Color Tex/7330 W. Fernwood Cir., Milwaukee	(414) 321-8979
Colorscreen, Inc./619 S. 70th St, Milwaukee	(414) 475-0580
Comess, Herb/540 Custer, Evanston	(708) 864-2456
Communi-Graphics, Inc./2483 N. Bartlett Ave., Milwaukee	(414) 962-6953
Conison, Joel/3201 Eastern, Cincinatti	(513) 241-1887
Copeland, Burns W./6651 N. Artesian, Chicago	(312) 465-3240
Coppock, Ron/Chicago	(312) 664-1824
Corporate Concepts/1300 N. Pennsylvania, Indpls.	(317) 635-2900
Corporate PhotoGroup/920 Race St., Cincinnati	(513) 241-8273
Cowan, Pat L./604 Division, Valparaiso	(219) 462-0199
Cowan, Ralph, Inc./604 Division Rd., Valparaiso	(219) 462-0199
Cox, D.E./22111 Cleveland, Dearborn	(313) 561-1842
Crofoot Photography/6140 Wayzata Blvd., Mpls.	(612) 546-0643
Crofton, Bill Photography, Inc./326-R Linden Ave., Wilmette	(708) 256-7862
Crosby Studio/1083 10th Ave. S.E., Mpls.	(612) 378-9566
Crowther Photography, Inc./1108 Kenilworth Ave., Cleveland	(216) 566-8066
Culbert-Aguilar, Kathleen/1338 W. Carmen, Chicago	(312) 561-1266
Curran, John/10835 Midwest Indust. Blvd., St. Louis	(800) 772-3330
Curtis, Lucky/1540 N. North Park Ave., Chicago	(312) 787-4422
Custom Photography, Inc./116 W. Sixth St., Cincinnati	(513) 381-7097
D'Orio, Tony/Chicago/(312) 421-5532	**pages 516-517**
D.J. Photography, Ltd./Northbrook	(708) 480-9336
DGM Studios/70 E. Long Lake Rd., Bloomfield Hills	(313) 645-2222
Dale, Darwin/2910 S. Deerfield Ave., Lansing	(517) 882-8149
Dale, Larry/7015 Wing Lake Rd., Birmingham	(313) 851-3296
Damien, Paul/180 N. 69th St., Milwaukee	(414) 259-1987
Danek, Ernie/1908 Grande Ave. S.E., Ceder Rapids	(319) 366-3816
Davis, Todd/St. Louis	(314) 533-6665
Davito, Dennis/638 Huntley Hts., Manchester	(314) 394-0660
Dayton Commercial Studio/5009 Nebraska Dr., Dayton	(513) 233-1070
Dayton Photographics/W. Carrollton	(513) 859-0180
De Marco Photographers/3152 N. Osceola, Chicago	(312) 622-8490
DeForest, Don Assoc./300 W. Lake St., Elmhurst	(312) 834-7200
Debacker, Michael/231 Ohio, Wichita	(316) 265-2776
Debolt, Dale/120 W. Kinzie St., Chicago	(312) 644-6264
Del Rey Communications/Chicago	(708) 655-0020
Denatale, Joe/2129 W. North Ave., Chicago	(312) 489-0089
Design Photography, Inc./1324 Hamilton Ave., Cleveland	(216) 687-0099
Detroit Photographic, Inc./1739 Coolidge, Berkley	(313) 543-5610
Deutch, Stephen Photography/525 Hawthorne Pl., Chicago	(312) 525-6723
Dickinson & Assoc./213 W. Institute Pl., Chicago	(312) 337-0453
Dieringer, Rick Photography/19 W. Court St., Cincinnati	(513) 621-2544
Ditlove, Michel Inc./18 W. Hubbard, Chicago	(312) 644-5233
Dooley, Mr. Studio, Ltd./212 Water St., Janesville	(608) 752-9201
Dorman, Paul/70 E. Long Lake Rd., Bloomfield Hills	(313) 645-2222
Doyle Studios/1550 E. Nine Mile Rd., Ferndale	(313) 543-9440
Drew, Terry/452 N. Morgan 2E, Chicago	(312) 829-1630
Dreyfus, Dan/2101 Locust St., St. Louis	(314) 436-1988
Drickey, Patrick/1412 Howard St., Omaha	(402) 344-3786

DuBroff, Don/Chicago	(312) 944-1434
Dublin, Rick/Mpls./(612) 332-8864	**page 505**
ETM Studios, Inc./9201 King St., Franklin Park	(708) 671-5150
Eagle, Lin/1725 W. N. Ave., Chicago	(312) 276-0707
Ebel Productions, Inc./1376 W. Carroll, Chicago	(312) 222-1123
Eckhard Photography, Inc./1306 S. 18th St., St. Louis	(314) 241-1116
Edmunds, Douglas/221 Division St., Madison	(608) 249-8448
Einhorn Photography/311 N. Desplaines St., Chicago	(312) 559-0401
Eisner, Scott/1456 N. Dayton, Chicago	(312) 642-2217
Eklof, Rolf/32588 Dequindre Rd., Warren	(313) 978-7373
Elden, David/253 Third Ave., Mpls.	(612) 332-7067
Eliasen, Steve /Image Studios/Appleton	(414) 739-7824
Elledge, Paul/Chicago/(312) 733-8021	**pages 474-475**
Emery Photography/222 S. Morgan, Chicago	(312) 226-2852
Engelhard, J. Verser/1278 N. Milwaukee, Chicago	(312) 235-4596
Engstrom, John/618 Washington Ave. N., Mpls.	(612) 332-4055
Ernst, Elizabeth/1020 Elm, Winnetka	(708) 441-8993
Ervin, Robert/4322 S. 50th St., Omaha	(402) 731-6010
Evanston Photographic Studios, Inc./2002 Maple Ave., Evanston	(708) 475-8871
Ewert, Steve/17 N. Elizabeth, Chicago	(312) 733-5762
Eye Blink Studios/546 S. Meridian, Indpls.	(317) 636-6363
Fairman & Schmidt/303 E. Wacker, Chicago	(312) 938-1452
Farber, Gerald/4925 Cadieux, Detroit	(313) 371-4161
Farret, Stanley E./1513 Collinsdale, Cincinnati	(513) 231-9278
Farrow, Charles/3488 Edgerton St., Vadnais Hts.	(612) 484-5367
Fegley, Richard/6083 N. Kirkwood, Chicago	(312) 685-8179
Feldkamp-Malloy, Inc./180 N. Wabash, Chicago	(312) 263-0633
Feldman, Ken/Chicago/(312) 337-0447	**pages 52-53, 570-571**
Feldman, Stephen/2705 W. Agatite, Chicago	(312) 539-0300
Felice, Nick/529 S. 7th St., Mpls.	(612) 338-8083
Ferderbar Studios, Inc./2356 S. 102nd St., Milwaukee	(414) 545-7770
Ferderbar Studios, Inc./62 W. Huron St., Chicago	(312) 642-9296
Ferguson, Ken/400 N. May St., Chicago	(312) 829-2366
Ferguson, Scott/710 N. Tucker Blvd., St. Louis	(314) 647-7466
Fiat, Randi & Assocs./Chicago/(312) 664-8322/784-2343	**pages 204-205, 500-503, 642-643**
Fichter, Russ/925 W. Cullom, Chicago	(312) 327-6793
Ficken, Bray/2605 Park Ave., Cincinnati	(513) 751-3311
Finlay, Charles/141 E. Main St., Ashland	(419) 323-0551
Firak, Tom/1043 W. Grand Ave., Chicago	(312) 421-2255
Fischer, Robert/230 N Michigan Ave., Chicago	(312) 263-1004
Fish, Peter/1151 W. Adams, Chicago	(312) 829-0129
Flash's/21 S. Broadway, Red Lodge	(406) 446-1940
Fleming, Larry/1029 N. Wichita, Wichita	(316) 267-0780
Fletcher, T. Mike/7467 Kingsbury Blvd., St. Louis	(314) 721-2279
Flood, Kevin/St. Louis	(314) 647-2485
Floyd, Bill/404 N. May St., Chicago	(312) 243-1611
Ford Graham, Jamie/21 Salem Ln., Evanston	(312) 679-4252
Ford, Madison/Troy	(313) 280-0640
Foto-Graphics, Inc./2402 N. Shadeland, Indpls.	(317) 353-6259
Fowler, Carl -Design Photography/1324 Hamilton Ave., Cleveland	(216) 687-0099
Frantz, Ken/415 W. Huron, Chicago	(312) 951-1077
Fredericks, Keith/527 N. 27th St., Milwaukee	(414) 342-6363
French, Robert E./1080 E. Post Rd., Marion	(319) 373-1431
Frerck, Robert/4158 N. Greenview, Chicago	(312) 883-1965
Frick, Ken/66 Northmoor Pl., Columbus	(614) 263-9955
Friedland, Paula Studio, Inc./112 S. 11th St., Omaha	(402) 345-2028
Friedman, Susan J./400 N. May St., Chicago	(312) 733-0891
Fritz, Tom/2930 W. Clybourn, Milwaukee	(414) 344-8300
Futran, Eric/3454 N. Bell, Chicago	(312) 525-5020
G-Photographic/10750 W. 9 Mile Rd., Oak Park	(313) 398-8822
G.S.P. Productions/156 N. Jefferson, Chicago	(312) 944-3000
Gage, Rob/Troy	(313) 280-0640
Gairy, John/419 S. Third St., Mpls.	(612) 375-1734
Gale, Bill/3041 Aldrich Ave. S., Mpls.	(612) 827-5858
Gallery 4/Dayton	(513) 449-9007
Galvan Photography, Inc./650 W. Grand Ave., Elmhurst	(312) 832-4464
Gaymont, Gregory, Inc./1812 W. Hubbard St., Chicago	(312) 421-3146
Gerlach, Monte H./705 S. Scoville, Oak Park	(708) 848-1193
Gerrior, Robert H./920 Race St., Cincinnati	(513) 651-2300
Getsug, Don Studios/Chicago/(312) 939-1477	**pages 482-483**
Giannetti Studio/119 N. 4th St., Mpls.	(612) 339-3172
Gillette, Bill/2917 Eisenhower, Ames	(515) 294-0503
Gillis, Greg/952 W. Lake St., Chicago	(312) 733-2340

MIDWEST 457

Gilmore, Susan/8415 Wesley Dr., Mpls. . . . . (612) 545-4608
Gilo, Dave/Chicago . . . . (312) 664-1824
Gilroy, John/2407 W. Main St., Kalamazoo . . . . (616) 349-6805
Girard, Connie/316 Telford Ave., Dayton . . . . (513) 294-2095
Girard, Jennifer & Roger lewin/1455 W. Roscoe, Chicago . . . . (312) 929-3730
Glenn, Chris W./1 E. Scott, Chicago . . . . (312) 787-4459
Glenn, Eileen/Chicago/(312) 666-7300 . . . . **pages 512-513**
Glenn, Chris W./Chicago/(312) 787-4459 . . . . **pages 628-629**
Gluth Foto Team/173 E. Grand Ave., Fox Lake . . . . (800) 243-3080
Goddard, Will/St. Paul . . . . (612) 645-9516
Goff, D.R./66 W. Whittier St., Columbus . . . . (614) 443-6530
Goldstein, Steven/343 Copper Lakes Blvd., St. Louis . . . . (314) 227-8797
Gondelman, Jay/Chicago . . . . (312) 280-5134
Gordon, Al/400 N. May, Chicago . . . . (312) 421-2223
Gordon, James/Bowling Green . . . . (419) 352-8175
Gorton, D./6533 Gracely Dr., Cincinnati . . . . (513) 941-5482
Goss, Jim/1737 McGee St., Kansas City . . . . (816) 471-8069
Goss, Michael/2444 W. Chicago Ave., Chicago . . . . (312) 235-4800
Gould, Christopher/1517 N. Elston Ave., Chicago . . . . (312) 527-3283
Gould, Ronald/216 N. Clinton St., Chicago . . . . (312) 454-0157
Graham-Henry, Diane/613 W. Belden, Chicago . . . . (312) 327-4493
Gray Photography, Inc./601 Main St., Cincinnati . . . . (513) 621-4936
Gray, Walter/1035 W. Lake, Chicago . . . . (312) 733-3800
Gregg, Bruce Productions/1500 N. Halsted, Chicago . . . . (312) 337-6508
Gregg, Robb/3300 N. Kenneth, Chicago . . . . (312) 283-3333
Griffith, Sam/345 N. Canal, Chicago . . . . (312) 648-1900
Grigar, Jim/3908 W. Dakin St., Chicago . . . . (312) 583-6273
Grigus, George/952 W. Lake, Chicago . . . . (312) 733-2340
Grimm, Mike/3123 Crooks Rd., Royal Oak . . . . (313) 435-4333
Grow, Jean/685 W. Ohio St., Chicago . . . . (312) 243-8578
Grubman, Steve/Chicago/(312) 226-2272 . . . . **pages 492-493**
Grunewald, Jeff/161 W. Harrison, Chicago . . . . (312) 663-5799
Gubin, Mark/2893 S. Delaware Ave., Milwaukee . . . . (414) 482-0640
Guyon, Craig/1835 Hampden Ct., Louisville . . . . (502) 893-6364
Gyssler, Glen/954 W. Washington, Chicago . . . . (312) 243-8482
Habermann, Mike/529 S. Seventh St., Mpls. . . . . (612) 338-4696
Haefner, James/Troy/(313) 583-4747 . . . . **pages 632-633**
Hall, Brian Photo/900 W. Jackson Blvd., Chicago . . . . (312) 226-0853
Haller, Pam Photography, Inc./935 W. Chestnut, Chicago . . . . (312) 243-4462
Hammarlund, Vern/135 Park St., Troy . . . . (313) 588-5533
Hanchett, Chet/735 Marshall Ave., St. Louis . . . . (314) 968-2327
Handley, Robert E./1920 E. Croxton Ave., Bloomington . . . . (309) 828-4661
Hansen, Art Photographic, Inc./3926 N. Fir Rd. #12, Mishawaka . . . . (219) 256-1818
Hanson, Jim/Chicago/(312) 337-7770 . . . . **pages 580-581**
Harding, Lew Studio/2076 N. Elston, Chicago . . . . (312) 252-4010
Harlib, Joel, Inc./Chicago/(312) 329-1370 . . . . **pages 472-477**
Harling Winer Graphics, Inc./2948 W. Central St., Evanston . . . . (708) 491-6304
Harmer, Mark/Troy . . . . (313) 280-0640
Harr, Bob/Chicago . . . . (312) 321-1151
Harrig, Rick/3316 S. 66th St., Omaha . . . . (402) 397-5529
Harris, Bart Photo., Inc./70 W. Hubbard, Chicago . . . . (312) 751-2977
Harrison Studio of Photo. & Design, Inc./7230 Forestate Dr., St. Louis . . . . . . (314) 621-0505
Hart, Bob Photography/125 S. Racine, Chicago . . . . (312) 939-8888
Hates, Kenn/4808 S. Union, Chicago . . . . (312) 924-8893
Hauser, Marc/Chicago/(312) 664-8322 . . . . **pages 502-503**
Hawker, Christopher/1025 W. Madison, Chicago . . . . (312) 829-4766
Hedblom, Scott/1939 Bryant Ave. S., Mpls. . . . . (612) 870-0814
Hedrich, Sandi/10-A W. Hubbard, Chicago . . . . (312) 527-1577
Hedrich-Blessing/11 W. Illinois, Chicago . . . . (312) 321-1151
Heiderer, F. Cody/1636 N. Wells, Chicago . . . . (312) 642-2188
Heil, Peter/913 W. Van Buren, Chicago . . . . (312) 666-1025
Hepler, Scott/Kansas City . . . . (816) 471-5488
Hermann, Dell/676 N. La Salle, Chicago . . . . (312) 664-1461
Hertzberg, Richard/432 N. Clark, Chicago . . . . (312) 836-0464
Hickson & Assoc./7790B N. Central Dr., Westerville . . . . (614) 548-5050
Hildebrand, R.F./5133 Hogsback Rd., Hubertus . . . . (414) 628-1413
Hill Studio/4040 W. River Dr., Comstock Park . . . . (616) 784-9620
Hill, John T./4234 Howard St., Western Spr. . . . . (708) 246-3566
Hill, Robert E. Pictures/5449 Daniel Dr., Brighton . . . . (313) 227-3666
Hirneisen, Richard/306 S. Washington, Royal Oak . . . . (313) 399-2410
Hirschfeld, Corson/316 W. Fourth, Cincinnati . . . . (513) 241-0550
Hix, Steve/517 Southwest Blvd., Kansas City . . . . (816) 421-5114
Hodes, Charles S./503 Crown Pt., Buffalo Grove . . . . (708) 215-3939

Hodge, Adele/Merchandise Mart, Chicago	(312) 472-6555
Hodges, Charles/934 W. North Ave., Chicago	(312) 664-8179
Hoffman, John/Chicago/(312) 222-0504	**pages 480-483**
Holcepl, Robert/2479 W. 11th, Cleveland	(216) 241-2479
Hollow, Elizabeth/Detroit/(313) 875-3123	**page 522**
Holtkamp, Jerome/5645 Montgomery Rd., Cincinnati	(513) 531-3864
Holzemer, Buck Photography/3448 Chicago Ave., Mpls.	(612) 824-2905
Honor, David/415 W. Superior, Chicago	(312) 751-1644
Howard Studio/4719 Vine St., Cincinnati	(513) 641-2525
Howrani, Ameen/Detroit/(313) 875-3123	**page 522**
Hoyt Studios, Ltd./2812 W. Devon Ave., Chicago	(312) 274-8151
Hrdlicka Photography/2057 Harney Rd., Omaha	(402) 346-3522
Huibregtse, Mike/Milwaukee/(414) 272-2929	**page 469**
Hulefeld Associates, Inc./333 E. Eighth St., Cincinnati	(513) 421-2210
Hummel, Dan/807 13th Ave. S., Mpls.	(612) 339-7438
Hurling, Robert/325 W. Huron, Chicago	(312) 944-2022
Hutson, David/8120 Juniper St., Prairie Vlg.	(913) 383-1123
Hynds, James/1220 W. Sixth St., Cleveland	(216) 771-6878
Iann-Hutchins, Inc./2044 Euclid Ave., Cleveland	(216) 579-1570
Icon Photographic Service/500 N. Ninth St., Lafayette	(317) 742-5405
Idea Design Technique/15936 Grand River Ave., Detroit	(313) 272-7338
Image Source, Inc. The/801 Front St., Toledo	(419) 697-1111
Image Studios/1100 S. Lynndale Dr., Appleton	(414) 738-4080
Imbrogno, James/Chicago	(312) 733-3650
Ingram, Russell/1000 W. Monroe St., Chicago	(312) 829-4652
Inwegen, Van/1422 W. Belle Pln., Chicago	(312) 477-8344
Irving, Gary/818 Cadillac Dr., Wheaton	(312) 653-0641
Itahara, Tets/676 N. La Salle, Chicago	(312) 649-0606
Izui Photography/Chicago/(312) 266-8029	**pages 518-519**
JMT/4549 Dickman Rd., Battle Creek	(616) 968-0044
Jackson, Brett/13900 Watt Rd., Novelty	(216) 338-3036
Jackson, David/1021 Hall St., Grand Rapids	(616) 243-3325
Jacobson, Scott Photography, Inc./3435 N. County Rd., Plymouth	(612) 546-9191
James, Phillip MacMillan/2300 Hazelwood Ave., St. Paul	(612) 777-2303
Janes, Lisa/Chicago/(312) 235-4613	**pages 532-533**
Janowiak Studio/16212 W. Rogers Dr., New Berlin	(414) 782-6550
Jelen, Tom/Arlington Heights	(708) 506-9479
Jensen, M./1101 Stinson Blvd. N.E., Mpls.	(612) 379-1944
Jilling, Helmut/3420-A Cavalier Trl., Cuyahoga Falls	(216) 928-1330
Jochim, Gary Photography/1324½ N. Milwaukee Ave., Chicago	(312) 252-5250
Joel, David Photography, Inc./1515 Washington Ave., Wilmette	(708) 256-8792
Johnson, Donald C./Northbrook	(312) 480-9336
Johnson, Jeff/529 S. Seventh St., Mpls.	(612) 339-7929
Johnson, Jim/802 W. Evergreen, Chicago	(312) 943-8864
Johnson, Wayne/614 E. 15th St., Mpls.	(612) 341-3035
Jones, Brent/9121 S. Merrill Ave., Chicago	(312) 933-1174
Jones, Dick Studios/325 W. Huron St., Chicago	(312) 642-0242
Jones, Duane/5605 Chicago Ave. S., Mpls.	(612) 823-8173
Jones, Harrison/Chicago/(312) 421-6400	**pages 470-471**
Jones, Jennie, Inc./1375 E. Ninth St., Cleveland	(216) 861-3850
Jordan, Jack/840 John St., Evansville	(812) 423-7676
Jordano, Dave/Chicago/(312) 280-8212	**pages 508-509**
Josephs, Alexander/1201 18th St., Denver	(303) 298-7791
Jungquist, Steve/Troy	(313) 583-2828
Justice/Patterson Studios/7609 Production Dr., Cincinnati	(513) 761-4023
K.I.T. Photos/1708 Logan, Cincinnati	(513) 721-0487
Kahn, Dick Studio, Inc./12425 Knoll Rd., Elm Grove	(414) 784-1996
Kalman & Pabst Photo Group/400 Lakeside Ave. N.W., Cleveland	(216) 574-9090
Kamin & Assocs./Chicago/(312) 787-8834	**pages 504, 508-509, 562-563, 604-605, 624-625**
Kansas City Photographic/1830 Main St., Kansas City	(816) 221-2710
Kapes, Jack & Assoc./233 E. Wacker Dr., Chicago	(312) 565-0566
Kaplan, Matthew/5452 N. Glenwood, Chicago	(312) 769-5903
Karant & Assocs./400 N. May St., Chicago	(312) 733-0891
Kauck, Jeffrey/Cincinnati	(513) 751-8515
Kauffman, Kim/444 Lentz Ct., Lansing	(517) 371-3036
Kazu Studio, Ltd./1211 W. Webster, Chicago	(312) 348-5393
Kean, Christopher/Park Ridge/(708) 292-1144	**pages 486-487**
Keeling, Robert/900 W. Jackson, Chicago	(312) 944-5680
Keisman & Keisman/518 W. 37th St., Chicago	(312) 268-7955
Kelly, Tony/828 Colfax St., Evanston	(312) 864-0488
Kelsey, Chris/18 W. Hubbard, Chicago	(312) 644-5233
Keltsch, Ann/Indpls./(317) 849-7723	**pages 514-515**
Kemmetmueller Photography, Inc./18336 MtKa Blvd., Deephaven	(612) 473-2142

MIDWEST

Kende, Benjamin/2118 W. Superior, Chicago .... (312) 929-0168
Kennedy, Layne C./Mpls. .... (612) 824-2999
Kerran, Jerry/Troy .... (313) 583-4747
Kessler Photography/34 W. Sixth St., Cincinnati .... (513) 651-5669
Ketchum, Art/1524 S. Peoria St., Chicago .... (312) 733-7706
Kienitz, Michael/Madison .... (608) 251-1642
Kinast, Susan/1504 N. Fremont, Chicago .... (312) 337-1770
King, Budde/5621 Golden Eagle Cir., Palm Beach Gardens .... (407) 796-7965
Kingsbury Photographics/700 N. Washington, Mpls. .... (612) 340-1919
Kirby, Tom/Troy .... (313) 583-2828
Klein Photography Inc./7900 N. Linder Ave., Morton Grove .... (708) 965-8618
Kloc, Howard/Berkley/(313) 541-1704 .... **pages 521, 523**
Klocworks/Berkley/(313) 541-1704 .... **pages 521, 523**
Knize, Karl/1920 N. Seminary, Chicago .... (312) 477-1001
Kogan, David/1242 W. Washington, Chicago .... (312) 243-1929
Kolbrener, Bob/12300 Ballas Woods Ct., St. Louis .... (314) 567-1361
Kolesar, Jerry/679 E. Mandoline, Madison Hts. .... (313) 589-0066
Kolorstat Studios/415 N. Dearborn, Chicago .... (312) 644-3729
Kondas Associates, Inc./1529 N. Alabama St., Indpls. .... (317) 637-1414
Kondor, Laszlo/2141 W. Lemoyne, Chicago .... (312) 642-7365
Konrath, Frank G./2445 N. Sayre Ave., Chicago .... (312) 622-7066
Korab, Balthazar, Ltd./5051 Beach Rd., Troy .... (313) 641-8880
Koralik, Connie/900 W. Jackson, Chicago .... (312) 944-5680
Kordela, David/3822 N. Janssen Ave., Chicago .... (312) 327-2937
Kramer, Ben/1242 W. Washington, Chicago .... (312) 666-2985
Krantz, Jim Studios, Inc./Omaha .... (402) 734-4848
Kranzten Studio, Inc./100 S. Ashland Ave., Chicago .... (312) 942-1900
Krejci, Don/3121 W. 25th St., Cleveland .... (216) 861-4730
Krider, Chas/1312 E. Broad St., Columbus .... (614) 253-1621
Krueger, Dick Studio/2625 S.W. Westlake Cir., Palm City .... (407) 286-9781
Kufrin, George/535 N. Michigan Ave., Chicago .... (312) 787-2854
Kulp, Curtis Prods., Inc./1255 S. Michigan Ave., Chicago .... (312) 786-1943
Kusel, Robert/2156 W. Arthur, Chicago .... (312) 465-8283
LK Photographic, Inc./1395 Wheaton, Troy .... (313) 680-8890
La Roche, Andre/32588 Dequindre, Warren .... (313) 978-7373
LaFavor, Mark/Mpls. .... (612) 388-1999
Lallo, Ed/7329 Terrace, Kansas City .... (816) 523-6222
Landau, Allan/1147 W. Ohio St., Chicago .... (312) 942-1382
Lane, Jack/815 N. Milwaukee, Chicago .... (312) 733-3937
Lanza, Scott/3200 S. Third St., Milwaukee .... (414) 482-4114
Larimer, Larry/Chicago .... (312) 280-2580
Lasersmith, The, Inc./1000 W. Monroe, Chicago .... (312) 733-5462
Lauth, Lyal Photography, Ltd./833 W. Chicago Ave., Chicago .... (312) 829-9800
Lawrence-Phillip Studios/343 S. Dearborn St., Chicago .... (312) 922-1945
Lawson, Jim -Design Photography/1324 Hamilton Ave., Cleveland .... (216) 687-0099
LeGrand, Peter/413 Sandburg St., Park Forest .... (312) 747-4923
Leavitt, Debbie/2029 W. Armitage, Chicago .... (312) 235-6777
Leavitt, Fred/916 W. Carmen, Chicago .... (312) 784-2344
Lecat, Paul Photography/820 N. Franklin, Chicago .... (312) 664-7122
Ledell, Steven/Chicago/(312) 787-8834 .... **page 504**
Lee II, Robert/1512 Northlin Dr., St. Louis .... (314) 965-5832
Lee, Mark/Troy .... (313) 583-2828
Lehn, John & Associates/2601 E. Franklin, Mpls. .... (612) 338-0257
Leick, James/1709 Washington Ave., St. Louis .... (314) 241-2354
Leinwohl, Steffens/1462 W. Irving Pk. Rd., Chicago .... (312) 975-0475
Lennon, Bausman & Fitzgerald/3625 Hampshire Ave. S., St. Louis Pk. ...... (612) 922-9522
Lerner, Frank & Assoc., Inc./392 Morrison Rd., Columbus .... (614) 864-8554
Lesnick, Mike/30500 Van Dyke, Warren .... (313) 573-7630
Levin, Jonathan/1035 W. Lake, Chicago .... (312) 226-3898
Levy, Burt/119 N. Fourth St., Mpls. .... (612) 339-0724
Lewandowski, Leon R./210 N. Racine, Chicago .... (312) 666-7646
Lieberman, Robert C.V./2076 N. Elston Ave., Chicago .... (312) 975-9229
Light Writer Photography, Inc./5991 Hampstead Ln., Columbus .... (614) 882-4013
Lightfoot, Robert M. III/311 Good Ave., Des Plaines .... (312) 297-5447
Lindholm, Robert/619 Sue Dr., Jefferson City .... (314) 893-3639
Lioce, Carl Photo/3649 W. 82nd Pl., Chicago .... (312) 735-0362
Livingston, Stanley/722 S. Seventh St., Ann Arbor .... (313) 665-6401
Lodder/Eastlight/6231 Montgomery Rd., Cincinnati .... (513) 351-1223
Longley's Studio/3809 Harrison Ave., Cincinnati .... (513) 661-5333
Lowe, Thomas/314 Fifth Ave. S., Mpls. .... (612) 375-1019
Lowry, Miles/Chicago .... (312) 664-1824
Lubzik, Wally/Grosse Pt. .... (313) 886-8130
Luce, Don/1547 St. Clair Ave., Cleveland .... (216) 781-1547

Ludwigs, David/3600 Troost Ave., Kansas City . . . . (816) 531-1363
Lulu Represents/70 W. Huron, Chicago . . . . (312) 951-2672
Lund, Kent/Troy . . . . (313) 583-4747
Lyles, David/855 W. Blackhawk, Chicago . . . . (312) 642-1223
MDI Photography & Design/142 E. Stafford, Worthington . . . . (614) 885-5591
MacTavish, David/4620 N. Winchester, Chicago . . . . (312) 334-2841
Mack, Richard Photography, Ltd./2331 Hartzell, Evanston . . . . (708) 869-7794
Maday, Tom/621 W. Randolph, Chicago . . . . (312) 648-1241
Magic Light Studio/214 E. Eighth St., Cincinnati . . . . (513) 381-3344
Magness, William/920 Race St., Cincinnati . . . . (513) 621-8988
Maki & Smith Photography,Inc./6156 Olson Memorial Hwy., Golden Valley . . . (612) 541-4722
Maloney, Tom & Assocs., Inc./Chicago/(312) 704-0500 . . . . **pages 534-535**
Malinowski, Stan/1150 N. State St., Chicago . . . . (312) 951-6622
Maloney Photography, Inc./231 W. 4th St., Cincinnati . . . . (513) 241-2208
Manarchy, Dennis/Chicago . . . . (312) 828-9117
Mandel, Avis/40 E. Cedar, Chicago . . . . (312) 642-4776
Mankus, Gary/835 N. Wood St., Chicago . . . . (312) 828-1120
Marino, Marlene/Chicago/(312) 666-7300 . . . . **pages 512-513**
Marshall, Don Photography/415 W. Huron, Chicago . . . . (312) 944-0720
Marshall, Paul/623 W. Randolph, Chicago . . . . (312) 559-1270
Marshall, Simeon/1043 W. Randolph St., Chicago . . . . (312) 243-9500
Marszalek, Sharon/213 N. Morgan, Chicago . . . . (312) 733-3118
Martin, Andrew/Chicago . . . . (312) 938-2148
Martin, Kathleen/10910 Whittier, Detroit . . . . (313) 521-7600
Marvy! Advertising Photography/Hopkins/(612) 935-0307 . . . . **pages 494-495**
Master Slide, Inc./118 E. Lockwood, St. Louis . . . . (314) 961-4463
Mathiowetz, Alan/1008 Nicollet Mall, Mpls. . . . . (612) 338-1999
Matusik, Jim/2223 W. Melrose, Chicago . . . . (312) 327-5615
Matz, Fred/6632 N. Sioux, Chicago . . . . (312) 792-0270
Mauney, Michael/1440 N. Dayton, Chicago . . . . (312) 266-6311
May, Sandy/18 N. Fourth St., Mpls. . . . . (612) 332-0272
Mayhew & Peper/615 Main St., Cincinnati . . . . (513) 421-0111
McCabe, Mark/1301 E. 12th St., Kansas City . . . . (816) 474-6491
McCall, Paul/Chicago . . . . (312) 280-2580
McCallum, John/935 W. Chestnut, Chicago . . . . (312) 829-8383
McCann & Co./15416 Village Woods Dr., Mpls. . . . . (612) 949-2407
McCann, Larry/666 W. Hubbard, Chicago . . . . (312) 942-1924
McCay, Larry Photography, Inc./3926 N. Fir Rd., Mishawaka . . . . (219) 259-1414
McDonald, Scott/Chicago . . . . (312) 321-1151
McGee Location Photography/3050 Edgewood St., Portage . . . . (219) 762-2805
McGuire, Joseph Studio, Inc./3148 N. Pennsylvania St., Indpls. . . . . (317) 923-1122
McHale Studio Inc./Cincinnati . . . . (513) 961-1454
McHugh & Associates/1200 N. Seventh St., Mpls. . . . . (612) 522-1031
McKay, Doug/512 S. Hanley, St. Louis . . . . (314) 863-7167
McKellar, William/Chicago/(312) 235-1499 . . . . **pages 534-535**
McLaughlin, Jim/St. Louis . . . . (314) 533-6665
McMahon, David/800 Washington Ave. N., Mpls. . . . . (612) 339-9709
McMahon, William Franklin/6010 N. Keating Ave., Chicago . . . . (312) 777-6770
McNaughton, Toni/233 E. Wacker, Chicago . . . . (312) 938-2148
McNichol, Greg/1222 W. Elmdale, Chicago . . . . (312) 973-1032
Meier, Don Photography/211 W. 9th St., Cincinnati . . . . (513) 721-2830
Melkus, Larry/679 E. Mandoline, Madison Hts. . . . . (313) 589-0066
Meoli/Lohbeck Studio Inc./710 N. Tucker, St. Louis . . . . (314) 231-6038
Merrick, Nick/Chicago . . . . (312) 321-1151
Merrill, Frank/2939 W. Touhy, Chicago . . . . (312) 764-1672
Messana, Joseph P./22500 Rio Vista, St. Clair Shores . . . . (313) 773-5815
Meyer, Aaron D./1302 W. Randolph, Chicago . . . . (312) 243-1458
Meyer, Fred/415 N. Dearborn, Chicago . . . . (312) 527-4873
Meyer, Gordon/216 W. Ohio, Chicago . . . . (312) 642-9303
Meyer, Jim/310 S. Holyoke, Wichita . . . . (316) 688-1116
Meyer, Robert E./2007 W. Division St., Chicago . . . . (312) 235-3686
Mid Coast Studio/2616 Industrial Row, Troy . . . . (313) 280-0640
Mignard & Assoc., Inc./1950-R S. Glenstone Ave., Springfield . . . . (417) 881-7422
Mihalevich, Michael/9235 Somerset Dr., Overland Pk. . . . . (913) 642-6466
Milgle, Tom/1931 Verniner Hwy., Cross Point Woods . . . . (313) 884-6310
Miller, Frank/6016 Blue Cir. Dr., Minnetonka . . . . (612) 935-8888
Miller, Jon/Chicago . . . . (312) 321-1151
Miller, Pat/420 N. Fifth St., Mpls. . . . . (612) 339-1115
Miller, Sandro/5275 Michigan Ave., Rosemont . . . . (708) 671-0300
Miller, Spider/833 N. Orleans, Chicago . . . . (312) 944-2880
Mills, Gary/Granger . . . . (219) 277-8844
Miracle Pictures/Merle Morris/2511 Lynn Ave., Mpls. . . . . (612) 926-8165
Mitchell, Mike Photog., Inc./137 30th St. Dr. S.E., Cedar Rapids . . . . (319) 366-1776

Mitchell, Rick/652 W. Grand Ave., Chicago . . . . (312) 829-1700
Montagano, David/405 N. Wabash Ave., Chicago . . . . (312) 527-3283
Morawski, Mike/679 E. Mandoline, Madison Heights . . . . (313) 589-8050
Morden, W.E./18555 Bainbridge, Southfield . . . . (313) 646-4813
Morgan, Dan /Straight Shooter/18628 Detroit Ave., Lakewood . . . . (216) 228-1100
Morioka, Gordon/1426 Shenandoah, Cincinnati . . . . (513) 821-7076
Morrison, Guy/32049 Milton, Madison Hts. . . . . (313) 588-6544
Morton & White Photography, Inc./Worthington . . . . (614) 885-8687
Moss, Jean/1255 S. Michigan Ave., Chicago . . . . (312) 786-9110
Moulton, George/527 N. 27th St., Milwaukee . . . . (414) 342-6363
Moustakas, Dan/1255 Rankin, Troy . . . . (313) 589-0100
Mowers, Laura/420 Fifth St. N., Mpls. . . . . (612) 339-4203
Moy, Willie/364 W. Erie, Chicago . . . . (312) 943-1863
Muresan, Jon/Dearborn . . . . (313) 581-5445
Murphey, Gregory/Chicago . . . . (312) 327-4856
Music, Ken/326 E. Fourth St., Royal Oak . . . . (313) 544-2441
Mutrux, John/5217 England, Kansas City . . . . (913) 722-4343
Mytech Images/29255 Orvylle Dr., Warren . . . . (313) 573-3820
Nano, Ed Studio Assoc./1452 Davenport Ave., Cleveland . . . . (216) 861-0148
Nardi, Bob/1335 N. Wells Ave., Chicago . . . . (312) 454-0286
Nawrocki, William S. ASMP/332 S. Michigan Ave., Chicago . . . . (312) 427-8625
Nelson, Herb/Middleton . . . . (608) 831-6174
Nelson, R.K./1024 W. Lincoln Ave., Milwaukee . . . . (414) 671-6191
Nelson, Tom/800 Washington Ave. N., Mpls. . . . . (612) 339-3579
Nelson-Curry, Loring/420 N. Clark St., Chicago . . . . (312) 644-2371
New View Studios/5275 Michigan Ave., Rosemont . . . . (708) 671-0300
Nible, Rick/905 Broadway, Kansas City . . . . (816) 221-6110
Nicholson, Rick/2310 Denison, Cleveland . . . . (216) 398-1494
Niedorf, Steve/700 Washington Ave. N., Mpls. . . . . (612) 332-7124
Nielsen Studios/1313 W. Randolph St., Chicago . . . . (312) 226-2661
Nienhuis, John/3623 N. 62nd St., Milwaukee . . . . (414) 442-9199
Nobart, Inc./1133 S. Wabash, Chicago . . . . (312) 427-9800
Northlight/32049 Milton, Madison Hts. . . . . (313) 588-6544
Nozicka, Steve/Chicago/(312) 787-8925 . . . . **pages 476-477**
Nugent, Wenckus, Inc./1100 Northwest Hwy., Des Plaines . . . . (708) 296-4443
Nykoruk, Mike/126 N. Wilson, Royal Oak . . . . (313) 547-5565
O'Barski, Don/17239 Parkside Ave., S. Holland . . . . (312) 596-0606
O'Connell, Tom/1546 N. Orleans, Chicago . . . . (312) 642-8715
Oakes, Kenneth/902 Yale Ln., Highland Pk. . . . . (708) 432-4809
Obata Design, Inc./1610 Menard St., St. Louis . . . . (314) 241-1710
Officer, Hollis/905 E. Fifth St., Kansas City . . . . (816) 474-5501
Olausen, Judy/213 N. Washington Ave., Mpls. . . . . (612) 332-5009
Ollis, K.R. Photography/1231 Superior Ave., Cleveland . . . . (216) 781-8646
Olsen, Dave/513 Washington Ave. S., Mpls. . . . . (612) 332-1084
Olsson/Baber Photography, Inc./215 W. Illinois, Chicago . . . . (312) 661-1800
Ontiveros, Don Photography/1837 W. Evergreen Ave., Chicago . . . . (312) 342-0900
Ores, Kathy/411 S. Sangamon, Chicago . . . . (312) 410-7139
Osburn, Ken/Farmington Hills . . . . (313) 855-0610
Osler, Spike/2616 Industrial Row, Troy . . . . (313) 280-0640
Owens, Corning/Fiberglass Twr., Toledo . . . . (419) 248-8041
Oxendorf, Eric/1442 N. Franklin St., Milwaukee . . . . (414) 273-0654
P.K. Photography/1832 E. 38th St., Mpls. . . . . (612) 729-8989
Pappas, Bill/1937 Prospect Ave., Cleveland . . . . (216) 861-7972
Parallel Productions/1008 Nicollet Mall, Mpls. . . . . (612) 338-1999
Parallel Productions/358 W. Ontario, Chicago . . . . (312) 280-1693
Paris, Rob/10805 Indeco Dr., Cincinnati . . . . (513) 891-9500
Park Photographic, Inc./1960 Thunderbird, Troy . . . . (313) 362-1550
Parker Photography/710 N. Second St., St. Louis . . . . (314) 621-8100
Parks, Jim/210 W. Chicago Ave., Chicago . . . . (312) 321-1193
Paulson, Bill/5358 Golla Rd., Stevens Pt. . . . . (715) 344-8484
Payne, John Photo Ltd./2250 W. Grand Ave., Chicago . . . . (312) 997-2288
Payne, Scott/5275 Michigan Ave., Rosemont . . . . (708) 671-0300
Pearson, James/2169 N. 54th St., Milwaukee . . . . (414) 442-7882
Perkins, Ray Photography/Chicago . . . . (312) 421-3438
Perman, Craig/1645 Hennepin Ave., Mpls. . . . . (612) 338-7727
Perno, Jack/Chicago/(312) 666-4345 . . . . **pages 192-193**
Perry, Eric/Troy . . . . (313) 280-0640
Perspective, Inc./2322 Pennsylvania St., Ft. Wayne . . . . (219) 424-8136
Perweiler, Gary/Chicago . . . . (312) 280-5134
Peterson, Glenn/7424 Washington Ave., Mpls. . . . . (612) 944-5750
Peterson, Kerry/Mpls./(612) 332-8864 . . . . **pages 505-506**
Peterson, Richard/7660 Washington Ave. S., Mpls. . . . . (612) 943-2404
Peterson, Vicki/Chicago/(312) 467-0780 . . . . **pages 432-433**

Petroff Photography/9 W. Hubbard, Chicago ... (312) 836-0411
Petrovich, Steve/679 E. Mandoline, Madison Hts. ... (313) 589-0066
Phillips, Les/Mpls. ... (612) 866-2155
Photo Comp Corporation/401 E. Main St., Brownsburg ... (317) 852-4377
Photo Concepts/11015 W. Layton Ave., Milwaukee ... (414) 425-4477
Photo Concepts, Inc./23042 Commerce Dr., Farmington Hills ... (313) 477-4301
Photo Group Photography, Inc./1945 Techny Rd., Northbrook ... (312) 564-9220
Photo Ideas, Inc./804 W. Washington Blvd., Chicago ... (312) 666-3100
Photo Reserve/2924 N. Racine, Chicago ... (312) 871-7371
Photo-One/Jorie Gracen Photography/7000 W. Carol Ave., Niles ... (708) 965-5289
PhotoDesign/815 Main St., Cincinnati ... (513) 421-5588
PhotoMark, Inc./323 Village Dr., Carol Stream ... (708) 690-9222
Photographers Assoc./719 S. 75th St., Omaha ... (402) 391-8474
Photography Unlimited, Inc./11600 W. Lincoln Ave., Milwaukee ... (414) 321-1600
Photos by Jeff/Palos Hts. ... (312) 448-2111
Pierce Photography, Ltd./917 N. Fifth St., Mpls. ... (612) 332-2670
Pieroni, Frank, Inc./2432 Oak Industrial Dr., Grand Rapids ... (616) 459-8325
Pintozzi Studio/42 E. Chicago, Chicago ... (312) 266-7775
PoKempner, Marc/1453 W. Addison, Chicago ... (312) 525-4567
Pohlman Studios/527 N. 27th St., Milwaukee ... (414) 342-6363
Polaski Photography/Nine W. Hubbard, Chicago ... (312) 944-6577
Poli, Frank/Chicago ... (312) 944-3924
Pomerantz, Ron/363 W. Erie St., Chicago ... (312) 787-6407
Pool, Linda/7216 E. 99th St., Kansas City ... (816) 761-7314
Pope, Carl/3722 N. Riley, Indpls. ... (317) 636-4428
Poplis, Paul/Columbus ... (614) 231-2942
Porth, Bob/Chicago ... (312) 321-1151
Portnoy, Lewis/Five Carole Ln., St. Louis ... (314) 567-5700
Potts, Carolyn/Chicago/(312) 944-1130 ... **pages 86-87**
Powell, Jim/326 W. Kalamazoo Ave, Kalamazoo ... (616) 381-2302
Powell, Victor/117 S. Morgan, Chicago ... (312) 738-1723
Presnall, Heather/53 W. Jackson, Chicago ... (312) 248-4880
Prestige Portaits Inc./2056 W. Irving Pk. Rd., Chicago ... (312) 248-4880
Przekop, Harry J./950 W. Lake St., Chicago ... (312) 829-8201
Pucci and Associates/18 W. Seventh St., Cincinnati ... (513) 621-0025
Puffer, David/213 W. Institute, Chicago ... (312) 266-7540
Puza, Greg Productions/Milwaukee ... (414) 271-1960
Quest Productions, Ltd./32000 Northwestern Hwy., Farmington Hills ... (313) 855-0610
Questudios, Inc./113 N. May, Chicago ... (312) 421-6400
Rabin, Bill & Assocs./Chicago/(312) 944-6655 ... **pages 256-257, 422-423**
Radencich, Michael/Kansas City ... (816) 756-1992
Ragan, Jake/3043 Carnegie, Cleveland ... (216) 391-4343
Randall, Robert/Chicago/(312) 235-4613 ... **pages 532-533**
Ransburg Studio/8620 Green Braes N. Dr., Indpls. ... (317) 291-6562
Rantala, Jim/932 Allston, Houston ... (713) 864-1585
Ray, Rodney/845 W. Grace, Chicago ... (312) 472-6550
Reames-Hanusin Studio/3306 Commercial Ave., Northbrook ... (312) 564-2706
Reed, Dick/1330 Coolidge, Troy ... (313) 280-0090
Reid, Ken/1651 W. North Ave., Chicago ... (312) 235-4343
Reiss, Ray/2144 N. Leavitt, Chicago ... (312) 384-3245
Remington, George/1455 W. 29th St., Cleveland ... (216) 241-1440
Renerts, Peter/633 Huron Rd., Cleveland ... (216) 781-2440
Renken, R.D./St. Louis ... (314) 394-5055
Ricco, Ron/117 W. Walker St., Milwaukee ... (414) 645-6450
Rice, Ted/2599 N. Fourth St., Columbus ... (614) 263-8656
Richardson, R.W./17 N. Elizabeth St., Chicago ... (312) 243-8764
Riverbed Studio/1678 Leonard, Cleveland ... (216) 241-1751
Robert, Francois/740 N. Wells St., Chicago ... (312) 787-0777
Rodney, Allen/375 W. Hickory Grv., Bloomfield Hills ... (313) 338-4586
Rogowski, Tom Photography, Inc./214 E. 8th St., Cincinnati ... (513) 621-3826
Rohde, Glen/Troy ... (313) 583-2828
Rohman, Jim/2254 Marengo, Toledo ... (419) 865-0234
Rossi & Assocs./4555 Emery Industrial Pky., Cleveland ... (216) 831-0688
Rothrock, Douglas/368 W. Huron, Chicago ... (312) 951-9045
Rott, Hans/1546 N. Orleans, Chicago ... (312) 642-8715
Rowley, Joe/401 N. Racine, Chicago ... (312) 829-2332
Rubin, Laurie/Chicago/(312) 664-8322 ... **pages 500-501**
Rung, D. Paul/1810 W. Grand, Chicago ... (312) 829-4064
Rush, Michael Photography/415 Delaware St., Kansas City ... (816) 471-1200
Rusk, Steve/4101 Parklawn Ave., Mpls. ... (612) 835-2520
Russell, Jim/811 W. Evergreen, Chicago ... (312) 642-0024
Russetti Camera Works/1260 Carnegie Ave., Cleveland ... (216) 687-1788
Rustin, Barry/934 Glenwood Rd., Glenview ... (708) 724-7600

MIDWEST 463

Ryan, Timothy/633 Huron Rd., Cleveland . . . . (216) 696-7926
Sacco Productions, Ltd./2035 W. Grand Ave., Chicago . . . . (312) 243-5757
Sacks, Andrew/20727 Scio Church Rd., Detroit . . . . (313) 475-2310
Sadin Photo Group Ltd./1420 W. Dickens, Chicago . . . . (312) 944-1434
Sadin, Abby/Chicago . . . . (312) 404-0133
Sadovsky, Bill/Troy . . . . (313) 583-4747
Saks Photography/Indpls./(317) 849-7723 . . . . **pages 514-515**
Salisbury, Mark/161 W. Harrison, Chicago . . . . (312) 922-7599
Salomon, Bob/3254 N. Clifton, Chicago . . . . (312) 472-3516
Salter, Al/685 Pallister Ave., Detroit . . . . (313) 874-1155
Saltzman, Ben/700 N. Washington, Mpls. . . . . (612) 332-5112
Sanders, Kathryn/411 S. Sangamon, Chicago . . . . (312) 829-3100
Sandoz Studios/Chicago . . . . (312) 733-0222
Sapecki, Roman/56 E. Oakland Ave., Columbus . . . . (614) 262-7497
Sato, A.Y./2470 N. Clark, Chicago . . . . (312) 975-9732
Sauer, Neil & Assoc., Inc./2844 Arsenal, St. Louis . . . . (314) 664-4646
Schabes, Charles/1220 W. Grace St., Chicago . . . . (312) 281-5403
Schanuel, Anthony/10901 Oasis Dr., St. Louis . . . . (314) 849-3495
Schewe, Jeff/Chicago/(312) 951-6334 . . . . **pages 484-485**
Schneider, Steve/2242 University Ave., St. Paul . . . . (612) 644-6588
Scholtes, Marc/726 Central Ave. N.E., Minneapolis . . . . (612) 378-1888
Schrempp, Erich/723 W. Randolph, Chicago . . . . (312) 454-3237
Schridde, Charles Photography/600 Ajax Dr., Madison Hts. . . . . (313) 589-0111
Schube-Soucek/1735 Carmen, Elk Grove . . . . (312) 439-0640
Schuemann, Bill/1591 S. Belvoir Blvd., Euclid . . . . (216) 382-4409
Schuessler, Dave/40 E. Delaware Pl., Chicago . . . . (312) 787-6868
Schulman, Bruce R./1421 Dobson, Evanston . . . . (708) 866-8666
Schultz, Karl/Chicago/(312) 454-0303 . . . . **pages 530-531**
Schultz, Tim, Photography, Inc./935 W. Chestnut, Chicago . . . . (312) 733-7113
Schutte, Bob/823 N. Second St., Milwaukee . . . . (414) 347-1113
Schwartz Studios, Inc./1113 Wayne, Dayton . . . . (513) 223-2277
Schwartz, Linda/2033 N. Orleans, Chicago . . . . (312) 327-7755
Schwelik Studios/1311 Main Ave., Cleveland . . . . (216) 579-1211
Scott Studios, Inc./500 N. Mannheim Rd., Hillside . . . . (312) 449-3800
Scott, Denis/216 W. Ohio St., Chicago . . . . (312) 467-5663
Secreto, Jim/2616 Industrial Row, Troy . . . . (313) 280-0640
Seed, Brian/7432 Lamon Ave., Skokie . . . . (708) 677-7887
Segal, Beth/1220 W. Sixth St., Cleveland . . . . (216) 771-7667
Segal, Mark A./Chicago . . . . (312) 236-8545
Segielski, Tony/1886 Thunderbird, Troy . . . . (313) 362-3111
Seng, Walt Photography/1220 W. 6th St., Cleveland . . . . (216) 861-3456
Sereta, Greg/2440 Lakeside Ave., Cleveland . . . . (216) 861-7227
Severson, Kent/637 Sexton Bldg., Mpls. . . . . (612) 375-1870
Seymour, Ronald, Inc./1625 N. Milwaukee Ave., Chicago . . . . (312) 235-0161
Shambroom, Paul/1607 Dupont Ave. N., Mpls. . . . . (612) 521-5835
Shanoor Photography/116 W. Illinois, Chicago . . . . (312) 266-0465
Shapiro, Terry/Chicago . . . . (312) 664-1824
Shaughnessy MacDonald Studio/1221 Jarvis, Elk Grove . . . . (708) 437-8850
Sheppard, Robbin/6858 Beechmont, Cincinnati . . . . (513) 231-3542
Shields, Kelly/1101 Stinson Blvd., Mpls. . . . . (612) 378-9454
Shigeta Associates, Inc./1546 N. Orleans, Chicago . . . . (312) 642-8715
Shimer, Bob/Chicago . . . . (312) 321-1151
Shirley, Thomas/1035 W. Lake St., Chicago . . . . (312) 243-9700
Shotwell/Chicago/(312) 929-0168 . . . . **pages 490-491**
Shoulders, Terry/676 N. La Salle, Chicago . . . . (312) 642-6622
Siede-Preis/1526 N. Halsted, Chicago . . . . (312) 787-2725
Sieracki, John/56 E. Oak, Chicago . . . . (312) 664-7824
Sigman, Gary/2229 W. Melrose, Chicago . . . . (312) 871-8756
Silker, Glen/5249-A W. 73rd St., Edina . . . . (612) 835-1811
Sills, Casey/411 N. La Salle, Chicago . . . . (312) 670-3660
Silver, Jared Straight Shooter/660 La Salle Pl., Highland Pk. . . . . (312) 433-3866
Silverstein, Dennis/411 Lathrop, Chicago . . . . (312) 771-4015
Sinkler, Paul/420 5th St. N., Mpls. . . . . (612) 343-0325
Skalak, Carl/4746 Grayton Rd., Cleveland . . . . (216) 676-6508
Skierski, Joseph/24040 Martha Washington, Southfield . . . . (313) 565-2341
Skillicorn Assocs./Chicago/(312) 856-1626 . . . . **pages 516-517**
Skrebneski, Victor/1350 N. La Salle, Chicago . . . . (312) 944-1339
Skutas/215 Second St., Downers Grove . . . . (708) 964-3535
Sladcik, William K./215 W. Illinois, Chicago . . . . (312) 644-7108
Slivinski, David/1035 W. Lake St., Chicago . . . . (312) 733-8008
Slocum, Paul/2616 Industrial Row, Troy . . . . (313) 280-0640
Smetzer, Don/2534 N. Burling, Chicago . . . . (312) 327-1716
Smith, Bill/600 N. McClurg Ct., Chicago . . . . (312) 787-4686

Smith, Doug, Inc./2911 Sutton, St. Louis	(314) 645-1359
Smith, Kevin/1609 N. Wolcott, Chicago	(312) 772-1113
Smith, Richard Hamilton/St.Paul/(612) 645-5070	**pages 480-481**
Smith, Richard L./1112 Brentwood Dr., Round Lake Beach	(708) 546-0977
Snook Studios, Inc./1433 W. Fullerton Ave., Addison	(708) 495-3939
Snow, Andy/Dayton	(513) 866-2424
Snowberger, Ann/Chicago	(312) 463-3590
Snyder, Don/3700 Superior Ave., Cleveland	(216) 881-5955
Snyder, John/811 W. Evergreen, Chicago	(312) 440-1053
Sokolik, Jim/Chicago/(312) 786-1560	**pages 526-527**
Sokolik, Jim/St. Louis/(314) 241-4014	**pages 526-527**
Soldat, Rick/432 N. Clark St., Chicago	(312) 661-1013
Solomon, Bob/Chicago	(312) 664-1824
Soluri, Tony/1147 W. Ohio St., Chicago	(312) 243-6580
Somlo, Carolyn/Chicago/(312) 226-2272	**pages 492-493**
Sorokowski, Richard/1015 N. Halsted, Chicago	(312) 280-1256
Spahr, Dick/1133 E. 61st St., Indpls.	(317) 255-2400
Spencer, G. Robert/3546 Dakota Ave. S., Mpls.	(612) 929-7803
Spiker, Scott Location Photography/824 S. Logan, Moscow	(208) 882-5102
Srenco Photography/5 Price Meadows, St. Louis	(314) 993-6548
Stage 3 Productions, Inc./32588 Dequlndre Rd., Warren	(313) 978-7373
Stansfield, Stanley/215 W. Ohio, Chicago	(312) 337-3245
Stark Production Assocs., Ltd./311 N. Deslpaines St., Chicago	(312) 648-1280
Starmark Photog./240 E. Ontario, Chicago	(312) 944-6700
Steele, Chas B./531 S. Plymouth Ct., Chicago	(312) 922-0201
Stege, Lynn Represents/441 E. Erie, Chicago	(312) 280-4771
Stein, Fredric/955 W. Lake St., Chicago	(312) 226-7447
Steinberg, Michael/2530 Superior, Cleveland	(216) 589-9953
Steinhardt, Dan/325 W. Huron St., Chicago	(312) 944-0226
Steinke, Jay/1831 E. Third St., Duluth	(218) 728-6046
Stemo Photography, Inc./1880 Holste Rd., Northbrook	(312) 498-4844
Stenberg, Pete/225 W. Hubbard, Chicago	(312) 644-6137
Stephens Studio/2001 Dalton Ave., Cincinnati	(513) 651-3456
Sterling, Joseph/2216 N. Cleveland, Chicago	(312) 348-4333
Stewart, Tom/2140 Austin Rd., Troy	(313) 689-0480
Stewart-Reiley/18 W. Seventh St., Cincinnati	(513) 241-7181
Stieber, Doug & Co./405 N. Wabash, Chicago	(312) 222-9595
Stille, George/2812 Harrison Ave., Cincinnati	(513) 661-4772
Stone, Tony Worldwide/233 E. Ontario, Chicago	(800) 234-7880
Stowell Studios, Inc./1255 S. Michigan Ave., Chicago	(312) 939-3337
Straus, Jerry/247 E. Ontario, Chicago	(312) 787-2628
Stringer, Tom/3842 W. Pine St., St. Louis	(314) 533-6665
Strong, Ron/5343 N. Adams, Bloomfield Hills	(313) 646-9233
Stroube, Greg/Chicago/(312) 786-1560	**pages 528-529**
Stroube, Greg/St. Louis/(314) 241-4014	**pages 528-529**
Struse, Perry L./232 Sixth St., W. Des Moines	(515) 279-9761
Studio 3/716 N. First St., Mpls.	(612) 338-4686
Studio 3, Inc./750 Forest, Birmingham	(313) 646-5550
Studio 3, Inc./Troy	(313) 689-0480
Studio Assoc., Inc./2204 Prudential Plz., Chicago	(312) 372-4013
Studio D, Inc./2857 E. Grand Blvd., Detroit	(313) 875-6617
Studio Plus, Inc./3025 S. 26th Ave., Broadview	(312) 344-1020
Studio R/3043 Carnegie, Cleveland	(216) 391-4343
Studio Rossi/4555 Emery Indust. Pky., Cleveland	(216) 831-0688
Studio on North Franklin, The/730 N. Franklin, Chicago	(312) 337-1490
Studio, The/Old Lake Rd., Baraboo	(608) 356-3761
Sudnik & Overhardt, Inc./700 Minnesota, Troy	(313) 588-1030
Sulla, Salavatore/59 W. Hubbard, Chicago	(312) 645-0714
Summers, Alan/153 W. Ohio, Chicago	(312) 527-0908
TPS Studios/4016 S. California Ave., Chicago	(312) 847-1221
TWC Illustrational Photography/Dearborn Hts.	(313) 561-9376
Taber, Gary/305 S. Green, Chicago	(312) 726-0374
Tann, Jasmin/3714 N. Racine, Chicago	(312) 248-3428
Tassone, Gary/2816 McKinley St., N.E., Mpls.	(612) 868-8600
Tate Jr., Ted M./1836 Euclid Ave., Cleveland	(216) 861-4230
Taverna, J.T. Assocs., Inc./344 M40 South, Allegen	(616) 673-3903
Taxel, Barney/4614 Prospect Ave., Cleveland	(216) 431-2400
Technigraph Studio/1212 Jarvis Ave., Elk Grove Vlg.	(312) 437-3334
Tepke, Janice/Chicago	(312) 348-5393
Terry's Photography/60 W. Superior, Chicago	(312) 943-2131
Teufen, Al/Medina	(216) 723-3237
Thill, Nancy/70 W. Huron, Chicago	(312) 944-7164
Thoen & Assoc. Adv. Photog., Inc./14940 Minnetonka Ind. Rd., Minnetonka	(612) 938-2433

Thomas, Tony/676 N. La Salle St., Chicago ..... (312) 337-2274
Thompson, Ken/215 W. Ohio St., Chicago ..... (312) 329-9363
Tilley, Ed/1121 Auburn Pl. N.W., Canton ..... (216) 493-7777
Tillis & Tillis, Inc./1050 W. Kinzie, Chicago ..... (312) 733-7336
Tokuno, Dean /Black Market/920 N. Franklin, Chicago ..... (312) 944-6104
Total Image Studios/332 Peterson Rd., Libertyville ..... (312) 816-3338
Tracy, Janis/213 W. Institute Pl., Chicago ..... (312) 787-7166
Trantafil, Gary/222 S. Morgan, Chicago ..... (312) 666-1029
Trepal Photography/2460 Lakeside Ave., Cleveland ..... (216) 781-3529
Trilla, Linda/Chicago ..... (312) 421-4446
Trinko, Genny/126 W. Kinzie, Chicago ..... (312) 670-0438
Trott, David/Troy ..... (313) 583-2828
Trujillo, Eduardo/345 N. Canal, Chicago ..... (312) 454-9798
Tucker, Bill Studio, Inc./Chicago/(312) 243-7113 ..... **pages 488-489**
Tucker, Mort/1616 St. Clair, Cleveland ..... (216) 696-4616
Tuke, Joni/325 W. Huron, Chicago ..... (312) 787-6826
Tull, Steve/Troy ..... (313) 583-4747
Tussing, Tim/700 N. Washington Ave., Mpls. ..... (612) 332-9165
Tytel Photography/500 S. Clinton, Chicago ..... (312) 739-5400
USAV Communications Group/Milwaukee ..... (414) 796-2000
Uhlmann, Gina/1611 N. Sheffield Ave., Chicago ..... (312) 642-6650
Umland, Steve/Mpls./(612) 332-1590 ..... **pages 498-499**
Upitis, Alvis/620 Morgan Ave. S., Mpls. ..... (612) 374-9375
Urba, Alexas/148 W. Illinois, Chicago ..... (312) 644-4466
Van De Velde, Mark/8965 Shannon, Sterling Hts. ..... (313) 254-9570
Van Dyne, Ken/3560 S. Old State Rd., Delaware ..... (614) 548-4349
Van Ingewen, Bruce/1422 W. Belle Plaine, Chicago ..... (312) 477-8344
Van Kirk, Deborah/855 W. Blackhawk, Chicago ..... (312) 642-7766
VanMarter, Robert/1209 Alstott Dr. S., Howell ..... (517) 546-1923
Vandenberg, Greg/119 N. Peoria St., Chicago ..... (312) 733-7007
Vander Lende, Craig/120 Commerce S.W., Grand Rapids ..... (616) 459-2880
Vander Veen Photography/Milwaukee ..... (414) 527-0450
Vaughan, Jim/321 S. Jefferson, Chicago ..... (312) 663-0369
Vaughn, Michael/6332 N. Guilford, Indpls. ..... (317) 255-0299
Vedros, Nick & Assocs./Kansas City/(816) 471-5488 ..... **pages 524-525**
Ventola, Giorgio Photography/Chicago ..... (312) 951-0880
Vergara, Carlos Photography/931 W. Liberty, Wheaton ..... (708) 690-7904
Vergos, Jim/122 W. Kinzie, Chicago ..... (312) 527-1769
Viernum, Bill/1629 Mandel Ave., Westchester ..... (312) 562-4143
Viewfinders, Inc./126 N. Third St., Mpls. ..... (800) 776-8171
Visser, James/4274 Shenandoah Ave., St. Louis ..... (314) 771-6857
Vizanko Adv. Photog./11511 K-Tel Dr., Minnetonka ..... (612) 933-1314
Vogue Wright/100 S. Ashland Ave., Chicago ..... (312) 942-1900
Vollan, Michael/117 S. Morgan, Chicago ..... (312) 997-2347
Von Dorn, John/685 W. Ohio St., Chicago ..... (312) 243-8578
Voyles, Dick & Assoc./2822 Breckenridge Ind. Ct., St. Louis ..... (314) 968-3851
Vuksanovich, Inc./318 N. Laflin St., Chicago ..... (312) 243-7464
Wagenaar, David/1035 W. Lake St., Chicago ..... (312) 944-6330
Waite, Tim/717 S. Sixth St., Milwaukee ..... (414) 643-1500
Wakefield's of Kansas City, Inc./5122 Grand Ave., Kansas City ..... (816) 531-8448
Walker, Jessie/241 Fairview, Glencoe ..... (312) 835-0522
Wans, Glen/Kansas City/(816) 931-8905 ..... **pages 478-479**
Ward, Les/Southfield/(313) 350-8666 ..... **page 536**
Warkenthien, Dan/117 S. Morgan, Chicago ..... (312) 666-6056
Warren Reynolds & Assoc., Inc./6401 Indian Hills Rd., Edina ..... (612) 941-2557
Warren, Lennie/Chicago ..... (312) 666-0490
Weeks, Christopher/1260 E. 31st Pl., Tulsa ..... (918) 749-8289
Weidemann, Skot/6621 Century Ave., Middleton ..... (608) 836-5744
Weiner, Jim/540 N. Lakeshore Dr., Chicago ..... (312) 644-0054
Weinstein, John/2413 N. Clybourn Ave., Chicago ..... (312) 327-8184
Weinstein, Philip/343 S. Dearborn, Chicago ..... (312) 922-1945
Welzenbach, John/Chicago ..... (312) 337-3611
Wend, Jim/Milwaukee ..... (414) 342-6363
West, Stu/430 First Ave. N., Mpls. ..... (612) 375-0404
Westerman, Charlie/Chicago/(312) 664-5837 ..... **pages 510-511**
Wetzler Studios/2240 Prospect, Cleveland ..... (216) 771-1554
Wheelock, Dana/800 Washington Ave. N., Mpls. ..... (612) 333-5110
Whit Anderson Photography/560 W. Lake St., Chicago ..... (312) 993-7644
Whitmer, Jim/125 Wakeman, Wheaton ..... (312) 653-1344
Whitson & Associates/7401 Manchester, St. Louis ..... (314) 781-7200
Wiand, Dennis/Troy ..... (363) 280-0640
Wigeland, Kaeti/3224 W. 204th St., Olympia Fields ..... (312) 747-9633
Wilder, Dave/411 W. St. Clair, Cleveland ..... (216) 771-7687

Willette, Brady/1030 Nicollet Mall, Mpls. .... (612) 338-6727
Williams, Wayne/1030 N. Beville, Indpls. .... (317) 637-7498
Wilson, Ellis V./Boise .... (208) 384-5220
Wilson, Tim Photo./1634 N. Milwaukee, Chicago .... (312) 486-0500
Withington, Troy/Milwaukee .... (414) 224-1055
Witte, Scott J./3025 W. Highland Blvd., Milwaukee .... (414) 933-3223
Woburn Studios/4715 N. Ronald, Harwood Hts. .... (312) 867-5445
Woit, Steve/6028 Kaymar Dr., Mpls. .... (612) 822-8619
Wolf, Bobbc/1101 W. Armitage, Chicago .... (312) 472-9503
Wolf, Don/3117 Merriam Ln., Kansas City .... (913) 384-9653
Wolff Studio, Inc./11357 S. Second St., Schoolcraft .... (616) 342-0666
Wolford, Ric/2300 E. Douglas, Wichita .... (316) 264-3013
Wolter, Stephen/117 S. Morgan, Chicago .... (312) 666-4772
Wong, Peter Poon On/510 First Ave. N., Mpls. .... (612) 340-0798
Wonsch, Dan/Troy .... (313) 280-0640
Wooden, John/219 N. Second St., Mpls. .... (612) 339-3032
Woodside, Mike/420 N. Fifth St., Mpls. .... (612) 338-5553
Woodward Photography Ltd./401 W. Superior, Chicago .... (312) 337-5838
Wright, John/642 Oakley, Topeka .... (913) 234-2770
Wyckoff Commercial Studio/Ten S. Waiola Ave., LaGrange .... (312) 354-2889
Yapp, Charles Studio, Inc./723 W. Randolph, Chicago .... (312) 558-9338
Yoder, Ken L./1510 S. Ironwood, Mishawaka .... (219) 288-8942
Zaitz, Dan/900 W. Jackson, Chicago .... (312) 489-7492
Zak, Rudy/500 S. Clinton, Chicago .... (312) 663-3654
Zake, Bruce/633 Huron Rd., Cleveland .... (216) 694-3686
Zamiar, Thomas/210 W. Chicago Ave., Chicago .... (312) 787-4976
Zann, Arnold/502 N. Grove, Oak Pk. .... (312) 386-2864
Zoom, Inc./DeLich Kitahara/304 W. Tenth St., Kansas City .... (816) 474-6699
Zukas, Rimantis/1244 W. Chicago, Chicago .... (312) 421-4446
Zwayer, Deborah & Assoc., Inc./308 W. Erie, Chicago .... (312) 664-1824

Huibregtse

Mike Huibregtse 414/272-2929 FAX/272-1502

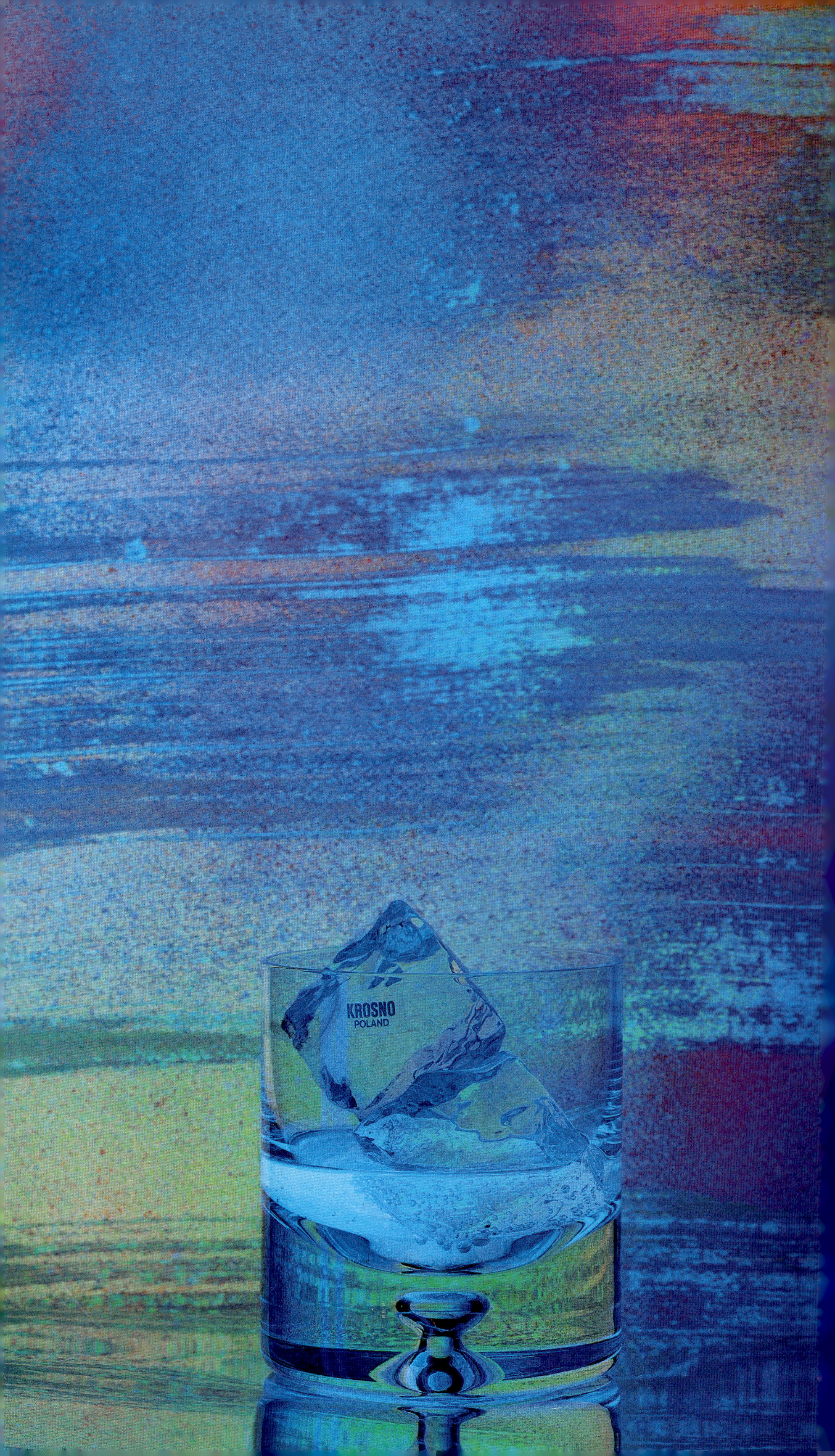
KROSNO
POLAND

HARRISON JONES

CHICAGO
312 421-6400
FAX 421-3391

AGENT
MARY ANN BARASA
312 464-7815

Bieber

Tim Bieber (312) 463-3590
In Chicago: Joel Harlib (312) 329-1370 Fax (312) 329-1397
In New York: Michael Ash (212) 807-6286

Paul Elledge Photography · 1808 West Grand Avenue · Chicago, Illinois 60622 · (312) 733-8021

Represented by: Joel Harlib (312) 329-1370
Outside Chicago: Ceci Bartels (314) 241-4014

Paul Elledge
PHOTOGRAPHY

NOZICKA

STEVE NOZICKA PHOTOGRAPHY LTD   314 W INSTITUTE PLACE   CHICAGO, IL 60610   312 787 8925
REPRESENTED BY JOEL HARLIB AND ASSOCIATES, INC   312 329 1370

477

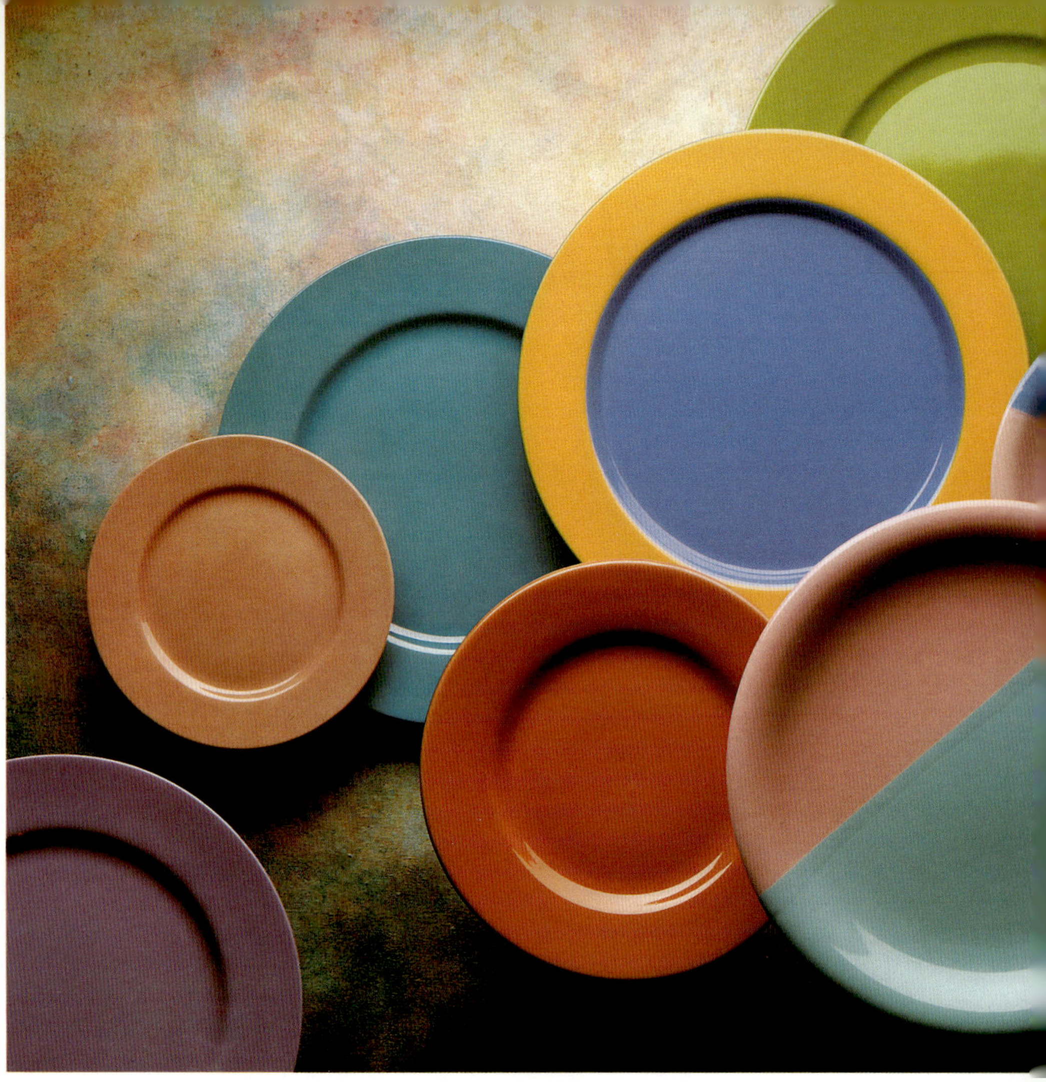

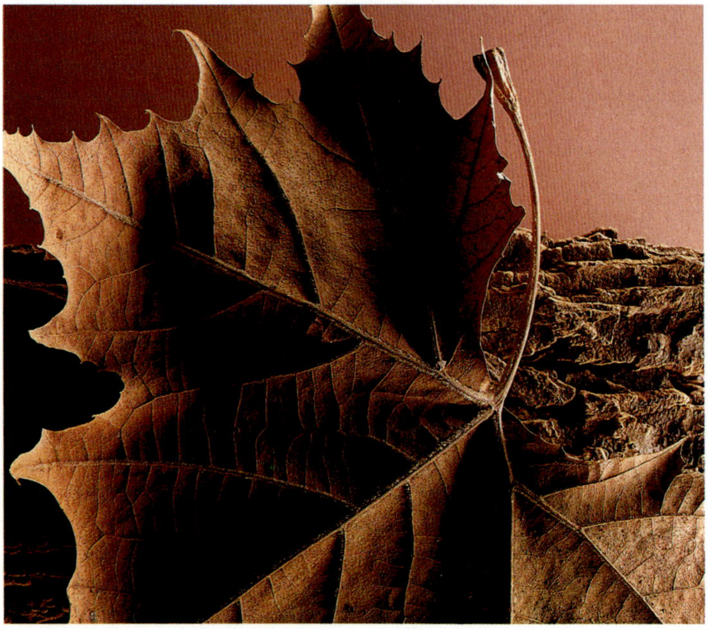

GLEN WANS

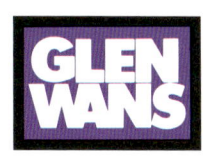

WANS STUDIO, INC.

325 West 40th Street
Kansas City, Missouri 64111
(816) 931-8905
FAX: (816) 931-6899

RICHARD HAMILTON SMITH

Richard Hamilton Smith 612-645-5070 Fax 612-645-8263

Agents: Mary Atols, John Hoffman 312-222-0504 Fax 312-222-0503

New York Agent: Susan Miller 212-905-8400

For stock call Jan Bliss 612-645-5070 Fax 612-645-8263

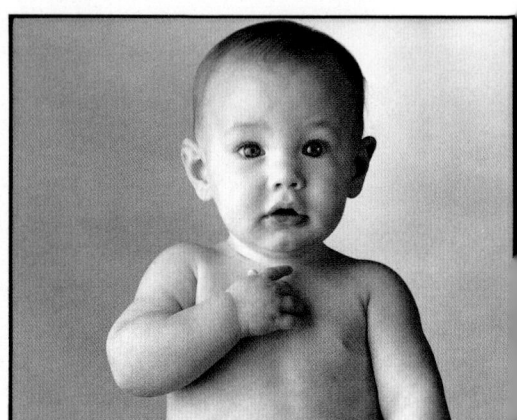

DON GETSUG STUDIOS, CHICAGO, 312/939-1477
AGENTS ▪ MARY ATOLS & JOHN HOFFMAN ▪ 312/222-0504

483

Concept

SCHEWE

Jeff Schewe Photography

624 West Willow

Chicago, Illinois 60614

312-951-6334

fax 312-787-6814

print and film assignments

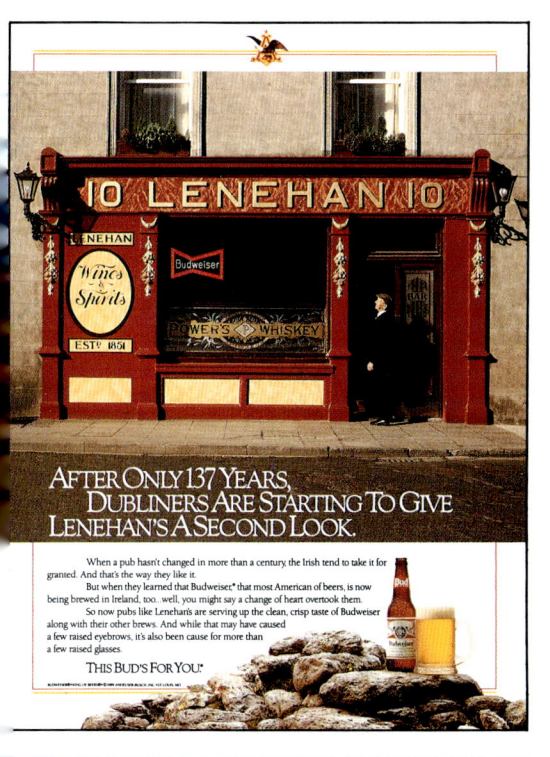

Execution

Christopher **Kean**

Pickwick Building
3 South Prospect
Park Ridge IL 60068 USA
Telephone 708 292 1144

Southwest Agents:
Larry & Andrea Lynch/Repertoire
Telephone 214 369 6990

How Bill Tucker Took The Cheese Out Of Childrens Photography

Stop by Bill's studio and you'll never once hear him ask his kids to smile. Because, after twenty years of shooting kids, Bill knows the more you ask a kid to do something, the more it looks like you asked a kid to do something. So instead, he does everything he can to make them feel comfortable. If the shot calls for a somber mood, he might just talk with them. If he wants a smile, he's been known to put on a puppet show or two. Only when everything's just right, will he let the camera do the rest.

And it's paid off, too. Bill's won every award from the Hatch to the Norma. Recently his work for Sears' McKids® stores helped Ogilvy & Mather take home the Gold Addy in Chicago. You see, any photographer can get a kid to say "cheese." But only a few have the sense to avoid asking.

Bill Tucker Studio, Inc. • 19 North May Street • Chicago, Illinois 60607 • (312) 243-7113 • Fax: (312) 243-9641

SHOTWELL
Studio 312-929-0168 Fax 312-929-1481

SHOTWELL
Studio 312-929-0168 Fax 312-929-1481

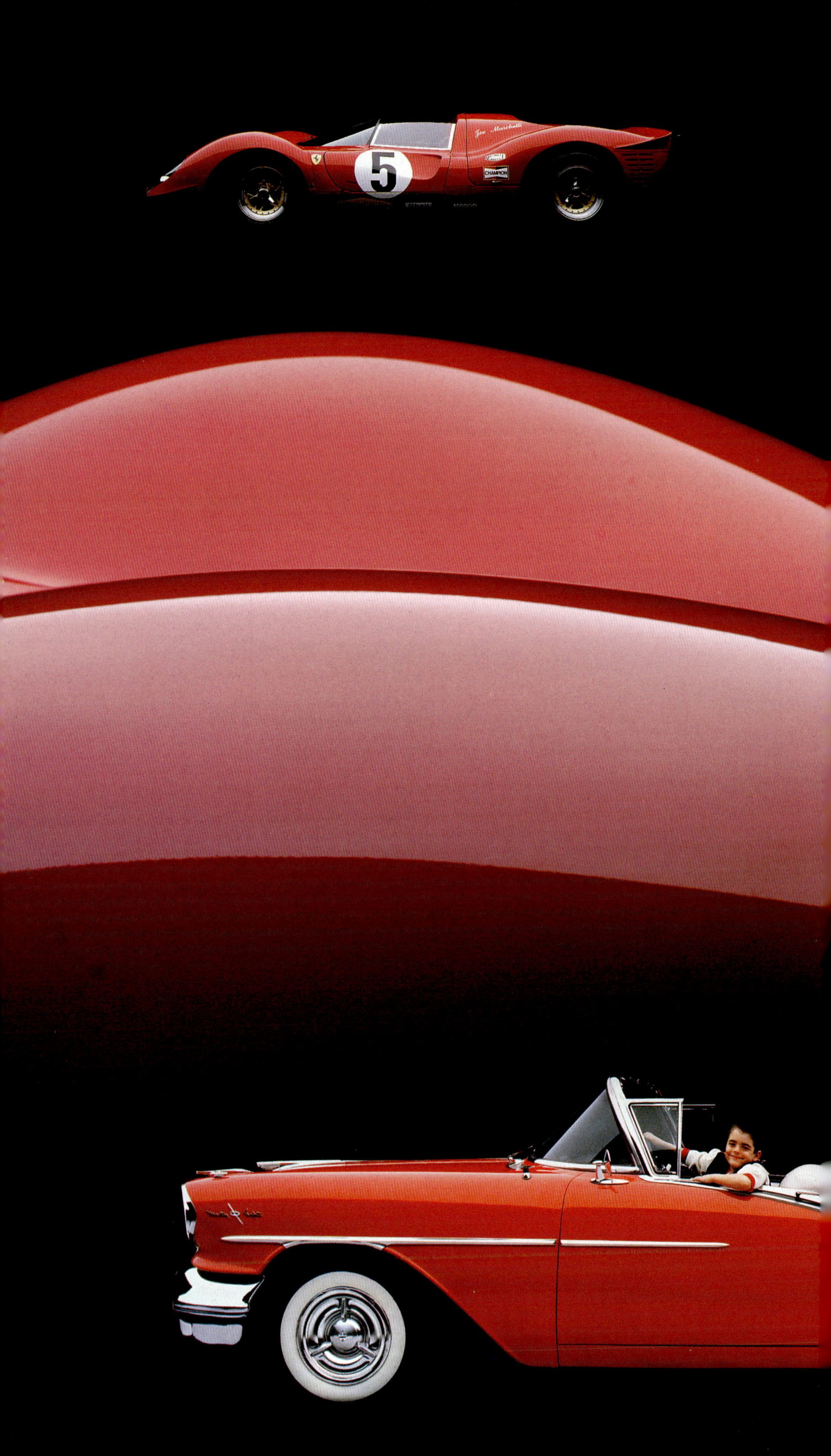
5
CHAMPION

GRUBMAN.

Steve Grubman Photography Inc.

456 North Morgan

Chicago IL 60622 (312) 226-2272

represented by Carolyn Somlo

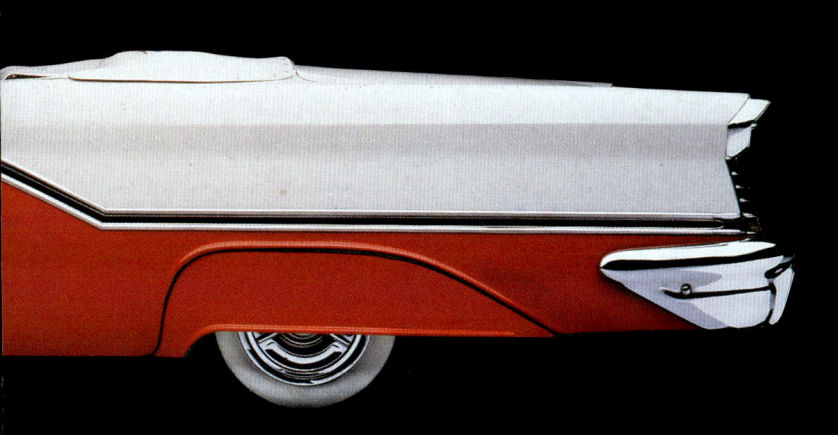

493

ART DIRECTION OF LeMOND PHOTOGRAPH BY PAUL KOERNER, BBDO, NEW YORK.

P E R F E C

MARVY! ADVERTISING PHOTOGRAPHY   41 TWELFTH AVENUE NORTH   HOPKINS, MINNESOTA 55343

TELEPHONE 612.935.0307   FAX 612.933.2061

©1990 MARVY! ADVERTISING PHOTOGRAPHY

T L Y MARVY!

GREG LeMOND, TWO-TIME TOUR de FRANCE WINNER PHOTOGRAPHED <u>IN STUDIO</u>

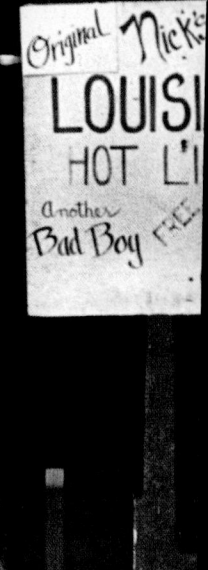

© 1990 Jim Arndt
Client: Lee Jeans
Art Director: Arty Tan

ARNDT
JIM ARNDT PHOTOGRAPHY

Umland

600 Washington Ave. N., Minneapolis, MN 55401
(612) 332-1590 FAX: (612) 332-6940

JOE HEMP / Carmichael Lynch

JAC COVERDALE / Clarity Coverdale Rueff

BOB KIESOW/Rumrill Hoyt

MARK JOHNSON/Fallon McElligott

MARK WOLF/CMF&Z

DESIGN FIRM: LISKA AND ASSOCIATES, INC.   CLIENT: INTERNATIONAL PAPER

Laurie Rubin

REPRESENTED BY RANDI FIAT AND ASSOCIATES   TELEPHONE 312-664-8322   FAX 312-787-9486

DESIGN FIRM: LISKA AND ASSOCIATES, INC.   CLIENT: INTERNATIONAL PAPER

Laurie Rubin

REPRESENTED BY RANDI FIAT AND ASSOCIATES   TELEPHONE 312-664-8322   FAX 312-787-9486

MARC HAUSER

REPRESENTED BY RANDI FIAT AND ASSOCIATES   612 NORTH MICHIGAN AVENUE, CHICAGO, ILLINOIS 60611   TELEPHONE 312-664-8322   FAX 312-787-9486

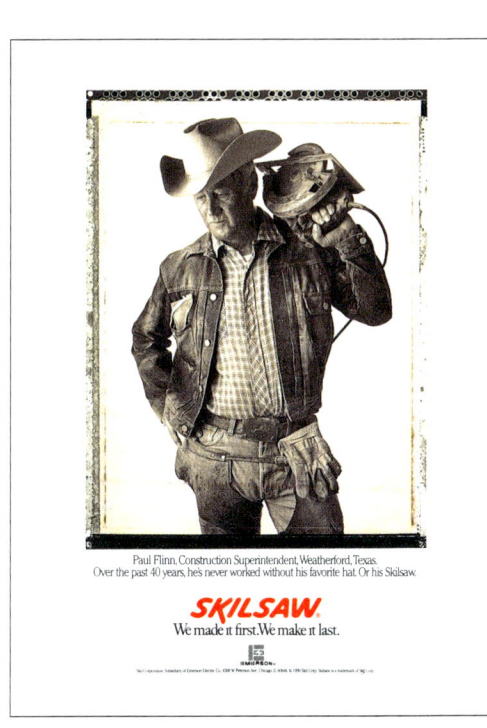

MARC HAUSER

FILM REPRESENTED BY SHERRY OWENS, GKO PRODUCTIONS, INC.   25 WEST HUBBARD, CHICAGO, ILLINOIS 60610   TELEPHONE 312-329-1877   FAX 312-527-2204
NEW YORK REPRESENTATIVE   ZARI INTERNATIONAL   SUITE 700   850 7TH AVENUE, NEW YORK, N.Y. 10019   TELEPHONE 212-765-8220   FAX 212-765-8221

REPRESENTED IN CHICAGO BY VINCENT KAMIN 312-787-8834

STEVEN
LEDELL

REPRESENTED IN CHICAGO BY VINCENT KAMIN 312-787-8834

KERRY PETERSON SHOOTS STILL LIFE.

To put the life back into your still life, use Kerry Peterson. Call (612) 332-8864 for still photography you'll flip over.

RICK DUBLIN SHOOTS ANIMALS.

No matter what the genus, Rick Dublin is a genius. Call (612) 332-8864 for animal photography you'll flip over.

KERRY PETERSON CAN STILL FOCUS AFTER 12 SHOTS OF BOURBON.
Call (612) 332-8864 for still life photography that goes down smooth.

"I shot the dog."

Mark Alexander Studio
412 Central Avenue, Cincinnati OH 45202, 513-651-5020 Fax: 651-0192

DAVE JORDANO PHOTOGRAPHY, NORTH WELLS, CHICAGO ILLINOIS 60610. 312.280.8212. FAX 312.280.1779

REPRESENTED BY VINCENT J. KAMIN & ASSOCIATES. 312.787.8834. FAX 312.787.8172

JORDANO

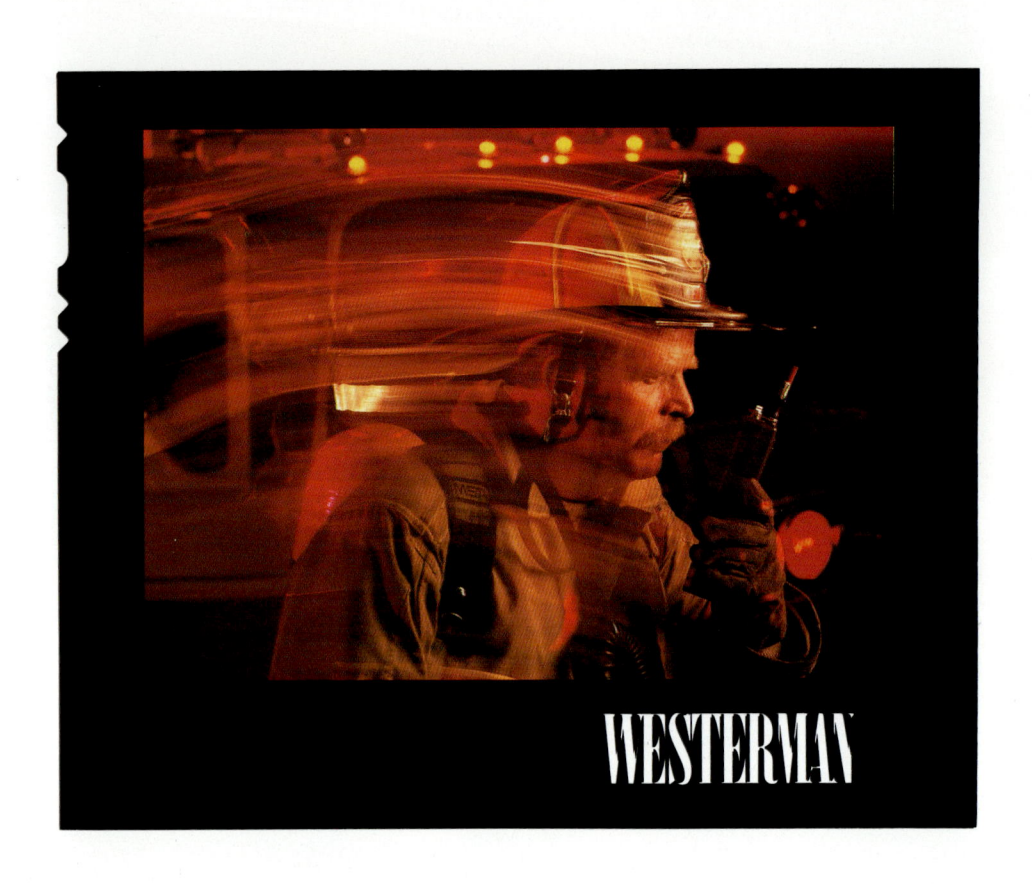

CHARLIE WESTERMAN • CHICAGO (312) 664-5837 • NEW YORK (212) 353-1235

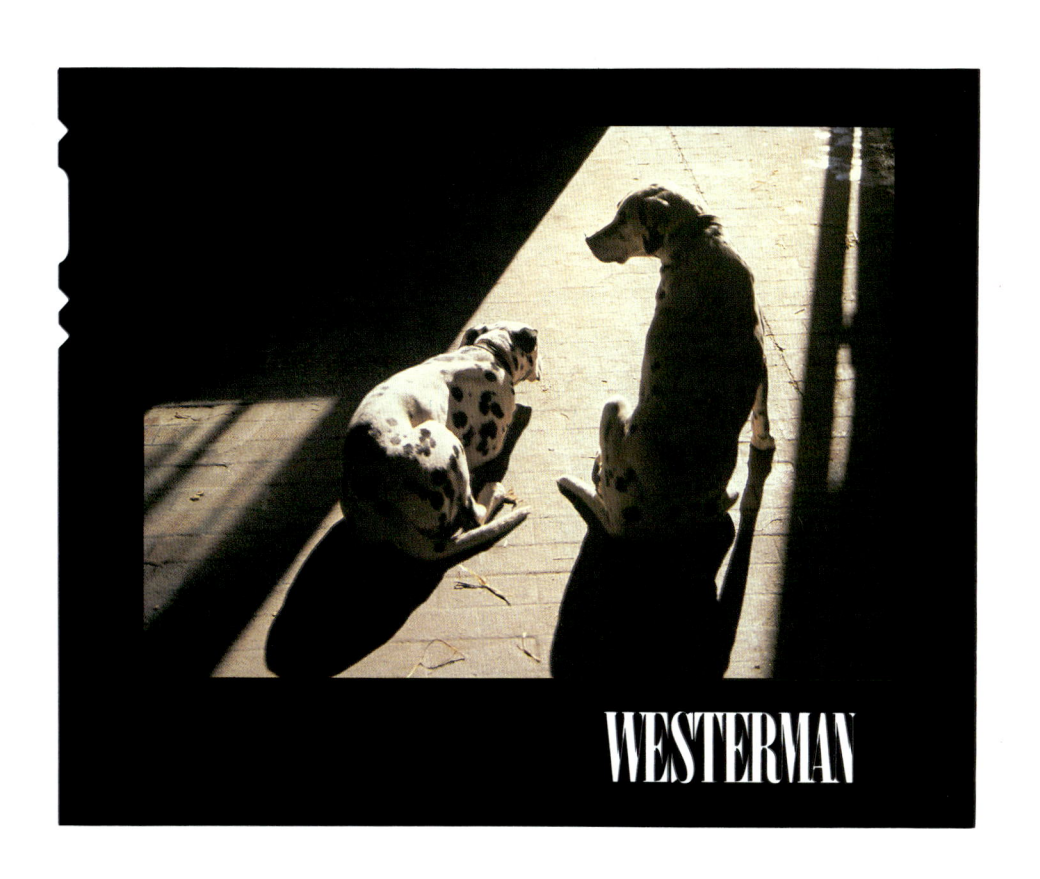

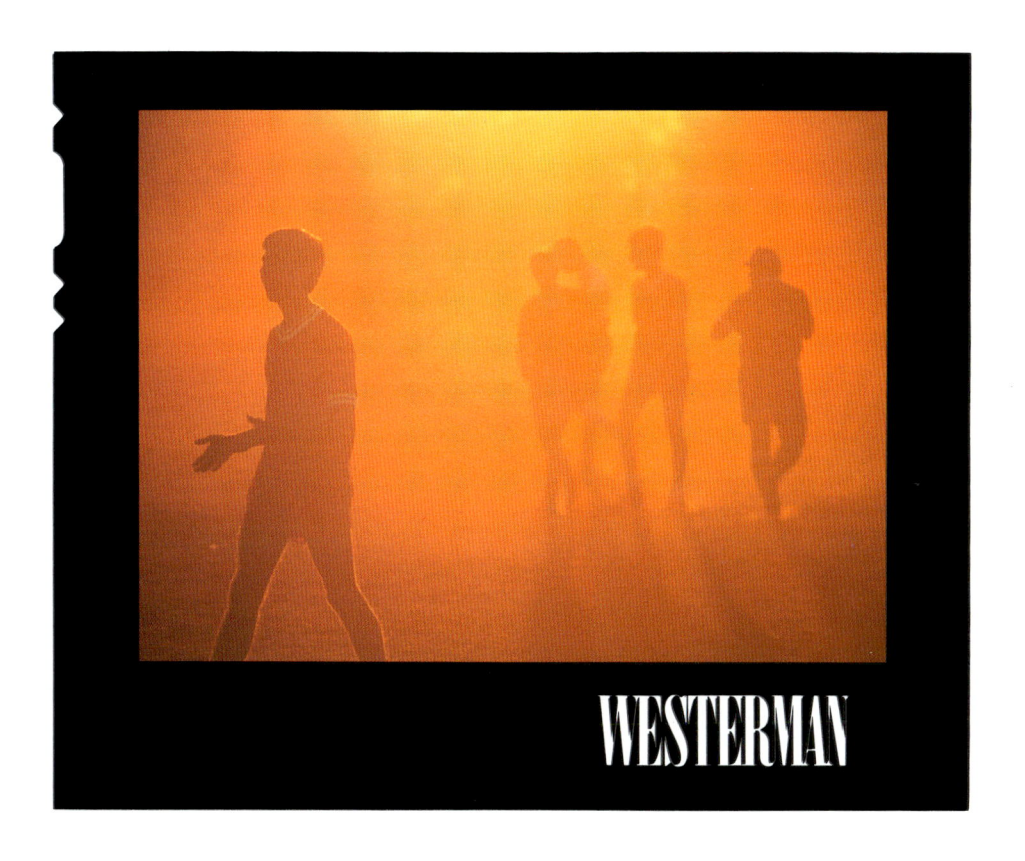

CHARLIE WESTERMAN • CHICAGO (312) 664-5837 • NEW YORK (212) 353-1235

Glenn Stern

Glenn Gemm

Photographic Illustration • 407 North Elizabeth Street, Chicago, Illinois, 60622 • Represented by Marlene Marino • (312) 666-7300

513

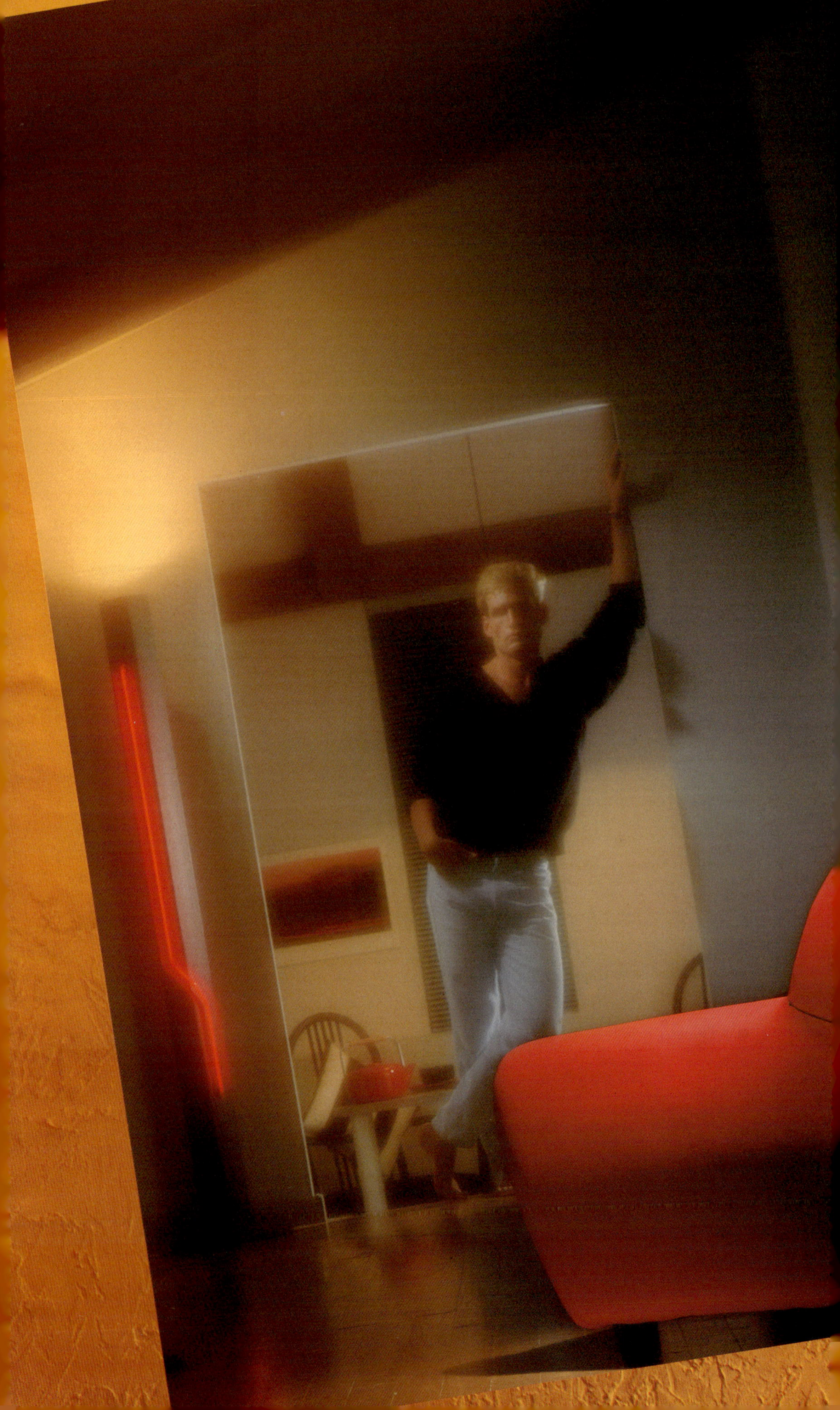

PHOTOGRAPHY
SAKS

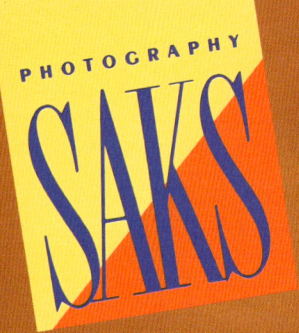

REPRESENTED BY ANN KELTSCH
317-849-7723
9257 CASTLEGATE DR.
INDIANAPOLIS, IN 46256
FAX-849-7885

D'Orio

Tony D'Orio Photography
312 421-5532

❖

Represented by Skillicorn Associates 312 856-1626 Fax 312 938-2072

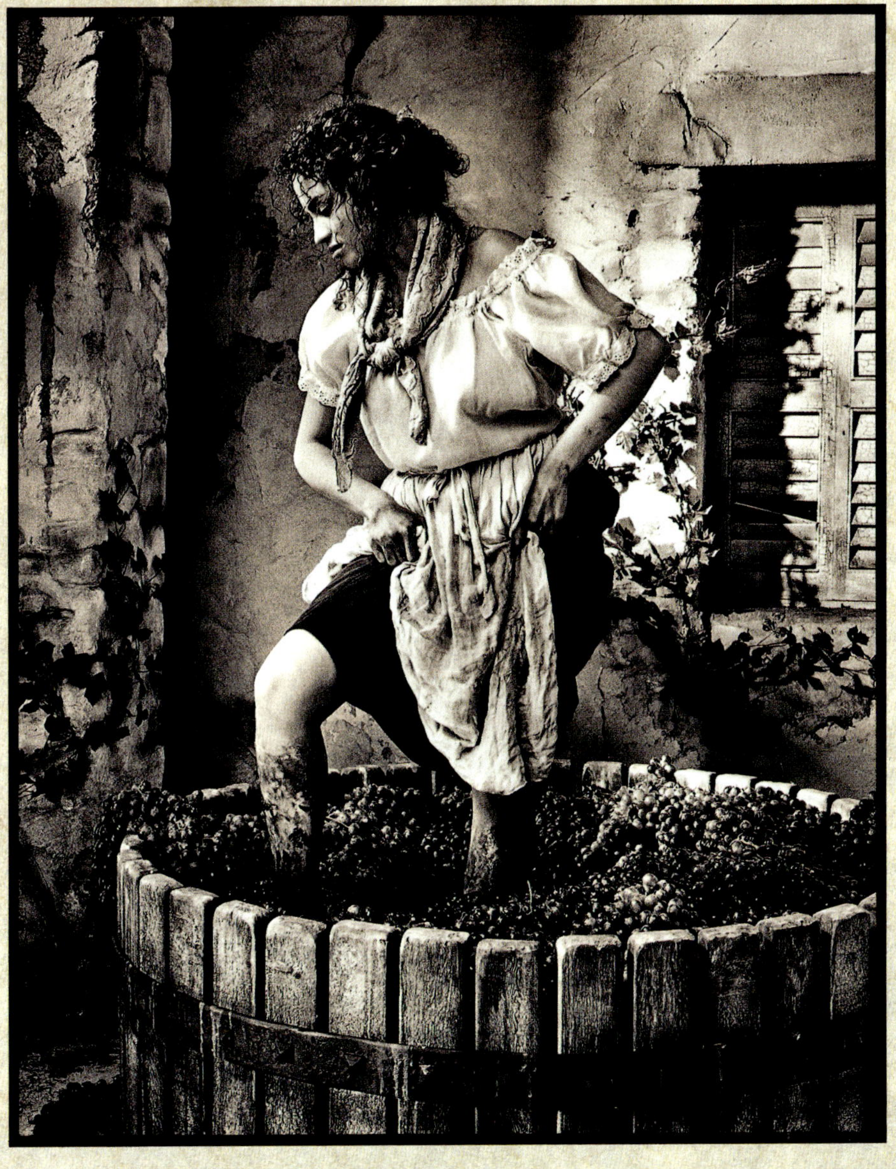

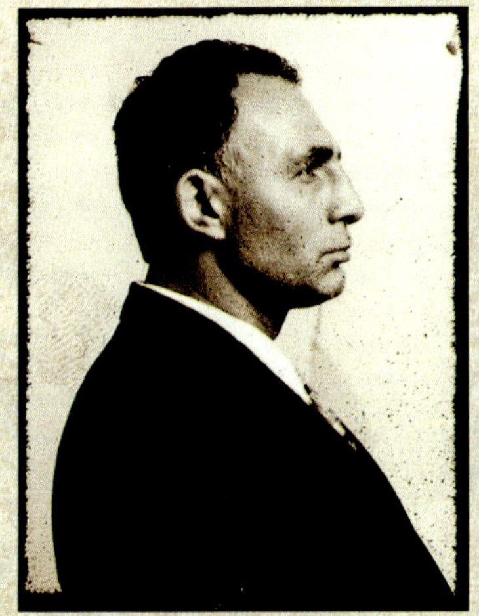

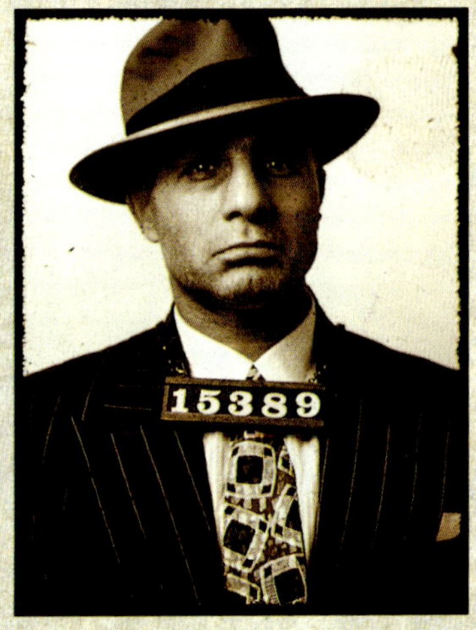
15389

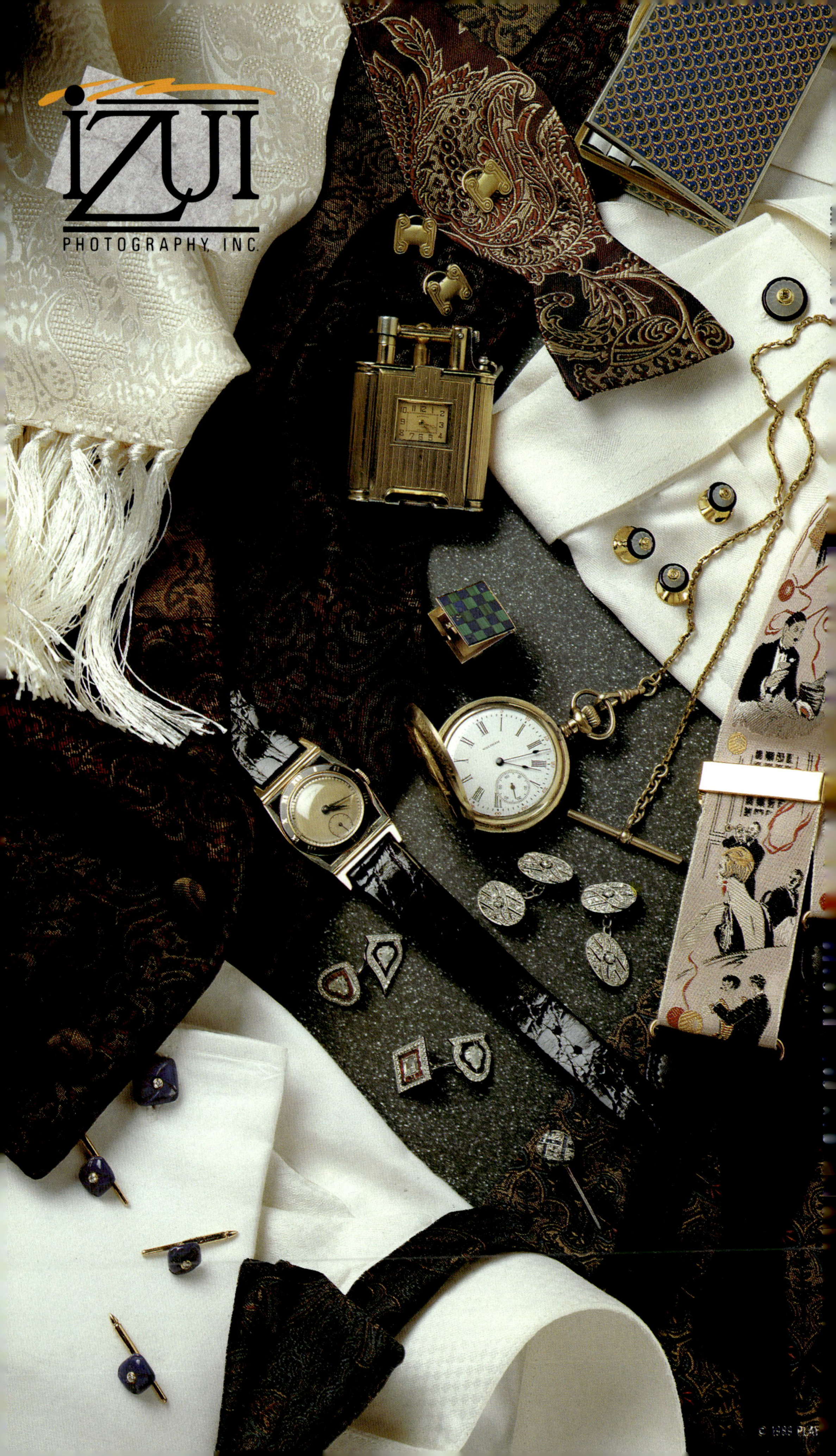
IZUI
PHOTOGRAPHY, INC.

COURTESY OF WILSON SPORTING GOODS

ZUI PHOTOGRAPHY
315 WEST WALTON
CHICAGO, IL 60610

Surface Lighting

HALO

© 1990 PLAYBOY

312.266.8029

FAX: 312.266.9430

STILLS AND FILM AVAILABLE UPON REQUEST

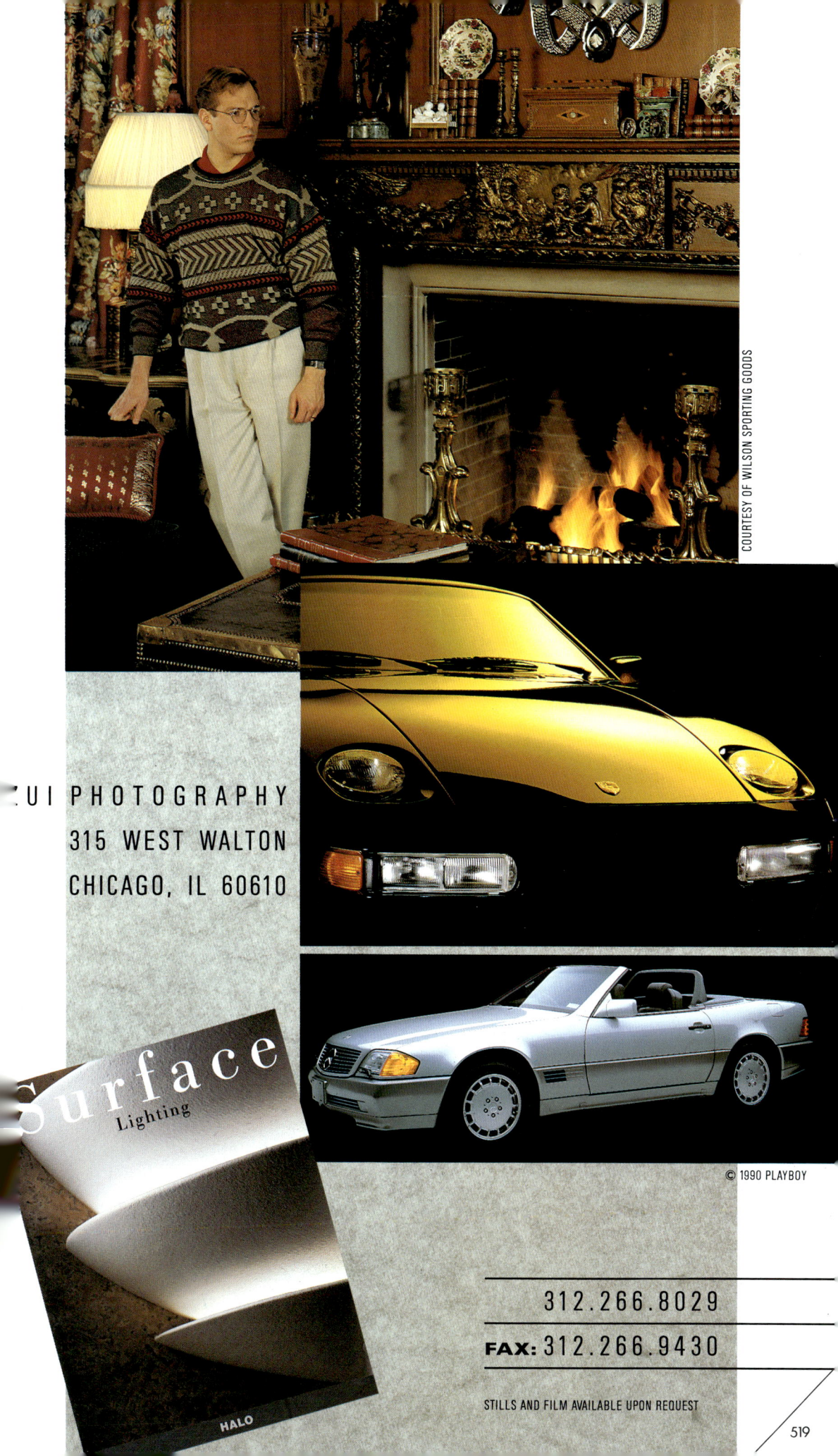

519

THE
ATKINSON
IMAGE

14 North Newstead
St. Louis Mo. 63108
(314) 535-6484
Fax (314) 535-9848
Phototographic art from
Gateways-Cookbook
PHOTO DESIGN BY
DAVID K. ATKINSON
Food styling by Joni.

HOWARD KLOC 313•541•1704

KLOCWORKS
PHOTOGRAPHY

Art Director-Bill Shea
Agency-McCann Erickson N.Y.

521

ROSS ROY

MICHAEL MOORER/AEGIS GROUP

AMEEN

AMEEN HOWRANI PHOTOGRAPHY REPRESENTED BY ELIZABETH HOLLOW
DETROIT: (313) 875-3123   FAX: 875-3134

HOWARD KLOC 313·541·1704

KLOCWORKS
PHOTOGRAPHY

VEDROS
& ASSOCIATES

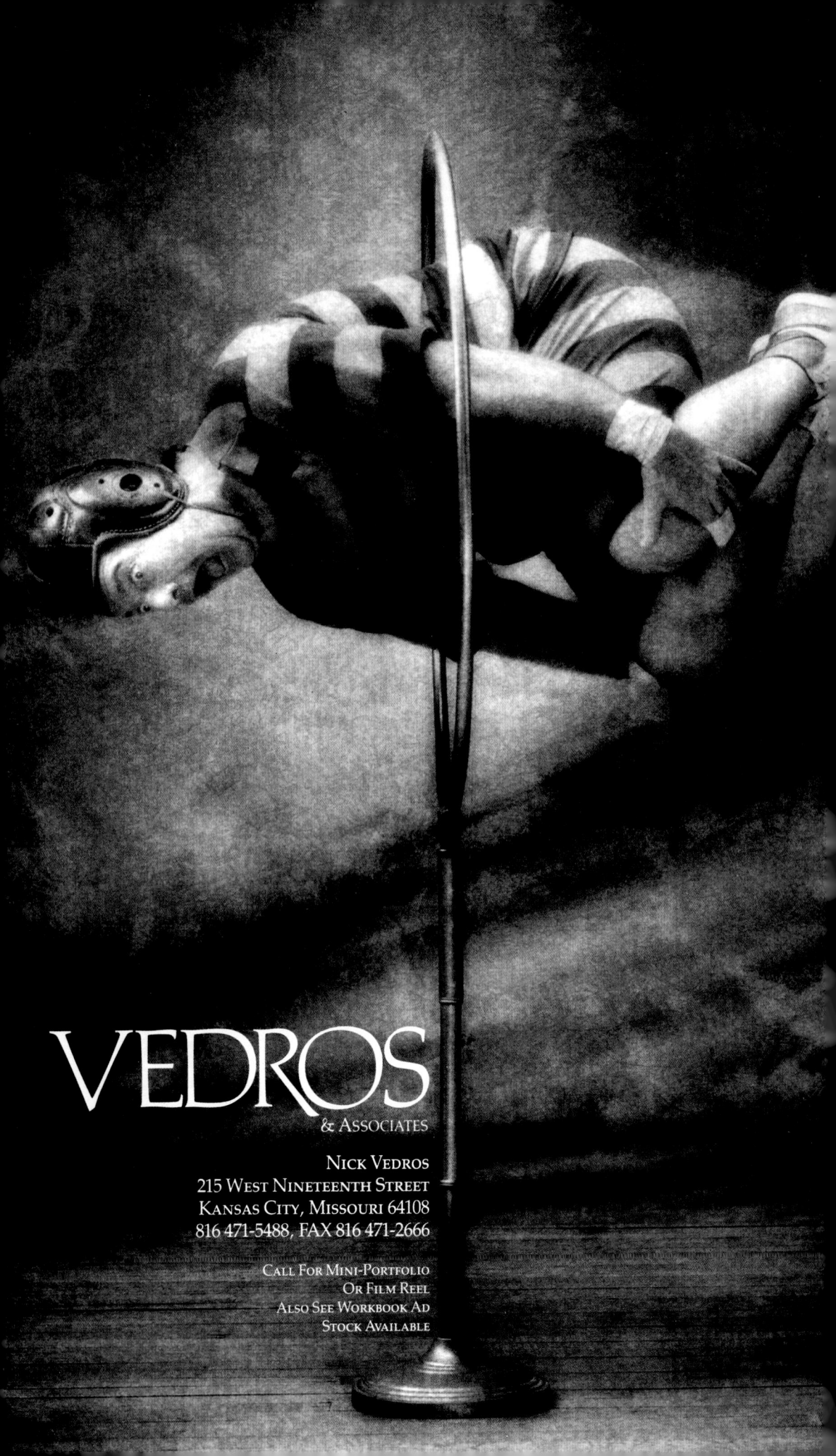

NICK VEDROS
215 WEST NINETEENTH STREET
KANSAS CITY, MISSOURI 64108
816 471-5488, FAX 816 471-2666

CALL FOR MINI-PORTFOLIO
OR FILM REEL
ALSO SEE WORKBOOK AD
STOCK AVAILABLE

© Nick Vedros, Vedros & Associates 1990

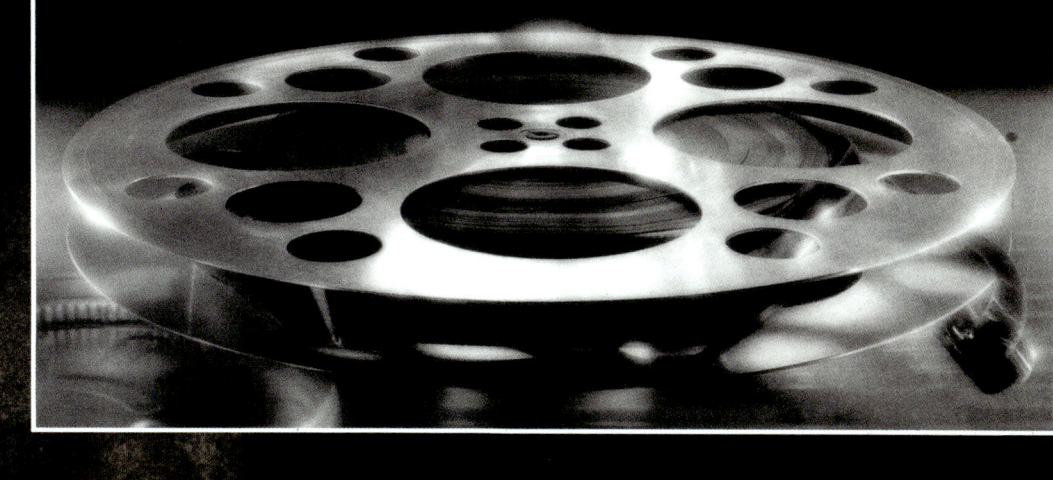

THE WINNING EXECUTION Finding the right artist, photographer or director is paramount to the winning execution your ideas demand.

If you had all the time in the world, you could search all the books and reels in the world. But time is precious.

You realize you must delegate the search to competent others.

At Ceci Bartels Associates we screen hundreds of portfolios and reels every year to represent to you only the best. By knowing you and knowing them, we're able to provide you with the talent you're looking for.

Rely on us to find the talent you need and you will inherit the time you need. Call us. Together we can turn your ideas into winning executions.

CECI BARTELS ASSOCIATES

1913 Park Ave. St. Louis, MO 63104 (314) 241-4014 STL (212) 912-1877 NYC (312) 786-1560 CHIC (314) 241-9028 FAX

314-241-4014 STL
212-912-1877 NYC
312-786-1560 CHIC
314-241-9028 FAX

JIM SOKOLIK
Represented by Ceci Bartels Associates

527

Prop by Janice TenBroek

Client: R. Valicenti THIRST

Client: Ralston Purina

Backgrounds and Surfaces by Rob Weaver

STROUBE

Greg Stroube Photography

For the complete portfolio call Ceci Bartels Associates ➤ St. Louis (314) 241-4014 ▼ Chicago (312) 786-1560 ➡ New York (212) 912-1877 ✳ FAX (314) 241-9028

529

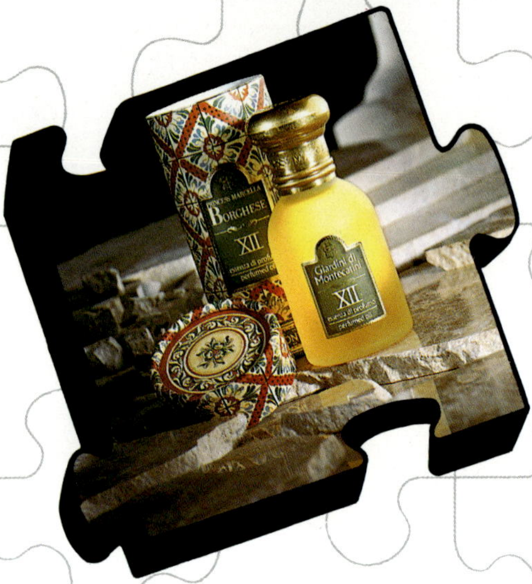

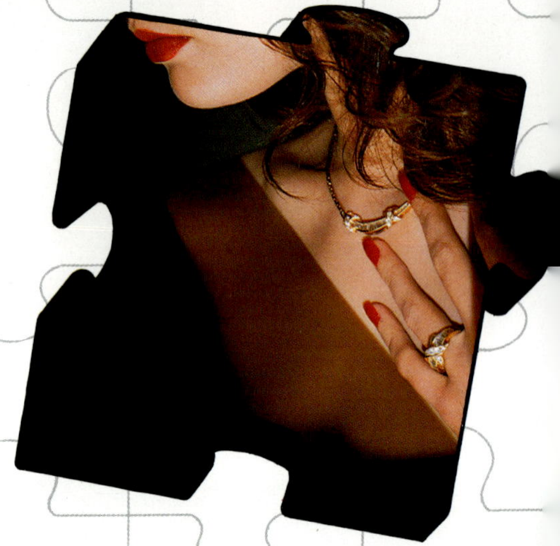

KARL SCHULTZ
ASSOCIATES INC.

740 WEST WASHINGTON
CHICAGO, ILLINOIS 60606

312•454•0303
FAX
312•454•0936

Robert Randall

REPRESENTED IN CHICAGO BY LISA JANES 312-235-4613

photography

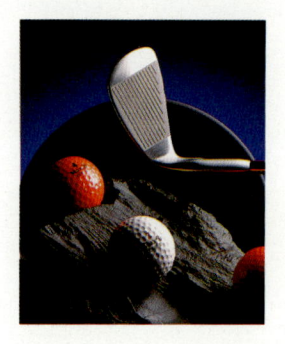

William McKellar Photography 1643 North Milwaukee Avenue, Chicago, IL 60647 (312) 235-1499
Agent: Tom Maloney & Associates, Inc. (312) 704-0500

McKELLAR

W

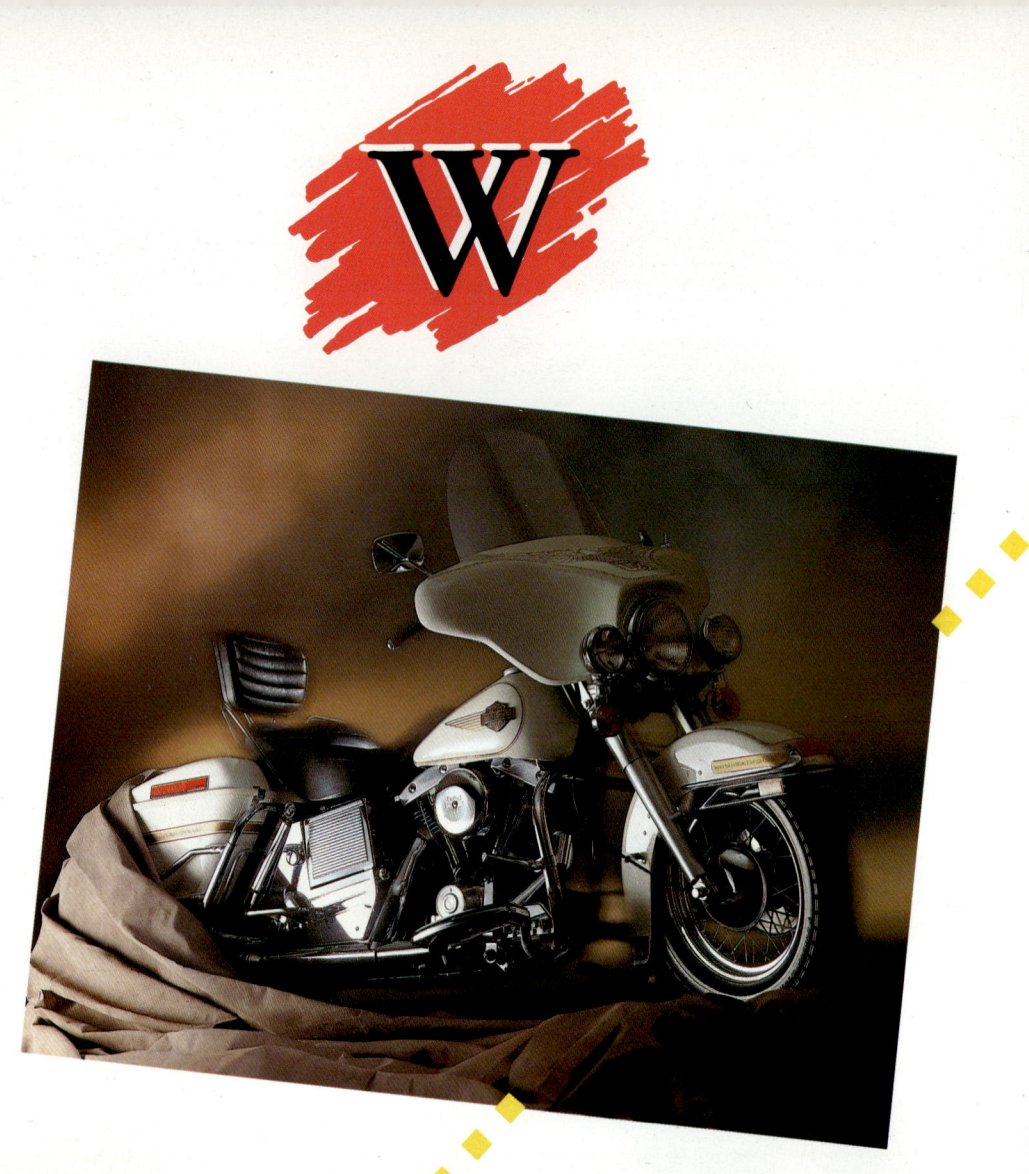

LES WARD PHOTOGRAPHY, INC.

21477 BRIDGE ST., SUITES C&D
SOUTHFIELD, MICHIGAN 48034
313-350-8666 / FAX 350-1019

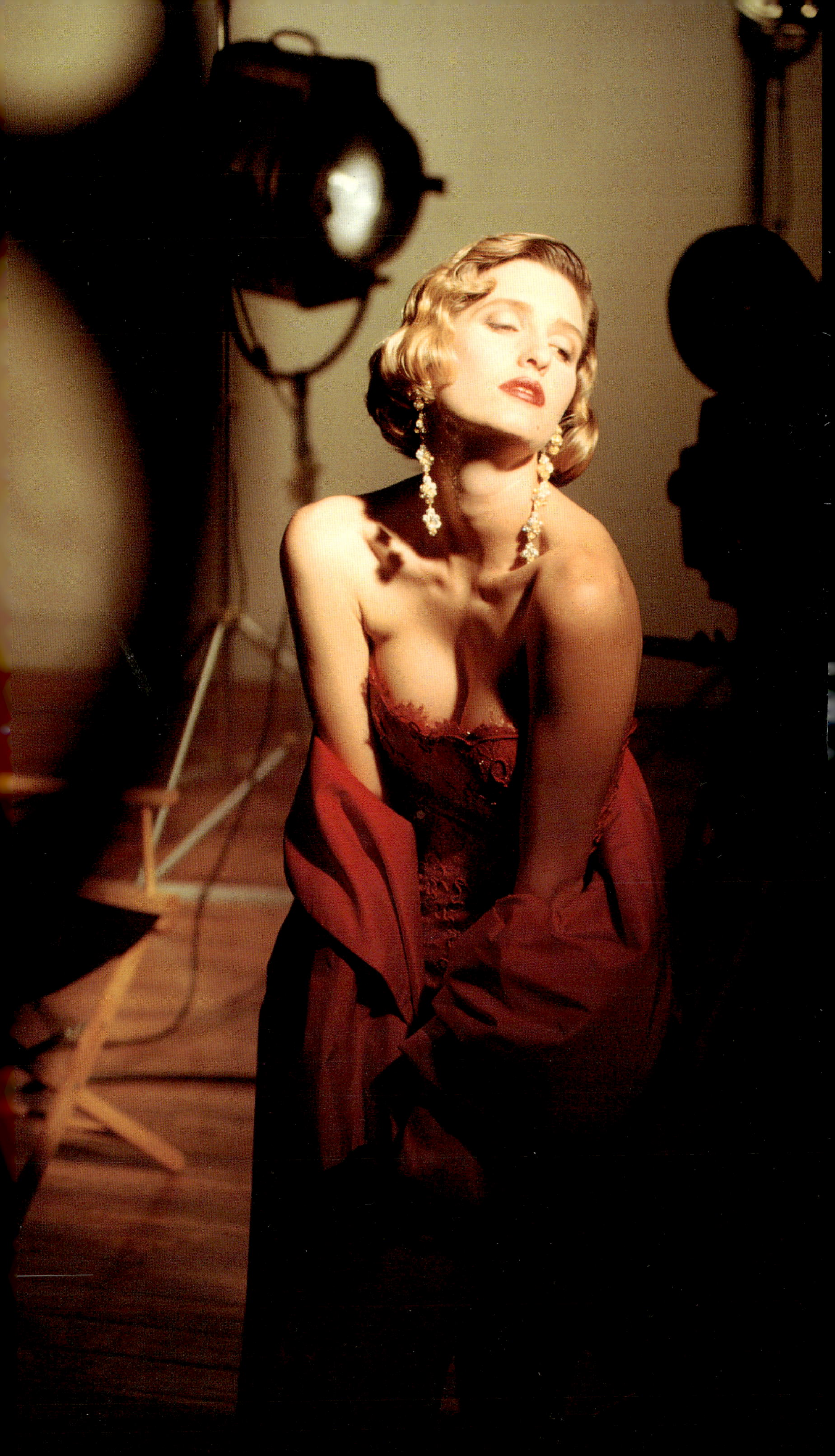

1924
Lewis W. Hine
Pennsylvania Railroad

The

developing

story

of the

20th century.

Kodak

PROFESSIONAL
PHOTOGRAPHY DIVISION

© Eastman Kodak Company, 1990. © Lewis W. Hine

WEST PHOTOGRAPHY

Listings 538
Ads 553

ALASKA
ARIZONA
CALIFORNIA
COLORADO
HAWAII
IDAHO
MONTANA
NEVADA
NEW MEXICO
OREGON
UTAH
VANCOUVER
WASHINGTON
WYOMING

WEST
PHOTOGRAPHY

A.B.L. Photographic Techniques/105-10 Ave. S.E., Calgary	(403) 266-6300
ARC Studios/21515 Hawthorne Blvd., Torrance	(213) 533-8060
Abecassis, Andree & Assocs./756 Neilson St., Berkeley	(415) 526-5099
Abraham, Russell/60 Federal St., S.F.	(415) 896-6400
Abramowitz, Alan/Seattle/(206) 621-0710	**pages 596-597**
Acronym Photographic/Tarzana	(818) 705-1470
Adams, Butch/1414 S. 700 W., Salt Lake City	(801) 973-0939
Adams, Michael/27216 Eastridge, El Toro	(714) 472-4559
Addor Photography/1456 63rd St., Emeryville	(415) 653-1745
Adler, Robert/33 Ellert St., S.F.	(415) 695-2867
Aerial Eye, Inc./17931-A Sky Park Cir., Irvine	(714) 250-4136
Agee, Bill/Corona del Mar	(714) 760-6700
Ahrend, Jay/L.A.	(213) 462-5256
Albers, Hans/3605 S. Broadway, L.A.	(213) 232-1525
Alexander, David/933 N. Highland, L.A.	(213) 464-8690
Aline, France, Inc./L.A.	(213) 933-2500
Allan/The Animal Photographers/3503 Argonne St., San Diego	(619) 270-1850
Allen, Charles S./537 S. Raymond Ave., Pasadena	(818) 795-1053
Allen, Don/1787 Shawn Dr., Baton Rouge	(504) 925-0251
Allen, Judson/839 Emerson St., Palo Alto	(415) 324-8177
Allen, Lincoln/1705 Woodbridge Dr., Salt Lake City	(801) 466-4677
Alpamayo Photography/1632 Francisco E., Berkeley	(415) 845-7535
Amedeo/L.A.	(213) 937-0300
Amkaut, Joel/444 Lincoln Blvd., Venice	(213) 559-7075
Amkraut, Joel/444 Lincoln Lincoln Blvd., Venice	(213) 599-7075
Andersen, Kurt/250 Newhall, S.F.	(415) 641-4276
Andersen, Welden/2643 S. Fairfax Ave., Culver City	(213) 559-0126
Anderson Studios, Inc./Tucson/(602) 881-1205	**pages 636-637**
Anderson, Gordon/5145 Crystal Park Rd., Manitou Spgs.	(719) 685-9139
Antisdel Image Group, Inc./3242 De La Cruz Blvd., Santa Clara	(408) 988-1010
Antrim Photography & Video/2300 Casa Grande, Pasadena	(818) 797-1100
Apton, Bill/1060 Folsom St., S.F.	(415) 861-1840
Arbogast, William/969 Matadero Ave., Palo Alto	(415) 494-6474
Archer, Mark/228 S. Madison St., Denver	(303) 399-5272
Arend, Chris/5401 Cordova, Anchorage	(907) 562-3173
Aristei, Sally/2867½ W. Seventh St., L.A.	(213) 937-9948
Arizona Land Co./Maersch, Michael/2631 N. 28th St., Phoenix	(602) 956-5552
Arnold, Steven/3316 Beverly Blvd., L.A.	(213) 384-9952
Aron, Jeffrey/17801 Skypark Cir., Irvine	(714) 250-1555
Aronovsky, James/San Diego	(619) 232-5855
Arsenault, Dan/L.A.	(213) 933-2500
Ashe/Photography/3430 E. 12th Ave., Denver	(303) 322-9325
Avery, Franklin L./S.F.	(415) 986-3701
Avery, Ron Studio/11821 Mississippi Ave., L.A.	(213) 477-1632
Aydelotte, John Studios/15747 E. Valley Blvd., City of Industry	(818) 961-2118
Ayeroff, Loretta/219 S. Stanley Dr., Beverly Hills	(213) 657-0256
Ayres, Robert Bruce/L.A.	(213) 837-8190
BAKO/BECQ Inc./3047 Fourth St. S.W., Calgary	(403) 243-9789
Bacon, Garth/18576 Bucknail Rd., Saratoga Spgs.	(408) 866-5858
Bak, Sunny/750 S. Spaulding Ave., L.A.	(213) 933-6986
Baker, Bill/265 29th St., Oakland	(415) 832-7685
Barkentin-Blackburn, Pamela/1218 N. La Cienega Blvd., L.A.	(213) 854-1941
Barnes, Craig/3109½ Beverly Blvd., L.A.	(213) 386-6939
Barnes, John/1129 A Folsom St., S.F.	(415) 631-5264
Baron, Dale Alison/519 Castro, S.F.	(415) 626-3131
Barros, Robert/1813 E. Sprague, Spokane	(509) 535-6455
Bartay Studio/66 Retiro Way, S.F.	(415) 563-0551
Barth, Chris/400 E. Pine St., Seattle	(206) 328-4450
Barton, Hugh G./33464 Bloomberg Rd., Eugene	(503) 747-8184
Bartone, Laurence/335 Fifth St., S.F.	(415) 974-6010
Bator, Joe/8245 Yarrow St., Arvada	(303) 425-0833
Bauer, Robert/1057 Winsor Ave, Oakland	(415) 763-4819
Baxter, Scott Photography/Phoenix	(602) 254-5879
Bayer, Dennis/130 Ninth St., S.F.	(415) 255-9467

Beals, Steven K./Portland	(503) 288-0550
Beaman, Quee Photography/430 Mountain View Ave., Mountain View	(415) 621-1109
Bean, Tom/Flagstaff	(602) 779-4381
Becker-Bishop/1830 17th St., S.F.	(415) 552-4254
Beebe, Morton/150 Lombard St., S.F.	(415) 362-3530
Beer, Rafael/14535 Arminta, Van Nuys	(818) 901-7864
Belcher, Richard/2565 Third St., S.F.	(415) 641-8912
Bell, Robert Photography/1360 Logan Ave., Costa Mesa	(714) 957-0772
Bell, Tony/Aspen	(303) 920-1431
Bencze, Louis/2442 N.W. Market St., Seattle	(206) 283-6314
Bennett, James/Corona Del Mar	(714) 494-6859
Bennett, Sue/Arizona	(602) 774-2544
Benoit, Tom/78 Shelly Dr., Mill Valley	(415) 381-0722
Benson, Hank/S.F./(415) 543-8153	**pages 422-423**
Berchert, James H./1020 W. Eigth Ave. Dr., Broomfield	(303) 466-7414
Bergman, Alan/8241 W. Fourth St., L.A.	(213) 852-1408
Berkun, Phillip/555 Prim St., Ashland	(503) 488-4486
Bernstein, Gary/Culver City/(213) 550-6891	**pages 558-561**
Berrett, Pat/2521 Madison N.E., Albuquerque	(505) 881-0935
Bertholmey, John/17962 Sky Park Cir., Irvine	(714) 261-0575
Best Graphics Group, The/1648 Flower St., Glendale	(818) 507-8730
Big City Visual Productions/1039 Seventh Ave., San Diego	(619) 232-3366
Big Time Productions/499 Alabama St., S.F.	(415) 864-7750
Biggs, Ken/1147 N. Hudson Ave., L.A.	(213) 462-7739
Bilecky Productions, Inc./5047 W. Pico Blvd., L.A.	(213) 931-1610
Birlauf & Steen, Inc./401 Delaware, Denver	(303) 629-0415
Birnbach, Allen/3600 Tejon St., Denver	(303) 455-7800
Bisignano, Gerard/L.A./(213) 458-7227	**pages 618-619**
Blakeley, Jim/1061 Folsom St., S.F.	(415) 558-9300
Blakeman, Robert Studios, Inc./710 Santa Fe Ave., L.A.	(213) 624-6662
Blattel Photography/4200 Burbank Blvd., Burbank	(818) 848-1166
Blau, Barry J. Photography/4133 East Blvd., L.A.	(213) 391-4468
Blaustein, John/S.F./(415) 525-8133	**pages 642-643**
Bleyer, Pete Studio, Inc./807 N. Sierra Bonita Ave., L.A.	(213) 653-6567
Blumensaat, Mike/306 Edna St., S.F.	(415) 333-6178
Boehm, Bernd/67591 Bolero Dr., Palm Spgs.	(619) 324-1500
Bolanos, Edgar/981 Prague St., S.F.	(415) 585-7805
Bond, Kevin/1930 Sacramento St., S.F.	(415) 771-6817
Bonini, Steve/S.F.	(415) 775-3366
Bonner, Tom/655 N. Harper Ave., L.A.	(213) 653-7041
Boudreau, Bernard/1015 N. Cahuenga Blvd., Hollywood	(213) 467-2602
Boulger & Kanuit/503 S. Catalina, Redondo Beach	(213) 540-6300
Boxer, Jeff/2414 Third St., S.F.	(415) 861-2215
Boyd, Jack/2038 Calvert Ave., Costa Mesa	(714) 556-8133
Boyer, Neil/1416 Aviation Blvd., Redondo Beach	(213) 374-0443
Braasch, Gary/Portland	(503) 368-5091
Brandeis, Robert/316 Escuela Ave., Mountain View	(415) 969-8529
Brandt Photography/500 W. Southern, Mesa	(602) 834-0203
Bray, Phil/3270 Ettie St., Oakland	(415) 658-9740
Breitborde, Steve/4027 Burbank Blvd., Burbank	(213) 849-4050
Breitrose, Howard/L.A./(213) 826-1332	**pages 240-241**
Britt, Jim/3221 Hutchinson Ave., L.A.	(213) 836-6317
Brooks, Bill/386 S. Burnside Ave., L.A.	(213) 857-6647
Brown, David L./280 Edgewood Ct., Prescott	(602) 445-2485
Brown, Dianne & Co., Inc./402 N. Windsor Blvd., L.A.	(213) 462-5598
Brown, Michael/L.A.	(213) 379-7254
Browne, Turner/10546 Greenwood Ave. N., Seattle	(206) 367-3782
Brownell, Gene/Phoenix	(602) 220-9331
Bubar, Julie/San Diego	(619) 234-4020
Buchanan, Craig/1026 Folson St., S.F.	(415) 861-5566
Buchanan, Michael B./Larkspur	(415) 383-7721
Buckley, Jim Productions/1310 Kawaihao St., Honolulu	(808) 538-6128
Buckner, Ken/5636 Melrose Ave., Hollywood	(213) 464-4003
Bufka, Aja & Assocs./9903 Santa Monica Blvd., Beverly Hills	(213) 391-1074
Burke/Triolo/940 E. Second St., L.A.	(213) 687-4730
Burkhart Photography/1408 Centinela, Inglewood	(213) 836-9654
Burr, Bruce/2867 W. Seventh St., L.A.	(213) 388-3361
Burt, Pat/1412 S.E. Stark, Portland	(503) 284-9989
Burton, Richard/1390 Market St., S.F.	(415) 626-2620
Bush, Charles William/940 N. Highland Ave., L.A.	(213) 466-6630
Busher, Dick/7042 20th Pl. N.E., Seattle	(206) 523-1426
Busselen/Bauer Photo Illustrators, Inc./Sacramento	(916) 452-2256
Bybee, Gerald/1811 Folsom St., S.F.	(415) 863-6346

C&I Photography, Inc./275 Santa Ana Ct., Sunnyvale	(408) 733-5855
C.H. Studios, Inc./13906 Ventura Blvd., Sherman Oaks	(818) 989-1088
Cable, Ronald/17835 Sky Park Cir., Irvine	(714) 261-8910
Cacitti, Stan/586 Howard St., S.F.	(415) 974-5668
Cahoon, John B. III/1419 Elliott Ave. W., Seattle	(206) 282-6111
Camacci, Pat/7735 Garland, Washington	(313) 781-4382
Cambon, Jim/216 Racquette Dr., Ft. Collins	(303) 221-4545
Camera Craft, Inc./2312 Second Ave., Seattle	(206) 682-0996
Camera Hawaii/875 Waimanu St., Honolulu	(808) 536-2302
Campbell, David/S.F.	(415) 864-2556
Campbell, Kathleen Taylor/315 W. Ninth St., L.A.	(213) 688-7865
Campbell, Marianne/S.F./(415) 227-0939	**pages 638-639**
Campbell, Tom & Assoc., Inc./7434 W. 91st St., L.A.	(213) 473-6054
Cannon, Bill/Seattle	(206) 682-7031
Cappello, Fred Studios/58 Brookmont St., Irvine	(714) 559-1365
Caputo, Tony/1040 N. Las Palmas, L.A.	(213) 464-6636
Cardin, Robert/142 Tenth St., S.F.	(415) 255-4546
Carey, Ed/438 Treat Ave., S.F.	(415) 621-2349
Carl's Dar;kroom/188 Jackson N.E., Albuquerque	(505) 268-5897
Carlson, Joe/901 El Centro St., S. Pasadena	(213) 682-1020
Carlson, John/S.F.	(415) 957-1339
Carofano, Ray Photography, Inc./1011¼ W. 190th St., Gardena	(213) 515-0310
Carriére, Lydia/Santa Cruz	(408) 425-1090
Carroon, Chip/S.F.	(415) 588-7790
Carson, Don/P.O. Box 416, Bolinas	(415) 868-2162
Casemore/Damon Productions/L.A./(213) 462-5256	**pages 616-617**
Casler, Christopher/1600 Viewmont Dr., L.A.	(213) 854-7733
Cason, Dean/2520 Field St., Denver	(303) 231-9948
Castaneda, Eduardo/976 Cunningham Dr., Whittier	(213) 336-1564
Casteel, Dave/Santa Cruz	(408) 475-8786
Catlett, Bill/1313 Zeus St., W. Covina	(818) 337-1964
Caulfield, Andy/L.A.	(213) 258-3070
Chaisson, Micheal/Beverly Hills	(213) 276-7648
Chamberlain, Harry/205 Pasadena Ave., South Pasadena	(213) 258-2277
Chaney, Brad/1750-H Army St., S.F.	(415) 826-2030
Charles, Cindy/631 Carolina St., S.F.	(415) 821-4457
Chen, James/1917 Anacapa St., Santa Barbara	(805) 569-1849
Chernus, Ken/9531 Washington Blvd., Culver City	(213) 838-3116
Chesley, Paul/Aspen	(303) 925-1148
Chesser, Mike/5290 W. Washington Blvd., L.A.	(213) 934-5211
Chiabaudo, Michael/4056 Wade St., L.A.	(213) 306-8948
Chiarot, Roy/846 S. Robertson Blvd., L.A.	(213) 659-9173
Chin, K.P./S.F.	(415) 282-3041
Christensen, David/321 Collingwood, S.F.	(415) 647-7442
Christine/L.A./(213) 938-9117	**pages 624-625**
Chung, Ken/L.A./(213) 938-9117	**pages 624-625**
Church, Jim & Cathy/Gilroy	(408) 842-9682
Clark, Casey/1225 Alta Vista, Aspen	(303) 925-8280
Clark, Stephen/1112 Beachwood, L.A.	(213) 465-5300
Clasen, Norm/160 Spring Creek Rd., Basalt	(303) 927-3043
Claudia/L.A./(213) 342-0226	**pages 564-565**
Clayton, John/160 S. Park, S.F.	(415) 495-4562
Clement, Michele/221 11th St., S.F.	(415) 558-9540
Clic, Oui & Assoc./3627 Fairesta St., La Crescenta	(818) 957-1008
Clifford, Geoffrey/Tucson/(602) 577-6439	**pages 144-145**
Cobb, Rick Studios/10 Liberty Ship Way, Sausalito	(415) 332-8739
Cobb, Vincent/Beverly Hills	(213) 558-3961
Cogen, Melinda/1112 N. Beachwood Dr., Hollywood	(213) 467-9414
Collector, Stephen/4209 N. 26th St., Boulder	(303) 442-1386
Collins, Denny/320 E. Rose Ln., Phoenix	(602) 277-4334
Colorific Photo Labs Ltd./195 W. Seventh Ave., Vancouver	(604) 879-1511
Colucci Jr., Martin A./136 Freelon St., S.F.	(415) 495-6763
Cook, Kathleen Norris/Laguna Hills/(714) 770-4619	**pages 576-577**
Cook, James A./Denver	(303) 433-4874
Cook, Jeff/450 Lincoln St., Denver	(303) 698-1734
Cook, Warren/Laguna Hills/(714) 770-4619	**pages 576-577**
Cornair, Mike/9582 Hamilton Ave., Huntington Beach	(714) 968-7288
Cornell, Kathleen/741 Millwood Ave., Venice	(213) 301-8059
Corning, Don/3204 Harvey Ct., Pleasanton	(415) 426-0230
Cornwell, David Prods., Inc./1311 Kalakaua Ave., Honolulu	(808) 949-7000
Cramer, John/San Diego	(619) 549-8881
Creative Eye Photography/668 W. Shaw Ave., Fresno	(209) 227-2979
Critchfield, Kim P./1413 Kimberly Rd., Twin Falls	(208) 734-5223

Crowley, Elliot/3221 Benda Pl., L.A.	(213) 851-5110
Crozat, Bruce Photography/Santa Monica	(213) 394-7984
Cruff, Kevin/2828 E. Van Buren, Phoenix	(602) 225-0273
Cummins, Jim/Seattle	(206) 322-4944
D'Aprix, Peter/Ojai	(805) 646-1991
Dahlquist, Roland/Phoenix	(602) 275-3563
Daniel, Jay/816 W. Francisco Blvd., San Rafael	(415) 459-1495
Daniels, Charles/905 N. Cole Ave., Hollywood	(213) 461-8659
Dannehl, Dennis/3303 Beverly Blvd., L.A.	(213) 388-3888
Dannen, Kent & Donna/851 Peak View, Estes Park	(303) 586-5794
Davidson, Dave/25003 S. Beeson Rd., Beavercreek	(503) 632-7650
Davidson, Jerry/3923 W. Jefferson Blvd., L.A.	(213) 735-1552
Davis, Tim/137 Park Ave., Palo Alto	(415) 327-4192
de Gennaro Assocs./902 S. Norton Ave., L.A.	(213) 935-5179
De Grood, Tim/Palos Verdes Estates, Palos Verdes	(213) 372-0930
De Lespinasse, Hank/2300 E. Patrick Ln., Las Vegas	(702) 798-6693
DeCruyenaere, Howard M./2417 N. Park Blvd., Santa Ana	(714) 997-4446
DeHoff, R.D./632 N. Sheridan, Colorado Spgs.	(719) 635-0263
DeLeon, Vince Photography/11734 Idalene St., Santa Fe Spgs.	(213) 929-1826
DeYoung, Skip/1112 N. Beachwood, L.A.	(213) 462-0712
Deliantoni, Richard/655 N. Harper Ave., L.A.	(213) 653-7041
Deligter, Harry/3866 Keeshen Dr., L.A.	(213) 398-4949
Denman, Frank B./1201 First Ave. S., Seattle	(206) 325-9260
Denny, Michael/2631 Ariane Dr., San Diego	(619) 272-9104
Der, Rick/50 Mendell St., S.F.	(415) 824-8580
Derhacopian, Ron/3109 Beverly Blvd., L.A.	(213) 388-6724
Deshong, Diane/Beverly Hills/(213) 275-2620	**pages 610-611**
Deshong, Howard/Beverly Hills/(213) 275-2620	**pages 610-611**
Diaz, Armando/19 S. Park, S.F.	(415) 495-3552
Diggs Photography/612 Alabama, S.F.	(415) 648-2266
Divine, Jeff/San Clemente	(714) 496-5922
Dixon, Phillip/1107 Fifth Ave., L.A.	(213) 392-1816
Dominick/833 N. La Brea, L.A.	(213) 934-3033
Donahue, Patrick J./1161 N. Highland Ave., Hollywood	(213) 463-4165
Dondero, Don/2755 Pioneer Dr., Reno	(702) 825-7348
Douglass, Dirk/2755 S. 300 W., Salt Lake City	(801) 485-5691
Dow, Carter/643 Seventh St., S.F.	(415) 431-3105
Dressler, Rick/Tustin	(714) 259-9113
Duckworth, Paul/736E Marine Dr., Sequim	(206) 683-8895
Duka, Lonnie/919 Oriole Dr., Laguna Beach	(714) 494-7057
Dull, Ed/1745 N.W. Marshall, Portland	(503) 224-3754
Dunbar, Clark/1260B Pear Ave., Mountain View	(415) 964-4225
Durke, Vernon/842 Folsom, S.F.	(415) 648-1262
EXTRA, Artists Management/130 S. Highland Ave., L.A.	(213) 937-0300
Eadon, Jack/28311 Kitano, Mission Viejo	(714) 770-4300
Earnest, Robert/1623 Boyd, Santa Anna	(714) 259-9190
Eastabrook, William R./3281 Oakshire Dr., Hollywood	(213) 851-3281
Edmunds, Dana/188 N. King St., Honolulu	(808) 521-7711
Edwardes, Gordon/S.F.	(415) 956-4750
Elias, Robert/L.A./(213) 460-2988	**pages 618-619**
Emberley, Gordon/1479 Folsom, S.F.	(415) 621-9714
Emerald Sea Photo Ltd./11551 Pelican Ct., Richmond	(604) 274-9432
Enger, Linda/915 S. 52nd St., Tempe	(602) 966-5776
Enkelis, Liane/764 Sutter Ave., Palo Alto	(415) 326-3253
Epstein, Rhoni/L.A./(213) 663-2388	**pages 598-599**
Esgro, Dan/L.A.	(213) 932-1919
Estel, Suzanne/2325 Third St., S.F.	(415) 864-3661
Evans, Bill/Smith Tower, Seattle	(206) 340-0655
Evans, Marty/6850 Vineland Ave., N. Hollywood	(818) 762-5400
Excalibur Photographics/Canoga Park	(818) 705-5026
Exley, Jonathan/1357 N. Spaulding Ave., L.A.	(213) 876-5923
Fabrick Photography/1320 Venice Blvd., Venice	(213) 822-1030
Fader, Bob/14 Pearl St., Denver	(303) 744-0711
Fay, John Spencer/6575 N.E. Windermere, Seattle	(206) 522-0044
Feldman, Marc/6442 Santa Monica Blvd., Hollywood	(213) 463-4829
Felzman, Joe/4504 S.W. Corbett Ave., Portland	(800) 545-7815
Fenton, Reed/922 N. Formosa, L.A.	(213) 850-1344
Fiess, Cliff/3131 Western Ave., Seattle	(206) 281-8798
Findysz, Mary/3550 E. Grant Rd., Tucson	(602) 325-0261
Finnegan, Kristin/3045 N.W. Thurman St., Portland	(503) 241-2701
Firebaugh, Steve/6750 55th Ave. S., Seattle	(206) 721-5151
Fischer, Curt/S.F.	(415) 552-4252
Fischer, David/S.F.	(415) 495-4585

Flavin, Frank/901 W. 54th Ave., Anchorage . . . . (907) 561-1606
Fletcher, Bruce/597 Guerrero St., S.F. . . . . (415) 864-6094
Flock, Mary/Scottsdale . . . . (602) 423-1500
Fogg, Don III/400 Treat Ave., S.F. . . . . (415) 553-4199
Forrester, Robert R./2700 Carmar Dr., L.A. . . . . (213) 657-5383
Forster, C. Bruce/431 N.W. Flanders, Portland . . . . (503) 222-5222
Forte, John Studio/7095 Hollywood Blvd., Hollywood . . . . (818) 981-0327
Four Eyes Photography/720 Iwilei Rd., Honolulu . . . . (808) 533-4662
Fowler, Brad/655 N. Harper Ave., L.A. . . . . (213) 653-7041
Fox & Spencer/L.A./(213) 653-6484 . . . . **pages 566-567**
Frandsen, Robert A./Denver . . . . (303) 355-2536
Frankel, Deborah/1110 N. Hudson Ave., L.A. . . . . (213) 461-2407
Frankel, Tracy/641 Bay St., Santa Monica . . . . (213) 396-2766
Franklin, Charly/3352-20th St., S.F. . . . . (415) 824-4000
Franz-Moore, Paul/421 Tehama St., S.F. . . . . (415) 495-6421
Frazier, Kim Andrew/P.O. 998, Lake Oswego . . . . (503) 697-8798
Freed, Jack/749 N. LaBrea Ave., L.A. . . . . (213) 931-1015
Freeman, Hunter/S.F./(415) 495-1900 . . . . **pages 594-595**
Freis, Jay/416 Richardson St., Sausalito . . . . (415) 332-6709
Friedlander, Ernie/275 Sixth St., S.F. . . . . (415) 777-3373
Frisch, Stephen/Industrial Ctr. Bldg., Sausalito . . . . (415) 332-4545
Fritz, Michael/San Diego . . . . (619) 281-3297
Fritz, Steve/3201 San Gabriel Ave., Glendale . . . . (818) 249-6719
Froussart, Beatrice/626 Broadway, Santa Monica . . . . (213) 451-8959
Fruchtman, Jerry/8735 Washington Blvd., Culver City . . . . (213) 839-7891
Fry, George B. III/Menlo Park . . . . (415) 323-7663
Fugate, Randy/6754 Eton Ave., L.A. . . . . (818) 887-2003
Fujioka, Robert Studios Inc./715 N. Shoreline Blvd., Mountain View . . . . (415) 960-3010
Fukuda, Steve/454 Natoma St., S.F. . . . . (415) 543-9339
Fukuhara, Inc./1032 W. Taft Ave., Orange . . . . (714) 998-8790
Fullerton, Claude/15190 Cobalt, Sylmar . . . . (818) 367-5190
Fulton, Dan/Jackson . . . . (307) 733-6179
Furuta, Carl/L.A. . . . . (213) 655-1911
G.M. Studios Ltd./59 W. Seventh Ave., Vancouver . . . . (604) 872-8277
Gallian, Dirk/Aspen . . . . (303) 925-8268
Galluzzi, John/427 S. Westminster, L.A. . . . . (213) 384-5574
Galván, Gary/L.A./(213) 667-1457 . . . . **pages 582-583**
Garcia, Elma/S.F./(415) 641-9992 . . . . **pages 588-591**
Gardner, Robert Studios, Inc./800 S. Citrus Ave., L.A. . . . . (213) 931-1108
Garfield Assoc./3540 S. Figueroa St., L.A. . . . . (213) 747-3888
Garnet, William/411 S. Fairfax Ave., L.A. . . . . (213) 931-0367
Gayle, Rick/2318 E. Roosevelt St., Phoenix . . . . (602) 267-8845
Gelineair, Val/n, L.A. . . . . (213) 937-0241
Gelineau, Val/1265 S. Cochran, L.A. . . . . (213) 937-0241
Gendreau, Raymond/300 Second Ave. W., Seattle . . . . (206) 285-1999
Genter, Ralph/6808 Academy Pky. E., Albuquerque . . . . (505) 334-1553
Gerba, Peter/50 Ringold St., S.F. . . . . (415) 864-5474
Gerczynski, Tom/2211 N. Seventh Ave., Phoenix . . . . (602) 252-9229
Gerdau, Vance & Assoc./1021 S. Fairfax Ave., L.A. . . . . (213) 937-7502
Gervase, Mark/L.A. . . . . (213) 877-0928
Giannetti Photography/730 Clementina St., S.F. . . . . (415) 864-0270
Gibson, Will/1420 Grand Ave., San Marcos . . . . (619) 744-7443
Giefer, Sebastian/3132 Hollyridge Dr., Hollywood . . . . (213) 461-1122
Gifford, Ed/Vancouver . . . . (604) 462-8612
Gildemeister Photographic Illustration/High Valley Foothill Rd., Union . . . . (503) 562-5687
Glenn, Joel/439 Bryant St., S.F. . . . . (415) 957-1273
Gluck, Barbara/314 Garcia St., Santa Fe . . . . (505) 983-6612
Goble, James/620 Moulton Ave., L.A. . . . . (213) 658-5463
Going, Michael/1117 N. Wilcox Pl., L.A. . . . . (213) 465-6853
Goldner, David/833 Traction Ave., L.A. . . . . (213) 617-7664
Goldstein, Deborah/1010 24th St., Sacramento . . . . (916) 448-1303
Gonzalez, Juan Antonio/2558 30th Ave., S.F. . . . . (415) 661-4286
Gorfkle, Gregory/1419C Elliot Ave. W., Seattle . . . . (206) 283-9703
Gornick, Alan/4200 Camino Real, L.A. . . . . (213) 223-8914
Gottlieb, Jane/629 N. Bundy Dr., L.A. . . . . (213) 471-4491
Gottlieb, Mark/1915 University Ave., Palo Alto . . . . (415) 321-8761
Grad, Wendy/Beverly Hills . . . . (213) 656-2220
Graham, Donald/L.A./(213) 656-7117 . . . . **pages 388-389**
Graves, Cory/1865 Rodney Dr., L.A. . . . . (213) 644-9712
Gray, Dennis/250 Newhall, S.F. . . . . (415) 641-4009
Gray, Dennis/8705 W. Washington Blvd., L.A. . . . . (213) 559-1711
Greenleigh, John/756 Natoma St., S.F. . . . . (415) 864-4147
Grigg, Robert L./1050 N. Wilcox Ave., Hollywood . . . . (213) 469-6316

Grison, Herve/4617 W. Washington Ave., L.A.	(213) 876-5434
Gross, Richard/434 Ninth St., S.F.	(415) 558-8075
Guilburt, David/L.A./(213) 930-1898	**pages 310-311**
Guiral, Ed/Oakland	(415) 839-8037
Gwynn, Cat/907 N. Maltman Ave., L.A.	(213) 660-5354
HBR Studios/Roger Reynolds/3310 S. Knox Ct., Denver	(303) 789-4307
HFWD/10545 Ayres Ave., L.A.	(213) 559-7742
Haefner, James/Carson/(213) 609-0160	**pages 632-633**
Hagopian, Jim/915 N. Mansfield Ave., Hollywood	(213) 856-0018
Hagyard, Dave/1205 E. Pike, Seattle	(206) 322-8419
Hailey, Jason/6700 W. Fifth St., L.A.	(213) 653-7710
Hall & Assocs./L.A./(213) 934-9420	**pages 604-605**
Hall, Bill Photography/917 20th St., Sacramento	(916) 443-3330
Hall, George/601 Minnesota St., S.F.	(415) 821-7373
Hall, Norman C./55 New Montgomery St., S.F.	(415) 543-8070
Halle, Kevin/San Diego	(619) 549-8881
Halpern, David/7420 E. 70th St., Tulsa	(918) 252-4973
Hamilton, David/511 The Almeda, San Anselmo	(415) 461-5901
Hamilton, Jeffrey M./6719 Quartzite Canyon Pl., Tuscon	(602) 299-3624
Hanauer, Mark/1153 N. Las Palmas, Hollywood	(213) 462-2421
Handelman, Doris/10108 Lovelane, L.A.	(213) 838-0088
Hands, Bruce/Seattle	(206) 938-8620
Hansen, Jim Photographic/2800 S. Main St., Santa Ana	(714) 545-1343
Hansen, Steve/Sedona	(602) 282-2443
Hanson, Robin Constable/3219 Sawtelle Blvd., L.A.	(213) 398-8100
Harleen, Carls/427 Bryant St., S.F.	(415) 543-9670
Harrington, Lewis/746 Ilaniwai, Honolulu	(808) 533-3696
Harrington, Marshall/San Diego/(619) 291-2775	**pages 634-635**
Harris, Alan/L.A.	(213) 653-7041
Harris, Mark/L.A./(213) 939-3979	**page 612**
Harvey, Bob/931 N. Highland, L.A.	(213) 934-5817
Harvey, Stephen/7801 W. Beverly Blvd., L.A.	(213) 934-5817
Hathaway, Steve/400 Treat Ave., S.F.	(415) 255-2100
Hauck, Kim/L.A./(213) 471-2412	**pages 602-603**
Haven, Carol/Anacortes	(206) 293-4525
Hawkins Productions/353 Dublin Dr., Cardiff	(619) 944-1646
Hawley, Larry James/6502 W. Santa Monica Blvd., Hollywood	(213) 466-5864
Healy, Bryan/541 Natoma St., S.F.	(415) 861-1008
Hedrich, David/4006 S. 23rd St., Phoenix	(602) 220-0090
Heffernan, Terry/S.F./(415) 626-1999	**pages 568-569**
Heide, Mark W. Photography/208 Alta Vista, Santa Fe	(505) 988-2980
Heinzen, Richard/West 1018 Shannon, Spokane	(503) 328-5020
Hellawell, Dennis/6015 E. 22nd Ave., Anchorage	(907) 338-2415
Henrichs, Joanne/1022 First Ave. S., Seattle	(206) 523-8828
Hernandez, Tony/1110 W. Heatherbrae, Phoenix	(602) 279-1042
Herrington-Olson/769 22nd St., Oakland	(415) 452-0501
Hershey Bruce/4790 Irvine Blvd. #105-220, Irvine	(714) 248-5288
Hess, Geri/134 S. Roxbury Dr., Beverly Hills	(213) 271-9092
Hicks, Jeff & Assocs./16 Lyndon Ave., Los Gatos	(408) 395-2277
Hill, Tracey/Phoenix	(602) 275-3563
Hines, Richard/734 E. Third St., L.A.	(213) 625-2333
Hirsch, Claudia/L.A./(213) 342-0226	**pages 564-565**
Hodges, Rose/2325 Third St., S.F.	(415) 550-7612
Hoffman, Davy/1923 Colorado Ave., Santa Monica	(213) 829-5158
Hoffman, Paul/4500 19th St., S.F.	(415) 863-3575
Hogg, Peter A./1221 S. La Brea, L.A.	(213) 937-0642
Holcomb, Mark/15½ Holcomb Ct., Walnut Creek	(415) 932-8126
Holden, Andrew A./17911 Sky Park Cir., Irvine	(714) 553-9455
Holland Productions/7338 Valjean Ave., Van Nuys	(213) 873-1717
Holland, Mary & Co./6638 N. 13th St., Phoenix	(602) 263-8990
Hollar, Thomas/441 E. Columbine, Santa Ana	(714) 545-4022
Hollis, Kenneth/5405 W. Pico Blvd., L.A.	(213) 937-4169
Holmes, Bob/S.F.	(415) 775-5110
Holt, David/1624 S. Cotner Ave., L.A.	(213) 478-1188
Honolulu Creative Group/Honolulu	(808) 924-2513
Hooke, Thomas/210 Third Ave. S., Seattle	(206) 682-0383
Hooper, R. Scott/825 Lacy La., Las Vegas	(702) 870-8653
Hopkins Photograpy & Production, Inc./1202 S. Boulder, Tulsa	(918) 583-2104
Horikawa, Michael/Honolulu/(808) 538-7378	**pages 584-585**
Howard, Arnold/Pahoa	(808) 965-8283
Huber, Vic/Santa Ana	(714) 261-5844
Hughes, April & Assoc./465 California St., S.F.	(415) 781-2773
Hunter, Jeff/L.A./(213) 669-0468	**pages 602-603**

Hurrell, George/6702 St. Clair Ave., N. Hollywood	(818) 764-0683
Husmann, Mark/201 S. Sante Fe Ave., L.A.	(213) 680-9999
Hussey, Ron/229 Argonne Ave., Long Beach	(213) 439-4438
Hylén, Bo/L.A./(213) 271-6543	**pages 566-567**
Hyun, Douglass/13601 Ventura Blvd., Sherman Oaks	(818) 789-4729
Identicolor, Inc./10950 Burbank Blvd., N. Hollywood	(818) 980-9730
Image Maker, The/3430 E. 12th Ave., Denver	(303) 322-9324
Imstepf, Charles/620 Moulton Ave., L.A.	(213) 222-8773
Infinity/3040 Lawrence Expy, Santa Clara	(408) 732-9903
Ingham, Stephen Photography/2717 Northwest St. Helens Rd., Portland	(503) 274-9788
Inocencio, David/2548 Greenwich, S.F.	(415) 563-8190
Inouye, Kaz/6568 Beachview Drive, Rancho Palos Verdes	(213) 544-2044
International, Tibor/3440 Airway Dr., Santa Rosa	(707) 579-1222
Ishikawa Photography/1650 Ala Moana Blvd., Honolulu	(808) 941-3277
Isom, Clarice/S.F./(415) 885-1563	**pages 556-557**
Ives, Thomas/2250 N. El Moraga, Tucson	(602) 743-0750
Japp, Lee/2012 Paseo del Mar, Palos Verdes Est.	(213) 375-7973
Jarrett, Michael Studios/16812 Redhill, Irvine	(714) 250-3377
Jasgur, Joseph/12228 Venice Blvd., L.A.	(213) 839-2455
Jay, Michael/One Zeno Pl., S.F.	(415) 543-7101
Jensen, John/449 Bryant St., S.F.	(415) 957-9449
Jew, Kim/1518 Girard N.E., Albuquerque	(505) 255-6424
Jim Felt/Studio 3, Inc./1316 S.E. 12th Ave., Portland	(503) 238-1748
Jo'elle/7581 Amador Valley, Dublin	(415) 829-2580
John-Paul Photography, Inc./20812 Vose St., Canoga Park	(818) 347-7719
Johnson, Chaz/2124 Third Ave. W., Seattle	(206) 284-6223
Johnson, Conrad/350 Sunset Ave., Venice	(213) 392-0541
Johnson, Edward/11823 Blythe St., North Hollywood	(818) 765-2890
Jonathon/Craig/132 E. Providencia Ave., Burbank	(818) 841-4050
Jones, Aaron/Santa Fe	(505) 988-5730
Jones, Dana/L.A.	(213) 937-0300
Jones, William B./5055 N. Harbor Dr., San Diego	(619) 224-9977
Joye, Clayton/L.A./(213) 957-1385	**page 608**
Joye, Clayton/S.F./(415) 362-9686	**page 608**
Kaiser, Dick/960 N. La Brea, L.A.	(213) 462-7432
Kaldor, Curt W./1011 Granview Dr., South S.F.	(415) 583-8704
Kallewaard, Susan/4450 Enterprise St., Fremont	(415) 651-7202
Kamens Photographic Design/333 Seventh St., S.F.	(415) 621-1888
Kapler, Jerry/1820 Harmon St., Berkeley	(415) 655-4351
Karageorge, Jim/610 22nd St., S.F.	(415) 648-3444
Karl Knox Images/P.O. Box 336, Novato	(415) 898-7632
Karody, Tony/300 E. Rustic Rd., Santa Monica	(213) 459-9984
Karr, Leo/9124 N. 66th Pl., Paradise Valley	(602) 953-1413
Kasmier, Richard/441 E. Columbine, Santa Ana	(714) 545-4022
Katano, Nicole/LA	(213) 655-1717
Keachie, Douglas/159 19th Ave., S.F.	(415) 751-1111
Keenan, Elaine Faris/3928 19th St., S.F.	(415) 621-2900
Keenan, Larry/421 Bryant St., S.F.	(415) 495-6474
Keith, Kelly/L.A./(213) 224-8288	**pages 592-593**
Keller, Bill/3930 N. Cactus Blvd., Tucson	(602) 881-7748
Keller, Tom/1186 S. La Brea, L.A.	(213) 934-2822
Kelley, Tom Studios, Inc./8525 Santa Monica Blvd., L.A.	(213) 657-1780
Kelly, John/140 Homestead, Basalt	(303) 927-4197
Kemper, Lewis/875 A Island Dr., Alameda	(415) 769-0570
Kennedy, Doug/432 Hillside, L.A.	(213) 454-9882
Kenny, Gill/6541 N. Camino Katrina, Tucson	(602) 297-7141
Kent, Tony/Santa Monica	(213) 458-7227
Kerns, Ben/1201 First Ave. S., Seattle	(206) 621-7636
Kersz, Valerie & Assoc./8281 Melrose Ave., L.A.	(213) 658-6616
Kessler, David/1306 N. Wilton Pl., Hollywood	(213) 462-6043
Ketchum, Robert Glenn/696 Stone Canyon Rd., L.A.	(213) 472-3681
Khoo Photography, Inc./671 S. La Brea Ave., L.A.	(213) 931-9393
Kiehl, Stuart Lee/Beverly Hills	(213) 659-2699
Kimball, Ron/1960 Colony St., Mountain View	(415) 969-0682
King, Jennifer Susan/9709 E. Jewell Ave., Denver	(303) 337-3137
Kingsbury, Robert/1730 Hastings Dr., Ft. Collins	(303) 223-5325
Kirsch Represents/7316 Pyramid Dr., L.A.	(213) 651-3706
Kissinger, Lee/655 N. Harper Ave., L.A.	(213) 653-7041
Kleinman, Kathryn/S.F.	(415) 331-5070
Klimek, Stan/6221 Orange St., L.A.	(213) 937-8924
Knable, Ellen & Assocs., Inc./1233 S. La Cienega Blvd., L.A.	(213) 855-8855
Knauer, Karen/688 S. Santa Fe, L.A.	(213) 623-0888
Knight, Gary/5666 La Jolla Village Dr., San Diego	(619) 286-0429

Knowles, Jim/10745 Kling St., Burbank	(818) 753-9655
Knudson, Kent/Phoenix	(602) 277-7701
Knutson, Kris/2475 Third St., S.F.	(415) 621-7367
Kodama & Moriarty Photo./4081 Glencoe Ave., Marina Del Ray	(213) 306-7574
Kohler Studios, Inc./125 Electric Dr., Pasadena	(818) 564-1130
Koosh, Dan/Westlake Village	(818) 991-2105
Korn, Barry/10530 Bradbury Rd., L.A.	(213) 836-7893
Korody, Tony/350 E. Rustic Rd., Santa Monica	(213) 459-9984
Koropp, Robert/901 E. 17th Ave., Denver	(303) 830-6000
Kosta, Jeff Studio/2565 Third St., S.F.	(415) 285-7001
Kramer, David/5527 W. Washington Blvd., L.A.	(213) 388-6747
Krasemann, Stephen J./265 Verde Valley School Rd., Sedona	(602) 284-9808
Krasner, Carin/3239 Helms Ave., L.A.	(213) 280-0082
Kraus, Gregor/439 S. Hamel Rd., L.A.	(213) 859-8379
Kravitz, Herb/959 N. Cole Ave., L.A.	(213) 461-9536
Krosnick, Alan/2800 20th St., S.F.	(415) 285-1819
Kubly, Jon/604 Moulton Ave., L.A.	(213) 224-8947
Kuhn, Chuck/Seattle/(206) 842-1996	**pages 570-571**
Kunkel, Larry/729 Minna Alley, S.F.	(415) 621-0729
Kurihara, Ted/601 22nd St., S.F.	(415) 285-3200
Kurisu, Kaz/819½ N. Fairfax Ave., L.A.	(213) 655-7287
Kurtz, Steve/16A Lyndon Ave., Los Gatos	(408) 395-8441
Kurzweil, Gordon M. Photography/211 Fifteenth St., Santa Monica	(213) 395-0624
Kuslich, Lawrence J./606 S. Church St., Dayton	(409) 258-2828
L.A. Models/8335 Sunset Blvd., L.A.	(213) 656-9572
LaRiche, Michael/17932 Sky Park Circle, Irvine	(714) 250-5997
LaTona, Kevin/159 Western Ave. W., Seattle	(206) 285-5779
Laidman, Allan/110 Free Silver Ct., Aspen	(303) 925-4791
Lamb & Hall, Inc./7318 Melrose Ave., L.A.	(213) 931-1775
Lamb, Deirdre/Mendocino	(707) 937-4606
Lamotte, Michael/S.F./(415) 777-1443	**pages 638-639**
Landau, Robert/7274 Sunset Blvd., L.A.	(213) 851-2995
Landecker, Tom/282 Seventh St., S.F.	(415) 864-8888
Landiscor/3816 N. Seventh St., Phoenix	(602) 248-8989
Lane, Bobbi/7213 Santa Monica Blvd., L.A.	(213) 874-0557
Langdon, Harry/8275 Beverly Blvd., L.A.	(213) 651-3212
Lanting, Frans/714-A Riverside Ave., Santa Cruz	(408) 429-9490
Larson, R. Dean/7668 Hollywood Blvd., Hollywood	(213) 876-1033
Lau & Assocs./4300 82nd St., Sacramento	(916) 451-0595
Lavadie, Martin/L.A.	(818) 243-8271
Lawder, John & Assoc./Santa Ana	(714) 557-3657
Lawlor on Location, Inc./3521 Berry Dr., Studio City	(818) 761-0091
Lawne, Judith/6863 Sunny Cove, Hollywood	(213) 874-3095
Lawrence, Buzz/12734 Branford St., Arleta	(818) 897-0064
Le Bon, David/8950 Ellis Ave., L.A.	(213) 204-1001
LeBon, David/8950 Ellis Ave., L.A.	(213) 204-1001
Leatart, Brian/520 N. Western Ave., L.A.	(213) 856-0121
Lee & Lou/L.A./(213) 287-1542	**page 646**
Lee, Larry/N. Hollywood	(805) 259-1226
Lee, Roger Allyn/1628 Folsom St., S.F.	(415) 861-1147
Lee, Sherwood/632 Alta Vista Cir., S. Pasadena	(213) 255-1338
Leeson, Tom & Pat/Vancouver	(206) 256-0436
Lefferts, Marshall/1050 Wilcox Ave., L.A.	(213) 469-6316
Lehman, Danny/L.A.	(213) 652-1930
Lekavich, Bill/4872 Oahu Dr., Huntington Beach	(714) 864-1283
Leng, Brian/L.A.	(213) 850-0995
Leonelli, Elisa/2614 Halm Ave., L.A.	(213) 559-1761
Lettich, Sheldon/6003 W. Sixth St., L.A.	(213) 939-0023
Levey, Al/9412 Swinton Ave., Sepulveda	(818) 893-0684
Levine, Kevin L./Berkeley	(415) 771-0303
Levy, Patricia Barry/3389 W. 29 Ave., Denver	(303) 458-6692
Levy, Paul/2830 S. Robertson Blvd., L.A.	(213) 838-2252
Lewin, Elyse/820 N. Fairfax, L.A.	(213) 655-4214
Lewine, Rob/8929 Holly Pl., L.A.	(213) 654-0830
Lidz, Jane/433 Baden St., S.F.	(415) 587-3377
Liles, Harry Prod., Inc./1060 N. Lillian Way, L.A.	(213) 466-1612
Lim, Henry/63 Bluxome St., S.F.	(415) 495-3666
Lincks, Randy/Vail	(303) 949-6564
Lind, Lenny/1559 Howard St., S.F.	(415) 563-2020
Linden, Randy/2638 Country Club Dr. #51, Cameron Park	(916) 677-5686
Lindstrom, Mel/2510 Old Middlefield Way, Mountain View	(415) 962-1313
Linn, Alan/11717 Sorrento Valley Rd., San Diego	(619) 455-0873
Linnett, Chris/1604 Via Lazo, Palos Verdes Estates	(213) 378-3559

Lipson, Mark/4121 Wilshire Blvd., L.A. .... (213) 383-6339
Lissy, David/14472 Applewood Ridge Rd., Golden .... (303) 277-0232
Little, Dane/2098 Lambert Dr., Pasadena .... (818) 577-1559
Livzey, John/1510 N. Las Palmas Ave., L.A. .... (213) 469-2992
Loftus, James/718 Echo Park Ave., L.A. .... (213) 482-8092
Logan, Ian/L.A. .... (213) 937-0300
Longwood, Marc/3045 65th St., Sacramento .... (916) 731-5373
Lopez, Bret/533 Moreno Ave., L.A. .... (213) 393-8841
Loven, Paul E./1405 E. Marshall, Phoenix .... (602) 253-0335
Lubrano, Dennis/2865 W. 7th St., L.A. .... (213) 384-1016
Lum, Raymond, Inc./1810 Pine St., Vancouver .... (604) 731-0131
Luna, Tony/819 N. Bel Aire, Burbank .... (213) 845-0533
Lund, John M./860 Second St., S.F. .... (415) 957-1775
Lung, Robert/5765 Rickenbacker Rd., L.A. .... (213) 933-7219
Luse, Eric/Three Atalaya Ter., S.F. .... (415) 387-0951
Lyon, Fred/237 Clara St., S.F. .... (415) 974-5645
Lyon, Laura Studio West/506 Arapahoe, Boulder .... (303) 449-4415
MK Communications/2737 Polk St., S.F. .... (415) 775-5110
MacGregor, Helen/381 Huntley Dr., L.A. .... (213) 659-9337
Maher, John/2408 N.E. 12th St., Portland .... (503) 238-3645
Maher, John Photography/2406 N.E. 12th Ave., Portland .... (503) 282-3815
Malphettes, Benoit/816 S. Grand Ave., L.A. .... (213) 629-9054
Marchand, Renaud/839 Wilcox Ave., L.A. .... (213) 462-0842
Marcus, Ken Studio, Inc./6916 Melrose Ave., L.A. .... (213) 937-7214
Markow Southwest/Phoenix/(602) 273-7985 .... **pages 606-607**
Markow, Paul/Phoenix/(602) 273-7985 .... **pages 606-607**
Marks, Stephen/4704-C Prospect N.E., Albuquerque .... (505) 884-6100
Marley, Stephen/1160 Industrial Rd., San Carlos .... (415) 595-4226
Marlow, Dave O., Inc./421 AABC, Aspen .... (303) 925-8882
Marra, Ben Studios/310 S. First, Seattle .... (206) 624-7344
Marriott, John F./1830 McAllister St., S.F. .... (415) 922-2920
Marsden, Dominic/3783 Cahuenga Blvd. W., Studio City .... (818) 508-5222
Marshutz, Roger/1649 S. La Cienega Blvd., L.A. .... (213) 273-1610
Martin, Hughes/Park City/(801) 649-1471 .... **page 621**
Martin, James/24 Ross Valley Dr., San Rafael .... (415) 459-8855
Martin, Tom/Aspen .... (303) 925-4483
Martinelli, Bill/1118 Cypress Ave., San Mateo .... (415) 347-3589
Marty, Alfred/559 Pacific Ave., S.F. .... (415) 397-6625
Masamori, Ron/5051 Garrison, Denver .... (303) 423-8120
Masho, William/1248 S. Fairfax, L.A. .... (213) 938-2481
Mason, Julia/5661 W. Pico Blvd., L.A. .... (213) 658-6299
Masterson, Edward/San Diego .... (619) 457-3251
Matsuda, Paul/920 Natoma, S.F. .... (415) 626-6146
Mayer, Dennis/1129A Folsom, S.F. .... (415) 864-2348
Mayer, Jeffrey/6541 Mammoth Ave, Van Nuys .... (818) 901-0703
McAfee, Lynn/12745 Moorpark St., Studio City .... (818) 761-1317
McAllister of Denver/Boulder .... (303) 444-9484
McCans, Michael/220 N. Juanita Ave., L.A. .... (213) 487-1822
McCollum, David/679 Arbor St., Pasadena .... (818) 793-4404
McCrary, Jim/211 S. La Brea, L.A. .... (213) 936-5115
McCreery, Nathan/2400 N. Prince, Clovis .... (505) 762-9856
McDermott, John/S.F. .... (415) 982-2010
McGuire, Gary/L.A./(213) 938-2481 .... **pages 630-631**
McIntyre, Gerry/3385 Lanatt Way, Sacramento .... (916) 736-2108
McLouth, Meredith/922 W. Roosevelt St., Phoenix .... (602) 253-4855
McMahon, Steve/L.A. .... (213) 546-5405
McRae, Michael/Salt Lake City/(801) 328-3633 .... **page 613**
McVay, Matthew/Seattle .... (206) 443-7700
Mears, Jim/1471 Elliott Ave. W., Seattle .... (206) 284-0929
Meisels, Penina Photography/521 Sixth St., S.F. .... (415) 541-9946
Mejia, Michael A./244 9th St., S.F. .... (415) 621-7670
Menzie, Gordon/2311 Kettner Blvd., San Diego .... (619) 234-4432
Merfeld, Ken/3951 Higuera, Culver City .... (213) 837-5300
Merken, Stefan/900 N. Citrus Ave., L.A. .... (213) 466-4533
Merrick, Mary/601 Minnesota Ave., S.F. .... (415) 821-3661
Merril, Olivie/655 N. Harper Ave., L.A. .... (213) 653-7041
Mertens, Nicolas/1821 Embudo Dr. N.E., Albuquerque .... (505) 298-4738
Meyer, Jeffrey/24018 Calbert St., Woodland Hills .... (818) 704-9964
Miles, Ian/20 Twenty Ninth Ave., Venice .... (213) 821-8730
Miles, Kent/465 Ninth Ave., Salt Lake City .... (801) 364-5755
Miles, Reid/Hollywood/(213) 462-6106 .... **pages 628-629**
Milkie Studio Inc./127 Boylston Ave. E., Seattle .... (206) 324-3000
Millar, Norman/301 Eighth St., S.F. .... (415) 861-4320

Miller Peter, Darley/L.A./(213) 460-4876 .... **page 620**
Miller, Bruce/Long Beach .... (213) 439-8775
Miller, Dennis/1467 12th St., Manhattan Beach .... (213) 546-3205
Miller, Donald/447 S. Hewitt St., L.A. .... (213) 680-1896
Miller, Edward L./106 Normandy Dr., Vacaville .... (707) 446-8515
Miller, Jim Studios, Inc./1122 N. Citrus Ave., L.A. .... (213) 466-9515
Miller, Jordan/506 S. San Vicente Blvd., L.A. .... (213) 655-0408
Miller, Karen/201 San Juan Ave., Venice .... (213) 827-5921
Miller, Peter Darley/959 N. Cole Ave., L.A. .... (213) 931-8481
Miller, Wynn, Inc./4083 Glencoe Ave., Marina Del Rey .... (213) 821-4948
Milne, Lee/3615 W. 49th Ave., Denver .... (303) 458-1520
Milroy/McAleer/Newport Beach/(714) 722-6402 .... **pages 586-587**
Minkowski, Steven/465 Kekaulike Hwy., Kula .... (808) 878-1953
Mirage Studios, Inc./8630 Hayden Pl., Culver City .... (213) 559-9893
Mishler, Clark/1238 G St., Anchorage .... (907) 279-8847
Mitchell, Charles/2865 W. 7th St., L.A. .... (213) 384-1016
Mitchell, David P./2302 Carleton St., Berkeley .... (415) 540-6518
Mitchell, Josh/1984 N. Main St., L.A. .... (213) 225-5674
Mizono, Robert/S.F./(415) 648-3993 .... **pages 562-563**
Mizuno, Kim/8560 Sunset Blvd., L.A. .... (213) 461-7186
Montagu, Geoffrey/L.A. .... (213) 465-1455
Montesclaros, Bob/1136 Howard St., S.F. .... (415) 864-7539
Moon, Batista/1620 montgomery St., S.F. .... (415) 777-5566
Moore, Gary/1125 E. Orange Ave., Monrovia .... (213) 359-9414
Morgan, Jay P./L.A./(213) 224-8288 .... **pages 592-593**
Morgan, Scott/612 C Hampton Dr., Venice .... (213) 392-1863
Mosgrove, Will/240 Newhall, S.F. .... (415) 282-7080
Mudford, Grant/5619 W. 4th Street, L.A. .... (213) 936-9145
Muench, David/Santa Barbara .... (805) 967-4488
Muna, R.J./S.F./(415) 468-8225 .... **pages 626-627**
Munk, David/410 Bullwinkle Cir., Aspen .... (303) 925-1945
Munns, John R./1339 Orange Ave., Coronado .... (619) 435-2131
Muresan, Lance Photography/Seattle .... (206) 481-0199
Murphy, Suzanne/Santa Monica .... (213) 399-6652
Murray, Bill/22213 N.E. 12th Pl., Redmond .... (206) 411-2154
Murray, Derik/1128 Homer St., Vancouver .... (604) 669-7468
Mustacchi, Michael & Assoc./1401 Illinois St., S.F. .... (415) 285-5252
Nadler, Jeff/520 N. Western Ave., L.A. .... (213) 467-2135
Nagler, Bernie/Playa Del Rey .... (213) 216-9559
Nakashima Tschoegl & Assoc., Inc./600 Moulton Ave., L.A. .... (213) 226-0506
Nease, Robert/441 E. Columbine, Santa Ana .... (714) 545-6557
Neill, William/Yosemite Nat'l Park .... (209) 379-2841
Neptune Films, Ltd./839 Linda Vista, Moss Beach .... (415) 728-5955
Ngan, Henry/1316 S.E. 12th Ave, Portland .... (503) 238-1748
Nicks, Dewey/5207 W 9th, LA .... (213) 467-3967
Nissing, Neil/711 S. Flower St., Burbank .... (213) 849-1811
Noble, Chris/8415 Kings Hill Dr., Salt Lake City .... (801) 942-8335
Noble, Richard/L.A./(213) 655-4711 .... **pages 644-645**
Normandin, Albert/Vancouver .... (604) 461-0766
Norwood, David/9023 Washington Blvd., Culver City .... (213) 204-3323
Noyle, Ric/Honolulu .... (808) 524-8269
Nyerges, Suzanne/413 S. Fairfax, L.A. .... (213) 938-0151
O'Brien, Tom/353 S. La Brea, L.A. .... (213) 938-2008
O'Looney, Doug/40 Hibbard Way, Helena .... (406) 449-5555
O'Rear, Chuck/St. Helena .... (707) 963-2663
O'Rouke, Gene/Honalula .... (808) 924-2513
Oliver, Peter/11660 Chenault St., L.A. .... (213) 476-1692
Olson, Dennis G./4-A Bayview Ave., Mill Valley .... (415) 388-7493
Oregon Scenics/24743 Bellfountain Rd., Monroe .... (503) 847-5582
Oriental Photo Dist., Co./3701 W. Moore Ave., Santa Ana .... (714) 432-7070
Oshiro, Jeff/2534 W. Seventh St., L.A. .... (213) 383-2774
Osta, Lisa/1090 Eddy, S.F. .... (415) 864-2755
Ostan Prentice Ostan Inc./L.A./(213) 826-1332 .... **pages 240-241**
Oswald, Jan/921 Santa Fe Dr., Denver .... (303) 893-8038
Otto, Glenn/10625 Magnolia Blvd., N. Hollywood .... (818) 762-5724
Oudkerkpool, Joyce/S.F. .... (415) 896-5181
Ouellette, J. Edouard/555 S. Alexandria Ave., L.A. .... (213) 387-3017
Ovregaard, Keith/765 Clementina St., S.F. .... (415) 621-0687
Owen, Owen/2071-A S. Beretania St., Honolulu .... (808) 943-6936
Oyama, Rick/1265 S. Cochran, L.A. .... (213) 937-0241
Pack, Bill /S.F./(415) 882-4460 .... **pages 556-557**
Pan, Richard/722 N. Hoover St., L.A. .... (213) 661-6638
Pannell, Tim/3301 E. Earll Dr., Phoenix .... (602) 954-6275

Paolini Corp./300 Fairview Ave. N., Seattle . . . . (206) 623-6640
Paris, Michael/L.A. . . . . (213) 851-4105
Parker Suzanne/2266 Vallejo St., S.F. . . . . (415) 931-7151
Parker, Linda Kane -Painted Photographs/62 Helens La., Mill Valley . . . . (415) 383-6288
Parks, Peggy/21 Broadview Dr., San Rafael . . . . (415) 457-5300
Parrish, Al/3501 Buena Vista Ave., Glendale . . . . (818) 957-3726
Pasley, Ray/418 Grande Ave., Davis . . . . (916) 753-0501
Pasquali, Art/L.A. . . . . (818) 785-9872
Pate, Hudson/812 E. Highland Ct., Upland . . . . (714) 985-3294
Patterson, Robert/915 N. Mansfield Ave., Hollywood . . . . (213) 462-4401
Pavol, David J./22320 Valerio St., Canoga Park . . . . (818) 992-8783
Payne, A.F./830 N. Fourth Ave., Phoenix . . . . (602) 258-3506
Peacock, Christian/930 Alabama St., S.F. . . . . (415) 641-8088
Pearson, Lee/1746 N. Ivan, L.A. . . . . (213) 461-3861
Peck, Michael/2046 Arapahoe St., Denver . . . . (303) 296-9427
Pendragon Studios/P.O. Box 9087, Canoga Park . . . . (818) 349-2776
Peregrine, Paul/1541 Platte St., Denver . . . . (303) 455-6944
Perez, James/16 Parkwood Ave., Mill Valley . . . . (415) 383-0316
Perry, David/Pioneer Sq. Station, Seattle . . . . (206) 932-6614
Persoff, Kathlene/211 S. La Brea, L.A. . . . . (213) 934-8276
Peterson, Abbo/32124 19th Lane S.W. Federal, Milton . . . . (206) 874-9339
Peterson, Bob/1220 42nd Ave. E., Seattle . . . . (206) 329-2299
Peterson, Bruce/2430 S. 20th St., Phoenix . . . . (602) 252-6088
Peterson, Bryan F./Gaston . . . . (503) 985-3276
Peterson, Darrell/84 University St., Seattle . . . . (206) 624-1762
Peterson, Jerry/416 N. Grand, Monrovia . . . . (818) 358-3902
Peterson, Richard/711 Eighth Ave., San Diego . . . . (619) 236-0284
Peterson, Rick/733 Auahi St., Honolulu . . . . (808) 536-8222
Petrucelli Assocs., Inc./17522 Von Karman Ave., Irvine . . . . (714) 250-8591
Pettee, Jack & Co./1501 Mission St., S. Pasadena . . . . (213) 682-1121
Pfuhl, Chris/Phoenix . . . . (602) 253-0525
Phelan, John/1632 Francisco E., Berkeley . . . . (415) 845-7535
Phillips, Ellen/433 Ocean Ave., Santa Monica . . . . (213) 393-3114
Phillips, Lee/1350 Pear Ave., Mountain View . . . . (415) 794-7447
Photography Northwest/1415 Elliott St., Seattle . . . . (206) 284-9810
Pierce, Corey Films, Inc./1503 W. Washington Blvd., Venice . . . . (213) 399-3313
Pinckney, Jim/Lake Buena Vista . . . . (407) 239-8855
Piscopo, Maria/2038 Calvert Ave., Costa Mesa . . . . (714) 556-8133
Pitcher, Don/2133 Grant, Berkeley . . . . (415) 843-9714
Pleasant, Ralph B./8755 W. Washington Blvd., Culver City . . . . (213) 202-8997
Ploch, Thomas A./30 S. Salinas, Santa Barbara . . . . (805) 965-1312
Plummer, Bil/S.F. . . . . (415) 284-1535
Porter, Alan/921 W. 21st St., Merced . . . . (209) 722-4911
Porter, James/3955 Birch St., Newport Beach . . . . (714) 852-8756
Portillo, Ralph/765 Minna St., S.F. . . . . (415) 255-9983
Pourmand, Tooraj/10804 Wilshire Blvd., L.A. . . . . (213) 583-1478
Powell, Alan/655 N. Harper Ave., L.A. . . . . (213) 653-7041
Powell, Todd/200 S. Ridge St., Breckenridge . . . . (303) 453-0469
Powers, David/2699 18th St., S.F. . . . . (415) 641-7766
Powers, Michael/3045 65th St., Sacramento . . . . (916) 451-5606
Powers, Rich/258 Imperial Dr., Pacifica . . . . (415) 355-0803
Prince, Norman/3245 25th St., S.F. . . . . (415) 821-6595
Pritzker, Burton/456 Denton Way, Santa Rosa . . . . (415) 626-3471
Professional Photog. Svcs./1011 Buenos Ave., San Diego . . . . (619) 276-4780
Puro, Steve/344 W. 200 S., St. George . . . . (801) 673-9159
Quick & Clean Tabletop Photo/1923 Colorado Ave., Santa Monica . . . . (213) 453-4661
Quinney, David Jr./423 E. Broadway, Salt Lake City . . . . (801) 363-0434
Quitslund, Garnie/Seattle . . . . (206) 842-2560
Rahn, Reed/655 N. Harper Ave., L.A. . . . . (213) 653-7041
Ramin Photography/5146 N. 76th Pl., Scottsdale . . . . (602) 945-4385
Randall, Bob/S. Pasadena . . . . (818) 441-1003
Ranson Photographers Ltd./26 Airport Rd., Edmonton . . . . (403) 454-9674
Rapoport, Aaron, Inc./3119 Beverly Blvd., L.A. . . . . (213) 738-7277
Rappaport, Rick/2725 N.E. 49th Ave., Portland . . . . (503) 249-0705
Rascona, Rodney/Phoenix/(602) 437-0866 . . . . **pages 554-555**
Rawcliffe, David/S.F. . . . . (415) 552-4252
Ray, Kathy/5701 Buckingham Pkwy., Culver City . . . . (213) 649-0202
Redmond, Frank/5332 S.W. Tualata Ct., Lake Oswego . . . . (503) 639-1924
Reed, May/Fair Oaks . . . . (916) 965-0456
Regua, Ernest/Phoenix . . . . (602) 275-3563
Reimers, Kevin/441 E. Columbine, Santa Ana . . . . (714) 545-4022
Reynolds, J.R./18537 Arrow Hwy., Covina . . . . (818) 339-2940
Reynosa, Carlos/Santa Monica . . . . (213) 458-7227

Ricketts, Mark/2809 N.E. 55th, Seattle	(206) 526-1911
Riggs, Robin/3785 Cahuenga Blvd. W., Hollywood	(213) 877-3753
Ritts, Herb/7927 Hillside Ave., L.A.	(213) 650-8880
Robbins, Bill/L.A./(213) 466-0377	**pages 598-599**
Roberts, Peggi/815 N. First Ave., Phoenix	(602) 257-0097
Robin Robin/7095 Hollywood Blvd., L.A.	(213) 933-2012
Robin, David Photography/818 Brannan St., S.F.	(415) 863-8900
Robin, David Photography/818 Brannan, S.F.	(415) 863-8900
Rogers, Ken/Beverly Hills	(213) 553-5532
Rokeach, Barrie/499 Vermont Ave., Berkeley	(415) 527-5376
Rolston, Matthew/8259 Melrose Ave., L.A.	(213) 658-1151
Rose, Peter/506 N.W. Pettygrove, Portland	(503) 228-1288
Rosenberg, Allan/963 N. Point St., S.F.	(415) 673-4550
Rosenberg, Dave/1545 Julian St., Denver	(303) 893-0893
Rosenman, Marjorie/Phoenix/(602) 273-7985	**pages 606-607**
Ross, Jeffrey B./195 N. Edison Way, Reno	(702) 329-1243
Ross, Jim/2565 Third St., S.F.	(415) 821-5710
Rothchild, Derek/N. Hollywood	(818) 508-7718
Rothman, Michael Kent/1816 N. Vermont, L.A.	(213) 662-9703
Rothman, Stewart F.M.P.A./921 Wood Way, Fairbanks	(907) 474-0685
Rouzer, Danny/7022 Melrose Ave., L.A.	(213) 936-2494
Rowell, Galen/1483 A Solano Ave., Albany	(415) 524-9343
Rubins, Richard/3268 Motor Ave., L.A.	(213) 287-0350
Ruppert, Michael/12130 Washington Pl., L.A.	(213) 938-3779
Rusing Photography/Phoenix	(602) 967-1864
Rusnak, Ron/Kona	(808) 329-4147
Russell, Gail/Taos	(505) 776-8474
Russell, John/Aspen/(303) 920-1431	**pages 640-641**
Russo, Anthony/1440 Bush St., S.F.	(415) 441-4881
Ryan, David/463 Eighth Ave., S.F.	(415) 752-8277
SFIDA/5872 W. Second St., L.A.	(213) 965-1984
Sabatini, Ken/915½ N. Mansfield, Hollywood	(213) 462-7744
Sachs, Joseph/259 Clara St., S.F.	(415) 543-3562
Sacks, Ron/Portland	(503) 641-4051
Sadlon, Jim/S.F.	(415) 775-5110
Saehlenou, Kevin/3478 W. 32nd Ave., Denver	(303) 455-1611
Safron, Marshal/1041 N. McCadden Pl., L.A.	(213) 461-5676
Sakai, Steve/L.A.	(213) 460-4811
Sal del Re/211 E. Columbine Ave., Santa Ana	(714) 432-1333
Salas, Michael/2310 Fairhill Dr., Newport Beach	(714) 722-9908
Salisbury, Sharon/116 W. Blithedale, Mill Valley	(415) 383-5943
Salome, Laura/San Diego/(619) 549-8881	**page 609**
Samerjan, Peter/743 N. Fairfax, L.A.	(213) 653-2940
Sanchez, Kevin/S.F./(415) 285-1770	**pages 622-623**
Sanders, Paul/L.A.	(213) 933-5791
Sandison, Teri/1545 N. Wilcox Ave., Hollywood	(213) 461-3529
Sandwich Isles Productions/Kaneohe	(808) 949-7000
Santullo, Nancy/L.A./(213) 874-1940	**pages 604-605**
Sargent, Sam/601 Minnesota Ave., S.F.	(415) 647-0921
Saruwatari, Craig/2865 W. 7th St., L.A.	(213) 384-1016
Scharf, David/2100 Loma Vista Pl., L.A.	(213) 666-8657
Schelling, Susan J./1440 Bush St., S.F.	(415) 441-3662
Schenker, Larry/2830 S. Robertson Blvd., L.A.	(213) 837-2020
Scherl, Ron/2121 Powell St., S.F.	(415) 391-9310
Schermeister, Phil/472 22nd Ave., S.F.	(415) 386-0218
Schiff Photography/8153 W. Blackburn Ave., L.A.	(213) 658-6179
Schlesinger, Terrence/Phoenix	(602) 957-7474
Schmidt, Dave/382 N. First Ave., Phoenix	(602) 258-2592
Schuster/16740 San Jose St., Granada Hills	(818) 368-2345
Schwortz, Barrie/2239 Vista Del Mar Pl., Hollywood	(213) 465-5451
Scott, Chris/351 Ninth St., S.F.	(415) 626-6905
Scott, Freda/S.F./(415) 621-2992	**pages 626-627**
Scott, Mark/L.A./(213) 931-9319	**page 553**
Sedam, Mike/Bothell	(206) 488-9375
Selig, Jonathan S./29206 Heathercliff Rd., Malibu	(213) 457-5856
Selland, George/461 Bryant St., S.F.	(415) 495-3633
Shanahan, Nancy/S.F./(415) 441-3769/243-8283	**pages 562-563, 580-581**
Shaneff, Carl/1200 College Walk, Honolulu	(808) 533-3010
Shapero, Don/225 Creekside Dr., Palo Alto	(415) 494-3731
Shimokochi Studio/L.A.	(213) 467-2135
Shirley, Ron/5757 Venice Blvd., L.A.	(213) 937-0919
Sholik, Stan/1946 E. Blair Ave., Santa Ana	(714) 250-9275
ShootingStar/Alameda	(415) 769-9767

WEST 549

Shorten, Chris/60 Federal St., S.F. .... (415) 543-4883
Shuman, Ron/One Menlo Pl., Berkeley .... (415) 527-7241
Siegel Photographic, Inc./224 N. Fifth Ave., Phoenix .... (602) 257-9509
Silva, Keith/S.F. .... (415) 863-5655
Silverman, Jay/Hollywood/(213) 466-6030 .... **pages 572-575**
Silvio Photography/9783 E. Camino Del Santo, Scottsdale .... (602) 860-0858
Simle, Jonathan/8859 Pickford St., L.A. .... (213) 854-6196
Simon, J. Harly/499 Alabama, S.F. .... (415) 552-1648
Simpson, Stephen/701 Kettner Blvd., San Diego .... (619) 239-6638
Sixth Street Studio/231 Sixth St., S.F. .... (415) 495-5990
Sjef's Fotographie/2311 N.W. Johnson St., Portland .... (503) 223-1089
Skelton, Keith Douglas/5129 Mt. Royal Dr., L.A. .... (213) 258-0851
Slattery, Chad/11869 Nebraska Ave., L.A. .... (213) 820-6603
Slaughter, Michael/2867 Seventh St., L.A. .... (213) 388-3361
Slaughter, Paul/1300 Calle Giraso, Sante Fe .... (505) 988-3179
Slenzak, Ron/7106 Waring Ave., L.A. .... (213) 934-9088
Slobodian, Scott, Inc./6519 Fountain Ave., L.A. .... (213) 464-2341
Smith, Derek/568 S. 400 W., Salt Lake City .... (801) 363-1061
Smith, Gil & Co./2865 W. Seventh St., L.A. .... (213) 384-1016
Smith, Grafton Marshall/0187 Lupine Dr., Aspen .... (303) 925-7120
Smith, Todd/7316 Pyramid Dr., L.A. .... (213) 651-3706
Snortum, Marty/382 N. 1st Ave., Phoenix .... (602) 252-1288
Snyder, Mark/2415 Third St., S.F. .... (415) 861-7514
Sokol, Howard/3006 Zuni St., Denver .... (303) 433-3353
Sokol, Mark/6518 Wilkinson Ave., N. Hollywood .... (818) 506-4910
Soloman, Marc/L.A. .... (213) 935-1771
Solzberg, David/655 N. Harper Ave., L.A. .... (213) 653-7041
Sornson, Bendt/401 Alston Rd., Santa Barbara .... (805) 969-1043
Spas, Dick Studio/Taos .... (505) 758-8418
Spitz, Harry/7723 Varna Ave., N. Hollywood .... (818) 376-1150
Spring, Bob & Ira/18819 Olympic View Dr., Edmonds .... (206) 776-4685
Springmann, Christopher/Pt. Reyes .... (415) 663-8428
St. John, Charles/1760 Lafayette, Denver .... (303) 860-7300
Staley, Bill/1160-21st St., West Vancouver .... (604) 922-6695
Stampfli, Eric J./50 Mendell, S.F. .... (415) 824-2305
Stanart Photography/1005 S. Granada Ave., Alhambra .... (818) 281-5423
Starr, Ashby/4416 Maycrest Ave., L.A. .... (213) 223-7247
Starr, Ron/S.F. .... (415) 541-7732
Stearns, Doug/1738 Wynkoop St., Denver .... (303) 296-1133
Steil, Rick/L.A. .... (213) 937-0300
Stein, Robert R./319 S. Robertson, Beverly Hills .... (213) 652-2030
Steinberg, John/10434 Corfu Ln., L.A. .... (213) 279-1775
Steiner, Glenn/3102 Moore St., San Diego .... (619) 299-0197
Steinheil Photography/26652 Granvia, Mission Viejo .... (714) 472-9041
Stevan Andrew Photography/610 22nd St., S.F. .... (415) 864-3009
Stevens, Ken/909 Yale Ave., Modesto .... (209) 523-5887
Stevens, Naomi/1627 W. Second Ave., Vancouver .... (604) 733-0211
Stevens, Robert/5701 Buckingham Parkway, Culver City .... (213) 645-1007
Stimson, Fred/3628 16th St., S.F. .... (415) 864-4729
Stone & Steccati/425 Second St., S.F. .... (415) 543-3827
Stone, Pete/L.A./(503) 224-7125 .... **pages 578-579**
Stott Shot/68177 Tumbleweed Rd., Montrose .... (303) 249-9036
Streano, Vince/Anacortes .... (206) 293-4525
Streshinsky, Ted/50 Kenyon Ave., Kensington .... (415) 526-1976
Strong, Aaron/Aspen/(303) 920-1431 .... **pages 640-641**
Studio 3, Inc./1000 Lenora, Seattle .... (206) 343-7002
Studio 3, Inc./1316 S.E. 12th Ave., Portland .... (503) 238-1748
Studio A/1665 Blake Ave, L.A. .... (213) 222-0735
Studio A Photographic Adv./6274 Peachtree St., L.A. .... (213) 721-1802
Studio B/17962 Sky Park Cir., Irvine .... (714) 261-0575
Studio Five, Inc./846 S. Robertson, L.A. .... (213) 652-5294
Su, Andrew/5733 Benner St., L.A. .... (213) 256-0598
Sugimoto, Norman/L.A. .... (213) 467-2135
Sullivan, Jeremiah S./2308 D. Kettner Blvd., San Diego .... (619) 236-0711
Sund, Harald/Seattle .... (206) 938-1080
Sunlit Ltd./1523 Montane Dr. E., Genesee .... (303) 526-1162
Sutton, John Photography/123 Townsend, S.F. .... (415) 974-5452
Svendsen, Linda/3915 Bayview Circle, Concord .... (415) 676-8299
Svoboda, John/3211-B S. Shannon, Santa Ana .... (714) 979-8992
Swarthout, Walter/370 Fourth St., S.F. .... (415) 543-2525
Sweet, Ron/S.F. .... (415) 473-1222
Sweitzer Photographs, Ltd./4800 Washington, Denver .... (303) 295-0703
Tafoya, Ron/6738 Elwood N.W., Albuquerque .... (505) 345-6351

Tanaka, Randall/8035 Airlane Ave., L.A.	(213) 670-9554
Tangen, Pete/2865 W. 7th St., L.A.	(213) 384-1016
Tao, Yoko/S.F.	(213) 274-3167
Tapp, Carlan/820 Industry Dr., Seattle	(206) 575-1775
Taub, Doug/Malibu	(213) 457-8600
Taylor, Luann/S.F./(415) 882-4460	**pages 556-557**
Taylor, Paul/N. Hollywood	(818) 763-4534
Team Russell/Aspen/(303) 920-1431	**pages 640-641**
Teke/Studio City	(818) 985-9066
Tevis, Peter E./Burbank	(213) 874-7656
Tezzuto, Allen/1822½ Newport Blvd., Costa Mesa	(714) 760-7171
Theo/Beverly Hiils	(213) 838-8811
Thimmes, Tim/8749 W. Washington Blvd., Culver City	(213) 204-6851
Thompson, Tomi/1448 Akamai St., Kailua	(808) 261-5367
Thonson, Sean/L.A./(213) 626-3686	**page 646**
Thornton, Tyler/4706 Oakwood Ave., L.A.	(213) 465-0425
Tilger, Stewart/Seattle	(206) 682-7818
Tise, David/975 Folsom St., S.F.	(415) 777-0669
Topalian, Carole/5223 San Feliciano Dr., Woodland Hills	(818) 703-7784
Towers, Clarence/499 Alabama St., S.F.	(415) 861-5150
Tradelius, Bob/738 Santa Fe Dr., Denver	(303) 825-4847
Trafficanda, Gerald/1111 N. Beachwood Dr., L.A.	(213) 466-1111
Trailer, Martin/San Diego/(619) 549-8881	**page 609**
Trank, Steven/706 W. Pico Blvd., L.A.	(213) 749-1220
Travis, Tom/1219 S. Pearl St., Denver	(303) 377-7422
Treaduny, Don/4617 W. Washington Blvd., L.A.	(213) 934-7016
Treadwell, Stephen/2161 Senasac Ave., Long Beach	(213) 596-6276
Tregeagle, Steve/2994 S. Richards St., Salt Lake City	(801) 484-1673
Tucker, Mark/601 Minnesota, S.F.	(415) 550-0303
Tunison, Richard/7829 E. Foxmore Ln., Scottsdale	(602) 998-4708
Turcotte, James/Long Beach	(213) 439-8775
Turner & de Vries/1200 College Walk, Honolulu	(808) 537-3115
Turner, John Terence/Seattle	(206) 325-9073
Tuschman, Mark/300 Santa Monica Ave., Menlow Park	(415) 322-4157
Twede, Brian/430 S. State St., Salt Lake City	(801) 534-1459
Undheim, Timothy/1039 Seventh Ave., San Diego	(619) 232-3366
Unger, Trudi/Mill Valley	(415) 381-5683
Vadasz, Bela/Norden	(916) 426-9108
Van Ackeren, Michael/214 Minor Ave. N., Seattle	(206) 625-1000
Vanderpoel, Fred/L.A./(213) 935-5695	**pages 600-601**
Vanderpoel, Fred/S.F./(415) 621-4405	**pages 600-601**
Vanguard Photography/3371 Cahuenga Blvd. W., L.A.	(213) 874-3980
Vano Photography/965 Mission St., S.F.	(415) 896-0624
Varela, Brent/875 Cheltenham, Santa Barbara	(805) 682-4459
Vaughn, Ray/7167 Woodmore Oaks Dr., Citrus Hts.	(916) 726-4530
Vega, Raul/3511 W. Sixth St., L.A.	(213) 387-2058
Veitch, Julie/5757 Venice Blvd., L.A.	(213) 936-4231
Veiwpoint Photographers/9034 N 23rd Ave., Phoenix	(602) 245-0013
Vereen, Jackson/570 Bryant St., S.F.	(415) 777-5272
Viarnes, Alex/33 Clementina, S.F.	(415) 543-1195
Villaflor/S.F.	(415) 921-4238
Visages/L.A./(213) 650-8880	**page 620**
Visual Images West, Inc./600 E. Baseline, Tempe	(800) 433-4765
Visual Impact/733 Auahi St., Honolulu	(808) 524-8269
Vogt, Laurie/17522 Von Karman, Irvine	(714) 250-8591
Wade, Harry/4216 Webster St., Oakland	(415) 652-1595
Wagner, Craig/1316 S.E. 12th Ave, Portland	(503) 238-1748
Wagner, Laura/2125 Lincon Way, S.F.	(415) 564-7772
Wahlberg, Chris/S.F./(415) 821-6906	**pages 614-615**
Wahlstrom, Richard/S.F./(415) 550-1400	**pages 580-581**
Waldon Photography-Aerials/2069 E. Third St., Long Beach	(213) 434-1782
Walker, Balfour /Mooney, Chris/1838 E. Sixth, Tucson	(602) 624-1121
Walker, Douglas/416 Duncan St., S.F.	(415) 821-4379
Wallace, Marlene/1624-B S. Cotner Ave., L.A.	(213) 826-1027
Waller, E.K./620 Moulton St., Studio 123, L.A.	(213) 223-0442
Ward Photo, Inc./1210 S. Jason, Denver	(303) 744-6301
Warren, William James & Assocs./509 S. Gramercy Pl., L.A.	(213) 383-0500
Warring, Ron/Phoenix	(602) 275-3563
Wasserman, David/S.F.	(415) 255-7393
Waterson, David/Seattle	(206) 365-9405
Watson, Stuart/620 Moulton Ave., L.A.	(213) 221-3886
Waz, Tony/1115 S. Trotwood Ave., San Pedro	(213) 548-3758
Weber, Joan/12532 Matterson Ave., L.A.	(213) 397-3408

Weisrer, Kris/Aspen	(303) 920-1431
Weiss, Stacey/L.A.	(213) 939-9797
Wells, Craig Photography/537 W. Granada Rd., Phoenix	(602) 252-8166
Welsh, Steve/1121 Grove St., Boise	(208) 336-5541
Wendt, Bobbi/S.F./(415) 495-1900	**pages 594-595**
Wenger, Greg/1330 Main St., Venice	(213) 399-5510
Wertz, Bill/732 N. Highland Ave, L.A.	(213) 469-2775
West, Greg/San Diego	(619) 549-8881
West, Randall G./Santa Fe	(800) 359-9777
West-Towne Studios/1447 11th St., Santa Monica	(213) 453-5000
Wexler, Glen/736 N. Highland Ave., L.A.	(213) 465-0268
White, Lee/1172 S. La Brea, L.A.	(213) 934-5993
Whitefield, Brent/816 S. Grand Ave., L.A.	(213) 624-7511
Whitfield, Brent/816 S. Grand Ave., L.A.	(213) 624-7511
Whitley, Dianna/453 Midvale Ave., L.A.	(213) 208-5594
Whittaker, Steve/111 Glenn Way, Belmont	(415) 595-4242
Wickes, Michael/Hailey	(208) 788-4923
Wickham, M.J./24 B Tenth St., Santa Rosa	(707) 526-4632
Wiener, Leigh/2600 Carman Crest, L.A.	(213) 876-0990
Wilcox, Bob Photography, Inc./515 E. Thomas Rd., Phoenix	(602) 264-2531
Wilcox, Shorty/Brechenridge	(303) 452-2511
Wildt, James W./9095 W. Wagontrail Dr., Littleton	(303) 972-8589
Wiley, John K./1916 Pike Pl., Seattle	(206) 448-4750
Wilhelm, Dave/2565 Third St., S.F.	(415) 826-9399
Willett, Larry/450 S. La Brea, L.A.	(213) 939-6047
Williams, Rene/1906 Griffith Pk. Blvd., L.A.	(213) 661-2908
Williams, Sandra/San Diego	(619) 283-3100
Williams, Steven Burr/8306 Wilshire Blvd., Beverly Hills	(213) 650-7906
Williford, Mark B./710 Spencer St., Honolulu	(808) 533-7083
Wilson, Bruce/1022 First Ave. S., Seattle	(206) 621-9182
Wilson, Doug/10133 N.E. 113th Pl., Kirkland	(206) 822-8604
Wilson, Gerry/6502 Santa Monica Blvd., L.A.	(213) 465-1532
Wimpey, Chris/627 Eighth Ave., San Diego	(619) 232-3222
Winegar, Ramon/118 Social Hall Ave., Salt Lake City	(801) 364-7482
Wittner, Dale/1916 Pike Pl., Seattle	(206) 623-4545
Wolf, Barbara/L.A.	(213) 466-4660
Wolfe, Dan Productions/39 E. Walnut St., Pasadena	(818) 584-4000
Wolfe, Toris Von/13906 Ventura Blvd., Sherman Oaks	(818) 995-1876
Wolin, Penny/2934 Nebraska Ave., Santa Monica	(213) 829-3631
Wong, Ken/3431 Wesley St., Culver City	(213) 836-3118
Wood, Earl/104 A Industrial Center Bldg., Sausalito	(415) 332-2307
Wood, James B./L.A.	(213) 461-3861
Wordal, Eric/3640 Keir Ln., Helena	(406) 475-3304
Worden, Kirk/3215 N. Zuni St., Denver	(303) 477-5621
Wortham, Robert/521 State St., L.A.	(818) 243-6400
Wray, Michael/18-A Reed St., Mill Valley	(415) 381-5161
Yarbrough, Carl/811 Mapleton Ave., Boulder	(303) 444-1500
Young & Robin/7095 Hollywood, L.A.	(213) 933-2012
Young, Pamela/3161 Cadet Crt., L.A.	(213) 851-6313
Yves Photography/6516 W. Sixth St., L.A.	(213) 655-2181
Zachary, Neil/4111 Lincoln Blvd., Marina Del Rey	(213) 399-5775
Zaitz, David/L.A./(213) 936-5115	**pages 256-257**
Zajack, Greg/Santa Ana	(714) 432-8400
Zak In the West/S.F.	(415) 781-1611
Zaruba, Jeff/911 E. Pike St., Seattle	(206) 328-9035
Zenuk, Alan/Vancouver	(604) 733-8271
Zimberoff, Tom/Sausalito	(415) 331-3100
Zimmerman, Dick/8743 W. Washington Blvd., L.A.	(213) 204-2911
Zimmerman, John/9135 Hazen Dr., Beverly Hills	(213) 273-2642
Zucchini Studios/121 Ocean View Blvd., Pacific Greene	(408) 372-9232
Zurek, Nikolay/276 Shipley St., S.F.	(415) 777-9210

Mark *Scott*

MARK SCOTT PHOTOGRAPHY LOS ANGELES / STUDIO 213.931.9319 FAX 213.931.9616

RODNEY
RASCONA

602.437.0866
fax 437.9015

PACK

BILL PACK PHOTOGRAPHY

SAN FRANCISCO REPRESENTATION

LUANN TAYLOR

415 882 4460

NATIONAL REPRESENTATION

CLARICE ISOM

415 885 1563

FACSIMLE 415 882 7394

PHOTO BY GARY BERNSTEIN • JEWELRY BY HARRY WINSTON • ©1988 PARFUMS INTERNATIONAL LTD.

Elizabeth Taylor's Passion For The Body And Soul.

Solitude. Serenity. A sensuous body and bath ritual.
Silkening and soothing the body.
Freeing the soul to its most beautiful imaginings.

ELIZABETH TAYLOR'S
PASSION
Body Riches

AVAILABLE AT
FILENE'S
To order call 1-800-FILENES

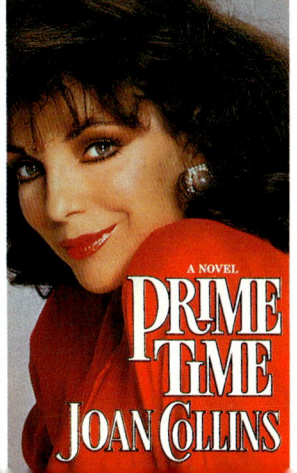

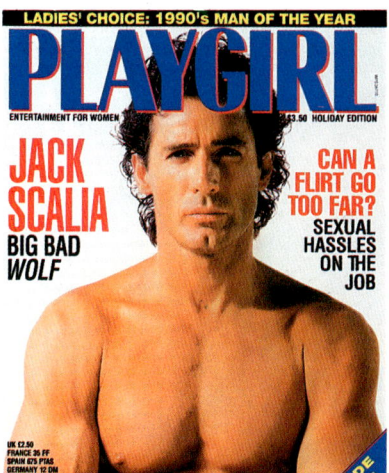

Gary Bernstein

559

Gary Bernstein

GARY BERNSTEIN STUDIO • GARY BERNSTEIN PRODUCTIONS
THE HELMS BUILDING, 8735 WASHINGTON BOULEVARD, CULVER CITY, CA 90230
PHONE: (213) 550-6891 • FAX: (213) 278-6706

Mizono

ROBERT MIZONO 650 ALABAMA SAN FRANCISCO, CA 94110 415/648-3993

VALLEJO, CA

563

CLAUDIA HIRSCH
L.A. 213·342·0226

moloko-plus

CLAUDIA

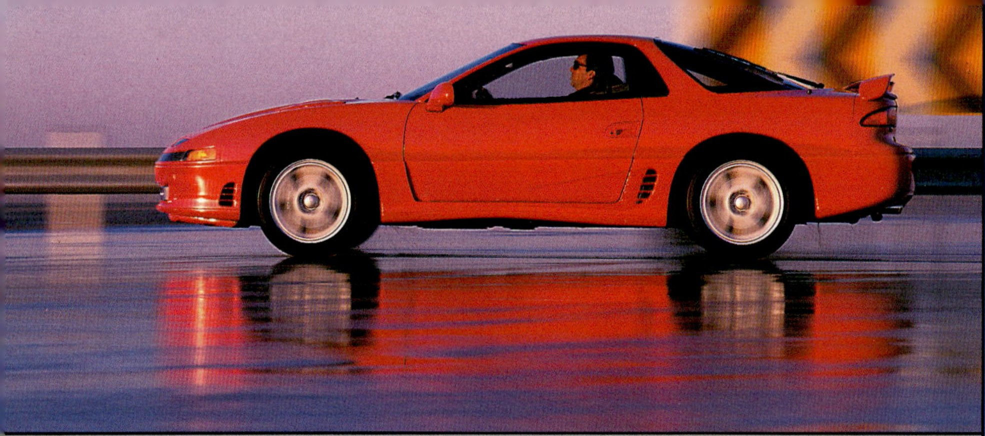
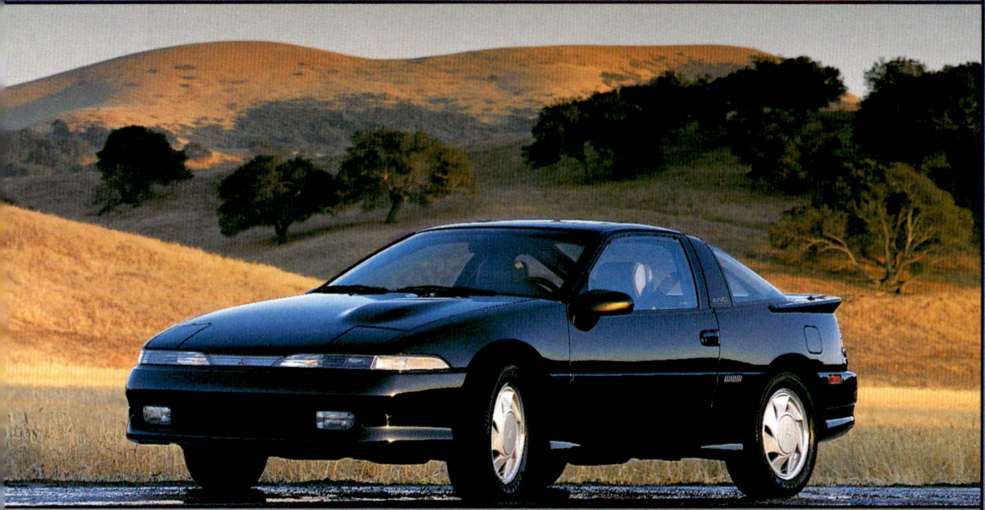
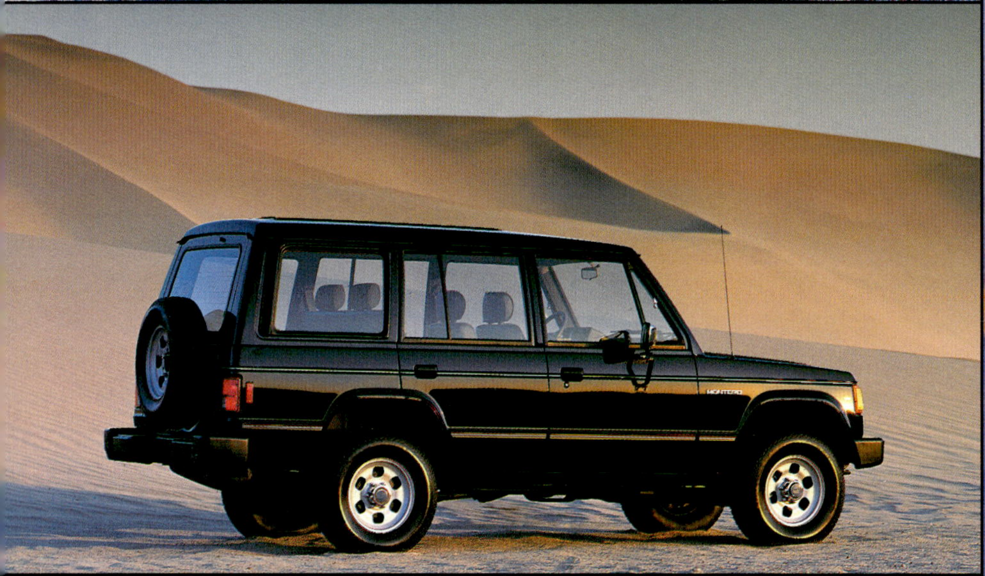
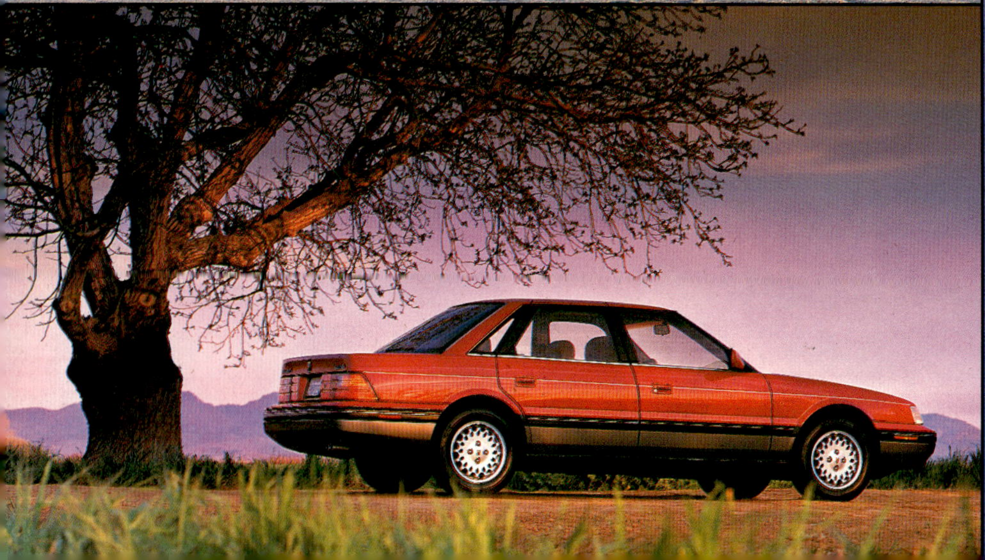

Bo Hylén

PHOTOGRAPHY
1640 S. La Cienega Blvd.
Los Angeles, CA 90035

For portfolio
and reel call
(213) 271-6543

REPRESENTATIVE
Fox & Spencer
(213) 653-6484

TELEFAX
(213) 271-6470

PRINT/FILM

HEFFERNAN

415.626.1999

CHUCK KUHN

Studio: 206-842-1996

Nike

Print: Represented in NY — Madeleine Robinson 212-243-3138   Chicago — Ken Feldman 312-337-0447

THE WEST

FAX: 206-842-1265

Marlboro/Leo Burnett/Chicago

Film: Van Ackeren Company 206-625-1000

571

Silver

Produced by **Kim Kelling** 213/466-6030   Studio FAX: 213/466-7139

man

CALL
FOR OUR
REEL

Jay Silverman Productions
920 North Citrus Avenue
Hollywood, CA 90038
213/466-6030

Not All Jews Retire To Miami.

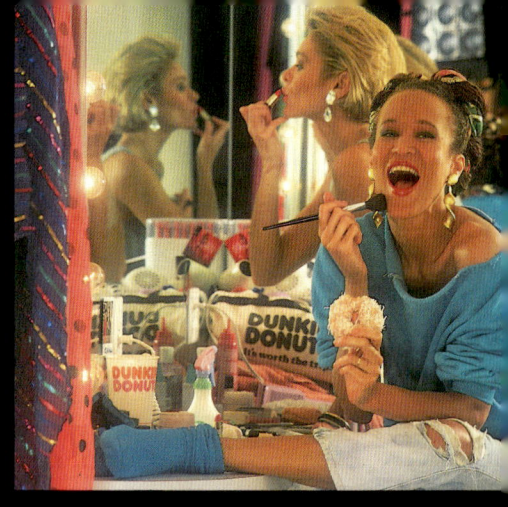

Silver

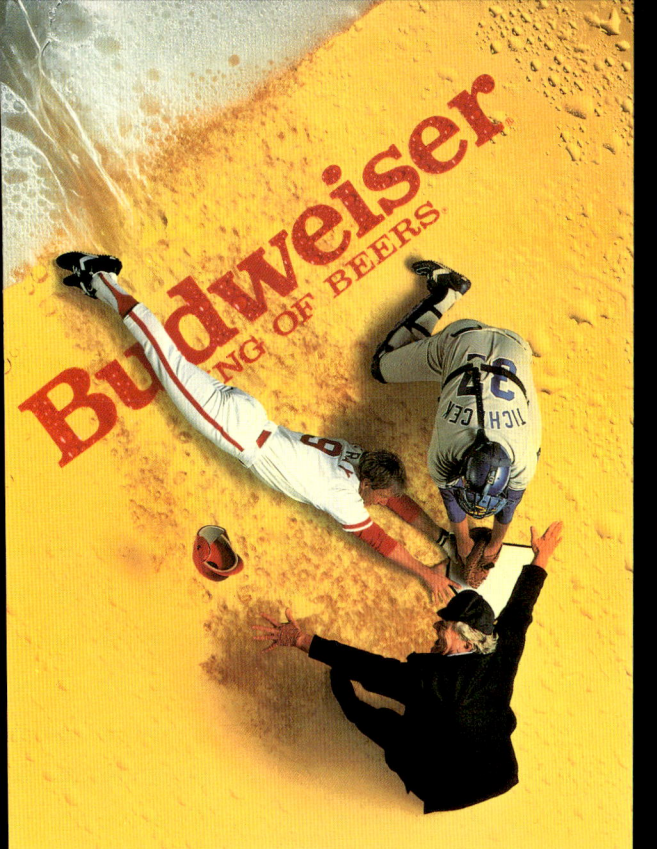

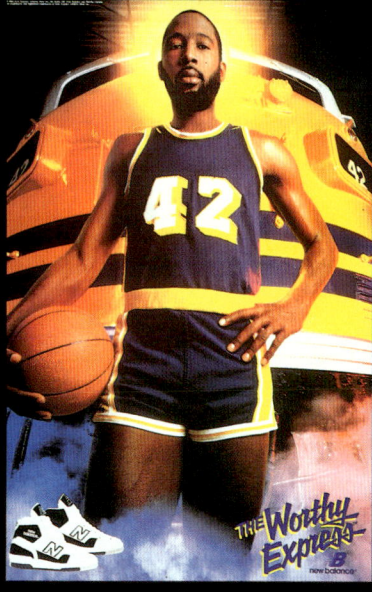

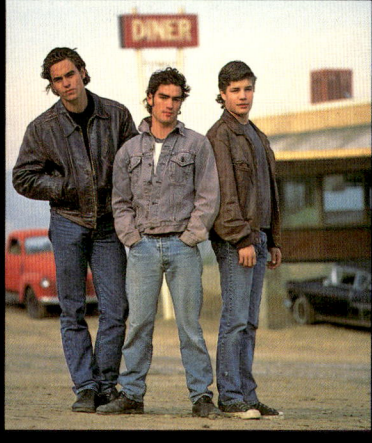

Produced by **Kim Kelling** 213/466-6030

Studio FAX: 213/466-7139

man

CALL FOR OUR REEL

Jay Silverman Productions
920 North Citrus Avenue
Hollywood, CA 90038
213/466-6030

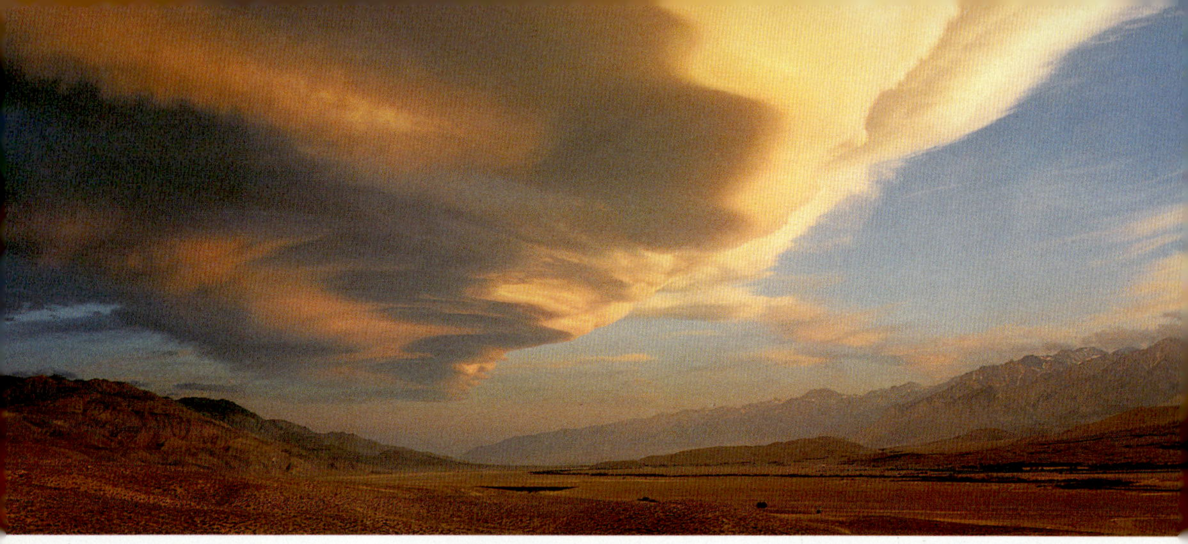

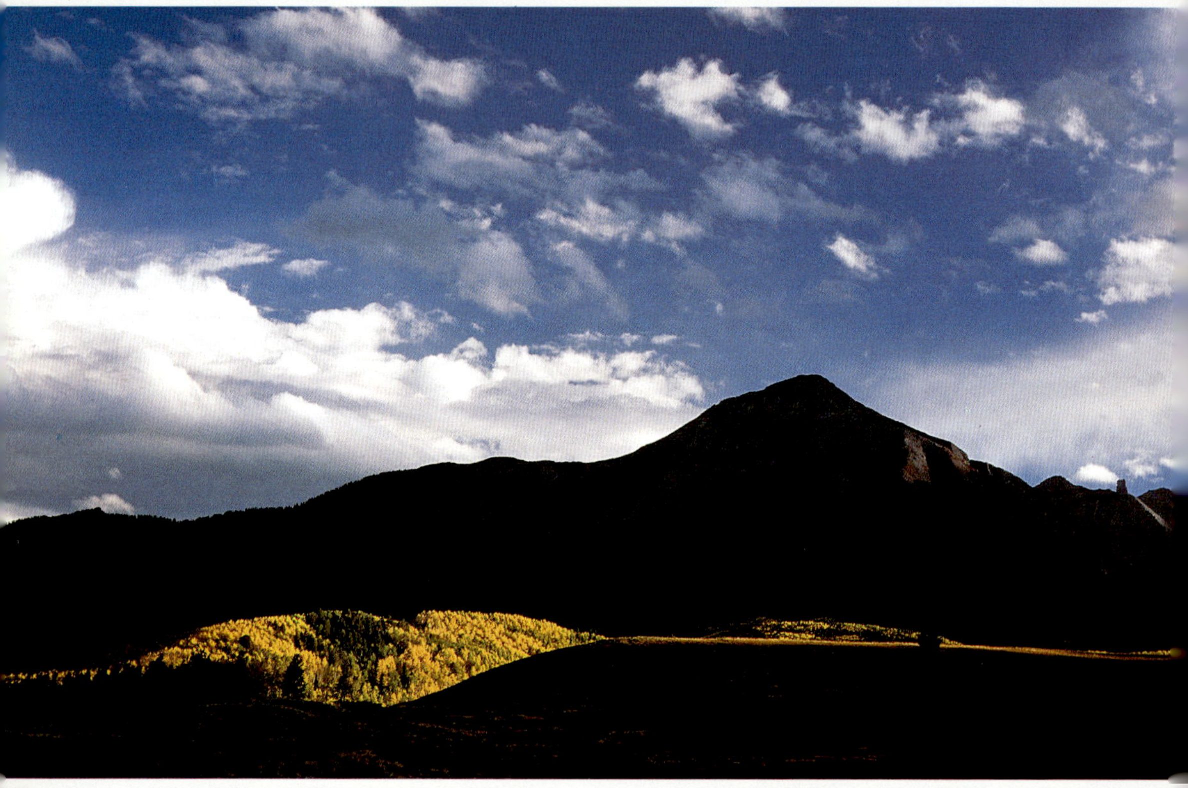

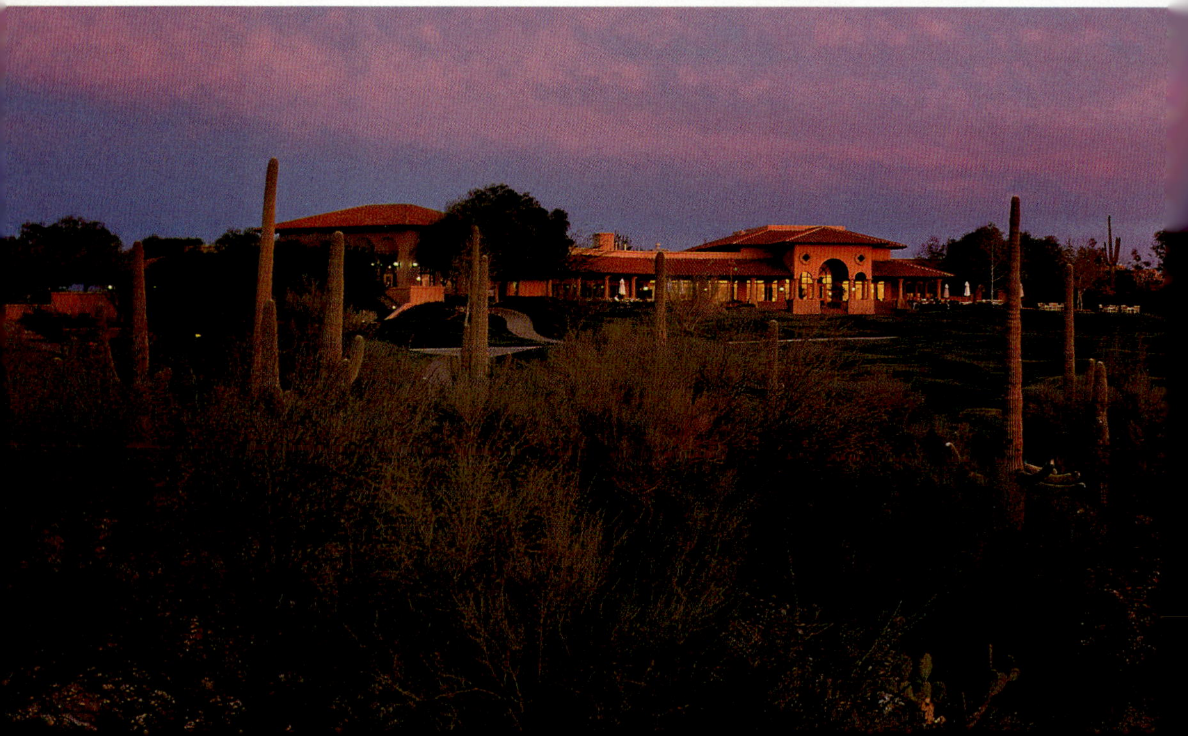

Kathleen Norris Cook

Assignment and Stock / Landscapes / Aerials / Panoramics

Represented by Warren Cook
(714) 770-4619

P.O. Box 2159
Laguna Hills, California 92654

For additional examples, see previous Showcase and Black Book volumes.
© 1990 Kathleen Norris Cook

PETE STONE

503·224·7125

REPRESENTED BY ROBIN DICTENBERG AND CHARLES BYRNES

BIG CITY PRODUCTIONS · 5 E 19TH STREET · NYC 10003   212·473·3366

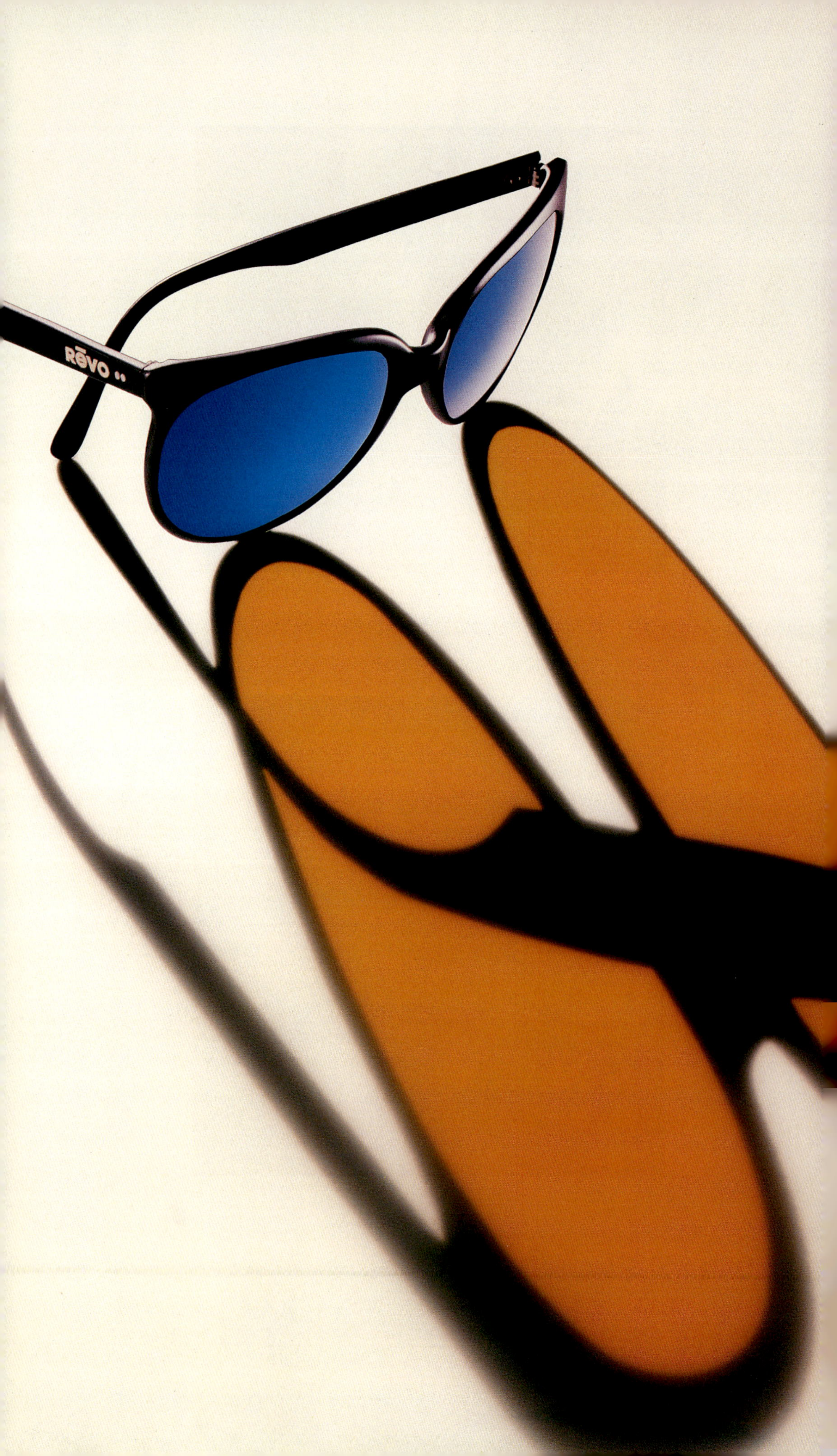

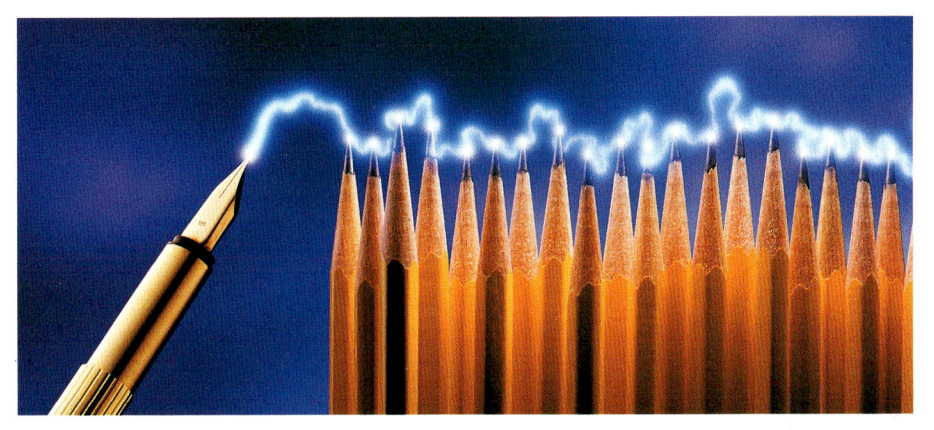

RICHARD WAHLSTROM

650 ALABAMA STREET
SAN FRANCISCO, CA 94110
TEL: 415 550 1400
FAX: 415 282 9133

DALLAS
PHOTOCOM 214 428 8781

SAN FRANCISCO
NANCY SHANAHAN 415 243 8283

CHICAGO
JIM HANSON 312 337 7770

GALVÁN

Gary Galván Studio
4626½ Hollywood Boulevard
Los Angeles, California 90027
213 667 1457   FAX 213 669 0493

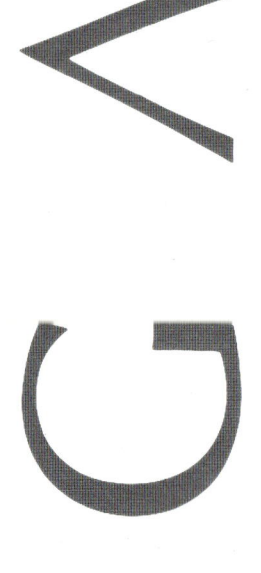

Partial Client List

AT&T
Century 21
Cover Girl
Disney
General Foods
Hilton Hotels
Levis
Reebok
Seagrams
Sears Savings Bank
Stroh Brewery
Pepsi-Co
Pacific Bell

583

MICHAEL HORIKAWA
shoots the best of Hawaii.

Luxury resorts, travel, fashion, product.
Location, studio and aerial.

Thanks to America West, American Hawaiian Cruises, AT&T, AMFAC, Aston Hotels, Catalina, Dole International, Eastern Airlines, Fuji Film, General Foods, Hawaiian Airlines, Hilton Hotels, Hyatt Hotels, Johnson & Johnson, Lever Brothers, Mauna Lani Resort, Mercedes-Benz (Europe), Nissan (Japan), Pan Am, Panasonic, Playboy, Sheraton Hotels, Shiseido, Toshiba, United Airlines, Westin Hotels and many others.

Studio: 508 Kamakee Street, Honolulu, Hawaii 96814
808 / 538-7378, Cellular 226-3256, Fax 528-2835

New York: Page Associates 212 / 772-0346

585

Milroy/McAleer

Milroy/McAleer Newport Beach Telephone: 714. 722. 6402 FAX: 714. 722. 6371

Elma Garcia
AMERICAN CLASSICS

*I first saw Darrell doing road work
for the county. When I asked him to be in a
picture, he said "Sure, as long as my
baby boy can be in it too."*

Darrell Thomas, Road Construction, Ben Wheeler, Texas

AN AMERICAN CLASSIC CAMPAIGN FOR THE MARTIN AGENCY AND WRANGLER JEANS

Elma Garcia
AMERICAN CLASSICS

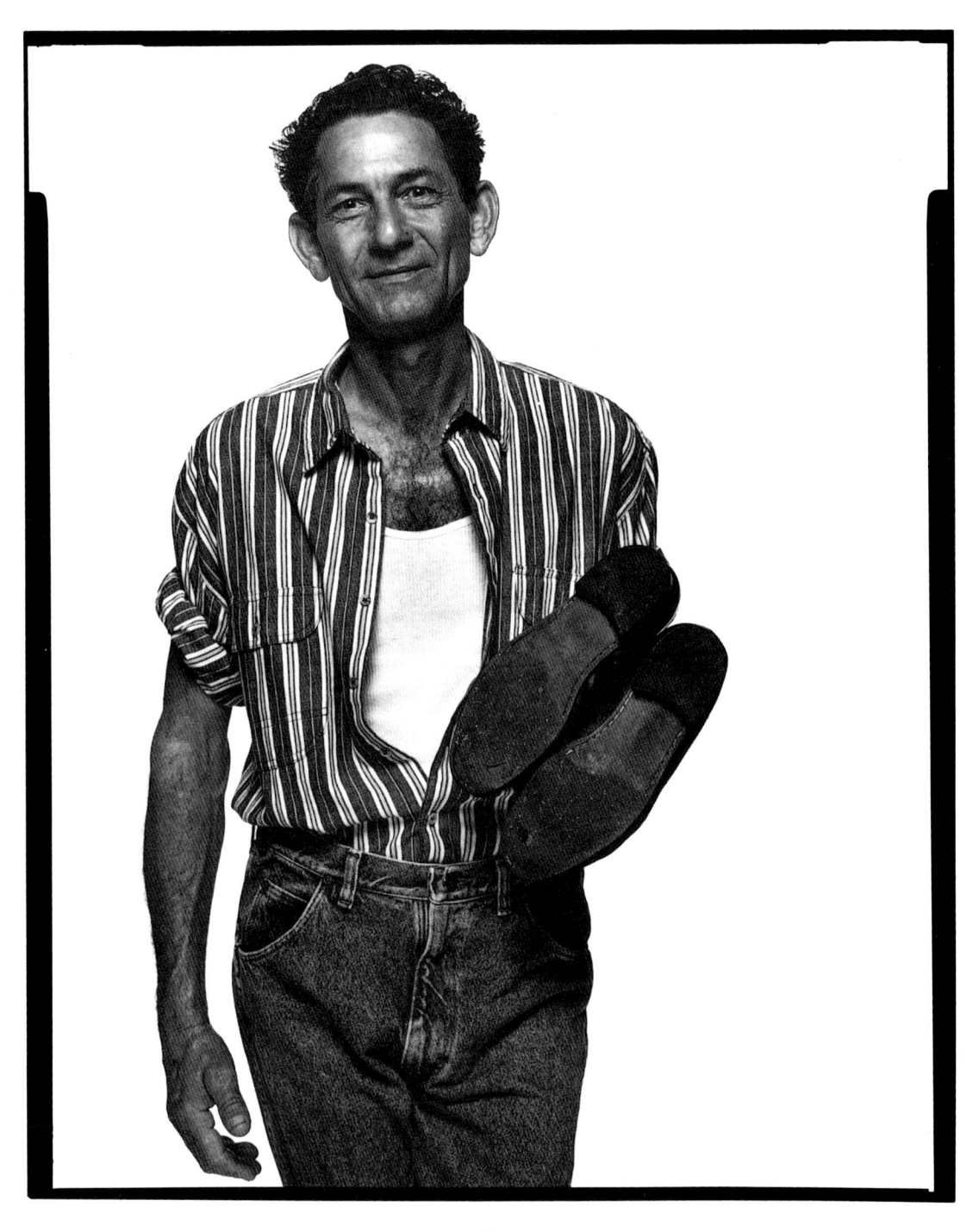

*I asked Elgin to bring his
favorite personal belonging to the shoot.
So he did—his dancing shoes.
"My wife and I love to dance!"*

Elgin Tibadaeux, Oil Field Worker, Houmma, Louisiana

ELMA GARCIA SAN FRANCISCO TELEPHONE (415)641-9992 FAX (415)641-0260

Elma Garcia
AMERICAN CLASSICS

*I asked Ed about winemaking.
He said his father had taught him, and that he too
would pass it down. "It's about heritage.
Traditional values keeps a family bonded."*

Ed Giobbi, Artist, Katonah, New York

AN AMERICAN CLASSIC CAMPAIGN FOR KETCHUM AND BEATRICE/HUNT/WESSON

Elma Garcia
AMERICAN CLASSICS

Karen is a homemaker.
She says that being a mom
is one of life's
greatest pleasures!

Karen Durrett, Homemaker, Portland, Oregon

ELMA GARCIA SAN FRANCISCO TELEPHONE (415)641-9992 FAX (415)641-0260

591

Fred/Alan Advertising/MTV

Austin-Kelley Advertising/Arvida

Hutchins, Y&R/Kodak

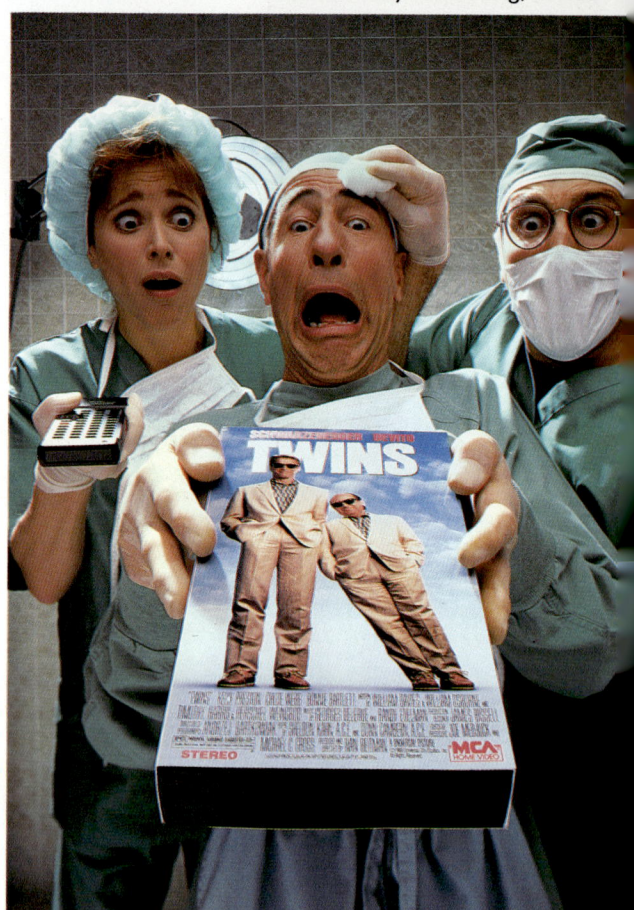

Foote Cone & Belding/MCA

RY&P/La Costa Hotel & Spa

Jay P. Morgan
PHOTOGRAPHY

2 1 3 - 2 2 4 - 8 2 8 8

Dial Communications

Jay P. Morgan Photography
618 D Moulton Ave., Los Angeles, CA 90031
Represented in Los Angeles by
Kelly Keith (213) 224-8288
FAX #(213) 224-8386

Call or write to add your
name to our mailing list.

Warner Bros./Van Dyke Parks

593

HUNTER FREEMAN PHOTOGRAPHY & FILM

HUNTER
FREEMAN
PHOTOGRAPHY
123 South Park St.
San Francisco,
Calif. 94107
Phone: (415) 495/1900
Fax: (415) 495/2594
REPRESENTED
BY: BOBBI
WENDT

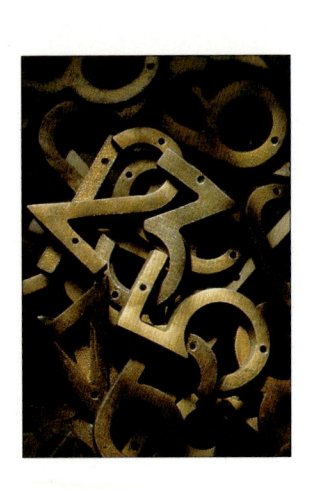

HUNTER FREEMAN PHOTOGRAPHY & FILM

HUNTER FREEMAN PHOTOGRAPHY & FILM

Whether it's a still life or real life, a visual should always be memorable. ~ A unique perspective that captures the essence of an object, the character of an individual. ~ That's how Hunter Freeman approaches both his photography and film work. ~ People who've shot with him know. ~ Whether their concept requires a human touch or a humorous touch, Hunter can translate it into an unforgettable image.

© 1990 Hunter Freeman Photography. All Rights Reserved.

Microsoft / Visible Images

A L A N A B R

(206) 621-0710 (206) 624-5713 (212) 472-1749
Seattle **Fax** **New York**

Partial Client List

United Airlines
Rockwell International
Xerox
McDonald's
Boeing
Microsoft

AMCA International
Meredith Corporation
Immunex
Flow Systems
DuPont
FMC
United Technologies

Ackerley Communications
Otis Elevator
Time/Life Books
Avon Products Inc.
Korry Electronics
Magnatek

Western Tugboat / Madsen Design

McDonald's / Leo Burnett USA

A   M   O   W   I   T   Z

Rockwell International Annual Report / Italy

597

BILL ROBBINS

Bill Robbins Photography 7016 Santa Monica Boulevard Los Angeles CA 90038
Studio 213.466.0377 FAX 213.465.8394 **Western States** Rhoni Epstein 213.663.2388
FAX 213.662.0035 **New York** Susan Miller 212.905.8400 FAX 212.427.7777

©1990. FRED VANDERPOEL. (213) 935-5695 (415) 621-4405.

©1990. FRED VANDERPOEL. (213) 935-5695 (415) 621-4405.

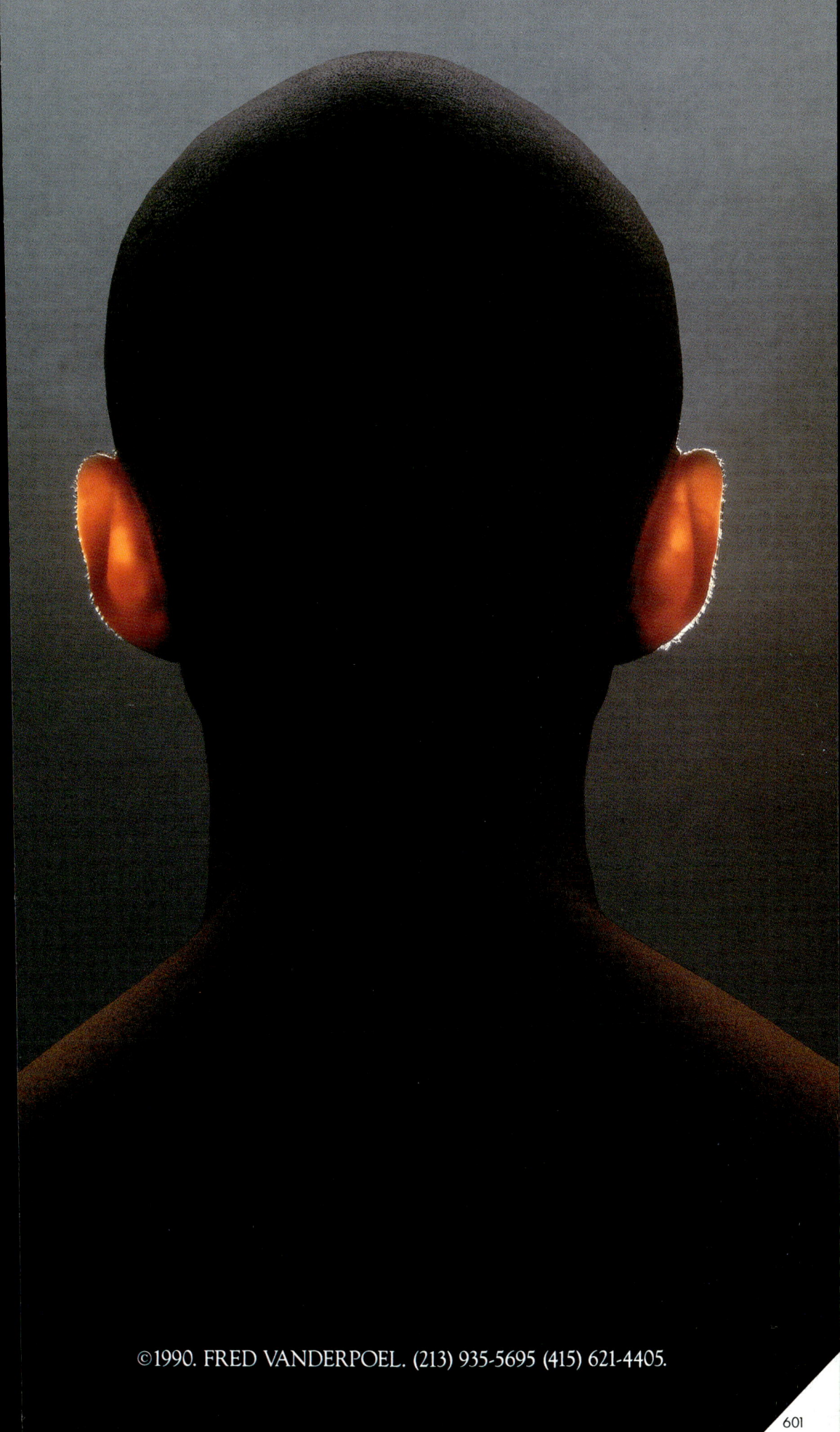

H U N

Clients include:

Knoll International
Allstate Insurance
Audi Automobile
Digital Equipment Corp.
Ethan Allen, Seaworld

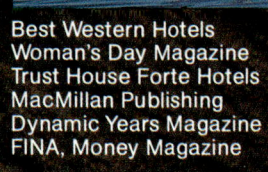

Best Western Hotels
Woman's Day Magazine
Trust House Forte Hotels
MacMillan Publishing
Dynamic Years Magazine
FINA, Money Magazine

American Funds Distributo
Great Western Financial
Capital Research and
  Management
Mexican Ministry of Tourisr
Seaworld, Hilton Hotels

©Copyright Jeff Hunter 1990

T E R

Stock Photography:
The Image Bank
For More Samples:
The Creative Black Book, 1990
The Workbook, 1990
Corporate Showcase, Volume 8
Call for our Portfolio

FAX: (213) 669-0493

Represented by **Kim Hauck**
(213) 471-2412

JEFF HUNTER
PHOTOGRAPHY

4626½ HOLLYWOOD BLVD.
LOS ANGELES, CA 90027
PHONE 213.669.0468

gue Magazine
lson Entertainment
e-Life, Allstate
es Entertainment
od Housekeeping
ersion Magazine

Prentice Hall
Reader's Digest
Stylus Furniture
Beneficial Life
Price Waterhouse
McGraw Hill

Giorgio, Clairol
Pepsi-Co., Yamaha
Westpoint Pepperell
AT&T Bell Labs
Eastman Kodak
John Deere

603

SANTULLO

7213	LOS ANGELES	STUDIO	IN CHICAGO	IN LOS ANG
SANTA MONICA	CALIFORNIA	TELEPHONE	VINCENT KAMIN	HALL & ASS
BOULEVARD	90046	213·874·1940	312·787·8834	213·934·9

SANTULLO

NANCY
SANTULLO
PHOTOGRAPHY

7213
SANTA MONICA
BOULEVARD

LOS ANGELES
CALIFORNIA
90046

STUDIO
TELEPHONE
213·874·1940

IN CHICAGO
VINCENT KAMIN
312·787·8834

IN LOS ANGELES
HALL & ASSOC.
213·934·9420

MARKOW SOUTHWEST

Paul Markow shoots for print, photomatics and stock on location. Anywhere. Represented in Phoenix by Marjorie Rosenman at 602/273-7985

FAX NUMBER: 602/273-6233

JOYE
PHOTOGRAPHY

CLAYTON JOYE
ASSIGNMENTS
WORLDWIDE

LOS ANGELES
213.957.1385
SAN FRANCISCO
415.362.9686

Partial list of clients: British Airways, Charles Schwab, Dole International, GTE Sprint, Levi's, Nissan, Pacific Bell

Determined   *Sensitive*   *Enthusiastic*

MARTIN PHOTOGRAPHIC INC TRAILER
619 549 8881 FAX 549 0758
Represented by Laura Salome

609

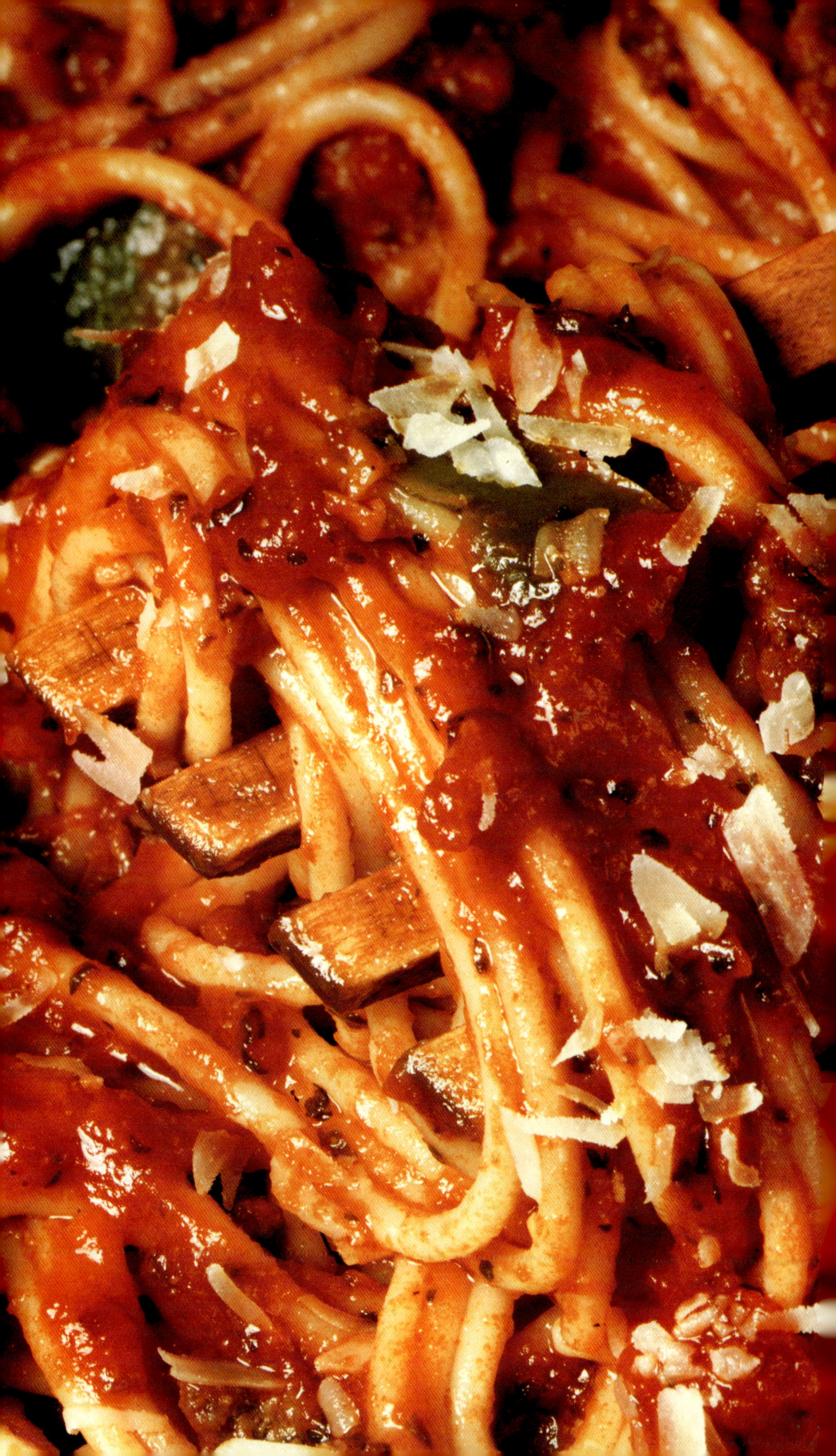

Bellissimo!

Deshong Studios
are represented
by Diane,
Tel. 213·275·2620
Fax.213·275·0543

PHOTOGRAPHY

MARK HARRIS

PHOTOGRAPHY
213/9393979

MICHAEL MCRAE

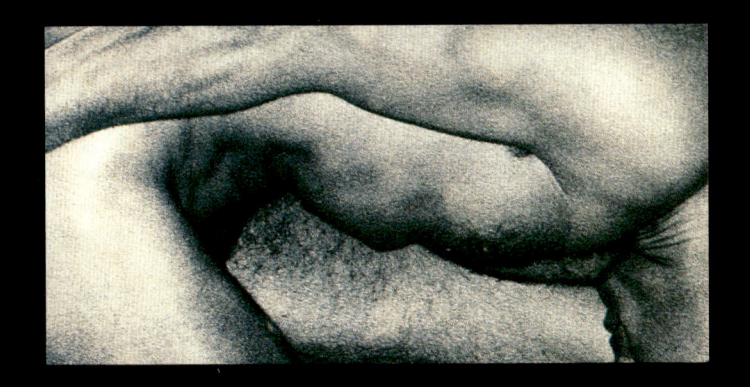

925 South West Temple · Salt Lake City · Utah 84101 · 801 328 3633

613

WAHLBERG

CHRIS WAHLBERG PHOTOGRAPHY
2660 Third Street   San Francisco, CA 94107   415-821-6906

615

CASEMORE

CASEMORE/DAMON PRODUCTIONS

Los Angeles
213-462-5256

Detroit
313-645-0741

CASEMORE/DAMON PRODUCTIONS

Los Angeles
213-462-5256

Detroit
313-645-0741

ROBERT ELIAS

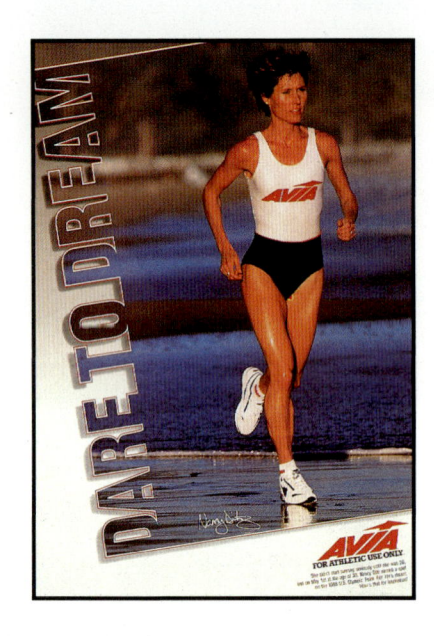

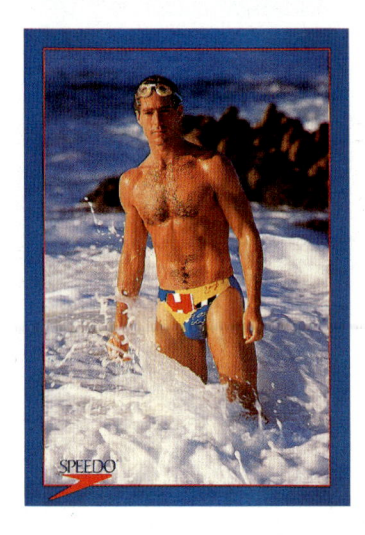

PARTIAL CLIENT LIST

COVER GIRL COSMETICS

CHRISTAN DIOR

VIDAL SASSON

MERLE NORMAN COSMETICS

AVON

SPEEDO NORTH AMERICA

CATALINA SWIMWEAR

TOO HOT BRAZIL SWIMWEAR

AVIA ATHLETIC

LANDS END

WHITE STAG

I. MAGNIN/BULLOCKS

LEVI STRAUSS CO

PENDLETON WOOLEN MILLS

SEARS

DAYTON'S

PARAMOUNT PICTURES

ROBERT ELIAS

Christian Dior
BEACHWEAR

959 N. COLE AVE. LOS ANGELES, CA. 90038
213-460-2988   FAX 213-460-4265
REPRESENTED BY GERARD BISIGNANO
2 1 3 - 4 5 8 - 7 2 2 7

619

PETER   DARLEY   MILLER   INC

Easy E

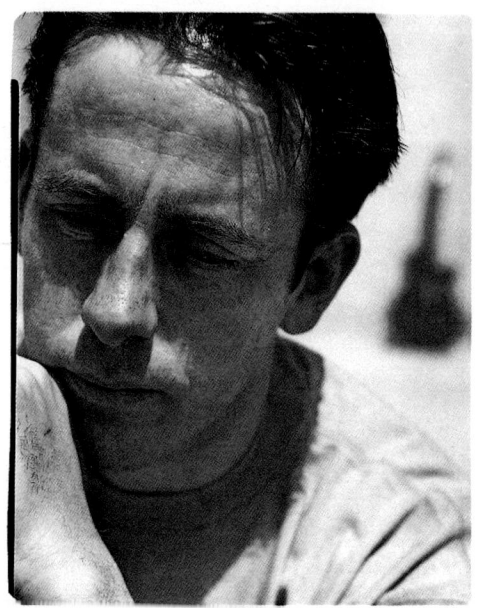

Luka Bloom

Buck Owens

Telephone   213 460 4876   Facsimile   213 460 4808

Representation   Print   Visages   213 650 8880
                  Film   Red Car Productions   213 960 2777

HUGHES MARTIN

HUGHES MARTIN
1408 WILLOW LANE
PARK CITY, UTAH 84060
PHN 801 649-1471
FAX 801 649-1491

FOR ADDITIONAL WORK
SEE 1991 AMERICAN
SHOWCASE

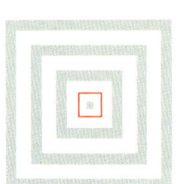

© 1990 HUGHES MARTIN

KEVIN SANCHEZ   415.285.1770

KEVIN SANCHEZ 415.285.1770

Catch A Glimps

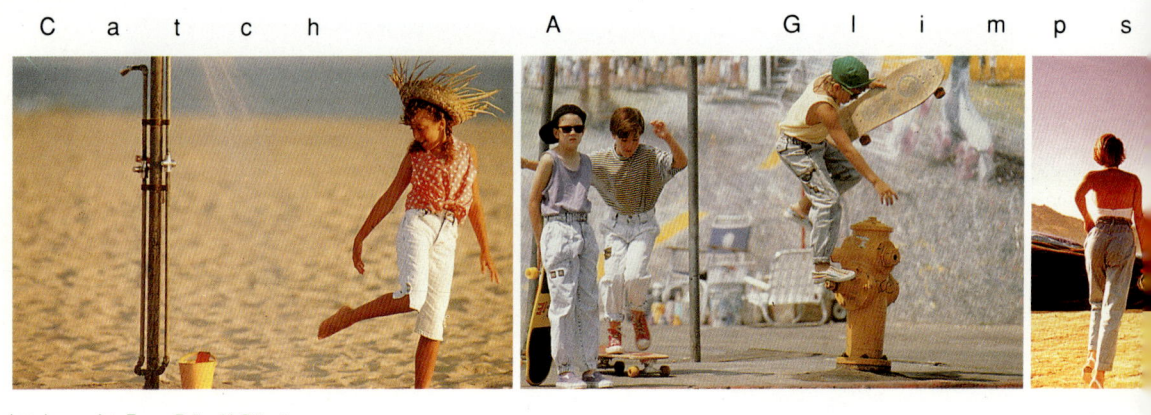

Lee Jeans   Arty Tan   Fallon McElligott

Visa   Jeff Rutherford   Broom & Broom   Izod / Cry

Kroger / Kodak   Jim Bohan   Campbell Mithun Esty   Ramada Inn   Rocky Pina   Della Famina Travisano   Premier

Hilton   Jim Huppenthal   Northwest Airline   Brian Bradshaw   Bausch & Lomb   Robert Meyer   Clothestime   Janis

O f   L i f e

Kroger / Kodak   Jim Bohan   Campbell Mithun Esty

US West   Don Anderson   Grey

Robert Meyer   Robert Meyer Design

Japanese Tabacco Co.   Minoru Murakoshi   BBDO / Asatsu

nola Hoddinot   JWT

Contempo Casuals   Janel Sobek

© Ken Chung 1991

Ken Chung

Represented By

East   **Joan Jedell**

☎ (212) 861-7861

Mid   **Vince Kamin**

☎ (312) 787-8834

West   **Christine**

☎ (213) 938-9117

📠 (213) 938-4306

5200 Venice Blvd

L.A.   CA 90019

625

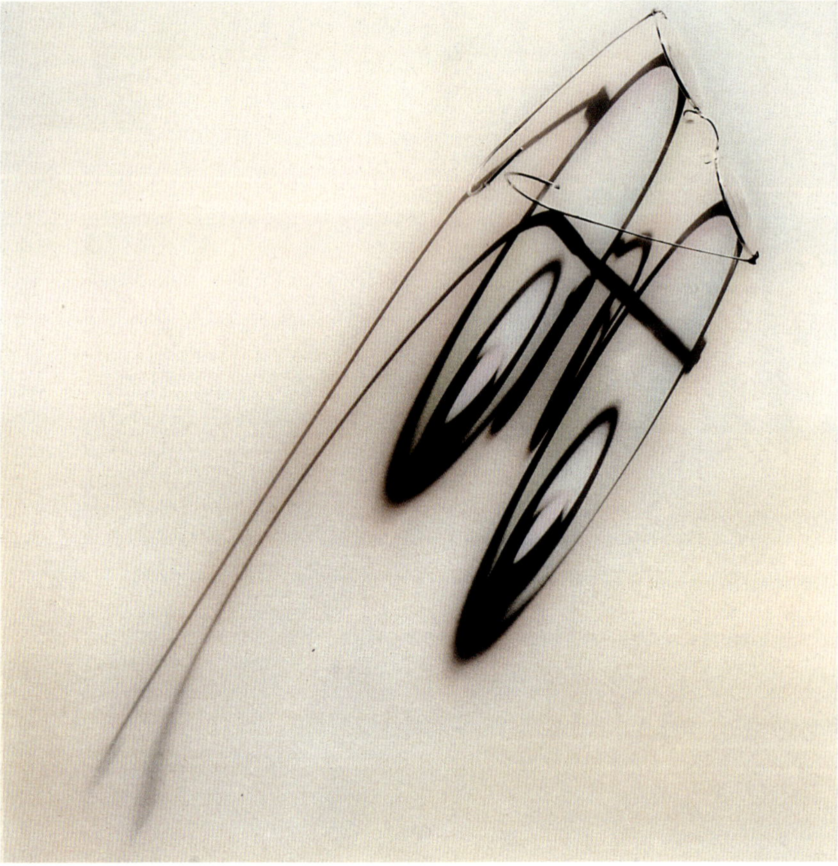

R J M u n a

Photography

415 - 468 - 8225

San Francisco

Represented by

Freda Scott

415 - 621 - 2992

The kids from E.T. all grown up with mom and Steven Spielberg bringing up the rear. Shot for Life Magazine.

Reid Miles, Inc.
1136 North Las Palmas
Hollywood, California 90038
Telephone (213) 462-6106
FAX 462-8816

Represented in Chicago by Chris W. Glenn (312) 787-4459
and now representing Europe Robert Toay, Jr. in London at (071) 829-8392

Reid Miles

McGuire

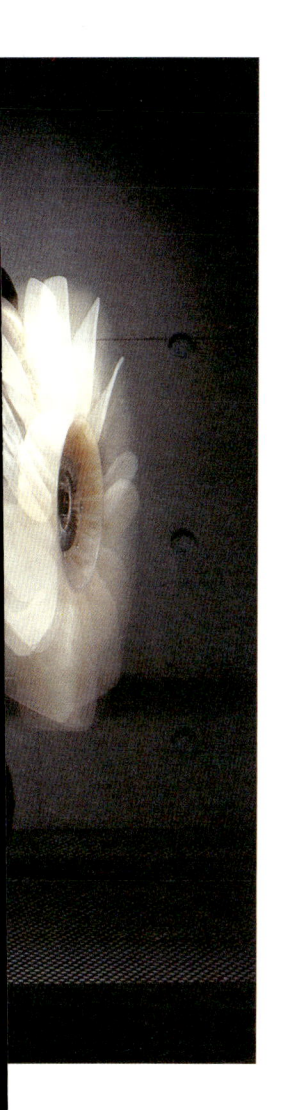

Gary McGuire Photography
1248 South Fairfax
Los Angeles, California 90019
213-938-2481
FAX 213-938-8420

631

JAMES HAEFNER PHOTOGRAPHY 213.609.0160 20434 S. SANTA FE AVE.

CARSON, CA 90810   313.583.4747   1307-C ALLEN DR.   TROY, MI 48083

MARSHALL HARRINGTON PHOTOGRAPHY

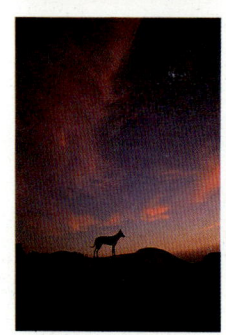

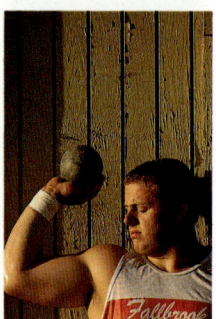

PHONE 619·291·2775
FAX 619·291·8466

Marshall Harrington Photography

2775 Kurtz St.
Studio Two
San Diego
California
92110

PHONE 619·291·2775
FAX 619·291·8466

635

...AND THEY LI

EDITORIAL, CORPORATE AND PEOPLE ILLUSTRATIVE PHOTOGRAPHY

3961 E. SPEEDWAY
SUITE 412
TUCSON, AZ 85712
(602) 881-1205

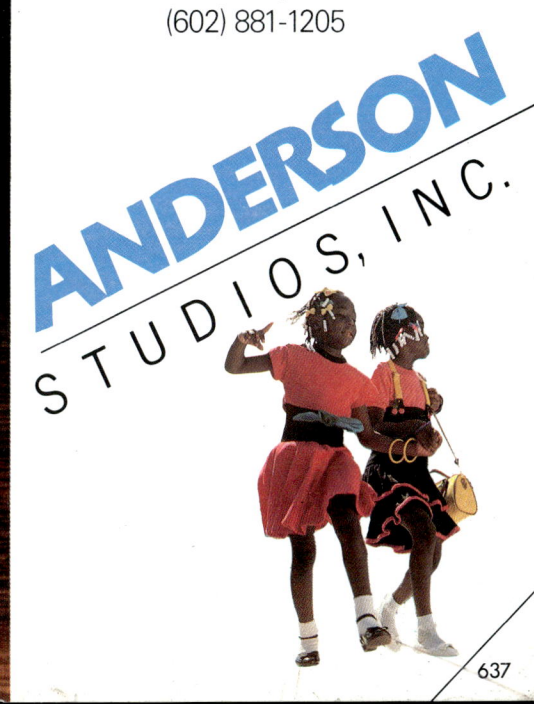

ANDERSON
STUDIOS, INC.

637

L^MOTTE

MICHAEL LAMOTTE PHOTOGRAPHY   SAN FRANCISCO   415 777 1443

L^MOTTE

Represented by Marianne Campbell   415 227 0939

KEN READ/SALOMON

LYNN HILL/PATAGONIA

WINDSURFERS/MAUI

TEAM RUSSELL

JOHN RUSSELL / AARON STRONG
P.O. BOX 4739 • ASPEN, COLORADO 81612

CHRIS EVERT/WORLD TENNIS

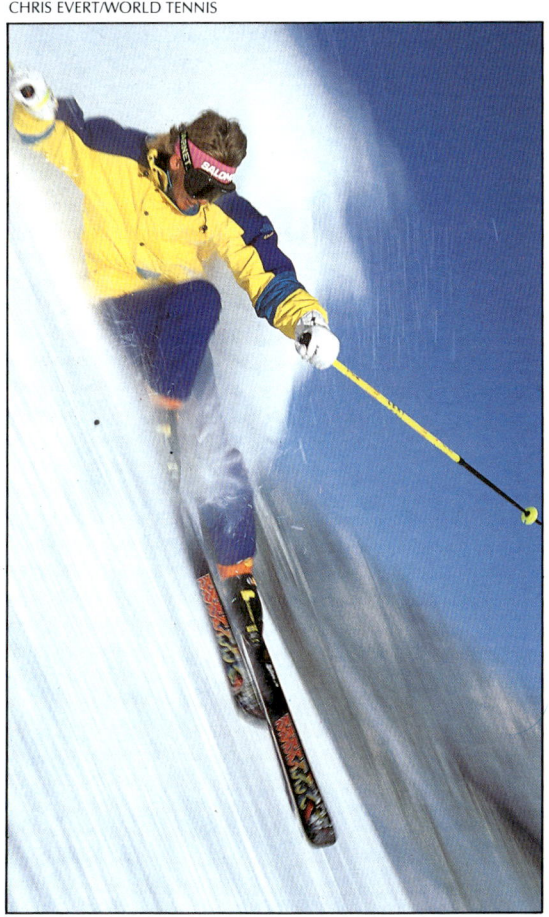

SCOT SCHMIDT/SALOMON

MONICA/KEY BISCAYNE

ASPEN
EXTENSIVE STOCK AVAILABLE
TEL: 303/920-1431 • FAX: 303/920-1432

JOHN BLAUSTEIN

(415) 525-8133
RANDI FIAT & ASSOCIATES (312) 664-8322

RICHARD NOBLE 213·6

JOE MONTANA

· 4711 FAX 213 · 874 · 0618

Sean Thonson

*940 East Second
Los Angeles, CA
90012*

*213.626.3686
Fax 213.626.8129*

*Represented in
Los Angeles
by Lee+Lou
213.287.1542*

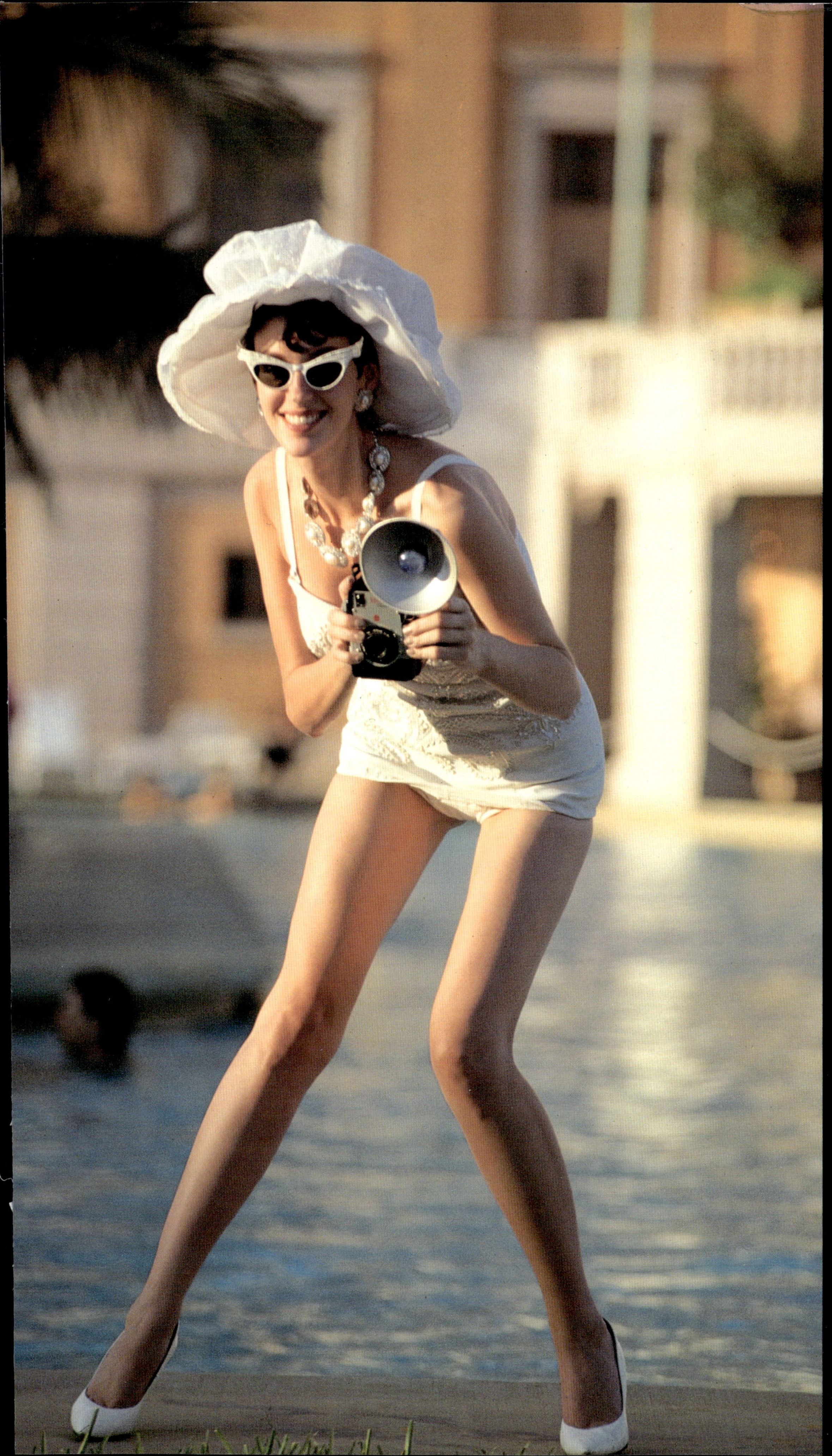

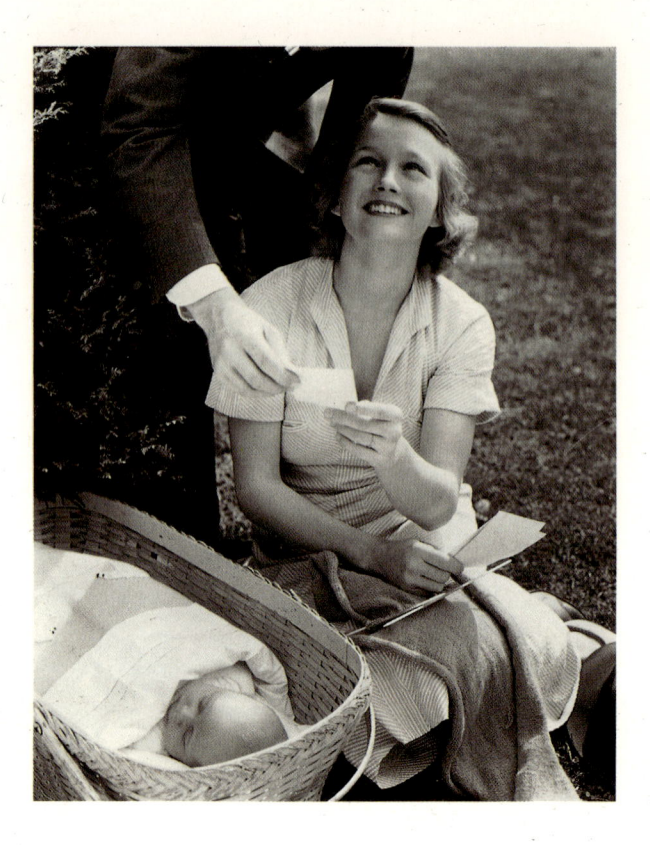

1933
Edward Steichen
Kodak Ad

The

developing

story

of the

20th century.

Kodak

PROFESSIONAL
PHOTOGRAPHY DIVISION

© Eastman Kodak Company, 1990. Reprinted with the permission of Joanna T. Steichen.

SOUTH
PHOTOGRAPHY

Listings 650
Ads 661

ALABAMA
ARKANSAS
FLORIDA
GEORGIA
KENTUCKY
LOUISIANA
MISSISSIPPI
NORTH CAROLINA
OKLAHOMA
SOUTH CAROLINA
TEXAS
TENNESSEE
VIRGINIA

SOUTH
PHOTOGRAPHY

API Photographers, Inc./3111 Stonebrook Cir., Memphis . . . . (901) 396-8650
Ads Photo-Graphix, Inc./2012 Farrington, Dallas . . . . (214) 742-9682
Akers, Charley/1200 Foster St., Atlanta . . . . (404) 352-5353
Aldhizer, Karen F./107 W. Gaines, Tallahassee . . . . (904) 488-8754
Alexander's Photographers/10,000 Memorial Dr., Houston . . . . (713) 682-6000
Alford, Jess/1800 Lear St., Dallas . . . . (214) 421-3107
Alterman, Jack/285 Meeting St., Charleston . . . . (803) 577-0647
Alvarez, Jorge/3105 W. Granada, Tampa . . . . (813) 831-6765
Amberger, Michael/128 River Rd., Lyme . . . . (603) 795-2645
Anderson, John H./650 N.E. 64th St., Miami . . . . (305) 758-9933
Andrews Photography/5662 Banana Rd., W. Palm Beach . . . . (407) 683-8956
Ansorg Prods./1006 Lincoln Rd., Miami Beach . . . . (305) 532-2351
Apogee Photographic/205 W. Davie Blvd., Ft. Lauderdale . . . . (305) 525-3686
Appel, Sandra/2951 N.W. 46th Ave., Ft. Lauderdale . . . . (305) 735-0731
Ashley, Constance/2024 Farrington, Dallas . . . . (214) 747-2501
Associated Photographic Svcs., Inc./516 Natchec St., New Orleans . . . . (504) 522-7503
Atkinson, Inc./1611 D. Colley Ave., Norfolk . . . . (804) 625-1594
Bachmann, Bill/Lake Mary . . . . (407) 322-4444
Badger, B./1355 Chemical St., Dallas . . . . (214) 634-0222
Baez, Carlos R. Productions/12168 S.W. 131st Ave., Miami . . . . (305) 252-4128
Baker, I. Wilson/1094 Morrison Dr., Charlestown . . . . (803) 577-0828
Baker, Jeff/3131 Premier Dr., Irving . . . . (214) 550-7992
Balbuza, Joseph T./25 N.E. 210th St., Miami . . . . (305) 652-1728
Baldridge, David/4096 Bent Oak Ct., Douglasville . . . . (404) 942-0262
Baldwin, Frederick C./1405 Branard, Houston . . . . (713) 524-9199
Ball, Roger/1402 A. Winnifered St., Charlotte . . . . (704) 335-0479
Baptie, Frank/1426 Ninth St. N., St. Petersburg . . . . (813) 823-7319
Baraban, Joe/Houston/(713) 526-0317 . . . . **pages 256-257**
Bardin, Keith Jr./P.O. Box 191241, Dallas . . . . (214) 686-0611
Barker, Kent/2919 Canton, Dallas . . . . (214) 760-7470
Barley, Bill & Assocs., Inc./Columbia . . . . (803) 755-1554
Barley, Michael/122 Parkhouse, Dallas . . . . (214) 255-4038
Barr, Ian/2640 S.W. 19th St., Ft. Lauderdale . . . . (305) 584-6247
Barreras, Anthony/1231-C Booth St., Atlanta . . . . (404) 352-0511
Barrs, Mike/Miami . . . . (305) 665-5518
Bassett, Donald W./9185 Green Meadows Way, Palm Beach Gardens . . . . . . (407) 694-1109
Beck, Charles/2721 Cherokee Rd., Birmingham . . . . (205) 871-6632
Beck, Gary/1438 Chattahoochee Ave., Atlanta . . . . (404) 352-8385
Becker, Joel/5121 Virginia Beach Blvd., Norfolk . . . . (804) 461-7886
Bedgood & Associates/1292 Logan Cir., Atlanta . . . . (404) 351-4852
Beebower Brothers/Dallas . . . . (214) 358-1219
Behrens, Bruce/762 Warrenton Rd., Winter Park . . . . (407) 657-5828
Belk, Michael & Co./1708 Peachtree St. N.E., Atlanta . . . . (404) 874-6304
Berg, Ron/Kansas . . . . (816) 471-5488
Berman, Bruce/140 N. Stevens St., El Paso . . . . (915) 544-0352
Beswick, Paul G./4479 Westfield Dr., Mableton . . . . (404) 944-8579
Bilby II, Glade/1715 Burgundy St., New Orleans . . . . (504) 949-6700
Blanco, Joe/3911 Farragut St., Hollywood . . . . (305) 962-9773
Blanton, Jeff/5515 S. Orange Ave., Orlando . . . . (407) 851-7279
Boatman, Mike, Photographer/3430 Park Ave., Memphis . . . . (901) 324-9337
Bollman, Brooks/1183 Virginia Ave. N.E., Atlanta . . . . (404) 876-2422
Bondy, Roger/309 N.W. 23rd St., Oklahoma City . . . . (405) 521-1616
Booke Communications/310 W. Fourth St., Winston-Salem . . . . (919) 748-1120
Bootes, Jeff/1013 Fairway Dr., Winter Pk. . . . . (305) 679-0622
Booth, Greg and Associates/1322 Round Table, Dallas . . . . (214) 688-1855
Borchelt, Mark/4938 D. Eisenhower Sq., Alexandria . . . . (703) 751-2533
Borum, Mike/Nashville . . . . (615) 259-9750
Bose, Patti K./707 Nicolet Ave., Winter Park . . . . (407) 629-5650
Bostick, Rick Photography/489 Semoran Blvd., Casselberry . . . . (407) 331-5717
Bostwick, Rick/489 Semoran Blvd., Casselberry . . . . (407) 331-5717
Bowman, Matt/1345 Chemical, Dallas . . . . (214) 637-0211
Bowyer, Cosby/209 Foushee St., Richmond . . . . (804) 643-1100
Boyd, Richard/819 Franklin Rd. S.W., Roanoke . . . . (703) 345-9144
Brackett, George/230 W. 49th St., Hialeah . . . . (305) 558-3131

Bradley, Matt/15 Butterfield Ln., Little Rock	(501) 224-0692
Bradshaw, Reagan/1700 S. Lamar, Ste.322, Austin	(512) 444-6767
Brady, Steve/Houston/(713) 660-6663	**pages 210-211**
Brasher/Rucker Photography/3373 Park Ave., Memphis	(901) 324-7447
Braun, Bob/Orlando	(407) 425-7921
Bravura Photography/3423 S. Blvd., Charlotte	(704) 525-2306
Brignolo, Joseph/11 Oak Gates Dr., Hendersonville	(704) 696-3374
Brill, David L./Fairburn	(404) 461-5488
Brinson, Rob/887-B W. Marietta St., Atlanta	(404) 874-2497
Britt, Ben/1345 Chemical St., Dallas	(214) 634-9846
Brooks Photography/800 Luttrell St., Knoxville	(615) 525-4501
Brooks, Charles/800 Luttrell, Knoxville	(615) 525-4501
Broomell, Peter/One S. Third St., Amelia Island	(904) 261-8557
Brousseau, Jay/2608 Irving Blvd., Dallas	(214) 638-1248
Brown, Richard & Assocs./144 Coxe Ave., Asheville	(704) 253-1634
Brown, Wesley David/5488 Fox Hollow Dr., Boca Raton	(407) 750-7976
Bryant Studios/6131 Luther Ln., Dallas	(214) 691-9335
Buettner, Rick/440 E. Nelson Ave., Alexandria	(703) 549-8455
Buffington, David/2401 S. Ervay, Dallas	(214) 428-8221
Bullock, David/Dallas	(214) 369-6990
Bumpass R.O./1222 N. Winnetka, Dallas	(214) 943-5411
Burkey, J.W./1526 Edison St., Dallas	(214) 746-6336
Burns, Jerry/331 Elizabeth St. N.E., Atlanta	(404) 522-9377
Busch, Scherley/4186 Pamona Ave., Miami	(305) 661-6605
Byrne, Kevin B./Centerville	(214) 536-2682
C&H Photography/Janes Creek Rd., S. Myrtle	(501) 937-4582
Cabluck, Jerry/Ft. Worth	(817) 336-1431
Caldwell, Jim/101 W. Drew, Houston	(713) 527-9121
Camera Graphics /Katie Deits/11663 Landing Pl., N. Palm Beach	(407) 844-3399
Cannedy, Carl/3333 Elm St., Dallas	(214) 748-1048
Canova, Pat/1575 S.W. 87th Ave., Miami	(305) 221-6731
Cardellino Photography/315 Ninth St., San Antonio	(512) 224-9606
Cardner, Kevin/1708 Rosewood, Houston	(713) 529-3012
Carpenter, Bernard J./7375 Brook Valley Rd., Rural Hall	(919) 969-5179
Carr, Fred/2331-D Wirtcrest, Houston	(713) 680-2465
Carriker, Ronald/Winston-Salem	(919) 765-3852
Carter, John/1184 14th Pl. N.E., Atlanta	(404) 875-3213
Caufield, Lin Photographers, Inc./2100 Arthur St., Louisville	(502) 636-3727
Cerny, Paul/5200 Wood St., Zephyrhills	(813) 782-4386
Chalfant, Flip/Atlanta/(404) 881-8510	**pages 670-671**
Chambers, Don/Atlanta/(404) 872-8117	**pages 678-679**
Chapple, Ron/501 N. College, Charlotte	(704) 377-4217
Chasing Rainbows/1026 San Jacinto 1721, Irving	(214) 402-9960
Chenn, Steve/6301 Ashcroft, Houston	(713) 271-0631
Chesler, Donna & Ken/6941 N.W. 12th St., Plantation	(305) 581-6489
Chisholm, Rich & Assocs./6813 Northampton Way, Houston	(713) 957-1250
Christian, Chris/Atlanta/(404) 872-8117	**pages 678-679**
Clair, Andre/11415 Chatten Way, Houston	(713) 465-5507
Clark, Marty Photography, Inc./1105 Peachtree St., N.E., Atlanta	(404) 873-4618
Clark, Robert C./1520-A Farrington Way, Columbia	(803) 731-0418
Clayton, Al/541 Edgewood Ave. S.E., Atlanta	(404) 577-4141
Clayton, Julie Ann/8123 B. Northboro Ct., W. Palm Beach	(407) 642-4971
Clevenger, David/658 11th St. N.W., Atlanta	(404) 876-1133
Clintsman, Dick/3001 Quebec, Dallas	(214) 630-1531
Cody Productions, Inc./Miami/(305) 666-0247	**page 661**
Cody, Dennie/Miami/(305) 666-0247	**page 661**
Cohen, Bernard/326 Nelson St. S.W., Atlanta	(404) 584-5500
Cohen, Stewart Charles/Dallas/(214) 421-2186	**pages 668-669**
Cohrssen, James/6704 McCrea Pl., Falls Church	(703) 534-9035
Cole, Ralph/615 E. Fourth St., Tulsa	(918) 585-9119
Coleman, Michael J./Alexandria	(703) 548-2353
Constantinos/Miami/(305) 467-3478	**pages 696-697**
Contorākes, George/Miami/(305) 661-0731	**pages 720-721**
Cook, Jamie/1740 DeFoor Pl. N.W., Atlanta	(404) 351-1883
Cooke, Bill/7761 S.W. 88th St., Miami	(305) 596-1348
Copeland, Jim/653 Ethel St. N.W., Atlanta	(404) 881-0221
Corry, Leon/4072 Park Ave., Miami	(305) 667-7147
Coste, Kurt/929 Julia St., New Orleans	(504) 523-6060
Cotter, Austin/1350 Manufacturing, Dallas	(214) 742-3633
Craft, Bill/2008 Laws St., Dallas	(214) 748-1470
Crane-McKee, Inc./4118 Commerce St., Dallas	(214) 823-4966
Crocker, Will/1806 Magazine St., New Orleans	(504) 522-2651
Cromer, Peggo/1206 Andora Ave., Coral Gables	(305) 667-3722

Crosby Images/307 Townes St., Greenville	(803) 232-4403
Crum, Lee/New Orleans/(504) 529-2156	**pages 440-441**
Culpepper, Mike Studios, Inc./1227 Sixth Ave., Columbus	(404) 323-5703
d'Arazien, Arthur/711 Hollybriar La., Naples	(813) 566-8511
Dakota, Michael/Miami/(305) 325-8727	**pages 682-683**
Dakota, Irene/Miami/(305) 674-9975	**pages 682-683**
Dale, John/576 Amour Cir. N.E., Atlanta	(404) 872-3203
Daniels, Mark/8413 Piney Branch Rd., Silver Spring	(301) 587-1727
Darlene's Total Photo/113 W. Marion Ave., Punta Gorda	(813) 639-6115
Dawson, Bill/289 Monroe, Memphis	(901) 522-9171
Dawson, Greg/Houston	(713) 862-8301
De Casseres, Joe/418 Calhoun St. N.W., Atlanta	(404) 872-2753
De la Houssaye, Jeanne/816 Foucher St., New Orleans	(504) 581-2167
DeVault, Jim/2400 Sunset Pl., Nashville	(615) 269-4538
Dean, Don/Dallas	(214) 939-0005
Debenport, Robb/2412 Converse, Dallas	(214) 631-7606
Debold, Bill/2320 Donley Dr., Austin	(512) 837-6294
Diaz, Fernando/8533 N.W. 66th St., Miami	(305) 594-7516
Diaz, Rick/Miami/(305) 264-9761	**pages 726-727**
Dickinson, Dick/1781 Independence Blvd., Sarasota	(813) 355-7688
Directions/119 E. Seventh St., Charlotte	(919) 373-0955
Dobbs, David/26 W. Harris St., Savannah, GA	(912) 238-2429
Doering, Douglas/2610 Catherine St., Dallas	(214) 946-6597
Doerr, D. Dean/11321 Greystone, Okla. City	(405) 751-0313
Doty, Gary/Ft. Lauderdale	(305) 928-0644
Douglas, Keith/405 N.E. Eighth St., Ft. Lauderdale	(305) 763-5883
Dressler, Brian/300-A Huger St., Columbia	(803) 254-7171
Driscoll, W.M./Dallas	(214) 363-8429
Duffley, Colleen/2724 N.W. 30th Ave., Ft. Lauderdale	(305) 731-3300
Duncan, Nena/5250 Gulfton, Houston	(713) 666-0474
Dyer, John/107 Blue Star, San Antonio	(512) 223-1891
E.P. Productions/602 Riverside Ave., Kingsport	(615) 246-7262
EDS Photography Services/4718 Iberia, Dallas	(214) 631-1157
Edelson, Michele/555 N.E. 15 St., Miami	(305) 271-3340
Edens, Swain Studio, Inc./1905 M. St. Mary's St., San Antonio	(512) 226-2210
Edwards, Jack/6250 Edgewater Dr., Orlando	(407) 291-7292
Edwards, Jim/418 Armour Ln. N.E., Atlanta	(404) 875-1005
Eibe, Bruce/11645 Strand Way, Cooper City	(305) 431-2533
Elam, Patrick/11201 Sundown Ln., Charlotte	(704) 543-9413
Engelmann, Suzanne J./1621 Woodbridge Lakes Cir., W. Palm Beach	(407) 969-6666
Enriquez, Arturo & Vallarie/1109 Arizona Ave., El Paso	(915) 533-9688
Epley, Paul/3110 Griffith St., Charlotte	(704) 332-5466
Erickson Photography, Inc./117 S. West St., Raleigh	(919) 833-9955
Erickson, Jim/Raleigh/(919) 833-9955	**pages 692-693**
Esquire Photographers, Inc./1802 N. Orange Ave., Orlando	(407) 898-2461
Evensen, Bruce M./7925 Fourth St. N., St. Petersburg	(813) 577-5626
Eyes, The, Inc./300 Viscaya Ave., Coral Gables	(305) 448-3048
Fancis, Pam Photography/2700 Albany, Houston	(713) 528-1672
Fawbush, Greg Photography/Miami	(305) 441-1881
Faye, Gary/2421 Barlett, Houston	(713) 529-9548
Feldott, Steven/1215 Diplomat Pkwy., Hollywood	(305) 925-7099
Fineman, Lewis T./1800 S.W. 98th Ct., Miami	(305) 226-5402
Fineman, Michael/7521 S.W. 57th Ter., Miami	(305) 666-1250
Fisher, Kurt/280 Elizabeth St., Atlanta	(404) 525-1333
Fisher, Ray/10700 S.W. 72nd Ct., Miami	(305) 665-7659
Fitzgerald, David G./100 W. Wilshire Blvd., Okla. City	(405) 840-0102
Flecther, Julie/1505 Palmetto Ave., Sanford	(407) 322-3148
Flip Minott Photographics/18469 Flamingo Rd., Ft. Myers	(813) 267-0060
Florida Photo, Inc./781 N.E. 125th St., Miami	(305) 891-6616
Fogleman, Owen/143 North Blvd., De Land	(904) 734-1133
Ford Jr., Gib/1048 Greymont Ave., Jackson	(601) 353-9675
Forer, Dan/Miami/(305) 949-3131	**pages 724-725**
Fort, Chris/111 23rd Ave. N., Nashville	(615) 327-9169
Fotoblitz Studio/562 Dutch Valley Rd., Atlanta	(404) 876-1331
Fowley, Douglas/103 N. Hite, Louisville	(502) 897-7222
Foxall, Steve/1605 Levee St., Dallas	(214) 824-1977
Francis, Pam/2700 Albany, Houston	(713) 528-1672
Frazier, Jeff/1025 Eighth Ave. S., Nashville	(615) 242-5642
Frederick's Commercial Photography/96 E. 48th St., Hialeah	(305) 822-1979
Freelance Pool/Springfield	(703) 451-5544
Freeman, Charlie/3333 Elm, Dallas	(214) 742-1446
Freeman, Tina/1040 Magazine St., New Orleans	(504) 523-3000
Friedman, Henry/3625 S. First St., Austin	(512) 445-5453

Friend & Johnson/Dallas/(214) 855-0055 .... **pages 728-731**
Frink, Stephen/Key Largo/(305) 451-3737/(800) 451-3737 .... **page 684**
Froneberger, Jean/HC-10, Junction .... (915) 446-2306
Fulton, George/1237 Gadsden St., Columbia .... (803) 779-8249
Gajano Photographers/892 Hialeah Dr., Hialeah .... (305) 885-8495
Gandy, Skip/302 E. Davis Blvd., Tampa .... (813) 253-0340
Gardella & Co./Atlanta/(404) 231-1316 .... **pages 708-709**
Gargala, Nick/932 Riverside Dr., Louisville .... (812) 282-2010
Garrison, Gary D./1052 Constance St., New Orleans .... (504) 588-9422
Gatz, Larry/5250 Gulfton, Houston .... (713) 666-5203
Gefter, Judith/1725 Clemson Rd., Jacksonville .... (904) 733-5498
Gelberg, Bob/Miami .... (305) 665-3200
Gemignani, Joe/13833 N.W. 19th Ave., Miami .... (305) 685-7636
Gerin Choiniere/1424 N. Tryon St., Charlotte .... (704) 372-0220
Gerlich, Fred S./1220 Spring St., Atlanta .... (404) 872-3487
Getz, Jacob Photography/87 Franklin St., NYC .... (212) 925-7376
Gilbert, Bruce/12335 Braesridge Dr., Houston .... (713) 728-4229
Gill Productions/15822 Laurel Heights Dr., Houston .... (713) 957-2575
Glaser Ken & Assoc./New Orleans/(504) 895-7170 .... **page 717**
Glentzer, Don/3814 S. Shepherd Dr., Houston .... (713) 529-9686
Gomel, Bob/10831 Valley Hills, Houston .... (713) 988-6390
Gomez, Rick/Miami/(305) 856-8338 .... **pages 686-689**
Gorham, John R./3221 Franklin, Waco .... (817) 753-3695
Graham, Curtis/648 First Ave. S., St. Petersburg .... (813) 821-0444
Graham, Larry L./1026 Kessler Pkwy, Dallas .... (214) 943-3553
Granberry Studios, Inc./578 Montogomery Ferry Dr., Atlanta .... (404) 874-2426
Graphics International/1930 Monroe Dr., Atlanta .... (404) 873-5271
Green, Mark/2406 Taft St., Houston .... (713) 523-6146
Greenhaus, Manny/9033 Garland Ave., Surfside .... (305) 865-0417
Greer, Elbert/111 Madison Ave., Memphis .... (901) 525-1194
Grigg, Roger Allen/Atlanta .... (404) 876-4748
Grill, Roger/5512 Lawrence Orr Rd., Charlotte .... (704) 535-6637
Grimes, Billy/Gainesville .... (404) 899-9975
Groendyke, Bill, Inc./6344 N.W. 201st Ln., Miami .... (305) 625-8293
Grossman, John/1752-B Branard St., Houston .... (713) 523-2316
Grove, Bob/210 N. Lee St., Alexandria .... (703) 548-3972
Gruby, Gary/353 W. Peachtree St. N.E., Atlanta .... (404) 525-4667
Guerrero, Charles/8301 Shoal Creek Blvd., Austin .... (512) 467-2797
Guggenheim, David/167 Mangum St., Atlanta .... (404) 577-4676
Guggenheim-Burnett & Assocs./167 Mangum St., Atlanta .... (404) 577-4676
Guider, John/517 Fairground Ct., Nashville .... (615) 255-4495
Gupton, Charles/5720-J Capital Blvd., Raleigh .... (919) 850-9441
Hale, Bruce Photography, Inc./2502 E. 12th St., Chatanooga .... (615) 629-2121
Hale, Butch/1319 Conant, Dallas .... (214) 637-3987
Hall, David/7035-E S.W. 47th St., Miami .... (305) 925-8186
Hall, Don/2922 Hyde Park St., Sarasota .... (813) 365-6161
Ham, Dan/1350 Manufacturing, Dallas .... (214) 742-8700
Hamblin, Steve/4718 Iberia, Dallas .... (214) 630-2848
Handel, Doug/3016 Selma Lane, Dallas .... (214) 241-9650
Hanks, Paul/506 Taylor St., Anderson .... (803) 226-3757
Hannau, Michael Enterprises/3800 N.W. 32nd Ave., Miami .... (305) 633-1100
Hannigan Photography/3459 Beech Dr., Decatur .... (404) 288-7915
Hansen, Eric/3005 Seventh Ave. S., Birmingham .... (205) 251-5587
Harness, Brian/1402 S. Montreal Ave., Dallas .... (214) 330-4419
Harrison, Michael/1124 S. Mint St., Charlotte .... (704) 334-8008
Hart, Michael/7320 Ashcroft, Houston .... (713) 271-8250
Hartman, Gary/911 S. St. Mary's, San Antonio .... (512) 225-2404
Hayden, Kenneth/1318 Morton Ave., Louisville .... (502) 583-5596
Haynes, Michael/10343 Best Dr., Dallas .... (214) 352-1314
Haynsworth, John/86½ Highland Park Vlg., Dallas .... (214) 559-3700
Heiner, Gary/1821 Levee, Dallas .... (214) 760-7471
Heit Photography, Inc./8502 Eustis Ave., Dallas .... (214) 324-0305
Helfer, Martin/3669 Victoria Dr., Stone Mountain .... (404) 292-1234
Heller, David/3225 S. MacDill, Tampa .... (813) 238-2166
Henderson Photography/6005 Chapel Hill Rd., Raleigh .... (919) 851-0458
Henderson, Eric Photography/1200 Foster St., Atlanta .... (404) 352-3615
Hendley, Arington/454 Irwin St. N.E., Atlanta .... (404) 577-2300
Henley & Savage Photography/113 S. Jefferson St., Richmond .... (804) 780-1120
Hepler, Scott/Kanasa .... (816) 471-5488
Heston, Ty/4505 131st Ave. N., Clearwater .... (813) 573-4878
Higgins, Neil Studio, Inc./1540 Monroe Dr., N.E., Atlanta .... (404) 876-3186
Hill, Jackson/New Orleans/(504) 861-3000 .... **page 705**
Hillyer, Jonathan Photography, Inc./450-A Bishop St., Atlanta .... (404) 351-0477

Hitt, Wesley ./518 W. Ninth St., Little Rock	(501) 375-5091
Hodge, Patsy F./1606 Milam St., Columbus	(409) 732-6241
Hoflich, Richard/544 N. Angier Ave. N.E., Atlanta	(404) 584-9159
Hogben, Steve/3180 Oakcliff Indust. St., Atlanta	(404) 266-2894
Holland, Ralph Photography, Inc./3706 Alliance Dr., Greensboro	(919) 855-6422
Holland, Robert/Miami/(305) 255-6758	**pages 710-711**
Hollenbeck, Phil/2833 Duval Dr., Dallas	(214) 331-8328
Holloway, Russ/27-R Waddell St., Atlanta	(404) 523-1511
Holt Group, The/403 Westcliff Rd., Greensboro	(919) 668-2770
Hood, Robin/Franklin/(615) 794-2041	**pages 676-677**
Hope, Christina/2720 3rd St. S., Jacksonville Beach	(904) 246-9689
Hopson, Melissa/2416½ McKinney, Dallas	(214) 747-3122
Horan, Eric/Hilton Head Is.	(803) 842-3233
Hornbacher, Inc./Big Pine Key	(305) 872-9091
Horne, Bill F.D.P.E./F.S.A/249 University Ave., Gainesville	(904) 377-6583
Hottelet, Mary/1100 Earl, Denton	(817) 382-2019
Howard, Dwight/464 Armour Dr. N.E., Atlanta	(404) 872-2488
Huff, Glenda/1222 Manufacturing St., Dallas	(214) 748-0502
Humphries, H. Gordon/1579 Broad River Rd., Columbia	(803) 772-3535
Hunter, Bud/1911 27th Ave. S., Birmingham	(205) 879-3153
Hursley, Timothy/1911 N. Markham, Little Rock	(501) 372-0640
Hutchinson, S. Scott/11,000-4 Metro Pky., Ft. Myers	(813) 275-6389
Image Int'l/3038 Golfcrest, Houston	(713) 641-2106
Impact Photographic Group, Inc./848 W. Fourth St., Winston-Salem	(919) 748-8267
Isgett, Neil/4303-D South Blvd, Charlotte	(704) 376-7172
Jackson, Robert N./520 N. Willow Ave., Tampa	(813) 254-6806
Jamison, Chipp/2131 Liddell Dr. N.E., Atlanta	(404) 873-3636
Jennings, Steve/2106 S. Atlanta Pl., Tulsa	(918) 745-0836
Jimison, Tom/New Orleans	(504) 522-7955
Johns, Douglas/2535 25th Ave. N., St. Petersburg	(813) 321-7235
Johnson, Forest/Miami/(305) 251-1300	**pages 694-695**
Johnson, George L./16603 Round Oak Dr., Tampa	(813) 963-3222
Johnson, Michael/830 Exposition, Dallas	(214) 824-9860
Jones, Bob Jr., Inc./1923 E. Franklin St., Richmond	(804) 783-0463
Jones, D. Photography/319 Westgate Dr., Greensboro	(919) 294-9060
Jones, Jerry/5250 Gulfton, Houston	(713) 668-4328
Jureit, Robert/916 Aguero Ave., Coral Gables	(305) 667-1346
Jurgens, Dan/202 S. 22nd St., Tampa	(813) 248-3636
Kaczmarek, Hans/3350 Ulmerton Rd., Clearwater	(813) 573-1015
Kaluzny, Zigy/4700 Strass Dr., Austin	(512) 452-4463
Kaplan Photography/McLean	(703) 893-1660
Katz, John/5222 Redfield, Dallas	(214) 637-0844
Katz, Shelly/3558 Chellen Dr., Dallas	(214) 247-0700
Kaufman, Len/740 Tyler St., Hollywood	(305) 920-7822
Kearney, Mitchell/301 E. Seventh St., Charlotte	(704) 377-7662
Kendrick, Robb/2700 Albany, Houston	(713) 528-4334
Kennedy, Eamon/4519 Maple Ave, Dallas	(214) 528-0632
Kennedy, William/3747 Chase Ave., Miami Beach	(305) 673-0000
Kenner, Jack/Memphis	(901) 527-3686
Kenny, D. Davis/4810 Greatland Ave, San Antonio	(512) 662-9882
Kent, David/7515 S.W. 153rd Ct., Miami	(305) 382-1587
Kern Photography of Palm Beaches/1243 N. 17th Ave., Lake Worth	(407) 582-2487
Kern, Geof/1337 Crampton, Dallas	(214) 630-0856
Kilborn Photography/109 E. New Haven, Melbourne	(407) 727-8290
Kinetic Photography/240 Distillery Commons, Louisville	(502) 583-1679
King, J. Brian/1267 Coral Way, Miami	(305) 856-6534
King, Jennifer Susan/4031 Green Bush Rd., Katy	(713) 392-8784
King, Sanoy/4212 San Felipe, Houston	(713) 869-8115
King, Tom/Orlando/(407) 856-0618	**page 685**
Kirkley, Kent/4906 Don Dr., Dallas	(214) 688-1841
Kirkwood Slide Svcs., Inc./2912 N. Pennsylvania Ave., Okla. City	(405) 524-2989
Klumpp, Don/804 Colquitt, Houston	(713) 521-2090
Knapp, Bevil S./118 Berverly Dr., Metairie	(504) 831-1496
Knibbs, Tom/5907 N.E. 27th Ave., Ft. Lauderdale	(305) 491-6263
Knight, Steve/1212 E. Tenth, Charlotte	(704) 334-5115
Koelsch, David Fotographik/526 Idaho, Okla. City	(405) 399-5212
Kohanim, Parish/1130 W. Peachtree St. N.W., Atlanta	(404) 892-0099
Kohler, Chris/1105 Peachtree St., Atlanta	(404) 876-1223
Koplitz, William/729 N. Lime Ave., Sarasota	(813) 366-5905
Kretchmar, Phil/2335 Valdina, Dallas	(214) 744-2039
Kroninger, Rick/717 W. Ashby, San Antonio	(512) 733-6128
Kufner, Gary/N. Carolina/(704) 387-2047	**pages 664-667**
Kufner, Gary/Miami/(305) 944-7740	**pages 664-667**

Kuhlman, Chris/12403-B Scarsdale Blvd., Houston	(713) 484-8600
Kuntz, Bryan/7700 Renwick, Houston	(713) 667-4200
Kuper, Holly/5522 Anita, Dallas	(214) 827-4494
Lackey, Larry Keith/4261 Sunnyslop, Memphis	(901) 725-0892
Lafayette, James/Hilton Head Is.	(803) 785-3201
Langoné, Peter/Ft. Lauderdale/(305) 467-0654	**pages 714-715**
Lanpher, Keith/865 Monticello Ave., Norfolk	(804) 627-3051
Larkin, Paul/Atlanta	(404) 872-8457
Lathem, Charlie & Assocs./559 Dutch Valley Rd., N.E., Atlanta	(404) 873-5858
Latorre, Robert/Dallas/(214) 630-8977	**pages 702-703**
Lauzon Photography/5170 N.E. 12th Ave., Ft. Lauderdale	(305) 771-0077
Lawrence, David Photography, Inc./2720 Stemmons Fwy., Dallas	(214) 637-4686
Lawson, Slick/3801 Whitland Ave., Nashville	(615) 383-0147
Lee, Wanda M. Represents/Atlanta	(404) 432-6309
Leenher, David/200 Boca Raton Rd., Boca Raton	(407) 391-1324
Leggett, Albert E. III/1415 Story Ave., Louisville	(502) 584-0255
Lemoine, Jim/1412 W. Alabama, Houston	(713) 524-1929
Lentz & Assoc./501 Washington St., Raleigh	(919) 828-6761
Levy, Sandy/6200 S.W. 108th Pl., Miami	(305) 595-4453
Lex, Debra/620 Harbor Cir., Miami	(305) 285-0999
Littlejohn, Dan/3390 Mary St., Cocunut Grove	(305) 447-1113
Llewellyn, Robert/Charlottesville	(804) 973-8000
Long, Lew/Miami	(305) 448-7667
Lorfing, Greg/1900 W. Alabama Rd., Houston	(713) 529-5968
Loumakis, Constantinos/Miami/(305) 467-3478	**pages 696-697**
Lowey Photo/Graphics, Inc./409 Spears Ave., Chatanooga	(61) 265-4311
Lucas, Jim/6009 N.W. 59th, Okla. City	(405) 721-3910
Lucas, Steve/16100 S.W. 100th Ct., Miami	(305) 238-6024
Luker, Tom/Coweta	(918) 486-5264
Luttrell, David/1500 Highland Dr., Knoxville	(615) 588-5775
Lynch, Larry & Andrea/Dallas/(214) 369-6990	**pages 486-487**
Lynch, Warren & Assoc./1324 E. Washington St., Louisville	(502) 587-7722
M&M Photography/533 S. Howard, Tampa	(813) 251-3774
Macuch, Rodger/Atlanta	(404) 876-7002
Majeski, Barry/2032 Harrison St., Hollywood	(305) 944-7740
Mangano, Chris/959A. Myers St., Richmond	(804) 358-4834
Mansfield, Eston/14111 N.W. 19th Ave., Miami	(305) 681-3005
Manske, Thaine/7313 Ashcroft, Houston	(713) 771-2220
Maratea, Ron/4338 Virginia Beach Blvd., Virginia Beach	(804) 340-6464
Markham, Jim/San Antonio/(512) 648-0403	**page 704**
Marks, Billy Inc./2451 Tuxedo La., Marietta	(404) 426-8778
Mason, Chuck/Miami/(305) 270-2070	**pages 706-707**
Massie, Wayne/3518 Wycliff, Dallas	(214) 526-4824
Maxham, Robert/San Antonio/(512) 223-6000	**page 716**
May, Clyde/1037 Monroe Dr. N.E., Atlanta	(404) 873-4329
Mayor, Randy/2007 15th Ave. S., Birmingham	(205) 933-2818
Mazey, Jon/2724 N.W. 30th Ave., Ft. Lauderdale	(305) 731-3300
McCann Co., The/Dallas/(214) 871-0353	**pages 668-669**
McCannon, Tricia/416 Armour Cir., Atlanta	(404) 873-3070
McCarthy, Tom/8960 S.W. 114th St., Miami	(305) 233-1703
McClure, Dan/320 N. Milledge Ave., Athens	(404) 354-1234
McCoy's Image Studio/2791 Shepherdsville Rd., Elizabethtown	(502) 769-5022
McCoy, Gary/9028 Redondo, Dallas	(214) 320-0002
McGee, E. Alan Photog., Inc./1816 Briarwood Ind. Ct., Atlanta	(404) 633-1286
McGukin, Douglas/5600 Glenridge Dr., Atlanta	(404) 252-7108
McKelvey, Michael/682 Greenwood Ave. N.E., Atlanta	(404) 892-8233
McNee Photo Communications/9261 Kirby, Houston	(713) 796-2633
McNeely, Burton/Land O'Lakes	(813) 996-3025
Meacham, Ralph/Franklin	(615) 794-1988
Mellette, Steve/112 N. Patrick St., Alexandria	(703) 548-9300
Melyana Assoc./Miami	(305) 673-0094
Messer, Alan/209 Broadway, Nashville	(615) 256-1019
Meyerson, Arthur/Houston/(713) 660-0405	**pages 662-663**
Meyler, Dennis/1412 W. Alabama, Houston	(713) 523-2731
Mikeo Photography/2189 N. Powerline Rd., Pompano Bch.	(305) 960-0485
Miller, Brad/3645 Stewart Ave., Coconut Grove	(305) 666-1617
Miller, Bruce/9401 S.W. 61st Ct., Miami	(305) 666-4333
Miller, Randy/Miami/(305) 667-5765	**pages 672-673**
Mills, Henry/5514 Starkwood Dr., Charlotte	(704) 535-1861
Mills, Jack Productions/4022-D N. MacArthur Blvd., Oklahoma City	(405) 787-7271
Mimms, Melissa/105 Lake Emerald Dr., Ft. Lauderdale	(305) 735-3739
Mims, Allen/107 Madison Ave., Memphis	(901) 527-4040
Minardi Photography/Tampa	(813) 251-1696

Mobley-Dozier Photography/3754 Gladney Dr., Atlanta	(404) 491-6364
Molina, Jose/Miami/(305) 443-1617	**pages 674-675**
Molnar, William Studios/Atlanta	(404) 350-8407
Molony, Bernard Charles/Atlanta	(404) 457-6934
Moore, Carolyn/930 N. Poplar St., Charlotte	(704) 335-1733
Moot, Kelly/2331-D Wirtcrest Ln., Houston	(713) 683-6400
Morris, Paul/Miami	(305) 758-8150
Morrison, Chet/2917 Canton St., Dallas	(214) 939-0903
Mouton III, Girard/3535 Buchanan St., New Orleans	(504) 288-4338
Mueller-Brown, Julie/Atlanta	(404) 875-1363
Murphy, Dennis/Dallas/(214) 651-7516	**pages 220-221**
Murray, Steve/Raleigh	(919) 828-0653
Myhre, Gordon/1310 Park Cir., Tampa	(813) 238-0360
Nance, David/8202 Fernbrook Ln., Houston	(713) 469-4757
Nehrenz, Paul/2673 LePage St., New Orleans	(504) 945-7107
Newby, Steve/4501 Swiss Ave., Dallas	(214) 821-0231
Newman, David/3319 Knight, Dallas	(214) 522-8612
Nolton, Gary/Dallas	(214) 369-6990
Norton, Michael/4917 W. Nassau, Tampa	(813) 289-8968
O'Connor, Michael/9041 Froude Ave., Surfside	(305) 861-3746
O'Dell, Dale/2040 Bissonnet, Houston	(713) 521-2611
Olivo, Tim/754 Piedmont Ave., Atlanta	(404) 872-0500
Olvera, Jim/235 Yorktown St., Dallas	(214) 760-0025
Oquendo, William Photography/4680 S.W. 27th Ave., Ft. Lauderdale	(305) 981-2823
Osborne, Mitchel/920 Frenchmen St., New Orleans	(504) 949-1366
Pantin, Tomás/1601 E. Seventh St., Austin	(512) 474-9968
Parrish, John/1218 Manufacturing, Dallas	(214) 742-9457
Parsley, Keith/801-K Atando Ave., Charlotte	(704) 331-0812
Payne, Richard/2029 Haddon St., Houston	(713) 524-7525
Payne, Tom/2425 Bartlett, Houston	(713) 527-8670
Pelosi & Chambers, Inc./Atlanta/(404) 872-8117	**pages 678-679**
Pelosi, Steve/Atlanta/(404) 872-8117	**pages 678-679**
Pepper Rose Productions/202 S. 22nd St., Tampa	(813) 248-3636
Petrey, John/670 Clay St., Winter Pk.	(407) 645-1718
Photo Associates, Inc./5205 N.W. 33rd Ave., Ft. Lauderdale	(305) 733-9400
Photocom, Inc./Dallas/(214) 428-8781	**pages 580-581**
Photographic Group/7407 Chancery Ln., Orlando	(305) 855-4306
Photographix, Inc./2335 Valdina St., Dallas	(214) 879-0000
Photography Unlimited, Inc./3662 S. Westshore Blvd., Tampa	(813) 839-7710
Pierce, Nancy/1715 Merry Oaks Rd., Charlotte	(704) 535-7409
Poissenot, Lloyd Prods./4602 E. Side Ave., Dallas	(214) 826-6262
Post, Andy Productions, Inc./4748 Algiers, Dallas	(214) 634-4490
Poulides, Peter/Dallas	(214) 350-5395
Prestige Unlimited Commercial Photography/Antioch	(615) 333-6825
Pumphrey, Steven/1309 Richcreek Rd., Austin	(512) 452-6865
Randolph, Bruce/132 Alan Dr., Newport News	(804) 874-2458
Rank, Don Photog., Inc./2265 Lawson Way, Atlanta	(404) 452-1658
Rasé, Stephen/1052-B St. Charles Ave. N.E., Atlanta	(404) 874-2678
Rathe, Robert/8451-A Hilltop Rd., Fairfax	(703) 560-7222
Raymond, Tom/2608 W. Market, Johnson City	(615) 928-2700
Redd, True & Co./2328 Farrington, Dallas	(214) 638-0602
Reens, Louis/4814 Sycamore, Dallas	(214) 827-3388
Reese, Donovan/3007 Canton Ave., Dallas	(214) 748-5900
Repertoire/Dallas/(214) 369-6990	**pages 486-487**
Ribar, Tim/807 66th Ave. N., Myrtle Beach	(803) 449-6115
Rickles, Tom/5401 Alton Rd., Miami Beach	(305) 866-5762
Rico, Paul/1506 Prytania St., New Orleans	(504) 529-2966
Riley, Richard/34 N. Ft. Harrison, Clearwater	(813) 446-2626
Robbins, Joe/7700 Renwick, Houston	(713) 667-5050
Robson, Howard/3807 E. 64th Pl., Tulsa	(918) 492-3079
Rodgers, Ted/544 Plasters Ave., Atlanta	(404) 892-0967
Roe, Cliff Photography/26734 IH-45 N., Spring	(713) 367-2520
Rogers, Brian/500 Bishop St. N.W., Atlanta	(404) 355-8069
Rogers, Chuck/2708 Janellen Dr., Atlanta	(404) 633-0105
Rose, Kevin C./146 Walker St., Atlanta	(404) 521-0729
Roth-Watts, Ronald/P.O. Box 4117, Ft. Lauderdale	(305) 763-5062
Rubio, Manny/1203 Techwood Dr., Atlanta	(404) 892-0783
Russell, John/High Point	(919) 887-1163
Rutherford, Michael W./Nashville/(615) 242-5953	**pages 700-701**
Ryan, Tom/Dallas/(214) 651-7085	**pages 728-729**
Salmon, George C./13354 Cain Rd., Tampa	(813) 961-8687
Salstrand, Duane/1639 Old Louisburg Rd., Raleigh	(919) 834-3434
Samaha, Sam/1526 Edison St., Dallas	(214) 746-6336

Sanacore, Steve/87 Westbury Close, W. Palm Beach .... (407) 795-1510
Sander, Neil/Leicester .... (704) 683-1854
Sanders, Bill/13903 Allamanda Ave., Miami Lakes .... (305) 821-5745
Santos, Roberto/15929 N.W. 49th Ave., Hialeah .... (305) 621-6047
Savant, Joseph/4756 Algiers St., Dallas .... (214) 951-0111
Savins, Mathew/101 Howell St., Dallas .... (214) 651-7516
Saxon, John/Dallas .... (214) 369-6990
Saylor, Ted/2312 Farwell Dr., Tampa .... (813) 879-5636
Schatz, Bob/112 Second Ave. N., Nashville .... (615) 254-7197
Schiavone, George/7340 S.W. 48th St., Miami .... (305) 662-6057
Schneps, Michael R./7700 Renwick, Houston .... (713) 520-8224
Schulke, Flip/Miami .... (305) 251-7717
Schuster, Elle/3719 Gilbert, Dallas .... (214) 526-6712
Schwartz, Alan/Miami .... (305) 387-4049
Scott, Ron/1000 Jackson Blvd., Houston .... (713) 529-5868
Scruggs, Jim/2410 Taft, Houston .... (713) 523-6146
Seeger, Stephen/2931 Irving Blvd., Dallas .... (214) 634-1309
Segrest, Jerry/1707 S. Ervay, Dallas .... (214) 426-6360
Seifried Photography/Decatur .... (205) 539-8191
Sellers, Dan/1317 Conant, Dallas .... (214) 631-4705
Sharpe, David/816 N. Saint Asaph St., Alexandria .... (703) 683-3773
Shaw, Bob/Powerhouse Productions/1723 Kelly St., Dallas .... (214) 428-1757
Sheridan, Phil, Inc./2024 Farrington St., Dallas .... (214) 760-8455
Sherman, Bob/1166 N.E. 182nd St., Miami .... (305) 944-2111
Sherman, Ron/Atlanta .... (404) 993-7197
Shook, Margaret/67 N. Market St., Asheville .... (704) 254-4166
Shooters/11321 Greystone, Okla. City .... (405) 751-0313
Simpson, Micheal/1415 Slocum St., Dallas .... (214) 761-0000
Sims/Boynton/Houston/(713) 522-0817 .... **pages 730-731**
Sims, Jim/Houston/(713) 522-0817 .... **pages 730-731**
Sims, Robert/Atlanta .... (404) 957-8351
Slater, Ed/3601 W. Commercial Blvd., Ft. Lauderdale .... (305) 486-7117
Slater, Greg/141 Mangum St., Atlanta .... (404) 584-6397
Sluder, Mark B./2819 Glendale Rd., Charlotte .... (704) 334-8797
Smiley Studio/Ft. Worth .... (817) 738-2175
Smiley's/2900 Smiley St., Ft. Worth .... (817) 738-2175
Smiley, Art/1413 Monte Sano Ave., Augusta .... (404) 731-0132
Smith Ottinger Graphics/1731 W. Main St., Richmond .... (804) 358-8667
Smith, F. Carter/818 Highland, Houston .... (713) 862-6272
Smith, Jackson R. Photography/1140 Burke St., Winston-Salem .... (919) 722-7053
Smith, Ralph/2211 Beall, Houston .... (713) 862-8301
Smith, Rich/1625 N.E. Third Ct., Ft. Lauderdale .... (305) 523-8861
Smith, Richard W./1007-B Norwalk St., Greensboro .... (919) 292-1190
Smith/Garner Studio/1114 W. Peachtree St. N.W., Atlanta .... (404) 875-0086
Snortum, Marty/2905 Pershing, El Paso .... (915) 562-1114
Southern Lights Studio/New Orleans/(504) 861-3000 .... **page 705**
Space Photos/2608 Sunset Blvd., Houston .... (713) 667-9668
Speidell, Bill/1030 McConville Rd., Lynchburg .... (804) 237-6426
Spielman, David/New Orleans .... (504) 899-7670
Squire, Terry/Raleigh/(919) 833-9955 .... **pages 692-693**
St. Gil, Marc/2230 Ashford Hollow Ln., Houston .... (713) 870-9458
St. John, Chuck/2724 N.W. 30th Ave., Ft. Lauderdale .... (305) 731-3300
Staartjes, Hans/Houston .... (713) 522-1488
Stansfield, Ross/4938 D. Eisenhower Ave., Alexandria .... (703) 370-5142
Stewart, Craig Studio/1900 W. Alabama, Houston .... (713) 529-5959
Strode, William Assocs./Louisville .... (502) 228-4446
Stroppe, Virginia/13 W. Main St., Richmond .... (804) 644-0266
Stroud, Dan/1350 Manufacturing, Dallas .... (214) 745-1933
Studio Masters, Inc./1398 N.E. 125th St., N. Miami .... (305) 893-3500
Studio Three/1021 Northside Dr. N.W., Atlanta .... (404) 875-0161
Suddarth, Robert/3402 73rd St., Lubbock .... (806) 795-4553
Sumner, Bill/1140 Cedar Hill Ave., Dallas .... (214) 948-6860
Sumpter, Will/Atlanta/(404) 874-2014 .... **pages 670-671**
Sussman, Bernard/1135 Gulf of Mexico Dr., Longboat Key .... (813) 383-5823
Sustendal, Michael F./147 Carondelet, New Orleans .... (504) 899-7255
Sutter, Frederick/411A E. Howell Ave., Alexandria .... (703) 549-2330
Swain Edens Studios/1905 N. St. Marys, San Antonio .... (512) 226-2210
Swann, David/Atlanta .... (404) 873-3003
Tapp, Eddie/955 Smoketree Dr., Tucker .... (404) 493-7233
Taylor, Belinda/2934 Country Pl. Dr., Carrollton .... (214) 323-9115
Taylor, Randy G./555 N.E. 34th St., Miami .... (305) 573-5200
Taylor, Rick/Atlanta .... (404) 634-8333
Tenney, Michael/2015 Ashland Ave., Charlotte .... (704) 372-7700

Terranova, Michael/1135 Cadiz St., New Orleans	(504) 899-7328
Terry, Phillip/1222 Manufacturing St., Dallas	(214) 823-4356
Tesh, John/904 A. Norwalk St., Greensboro	(919) 299-1400
Thatcher, C., Inc./2410 Farrington St., Dallas	(214) 823-4356
Thayer, Evin Studios, Inc./2643 Colquitt, Houston	(713) 524-0199
Thomas, Bruce Studio/7925 Fourth St. N., St. Petersburg	(813) 577-5626
Thomas, Clark/235 Lauderdale Rd., Nashville	(615) 269-7700
Thomas, Jason Photography/233 N.E. 21st Ct., Fort Lauderdale	(305) 563-7666
Thomas, Larry/1212 Spring St. N.W., Atlanta	(404) 881-8850
Thompson & Thompson/5180 N.E. 12th Ave., Ft. Lauderdale	(305) 772-4411
Thompson, Darrell/124 Rhodes Dr. S.E., Marietta	(404) 565-9865
Thompson, Keith & Jody/Lighthouse Pt.	(305) 428-2080
Thompson, Kern, Inc./6990 F. Peachtree Indust. Blvd., Norcross	(404) 441-1144
Thompson, Rose/1802 N.W. 29th St., Oakland Park	(305) 485-0148
Thompson, Tommy L./1317 N. Highland Ave. N.E., Atlanta	(404) 892-3499
Thompson, Wes/Dallas	(241) 438-7762
Those 3 Reps/Dallas/(214) 871-1316	**pages 210-211**
Three Score, Inc./5150 N. Royal Atlanta Dr., Atlanta	(404) 934-1224
Tiffany Photo/948 N.E. 20th Ave., Ft. Lauderdale	(305) 764-0662
Tilley, Arthur/1925 College Ave., Atlanta	(404) 371-8086
Tobias, Jerry/Miami/(305) 685-3003	**pages 680-681**
Tomlinson, Doug/5651 E. Side Ave., Dallas	(214) 821-1192
Transphoto, Inc./823 Virginia Dr., Orlando	(407) 896-1776
Traves, Stephen C./360 Elden Dr., Atlanta	(404) 255-5711
Tri-Photo, Inc./1100 S. Dixie Hwy. W., Pompano Beach	(305) 941-1368
Turnau, Jeffrey/4950 S.W. 72nd Ave., Miami	(305) 666-5454
Turner, Danny/1821 Levee, Dallas	(214) 760-7472
Urban, Linda/2931 Irving Blvd., Dallas	(214) 634-9009
Van de Zande, Doug/307 W. Martin St., Raleigh	(919) 832-2499
Vance, David/150 N.W. 164th St., Miami	(305) 354-2083
Vance, Neal/Dallas	(214) 761-9990
Vaughn, Marc/11140 Griffing Blvd., N. Miami	(305) 845-5790
Verlent, Christian/9003 Park Dr., Miami Shores	(305) 751-3385
Vine, Terry/Houston/(713) 664-2920	**pages 698-699**
Von Guttenberg Photographics/417 S. Pineapple Ave., Sarasota	(813) 955-6065
Von Helms, Michael/4212 San Felipe, Houston	(713) 666-1212
Vracin, Andy/4906 Don Dr., Dallas	(214) 688-1841
Vullo, Phillip S./565 Dutch Valley Rd. N.E., Atlanta	(404) 874-0822
Wagnon, Ken/Dallas	(214) 637-2800
Waine, Michael Studio, Inc./1923 E. Franklin St., Richmond	(804) 644-0164
Wallace, Jimmie/19 N. Sheridan Rd., Louisville	(502) 459-3630
Walpole, Gary/284 N. Cleveland, Memphis	(901) 726-1155
Walters, Tom/3108 Airlie St., Charlotte	(704) 537-7908
Washington, Dick/717 W. Ashby, San Antonio	(512) 733-6128
Waters, Bruce/3741 Edgewater Dr., Nashville	(615) 361-6979
Webb Photography/2023 Kenilworth Ave., Louisville	(502) 459-7081
Webb, Clem/2415 Laurel Ave., Beaumont	(409) 832-2749
Webb, Jon Photography/Louisville	(502) 459-7081
Weber, C.F., Inc./516 Natchez St., New Orleans	(504) 522-7503
Welsch, Diana/Austin	(512) 469-0958
Wergeles, Ed/15 Crossroads Ctr., Sarasota	(813) 351-5020
Werre, Bob/2437 Bartlett St., Houston	(713) 529-4841
West, Michael/1157 W. Peachtree St., Atlanta	(404) 892-6263
Whalen, Judy/Dallas/(214) 828-1226	**pages 702-703**
Wheeler, Don/1933 S. Boston, Tulsa	(918) 587-3808
Wheless, Rob Studio, Inc./3039 Amwiler Rd., Atlanta	(404) 729-1066
White, Alberto Productions, Inc./1050 Glenwood Ave. S.E., Atlanta	(404) 627-2431
White, Frank/2702 Sackett, Houston	(713) 524-9250
Whitehead, John H./13 S. Foushee St., Richmond	(804) 648-3219
Whitlock, Neill/122 E. Fifth St., Dallas	(214) 948-3117
Wile, Dennis/1812 Ashwood Ave., Nashville	(615) 383-3412
Willard, W.W. & Assoc./1045 S.E. Ninth Ct., Hialeah	(305) 885-1110
Williams, Jeff/Miami/(305) 856-8338	**pages 690-691**
Williams, Jimmy/Raleigh/(919) 832-5971	**pages 712-713**
Williams, Sonny Photography, Inc./741 Monroe Dr. N.E., Atlanta	(404) 892-5551
Williamson, Tom/10830 N. Central Expressway, Dallas	(214) 373-4999
Willis, Joe/Miami/(305) 485-7185	**pages 718-719**
Willis, Molly/7314 Muirwood Ln., Houston	(713) 937-1881
Wilson, Andrew/1640 Smyra-Roswell Rd. S.E., Atlanta	(404) 436-7553
Winner, Alan/20151 N.E. 15th Ct., Miami	(305) 653-6778
Wöhrman, Scott/Coral Springs/(305) 752-6297	**pages 722-723**
Wolkis, Ed/Atlanta	(404) 266-1070
Wollam, Les/5215 Goodwin Ave., Dallas	(214) 760-7721

Wood, Keith/1308 Conant, Dallas .... (214) 643-7344
Woodbury & Assocs./6801 N.W. Ninth Ave., Fort Lauderdale .... (305) 977-7045
Woodson, Richard/Raleigh .... (919) 833-2882
Yeung, Ka-Chuen/4901 W. Lovers Ln., Dallas .... (214) 350-8716
Young, Chuck Photography, Inc./1199-R Howell Mill Rd., Atlanta .... (404) 351-1199
Zagarino, Frank/3620 Palmarito St., Coral Gables .... (305) 448-4881
Ziegler, Rob/321 S. Randolph St., Richmond .... (804) 358-4835
Zillioux, John/663 Woodcrest Rd., Miami .... (305) 361-0368
Zimmerman, Michael/4054 N. 30th Ave., Hollywood .... (305) 963-6240

CODY

MIAMI

©1991 Dennie Cody, Photographer • 5880 SW 53 Terrace, Miami, FL 33155
(305) 666-0247 • Fax (305) 669-0110
Chromes by Color Lab Miami

6:33 **A.M.**

SAN FRANCISCO, CA

Mothers,

there's a mad man

running in the

streets,

And he's

humming a tune,

And he's

snarling at dogs,

And he still

has

four

more

miles

to go.

Just do it.

Arthur Meyerson Photography
For assignments and stock, phone 713-660-0405 or fax 713-660-9561

GARY KUFNER

REPRESENTED
IN NEW YORK BY
JOE DiBARTOLO AND
LAURA LEMKOWITZ
(212) 297-0041

STUDIOS IN MIAMI AND NORTH CAROLINA

GARY KUFNER STUDIO (305) 944-7740
STOCK: SHARPSHOOTERS 800-666-1266 • FAX 305-940-4011

SOUTH
FLORIDA

665

GARY KUFNER

REPRESENTED
IN NEW YORK BY
JOE DiBARTOLO AND
LAURA LEMKOWITZ
(212) 297-0041

STUDIOS IN NORTH CAROLINA AND MIAMI

GARY KUFNER STUDIO (704) 387-2047
STOCK: SHARPSHOOTERS 800-666-1266 • FAX 305-940-4011

NORTH CAROLINA

667

STEWART
CHARLES
COHEN

The Difference Between Taking Pictures And Making Pictures.

STEWART CHARLES COHEN
PHOTOGRAPHY
2401 SOUTH ERVAY SUITE 206
DALLAS, TEXAS 75215
214-421-2186
FAX: 214-565-0623

REPRESENTED BY:
THE McCANN COMPANY
214-871-0353

STOCK AVAILABLE

DUPES BY BWC PHOTOLABS • DALLAS

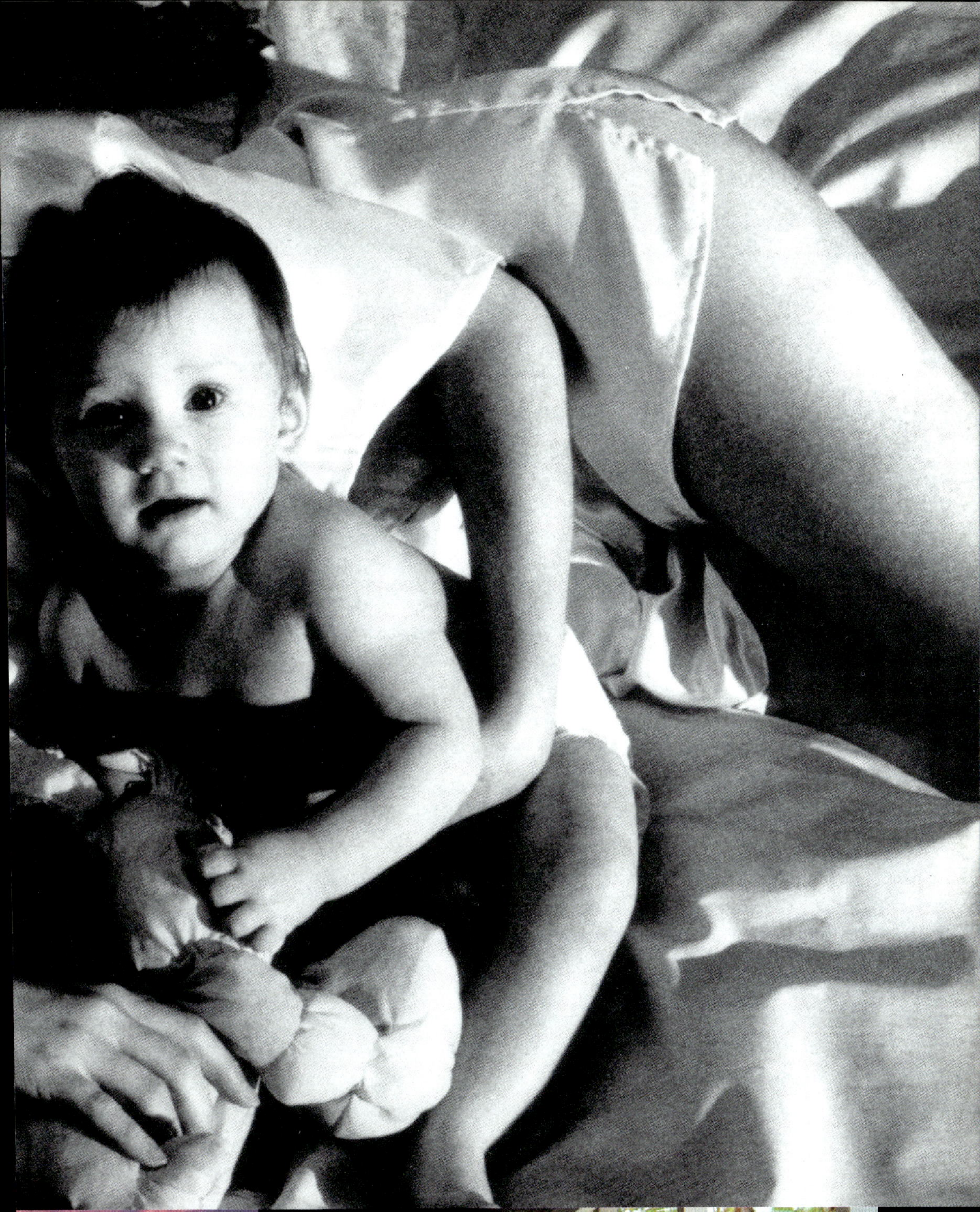

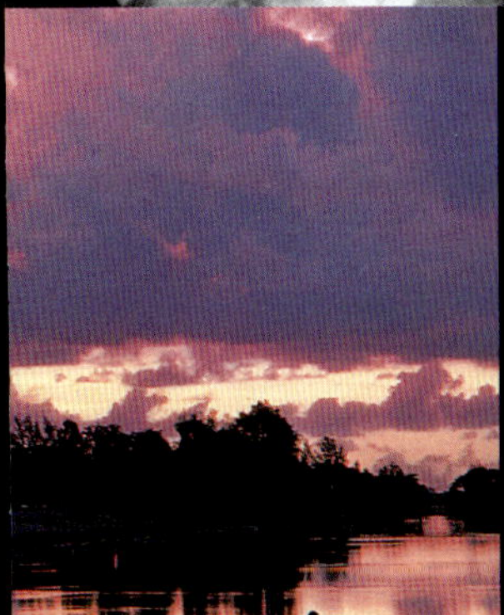

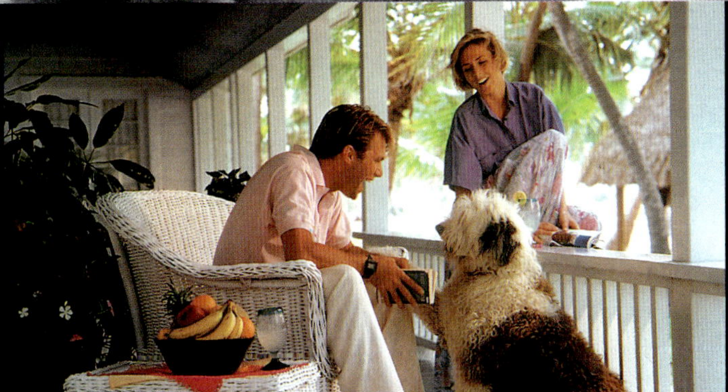

FLIP CHALFANT

Represented by

Will Sumpter

404/874-2014

Fax. 404/874-8173

1728 N. Rock Springs Rd.

Atlanta, Ga. 30324

Studio 404/881-8510

All photos © 1990 Flip Chalfant

R A N D Y

Palm Studio / 6666 S.W. 96th Street, Miami, Florida 33156

Richard Foster/Hill Holiday

Rick McQuiston/Weiden & Kennedy

Stouffers Hotels

Dick Henderson/Ritz Carlton

Now comes millisecond time.

A mere fraction of a second. Gain one, and it could mean victory; lose one, and you've had it. Just a little something we kept in mind when designing the Speedo Optic. A suit so hot it'll electrify the water. Not to mention the crowd.

SPEEDO

MILLER

(305) 667-5765/Fax: (305) 667-0892

onis Gold/Smith, Greenland Agency

"He squeezes the toothpaste from the bottom.
And he drinks Johnnie Walker Red."

Good taste is always an asset.

Harry Baldwin/McCann-Erickson

Can't Beat The Feeling!

Grant Richards/The Richards Group

673

3 0 5 · 4 4 3 · 1 6 1 7

MOLINA

Hal Riney / Saturn

Dudnyk / Pfizer

Robin Hood
(615) 794-2041

Hal Riney / Saturn

Leo Burnett / Phillip Morris

Robin Hood
(615) 794-2041

PELOSI &

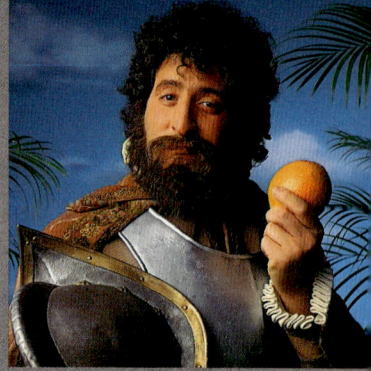

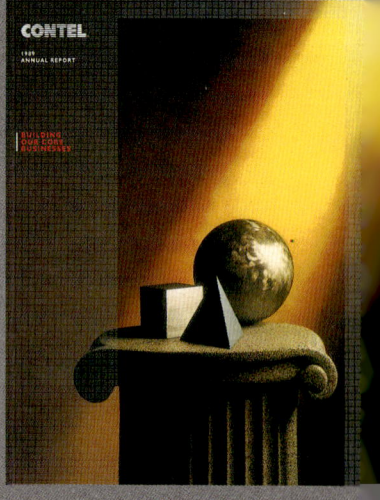

**Steve Pelosi & Don Chambers
Print and Film**

684 Greenwood Ave. NE
Atlanta, Georgia 30306
Telephone: 404-872-8117
Fax: 404-872-2992

Clients include:
American Express, Coca-Cola,
Delta, Marriott Hotels, Ryder Trucks,
R.J. Reynolds

Represented by Chris Christian

CHAMBERS

JERRY Tobias

MIAMI, FLORIDA
305 685 3003
FAX: 305 685 3008

DUPES BY COLOR LAB MIAMI   STOCK: SHARPSHOOTERS 1-800-666-1266

Represented in Europe by **AGNES SCHWENZEL**
Tel. 0911/35 33 66   Fax 0911/36 16 24

USA

Da

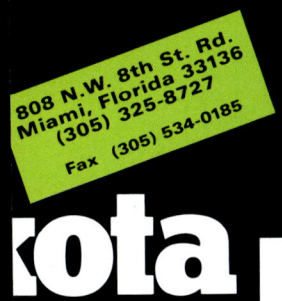

808 N.W. 8th St. Rd.
Miami, Florida 33136
(305) 325-8727
Fax (305) 534-0185

kota

MIAMI

Represented by **IRENE DAKOTA** (305) 674-9975

UNDERWATER

THINK
·
FRINK
·
UNDER
·
WATER

TROPICAL

Stephen Frink

· P.O. BOX 2720 · KEY LARGO, FLORIDA 33037
· TOLL FREE: (800) 451-3737
· FAX: (305) 451-5147
· PHONE: (305) 451-3737

STOCK

ASSIGNMENT

P H O T O G R A P H E R

Tom King, Inc.

7401 Chancery Lane • Orlando, Florida 32809
407-856-0618 • FAX 407-876-0210
In New York: Rich Kane 212-496-9670 • Stock: The Image Bank

Some Like It Hot!

Hot Prices. Hot Places. Florida And The Caribbean.
EASTERN

2545 TIGERTAIL AVENUE
MIAMI, FLORIDA 33133
305 - 856 - 8338

©RICK GOMEZ

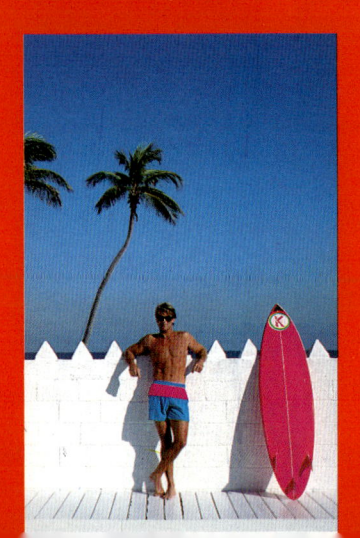

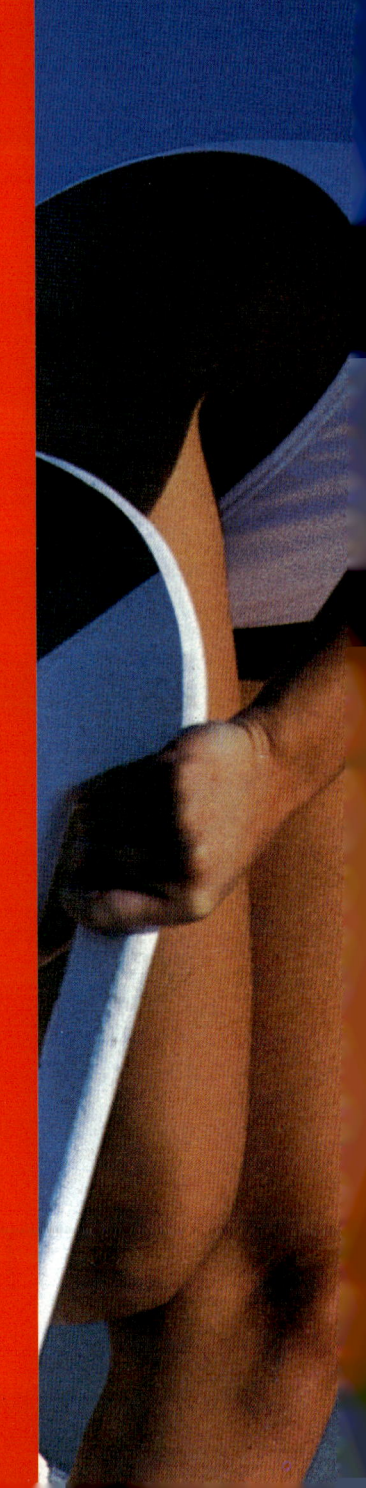

Stock/Sharpshooters (800)666-1266

KODAK STUDIO LIGHT

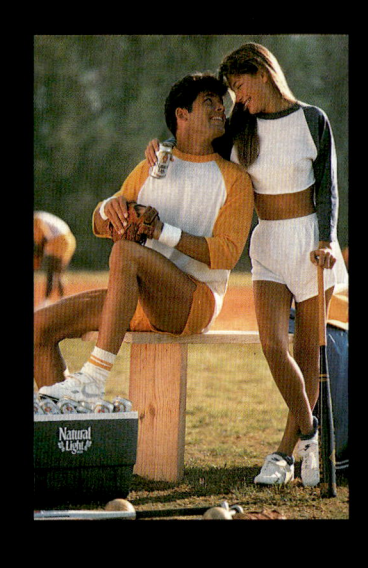

Stock/Sharpshooters (800)666-1266

2545 TIGERTAIL AVENUE
MIAMI, FLORIDA 33133
305 - 856 - 8338

RICK GOMEZ

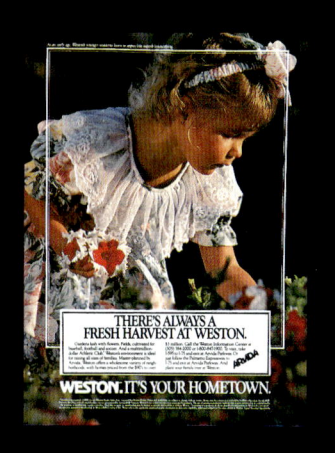

Stock/Sharpshooters (800)666-1266

JEFF WILLIAMS

*In association with
Rick Gomez Studio*

2545 Tigertail Avenue
Miami, Florida 33133
305 - 856 - 8338

The second greates

Call 919-833-9955 for the boo

Book in the Bible Belt.

Jim Erickson represented by Terry Squire.

FOREST J

7200 SOUTHWEST 129 STREET, MIAM

OHNSON

FLORIDA 33156 PHONE 305/251-1300

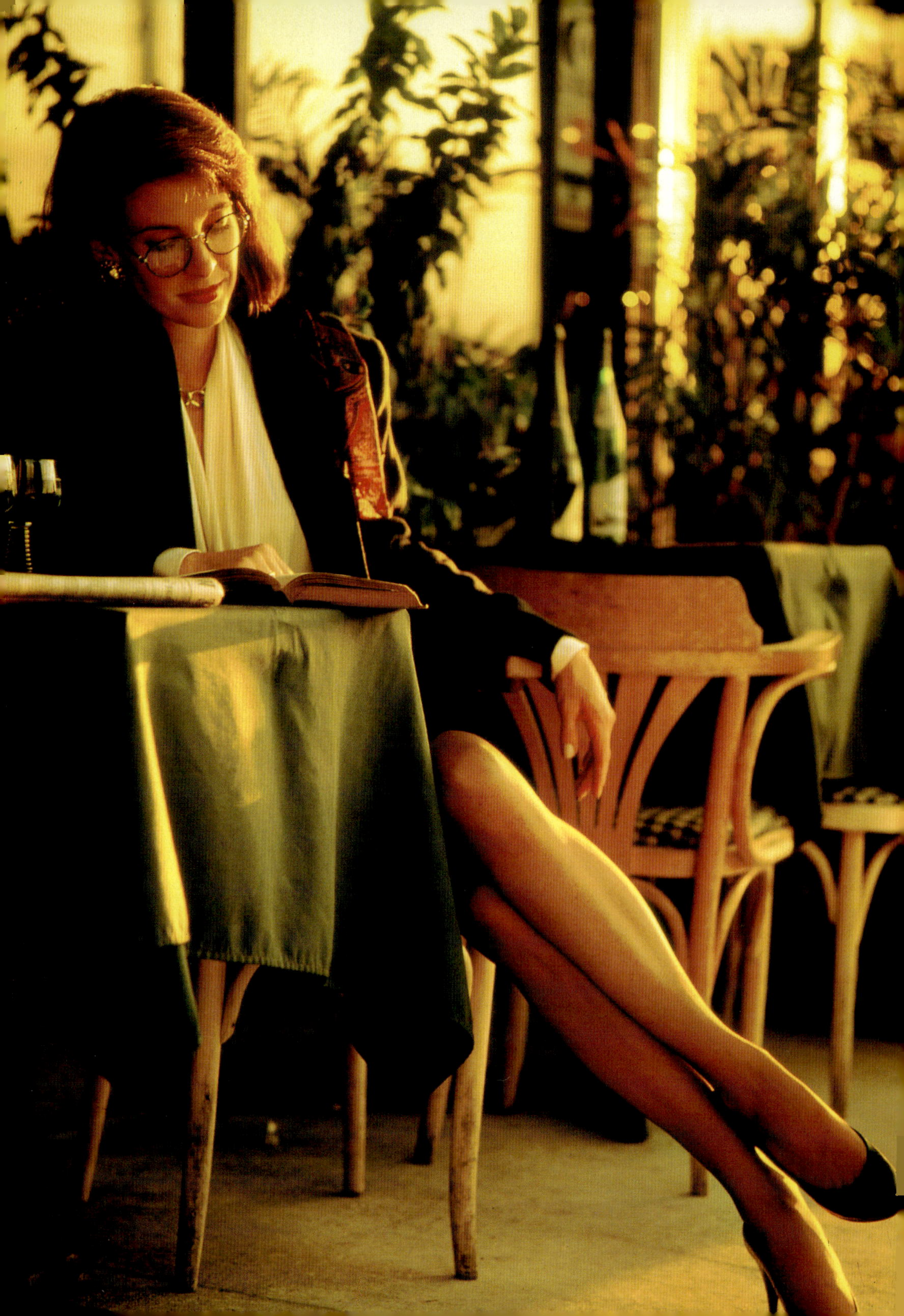

CONSTANTINOS
PHOTOGRAPHY

305/467-3478

YO HO HO
POOR RICHARD'67
CACACA 87 BRASIL
JEAN H. '79
SEA-BIRD A. OLSON 1913
JOPER-83
KATRINA
GLÁUCIA 78-79
BRAZIL
HELENA
ANA CLÁUDIA 87
MARLENE-PLINIO-85
MARIA 81 182
Adams '80
CAIRNS 80-82-83
85-7-8
BRUNETTE 72-88
BUD+FLO
JAN+LAR '82-83
'82, '88

Terry Vine

713·664·2920

Houston

MICHAEL W. RUTHERFORD · 615-242-5953

After all those year

MICHAEL W. RUTHERFORD · 615-242-5953

ie shooting hasn't stopped.

2336 FARRINGTON   DALLAS, TEXAS   75207   214-630-8977   R

LATORRE

CALL FOR OUR Film REEL

ENTED BY JUDY WHALEN 214-828-1226   FAX 214-638-3319

JIM MARKHAM
2739 S.E. Loop 410 San Antonio, TX. 78222
(512) 648-0403

≈≈Jackson Hill

SOUTHERN LIGHTS STUDIO ≈≈≈ 504.861.3000 Fax 504.861.3019

New Orleans ≈≈

MASON

PHOTOGRAPHY

CHUCK MASON

305·270·2070

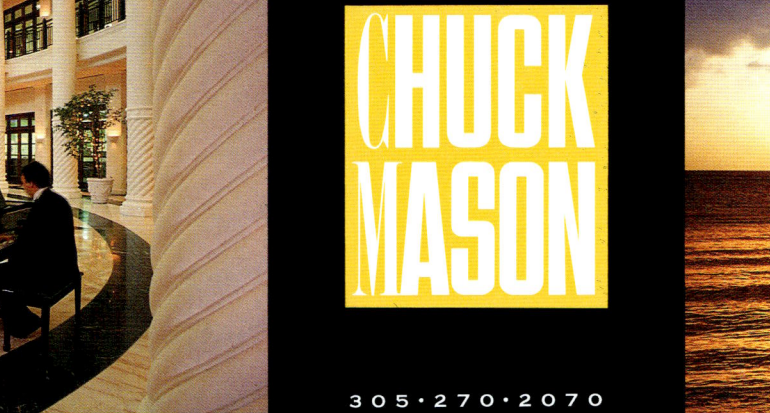

THE PRESIDENTIAL

COLONNADE HOTEL

CONTINENTAL HOTELS

XANADU RESORT BAHAMAS

MIAMI

707

781 Miami Circle, N.E., Atlanta, Georgia 30324   (404) 231-1316 / FAX (404) 231-1318

Gardella
AND COMPANY

Robert Holland Phone: 305-255-6758 Stock: The Image Bank
Miami   Fax: 305-254-9062   Dupes: Color Lab Miami

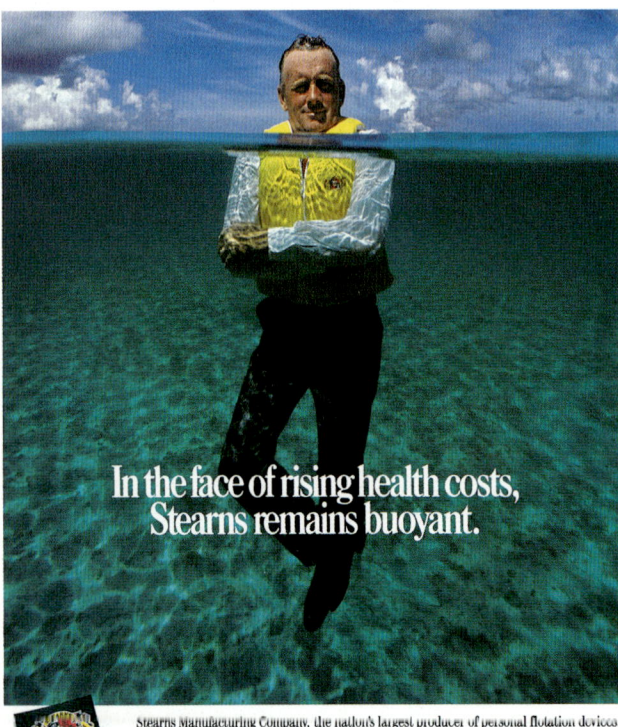

HOLLAND

© 1991 ROBERT HOLLAND

A BRILLIANT
TO BIG-CITY O

ALTERNATIVE
TO OVEREXPOSURE.

Jimmy Williams

3801 Beryl Road · Raleigh, North Carolina 27607 · (919) 832-5971

LANGONE

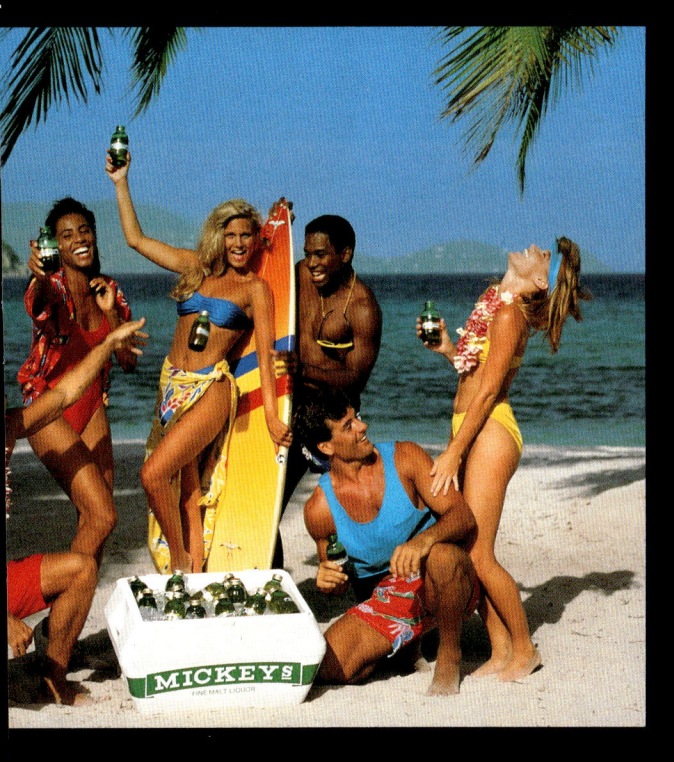

PETER LANGONĒ

516 Northeast 13th Street
Fort Lauderdale, Florida 33304
(305) 467-0654
FAX: (305) 522-2562

Complete production services

For additional work see American Showcase volumes 8-13.

Stock Photography Call:
INSTOCK (305) 527-4111

New York
Representative
Bruce Levin Associates
Phone: (212) 832-4053
Fax: (212) 355-4608

MAXHAM

Robert Maxham Studio   223 Howard   San Antonio, TX 78212
(512) 223-6000 FAX 223-6192
Call for portfolio.

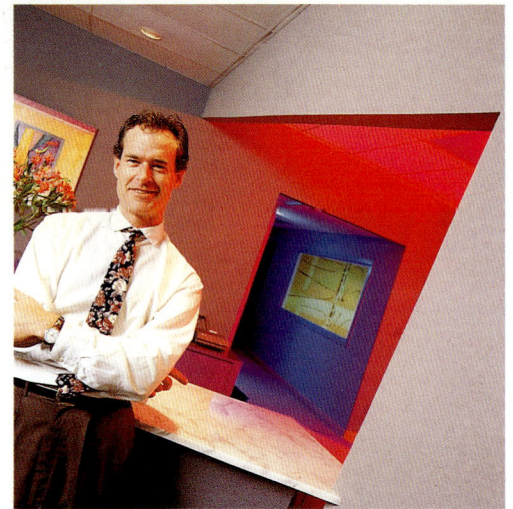

On location for Texas Monthly Magazine

On location for Sunbelt Sportswear catalog

In Studio for Rawlings Sports Equipment

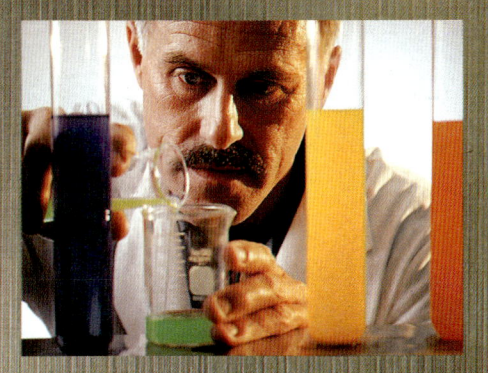

KEN GLASER

NEW ORLEANS, LA 504.895.7170

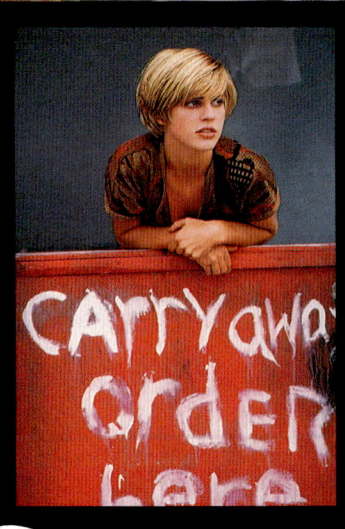

WILLIS

Joe Willis Photography
Miami (305) 485-7185

AT&T
ALAMO RENTAL CARS
BOCA RATON HOTEL & CLUB
BUDGET AUTO RENTAL
CAPITOL BANK
CONTINENTAL AIRLINES
COOPER TOOLS
COPPERTONE
CORDIS-DOW
DANIEL MINK
DIBARTOLO CORP.
DORAL RESORT
EASTERN AIRLINES
EXXON CORP.
FLORIDA KEYS TOURISM BOARD
FLORIDA POWER & LIGHT
HAWK'S CAY RESORT
HERTZ
HILTON HOTELS

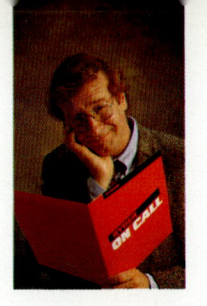

HOLLAND AMERICA LINES
HOLIDAY INNS
HOMELITE
IBM
LONGBOAT KEY RESORT
MILLER BREWING COMPANY
MORABITO PERFUME
MINUTE MAID

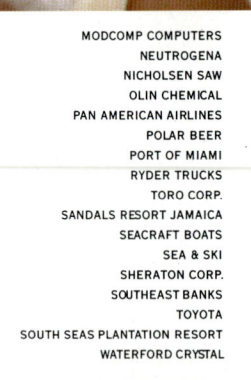

MODCOMP COMPUTERS
NEUTROGENA
NICHOLSEN SAW
OLIN CHEMICAL
PAN AMERICAN AIRLINES
POLAR BEER
PORT OF MIAMI
RYDER TRUCKS
TORO CORP.
SANDALS RESORT JAMAICA
SEACRAFT BOATS
SEA & SKI
SHERATON CORP.
SOUTHEAST BANKS
TOYOTA
SOUTH SEAS PLANTATION RESORT
WATERFORD CRYSTAL

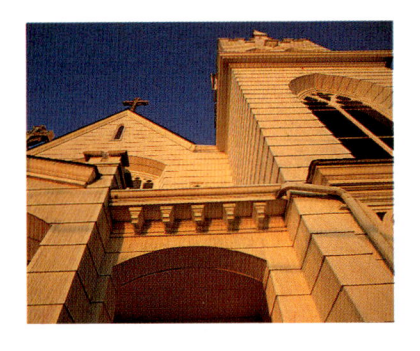

MIAMI

GEORGE

CONTORAKES

(305)

661-0731

FAX

(305)

662-5752

CONTORÄKES

721

wöh

Scott Wöhrman • P.O. Box 9728 • Coral Springs, Florida 33075 • (305) 752-6297
South Florida and the Caribbean

rman

D A N F O R E R

Miami

305.949.3131

Courtesy Architectural Digest

725

RICK

For Additional Work
See Black Book
'84 thru '89.

DIAZ *miami*

Rick Diaz Photography Inc.
4884 S.W. 74th Court
Miami, Florida 33155
Phone 305 264 9761
Fax 305 661 7175

Stock through
SharpShooters
Miami, Florida
305 666 1266

2919 Canton

Dallas, Texas 75226

214 651 7085

TOM
RYAN

Represented by

Friend & Johnson

214 855 0055

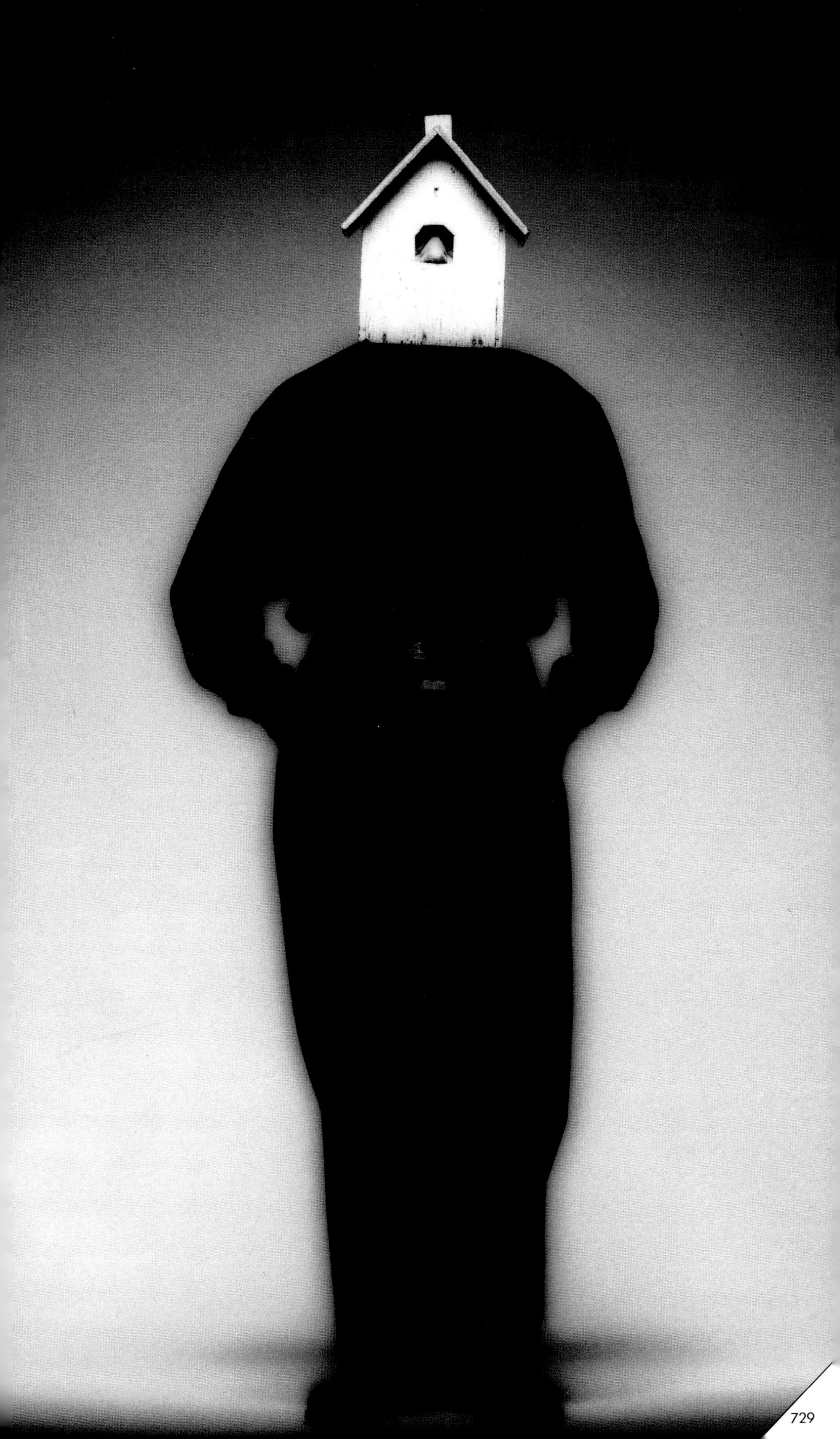

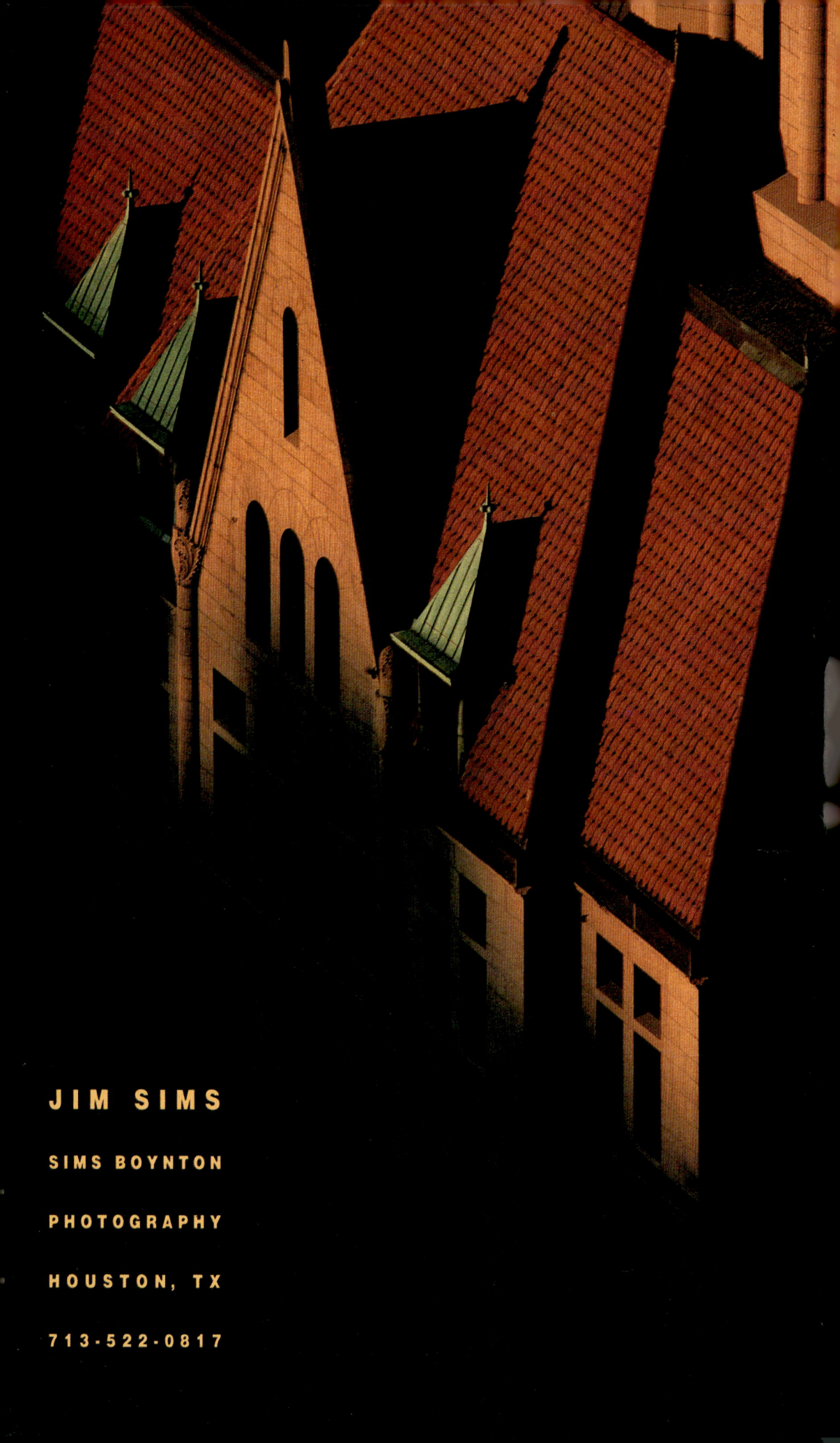

JIM SIMS

SIMS BOYNTON

PHOTOGRAPHY

HOUSTON, TX

713-522-0817

JIM SIMS

REPRESENTED BY

FRIEND & JOHNSON

DALLAS, TX

214·855·0055

NORTH AMERICA STOCK PHOTOGRAPHY

Listings 734
Ads 737

NORTH AMERICA
STOCK PHOTOGRAPHY

3-M/Salt Lake City .... (801) 359-8183
ALLSPORT Photography/6160 Fairmaount Ave., San Diego .... (619) 280-3595
AdStock Photo/6219 N. 9th Place, Phoenix .... (602) 277-5903
All-Sport Photography/320 Wilshire Blvd., Santa Monica .... (213) 395-2955
AllStock/1530 Westlake Ave. N., Seattle .... (206) 282-8116
Ambrose, Paul Studios/Durango .... (303) 259-5925
American Stock Photography/6255 Sunset Blvd., Hollywood .... (213) 469-3900
Arnold, Peter, Inc./1181 Broadway, NYC .... (212) 481-1190
Art Resource/65 Bleecker St., NYC .... (212) 505-8700
Baraban, Joe/Houston/(713) 526-0317 .... pages 256-257
Barton, Paul/NYC/(212) 691-1999 .... pages 134-135
Bergman, L.V. & Assocs./E. Mountain Rd., Cold Springs .... (914) 265-3656
Bettmann/902 Broadway, NYC .... (212) 777-6200
Blecker, Charles/NYC/(212) 242-8390 .... pages 238-239
Bliss, Jan/St. Paul/(612) 645-5070 .... pages 480-481
Bowen, Paul/Wichita/(316) 263-5537 .... page 740
Brandt, Peter/73 Fifth Ave., NYC .... (212) 242-4289
Breitrose, Howard/E. Elmhurst/(800) 873-7862 .... pages 240-241
Brown, Nancy/NYC/(212) 924-9105 .... page 358
Bryant, D. Donne/4036 Irving St., Baton Rouge .... (504) 387-1620
Camerique Inc. Int'l./1701 Skippack Pike, Blue Bell .... (215) 272-4000
Camerique Stock Photography/3102 N. Habana Ave., Tampa .... (813) 876-1868
Caswell Marine Photography/2732 Tucker Ln., Los Alamitos .... (213) 598-0782
Charlton Photos/11518 N. Pt. Washington Rd., Mequon .... (414) 241-8634
Cohen, Stewart Charles/Dallas/(214) 421-2186 .... pages 668-669
Comstock, Inc./30 Irving Pl., NYC .... (212) 353-8600
Cook, Kathleen Norris/Laguna Hills/(714) 770-4619 .... pages 576-577
Culver Pictures, Inc./150 W. 22nd St., NYC .... (212) 645-1672
Custom Medical Stock Photo/3819 N. Southport Ave., Chicago .... (800) 373-2677
Cyr Color Photo Agency/73 Benedict St., Norwalk .... (203) 838-8230
de Wys, Leo/NYC .... (212) 889-4932
DPI/19 W. 21st St., NYC .... (212) 627-4060
DRK Photo/265 Verde Valley School Rd., Sedona .... (602) 284-9808
Davidson, Josiah/8936 N. Ferber Ct., Tucson .... (800) 537-7810
Design Conceptions/112 Fourth Ave., NYC .... (212) 254-1688
Design Photographers Int'l., Inc. (DPI)/19 W. 21st. St., NYC .... (212) 627-4060
Devaney Stock Photos/755 New York Ave., Huntington .... (516) 673-4477
Dot Picture Agency/253 W. 73rd St., NYC .... (212) 769-0158
Duomo Photography Inc./133 W. 19th St., NYC .... (212) 243-1150
E.P. Jones Co./45 Newbury St., Boston .... (617) 267-6450
EKM-Nepenthe/El Rito .... (505) 984-9719
Earth Images/682 Winslow Way E., Bainbridge Island .... (206) 842-7793
Eastern Photo Service/1170 Broadway, NYC .... (212) 689-5580
Ellis Wildlife Collection/69 Cranberry St., Bklyn. Heights .... (718) 935-9600
Envision/220 W. 19th St., NYC .... (212) 243-0415
Ergenbright, Ric/Bend .... (503) 389-7662
Esto Photographics/Mamaroneck .... (914) 698-4060
Ewing Galloway/100 Merrick Rd., Rockville Ctr. .... (516) 764-8620
Eyerman, J.R. Archives/475 17th St., Santa Monica .... (213) 393-2351
FPG International/251 Park Ave. S., NYC .... (212) 777-4210
Fashions In Stock/21-45 78th St., E. Elmhurst .... (800) 873-7862
Florida Image File, Inc./526-11 Ave. N.E., St. Petersburg .... (813) 894-8433
Focus on Sports, Inc./NYC/(212) 661-6860 .... page 741
Fotograf/Headhunters/2619 Lovegrove St., Balt. .... (301) 338-1820
Four By Five Photography, Inc./512 King St. E., Toronto .... (416) 860-1518
Friedman, Todd/Beverly Hills .... (213) 474-6715
Frink, Stephen/Key Largo/(305) 451-3737/(800) 451-3737 .... page 684
Frozen Images/400 First Ave. N., Mpls. .... (612) 339-3191
Fundamental Photographs/210 Forsyth St., NYC .... (212) 473-5770
Garber, Bette/2110 Valley Dr., W. Chester .... (215) 692-9076
Gartman, Marilyn Photo Agency/510 N. Dearborn, Chicago .... (312) 661-1656
Globe Photos, Inc./275 Seventh Ave., NYC .... (212) 689-1340
Golfoto/224 N. Independence, Enid .... (800) 338-1656
Gottlieb, Dennis M./NYC/(212) 620-7050 .... pages 44-45

Hanover Direct, Inc./1500 Harbor Blvd., Weehauken	(201) 863-7300
Hathon, Elizabeth/NYC/(212) 219-0685	**pages 330-331**
Hayes, Eric/836 LaHave St., Bridgewater	(902) 543-0256
Hayes, Robert Cushman/7350 Gracely Dr., Cincinnati	(513) 941-2447
Heilman, Grant Photography, Inc./506 W. Lincoln Ave., Lititz	(800) 622-2046
Heyl, Fran Assocs./230 Park Ave., NYC	(212) 581-6470
Hillstrom Stock Photo, Inc./5483 N. Northwest Hwy., Chicago	(312) 775-4090
Hillstrom, Ray F./5483 N. Northwest Hwy., Chicago	(312) 775-4090
Historical Pictures Service/921 W. Van Buren, Chicago	(312) 346-0599
Holland, Robert/Miami/(305) 255-6758	**pages 710-711**
Hormuth, Susan/1400 C St. N.E., Washington	(202) 398-3227
Hot Shots/309 Lesmill Rd., Don Mills, Canada	(416) 441-3281
Hughes, Karen/4602 E. Side Ave., Dallas	(214) 826-6262
IBID, Inc./935 Chestnut St., Chicago	(312) 733-8000
Image Bank, The/Atlanta/(404) 233-9200	**pages 358, 602-603, 685, 710**
Image Bank, The/Boston/(617) 267-8866	**pages 358, 602-603, 685, 710**
Image Bank, The/Chicago/(312) 329-1817	**pages 358, 602-603, 685, 710**
Image Bank, The/Dallas/(214) 528-3888	**pages 358, 602-603, 685, 710**
Image Bank, The/Detroit/(313) 524-1850	**pages 358, 602-603, 685, 710**
Image Bank, The/Houston/(713) 668-0066	**pages 358, 602-603, 685, 710**
Image Bank, The/L.A./(213) 930-0797	**pages 358, 602-603, 685, 710**
Image Bank, The/Mpls./(612) 332-8935	**pages 358, 602-603, 685, 710**
Image Bank, The/NYC/(212) 529-6700	**pages 358, 602-603, 685, 710**
Image Bank, The/Naples/(813) 566-3444	**pages 358, 602-603, 685, 710**
Image Bank, The/S.F./(415) 788-2208	**pages 358, 602-603, 685, 710**
Image Finders Photo Agency Inc./501-134 Abbott St., Vancouver	(604) 688-9818
Image Imagination/4111 Lincoln Blvd., Marina Del Rey	(213) 392-4505
Image Resources, Inc./224 W. 29th St., NYC	(212) 736-2523
Impact/26 Airport Rd., Edmonton	(403) 454-9676
Index Stock International, Inc./126 Fifth Ave., NYC	(212) 929-4644
Instock Picture Agency/Ft. Lauderdale/(305) 527-4111	**page 714-715, 738**
Johnston, Greg Travel Photography/Miami	(305) 382-5535
Jones, Dawson L./44 E. Franklin St., Dayton	(513) 435-1121
Jones, Edgar T./43 Westbrook Dr., Edmonton	(403) 436-5327
Kesser Stock Footage Library/21 S.W. 15th Rd., Miami	(305) 358-7900
Ketchum Stock Photos/1524 S. Peoria St., Chicago	(312) 733-7706
Keystone Press Agency, Inc./202 E. 42nd St., NYC	(212) 924-8123
Klass, Rubin & Erika/5200 N. Federal Hwy., Ft. Lauderdale	(305) 565-1612
Kramer, Joan & Assocs./248 Westminster Ave., Venice	(213) 314-8111
Kramer, Joan/NYC/(212) 567-5545	**page 739**
Kramer, Joan/Great Neck/(516) 466-5582	**page 739**
LGI Photo Agency/241 W. 36th St., NYC	(212) 736-4602
Lavenstein, Lance/348 Southport Cir., Virginia Beach	(804) 499-9959
Lewis, Frederic Stock Photos/530 W. 25th St., NYC	(800) 688-5656
Life Picture Service/Time & Life Bldg., NYC	(212) 522-4800
Lightwave/1430 Mass. Ave., Cambridge	(617) 628-1052
MacLaren, Mark, Inc./430 E. 20th St., NYC	(212) 674-8615
Madison, David/2330 Old Middlefield, Mountain View	(415) 961-6297
Magnum Photos, Inc./72 Spring St., NYC	(212) 966-9200
Maisel, Jay/NYC	(212) 431-5157
McLaughlin, Herb & Dorothy/2344 W. Holly, Phoenix	(602) 258-6551
McVicker, Sam/324 Scotland St., Dunedin	(813) 734-9660
Mead, Joyce/Palisades Park/(201) 568-1412	**page 737**
MediChrome/NYC/(212) 679-8480/(800) 233-1975	**pages 742-743**
Meyers, Jonathan A./3431 Anderson S.E., Albuquerque	(505) 268-9284
Meyerson, Arthur/Houston/(713) 660-0405	**pages 662-663**
Miller Comstock/180 Bloor St. W., Toronto	(416) 925-4323
Mug Shots/30 Rockledge Rd., W. Redding	(203) 938-3246
Murray's J2/4136 Hillcrest Ave. S.W., Seattle	(206) 937-9235
NFL Photos/6701 Center Dr. W., L.A.	(213) 215-1606
National Stock Network/8960 S.W. 114th St., Miami	(305) 233-1703
Natural Selection Stock, Inc./183 St. Paul St., Rochester	(716) 232-1502
Nawrocki Stock Photo,Inc./332 S. Michigan Ave., Chicago	(312) 427-0178
New Image Stock Agency, The, Inc./38 Quail Ct., Walnut Creek	(415) 934-2405
Pacific Stock/Honolulu	(808) 922-0975
Panoramic Stock Images/230 N. Michigan Ave., Chicago	(312) 236-8545
Pantages, Tom/Three Raymond St., Gloucester	(508) 525-3678
Peebles, Douglas/445 Iliwahi Loop, Kailua	(808) 254-1082
Photo Agents Ltd./113 E. 31st St., NYC	(212) 683-5777
Photo Network/1541-J Parkway Loop, Tustin	(800) 548-0199
Photo Researchers, Inc./NYC	(212) 758-3420
Photo Resources/511 Broadway, Saratoga Spgs.	(800) 627-4686
Photo Stock Unlimited/7208 Thomas Blvd., Pittsburgh	(215) 242-5070

PhotoBank, Inc./17952-B Skypark Cir., Irvine	(714) 250-4480
PhotoSource International/Pine Lake Farm, Osceola	(715) 248-3800
Photophile/2311 Kettner Blvd., San Diego	(619) 234-4431
Photovault/1045 17th St., S.F.	(415) 552-9682
Photri, Inc./3701 S. George Mason Dr., Falls Church	(800) 544-0385
Pictorial History Research/565 Meadow Rd., Winnetka	(708) 446-5987
Picture Agency Council of America/4203 Locust St., Phila.	(215) 386-8681
Pictures in Color/Austin	(512) 469-0958
Picturesque/1520 Brookside Dr., Raleigh	(919) 828-0023
Poehlman, J./18306 Olympic View Dr., Edmonds	(206) 774-3097
Positive Images/317 N. Main St., Natick	(508) 653-7610
Prever, Tracey/Walnut Creek/(415) 398-7148	**page 737**
Reference Pictures/900 Broadway, NYC	(212) 254-0008
Roberts, H. Armstrong, Inc./1181 Broadway, NYC	(212) 685-3870
Robinson, James/NYC/(212) 580-1793	**page 156**
Roof Bin Inc./13 E. 17th St., NYC	(212) 929-0008
Rotkin Review, The/1697 Broadway, NYC	(212) 757-9255
Sharpshooters/Miami/(305) 666-1266	**pages 664-667, 680-681, 686-691, 726-727**
Sharpshooters/Miami/(800) 666-1266	**pages 664-667, 680-681, 686-691, 726-727**
Silverstein, Roy/1604 Gary St., E. Meadow	(212) 941-7497
Simowitz, Carol/16 Cazneau St., Sausalito	(415) 331-0278
Snyder, Lee F./112th Terrace N., Clearwater	(813) 573-2332
Southern Stock Photos/3601 W. Commercial Blvd., Ft. Lauderdale	(305) 486-7117
Spectra-Action, Inc./Five Carole Ln., St. Louis	(314) 567-5700
Spectrum/115 Sansome St., S.F.	(415) 340-9811
SportsChrome East/West/Palisades Park/(201) 568-1412	**page 737**
SportsChrome East/West/Walnut Creek/(415) 398-7148	**page 737**
Sports File/1674 Meridian Ave., Miami Beach	(305) 672-1674
Sports Illustrated Pictures/Time & Life Bldg., NYC	(212) 522-4781
Starlight Photo Agency/61 Hill St., Southampton	(516) 283-6183
Stock Advantage, The/213 N. 12th St., Allentown	(215) 776-7381
Stock Boston, Inc./36 Gloucester St., Boston	(617) 266-2300
Stock Broker, The/450 Lincoln St., Denver	(303) 698-1734
Stock Imagery/711 Kalamath, Denver	(800) 288-3686
Stock Market Inc., The/93 Parliament St., Toronto	(416) 362-7767
Stock Market, The/1181 Broadway, NYC	(212) 684-7878
Stock Photos Hawaii/1128 Nuuana Ave., Honolulu	(808) 538-1389
Stock Shop, Inc., The/NYC/(212) 679-8480/(800) 233-1975	**pages 742-743**
Stock Solution, The/6640 S. 2200 W., Salt Lake City	(801) 569-1155
Stock, Richard/1205 Raintree Cir., Culver City	(213) 559-3344
Stockhouse, The, Inc./9261 Kirby, Houston	(713) 796-8400
Stockphotos, Inc./373 Park Ave. S., NYC	(212) 686-1196
Super Stock/Four By Five/11 W. 19th St. ., NYC	(800) 828-4545
Superstock International, Inc./Ten W. 20th St., NYC	(212) 633-0200
TSW/After Image/L.A.	(213) 938-1700
Take Stock /Generic Photos/66 Broadway, S.F.	(415) 296-0902
Taurus Photos/NYC	(212) 683-4025
Team Russell/Aspen/(303) 920-1431	**pages 640-641**
Telephoto/8 Thomas St., NYC	(212) 406-2440
Third Coast Stock Source/Milwaukee	(414) 765-9442
Thompson, William/15566 Sandy Hook Rd., Poulsbo	(206) 621-9069
Uniphoto Picture Agency/3205 Grace St. N.W., Wash. D.C.	(202) 333-0500
Vedros, Nick & Assocs./Kansas City/(816) 471-5488	**pages 524-525**
View Finder/2310 Penn Ave., Pittsburgh	(412) 391-8720
Viewfinders, Inc./126 N. Third St., Mpls.	(800) 776-8171
Visual File/1039 Seventh Ave., San Diego	(619) 724-5761
Visual Media, Inc./1877 Purdue Dr., Reno	(702) 322-8868
Von Ehrenpreis Studio/102 A South Main St., New Hope	(215) 862-0790
WaterHouse, The Inc./Mile Marker 102.5, U.S. #1, Key Largo	(800) 451-3737
West Light/2223 S. Carmelina Ave., L.A.	(213) 820-7077
West Stock, Inc./83 South King St., Seattle	(800) 821-9600
Westlight/2223 S. Carmelina Ave., L.A.	(213) 820-7077
Wheeler Pictures/145 W. 28th St., NYC	(212) 564-5430
Woodfin Camp & Assocs., Inc./NYC	(212) 481-6900
Yuter, Mona/317 W. 93rd St., NYC	(212) 316-9101
Zehrt, Jack/18920 Deer Creek Rd., Pacific	(314) 458-3600
Zoological Society of San Diego Photo Lab/San Diego	(619) 231-1515

In Sports Photography...
We're in a League by Ourselves!

PICTURE AGENCY - STOCK PHOTO LIBRARY

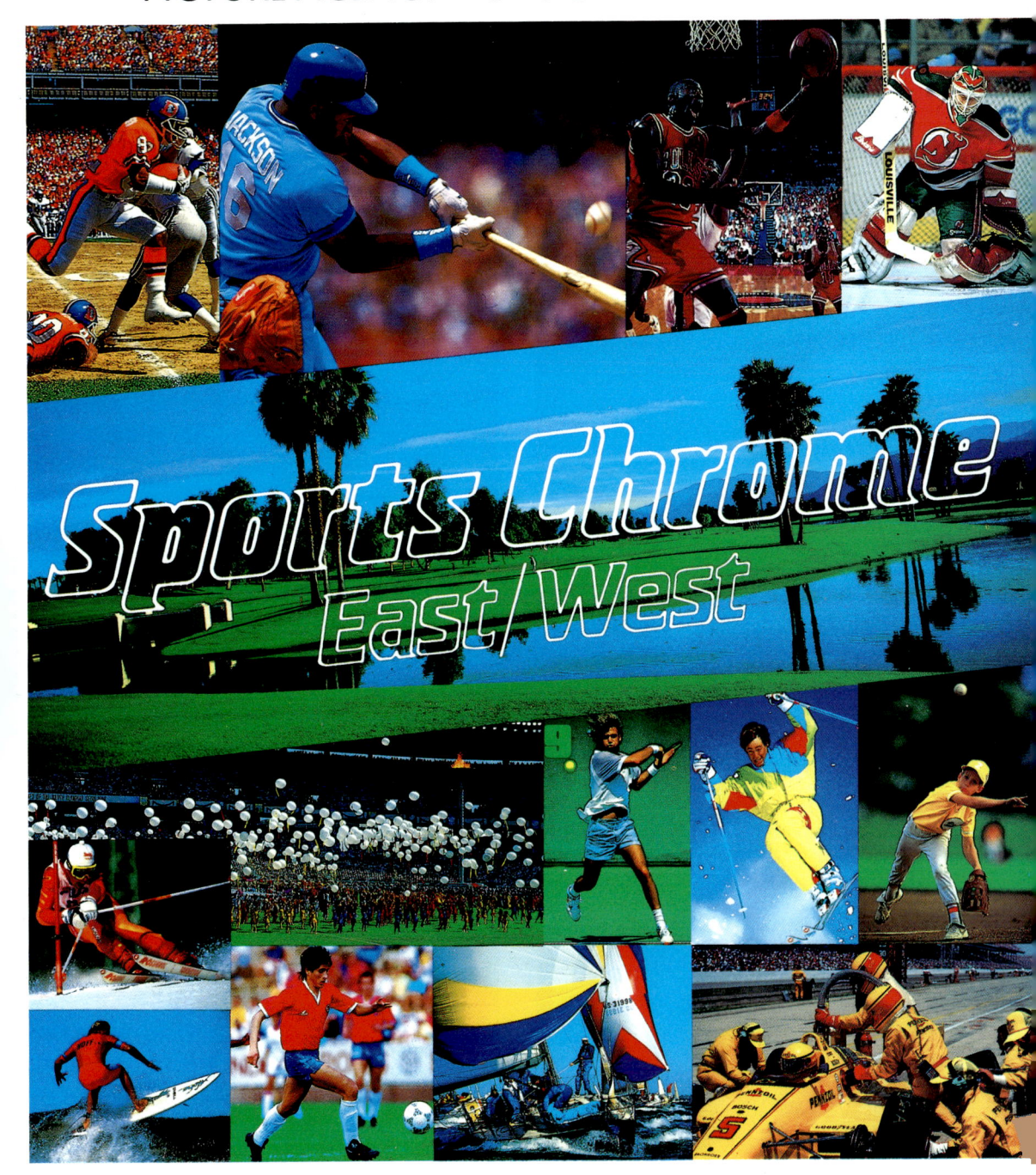

Original Slides For Original Thinkers

IN THE EAST: JOYCE MEAD
10 BRINKERHOFF AVENUE
PALISADES PARK, NEW JERSEY 07650
(201) 568-1412 FAX: (201) 944-1045

IN THE WEST: TRACEY PREVER
38 QUAIL COURT
WALNUT CREEK, CALIFORNIA 94596
(415) 398-7148 FAX: (415) 256-7754

Design and Color Separation by NEW LIFE COLOR REPRODUCTION, INC., 610 Broad Avenue, Ridgefield, N.J. 07657 (201) 943-7005 FAX: (201) 943-7010

iNSTOCK

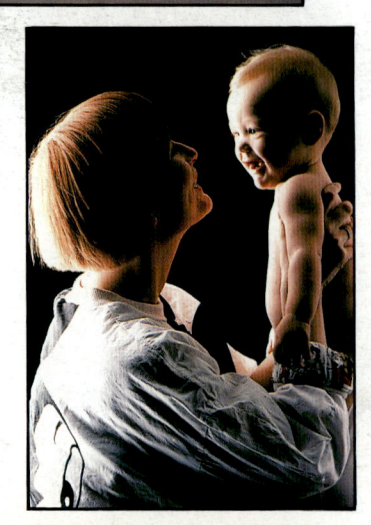

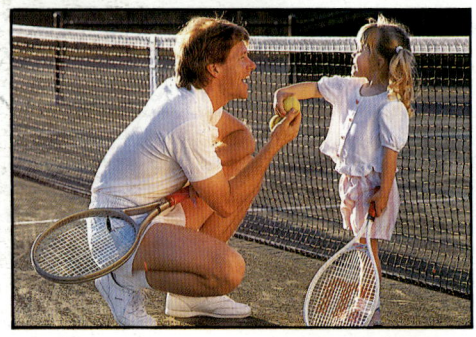

PICTURE AGENCY
516 Northeast 13th Street
Fort Lauderdale, Florida 33304
(305) 527-4111

Fax us your layout
Fax No. (305) 522-2562

TOO BEAUTIFUL TO BE STOCK?

Joan Kramer AND ASSOCIATES 
© John M. Russell

Joan Kramer AND ASSOCIATES 
© Glen R. Steiner

Joan Kramer AND ASSOCIATES 
© Ed Simpson

Joan Kramer AND ASSOCIATES 
© Clark M. Dunbar

Joan Kramer AND ASSOCIATES 
© David Cornwell

Joan Kramer AND ASSOCIATES 
© Stephen Frink

Joan Kramer AND ASSOCIATES 
© Ed Simpson

Joan Kramer AND ASSOCIATES 
© Bill Bachmann

Joan Kramer AND ASSOCIATES 
© Simpson/Flint

CALL JOAN KRAMER AND ASSOCIATES

Thousands of photographs—all model released.
If you're in the market, we've got the stock.

(212) 567-5545 or (516) 466-5582

stock photography-photo assignments

© 1991 Joan Kramer & Associates, Inc.

BOWEN:WICHITA

PAUL BOWEN PHOTOGRAPHY INC.
2300 East Douglas • Wichita, Kansas 67201
(316) 263-5537 • Fax (316) 264-3013

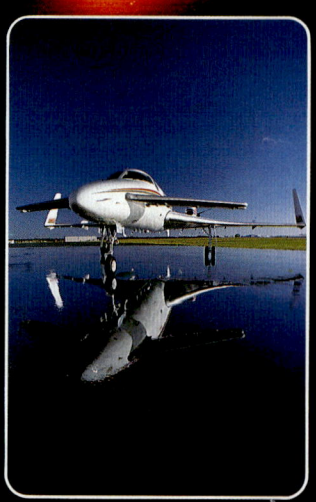

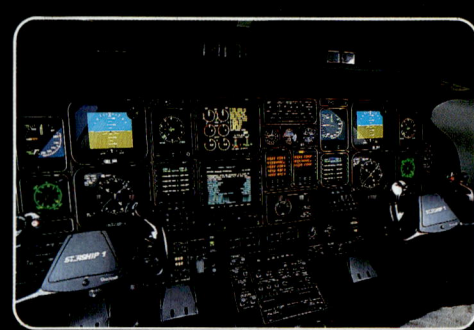

The Stock Shop Inc.

MediChrome

232 Madison Avenue
New York, NY 10016
call for our free catalog
212/679-8480
800/233-1975
Fax/532-1934

FOCUS ON SPORTS, INC.

You've seen our images...
now you know our name.

FOCUS ON SPORTS, INC.
222 East 46 Street, New York, NY 10017
(212) 661-6860   Fax: (212) 983-3031

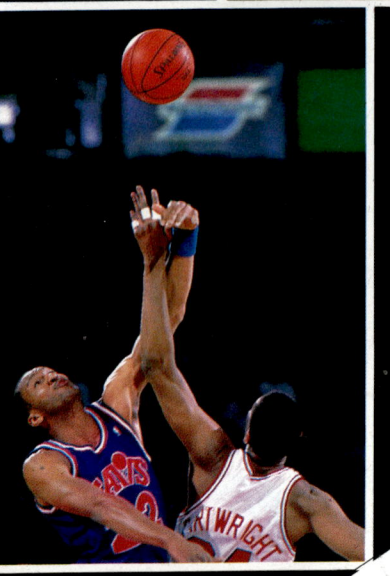